LAND LAW

AUSTRALIA
LBC Information Services Ltd
Sydney

CANADA and USA
Carswell
Toronto

NEW ZEALAND
Brooker's
Auckland

SINGAPORE and MALAYSIA
Thomson Information (S.E. Asia)
Singapore

LAND LAW

Sweet & Maxwell's Textbook Series

John Stevens
Lecturer in Law, University of Birmingham

and

Robert Pearce
Professor of the Law of Property and Equity and
Pro-Vice Chancellor, University of Buckingham

LONDON
SWEET & MAXWELL
1998

Published in 1998 by
Sweet & Maxwell Limited of
100 Avenue Road, London NW3 3PF
(http://www.smlawpub.co.uk)
Typeset by Dataword Services Limited of Chilcompton
Printed in Great Britain by
Redwood Books, Trowbridge, Wiltshire

Reprinted 1999 (twice)

No natural forests were destroyed to make this product;
only farmed timber was used and replanted

A C.I.P. catalogue
record for this book
is available from
the British Library

ISBN 0–421–571–705

Preface

"Of the making of many books there is no end:" so why the need for another to join the existing ranks of Land Law texts? In common with all the contributions to the new Sweet & Maxwell Textbook Series the authors are of the view that in the light of recent changes in university course structures and student working practices many existing works fall into one of two camps. Some older and established works, despite their undisputed academic quality, are increasingly too detailed and inaccessible for the majority of students, and provide coverage well in excess of that required by modern courses. Many of their more recent competitors are too shallow to serve as main course texts, providing students with over simplifications of complex issues and insufficient information and interaction with primary source materials and academic debate.

This book is intended to serve as a comprehensive student textbook providing coverage of the range of topics studied in the vast majority of undergraduate Land Law modules in sufficient depth to serve as a course text. We have sought to explain the basic concepts and principles of English Land Law simply and straightforwardly to aid student comprehension of the fundamentals, but also to raise and discuss areas of academic debate, examine the policy background to the present law and evaluate proposals for reform.

Two aspects of our approach are perhaps worthy of particular note. First in our combined experience of teaching the subject we have felt that students are often expected to grasp the principles governing issues of priority between interests in registered and unregistered land before they have any real understanding of what those interests are. We feel that this is often to put the cart before the horse. For this reason we have provided only an overview of those issues in the introductory chapters and have left until the end the task of providing an integrated exposition of the operation of the registered land system and the rules operating in the residual rump of unregistered land. To some extent this has involved a degree of repetition in the text. This is deliberate, and we hope that as issues of priority are discussed in increasing depth in the context of specific rights and interests, and culminating in the final chapters, the readers' understanding will be sharpened. Secondly, we are of the opinion that students should be exposed to the primary source material of statutory provisions and caselaw, and not merely to our distilled interpretation, to enable them to form their own judgments and develop the skills of critical analysis. For this reason, where appropriate, we have made use of extensive quotations. This is not intended to take the place of first-hand reading, or even of a casebook, but to expose students, and especially those who may be studying Land Law at an early stage of their legal education, to the importance of such primary material and to enable them to enter their libraries with a little less trepidation.

Land Law has been the subject of much recent development, both by statutory reform and judicial decision. The two major legislative reforms introduced by the Landlord and Tenant (Covenants) Act 1995 and the Trusts of Land and Appointment of Trustees Act 1996 have purported to simplify the law and remedy a number of long-recognised weaknesses. However, since both leave the pre-existing systems in place, they have made the presentation of the law more complex, requiring an explanation of both the old and the new regimes. Each unfortunately requires an extensive exposition of the old law in order to make sense of the reforms.

As ever we are extremely grateful to those who have provided us with support and encouragement as we have prepared this text. Our thanks are due to Sweet & Maxwell for their efficiency and patience while the manuscript was prepared, and also to our families, colleagues and friends for their tolerance of us while writing. Special thanks are due to Jonathan for his stimulating comments on Land Law over many lunchtimes in Birmingham and to Panos, Sophie, Magali and Annie for their friendship, which has proved resilient despite listening to so much talk about a subject which is not their own.

Needless to say all errors are ours alone. We have attempted to state the law as it stood on September 1, 1997.

John Stevens
Robert Pearce
September, 1997

Table of Contents

Table of Cases

Table of Statutes

Part I

Introductory

Chapter 1

ORIENTATION

WHAT IS PROPERTY?

1 Property concerns the ownership of things

At a basic level everyone is familiar with the idea of property, since they have some experience of owning things. For example if Damon is given a car by his parents for his eighteenth birthday he becomes its owner, and it can be said to belong to him. As a consequence of his ownership he is able to do whatever he wants with it. He can make use of it himself and enjoy the privileges of his ownership. He can decide to lend the car to a friend, or perhaps offer it for hire. He can decided to sell it and thus realise its value in money. He can decide to destroy it if he so chooses. All of these options are made possible by the fact that he owns the car. Integral to his ownership of the car is the fact that his rights in relation to it are exclusive, and that other people have no rights in it. For example, if Murray takes the car without permission and sells it to Frank, it is clear that Frank should not become the owner of the car. Murray had no right to the car himself and cannot pass to Frank a better right than he himself possessed. Even though the car may now be in the possession of Frank this does not mean that he owns it. It still belongs to Damon and he can insist on its return to him.

2 A wide variety of "things"

If property is concerned with the ownership of things it should be obvious that there is a wide variety of things which can be owned. For example a person may own money, clothes, shares in a company, a ticket to a pop concert, a house or flat. These are all different types of "thing" which may be owned. An important distinction is drawn between tangible and intangible property. Tangible property consists of things which are physical in nature, for example a car. Intangible property consists of things which are not physical in nature but which are regarded as property because they are capable of ownership. For example, shares in a company are property which may be owned and traded but which are not physical. Although the share certificates are in some sense "physical" these are only evidence of the existence of the property right to which they relate, namely the notional share of the ownership of the company and its assets.

Other examples of intangible property are intellectual property rights such as copyrights and patents.

3 Proprietary rights

(a) The nature of proprietary rights

A proprietary right is a right which exists in relation to a thing, whether tangible or intangible. The most important proprietary right is that of ownership, but this is by no means the only right which may exist in relation to a thing. For example, a house which is owned by one person may be leased to a tenant and mortgaged to a building society. In this case the owner, the tenant and the building society will all enjoy proprietary rights in the house. An important distinction is drawn between rights which are proprietary in nature and rights which are purely personal. A personal right is an entitlement which a person enjoys against another specific individual, and its central characteristic is that it can only be enforced against that specific person. It is often referred to by latin terminology as a right *in personam.* In contrast, a proprietary right is a right existing "in" the item of property, or thing, to which it relates. The right is enforceable against the thing irrespective of who possesses or owns it at the time that the right is sought to be enforced. Such rights are described as rights *in rem,* which translated means "in the thing itself". The central characteristic of a proprietary right is that it is capable of enduring through changes in ownership of the property to which it relates, so that it will be enforceable against the new owner.

(b) An illustration of personal rights

Imagine that Andy goes up to read law at the University of Barsetshire. He is in need of accommodation and answers an advert in a local newspaper placed by Beryl, an elderly lady, who takes in students as lodgers at a rent of £25 per week. If Beryl and Andy agree that he can use a room in her house for his first year, his right to live there will be founded upon a contractual agreement between himself and Beryl and will be purely personal in nature. He will not be a trespasser on her land because she has granted him permission to be there, but he in no sense owns the land, nor does he enjoy any proprietary right in it. His right is technically termed a licence. Unless Beryl has agreed not to terminate his licence before the end of the year she will be entitled to withdraw her permission for him to live in her room at any time. If she does tell him to leave he may well be entitled to a remedy against her for breach of contract, for which he would be entitled to damages to compensate him for any loss he suffered as a result of the breach, but he is not entitled to continue living in the house, and if he attempts to do so he will be committing a trespass. He cannot transfer his right to anyone else, for example he cannot decide that after the first week he is going to return home and allow Charlotte to take over his licence and insist on living in the house. More importantly, if Beryl decides to sell the house to David, Andy will not be entitled to assert his contractual right to live in the room against David. David will be entitled to take the house free from any rights of Andy, since his rights do not exist in the house as such but only against Beryl personally. Similarly if Beryl were to mortgage the house to the bank and it subsequently turned out that she was unable to keep up the repayments so that they intended to repossess it, Andy would not be able to assert his right to occupy against the Bank to prevent the repossession.

(c) An illustration of proprietary rights

If, however, rather than taking Andy as a lodger into her house Beryl owned a single bedroom flat and agreed to grant him a lease for a year at a rent of £100 a month, Andy's interest would no longer be purely personal, but his lease would constitute a proprietary interest in the flat. Unless Andy committed a breach of the terms of his lease entitling Beryl to forfeit his interest she would not be able simply to decide that she no longer wanted him to live there. He would be entitled to remain for as long as the term he had been granted. Unless the lease specifically prevented him from so doing he would be able to transfer his right to occupy to someone else, such as Charlotte, who would then be entitled to occupy the flat in his stead. If Beryl were to sell the flat to David, or to mortgage it to the bank, Andy's interest would be enforceable against both David and the bank because they would have acquired the thing subject to his pre-existing right to occupy it.

CENTRAL CONCERNS OF THE LAW OF PROPERTY

1 Function of the law of property

The law of property comprises the range of legal rules and principles which regulate proprietary rights in things. It is an analytically coherent body of law as, for example, is criminal law which concerns itself with how the law determines if conduct is criminal in the eyes of the state, or the law of contract which comprises the legal rules regulating obligations voluntarily entered into by consensual agreement. Although there is an inevitable overlap with other subject areas a number of prime concerns may be identified which property law addresses. It is not intended at this stage to attempt to answer these questions but merely to raise them.

2 Ownership

One of the central questions of property law concerns the ownership of things. Who is the owner of a particular thing, whether tangible or intangible. For example, if a wallet is found in the street containing a large quantity of money who is the owner? Does it belong to the finder, the state or to the person who lost it? Central to issues of ownership are the questions as to how the ownership of property can be acquired and transferred. For example, if Damon agrees to sell his car to Frank, at what point does Damon cease to be the owner of his car and Frank become the new owner. By what mechanism is the ownership transferred from Damon to Frank. Alternatively, if Beryl agrees to grant Andy a lease of her flat at what point does he become entitled to a lease and the concomitant right to occupy it? If Charlotte owns shares in Marks & Spencer and merely gives the share certificates to David for his birthday does this transfer the ownership of them to her? If Edward owns an estate in Cornwall but for the last five years a group of travellers led by Francesca have been living there have they acquired the ownership by virtue of their possession for that period? In many cases the transfer of property might require special formalities or procedures to be observed and the transfer will be ineffective if they have not been followed.

3 Creation of subsidiary interests

A second major issue is whether there are any lesser, or subsidiary, rights existing in a thing which is owned by someone else. For example, a car may have been purchased by Frank but he has pledged it as security for a loan from Murray. What sort of right, if any, does Murray have in the car? Such subsidiary rights and interests are common in relation to land. As has been seen, a house or flat may be owned by one person, leased to another, mortgaged to a bank. How and when are such subsidiary interests as leases and mortgages created over the land? What do they entitle the holder of the subsidiary right to do in relation to the thing in which they exist?

4 Priorities between competing interests

A third major issue addressed by the law of property is that of determining which of several competing proprietary rights in the same thing should have priority over the others. For example, if Beryl owns a flat and on Monday grants a lease for a year to Andy and then on Wednesday grants a lease for a year to Charlotte, which of these two proprietary rights will have priority over the other, since it is impossible for both to be enjoyed simultaneously? Similarly, if Beryl granted a lease for a year to Andy last month and this month sold her house to Charlotte who did not know of the existence of David's interest, will David's right enjoy priority over Charlotte's, or will Charlotte's ownership enjoy priority so that she can effectively evict David? Will it make any difference if Charlotte was merely given the house by Beryl rather than purchasing it?

LAND LAW

1 The distinction between real and personal property

In English law a fundamental distinction was made between what was termed "real property" and "personal property." At its simplest real property consists of what today would be called "land" and personal property is all property which is not land. Historically there were significant distinctions between the regimes applicable to each, especially as to the law of succession. Despite the more recent objective of harmonising unnecessary distinctions between the two types of property the difference between land and personal property is still important, especially as legislation has introduced a statutory framework governing many of the important property issues which is exclusive to land. The following chapter will consider what is meant by "land" in the technical sense.

2 The social and cultural context of land law

(a) Background

Land law therefore comprises the body or law which regulates proprietary issues concerning that which is classified as "land". The content of such law is obviously of tremendous social significance, since the ownership and exploitation of land is of fundamental importance to society and its functioning. No one can live without reference to land, as their home, providing their place of work and for recreation. The nature of land ownership has changed dramatically over the centuries. Initially land was owned by a small number of people for whom it was a source of power and income, and the majority of the population had no real rights at all. As a consequence of industrialisation and the agricultural revolution land gradually became less significant as a source of revenue and other forms of investment emerged. There has been a gradual increase in the number of people buying land of their own, so that today a majority of people own land which provides their home. For many people their home is their greatest asset in terms of value, and it has usually been acquired by the use of a mortgage.

(b) Key principles underlying English land law

Given the social background a number of central principles underlie English land law and have influenced its development and structures. There is nothing necessarily objectively correct about these principles but they are a reflection of the cultural background within which English land law has evolved.

(i) The individual ownership of land: Unlike other cultures which may emphasise tribal, family, or state ownership of land, English land law regards land as primarily an individual asset. This is closely related to the concepts of freedom and self-determination so that the owner is entitled to use his land as he chooses, or indeed to fail to use it, no matter how little benefit this may bring to others or how much more effectively the land could be used. He can transfer it to whoever he wants, and on death he can leave it by will to whoever he wants. Closely allied to this is the fact that English law will protect an owner's land from any interference by others. He is entitled to exclude whoever he wants. It is a truism that an "Englishman's home is his castle," no matter how small the particular castle may be!

(ii) Facilitation of the use of land: At the same time as emphasising individual ownership as a cardinal principle English land law aims to facilitate the efficient use of land by enabling the owner to create subsidiary interests which will benefit himself and others. If he does not wish to inhabit land himself he may wish to grant a lease to someone else, entitling them to the benefit of occupation and him to the benefit of rent. Similarly, if a neighbouring landowner wishes to start industrial production on his land which will necessitate a means of access that he does not otherwise possess, he will be able to grant a right of way in return for the payment of an appropriate price. Thus the variety of subsidiary interests which may be created in land and are enjoyed by someone other than the owner are a means by which efficient use may be made of what is a scarce resource.

(iii) Free marketability of land: A further objective is to ensure that land remains a readily tradable market commodity. English land law has sought to reduce the difficulties inherent in the buying and selling of land, in particular by seeking to ensure that a prospective purchaser can be confident that the vendor is entitled to sell him the land in question, and by providing that he is not taken unawares by the existence of subsidiary interests which affect the value of the land to him. In more recent years many developments in land law have been affected by the need to ensure that mortgage lenders are able to lend without risk that their security will be subsequently compromised by undiscovered third party interests in the land. Without the willingness of lenders to provide purchase money on the security of land the housing market would grind to a virtual standstill, since there are relatively few buyers who are able to raise the purchase price from their own resources alone.

(iv) Fair protection of third party interests: A further objective is to ensure that subsidiary interests in land enjoy fair protection when the land is transferred, so that they are not easily defeated by a mere transfer of the land to a new owner. However, this is balanced against the desire to ensure that a transferee, and especially a purchaser of the land, is not unfairly burdened by subsidiary interests in the land of which he was unaware, and perhaps could not have been aware, at the time when he acquired the land.

INTRODUCTION TO THIS BOOK

It is not the object of this book to provide a detailed and comprehensive guide to every issue that may arise in relation to land and its use and ownership. It is intended to provide a guide to the most important concepts and mechanisms in English land law. The book is divided into five parts, of which this is the introductory section providing brief commentary on some of the most important concepts and structures of English land law. Part II "The Ownership of Land" will examine the various types of ownership of land which can be enjoyed and how they may be acquired and transferred. Freehold, leasehold and equitable ownership will be considered in detail. Part III "Subsidiary Interests in Land" will examine the most important of the various subsidiary interest in land, including easements, restrictive covenants, mortgages, licences and estoppel interests. It will be considered how such interests can be acquired and what rights they confer upon the holder. Part IV "Registered Land" will examine the system of land registration as it operates in detail, and especially how it determines issues of priority between interests in land. Reference will also be made to the system of land registration which was introduced in 1925 throughout the preceding two sections. Since it is not yet the case that all land has been brought within the ambit of a universal scheme of registration Part V, "Unregistered Land," will examine the law relating to the residue of land remaining outside of it. By necessity this is an area of constantly diminishing significance, which is why it has been placed last. Again particular attention will be devoted to how issues of priority are resolved between competing interests in unregistered land.

Chapter 2

What is Land?

Land as the Physical Ground

The majority of laymen would naturally define "land" in terms of the physical ground. There is a scene in Woody Allen's film "Love and Death" where it is announced that the central character's Uncle Boris owns a small piece of land. The said uncle is then shown holding a piece of turf in his hands and the rest of the family rejoicing around it. Somewhat later in the film it is announced that Uncle Boris has gone into hotel development, and he is shown holding the same piece of turf but with a minute monopoly style hotel placed in the middle. Many people conceive of their "land" in a similar way, and although this is not wrong in itself, it is inadequate from a legal point of view because "land" enjoys a wider technical meaning.

The Legal Concept of Land

1 A statutory definition

"Land" is given a wider meaning by section 205(1)(ix) of the Law of Property Act 1925, which provides that:

> "'Land' includes land of any tenure, and mines and minerals, whether or not held apart from the surface, buildings or parts of buildings (whether the division is horizontal, vertical or made in any other way) and other corporeal hereditaments; also a manor, an advowson, and a rent and other incorporeal hereditaments; and an easement, right privilege, or benefit in, over or derived from land . . ."

Although many of the terms used in this section are as yet unfamiliar, it is clear that land is not regarded as the mere ground, but is a category describing a whole range of rights associated with the ground. The section distinguishes between two very important categories of rights which comprise land, namely corporeal and incorporeal hereditaments.

2 Corporeal hereditaments

Corporeal hereditaments are the physical features of land, and consist of the physical surface and everything attached to the land. For example, minerals found in the ground beneath the surface belong to the land and are corporeal hereditaments, as are buildings attached to the surface, and any plants or trees growing[1] on the land.

3 Incorporeal hereditaments

In contrast incorporeal hereditaments are intangible rights existing in the land as a physical entity. Thus proprietary rights in land are themselves classified as "land", in the sense that they are regulated by the rules appropriate to land rather than personal property. Thus such rights as a lease, an easement or a mortgage will be regarded as "land."

OWNERSHIP OF THE SURFACE OF LAND CARRIES WITH IT RIGHTS ABOVE AND BELOW THE SURFACE

1 The traditional maxim

It is clear that ownership of the surface of land carries with it rights to what is below the surface and to control of the airspace above. Historically it was said that "cuius est solum, eius est usque ad coelum et ad inferos" (whoever owns the soil owns everything up to the heavens and down to the depths of the earth). Although this may well have proved practical when there was virtually no possibility of the exploitation of the airspace above land it has had to be substantially modified in the light of the evolution of flight to strike a sensible balance between the rights of the surface owner and the right to overflight of land.

2 Rights below the surface of land

(a) Rights to mineral deposits

The owner of land is prima facie entitled to the ownership of any mineral deposits found beneath the surface. However, even this right is qualified in the national interest. At common law any unmined gold and silver belongs to the Crown as a prerogative right.[2] By statute ownership of oil, coal and natural gas also belong to the Crown.[3]

(b) Right to spaces below the surface

Space below the surface, whether natural or man-made, is land and capable of ownership and protection from intrusion by trespassers. In *The Metropolitan Railway*

[1] See: *Stukeley v. Butler* (1615) Hob. 168.
[2] *Case of Mines* (1567) 1 Plowd. 310; *Attorney-General v. Morgan* [1891] 1 Ch. 432.
[3] Petroleum (Production) Act 1934, s.1; Coal Industry Act 1994, s.9.

Co. v. Fowler[4] it was held that ownership of a tunnel was to be regarded as ownership of an interest in land so as to attract the equivalent of rates. In *Grigsby v. Melville*[5] the Court of Appeal held that the owner of a house also owned a cellar underneath it, even though he could not gain access to it from his own land, and that he was entitled to an injunction to prevent his neighbour, who did have a means of access, from using it for storage without permission, which would constitute a trespass.[6]

(c) Rights to items found in the land

The owner of land is also entitled to the ownership of any lost items of property found in the land, unless they are treasure trove, in which case ownership will vest in the Crown.[7] For example, in *Elwes v. Brigg Gas Company*[8] when the tenant of land unearthed a pre-historic boat it was held to belong to the landowner. More recently in *Waverley Borough Council v. Fletcher*[9] the Court of Appeal held that a brooch unearthed by a metal detecting enthusiast in a public park belonged to the Council which owned the land.

3 Rights to the airspace above the land

The owner of the physical surface also owns the airspace above the land, and is entitled to assert his rights in relation to it and to restrain others from trespassing into it. For example, in *Kelson v. Imperial Tobacco*[10] an owner of the surface of land was granted an injunction to restrain a trespass by the neighbouring landowner who had erected a sign which projected into the airspace above his land by some four inches. In such cases an injunction is available even thought the infringement causes no damage because trespass is actionable *per se.* However, it is now clear that the owner of the surface does not enjoy rights over the superjacent airspace to an unlimited height. In *Bernstein v. Skyviews and General Ltd*[11] a landowner claimed that there had been a trespass when a light aircraft had overflown his land to take an aerial photograph at a height of some hundreds of feet. The landowner relied on the maxim "cuius est solum, eius est usque ad coelum et ad inferos" to justify a remedy, but Griffiths J. held that no actionable trespass had occurred. He concluded that in the light of the scientific developments enabling use of airspace the maxim was incapable of balancing the rights of landowners against the rights of the public. Instead he held that the rights of a landowner to the airspace above his land should be restricted "to such a height as is reasonably necessary for the ordinary use and enjoyment of his land and the structure upon it" and that "above that height he has no greater rights in the air space than any

[4] [1892] 1 Q.B. 165.
[5] [1974] 1 W.L.R. 80.
[6] See also: *Edward's v. Lee's Administrator* (1936) 96 S.W.2d 1028.
[7] At common law an item was only treasure trove if it contained a substantial quantity of gold or silver and it had been hidden rather than lost. The scope of treasure trove has been widened by the Treasure Act 1996, the provisions of which are too technical for detailed discussion here. See also: *Attorney-General v. Trustees of the British Museum* [1903] 2 Ch. 598; *Attorney-General of the Duchy of Lancaster v. G. E. Overton (Farms) Ltd* [1982] Ch. 277.
[8] (1886) 33 Ch.D. 562.
[9] [1995] 4 All E.R. 756; [1996] Conv. 216 (Stevens).
[10] [1957] 2 Q.B. 334.
[11] [1978] Q.B. 479.

other member of the public." Thus the extent to which a landowner enjoys rights to the airspace above his land is dependent upon the nature and use to which he has put his land. Statute has also intervened, so that overflight by aircraft is not actionable if they were flying at a height reasonable in the circumstances.[12] In *Anchor Brewhouse Developments Ltd v. Berkley House Ltd*[13] a developer allowed the jib of a tower crane to swing over the plaintiff's property. Scott J. granted them an injunction to restrain the trespass.[14]

4 Possible division of land into horizontal strata

The fact that "land" extends to rights enjoyed to the space above and below the physical surface opens the possibility of the horizontal division of land into strata capable of ownership by different persons. This is most clearly seen in the case of flats, where the owners of a fourth floor flat do not own the surface itself. The possibility of such horizontal division of land is expressly recognised in the definition of land in section 205(1)(ix) of the Law of Property Act 1925.

5 Protection from illegitimate entry and interference

(a) Protection from unauthorised entry

Since the ownership of land carries with it rights to the space both above and beneath the owner, or a person enjoying exclusive possession as a tenant under a lease, enjoys protection from illegitimate entry. Any unauthorised physical intrusion onto his land, whether on the surface, under the surface, or into the airspace at a height below that necessary for the reasonable use and enjoyment of the land, will constitute a trespass. Such a trespass is actionable *per se* without the need for the landowner to demonstrate that he has suffered any loss. The court will usually grant an injunction to remove any continuing trespass and damages for any loss which has been caused. In some circumstances the court may be prepared to grant damages in lieu of an injunction. The vigour with which a landowner's rights will be defended is well illustrated by *John Trenberth Ltd v. National Westminster Bank Ltd.*[15] The defendant bank owned a building fronting a highway which they were under a statutory duty to maintain in a safe condition. It needed to be repaired but the repairs could only be completed by the erection of scaffolding on the plaintiff's neighbouring land. After some months of inconclusive negotiations in which the defendants sought permission to erect the scaffolding they went ahead without their consent. Walton J. held that despite the fact that the refusal of permission was irrational an injunction was appropriate because there had been a flagrant invasion of the plaintiff's land. He commented that the protection of the rights of a land owner was so comprehensive that the defendants

[12] Civil Aviation Act 1982, s.76(1).
[13] [1987] E.G.L.R. 172.
[14] Compare: *Woolerton and Wilson v. Costain* [1970] 1 W.L.R. 411 where an injunction was suspended by Stamp J. in a similar case, but this decision was doubted in *Charrington v. Simons Ltd* [1971] 1 W.L.R. 598 and *John Trenberth Ltd v. National Westminster Bank* (1979) 39 P. & C.R. 104.
[15] (1979) 39 P. & C.R. 104.

might have to demolish and rebuild their building if permission could not be obtained. Although the general principle of the protection of private property still stands, the position of persons such as the defendants has been ameliorated by the intervention of statute. The Access to Neighbouring Land Act 1992 entitles a person requiring access to neighbouring land for carrying out specified works to apply to the court for an access order entitling him to enter the land for that purpose.

(b) Protection from unauthorised interference with use

A landowner is also entitled to protection from illegitimate interference with his use and enjoyment of his land occasioned by the activities of another landowner on his own land, for example because they emit noise, smell or smoke. A person's activities will be actionable in tort as a nuisance if they cause physical damage or amount to an unreasonable interference with the use of the land. For example, in *St Helens Smelting Co. v. Tipping*[16] it was held that a nuisance had been committed when noxious gases and vapours from the defendant's smelting works damaged trees and hedges on the plaintiff's land. Clearly what constitutes an unreasonable interference will depend upon the circumstances of the land affected, and especially its location. As Thesiger L.J. said in *Sturges v. Bridgman*[17] "what would be a nuisance in Belgrave Square would not necessarily be so in Bermondsey," which was known for its air polluting tanneries. Not every possible use of land is subject to protection from interference. In *Hunter v. Canary Wharf Ltd*[18] the House of Lords held that interference with potential television reception by the building of a tower block was not actionable as a nuisance,[19] in just the same way that the erection of a building which obscures a view is not a nuisance.[20] Where an actual nuisance has occurred the landowner may be entitled to an injunction or damages.

OWNERSHIP OF THE SURFACE OF LAND CARRIES WITH IT THE OWNERSHIP OF THINGS ATTACHED TO IT

1 The general principle

A second latin maxim provides "quicquid plantatur solo, solo cedit" (whatever is attached to the soil becomes part of it). This provides the rationale for the principle that items of personal property, known as chattels, become land if they are attached to it so as to become part of it. Chattels which have become attached so as to form part of the land are known as fixtures. Whether an item has become a fixture will be especially important in two contexts. First, where the land is transferred a conveyance of the land will transfer with it all the fixtures which are not expressly excluded.[21] Even more importantly from the very moment that an owner of land has entered into a

[16] (1865) 11 E.R. 1483.
[17] (1879) 11 Ch.D. 852, 865.
[18] [1997] 2 All E.R. 426.
[19] See also: *Bridlington Relay Ltd v. Yorkshire Electricity Board* [1965] Ch. 436.
[20] See: *A-G v. Doughty* (1752) 2 Ves. Sen. 453; *Fishmongers' Co. v. East India Co* (1752) 1 Dick 164.
[21] Law of Property Act 1925, s.62.

contract to sell it he is no longer entitled to remove fixtures since they belong to the purchaser along with the land from that time.[22] Secondly, where land is subject to a lease any chattels which the tenant attaches to the land so as to become fixtures will belong to the landlord, and prima facie the tenant will not be entitled to remove them when the lease comes to an end. However, as will be seen, the law has developed to allows a tenant to remove specific categories of fixture he added to the land.

2 When does a chattel become a fixture?

(a) Chattel attached to the land

Prima facie a chattel will become a fixture when it is physically attached, or annexed, to the land. In *Holland v. Hodgson*[23] the owner of a mill installed looms which were attached to the stone floor by means of nails driven through holes in their feet. Blackburn J. held that by virtue of this attachment, despite the fact that they could be easily removed, the looms had become fixtures and therefore passed with the land when it was repossessed under a mortgage which had not been repaid. He stated the general principle:

> "an article which is affixed to the land even slightly is to be considered as part of the land, unless the circumstances are such as to shew that it was intended to all along to continue a chattel, the onus lying on those who contend that it is a chattel."

This suggests that the mere fact that an item has been attached to the land will prima facie indicate that it has become a fixture, but with the qualification that such attachment is not always a conclusive indication of a fixture. As Blackburn J. indicated earlier in his judgment there are two relevant factors to be take into account, namely "the degree of annexation and the object of the annexation." In practice what this has meant is that chattels which are attached to the land merely to enable them to be better enjoyed as chattels will not be regarded as fixtures and will retain their status as personal property. For example, in *Leigh v. Taylor*[24] the tenant for life of a mansion house had hung valuable tapestries in a drawing room. Although they were affixed to the land the House of Lords held that they remained chattels because they were never intended to form part of the structure of the house and were only attached to enable them to be better enjoyed as ornamental decoration. This can be contrasted with *D'Eyncourt v. Gregory*[25] where tapestries were held to be fixtures because they were as integral to the decoration of the room where they were attached as wallpaper or frescos. In *Leigh v. Taylor* Lord Halsbury suggested that the difference between these two cases was not one of law but as to the facts, and that fashions had changed so that attitudes to styles of ornamentation were different. In *Berkley v. Poulett*[26] the Court of Appeal indicated that the "purpose of annexation" test was pre-eminent over the fact

[22] The contract operates to transfer the equitable ownership of the land to the purchaser immediately.
[23] (1872) L.R. 7 C.P. 328.
[24] [1902] A.C. 157.
[25] (1866) Law Rep. 3 Eq. 382.
[26] (1976) 241 E.G. 911.

of physical attachment, but Scarman L.J. noted that there was a close relationship between the two:

> "If the purpose of the annexation be for the better enjoyment of the object itself, it may remain a chattel, notwithstanding a high degree of physical annexation. Clearly, however, it remains significant to discover the extent of physical disturbance of the building or the land involved in the removal of the object. If an object cannot be removed without serious damage to, or destruction of, some part of the realty, the case for its having become a fixture is a strong one."

The vendor of land had removed a number of pictures affixed by screws into panelling of the dinning room after contracting to sell, and the purchaser claimed that these had been fixtures. The Court held that although they were attached to the wall they had retained their character as mere chattels because they had been fixed so that they could be better enjoyed as pictures, and they were not part of an overall design for the room which would be lost if they were removed. They could easily be replaced by other pictures. The operation of the two tests can also been seen in the contrast between two cases involving cinema chairs. In *Lyon & Co. v. London City and Midland Bank*[27] chairs were hired and fastened to the floor of a cinema with screws. It was held that they remained chattels despite their annexation to the land because they had only been installed for a temporary duration of twelve weeks and they were easily removable without causing damage to the premises. In *Vaudeville Electric Cinema Ltd v. Muriset*[28] it was held that cinema chairs attached to the floor had become fixtures and therefore passed to a person who enjoyed a mortgage over the land. The central difference seems to have been that here the chairs were part of the permanent equipment of the building and the annexation was not merely for a temporary use. In *Elitestone Ltd v. Morris*[29] the House of Lords stressed that the "purpose of annexation" test did not mean that the subjective intentions of the owners of the land or chattels attached were determinative of their status. Lord Lloyd stated:

> "the intention of the parties is only relevant to the extent that it can be derived from the degree and object of the annexation. The subjective intention of the parties cannot affect the question whether the chattel has, in law, become part of the freehold, any more than the subjective intention of the parties can prevent what they have called a licence from taking effect as a tenancy, if that is what the law is."[30]

This principle had been applied by the House of Lords in *Melluish (Inspector of Taxes) v. BMI (No. 3) Ltd*[31] which concerned the question whether various items, including central heating installed in council flats, lifts in council car parks, cremators in a council crematorium and a filtration plant in a council swimming pool, had become fixtures and were therefore owned by the councils, or remained chattels so that they

[27] [1903] 2 K.B. 135.
[28] [1923] 2 Ch. 74.
[29] [1997] 2 All E.R. 513.
[30] *ibid.* at 519.
[31] [1995] 4 All E.R. 453.

were owned by companies which had leased them to the councils. Lord Browne-Wilkinson explained that it was irrelevant that the lease demonstrated a common intention of the parties that the chattels should continue to belong to the companies fixing them to the land. Such a contractual agreement may regulate the right to sever the chattels from the land between the parties, but it cannot prevent the chattel, once fixed, becoming in law part of the land, and as such owned by the owner of the land so long as it remains fixed.

(b) Chattel resting on land

The corollary to the presumption that a chattel attached to the land becomes a fixture is that a chattel which is not attached to the land retains its status as such. As Blackburn J. stated in *Holland v. Hodgson*[32]:

> "articles not otherwise attached to the land than by their own weight are not to be considered as part of the land, unless the circumstances are such as to shew that they were intended to be part of the land, the onus of shewing that they were so intended lying on those who assert that they have ceased to be chattels."

The general rule was applied in *Jordan v. May*[33] where the issue was whether an electric motor and batteries were fixtures. It was held that as the motor was sunk in concrete it was attached to the land and a fixture, but the batteries remained chattels because they were resting by their own weight. However, the purpose for which the chattels are allowed to remain on the land by their own weight is again the pre-eminent test so that the mere fact that there is no attachment does not prevent a chattel becoming a fixture. In *Hamp v. Bygrave*[34] the vendors of land removed a number of items from their garden after entering into a contract with the purchasers, including a stone statue and other stone ornaments in the garden. It was held that these were fixtures despite the fact that they merely rested by their own weight because they formed "part and parcel of the garden" and had been installed primarily to improve the land. Similarly it had been held in *D'Eyncourt v. Gregory*[35] that ornamental statues of lions in the garden and house were fixtures because they were a integral part of the overall architectural design of the land. In *Berkley v. Poulett*[36] the vendor of land removed a half-ton statute of a Greek athlete from the garden which the purchaser claimed had been a fixture. The Court of Appeal held that it had remained a chattel since it was not part of an architectural design to improve the land, as evidenced by the fact that a different ornament had previously stood in the same place.

(c) Buildings

In *Billing v. Pill*[37] Lord Goddard C.J. stated:

> "What is a fixture? First, the commonest fixture is a house. A house is built into the land, so the house, in law, is regarded as part of the land; the house and the land are one thing."

[32] (1872) L.R. 7 C.P. 328.
[33] [1947] K.B. 427.
[34] (1982) 266 E.G. 720.
[35] (1866) Law Rep. 3 Eq. 382.
[36] (1976) 241 E.G. 911.
[37] [1954] 1 Q.B. 70, 75.

Although a house attached to the land by its foundations will clearly be a fixture, greater problems have arisen in connection with buildings resting on the land by their own weight. In a number of early cases wooden buildings resting on land were held to have remained chattels.[38] In *Webb v. Frank Bevis Ltd*[39] a large shed attached to a concrete floor by iron straps was held to have become part of the land, although as a trade fixture the tenant was entitled to sever it at the end of his tenancy. In the recent case *Elitestone Ltd v. Morris*[40] the House of Lords was called to resolve the question whether a bungalow which rested on concrete foundation blocks by its own weight was a fixture or a chattel. It was held that although it rested by its own weight it had become part of the land. The central factor in determining whether it had become part of the land was whether it was capable of being removed without demolition. Lord Lloyd referred to the two tests outline by Blackburn J. in *Holland v. Hodgson*[41] and concluded:

> "These tests are less useful when one is considering the house itself. In the case of the house the answer is as much a matter of common sense as precise analysis. A house which is constructed in such a way so as to be removable, whether as a unit or in sections, may well remain a chattel, even though it is connected temporarily to mains services such as water and electricity. But a house which is constructed in such a way that it cannot be removed at all, save by destruction, cannot have been intended to remain as a chattel. It must have been intended to form part of the realty."[42]

He therefore held that the bungalow had become part of the land because it could not be taken down and re-erected elsewhere without demolition. However, such buildings as portacabins, mobile homes and pre-fabricated buildings are capable of retaining their status as chattels.

3 Rights to remove fixtures

(a) Severance of fixtures by the owner of land

If a chattel has become a fixture it is perfectly possible for it to be severed from the land so as to regain its status as a chattel. The owner of land can clearly sever any fixtures whenever he wishes.

(b) Severance of fixtures by the vendor of land

It has already been noted that the effect of a contract to sell land is to pass the ownership of the land to the purchaser immediately.[43] From that time the vendor is

[38] *Elwes v. Maw* (1802) 3 East. 38; *R v. Otley (Inhabitants)* (1830) 1 B. & Ad. 161; *Wansbrough v. Maton* (1836) 4 Ad. & E. 884; *Wiltshear v. Cottrell* (1853) 1 E. & B. 674.
[39] [1940] 1 All E.R. 247.
[40] [1997] 2 All E.R. 513.
[41] (1872) L.R. 7 C.P. 328.
[42] *ibid.* at 519.
[43] As will be seen the ownership which passes in this situation is the equitable ownership of the land and the vendor retains the legal ownership.

only entitled to remove such fixtures as the contract entitles him to sever from the land. As has been noted a number of the cases discussed above involved claims by the purchasers of land that fixtures had been wrongly removed.[44]

(c) Severance of fixtures by a tenant of land on the termination of his lease

Where a tenant of has attached chattels to the land he is leasing so that they become fixtures, they thenceforth belong to the landlord who owns the land. However, the common law and statute have intervened so that the tenant is entitled to remove some categories of fixtures which he adds to the land, to prevent the landlord unjustifiably gaining the benefit of them. In all cases such fixtures can only be severed from the land if they can be removed without causing severe structural damage, and the severing tenant is required to make good any damage that their removal causes.

(i) Tenant's right to remove ornamental and domestic fixtures: A tenant is entitled to remove fixtures which he added to the land purely for decoration or ornament. For example in *Spyer v. Phillipson*[45] a tenant who had installed antique panelling in the room of a house to give it a Jacobean appearance was held entitled to remove it because it was only attached by screws and was readily removable.

(ii) Tenant's right to remove trade fixtures: It has long been recognised that a tenant is entitled to remove fixtures installed during the term of his lease for the purpose of carrying on his business.[46] For example, in *Smith v. City Petroleum*[47] it was held that a tenant could remove petrol pumps from the land because they were trade fixtures and could be easily removed since they were only bolted to the land. However it was held that the petrol tanks could not be removed because they had become an integral part of the land and could not easily be detached. In *Young v. Dalgety plc*[48] a tenant had installed light fittings and a carpet which had become fixtures by virtue of their attachment to the land, but the Court of Appeal held that they were trade fixtures and removable because they were attached to render the premises convenient for the tenant's business use. In *Mancetter Developments Ltd v. Garmanson Ltd*[49] it was held that a tenant was entitled to remove an extractor fan from a wall of premises used for their chemical business.

(iii) Agricultural tenant's right to remove fixtures: Historically fixtures installed by a tenant of agricultural land could not be removed because they were not categorised as "trade fixtures".[50] However statute has intervened so that an agricultural tenant is entitled to remove fixtures added during the term, either before the termination of the tenancy or within two months thereof.[51]

(iv) Duty of tenant removing fixtures to make good any damage to the land: A tenant who legitimately severs any fixtures from the land is under a duty to make good the damage that may be caused by such removal. This principle was recognised by the Court of Appeal in *Mancetter Developments Ltd v. Garmanson Ltd*[52] where the tenants

[44] For example see *Berkley v. Poulett* (1976) 241 E.G. 911 and *Hamp v. Bygrave* (1983) 266 E.G. 720.
[45] [1931] 2 Ch. 183.
[46] *Poole's Case* (1703) 1 Salk. 368.
[47] [1940] 1 All E.R. 260.
[48] [1987] 1 E.G.L.R. 116.
[49] [1986] Q.B. 1212.
[50] See: *Elwes v. Maw* (1802) 3 East 38.
[51] Agricultural Holdings Act 1986, s.10.
[52] [1986] Q.B. 1212.

who had removed the extractor fan had failed to fill in the holes left in the wall. Dillon L.J. stated:

> "The analysis of the liability at common law is, in my judgement, that the liability to make good the damage is a condition of the tenant's right to remove tenant's fixtures: therefore removal of the fixtures without making good the damage, being in excess of the tenant's right of removal, is waste, actionable in tort, just as much as removal by the tenant of a landlord's fixture which the tenant has no right to remove is waste."[53]

The tenant who fails to make good damage to the land occasioned by the legitimate removal of fixtures will therefore be liable to compensate the owner for the loss suffered. However, Dillon L.J. also noted that such things as holes left by the removal of screws or nails are *de minimis* and unlikely to be actionable, and in *Re de Falbe*[54] it was held that a tenant was not obliged to redecorate a wall after the removal of a fixture.

4 Ownership of chattels found on land

It has already been noted that items of personal property found buried in land will belong to the landowner if they are not treasure trove. The position in relation to such items found on the surface of land is different, and they do not automatically belong to the landowner. If a chattel is found on the surface of land and its original owner cannot be found and it is not treasure trove, the central question is whether it belongs to the finder or to the occupier of the land, whether the occupier be the owner, or a tenant. The principles were considered by the Court of Appeal in *Parker v. British Airways Board,*[55] where a passenger had found a gold bracelet in the executive lounge at Heathrow airport. Donaldson L.J. held that unless the finder was a trespasser, in which case the occupier of the land where the chattel was found would always have a better entitlement to it than the finder, the occupier of the land would only have a better right to the item than the finder if he had manifested a sufficient intention to exercise control over the land and anything which might be found on it. He considered that a bank would certainly exercise sufficient control over a bank vault to gain a better entitlement to a chattel found there than the finder, and that the owner of a public park clearly would not have exercised such control. However, there remains a wide area between these extremes where it is unclear whether sufficient control is exercised, for example if a chattel is found on a petrol station forecourt, the public part of a supermarket,[56] or a private front garden. Although British Airways exercised a degree of control over the airport lounge, admitting only those with appropriate business class tickets and seeking to exercise a right to refuse entry where necessary, it was held that their control was not sufficient to give a right to the found property superior to the finder who was not a trespasser. It therefore seems that only in cases where an

[53] *ibid.* at 1219.
[54] [1901] 1 Ch. 523.
[55] [1982] Q.B. 1004.
[56] See: *Bridges v. Hawkesworth* (1851) 21 L.J. Q.B. 75.

occupier of land exercises a very high degree of control over it will they gain a better entitlement to lost chattels than a finder who is legitimately present on the land. In all cases there is an obligation on the finder or occupier to take reasonable steps to return the found item to its true owner.

Chapter 3

Foundational Concepts

Feudal Beginnings

1 Ownership by the King

Modern land law has developed by a process of evolution over a period of some thousand years. The shape of the present law is far removed from that of the medieval period, but some of the fundamental concepts which make up the framework of English land law, and in particular concepts of the ownership of land, are derived from that time. It is commonly assumed today that land is "owned" by those who hold title to it. Although this may be true for all practical purposes, historically English law was founded upon the premise that all land was owned by the King.[1] His subjects were merely permitted to make use of it, holding it on the basis of some form of tenancy, either from the King directly, or indirectly through a chain of others deriving their holding ultimately from the King himself. Those who held their land directly from the King were known as tenants *in capite*. They were then able to grant what were in effect sub-tenancies of the land they themselves held, and their sub-tenants were know as *tenants in demesne*. By means of such sub-grants a feudal ladder was constructed of persons who held their land as tenants of their immediate overlord, who would in turn hold the land as tenant of their lord, until the ladder culminated in the tenants *in capite* who held directly from the King. The intermediate lords between the King and the person actually enjoying the tenure of the land were know as *mesne* lords. Crucial to an understanding of this feudal structure of land holding were the twin doctrines of tenures and estates.

2 The doctrine of tenure

(a) Meaning of tenure

Since no one within the feudal system owned land except the king, those who enjoyed its use did so only as tenants. The terms under which they enjoyed the right to a

[1] See: Pollock and Maitland, *History of English Law* (2nd ed), Vol. i, p. 237.

tenancy of the land were known as *tenure*. Tenure is therefore best understood as the terms under which a person held land as either a tenant *in capite* of the king or as the tenant *in demesne* of their immediate overlord. Generally tenure required the tenant to perform services for the king or his overlord. There were a wide variety of tenures, differing according to the nature of the services that had to be performed.

(b) Free and unfree tenures

In the system of tenure two types of tenants should be distinguished. Some tenants enjoyed tenure of land in their own right, and therefore enjoyed a place on the feudal ladder that stretched from the relatively minor and insignificant lords through the nobility to the king himself. Such persons enjoyed what is known as free tenure. However, the ordinary common people enjoyed no such place on the feudal ladder and only occupied their land on behalf of their lords, rather than in their own right, and it was the lord who was regarded by law as having the possession, technically the *seisin*, of the land. This was known as unfree tenure or villeinage. In more recent times unfree tenure was known as "copyhold tenure". Only those who enjoyed free tenure could be regarded as having an interest in land which they could transfer to others.

(c) Types of free tenure

The terms under which land was held by those enjoying free tenure varied, though they were intended to ensure that the country's military, spiritual and agricultural needs were met. The majority of those whose held their tenure directly from the king as tenants *in capite* did so on the basis of knights' service, a tenure in chivalry, which required them to provide the king with a specified number of armed horsemen for a number of days each year. This was the means by which the army was raised. Other forms of tenure included "frankalmoign" and "divine service" where the land was held in return for the performance of religious functions and "tenure in socage" where the tenant was required to perform agricultural services for his lord. From an early stage those enjoying tenure of land on the basis of knights' service were required to pay the king a sum of money, known as scutage, rather than provide actual horsemen. It is important to realise that tenure did not merely mean that the tenant was obliged to perform services for his lord, but that he also enjoyed certain privileges attached to his tenure, know as the "incidents" of tenure, which represented a valuable means of obtaining wealth from the land.

(d) Transfer of tenure: Subinfeudation and the Statute of Quia Emptores

Under a fully developed feudal system of land holding one question which arises is how a tenant can transfer his interest in land to another person. One means was by the grant of new sub-tenancies and tenure, thus adding further rungs of *mesne* lords to the feudal ladder. This process of transfer through the creation of new tenancies was known as subinfeudation, and was common until prohibited by the Statute Quia Emptores of 1290, which had the effect that only the King was entitled to grant new tenures. From that time tenure to land was transferred by the substitution of a new tenant for the old in the place that he had enjoyed on the feudal ladder. This, in essence, is the same means by which land is transferred today, where one owner (tenant) is substituted by another who takes over his tenure.

(e) Modern relevance of tenure

Although of historical importance the doctrine of tenure has virtually no practical significance in modern land law. The Tenures Abolition Act 1660 converted most free tenures into tenure in socage, so that the only remaining tenures were socage and copyhold. Copyhold tenure was finally abolished by the Law of Property Act 1922 and converted into freehold tenure in socage. Today all land is held by its owners as tenant of the Crown in socage. It no longer has any practical impact on the owner or how he can make use of his land.

3 The doctrine of estates

(a) The meaning of an estate in land

Since ultimate ownership of land remained with the king it was clear that tenants did not own the land itself. Instead what the tenant was regarded as enjoying was a right to possession, or *seisin* of the land. The common law would protect the tenant's right to seisin of the land against everyone except a person who had a better right to the land. Instead of speaking of ownership of the land the person who enjoyed the right to seisin enjoyed an estate in the land. The estate is best understood as the grant of a right of seisin, or proprietorial rights, over the land for a period of time. Whereas the doctrine of tenures refers to the terms under which a tenant enjoys his right to the land, the doctrine of estates relates to the period of time during which his rights to the land will last. Rather than owning the land itself the doctrine of estates means that a person enjoys a notional period of time in the land, during which period he is entitled to enjoy tenure of it. By means of the doctrine of estates English land law fundamentally distinguishes between the ownership of the land itself and the enjoyment of rights to use and enjoy land to the exclusion of all others. As was stated in *Walsinghams Case*[2]:

> "the land itself is one thing, and the estate in the land is another thing, for an estate in the land is a time in the land, or land for a time, and there are diversities of estates, which are no more than diversities of time . . ."

As is noted in this comment, English law recognised a number of different types of estate in land, and the key distinguishing feature between them is the period of time for which the grant of the land may be enjoyed. The relationship between the doctrines of tenures and estates was therefore that tenure represented the terms under which a person enjoyed rights to the land and the estate was the period of time for which such rights were to endure.

(b) Freehold estates in land

There were three main types of freehold estate, each of which differed in the length of time for which the grant of the land would last.

(i) Fee simple estate: The first and most important of the estates was the fee simple. This is a perpetual grant of proprietorial rights over land, meaning that the grant can never come to an end. The person who enjoys a fee simple in the land is technically a tenant *in capite* of the Crown, but since the interest can never end it is tantamount to absolute ownership of the land for all practical purposes. In *Walsingham's Case*[3] an

[2] (1573) 2 Plowd. 547 at 555.
[3] (1573) 2 Plowd. 547.

estate in fee simple was described as "a time in the land without end". The estate in fee simple may be transferred to others and on death will pass as part of the owner's estate, either by will or in the absence of a will following the rules of intestacy.

(ii) Fee-tail estate: The fee tail, or entailed estate, was a grant of land which can only pass to the lineal descendants of the original grantee. Therefore if the family to which the land was granted dies out, it will revert back to the Crown. In *Walsingham's Case* the fee tail was described as "time in the land . . . for as long as [the grantee] has issues of his body". The precise terms of the fee tail could vary, so that in some cases the land was granted only so long as the original grantee had male lineal descendants, or in some rare cases female lineal descendants. Obviously the fee tail is not as durable an interest in land as the fee simple, and therefore it is possible to convert the fee tail into a fee simple by means of "barring the entail". This may be done by the tenant in possession by will[4] or through an *inter vivos* declaration by deed that he is henceforth holding the land as a tenant in fee simple. The Trusts of Land and Appointment of Trustees Act 1996 has recently amended the law so that it is impossible to create an entailed estate. A grant of such an interest in land will instead take effect as an absolute interest under a trust of the land.[5]

(iii) Life estate: A life estate is a grant of the land for the lifetime of the grantee only, and it automatically comes to an end on his death. The life interest is transferrable, but the estate will still come to an end on the death of the original grantee and not on the death of the transferee. In the modern law a life estate can only take effect behind a trust of the land.[6]

(c) Flexibility of land ownership through estates

The concept of the estate has enabled English law to develop a complex and flexible means of land ownership, since a person does not own the land itself, but an abstract estate in the land. It is possible for a lesser estate to be carved out of a greater estate. For example, a person holding an estate in fee simple of the land can grant a life interest out of his estate to another. The holder of the life interest will then be entitled to enjoy immediate possession and use of the land for the period of his life, at which point the holder of the fee simple will be entitled to enjoy his full unencumbered rights over the land again. Thus a number of people may enjoy different rights in the same piece of land at the same time, and different people may be regarded as "owners" of the same piece of land at the same time because the nature of their "ownership" varies. As between themselves the rights of such "owners" will depend upon who has the better right to immediate possession of the land, and their relationship *inter se* will be regulated by the incidents of their various rights of ownership.

(d) Leasehold estates in land

As well as the freehold estates in land English law also recognised leasehold estates, which are created by leases. Historically leasehold estates were not regarded as items of real property but as personal proprietary interests where the freehold owner of land had granted a tenant a right to occupy the land for a period of time, usually in return

[4] Law of Property Act 1925, s.176.
[5] Sched. 1, para. 5(1).
[6] See Chap. 9.

for the payment of rent. The leasehold estate therefore enables a separation between the ownership of the land and its use, since the landlord remains the true owner whilst the tenant under the lease is entitled to the exclusive use of the land. In the modern law leases, which take a very wide range of forms and lengths, provide an important means of enjoying interests in land, and in the case of very long leases are almost equivalent to actual ownership.

COMMON LAW AND EQUITY[7]

1 Introduction

Another important factor which underpins much of the language used to describe rights and interests in land is the distinction between Common Law and Equity. Due to historical factors English Law developed two completely separate jurisprudential systems, each of which recognised its own body of rights and interests, enforced and protected in its own courts. One body of law was the Common Law, which was administered by the common law courts and the other was Equity, which was administered by the Courts of Chancery.

2 The Common Law

The Common law was the system of justice which emerged after the Norman Conquest and was administered by the Royal Courts. By 1234 the origins of the two common law courts, the Court of Common Pleas and the King's Bench had emerged. The common law courts naturally applied the common law and protected the interests in land which it recognised. However, the common law system was subject to a number of important defects. First, in order to start an action it was necessary to obtain a writ. As a consequence of the Provisions of Oxford in 1258 it was no longer possible for the courts to create new writs, and therefore actions had to be brought within the narrow range of writs that were available. The common law also had a limited variety of remedies available.

3 The development of equity

(a) Motivations for the development of equity

Equity was a parallel system of law which developed initially to remedy the defects of the common law system. The equity jurisdiction had its origins in appeals by aggrieved parties directly to the King, and the delegation of this appellate role to the King's Council and ultimately to the Chancellor acting in his own right. The Court of Chancery developed as a court of "conscience" where justice would be done between the parties. Actions were started by means of a simple *subpoena* which avoided the

[7] See: Holdsworth, *A History of English Law* (7th ed, 1956), Vol. 1, Chap. V; J. H. Baker, *An Introduction to English Legal History*, (2nd ed., 1979), Chap. 6.

need for a writ. Although the Chancery Court initially operated as a court of conscience over a period of time Equity began to develop its own body of rights, rules and principles which it would enforce. Its relationship with the common law was a matter of ongoing argument, which was finally settled in 1616 when James I ordered that the Chancery courts were entitled to grant "common injunctions" which had the effect of restraining a person from pursuing an action at common law or from enforcing a judgment which had been given by the common law courts. This had the practical effect of enabling the Chancery Court to establish its primacy over the common law and thus to achieve the supremacy of Equity.

(b) Equity prior to the Judicature Acts

By the middle of the nineteenth century Equity was an established body of law recognising and protecting its own rights and interests in property, including interests in land. There were in effect two separate court systems operating side by side, the common law courts where a plaintiff could obtain remedies to enforce his common law rights and the Chancery Courts, where a plaintiff could enforce his rights in equity. It was not possible to obtain equitable relief in a common law court, nor common law remedies in the Court of Chancery. In order to overcome the administrative difficulties of having two parallel systems of law administered by different courts the structure of the English legal system was radically reshaped by the Judicature Acts of 1873 and 1875.

(c) Effect of the Judicature Acts

The central effect of the Judicature Acts was to create a single Supreme Court from the common law and Chancery courts, where the judges possessed both common law and equitable jurisdiction.[8] This Supreme Court comprises the High Court and the Court of Appeal, and although the court is organised into divisions, such as the Queen's Bench and Chancery Division, these are divisions of administrative convenience rather than of jurisdiction. The amalgamation of the courts meant that it was no longer necessary to start separate actions in separate courts to obtain both common law and equitable relief. The Act also incorporated the supremacy of equity in section 25 of the Judicature Act 1873, which provided that in matters where there was a conflict between the rules of equity and the rules of the common law the rules of equity were to prevail.[9] It has long been a question of debate whether the Judicature Acts brought about a fusion of the common law and equity into a single body of law, or whether there was merely a fusion of administration, so that they remained essentially separate systems, but administered by the same court. Although the traditional view has been that there was merely a fusion of administration, well expressed by Ashburner's famous fluvial metaphor that "the two streams of jurisprudence, though they run in the same channel, run side by side and do not mingle their waters," more recent cases take the view that there has been a substantive fusion to produce a single body of law.[10] This does not mean that as labels the distinction between legal and

[8] Judicature Act 1873, s.24; See now Supreme Court Act 1981, s.49(1).

[9] See: *Walsh v. Lonsdale* (1882) 21 Ch.D. 9; *United Scientific Holding v. Burnley B.C.* [1978] A.C. 904.

[10] See: *United Scientific Holdings Ltd v. Burnley Borough Council* [1978] A.C. 904; *Aquaculture Corp v. New Zealand Green Mussel Co. Ltd* [1990] 3 N.Z.L.R. 299; *Canson Enterprises Ltd v. Broughton & Co.* (1993) 85 D.L.R. (4th) 129; *Tinsley v. Milligan* [1993] 3 All E.R. 65.

equitable rights and interests in land are unimportant, and it may still be essential to distinguish between them since their character may determine whether such rights are binding upon a particular person claiming interests in the land to which they relate.

THE DEVELOPMENT OF THE TRUST

1 The nature of a trust

One of the most important creations of equity is the trust. This is best defined as a means by which property may be held by one person for the benefit of another. For example, if a famous pop star wants to purchase a house in a village without it being known that he is the owner, he may wish someone else to appear to be the owner. He may ask his friend to purchase the house with money that he provides. Here the friend will appear from the legal documents to be the owner of the house, but the reality behind that "front" is that the pop star is the true owner. The friend cannot treat the house as if it were his own property but must instead treat it as the property of the star. As the paper owner he will have the power to deal with the property, but he must do so not in his own interests but on behalf of the star. The essence of a trust is therefore a separation of the ownership of property into two distinct types, namely the legal ownership and the equitable or beneficial ownership. The legal ownership is the ownership which would have been recognised by the common law, and the legal owners are the trustees of the property. This means that they have all the powers over the property that are the proper incidents of legal ownership, including the power to transfer title to the property. However, although they hold these powers by virtue of their ownership, they are not entitled to use them for their own advantage, since the persons who are the "real" owners of the trust property are the beneficiaries. The trustees must always act in the interests of the beneficiaries, and if they fail to do so the beneficiaries will be entitled to remedies against them for breach of trust. The beneficiaries are regarded as the owners of the property held on trust for them and under the rule in *Saunders v. Vautier*[11] are entitled to demand that the trustees transfer the legal title to them, provided that they are unanimous in their demand and are all of age and legally competent. Trusts may be created of all types of property, personal property, intellectual property and land, and they provide a vital means of facilitating flexible arrangements for the ownership and management of property. The nature of a trust is well illustrated by the facts of *Tinsley v. Milligan*.[12] A house was purchased by a lesbian couple who both contributed equally to the purchase price. The house was purchased in the name of Tinsley alone, so that she was the sole legal owner, with the object of ensuring that Milligan would appear to be a lodger in the house to enable her to continue claiming housing benefit from the department of social security. However, the consequence of her contribution to the purchase price was to give rise to a special type of trust called a resulting trust. In consequence although Tinsley was the sole legal owner she held the house as trustee on trust for herself and Milligan in equal shares. Therefore Milligan enjoyed a beneficial interest in a half share of the property.

[11] (1841) 4 Beav. 115.
[12] [1993] 3 All E.R. 65.

2 The importance of trusts to the ownership of land

Although trusts may be created over any type of property, they form a vital aspect of modern land law. For reasons which will be explained more fully in Chapter 7 every situation where there is co-ownership of land will take place behind a trust of land, as do life interests and other successive interests.[13] Only where land is owned by a single absolute owner for his own sole benefit will the land be free from the existence of a trust.

3 Historical origins of the trust

(a) The development of the "use"

The modern concept of the trust began with the development of the "use" in the medieval period to avoid some of the difficulties associated with the feudal system of landholding. It was common for land to be conveyed to X "to the use of Y" so that X was not to enjoy the property for his own benefit but was to apply it for the benefit of Y. X was known as the *feoffee* and Y as the *cestui que use*. The legal ownership of the land was vested in the feoffee. One advantage of the use included the ability to give property to religious orders that were prevented from owning property, such as the order of St Francis. More importantly, they enabled a landowner to avoid the strict rules of inheritance by enabling them to direct the feoffees by will how the property should be held on their death, and to avoid the payment of feudal dues payable on inheritance by ensuring that the land was perpetually held by a group of feoffees, so that there was no succession to the legal title. The death of the *cestui que use* did not require the payment of such dues. A use was also a means of avoiding forfeiture of land to the Crown if the tenant committed high treason. The use was not recognised by the common law but they were enforced by the Chancellor who would act against feoffees who did not observe the rights and interests of the *cestui que use*. The development of the use therefore marked the beginning of the distinction between legal and equitable ownership.

(b) Statute of Uses 1535

The development of the use was so successful that by 1500 the majority of land was held in use, with consequent detrimental effects on the revenue of the Crown through the avoidance of the feudal dues. To reverse this reduction in revenue the King attempted to abolish the use by legislation by the Statute of Uses 1535, which had the effect of executing the use by statutorily vesting legal ownership in the *cestui que use*, thus bringing it to an end. However, the statute did not abolish all uses, and those where the feoffees had active duties to perform, for example the collection and distribution of profits and the management of an estate, were excluded. The effects of the statute could also be avoided by means of a "use upon a use", where property was conveyed "to X to the use of Y, to the use of Z." The Statute of Uses only executed the first use, and equity was prepared to accept that Y was holding the land to the use of Z. Recognition of the second use had originally been rejected by both the common

[13] See Chap. 8.

law[14] and equity, but by the later part of the sixteenth century the "use upon the use" was recognised in equity in order to give effect to the transferor's intentions.[15] This second use was referred to as a "trust", which is the origin of the modern terminology.[16] A simple conveyance of land "upon trust" was effective to create a trust of the land without any mention of the first use, under which the trustee received the legal title to the land and the beneficiary enjoyed the equitable ownership.

4 Legal and equitable ownership compared

By means of the trust English law has developed a system of dual ownership of property, including land. It is important to recognise that the beneficiary of a trust of land is in a real sense an owner of it. There has been some debate as to whether the interest of a beneficiary is to be regarded as a proprietary interest *in rem* or a personal interest *in personam*. Those who have argued that the beneficial interest is a right in personam have done so on the grounds that, as with all equitable rights, it was enforced *in personam*[17] by the Chancery Court ordering the trustee to observe the trust and that it was liable to be defeated by the interest of a person who purchased the legal title from the trustees bona fides without notice of the existence of the trust, at which point the beneficiary would be restricted to his remedies against the trustee for breach of trust. This was a consequence of the operation of the doctrine of notice which will be considered more fully below. In *Webb v. Webb*[18] the Court of Justice of the European Community held that for the purposes of jurisdiction under the Convention on Jurisdiction and the Enforcement of Judgements a father's claim that his son held an apartment in France on resulting trust for him was an issue *in personam* and not an issue *in rem* to immoveable property, which would have meant that the French courts had exclusive jurisdiction over the proceedings. However, it is inappropriate to draw conclusions as to the characterisation of an issue in domestic law from characterisation of the nature of the claim for the purposes of private international law, where English concepts of property have to interact with those of civilian systems of law.[19] The better view seems to be that the rights of the beneficiary of a trust, including a trust of land, should be regarded as proprietary rights, although of a special character. As Lord Browne-Wilkinson observed in *Tinsley v. Milligan*[20]:

> "Although for historical reasons legal estates and equitable estates have differing incidents, the person owning either type of estate has a right of property, a right in rem and not merely a right *in personam*."

The reality of the proprietary status of the equitable interest is evidenced by the fact that the beneficiary can deal with it in much the same way as he could deal with other

[14] *Jane Tyrrel's Case* (1557) 2 Dyer 155a.
[15] See for example, *Sambach v. Dalston* (1635) Toth. 188.
[16] Although the term trust had also been used for a single use prior to the development of the "use upon a use.
[17] It is one of the maxims of equity that "equity acts *in personam*".
[18] [1994] 3 All E.R. 911.
[19] Civilian systems tend to differentiate between moveable and immoveable property, unlike English law which differentiates between real and personal property.
[20] [1993] 3 All E.R. 65 at 86.

property. It is an asset which he can transfer to others, provided that the appropriate formalities required by the Law of Property Act 1925, s.53(1)(c), namely that the disposition of the subsisting equitable interest is made in writing signed by the person disposing of it, are satisfied. He can dispose of it by will, or in the event of his intestacy it will devolve to his heirs. He can use his interest as security for a loan, and he may incur tax upon its value. With the exception of a purchaser protected by the doctrine of notice the equitable interest behind a trust is capable of enduring through changes in the legal ownership of the property. However, the beneficiary clearly cannot transfer a title better than that which he himself enjoys, so that he is not able to transfer the full legal title to the land. Equitable ownership behind a trust is also, as has been noted above, less durable than legal ownership, since it is liable to be defeated by the rights of a person who acquires the legal title bona fides without notice of its existence.

5 The creation of trusts of land

There are three main ways that a trust of land may come into being. These will be examined in detail in Chapter 6, but here an outline is provided.

(a) Express trusts

As the name suggests, express trusts are those which are created by the deliberate acts of the legal owner of the land. He may either declare himself to be a trustee in favour of the beneficiary, at which point he will retain the legal title himself but only in the capacity as trustee for the beneficiary, or alternatively he may transfers the land to a person who has agreed to take it as trustee. According to the Law of Property Act 1925, s.53(1)(b) an *inter vivos* declaration of trust of land must be evidenced by writing, signed by the person creating the trust or his agent.

(b) Resulting trusts

Resulting trusts are trusts which arise automatically in certain circumstances. The most important situation is where one person has contributed to the price of land purchased in the name of another. This was the case in *Tinsley v. Milligan*[21] noted above. By Law of Property Act 1925, s.53(2) there are no formal requirements for the creation of resulting trusts. Under a resulting trust of land the equitable ownership of land will be held in the same proportions as the contributions that have been made to the purchase price.

(c) Constructive trusts

Constructive trusts are trusts which arise as a result of the conduct of the parties. The principles were laid down by the House of Lords in *Lloyd's Bank plc v. Rosset*,[22] namely that where the legal ownership of land is held in the name of one person, but there was a common intention[23] that someone else was to enjoy a share of the ownership a constructive trust will arise if the person claiming a share had acted to their detriment on the basis of the common intention. Again by virtue of the Law of Property Act

[21] [1993] 3 All E.R. 65.
[22] [1991] 1 A.C. 107.
[23] The common intention may be express or implied from the facts of the parties dealings with each other.

1925, s.53(2) there is no necessity for writing. The parties respective shares of the equitable ownership will be determined in accordance with their common intention.

LEGAL AND EQUITABLE RIGHTS AND INTERESTS IN LAND

1 Subsidiary rights and interests in land

Although ownership, whether legal or equitable under a trust, is the most important right that a person may enjoy over land there are many other lesser interests or rights in land which a person may enjoy. For example, a person may have a right of way to cross another's land, which right is known as an easement. A person may have borrowed money on the security of his land by means of a mortgage, or he may have granted a tenant a lease of his land. Many of these subsidiary rights or interests in land may exist with either legal or equitable status. Lord Browne-Wilkinson's statement in *Tinsley v. Milligan*[24] that English law "has one single law of property made up of legal and equitable interests" is an appropriate description.

2 The origin of equitable interests in land

Common law rights and interests in land were those which were historically recognised and enforced by the common law courts prior to the Judicature Acts. Equitable rights and interest were those which were recognised and enforced by the Chancery Courts. One of the main examples of circumstances in which an equitable right arose is where there was a contract to create a legal right but the necessary formalities had not been observed, generally because no deed had been executed. However, equity, following the maxim that "equity treats as done that which ought to be done", was willing to treat a specifically enforceable contract to create an interest in land as effective to create an equitable interest on equivalent terms to those agreed in the contract. The operation of this principle can be illustrated from the facts of *Walsh v. Lonsdale*.[25] The defendant had entered into a contract to grant the plaintiff a lease of his land under the terms of which the rent was to be payable yearly in advance. No lease was ever granted by the defendant by means of a deed, so that there was no legal lease. However, since there was a valid and enforceable contract, it was held that there was an equitable lease on the same terms as the contract, namely requiring the rent to be paid in advance. The operation of this principle that equitable rights are generated on the basis of contract where the requisite common law formalities have not been observed is also applicable to easements and mortgages.

3 The modern distinction between legal and equitable estates and interests in land

Today the question whether estates and interests in land are legal or equitable in character is not determined by their historical origins, but is fixed by means of the

[24] [1993] 3 All E.R. 65 at 86.
[25] (1882) 21 Ch.D. 9.

statutory definition of the Law of Property Act 1925 section 1. This section outlines the categories of estates and interests which are capable of assuming legal character, and by a process of elimination all other estates and interests are deemed equitable. A fuller consideration of this section and its effects is given below, but it is to be noted that although an interest may be capable of enjoying legal status whether it is in fact legal will often depend on whether the appropriate formalities have been followed for its creation.

HISTORIC RULES GOVERNING PRIORITY OF LEGAL AND EQUITABLE RIGHTS

1 The problem of priority and interests in land

One of the central issues with which land law has to grapple is the problem of determining priorities between competing interests in land. This difficulty arises in particular where a person purchases land and there are third parties who held interests in it prior to the purchase. Is the purchaser to be bound by those pre-existing third party interests? For example, imagine a situation where Mark is the legal owner of a house. He may have granted Norma a three year lease of the house so that she could live there while she studies at a local university. Owen may enjoy a right of way across the drive of the house so that he can have access to his own garage. Penelope, who owns land at the back of the house, may enjoy the benefit of a restrictive covenant entered by Mark agreeing that he will not use his land for business purposes. Mark may have declared himself a trustee of a half share of the house in favour of his girlfriend Roberta. In this situation Norma, Owen, Penelope and Roberta all have proprietary interests in the house owned by Mark. No doubt their interests are valid and enforceable against him but the question arises as to what happens if he decides to sell the house to Stephanie. When the house is transferred into her name is she still bound to observe their interests? This will depend upon whether their interests have priority over the interest in the house she has acquired. If they do, then she will be bound by them. If not she will take the land free from them. The same question would arise if, for example, instead of selling the house to Stephanie Mark merely transferred it to her as a gift, or alternatively if he decided to grant a mortgage over the house to Floyd's Bank to secure a loan.

2 Rules of priority governing legal rights

In relation to legal rights the priority rule was simply that they were indefeasible, expressed in the maxim that "legal rights bind the world." A legal right would always gain priority over any subsequent rights acquired in the land, whether legal or equitable. To return to the example cited above, if Mark owned the fee simple of a house and had granted Norma a legal lease for three years and then sold the house to Stephanie, Stephanie would be bound by Norma's lease because it was a legal interest and gained priority over Stephanie's subsequent acquisition of the house. Legal interests were not, therefore, defeated by changes in the ownership of the land or by the acquisition of other interests. If Mark had granted a legal mortgage to Floyd's Bank they would take their security subject to Norma's legal lease and would not gain priority over it. Whether the person acquiring the subsequent interest in the house knew about the subsisting legal interest was irrelevant. They would be bound by it even if they had no idea that it existed.

3 Rules of priority governing equitable rights

(a) The doctrine of notice

As has been noted above in the context of the difference between legal ownership and equitable ownership under a trust, equitable interests were not so durable as legal interests and did not bind the world automatically. As between themselves, priority to equitable interests was governed by the order of their creation, so that pre-existing equitable interests took priority to those which were created subsequent to them. However, in relation to legal interests it was not necessarily the case that a pre-existing equitable interest would have priority over a subsequently created legal interest. In a sense legal interests had the ability to operate as "trump" cards which could defeat pre-existing equitable interests. However, it was not inevitable that they would do so. The principle, known as the doctrine of notice, was that equitable interests took priority to all subsequently created interests except those of a person who had purchased a legal estate in the land bona fides for valuable consideration without notice of the existence of the equitable interest. The element of notice is the most significant, and means that if in the circumstance the purchaser knew, or should have known of the existence of the equitable interest he cannot acquire his legal estate free from it. He knew what he was getting. Returning to the example above, if Norma enjoyed only an equitable lease then Stephanie would take free from it only if she was a bona fide purchaser of a legal estate without notice.

(b) Requirements of the doctrine of notice

For a person to take free from equitable interests they must have fallen within the scope of the doctrine of notice. The constituent elements can be examined individually.
(i) Bona fides: This amounts to a general requirement that the person claiming to take advantage of the doctrine of notice must have acted in good faith, and it adds little in substance to the requirements.
(ii) Purchaser of a legal estate: Only a person who has purchased a legal estate in the land can take advantage of the doctrine of notice. The modern definition of a legal estate will be considered below.
(iii) Purchaser for value: A person will only obtain the protection of the doctrine of notice if they have purchased a legal estate in return for valuable consideration. This means consideration which is recognised by equity and includes marriage consideration but not nominal consideration. The donee of a gift of land will not therefore obtain the protection of the doctrine of notice, nor will a person who inherits the land on the death of the owner. In *Midland Bank Trust Co v. Green*[26] the House of Lords held that the requirement that consideration must be valuable did not mean that it had to be

[26] [1981] A.C. 517.

adequate, so that a payment of £500 to purchase a legal estate in farmland which was worth hundreds of times more was still treated as "valuable consideration."

(iv) Without notice: The most important element of the doctrine of notice is that the purchaser of the legal estate must have no notice (sometimes referred to as "knowledge") of the existence of the equitable right. The foundation of this principle is that if the purchaser knows of the equitable interest their conscience is affected and they should not have gone ahead with the purchase if they had not wanted to be bound by the interest. However, if they did not know that it existed their conscience was not affected and there is no reason why they should be bound by it. Notice comprises three different types of knowledge, which are referred to in the Law of Property Act 1925, s.199(1). "Actual knowledge" means knowledge that the purchaser actually has of the interest. He is consciously aware of its existence. "Constructive knowledge" is knowledge which the purchaser does not consciously have but which he would have had if he had taken all the steps to make "such inquiries and inspections . . . as ought reasonably to have been made by him." This imposes an objective standard so that the purchaser cannot avoid knowledge by failing to do what a reasonable man would have done. "Imputed knowledge" means that the purchaser is imputed with the knowledge of his agent, whether that knowledge was actual or constructive. This prevents the purchaser from denying knowledge on the grounds that his agent knew of the interest but he did not. The most important in practice is often constructive notice. A person proposing to purchase land is expected to make a reasonable inspection of the land itself and will therefore have constructive notice of everything that would have come to light from such an inspection. However, a person claiming that another is bound by his equitable interest by reason of constructive notice may be estopped from so relying if he deliberately withheld information about his interest, as was held in *Midland Bank v. Farm Pride Hatcheries Ltd.*[27]

(c) Effects of the doctrine of notice on equitable interests

Where an equitable interest is defeated by application of the doctrine of notice the interest is completely destroyed and is not resurrected even if the land is subsequently purchased by someone who had actual notice of its existence.[28] To return to the example outlined above, if Norma enjoyed an equitable lease over Mark's house and Stephanie was a bona fide purchaser for value without notice of a legal estate in the house then the consequence would be that Stephanie would take the house free from Norma's equitable interest. That equitable interest would therefore be destroyed and if Stephanie subsequently sold the house to Timothy it would not revive to bind him even, even though he had actual knowledge that Norma's had enjoyed an equitable lease.

OUTLINE OF THE PROPERTY LEGISLATION OF 1925

1 Objectives of the reform

As has been seen the system of land law in place before the intervention of statutory reform was characterised by the existence of legal and equitable estates and interests in

[27] (1981) 260 E.G. 495.
[28] See, for example, *Wilkes v. Spooner* [1911] 2 K.B. 473.

land and issues of priority were governed by the doctrine of notice. The reform of the law of property, which culminated in the legislation of 1925, was intended to reshape the system so that unnecessary complications and difficulties were removed, through the establishment of a central, state-maintained, Land Registry, which would govern the ownership and transfer of land and replace the doctrine of notice as a means of determining issues of priority.

2 Facilitating the transfer of land

One of the prime objectives was to reduce the difficulties encountered in the transfer of land through the existence of a multiplicity of legal estates and the doctrine of notice, thus making conveyancing a simpler and safer process. In order to achieve this end the legislation introduced a number of key reforms.

(a) Reduction in the number of legal estates

By section 1(1) of the Law of Property Act 1925 the number of legal estates that could exist in land was reduced to two, the fee simple absolute in possession and the term of years absolute.

(b) Maximum number of trustees of the legal title

Since it is the legal owners of the land who are capable of transferring the title to effect a transfer of the land, the Trustee Act 1925, s.34(2) had the effect that there could be a maximum of only four co-owners of the legal title to land. Although this did not limit the number of co-owners that could share entitlement to it in equity through the mechanism of a trust, it did have the effect of making a transfer of the land less complicated since a potential transferee would only have to deal with a limited number of legal owners.

(c) Title to be constituted by registration

The ultimate object of the legislation was to introduce a universal system of land registration under the Land Registration Act 1925, whereby title to land would be constituted by being registered as the owner by a central land registry. Therefore anyone who needed to establish the identity of the legal owners of the land could find out by simply looking at the register. The two legal estates defined in the Law of Property Act 1925, s.1(1) form the foundations of the system since they constitute the interests (known as titles) which must be registered as distinct entries on the register.

(d) Equitable trust interests to be kept off the register

A further objective was that whereas the legal ownership of land was to be constituted by means of a register, equitable trust interests in the land were not to form a part of the register so that a potential transferee did not need to concern himself about their possible existence. This was to be achieved through the mechanism of overreaching, which was a statutory means by which any equitable trust interests in land were to be converted into trust interests in the same proportions in the purchase money that a transferee of the land paid to the legal owners. This would mean that provided the purchase moneys were paid the purchaser would know that he took the land free from any existing trust interests affecting it, even if he had notice of their existence. The statutory conditions for overreaching was that the purchase moneys must be paid to at least two trustees. This means that the only circumstance in which a purchaser could not be guaranteed of taking the land free from any equitable trust interests was if he purchased it from a sole legal owner, in which case he would have to be more careful to make sure that there were no such adverse interests that would bind him. If a beneficiary's trust interest was overreached, their remedies would lie not against the purchaser but against the legal owners of the land who had acted as trustees for them.

3 Providing protection for third party interests

The creation of a system of land registration was not merely intended to facilitate simpler conveyancing, but also to provide a mechanism by which third party subsidiary rights and interests in land could be protected. The essence of the system of registration is that third party rights can be protected on the Land Register against the title of the land to which they relate. A person who is contemplating a purchase of the land will be able to find out if there are any adverse interests affecting it by simply looking at the register, a process known as a search. Rather than being governed by the doctrine of notice the purchaser would only be bound by those interests which were properly protected by means of an entry on the register, irrespective of whether he knew of them or not. As was recognised by the House of Lords in *Midland Bank Trust Co v. Green*[29] this system firmly places the burden of protecting interests in land on those who hold them. It is their responsibility to ensure that they are properly protected by registration and they take the risk that they will loose priority to a subsequent purchaser if they have failed to do so. However, this general rule is subject to the exception that certain interests in land, which are known as overriding interests and are defined by statute,[30] are binding on a person who purchases the land even though they do not appear on the register. The presence of such overriding interests has proved one of the most important and controversial aspects of the scheme of land registration. In the registered land system there is no continuing place for the doctrine of notice.

4 A temporary reprieve for the doctrine of notice

(a) Unregistered land

Although the ultimate intention of the legislation of 1925 was to introduce a universal scheme of registration replacing the doctrine of notice, it was obviously not possible for this to be introduced overnight. Therefore the system was introduced gradually by designating geographical areas to be areas of compulsory registration, with the consequence that the land would have to be registered when next transferred. By this means a piece meal process or registration was set in motion. The legislators anticipated in 1925 that full registration would take some thirty years, although it was not until the Registration of Title Order 1989[31] that the whole of England and Wales

[29] [1981] A.C. 513.
[30] Law of Property Act 1925, s.70(1).
[31] S.I. 1989 No. 1347.

was finally designated an area of compulsory registration. To ameliorate for the problems of an interim period the original legislation made provision for a special regime for land that had not yet been registered. Such land is known as unregistered land, and although many of the reforms outlined above, for example the limitation of the maximum number of legal owners and the principles of overreaching, apply to it there was no system of registration of legal ownership and no generalised scheme of registration for the protection of third party interests.

(b) A limited scheme of registration for some third party interests in land

Although there was no universal scheme of registration for unregistered land, the legislation did introduce a limited scheme for the registration of the most important types of interest in the Land Charges Act 1925.[32] In a sense therefore, unregistered land may be regarded as a form of semi-registered land. For those interests designated land charges by the Land Charges Act the doctrine of notice has been replaced by registration, so that a purchaser of the land will only be bound by those land charges which have been properly registered. Unlike the full system of land registration where third party interests in the land are protected against the title of the land to which they relate, land charges are protected on the separately maintained Land Charges Register against the name of the estate owner of the land which they affect. The names based nature of this register has been the cause of difficulties which have arisen because the interim system was only intended to have a limited life span.

(c) Survival of the doctrine of notice

Interests which do not fall within the categories of statutory land charges are not registrable, and continue to be governed by the doctrine of notice, which therefore retains some residual significance in English land law. The doctrine of notice governed the issues of priority over a wife's equitable trust interest in unregistered land in *Kingsnorth Finance Co. Ltd v. Tizard*[33] and to an estoppel easement in *E R Ives Investments Ltd v. High*.[34]

DISTINGUISHING BETWEEN LEGAL AND EQUITABLE ESTATES AND INTERESTS IN LAND

1 Section 1 of the Law of Property Act 1925

As has already been noted, the Law of Property Act 1925, s.1 defined which estates and interests in land are capable of enjoying legal character. Section 1(1) defines the only two estates which are "capable of subsisting or of being conveyed or created at law" and section 1(2) the five legal interests and charges, of which only three are of any practical significance. By means of a definition by exclusion in section 1(3) all other estates, interests and charges in land "take effect merely as equitable interests."

[32] Now replaced by the Land Charges Act 1972.
[33] [1986] 1 W.L.R. 783.
[34] [1967] 2 Q.B. 379.

2 Legal estates

(a) Fee simple absolute in possession

In section 1(1)(a) the first of the two legal estates is "an estate in fee simple absolute in possession." This is a freehold estate and as has been noted above it is an estate which has perpetual duration. The limitation that the estate must be "absolute" is intended to differentiate it from conditional and determinable fee simples, and the requirement that it must be in possession is intended to distinguish reversionary or remainder interests. These distinctions will be will be considered in detail in Chapter 4.

(b) Term of years absolute

Section 1(1)(b) states that the second of the legal estates is the term of years absolute. This is a lease, and therefore it constitutes the legal leasehold estate in land. The nature of leasehold interests will be considered in detail in Chapter 5.

3 Legal interests and charges

(a) Easements

By section 1(2)(a) easements which are granted for a period equivalent to the duration of either of the two legal estates is capable of being a legal easement. This means, for example, that a right of way will only be capable of legal status if it is granted perpetually for a specified period of time. A grant of an easement for life would not qualify for legal status. Whether an easement is in fact legal will also be dependent upon the manner of its creation. Easements are examined in detail in Chapter 9.

(b) Rentcharges

A rentcharge is a entitlement to be paid a periodic sum by the owner of a piece of land, which is neither the rent payable under a lease nor payments due under a mortgage. In common with easements they are only capable of attaining legal status if created for a period equivalent to either of the two legal estates. Rentcharges are of limited significance since the Rentcharges Act 1977 prohibits the creation of new rent charges and those existing as of the date of the act will ultimately be extinguished.

(c) Charges by way of legal mortgage

Where a mortgage, which is a security interest over land, is created in the appropriate form as a charge by way of legal mortgage, it is capable of existing as a legal interest. Mortgages are considered in detail in Chapter 11.

(d) Miscellaneous charges

Section 1(2)(d) provides that similarly charges to those by way of legal mortgage which are "not created by an instrument" are also capable of legal status. This category contained predominantly statutory charges and is now of limited significance.

(e) Rights of entry

Rights of entry are the means by which a lease is forfeited if the tenant is in breach of its terms. An estate may also be forfeited if the terms of a rentcharge to which it is subject have been broken. The legal quality of a right of entry is dependant upon the legal quality of the lease or rentcharge to which it relates.

Part II

The Ownership of Land

Chapter 4

FREEHOLD OWNERSHIP OF LAND

THE IMPORTANCE OF FREEHOLD OWNERSHIP

Freehold equivalent to ownership

The most important interest in land which can be held by a person is the freehold. This is the interest which is tantamount to the actual ownership of the land. Although such ownership prima facie carries with it the right of the freeholder to do whatever he wants with his land, in reality his freedom is circumscribed by state intervention. It has been seen in the previous chapter that the ownership of certain valuable minerals in his land is vested in the Crown. More significantly his ability to develop and build on his land, and the use to which he may put it, are regulated by planning controls.

2 The relationship between the freehold and other rights and interests in land

The freehold interest is also the most fundamental interest in land since all other lesser rights and interests in the land are derived from it. For example, where a lease has been granted of land the leasehold interest is simply carved out from the landlords freehold interest. Similarly, where there is a trust of land, the equitable interest is enjoyed by the beneficiaries of the trust but the freehold is generally held by the trustees. It follows that the freehold interest in every piece of land will be held by someone, although that person's rights will be qualified to the extent that third parties enjoy interests in that land which detract from his right to enjoy the freehold for himself.

THE FREEHOLD AS A LEGAL ESTATE IN LAND

1 Law of Property Act 1925

As a consequence of the Law of Property Act 1925 the freehold ownership in land is capable of exisiting as a legal estate. Section 1(1)(a) provides that "an estate in fee simple absolute in possession" is "capable of subsisting or of being conveyed or created at law." The purpose of this definition is to differentiate freehold estates which are capable of attaining legal status from those which are not. If a fee simple estate fails to satisfy all three requirements it cannot take effect as a legal estate but only as an equitable interest behind a trust.

2 "Fee simple"

As was noted in Chapter 3 the fee simple is one of the estates in land which was recognised in English law. The essence of the fee simple is that it is a perpetual grant of the land which cannot be brought to an end, in contrast to the estate in fee tail and the life interest.

3 "Absolute"[1]

(a) Meaning of the requirement

The requirement in section 1(1)(a) that a freehold interest in land must be absolute in order to enjoy legal status is intended to exclude all grants of a fee simple estate where there is some possibility that the grant may fail in the future. This will generally be the case if the owner of a fee simple has transferred it to another person subject to a condition, so that in the event of the condition occurring the estate would revert back to him. In this way he has not fully divested himself of all his interests in the land, since there is a possibility that it will revert to him if the condition occurs, and the recipient cannot be said to enjoy an unqualified perpetual entitlement to the land. The requirement that the fee simple be absolute would be expected to exclude conditional and determinable fee simples from the class of legal estates. However, it should be noted that legislation intervenes to accord legal status to many conditional fee simples, so that generally only determinable fee simples are incapable of enjoying legal status.

(b) Conditional fee simple

(i) Defintion: A conditional fee simple will arise whenever a fee simple is transferred subject to the provision that it will fail on the happening of a condition subsequent.[2] For example, the freehold owner of land may transfer it to his mistress "as long as she does not marry"; to his son "unless he becomes a Roman Catholic;" or to to his daughter "provided that she does not become a doctor."

(ii) Effect of the occurrence of the condition subsequent: If the conditon occurs this does not have the effect of revesting the land automatically back into the hands of the grantor, thus leaving the grantee with not interest. Instead, the occurence of the condition gives the grantor the right to terminate the interest by "re-entering" the land.[3]

(iii) Void conditions: Although generally the grantor of land is free to restrict a grant of land with whatever conditions he chooses, the law has always intervened to strike

[1] See: Cheshire & Burn, *Modern Law of Real Property* (14th ed.), Chap. 15; Pearce & Stevens, *The Law of Trusts and Equitable Obligations*, (1995), pp. 272–276.

[2] In the case of a condition precedent the interest will not take effect until the condition is satisfied.

[3] See Challis's *Real Property*, (3rd ed., 1911), pp. 219, 261.

out conditions which are regarded as contrary to public policy. The reason for this is that the impositon of a condition is a powerful means of exercising control over the behaviour of the grantee, since he will not wish to lose his interest in the land. The law has always regarded as void conditions which impose a complete restriction on the ability of the grantee to sell or transfer the land to others.[4] Technically such conditions are said to restrict his ability to alienate the land. In *Re Brown*,[5] a father left his freehold interest in land by will to his four sons subject to the condition that they were only to alienate their shares to each other. Harman J. held that as they were a small and diminishing class this amounted to a general restriction on alienation and was therefore void. In contrast in *Re Macleay*[6] a condition not to alienate land other than within "the family" was upheld since this was a large group of people which would be increasing in size. Conditions which are in complete restraint of marriage are regarded as contrary to public policy.[7] However, conditions which restrain the freedom to remarry have been upheld,[8] as have conditions which restrict the right of the grantee to marry a particular individual[9] or persons from a specified group. For example, in *Jenner v. Turner*[10] a condition imposed by a sister on her brother that he should not marry a "domestic servant" was upheld by Bacon V.-C. Similarly, a condition that the grantee not marry a "Papist" was upheld in *Duggan v. Kelly*[11] as was a condition not to marry a "Scotchman" in *Perrin v Lyon*.[12] Conditons which encourage the separation or divorce of a husband and wife,[13] seek to separate a parent from child,[14] or which interfere with the exercise of parental duties in relation to their children[15] have also been held to be void. However, conditions which restrict the religion of the grantee have never been held to be contrary to public policy and such a restriction was upheld by the House of Lords in *Blathwayt v. Baron Cawley*.[16] Conditions will also be regarded as void if they are uncertain, since as Lord Cranworth stated in *Clavering v. Ellison*[17] the court must be able to "see from the beginning, precisely and distinctly, upon the happening of what event it was that [the gift] was to determine." In *Clayton v. Ramsden*[18] it was held that a condition forfeiting an interest in the event of marriage to a person "not of Jewish parentage" was void on the grounds of uncertainty.

[4] See: *Muschamp v. Bluett* (1617) J. Bridge 132; *Hood v. Oglander* (1865) 34 Beav 513; *Re Rosher* (1884) 26 ChD 801; *Corbett v. Corbett* (1888) 14 PD 7; *Re Dugdale* (1888) 38 Ch.D. 176; *Re Cockerill* [1929] 2 Ch. 131.
[5] [1954] Ch. 39.
[6] (1875) L.R. 20 Eq. 186.
[7] *Long v. Dennis (1767)* 4 Burr 2052; *Low v. Peers* (1770) Wilm 364.
[8] *Jordan v. Holkham* (1753) Amb. 209. Contrast the Irish case of *Duddy v. Gresham* (1878) 2 L.R.Ir. 442 where a condition in the testator's will that his wife should not remarry but enter a convent of her choice was held void.
[9] *Re Bathe* [1925] Ch. 377; *Re Hanlon* [1933] Ch. 254.
[10] (1880) 16 Ch.D. 188.
[11] (1848) 10 I Eq. R. 295.
[12] (1807) 9 East. 170.
[13] *Wren v. Bradley* (1848) 2 de G & Sm 49; *Re Moore* (1888) 39 Ch.D. 116; *Re Caborne* [1943] Ch. 224; *Re Johnson's Will Trusts* [1967] Ch. 387.
[14] *Re Morgan* (1910) 26 T.L.R. 398; *Re Sandbrook* [1912] 2 Ch. 471; *Re Boulter* [1922] 1 Ch. 75; *Re Piper* [1946] 2 All E.R. 503.
[15] See *Re Borwick* [1933] Ch. 657, where a condition that a child would forfeit her interest if she became a Roman Catholic was held void as it interfered with a parent's duty to provide his children with religious instruction.
[16] [1976] A.C. 397.
[17] (1859) 7 H.L. Cas. 707 at 725.
[18] [1943] A.C. 320.

(iv) Consequence of a void condition subsequent: Where a conditional fee simple is granted but the condition is held to be void the grantee takes his interest in the land free from the condition.[19] He therefore receives a fee simple absolute. This result will also follow if the condition is impossible and cannot possibly occur.[20]

(v) Status of a conditional fee simple: Although section 1(1)(a) of the Law of Property Act 1925 would seem to indicate that a conditional fee simple cannot rank as a legal estate in land, section 7 has the effect that most conditional fee simples will enjoy legal status. The section, which was introduced by the Law of Property (Amendment) Act 1926[21] has the effect that:

> "a fee simple subject to a legal or equitable right of entry or re-entry is for the purposes of this Act a fee simple absolute."

As has already been noted the interest under a conditional fee simple does not automatically terminate if the condition occurs but must be forfeited by means of the exercise of a power of re-entry. Therefore the majority of conditional fee simples will fall within the ambit of section 7.

(c) Determinable fee simple

(i) Definition: The distinction between a fee simple which is subject to a condition subsequent and a fee simple which is determinable is extremely fine, and was described in *Re King's Trusts*[22] as "little short of disgraceful to our jurisprudence" and in *Re Sharp's Settlement*[23] as "extremely artificial". The essence of the distinction seems to be that in the case of a determinable fee simple the grant of the land is never contemplated as being absolute, but only as lasting until the determining event occurs. The grant is only absolute in practice because the determining event never occurs. In the case of a conditional gift the grant is of a prima facie absolute interest in the land but which will be cut short if the condition occurs. The difference between the two often comes down to a matter of the language that has been used to phrase the gift.[24] If the grant is said to be "until", "so long as", "whilst" or "during" the general conclusion is that it is determinable. In contrast if phrases such as "on condition that", "provided that", and "if" are used the grant will be conditional in form. Therefore a grant of a fee simple to Peter "until he becomes a fighter pilot" will be determinable, but a grant "unless he becomes a fighter pilot" will be conditional. The problems occassioned by the artificiality of this distinction are compounded by the fact that the distinction is not trivial and has important consequences for the natrue of the interest which is enjoyed by the grantee.

(ii) Effect of the occurence of the determining event: If the event which is stipulated as the determining event of a determinable fee simple occurs, the consequence is that the

[19] *Re Croxon* [1904] 1 Ch. 252.
[20] *Re Turton* [1926] Ch. 96.
[21] The section was introduced because in some parts of the country the purchaser of land did not pay the seller the price of the land but instead granted a perpetual annual landcharge over it. In the event of the failure to repay the seller could re-enter the land and reacquire the fee simple. The section was intended to prevent the inconvenience of the fee simple not enjoying the status of a legal estate in such arrangements.
[22] (1892) 29 L.R.Ir. 410 at 410, *per* Porter M.R.
[23] [1973] Ch. 331 at 340, *per* Pennycuick V.-C.
[24] See: Challis, *Law of Real Property*, (3rd ed.), p. 283.

grant is automatically brought to an end and the fee simple revestes in the grantee.[25] Unlike a conditional fee simple there is no need for the grantee to take the intiative to forfeit the interest by exercise of a right of re-entry.

(iii) Effect if the determining event is held void: As was noted above certain conditions are liable to be held void for reasons of public policy. If a determining event is held void the grant itself fails and the interest reverts back to the grantee. For example, in *Re Moore*[26] a trust to pay a weekly sum to a woman "whilst..living apart from her husband" was held to be void since the determining event was void. This is an exactly opposite result to the consequence where a condition subsequent is held void and the grant becomes absolute.

(iv) Effect if the determining event becomes impossible: If the determining event becomes impossible, so that it will never happen, the interest automatically becomes absolute.[27]

(v) Status of a determinable fee simple: Unless a determinable fee simple is accompanied by a right of re-entry, it will fall outside the scope of the Law of Property Act 1925, s.7 and cannot enjoy the status of a legal estate, and can only take effect as an equitable interest behind a trust.

3 "In possession"

(a) Definition

The meaning of the limtiation that the fee simple must be "in possession" is not that the fee simple owner must necessarily be enjoying the actual use and possession of the land. For example, a freehold owner who has let his land does not enjoy the factual possession since the tenant has the right to "exclusive possession" of the land for the duration of the lease.[28] The requirement therefore refers to the fact that the holder of the fee simple is entitled to immediate enjoyment of his full rights as owner of the land, differentiating it from circumstances where he will only come to enjoy his full rights in the future. As Viscount Dilhorne stated in *Pearson v. IRC*[29] an estate in possession gives "a present right of present enjoyment."

(b) Fee simple estates in remainder

A person will not be entitled to a fee simple absolute in possession if he holds a mere remainder interest in the land. This means that for the present someone else enjoys immediate rights over the land and that the fee simple owner will only become entitled to his full rights when those immediate rights are exhausted. For example, if James transferred the fee simple in his land to Karen, subject to a life interest for Leon, Karen's interest would be an interest in remainder since she would not be entitled to immediate enjoyment of her rights over the land but only on the death of Leon. It is not that the person with a remainder interest has no present rights in the land, the

[25] *Re Evans's Contract* (1920) 2 Ch. 469.
[26] (1888) 39 Ch.D. 116.
[27] *Re Leach* [1912] 2 Ch. 422.
[28] See Law of Property Act 1925, s.205(1)(xix) where "possession" includes the "receipt of rents or profits or the right to receive the same."
[29] [1981] A.C. 753 at 772.

remainder interest is itself a present interest which can be transferred, but that his rights over the land will only come into full effect in the future.

(c) Fee simple estates in reversion

An estate in reversion is similar to a remainder interest in that the estate owner's rights will not be fully enjoyed until the future. Reversionary interests generally arise where the original fee simple owner of land has failed to divest himself fully of his interests in the land, leaving the possibility that the estate will revert to him. For example, if instead of transfering the fee simple to Karen James had simply granted Leon a life interest over his land James would himself retain the reversionary interest, since on the death of Leon he would again be entitled to exercise his immediate rights as the fee simple owner.

DETERMINING FREEHOLD OWNERSHIP

1 Introduction to freehold title

Having examined the theoretical nature of the freehold interest in the form of a fee simple absolute in possession, the question arises as to who actually enjoys the freehold ownership, or title, to a particular piece of land. What constitutes good title will depend upon whether the land is registered or unregistered, and is subject to the qualification that a person who has adversely possessed the land may have gained a title which displaces that of the paper owner.

2 Freehold title in unregistered land

Where land is unregistered ownership of the freehold is not constituted by the possession of any particular document or piece of paper. Title is constituted by being able to demonstrate an entitlement to the ownership of the land which is superior to the claims of any others. The most important means by which a person can establish such a title is by showing that he has derived his interest from a good root of title. This is done by showing that the land was transferred to him by a person who himself enjoyed a good title and was entitled to transfer it. Such a transfer is described as a conveyance, and by the Law of Property Act 1925, s.52(1) must be made by deed. What are known as the "title deeds" of unregistered land are simply a collection of the conveyances of the land which demonstrate how the title to the land has been derived. It is only necessary for a person claiming the land to demonstrate a good root of title stretching back twelve years, since if he has possessed the land for that period he will have gained a title good against anyone else by means of adverse possession.

3 Freehold title in registered land

(a) Registration of title

One of the most significant reforms of the Land Registration Act 1925 was to establish a system of land registration, so that it is no longer necessary to constantly demonstrate a good root of title.

Instead legal ownership of land is definitively constituted by being registered as the "registered proprietor" of the land at the centrally maintained Land Register.

(b) Fee simple as a registrable title

According to the Land Registration Act 1925, s.2(1) the only interests in land which can be registered in their own right, and thus receive an individual title number, are those estates in land "capable of subsisting as legal estates." This clearly includes the fee simple absolute in possession.[30] The entry for each registrable interest at the land registry includes a "Property Register" which identifies the plot of land to which the title relates, including a map, and a "Prioprietorship Register" which indicates the name and address of the current registered proprietor.

(c) Time when title must be registered

Because the system of land regsitration could not be introduced immediately, registration of title was introduced by means of the designation of geographical areas as areas of compulsory registration. In 1989 the entire country was so designated by the Registration of Title Order.[31] The consequence of this designation is that if title to freehold is presently unregistered it must be registered on the first "qualifying conveyance" of the freehold estate.[32] This means that whenever a freehold estate in unregistered land is transferred,[33] whether for valuable consideration, as a gift or in pursuance of an order of the court,[34] title must be registered by the transferee proving his title to the Land Registrar, who will then create a new title for the land.

(d) Qualities of title which may be awarded on first registration

When the freehold title is first registered the person claiming to be registered as the proprietor must demonstrate that he enjoys title to the land to the Land Registrar. The degree to which he has been able to prove his entitlement will determine the quality of title that the Land Registrar is prepared to award him.
(i) Absolute title: If the person seeking registration has demonstrated that he has good title to the land to the satisfaction of the registrar he will be registered as proprietor of the land with absolute title. The effect of registration with absolute title is stated in the Land Registration Act 1925, s.5:

> "Where the registered land is a freehold estate, the registration of any person as first proprietor thereof with an absolute title shall vest in the person so registered an estate in fee simple in possession in the land, together with all rights, privileges and appurtenances belonging to or appurtenant thereto."

The registered proprietor takes the land subject only to any third party interests appearing on the register[35] and to overriding interests which affect the registered land.[36] Additionally, if the registered proprietor holds the land on trust he also takes

[30] Law of Property Act 1925, s.1(1)(a).
[31] Registration of Tile Order 1989 (S.I. 1989 No. 1347).
[32] Law of Property Act 1925, s.123(1)(a) as amended by Land Registration Act 1997, s.1.
[33] A transfer of land for other land is excluded: *Re Westminster Property Group Plc* [1985] 1 W.L.R. 676.
[34] Law of Property Act 1925, s.123(6).
[35] s.5(a).
[36] s.5(b).

the land subject to any minor interests of which he has notice.[37] Where a person is registered as the first registered proprietor of the land with absolute title the effect of registration is to invest him with the legal fee simple estate in the land even if his title was defective and someone else was in fact entitled to the land. For example in, *Re 139 High Street Deptford*[38] it was held that registration invested the registered proprietor with legal title to land although the vendor from whom he had purported to purchase it had no title. However, in such cases it may be possible for the register to be rectified, or for the person who has suffered loss as a consequence of the incorrect registration to receive an indemnity. Once the land has become registered the freehold can only be transferred by the registration of a substitute freehold owner as the proprietor.
(ii) Possessory title: Where a person is unable to demonstrate a good root of title to land he may still be registered as proprietor with mere possessory title. As will be seen below, a person can acquire good freehold title to land if he takes possession of it adverse to the true owner for a sufficient period of time. Where a person is registered with possessory title, Land Registration Act 1925, s.6 provides that such registration shall not affect or prejudice the enforcement of any estate, right or interest adverse to or in derogation of the title of the first proprietor, and subsisting or capable of arising at the time of registration of that proprietor. This means that the person registered as proprietor with possessory title will always take the land subject to the interests of the true owner if he was not in fact entitled to the land at the date of registration. A registration with possessory title may be converted to absolute title if in the future the Land Registrar is "satisfied as to the title" of the proprietor.[39] If the proprietary with possessory title remains in possession for twelve years after the registration he has the right to be registered with absolute title since after that period the ownership of any other person in the land will have been extinguished by adverse possession.[40]
(iii) Qualified title: If the person seeking registration can only establish his title for a limited period, or subject to exceptions, he may be registered as proprietor with qualified title. The proprietor with qualified title will take the land subject to the estates rights and interests excepted by the register.[41]

(e) Effect of failure to register when compulsory

First registration is compulsory on the first "qualifying conveyance." However, if registration is not effected within two months from the date of the conveyance section 123A(5) of the Land Registration Act 1925[42] provides that the conveyance is void as regards the transfer of the freehold estate in the land. Section 123A(5)(a) provides that in such circumstances the title will revert to the transferor "who shall hold that estate on a bare trust for the transferee." Rather than enjoying the legal freehold ownership of the land the transferee will enjoy the equitable ownership only.

[37] s.5(c).
[38] [1951] Ch. 884.
[39] Land Registration Act 25, s.77(2)(a).
[40] s.77(2)(b).
[41] Land Registration Act 1925, s.7(2).
[42] As amended by Land Registration Act 1997, s.1.

ACQUISITION OF THE FREEHOLD TITLE TO LAND BY TRANSFER FROM THE EXISTING FREEHOLD OWNER

1 General principles

The most important means by which a person can obtain the freehold ownership of land is through a valid transfer from the present freehold owner. There is therefore a transfer of the freehold estate from the transferor to the transferee. The transfer may either be voluntary, or as a result of a contract that has been entered between the parties, for example for the sale and transfer of the land. The principles governing transfers of the freehold ownership differ depending upon whether the land in question is registered or unregistered. The process by which the ownership is transferred is known as conveyancing.

2 Transfer of freehold ownership in unregistered land

Where land is unregistered the freehold may be transferred by means of a conveyance from the transferor to the transferee. By section 52(1) of the Law of Property Act 1925 a conveyance of land is "void for the purpose of conveying or creating a legal estate unless made by deed."[43] In every case the transfer will have to be completed by registration.

3 Transfer of freehold ownership in registered land

Where land is registered and title to the freehold is therefore constituted by registration as proprietor, the freehold ownership can only be transferred by the entry of the transferee as the new registered proprietor of the land at the Land Registry.[44] The transferor of the freehold completes a land transfer form authorising the land registrar to alter the register entry, which form is then passed to the transferee who completes it by entering his own details. The form is then forwarded to the land registry and the register is amended.[45]

4 Transfer of freehold ownership on sale

(a) The conveyancing process

By far the most common circumstance in which the freehold ownership of land will be transferred is where the land is sold. In the case of unregistered land this will give rise to the need to register the title. Ultimately in the case of both registered and unregistered land a sale will only effect a transfer of the legal freehold ownership through registration of the transferee as registered proprietor. Although the means by

[43] Law of property (Miscellaneous Provisions) Act 1989, s.1.
[44] Land Registration Act 1925, ss.19(1) and 22(1).
[45] See: *Mascall v. Mascall* (1984) 50 P. & C.R. 119.

which freehold ownership is transferred is by registration of the transferee, the process of conveyancing where there is a sale is complex because of the interrelationship between the contract entered into by the parties and their proprietary entitlements to the land. This section will outline the key stages of the conveyancing process and the effects that they have on the rights and entitlements of the parties.[46]

(b) Distinguishing contract and transfer

(i) Entering a binding contract for sale: Where land is transferred by sale there are a number of important steps involved in conveying the land from the vendor to the purchaser. Two separate elements of such a transaction must be distinguished. First, there is the contract between the purchaser and the vendor which constitutes a binding agreement to sell and transfer the land in return for the payment of an agreed price. One issue to be considered is the stage at which such a binding contract comes into existence between the parties, and different rules apply to contracts for the sale of land than the ordinary rules of offer and acceptance governing conventional contracts. The contract does not usually come into being at the moment an offer from the purchaser is accepted by the vendor, since an offer is usually accepted "subject to contract". The contract between the parties only becomes binding when there is an exchange of contracts.

(ii) Transferring the ownership of the land: However, the mere entering of a binding contract is not itself sufficient to transfer the ownership of the land from the vendor to the purchaser. A second stage to the transaction is required when the ownership is actually transferred by means of a conveyance. This is described as "completion" of the contract. In registered land this transfer is only effective when the purchaser is actually entered on the register as the new owner of the land. Therefore the transfer is not technically completed until such registration has taken place.

(c) Reaching agreement "subject to contract"

A vendor seeking to sell land will obviously seek a buyer, probably through the services of an estate agent, and advertise the land as available for purchase stipulating an expected price. Potential buyers offer a price they are willing to pay. When an offer is made it is for the vendor to decide whether to accept or reject it. Although in conventional bargains the contract comes into existence and is binding on the parties at the moment that an offer is accepted, in conveyancing the offer is usually accepted by the vendor "subject to contract". This operates as a provisional acceptance of the offer, signifying that the vendor is willing to sell at that price, but without creating a binding agreement. Both parties remain free not to go ahead with the transaction and they will have no remedies if the other decides not to go ahead with the sale. This "sale" may fall through for a number of common reasons, for example if the vendor accepts and subsequently receives a higher offer from someone else, a practice known as gazumping. Alternatively, if the price of property is falling the purchaser may wish to pull out of the sale if he feels the offer is too high. During the period between acceptance subject to contract and exchange of contracts the purchaser will have opportunity to make inquiries concerning the land including to determine whether

[46] For a full discussion of the conveyancing process see: Thompson, *Barnsley's Conveyancing: Law and Practice*, (4th ed., 1996).

there are any third party interests which affect it. The basic rule remains *caveat emptor* so the burden falls on the purchaser to satisfy himself of what he is getting.

(d) Exchange of contract

(i) Effect of exchange: Exchange is the moment at which a fully binding contract comes into being between the parties. Neither party can then withdraw from the sale without committing a breach of contract. If one party does breach their contract the other will be able to seek a remedy from the courts. Since the property involved is land, which is unique, the equitable remedy of specific performance will generally be available so that the other party can compel the party in breach to perform the contract. As Lord Diplock said in *Sudbrook Trading Estate Ltd v. Eggleton*[47] damages alone would "constitute a wholly inadequate and unjust remedy for the breach" and therefore "the normal remedy is by way of specific performance." However as an equitable remedy specific performance is discretionary and may be unavailable if the party seeking it has acted unconscionable, if the award would prejudice the interests of third parties, or if it would cause a hardship amounting to an injustice. For example, in *Patel v. Ali*[48] Mr and Mrs Ali had entered a contract to sell their house to Mr and Mrs Patel. Mr Ali was then adjudicated bankrupt and spent a year in prison. Mrs Ali was diagnosed as suffering from cancer and had a leg amputated just before the birth of her second child and then subsequently had a third child. Goulding J. refused an order for specific performance on the ground of undue hardship, but emphasised that "only in extraordinary and persuasive circumstances can hardship supply a excuse for resisting performance of a contract for the sale of [land]."

(ii) Formalities required for the creation of contracts for the sale of land: A contract for the sale of land will be void unless the requisite formalities have been satisfied. For contracts entered after September 27, 1989 the formal requirements are stipulated in the Law of Property (Miscellaneous Provisions) Act 1989. Section 2(1) provides that:

> "A contract for the sale or other disposition of an interest in land can only be made in writing and only by incorporating all the terms which the parties have expressly agreed in one document or, where contracts are exchanged, in each."

Where a prior valid contract has granted a person an option to purchase land Hoffman J. held in *Spiro v. Glencrown*[49] that there was no need for a notice exercising the option to comply with section 2. This follows from the fact that an option is exercised by the grantee and it is unrealistic to expect the grantor to sign such a notice. Contracts made prior to September 27, 1997 merely needed to be evidenced in writing by the Law of Property Act 1925, s.40. If there was no writing the contract was unenforceable unless it there had been some act of part performance by the parties, such as entering into possession of the land, in which case it would be enforceable in equity. The fact that a contract which does not comply with the formalities requirements of Law of Property (Miscellaneous Provisions) Act 1989 is rendered void has abolished the doctrine of part performance and it is no longer applicable.

[47] [1983] 1 A.C. 444 at 478.
[48] [1984] Ch. 283.
[49] [1991] Ch. 537.

(iii) Mechanism of exchange: Exchange consists of the vendor signing and passing a copy of the contract to the purchaser, and the purchaser signing and passing a copy of the contract to the vendor. This may be effected by post, in which case the contractual postal rule[50] will apply, by telephone,[51] or in person. Customarily a deposit is paid by the purchaser when the contracts are exchanged.

(iv) Contract for sale constitutes an interest in land: Since the contract for sale of land involves the transfer of property the contract itself has proprietary consequences. The contract is itself regarded as a type of interest in land, which is known as an estate contract. Since it falls outside of the scope of the Law of Property Act 1925, s.1(2) the estate contract is merely an equitable interest in the land.[52] If the land is wrongly conveyed to someone other than the purchaser by the vendor it is possible that that third person will be bound by the purchaser's estate contract. This will be a question of priorities. In the case of registered land it will depend upon whether the estate contract was properly protected on the register, or whether he was in actual occupation of the land he had contracted to buy in which case his estate contract will be an overriding interest. In the case of unregistered land an estate contract is a land charge and whether it binds the third party transferee will depend on whether it was properly protected on the land charges register.[53]

(v) Contract gives rise to a constructive trust: Although entering a binding contract does not itself effect the transfer of the freehold ownership of the land to the purchaser, the equitable ownership of the land passes to the purchaser by means of a constructive trust as soon as the contract is entered because the contract is specifically enforceable and "equity treats as done that which ought to be done. As Jessel MR said in *Lysaght v. Edwards*[54]: "the moment you have a valid contract for sale the vendor becomes in equity a trustee for the purchaser of the estate sold." One consequence of this is that from the moment of contract the purchaser is required to insure the land since the risk passes to him when he obtains the equitable ownership of the land.

(e) Completion

Completion is the final stage of the transfer where the legal title is transferred from the vendor to the purchaser. The mere fact that the new freehold owner has taken possession of the land in pursuance of the contract is not itself effective to transfer title. In the case of unregistered land the conveyance is executed after the purchaser has paid over the purchase moneys and the appropriate title deeds are then handed over. In the case of registered land the vendor hands over the form of transfer which must be completed and sent to the Land Registry. Completion is the time at which the purchaser is entitled to enter into the land being transferred, so that in the case of a transfer of domestic accommodation it usually equates with the date of moving.

(f) Registration

As has been noted above the legal title is not technically transferred by conveyance but by registration of the transferee as the new proprietor of the land, a first registration if

[50] *Adams v. Lindsell* (1818) 1 B. & Ald. 681; *Household Fire and Carriage Accident Insurance Co Ltd v. Grant* (1879) 4 Ex.D. 216; *Henthorn v. Fraser* [1892] 2 Ch. 27. See also: *Entores v. Miles Far East Corp* [1955] 2 Q.B. 327; *Brinkibon Ltd v. Stahag Stahl* [1983] A.C. 34.

[51] *Domb v. Isoz* [1980] Ch. 548.

[52] s.1(3).

[53] *Midland Bank Trust Co v. Green* [1981] A.C. 513

[54] [1876] 2 Ch.D. 499.

the land was previously unregistered. Inevitably this process takes time and it is unlikely that the purchaser will be registered at the time that completion takes place. The gap between the date of completion and the date at which the purchaser is registered as the new owner is referred to as the registration gap. By the Law of Property Act 1925, s.123A(3)registration should occur within two months of the date of the transfer of the land, but the land registrar has the discretion to extend the period on the application of any interested person if satisfied "that there is good reason for doing so."

ACQUISITION OF THE FREEHOLD TITLE TO LAND BY ADVERSE POSSESSION

1 Meaning of adverse possession

In the previous section it has been seen how the usual means of acquiring the freehold ownership of land is by effective transfer from the present freeholder. However, it is also possible for a person to gain title to the land which is effective against the whole world, including the true owner, merely by taking possession of it for a sufficient period of time. By this means a squatter may in effect "steal" land from its true owner, who will be incapable of recovering it back. Such a person is said to have acquired his title to the land by adverse possession.

2 Rationale of adverse possession

Although it might initially seem to be against public policy to allow persons to acquire ownership to land merely by taking possession of it as this might encourage squatting, the law regards the owner of land as being under a duty to protect his own interests. If the land is occupied by squatters he is not expected to stand by and do nothing to have them removed but to seek his rightful remedies to remove them as trespassers from his land. If he does not take advantage of the remedies that are available to him the law supposes that he does not particularly value the land that is adversely possessed, or at least not sufficiently to take action to protect his rights. This rational was articulated in *R.B. Policies at Lloyd's v. Butler*[55] where it was said that landowners should not "go to sleep on their claims" and cannot then expect the assistance of the courts in recovering their land if they do so. The inherent limitations in the operation of the principles of adverse possession mean that only in extreme cases will squatters qualify to oust the rights of landowners.

3 Requirements of adverse possession

There are three main requirements which a person must satisfy before he is able to defeat the rights of the freehold owner of land. First, he must show that he had the

[55] [1950] 1 K.B. 76.

necessary factual possession of the land. Secondly, he must show that he possessed the land with the necessary intention to defeat the interests of the owner. Thirdly, he must be able to demonstrate that he enjoyed such factual possession with the necessary intention for the requisite period of time. Only when all three requirements are satisfied will the adverse possessor gain title to the land which was described in *Buckinghamshire County Council v. Moran*[56] by Nourse L.J. as "impregnable . . . a title superior to all others."

(a) Factual possession of the land

(i) Factual possession a necessity: A person will only be able to claim adverse possession if he has in fact taken physical possession of the land. Under the provisions of the Limitation Act 1980 a person claiming an interest by way of adverse possession will only be entitled to claim that his possession was adverse from the date that the true owner was dispossessed or discontinued his possession.[57] In *Treloar v. Nute*[58] Sir John Pennycuick stated that the requirement was that: "the person claiming by possession must show either (1) discontinuance by the paper owner followed by possession or (2) dispossession (or as it is sometimes called "ouster") of the paper owner."

(ii) What constitutes factual possession of land: The question whether a person has taken factual possession of the land is complex since what will be sufficient to constitute such possession will depend upon the nature of the land concerned.[59] What seems to be required is that the possessor must have taken exclusive physical control of the land. However, what will be sufficient to constitute control will itself vary with nature of the land. As was stated by Slade J. in *Powell v. McFarlane*[60]: "what act constitutes a sufficient degree of exclusive physical control must depend on the circumstances, in particular the nature of the land and the manner in which land of that nature is commonly used or enjoyed." It is clear that physical fencing of land will generally be regarded as amounting to factual possession.[61] In *Seddon v. Smith*[62] Cockburn C.J. said that "enclosure is the strongest possible evidence of adverse possession."[63] Therefore there was no doubt that land had been factually possessed in *Buckinghamshire County Council v. Moran*[64] where the claimant had completely enclosed an area belonging to the council with fences and hedges and incorporated it as part of his garden by adding a new gate and lock. However, the enclosure of the land is not a necessary requirement for factual possession and in some cases has been held to be insufficient,[65] for example where a fence was erected for only 24 hours,[66] or for the purpose of preventing a senile family member from straying.[67] In many cases it

[56] [1990] Ch. 623 at 644.
[57] s.15(6), Sched. 1, para. 1.
[58] [1976] 1 W.L.R. 1295.
[59] *Lord Advocate v. Lord Lovat* (1880) 5 App. Cas. 273 at 288, *per* Lord O'Hagan.
[60] (1979) 38 P. & C.R. 452 at 471.
[61] See for example: *Williams v. Usherwood* (1983) 45 P. & C.R. 235.
[62] (1877) 36 L.T. 168.
[63] In *Mulcahy v. Curramore Ltd* [1974] 2 N.S.W.L.R. 464 fencing was described as "useful evidence of occupation to the exclusion of others."
[64] [1990] Ch. 623.
[65] See: *Basildon District Council v. Manning* (1975) 237 E.G. 879; *Boosey v. Davis* (1987) 55 P. & C.R. 83.
[66] *Marsden v. Miller* (1992) 64 P. & C.R. 239.
[67] *Fruin v. Fruin* [1983] C.A. (unreported).

has been held that factual possession has been established even without fencing or otherwise enclosing the land. In *Treloar v. Nute*[68] grazing cows and storing timber on land was held to amount to factual possession. In *Red House Farms (Thorndon) Ltd v. Catchpole*[69] shooting over marshy ground was also held to be sufficient. In *Leigh v. Jack*[70] Bramwell L.J. suggested that building on land or cultivating it could constitute factual possession. However, the performance of purely trivial acts will not generally constitute factual possession of the land. In *Tecbild v. Chamberlain*[71] it was held that children who had played on land and tethered and exercised their ponies there had not done sufficient to establish factual possession.[72]

(iii) Possession must be adverse to the interests of the owner: This means that the claimant must be exercising factual possession of the land as a trespasser, rather than as someone who is entitled because he has the permission of the owner to occupy the land. Therefore a tenant[73] of the freeholder or a person to whom he has granted a licence[74] cannot maintain that his possession was adverse. However, his possession may become adverse if it continues beyond the time when his lease or licence[75] has come to an end. As was stated by Slade L.J. in *Buckinghamshire County Council v. Moran*[76]:

> "Possession is never "adverse" . . . if it is enjoyed by lawful title. If, therefore, a person occupies or uses land by licence of the owner with the paper title and his licence has not been duly determined, he cannot be treated as having been in "adverse possession" as against the owner of the paper title."

Prior to the Limitation Act 1980 a licence would generally be implied whenever the owner of land left it unoccupied because he had no present use for it but intended to make some use in the future. For example, in *Wallis's Cayton Bay Holiday Camp Ltd v. Shell Mex and BP Ltd*,[77] where squatters took possession of land which a petroleum company intended to use for the construction of a road in the future, Lord Denning M.R. held that there was an implied licence so that they had not defeated the company's title to the land. Such implication of licences made it extremely difficult to establish adverse possession of unoccupied land.[78] In *Buckinghamshire County Council v. Moran*[79] Nourse L.J. described the implied licence theory introduced by Lord Denning as "an original heresy of his own," and the law was reformed by the Limitiation Act 1980 which provides that a licence will not be implied "merely by virtue of the fact that [the claimant's] occupation is not inconsistent with the [owner's] present or future enjoyment of the land."[80] This provision expressly does not prevent

[68] [1976] 1 W.L.R. 1295.
[69] (1977) 244 E.G. 295.
[70] (1879) 5 Ex.D. 264.
[71] (1969) 20 P. & C.R. 633.
[72] See also: *Bills v. Fernandez-Gonzalez* (1981) 132 N.L.J. 60; *Boosey v. Davis* (1987) 55 P. & C.R. 83; *Wilson v. Marton's Executors* [1993] 24 E.G. 119.
[73] *Colchester B.C. v. Smith* [1991] Ch. 448.
[74] *BP Properties v. Buckler* [1987] 2 E.G.L.R. 168.
[75] *Colchester B.C. v. Smith* [1991] Ch. 448.
[76] [1990] Ch. 623 at 626.
[77] [1975] Q.B. 94.
[78] See also: *Gray v. Wykeham Martin & Goode* (unreported) January 17, 1977.
[79] [1990] Ch. 623.
[80] s.15(6), Sched. 1, para. 8(4).

the court from finding that there was an implied licence "where such a finding is justified on the actual facts of the case."[81]

(iv) Possession must be open: The adverse possession of the land must be open, notorious and unconcealed. This requirement means that the period of adverse possession cannot start running against a true owner where he would not have been able to observe that the land was being possessed. The Limitation Act 1980, s.32 provides that any actions of the possessor which were fraudulent or deliberately concealed from the owner do not cause the limitation period to run until the owner discovered, or should reasonably have discovered, the fraud or concealment.

(b) Intention to possess the land

(i) Requisite intention a necessity: The mere fact that a person enjoys factual possession of the land adverse to the owner is not itself sufficient to entitle him to defeat the owner's title. This elusive quality of the requisite intention has also been known as the *animus possidendi*. Historically, it was thought that the necessary intention was actually an intention to own the land, but recent cases have held that this is not the case.

(ii) An intention to exclude: It is clear from the decision of the Court of Appeal in *Buckinghamshire County Council v. Moran*[82] that it is not necessary for a person claiming adverse possession to demonstrate that they took possession of the land with an intention to own it. Although there are dicta in some cases which seem to suggest such an approach,[83] Slade L.J. stated that what was needed was "an intention for the time being to possess the land to the exclusion of all other persons, including the owner with the paper title." This re-iterated his decision in the earlier case of *Powell v. Macfarlane*[84] where he had stated that a failure by the adverse possessor to make it "perfectly plain to the world at large by his actions or words that he has intended to exclude the owner as best he can" will mean that he does not have the requisite *animus possidendi*. In *Powell v. Macfarlane* a claim of adverse possession was made when a boy had started grazing his cow on the land at the age of fourteen. Slade J. held that in these circumstances he did not have the necessary intention to exclude the true owner from the land.

(iii) Requisite intention where the true owner has a future use for the land: The question of intention has generally arisen in the context of adverse possession where the possessor was aware that the true owner of the land did not intend to make use of it immediately, but intended to do so in the future. In *Leigh v. Jack*[85] the claimant had stored scrap metal on land which he knew was intended to be used in the future by the owners for the construction of a street. It was held that he had not dispossessed the true owner and Cockburn C.J. stated that his knowledge of the future intended use meant that he did not intend to act as a trespasser. However, in *Buckingham County Council v. Moran*[86] the Court of Appeal rejected the view that *Leigh v. Jack* meant that

[81] See: (1980) 96 L.Q.R. 333 (P. Jackson); [1986] Conv. 434 (G. McCormack).
[82] [1990] Ch. 623.
[83] *Littledale v. Liverpool College* [1900] 1 Ch. 19 at 23 *per* Lindley M.R.; *George Wimpey & Co Ltd v. Sohn* [1967] Ch. 487 at 510 *per* Russel L.J.
[84] (1977) 38 P. & C.R. 452; (1980) 96 L.Q.R. 333 (P. Jackson); [1982] Conv. 256, 345 (M. Dockray).
[85] (1879) 5 Ex.D. 264.
[86] [1990] Ch. 623.

there could never be sufficient intention to possess where the possessor was aware of a future intended use of the land. Slade L.J. considered:

> "it must . . . be too broad a proposition to suggest that an owner who retains a piece of land with a view to its utilisation for a specific purpose in the future can never be treated as dispossessed, no matter how firm and obvious the intention to dispossess, and however drastic the acts of dispossession of the person seeking to dispossess him may be."

The defendant had incorporated a plot of land owned by the Council into his garden and by means of the addition of a new gate and lock had ensured that access to the land could only be made through his own land. He had also cultivated and maintained the plot as part of the garden, planting bulbs and daffodils in the grass, and trimming the hedges. The council had intended to use the incorporated plot for a road diversion scheme. In 1975 the Council wrote to him asking why he was exercising rights over the land and he replied "without prejudice" that he intended to keep the land unless and until the road was built. By the time that the council sought possession of the plot in 1985 the limitation period for adverse possession had passed. The Court of Appeal held that the defendant was entitled to adverse possession of the land since he had clearly acquired "complete and exclusive physical control of the land."

(iv) Intention of the true owner irrelevant? Although the future intentions of the landowner did not defeat the defendant's claim to adverse possession in *Buckinghamshire County Council v. Moran* this does not mean that such an intention is always irrelevant. Slade L.J. was careful to point out that in such cases the court should be "slow to make a finding of adverse possession." Nourse L.J. stated that although in most cases the intention of the true owner is irrelevant in practice there was one exception:

> "If an intention on the part of the true owner to use the land for a particular purpose at some future date is known to the squatter, then his knowledge may affect the quality of his own intention, reducing it below that which is required to constitute adverse possession."

(v) Finding the necessary intention from enclosure: The difficulty of establishing the precise intentions of a person who has taken possession of land means that there is a very close relationship between the requirement of an intention to possess and the fact of possession. In *Buckinghamshire County Council v. Moran* the Court of Appeal took the view that the fact of physical enclosure of land "itself prima facie indicates the requisite animus possidendi." Slade L.J. cited the judgment of Lord Halsbury L.C. in *Marshall v. Taylor*[87] who stated in relation to the piece of land in question:

> "The true nature of this particular strip of land is that it is enclosed. It cannot be denied that the person who now says he owns it could not get to it in any ordinary way. I do not deny that he could have crept through the hedge, or, if it had been a brick wall, that he could have climbed over the wall; but that was not the ordinary and usual mode of access."

[87] [1895] 1 Ch. 641 at 645.

The same could be said of the land at issue in *Buckinghamshire County Council v. Moran*.

(vi) Finding the necessary intention where there has been no enclosure: The difficulties of establishing the requisite intention to possess will therefore be most apparent where the claimant has taken factual possession of the land other than by enclosure. In *Powell v. Macfarlane*[88] Slade J. considered that compelling evidence was necessary to establish the intention where the claimant's use of the land did not itself indicate such an intention.

(vii) Too strict a requirement? It has been argued by some that the requirement of an intention to possess has been set too highly.[89] However, it should be noted that the effect of adverse possession is to allow a person to acquire such a valuable asset as land without providing the true owner with any consideration for his loss of title and consequent wealth, by nothing more than taking possession of it. Surely the law is correct to strongly protect the rights of true owners and not to allow squatters to gain title to land too easily. It seems somewhat unfair that in *Buckinghamshire County Council v Moran*[90] the defendant was enabled to claim land which he had known the council intended to use. However, his success must be judged against the failure of the council to take steps to protect their interests when they were aware of the fact of his possession.

(c) Possession for the necessary period

(i) A twelve year limitation period: The Limitation Act 1980 lays down the period of time after which a true owner will no longer be able to assert his rights against an adverse possessor. Section 15(1) provides that:

> "No action shall be brought by any person to recover any land after the expiration of twelve years from the date on which the right of action accrued to him or, if it first accrued to some person through whom he claims, to that person."

The effect of this provision is that if land is adversely possessed for a period of twelve years or more the true owner will not be entitled to recover his land from the adverse possessor, who will thereby gain ownership of the land.

(ii) Continuous possession for twelve years: The claimant will only be entitled to defeat the title of the paper owner if he can demonstrate that he enjoyed a continuous period of adverse possession for 12 years. If at any point the true owner regained possession and broke the continuity of the period of adverse possession then the claimant will be unable to defeat his title.

(iii) Cumulative periods of adverse possession: Limitation Act 1980 expressly anticipates that the 12 year period may comprise the cumulation of several persons' adverse possession, possessors, provided there is no break in the chain of possession. For example if Peter began to possess land in 1980 and Quentin joined him in 1987 and then Peter left the land in 1991, Quentin will be able to claim adverse possession as

[88] (1977) 38 P. & C.R. 452 at 476.
[89] See: (1980) 96 L.Q.R. 333 (P. Jackson).
[90] [1990] Ch. 623.

theirs is a continuous period of more than 12 years even though personally he has only possessed the land for eight years. However, the 12 year period of adverse possession must be continuous, so that if Peter began to possess the land in 1980, abandoned his possession in 1986, and Quentin then took possession in 1987 Quentin would not be able to assert a right to adverse possession.[91]

4 Operation of adverse possession

(a) Paper owner unable to assert his title

When the requirements of adverse possession have been satisfied the paper owner of the land is no longer entitled to assert his rights against the adverse possessor as the adverse possession extinguishes his better title.[92] However, the mere fact of the extinction of the paper owner's title does not mean that the adverse possessor is automatically invested with the freehold ownership himself. It is true to say that there is no-one in the entire world who can assert a better claim than his to the land, but formal steps are necessary for him to be vested as the freeholder and to become the new paper owner. The precise process necessary will depend upon the type of land that is in issue, and in the case of registered land the nature of the adverse possessor's interest in the intervening time between the expiry of the 12 year period and his registration as the registered proprietor is determined by statute. However, even before such a process is completed the adverse possessor has acquired an interest in the land which he is entitled to transfer to others, either *inter vivos*, by assignment, or on death by will.[93]

(b) Adverse possession of unregistered land

If the land which has been adversely possessed is unregistered the mere fact of adverse possession does not effect a transfer of the fee simple of the land to the adverse possessor. However, the adverse possessor is entitled to claim a new title of his own. He will not be able to prove his title through title deeds, but will have to rely on the fact of his adverse possession for 12 years or more. Such an adverse possessor will take his freehold interest in the land subject to all other third party interests which affect the land since he is not a purchaser.

(c) Adverse possession of registered land

Where the land which has been adversely possessed is registered the paper owner will remain registered as the proprietor of the land at the Land Registry even after the completion of the 12 year period. The adverse possessor can only obtain the freehold title to the land by being registered as proprietor himself. Under the Land Registration Act 1925, s.75(2) the adverse possessor is entitled to be registered as proprietor of the land by virtue of his adverse possession, and that registration will effect a transfer of the ownership to him. In the interim period before such registration section 75(2)

[91] See Limitation Act, s.15(6) Sched. 1, para. 8(2); *Trustees Executors and Agency Co Ltd v. Short* (1888) 13 App. Cas. 793; *Willis v. Earl Howe* [1893] 2 Ch. 545; *Samuel Johnson and Sons Ltd v. Brock* [1907] 2 Ch. 533; *Mulcahy v. Curramore Pty Ltd* [1974] 2 N.S.W.L.R. 464.

[92] *St Marylebone Property Co Ltd v. Fairweather* [1963] A.C. 510.

[93] *Asher v. Whitlock* (1865) L.R. 1 Q.B. 1.

provides that the registered proprietor holds the land on trust for him. Although this interest is not as strong as the freehold ownership itself, the adverse possessor's interests cannot be defeated as his rights constitute an "overriding interest" under section 70(1)(f), which means that they will bind any transferee of the land.

(5) Adverse possession of freehold of land subject to a lease[94]

(a) No adverse possession of the freehold title while the lease is in force

Where land is subject to a lease the tenant enjoys possession of the land whilst the landlord retains the freehold title. Any adverse possession is only therefore adverse to the interests of the tenant and not of the freeholder whilst the lease remains in force. If the adverse possessor completes 12 years continuous possession the tenant can no longer assert his right to possession against him. The landlord cannot himself seek possession until the lease is determined, since he is not entitled to possession until that point. The landlord cannot enforce the leasehold covenants against the adverse possessor. However, where a tenant is no longer able to assert his rights against an adverse possessor because the land has been possessed for the 12 year period it was held in *St Marylebone Property Co Ltd v. Fairweather*[95] that he may voluntarily surrender his lease to the landlord, which has the effect of bringing the lease to an end enabling the landlord to recover possession from the adverse possessor because the adverse possession does not defeat the rights of the landlord as the freehold owner. This conclusion is open to question because when an adverse possessor has defeated the interest of the tenant, the tenant has no lease which can be surrendered to the landlord as his rights have passed to the possessor. *St Marylebone Property Co. Ltd v. Fairweather* concerned unregistered land and the principle was not applied to registered land in *Spectrum Investment Co. Ltd v. Holmes*[96] since the adverse possessor of leasehold land is entitled to be registered as proprietor after extinguishing the tenant's rights. After registration as proprietor the previous tenant has nothing to surrender.

(b) Adverse possession against the landlord's freehold title once the lease has come to an end

The adverse possessor will only defeat the freehold title of the landlord if he remains in adverse possession of the land for 12 years after the expiry of the lease, since the limitation period runs against the freeholder from the expiry of the lease.[97] If he completes the necessary period he will extinguish the freehold title.

ACQUISITION OF THE FREEHOLD TITLE TO LAND BY PROPRIETARY ESTOPPEL

A further means by which a person may acquire the freehold title of land is if the court orders that it should be transferred to him as a remedy where he has established an

[94] See also Chap. 5.
[95] [1963] A.C. 510.
[96] [1981] 1 W.L.R. 221.
[97] Limitation Act 1980, Sched. 1, para. 4.

entitlement by way of proprietary estoppel. The general doctrine of proprietary estoppel is examined in detail in Chapter 13 below. The essence of the doctrine is that if the owner of land has made an assurance to someone else that they are, or will become, entitled to some interest in the land, they will be estopped from denying that person any interest if they have subsequently acted to their detriment in reliance upon the assurance. A person who fulfils the requirements of an assurance, reliance and detriment will enjoy an estoppel "equity" which the court will "satisfy" by the award of an appropriate remedy. In circumstances where the nature of the assurance is that the person will receive the ownership of the land the court may satisfy the equity by ordering the owner to transfer the freehold title to the claimant.[98] For example, in *Pascoe v. Turner*[99] the plaintiff and defendant lived together in a house owned by the plaintiff. He had told her that the house was hers, and in reliance on this representation she spent money redecorating and improving the property, and purchased furniture and furnishings. When their relationship ended the plaintiff purported to determine any licence the defendant might have to occupy the property and sought possession. The Court of Appeal held that defendant had established an entitlement to an estoppel equity since she had clearly acted to her detriment in reliance upon the plaintiff's assurances, and that the appropriate remedy for the satisfaction of that equity was to order the plaintiff to fulfil the defendant's expectations by transferring the freehold ownership to her.

[98] See: *Dillwyn v. Llewelyn* (1862) 4 De G. F. & J. 517.
[99] [1979] 1 W.L.R. 431.

Chapter 5

Leasehold Ownership

The Nature of Leasehold Ownership

1 Essence of leasehold ownership

In the previous chapter it has been seen that the closest concept to the absolute ownership of land in English law is offered by the legal freehold. However, it is not always the case that the freehold owner of land wishes to use and occupy it himself, and leasehold ownership provides a mechanism by which the freeholder can grant another person the right to occupy and use the land that he owns. Generally, such a right is granted in return for the payment of rent which enables the freeholder to economically exploit his land by in effect selling the right of occupation and use to someone else. The person who grants a lease becomes the landlord and the person who enjoys the leasehold interest in the land is the tenant. The landlord who creates a leasehold interest does not lose all entitlement to the land. He retains his ownership subject to the rights of the tenant, and his interest is known as the freehold reversion. When the lease comes to an end, either through the passage of time or if it is forfeited for some reason, the full unencumbered freehold title to the property will return to him. It is also possible for a new leasehold interest to be carved out of an existing leasehold. For example, if David enjoys a 99 year lease of a house he may, subject to any limitations in his own lease, grant a 12 months tenancy to Elizabeth. Such a lease is described as a "sub-lease" whereas the lease between David and the fee simple owner is the "head-lease."

2 Varieties of leasehold ownership

The concept of leasehold title has proved extremely flexible as a means of facilitating a separation between the ownership and use of land. Leases may be granted for any period of time, and it is not uncommon for a lease to be granted for 999 years or more. On the other hand leases can also be granted for very short periods of time and students often rent houses during their university studies for periods of six months or a year. Leasehold interests are significant in commercial contexts, for example the majority of shops in modern developments are granted leases of their premises, but also residentially, whether in the private sector or public council housing.

3 Leasehold interests confer the right to "exclusive possession"

The leasehold interest is not the only means by which an owner can enable another person to use and occupy his land. A person who enters onto land owned by another without permission is a trespasser. However, if the owner has granted him permission to enter his land then no trespass will be committed if he does so. An owner may therefore grant a person permission to enter and to use his land. Such a permission is known as a licence. However, the central distinction between a lease and a licence is that a lease confers the right to "exclusive possession" on the tenant, whereas a licence does not confer such a right on the licensee. The right to exclusive possession means the right to exclude all persons from the land, including the landlord who has granted the lease. The tenant is therefore entitled to refuse the landlord entry to the land and if the landlord attempts to enter without permission he will stands as a trespasser vis-à-vis the tenant, who will be entitled to seek appropriate relief. However, a licensee enjoys a mere permission to be present on the licensor's land and has no right to exclude the licensor. If the licensor enters the land without the licensee's permission he will not commit a trespass and there are no remedies available to the licensee. Whether exclusive occupation has been granted or not provides the central test whether a right which has been granted to occupy land is to be characterised as a lease or a licence.

4 Leasehold interests as proprietary interests in land

A further central distinction between leasehold interests and licences is that only leasehold interests are proprietary rights in land. A licence confers a purely personal right on the licensee as against the licensor. As such the licence is incapable of enduring through changes of ownership of the land, so that if the owner/licensor transfers or sells the property to a third person, that third person will not be bound by the licence previously granted by the owner. Despite a number of attempts by Lord Denning to elevate contractual licences to a proprietary status, the purely personal character of licences was categorically affirmed by the Court of Appeal in *Ashburn Anstalt v. Arnold*.[1] In some exceptional circumstances a licence may be binding on a transferee of the land by means of a constructive trust, but this is as result of the conduct of the transferee rather than as a consequence of the inherent nature of the licence itself.[2]

5 Leasehold as a legal estate

Leasehold interests are also capable of enjoying the status of legal estates in land. By section 1(1)(b) of the Law of Property Act 1925 a "term of years absolute" is capable of existing as a legal estate in land. The definitions section of the Act makes clear that a "term of years" includes a lease for a period of less than a year,[3] so that leases of any

[1] [1989] Ch. 1.
[2] See Chap. 12.
[3] Law of Property Act 1925, s.205(1)(xxvii).

duration are capable of creating a legal estate in the land. However, as will be seen below, whether a lease in fact creates a legal estate or merely an equitable interest will depend upon whether the appropriate formalities for its creation have been followed.

6 Leasehold as a registrable interest

As well as potentially constituting a legal estate, leasehold ownership forms one of the twin foundation interests of the system of land registration, since by the Land Registration Act 1925, s.123 a term of years absolute for more than 21 years is a registrable interest, and will therefore, when registered, form a title against which other subsidiary interests in land can be protected.

7 Transferability of leasehold ownership

Just as the fee simple interest in land may be transferred from one person to another so the interest of both the landlord and the tenant may be transferred. The landlord's "freehold reversion" and the tenant's leasehold interest may be transferred by assignment, subject to any provisions in the lease.

8 Terms of the leasehold relationship

As has been noted, leasehold interests arise in a wide range of circumstances. Although in all cases a relationship is established between the landlord and the tenant it is obvious that the terms of that relationship will also widely differ. The terms of the relationship between the landlord and tenant are described as the covenants of the lease, and they consist of the agreements of the parties as to their respective roles. A simple covenant entered by the tenant is the obligation to pay rent to the landlord. The landlord may promise to keep the premises in good repair. Some covenants will be implied into leases by either statute or the common law. A number of the most common and important covenants will be examined below, although a full analysis is outside of the scope of this book and is more properly the subject of the Law of Landlord and Tenant. Since the covenants of a lease are essentially contractual provisions entered into by the landlord and tenant difficulties arise as to their enforceability if the freehold reversion or the tenancy is transferred to another person, since that person will not have been privy to the original contract. In order to deal with the difficulties caused by this interface between the property and contract special rules have developed to govern the enforceability of leasehold covenants between successors in title to the original landlord and tenant. The general principles which govern such enforceability will be examined in detail below.

9 State regulation of leasehold ownership

(a) The need for state intervention

When an owner of land agrees to grant a lease to a tenant they effectively enter into a contractual bargain. However, there is generally a disparity between the relative bargaining strengths of the parties, so that the landlord is in a stronger position and is able to dictate the terms of the lease. The tenant is usually much more vulnerable since he needs to find somewhere to live. If the law merely allowed unrestrained freedom of contract to operate tenants would be open to unmitigated exploitation by landlords imposing extremely harsh terms upon them. In particular they would be able to charge unacceptably high rents, securing compliance by the threat of termination of the lease and eviction. Given the potential vulnerability of the tenant to exploitation the state has intervened to regulate the relationship of landlord and tenant. This state control has had a marked impact on the development of the law relating to leases, as will be seen below. A detailed analysis is beyond the scope of this book and only a brief outline of the most important legislation will be given here by way of introduction.[4]

(b) Security of tenure and rent control

From the First World War tenants were protected against poor quality housing, and the Rent Acts enacted after the Second World War provided them with security of tenure, so that they could not be easily removed, and rent control so that they could not be charged excessive rents. Leases granted before January 15, 1989 are still capable of enjoying status as a "protected" or "statutory" tenancy under the Rent Act 1977. A tenancy is a "protected tenancy" during the contractually agreed term and a "statutory tenancy" arises when the contractual agreed term has come to an end.[5] The landlord cannot terminate the tenancy without a court order and this will only be given in limited circumstances, such as the non-payment of rent or neglect causing the condition of the premises to deteriorate.[6] In a Rent Act tenancy the rent is also controlled so that the tenant is only obliged to pay a "fair rent," which overrides any rent agreed by the parties and is often lower than the market rent for the property. However during the 1980s government policy considered that the Rent Acts provided too much protection to tenants with the effect that they operated as a disincentive to private landlords letting their property, thus stultifying the private rented sector. The Housing Act 1988 therefore introduced a reduced level of protection with the objective of encouraging landowners to grant leases without the fear that they would be stuck with a tenant paying uneconomic rent who could not be removed. Tenancies created after January 15, 1989 may take the form of an "assured tenancy." A tenant under an assured tenancy enjoys similar protection from eviction but there is no provision for payment of a fair rent. There is no control of initial rents except where a landlord serves notice to increase the rent under an assured periodic tenancy, in which case a rent assessment committee can determine the rent that the landlord might reasonably be expected to have obtained on the open market.[7] The Act also introduced the "assured shorthold tenancy," which is a lease for a specified period of not less than six months where the landlord has served notice on the tenant that the tenancy will be an assured shorthold. The chief difference is that the assured shorthold does not offer security of tenure, so that at the end of the fixed term a new shorthold tenancy arises which can be terminated by the landlord giving two months notice. The tenant is

[4] For further information see: Bright & Gilbert, *Landlord and Tenant Law: The Nature of Tenancies* (1995).
[5] Rent Act 1977, s.2.
[6] See: Rent Act 1977, Sched. 15.
[7] Housing Act 1988, s.14(1).

entitled to refer the initial rent of a shorthold tenancy to a rent assessment committee, but the committee is only entitled to make a determination if the rent is "significantly higher than the landlord might reasonably be expected to obtain having regard to the rents payable under assured tenancies of similar houses in the locality.[8] Assured shorthold tenancies therefore provide relatively little protection for tenants in terms of rent control or security of tenure and have proved popular with landlords as a means of facilitating short term letting. The majority of students renting private housing during their courses will do so on the basis of such an assured shorthold tenancy. The Housing Act 1996 has recently amended the law so that a tenancy will be an "assured shorthold" unless the landlord serves notice on the tenant that it is an "assured tenancy" conferring greater security, and there is no requirement of a fixed term.[9] However, where such an assured shorthold tenancy is not for a fixed period the landlord is not entitled to recover possession until at least six months has elapsed from the grant of the tenancy.[10]

THE ESSENTIAL REQUIREMENTS OF A LEASE

1 The three *Street v. Mountford* criteria

One of the most difficult issues of the post-war period has been to satisfactorily differentiate between leases and licences. In the leading case of *Street v. Mountford*[11]. Lord Templeman propounded a definition of a lease which included three essential criteria. He stated that "to constitute a tenancy the occupier must be granted exclusive possession for a fixed or periodic term certain in consideration of a premium or period payments."[12] The three elements are therefore (i) the grant of exclusive possession; (ii) for a time period which is certain and (iii) the payment of rent. As these are examined it will be seen that the crucial criteria is often the presence or absence of exclusive possession.

2 Exclusive Possession

(a) Differentiating leases and licences

As has already been noted above the central difference between a lease and a licence is that a lease confers exclusive possession on the tenant whereas a licence confers merely a right to occupation of the land. Difficulties arose because of the attempts of landowners to avoid the protection afforded to tenants under the Rents Acts by instead granting mere licences which would not fall under the statutory protection. It therefore became common for landowners to grant rights of occupancy which were in practice leases but which were stated by the parties to be mere licences. Initially, the

[8] Housing Act 1988, s.20.
[9] Housing Act 1988, s.19A as introduced by, Housing Act 1996, s.96.
[10] Housing Act 1996, s.21(5) as amended by, Housing Act 1996, s.99.
[11] [1985] A.C. 809.
[12] *ibid.* at 818.

courts responded to these attempts by adopting a clear policy of refusing to allow property owners to avoid Rent Act provisions by framing their agreements as licences. For example, in *Facchini v. Bryson*[13] it was held that a tenancy had been created even where the agreement between the parties was stated to be a licence and it contained the provision that "nothing in this agreement shall be construed to create a tenancy." The policy was stated by Denning L.J.:

> "The occupation has all the features of a tenancy, and the parties cannot by the mere words of their contract turn it into something else. Their relationship is determined by the law and not by the label which they choose to put on it . . . It is most important that we should adhere to this principle, or else we might find all landlords granting licences and not tenancies, and we should make a hole in the rent acts through which could be driven — I will not say in these days a coach and four — but an articulated vehicle."[14]

However, in a growing number of cases through the seventies the courts came to give primacy to the parties' intentions rather than to the objective nature of what had been created. This may have been reflective of a feeling that the Rent Acts, rather than providing protection for vulnerable tenants as had been the case in the post war period, were an increasing burden to landlords and badly distorted the private rented market in property. In marked contrast to his comments on the policy of preventing avoidance of the Rent Acts in *Facchini v. Bryson*[15] Lord Denning M.R. recognised in *Shell-Mex and BP Ltd v. Manchester Garages Ltd*[16] that giving primacy to the parties intentions would enable landlords to avoid the protection offered by the Rent Acts but commented: "I realise that this means that the parties can, by agreeing on a licence, get out of the Act; but so be it; it may be no bad thing." This new approach was exemplified by the decision of the Court of Appeal in *Somma v. Hazelhurst.*[17] An unmarried couple entered into an agreement with the owner of a house for the use of a double bed-sitting room. The agreement stated that it was a licence, and the two partners were required to sign separate agreements and the licence fee was paid separately by each of them to the owner. It was a term of the agreement that the licensees share the room with "such other licensees or invitees whom the licensor shall from time to time permit to use the room." Although it was patently clear that in reality the couple in fact enjoyed an exclusive occupancy of the room, the casting of the agreement as a licence was intended to avoid the consequences of Rent Act control of the rent payable. The couple subsequently claimed that the agreement in fact created a tenancy and sought Rent Act protection, but the Court of Appeal held that a mere licence had been created, a conclusion which would not be likely on the same facts following the House of Lords decision in *Street v. Mountford.*[18]

[13] [1952] 1 T.L.R. 1386.
[14] *ibid.* at 1389–1390.
[15] [1952] 1 T.L.R. 1386.
[16] [1971] 1 All E.R. 841 at 845.
[17] 1978] 1 W.L.R. 1014.
[18] [1985] A.C. 809, 826 where Lord Templeman expressly disapproved of the decision of the Court of Appeal in *Somma v. Hazelhurst.*

(b) A subjective approach to differentiating between leases and licenses

The decision of the Court of Appeal in *Somma v. Hazelhurst*[19] is best explained as the consequence of taking a subjective approach to the issue of differentiating between leases and licences. The prime factor to be taken into consideration is the expressed intentions of the parties, not the substantive and objective reality of what they created.[20] Cumming-Bruce L.J. took the view that the agreement was clearly in the form of a licence and that the terms of the agreement were consistent with there being a licence and not a lease. Although some of the provisions of the agreement, especially in relation to sharing the room with other occupants, may prove unattractive there was no reason to undo the bargain that the parties had knowingly entered. He stated:.

> "We can see no reason why an ordinary landlord . . . should not be able to grant a licence to occupy an ordinary house. If that is what both he and the licensee intend and if they can frame any written agreement in such a way as to demonstrate that it is not really an agreement for a lease masquerading as a licence, we can see no reason in law or justice why they should be prevented from achieving that object. Nor can we see why their common intentions should be categorised as bogus or unreal or as sham merely on the ground that the court disapproves of the bargain."[21]

However, although this approach may be said to uphold the complete freedom of contract of the parties, the reality is surely that the characterisation of the interest as a licence is somewhat disingenuous. The room which was occupied by the couple was a mere 22 feet by 18 feet, and the suggestion that the owner had the right to impose other occupiers on them is ridiculous. Similarly the licence contained terms that if either of the couple left the owner was entitled to impose another occupier on the remaining licensee. As was pointed out this could mean that if one of the couple left the owner could introduce another person of a different sex to occupy the same room. Although the court concluded that these provisions were not a sham, again the reality would seem to be that the landlord never had any intention of introducing additional or replacement occupiers, but that the whole purpose of the provisions was to ensure that the agreement appeared to have the character of a licence rather than a lease.

(c) An objective approach to differentiating between leases and licences

The primacy of the subjective approach, which paid closer attention to the parties' expressed intention than the reality of their arrangement, was finally ended by the decision of the House of Lords in *Street v. Mountford*.[22] The facts were that the owner, Mr Street, granted Mrs Mountford a licence to occupy furnished rooms in a house. The agreement was stated to be a licence and a "licence fee" of £37 per week was payable. Mrs Mountford then claimed that the agreement created a Rent Act

[19] [1978] 1 W.L.R. 1014.
[20] See also: *Aldrington Garages Ltd v. Fielder* (1978) 37 P. & C.R. 461; *Sturolson and Co. v. Weniz* (1984) 17 H.L.R. 140.
[21] *ibid.* at 1025.
[22] [1985] A.C. 809.

protected tenancy. The House of Lords, whose judgment was delivered by Lord Templeman, concluded that in reality a tenancy had been created. Central to his conclusion was the adoption of an objective approach to determining what had been created by the parties' agreement. The key elements of a tenancy were identified as "exclusive possession at a rent for a term." If these factors were present then a tenancy had been created and not a mere licence, irrespective of what the parties had chosen to call it. He stated the general principle:

> "In my opinion in order to ascertain the nature and quality of the occupancy . . . the court must decide whether upon its true construction the agreement confers on the occupier exclusive possession. If exclusive possession at a rent for a term does not constitute a tenancy then the distinction between a contractual tenancy and a contractual licence of land becomes wholly unidentifiable."[23]

The description given by the parties to their agreement is not therefore determinative of its legal character. As he stated:

> "[T]he consequences in law of the agreement, once concluded, can only be determined by consideration of the effect of the agreement. If the agreement satisfied all the requirements of a tenancy, then the agreement produced a tenancy and the parties cannot alter the effect of the agreement by insisting that they only created a licence."[24]

He expressed the objective nature of the test in the memorable aphorism that "the manufacture of a five-pronged implement for manual digging results in a fork even if the manufacturer, unfamiliar with the English language, insists that he intended to make and has made a spade."[25] The objective approach had also been adopted by the High Court of Australia in *Radaich v. Smith*[26] where Windeyer J., whose sentiments were approved by Lord Templeman,[27] had held that it was inherently contradictory to say that a man who had by agreement been granted a right of exclusive possession of land was not a tenant but a mere licensee. In the later case of *Antoniades v. Villiers*[28] Lord Templeman re-emphasised this objective approach: "an express statement of intention is not decisive and . . . the court must pay attention to the facts and surrounding circumstances and to what people do as well as to what people say." The objective approach is not confined to residential leases but also applies to leases of commercial property. In *Rochester Poster Services Ltd v. Dartford Borough Council*[29] the plaintiffs had made an agreement for the use of a poster site at the perimeter of business premises under an agreement described as a licence. Despite this nomenclature it was held that the agreement in fact conferred exclusive possession of the site and therefore their interest was in the nature of a tenancy.

[23] *ibid.* at 825.
[24] *ibid.* at 819.
[25] *ibid.* at 819.
[26] (1959) 101 C.L.R. 209.
[27] [1985] A.C. 809 at 827.
[28] [1990] 1 A.C. 417.
[29] (1991) 63 P. & C.R. 88.

(d) Advantages of the objective approach

The objective approach adopted by the House of Lords in *Street v. Mountford* prevents the use of false agreements to avoid the provisions of the Rent Acts. The Rent Acts were put in place for the very purpose of protecting vulnerable tenants with little bargaining power against the might of landlords, and to allow such protection to be avoided by the simple device of licence agreements was unacceptable. Such cases as *Somma v. Hazelhurst* would clearly be caught by the objective approach. Lord Templeman disapproved of the decision, holding that the "court should be astute to detect and frustrate sham devices and artificial transactions whose only object is to disguise the grant of a tenancy and to evade the Rent Acts."[30]

(e) Difficulties in applying the objective approach

However, despite the advantages of preventing easy avoidance of the rent acts, the objective approach in *Street v. Mountford* does not provide a comprehensive and easy solution to the problem of determining whether an agreement creates a lease or a licence. The heart of the problem is that although attention is now focused on the factual nature of the parties occupancy rather than on their agreement, the essential characteristic of leases, namely "exclusive possession" is essentially a legal rather than a factual concept. It is perfectly possible for a person to in fact enjoy exclusive occupation of premises whereas they have no legal entitlement to exclusive possession. For example, if an owner of a house goes abroad for a year and allows a friend to live in his house for that time, the friend may in fact enjoy the exclusive use of the house for the time the owner is away, but this does not mean that he enjoys the right to exclude the owner from the house. If the owner were to return to the house for the Christmas holiday without the friend's permission he would not be a trespasser. Therefore, the mere fact of exclusive occupation will not always mean that there is also a right to exclusive possession in law, and therefore a tenancy. However, the existence of factual exclusive occupation is the essential starting point to the determination whether there is exclusive possession. Where there is exclusive occupation there may also be exclusive possession, but where there is no exclusive occupation there cannot be exclusive possession and any interest must only constitute a licence. The difficulties were identified by Lord Donaldson M.R. in *Aslan v. Murphy*[31] where he noted that:

> "The occupier has in the end of the day to be a tenant or a lodger. He cannot be both. But there is a spectrum of exclusivity ranging from the occupier of a detached property under a full repairing lease, who is without doubt a tenant, to the overnight occupier of a hotel bedroom who, however upmarket the hotel, is without doubt a lodger. The dividing line — the sorting of the forks from the spades — will not necessarily or even usually depend upon a single factor, but upon a combination of factors."

[30] *ibid.* at 825.
[31] [1990] 1 W.L.R. 766, at 770.

(f) Identifying exclusive occupation

(i) Exclusive occupation in fact: Exclusive occupation is a purely factual state. It simply means that as a matter of fact a person, or number of persons, enjoy the sole and exclusive use of premises. For example, in *Somma v. Hazelhurst*[32] it could be said that the couple in question in fact enjoyed the exclusive occupancy of their double room. Similarly in *Street v. Mountford*[33] Mr and Mrs Mountford enjoyed the exclusive occupancy of their two rooms. In other cases it is clear that there is no exclusive occupancy, for example if an elderly lady in a university town allows a student to live in one of her spare rooms as a lodger. In such circumstances the lodger cannot be said to exclusively occupy the house.

(ii) Shared occupation of premises: The mere fact that a number of people occupy the same premises does not necessarily mean that there is no exclusive occupancy, since they may jointly occupy the premises. For example if a group of students join together and share a house which they rent although they do not individually enjoy exclusive occupation, jointly they are the exclusive occupiers of the house. However, particular difficulties have arisen in determining whether shared occupation of premises constituted a genuine joint tenancy or the grant of separate licences to the individual occupiers. In *A G Securities v. Vaughan*[34] an owner of a four-bedroomed flat entered into separate agreements with the four occupiers each expressed to be licences. The agreements contained provisions requiring the individual licensees to share the flat with all the other occupiers granted licences by the owner. The flat was kept fully occupied over a period of time so that whenever one occupier left another would be granted a licence by the owner. Such licensees had the sole use of a bedroom and shared use of the lounge, kitchen and bathroom. The House of Lords held that in these circumstances the occupiers were licensees and not joint tenants. Lord Templeman explained the crucial factors which led to this conclusion:

> "In the present case, if the four [occupiers] had been jointly entitled to exclusive occupation of the flat then, on the death of one of [them] the remaining three would be entitled to joint and exclusive occupation. But, in fact, on the death of one [occupier] the remaining three would not be entitled to joint and exclusive occupation of the flat. They could not exclude a fourth person nominated by the [owner]."[35]

In contrast, in *Antoniades v. Villiers*,[36] which was decided at the same time, the House of Lords found that there was a joint tenancy rather than individual licences. A couple occupied a flat and enjoyed exclusive occupation of it in fact. However, the owner had required them to enter separate agreements with himself described as licences and required them to separately undertake to pay half the rent. The licence also contained a clause reserving the owner the right to go into occupation of the flat with the couple or to nominate others to occupy it with them. The House of Lords took the view that

[32] [1978] 1 W.L.R. 1014.
[33] [1985] A.C. 809.
[34] [1990] 1 A.C. 417.
[35] *ibid.* at 460.
[36] [1990] 1 A.C. 417.

this provision in the agreements was a pretence and that there had never been any real intention on the part of the owner to enter occupation himself or impose any other occupiers on the couple. The couple were therefore held to be tenants in joint possession.[37]

(iii) Landlord's retention of keys?: The mere fact that a landlord retains the keys to premises does not mean that the occupiers do not enjoy exclusive occupation. In *Aslan v. Murphy*[38] the owner of premises had entered into a "licence" agreement which included a term that he, as the licensor, would "retain the keys and has absolute right of entry at all times." The Court of Appeal rejected the argument that of itself the retention of the keys prevented the finding of a tenancy. The principles were stated by Lord Donaldson M.R.:

> "What matters is what underlies the provision as to keys. Why does the owner want a key, want to prevent keys being issued to the friends of the occupier or want to prevent a lock being changed? A landlord may well need a key in order that he may be able to enter quickly in the event of emergency: fire, burst pipes or whatever. He may need a key to enable him or those authorised by him to read meters or do repairs which are his responsibility. None of these underlying reasons would of themselves indicate that the true bargain between the parties was such that the occupier was in law a lodger."[39]

In contrast, if the keys were retained to enable the landlord to provide such services as cleaning or bed-making then the retention would indicate that a tenancy was not granted.

(iv) Exclusive occupation of business premises: Just as in residential premises the absence of exclusive occupation will prevent the finding of a tenancy, the absence of exclusive occupation will render an agreement to occupy business premises a mere licence. In *Shell-Mex and BP Ltd v. Manchester Garages Ltd*[40] the plaintiffs owned a petrol-filling station and granted the defendants the right to occupy for a year under an agreement called a licence. The defendants claimed that they were tenants. However, the agreement restricted the defendants to selling the plaintiff's brand of petrol and allowed the plaintiff's to enter the premises whenever they wanted to alter the layout, decoration or equipment of the premises. In these circumstances the Court of Appeal held that there was no tenancy.

(g) Situations where there is no exclusive occupation

(i) Consequence of no exclusive occupation: Since exclusive occupation is a factual pre-requisite of exclusive possession, in certain well-recognised cases where there is no exclusive occupation there cannot be a lease but merely a licence.

[37] See also: *Hadjiloucas v. Crean* [1988] 1 W.L.R. 1006, where sharing occupiers were found to be tenants; *Stribling v. Wickham* [1989] 2 E.G.L.R. 35 where there was held to be a licence.
[38] [1990] 1 W.L.R. 767.
[39] *ibid.* at 773.
[40] [1971] 1 All E.R. 841.

(ii) Lodgers: It is clear that lodgers cannot enjoy the status of tenants but are mere licensees of the premises in which they lodge. As Lord Templeman stated in *Street v. Mountford*[41]:

> "In the case of residential accommodation there is no difficulty in deciding whether the grant confers exclusive possession. An occupier of residential accommodation at a rent for a term is either a lodger or a tenant. The occupier is a lodger if the landlord provides attendance or services which require the landlord or his servants to exercise unrestricted access to and use of the premises. A lodger is entitled to live in the premises but cannot call the place his own."

The central feature of lodgers is therefore their inability to refuse access to the premises they occupy to the owner or his servants acting on his behalf. For example, in the example suggested above of the student living with the elderly lady, the student does not enjoy the right to exclude her from the premises, and even though he may not wish it she remains entitled to enter his room whenever she wishes.

(iii) Provision of attendance: One of the most common factors which will mitigate against the finding of exclusive occupation is if the owner of the occupied property has agreed to provide regular services on behalf of the occupier. Such services are described as attendance, and what is meant are only those services which are personal to the occupiers use of the premises he is occupying, and not services in regard to the common areas.[42] For example, the owner may agree to provide an occupier with daily cleaning of his room. This would constitute such attendance, whereas the agreement to clean the common staircase of a house divided into separate flats would not. An example of a case where occupants were found to be lodgers and not tenants because of the provision of attendance services is *Marcou v. De Silvesa*.[43] A number of persons occupied flats in a house on the basis of agreements with the owner described as a licences. These agreement included provisions that the licensor would retain keys to the flats and enjoy the absolute right of entry at all times; that the licensor could require the licensees to vacate their flat at any time and move to another flat of comparable size in the house; and that the licensor would provide attendance for the licensees, including acting as housekeeper, cleaning the flats, collecting rubbish and cleaning windows. In these circumstance the Court of Appeal held that the occupiers did not enjoy exclusive occupation and were therefore mere lodgers and not tenants.

(iv) Sham or pretence provisions: However, the mere presence of provisions in an agreement which seem to suggest that exclusive occupation is not enjoyed will not be conclusive if they can be shown to be a sham.[44] In other words, if the agreement contained terms which the owner had inserted not because he wished to continue to enjoy a right of access to the premises but merely to ensure that the agreement appeared in substance to be a licence rather than a tenancy, the Court will look to the reality of what the parties do, rather than to the mere terms of the agreement and what they are technically allowed to do. As Lord Templeman stated in *Street v.*

[41] [1985] A.C. 809, at 818.
[42] See: *Pasler v. Grinling* [1948] A.C. 291; *Marchant v. Charters* [1977] 1 W.L.R. 1181.
[43] (1986) 52 P. & C.R. 204.
[44] In *Antoniades v. Villiers* [1990] 1 A.C. 417, Lord Templeman preferred to use the term "pretense."

Mountford[45], commenting on the decision of the Court of Appeal in *Somma v. Hazelhurst*[46]: "the court should, in my opinion, be astute to detect and frustrate sham devices and artificial transactions whose only object is to disguise the grant of a tenancy and to evade the Rent Acts." In *Marcou v. De Silvaesa*[47] it was argued that the agreements between the occupiers and the owner were sham provisions. In particular there was a provision that the licensees were not entitled to use the premises between 10.30am and 12.00am each day and a provision that the licensor was entitled to remove and substitute furniture in the flats. It was held that although this provision might itself be a sham provision, this did not mean that the agreement as a whole was a sham, since the other terms of the agreements did envisage the performance of attendance and services which detracted from exclusive occupation. In contrast, in the very similar case of *Aslan v. Murphy*[48] the Court of Appeal held that an agreement did contain sham provisions which were to be ignored and held that there was a tenancy. The occupier had entered into a licence agreement for a small basement room which included the provision that the licensee had no right to use the room between 10.30am and 12.00am and that the licensor would retain the keys to the room. Lord Donaldson M.R. took the view that "both provisions were wholly unrealistic and were clearly pretences," since no services had been provided. The occupancy was therefore a tenancy.

(v) Long-term hotel residents: It seems clear that a person who is a long-term hotel resident does not enjoy a tenancy of the room they occupy. In *Appah v. Parncliffe Investments Ltd*[49] a woman occupying a room at the "Emperor's Gate Hotel" was held to be a licensee and not a tenant. The provision of cleaning, bed making and linen by the owners all necessitated entry which was inconsistent with exclusive occupation.[50] The large numbers of persons now housed in bed and breakfast accommodation rather than council housing do not therefore enjoy tenancies but are mere licensees.

(vi) Residents of homes for the elderly: It is also clear that a resident of a home for the elderly will not enjoy a tenancy. In *Abbeyfield (Harpenden) Society v. Woods*[51] a man of 85 occupied a room at a home for old people in return for a weekly payment. A letter he received stated that he was entitled to "sole occupation" of his room, and that the society would provide service, meals, heating, lighting and a resident housekeeper. When the man was asked to leave he refused and claimed that he enjoyed exclusive possession and was entitled to Rent Act protection from eviction. The Court of Appeal held that he enjoyed a mere licence, with the central factors taken into consideration the provision of services and the entirely personal nature of the arrangement between the man and the society.

(vii) Hostel accommodation: Occupation of hostel accommodation is also unlikely to give rise to the exclusive occupation which is a necessary pre-requisite of a tenancy. In

[45] [1985] A.C. 809 at 825.
[46] [1978] 1 W.L.R. 1014.
[47] (1986) 52 P. & C.R. 204.
[48] [1990] 1 W.L.R. 766.
[49] [1964] 1 W.L.R. 1064.
[50] See also: *Luganda v. Service Hotels Ltd* [1969] 2 Ch. 209; *Mayflower Cambridge Ltd v. Secretary of State* (1975) 30 P. & C.R. 28.
[51] [1968] 1 W.L.R. 374.

R. v. South Middlesex Rent Tribunal, ex p. Beswick[52] a lady who lived in a room at a YWCA hostel was held to be a licensee and not a tenant. In *Westminster City Council v. Clarke*[53] the House of Lords considered the case of a man who was housed in a hostel containing thirty-one single rooms for homeless men. Their agreement entitled the council to change the accommodation without notice and to require the occupant to share. The occupier was required to be in his room by 11pm and not to entertain visitors after that time. The House of Lords held that in these circumstances the grant of exclusive possession would have been inconsistent with the purposes for which they provided the accommodation, and that the occupants were licenses and not tenants.

(viii) Occupancy of furnished rooms: In general a person who occupies furnished rooms will be characterised as a lodger rather than a tenant. In *Marchant v. Charters*[54] a man occupied what had been described as an "attractive bachelor service apartment," which comprised a bed-sitting room. The owner provided regular services, including daily cleaning and weekly provision of clean linen. In these circumstances the Court of Appeal held that the occupier was a mere licensee. In relation to the provision of attendance it was held irrelevant that on some occasions he had refused the services. For similar reasons students who occupy rooms in a university halls of residence will not be regarded as tenants, since the university requires access for cleaning and the provision of other services.

(h) Exclusive occupation which does not indicate exclusive possession

(i) General principles: Although in the absence of exclusive occupation there cannot be a lease but merely a licence, the presence of exclusive occupation in fact does not conclusively indicate the presence of exclusive possession. Once such factual exclusive occupation has been established the question becomes one of considering whether there are any features of the circumstances of the occupancy or of the relationship between the owner and occupier which would indicate that any agreement was not intended to confer the right to exclusive possession. As Lord Templeman stated in *Street v. Mountford*[55]:

> "Sometimes it may be difficult to discover whether, on the true construction of an agreement, exclusive possession is conferred. Sometimes it may appear from the surrounding circumstances that there was no intention to create legal relationships. Sometimes it may appear from the surrounding circumstances that the right to exclusive possession is referable to a legal relationship other than a tenancy. Legal relationships to which the grant of exclusive possession might be referable and which would or might negative the grant of an estate or interest in the land include occupancy under a contract for the sale of the land, occupancy pursuant to a contract of employment or occupancy referable to the holding of an office."

[52] *The Times,* March 26, 1976.
[53] [1992] 2 A.C. 288.
[54] [1977] 1 W.L.R. 1181.
[55] [1985] A.C. 809 at 826.

It is clear from these comments that there are a number of well recognised circumstances where the grant of exclusive occupation will not be taken to amount to the grant of a tenancy. However, where the only circumstances are that residential accommodation is offered and accepted with exclusive occupation for a term, at a rent, a tenancy will definitely result. This approach of establishing factual exclusive occupation and then looking to see if there are any other factors which indicate that a tenancy was not intended are an echo of the approach advocated by Denning L.J. in *Facchini v. Bryson*[56] where he stated:

> "In all the cases where an occupier has been held to be a licensee there has been something in the circumstances, such as a family arrangement, and act of friendship or generosity or such like to negative any intention to create a tenancy. In such circumstances it would be unjust to saddle the owner with a tenancy, with all the momentous consequences that that entails nowadays, when there was no intention to create a tenancy at all."[57]

(ii) Service occupancy: An occupier who enjoys exclusive occupation of premises as a consequence of his employment will not enjoy a tenancy if his occupancy is characterised as "service occupancy." The general principles were stated by Lord Templeman in *Street v. Mountford*[58] who stated that:

> "A service occupier is a servant who occupies his master's premises in order to perform his duties as a servant. In those circumstances the possession and occupation of the servant is treated as the possession and occupation of the master and the relationship of landlord and tenant is not created."[59]

Where a person is required to occupy premises by his employer his occupation is likely to be a service occupancy and a licence rather than a tenancy. In *Smith v. Seghill Overseers*.[60] Mellor J. propounded as the relevant test whether the servant is required to occupy premises in order to better perform his duties as a servant. For example, a school housemaster who occupies a school house within the school grounds is unlikely to enjoy a tenancy and will be a mere licensee of the school since his occupancy is to enable him to more effectively act as a housemaster. Other common examples of service occupancies include farm workers, police officers and members of the armed forces. It does not have to be strictly necessary for the employee to occupy the premises provided he is required to do so with a view to the more efficient performance of his duties. For example, in *Fox v. Dalby*[61] a sergeant required to occupy a particular house by his commanding officer was held not to be a tenant. In *Glasgow Corporation v. Johnstone*[62] the question was whether a non-conformist clergyman, who

[56] [1952] 1 T.L.R. 1386.
[57] *ibid.* at 1389.
[58] [1985] A.C. 809 at 818.
[59] See: *Mayhew v. Suttle* (1854) 4 El. & Bl. 347.
[60] (1875) L.R. 10 Q.B. 422 at 428.
[61] (1874) L.R. 10 C.P. 285.
[62] [1965] A.C. 609.

occupied a house which was part of the church building, was a tenant or whether the church could itself be said to occupy the building.[63] The minister's duties included attending the services, counting the collection and acting as caretaker of the church. The House of Lords held that although it was not strictly necessary for him to reside in that house, since he could still have performed his duties if he had lived a short distance away though with some loss of efficiency, he was not a tenant because he was required to live there which was of material assistance to the carrying out of his duties.[64] However, if the occupancy was in no sense required by the nature of his employment it is unlikely to constitute a service occupancy. In *Murray Bull & Co Ltd v. Murray*[65] the defendant was appointed managing director of the plaintiff chemical research company and was granted a lease of a flat in the company's premises which enjoyed independent access to the street but also had direct access to the company's offices and laboratory. McNair J. held that in these circumstances his occupancy was not a service occupancy because the defendant was never required by the terms of his service to live in the flat and he did so only because it was convenient for both parties. Similarly in *Facchini v. Bryson*[66] an ice-cream manufacturer allowed his assistant to enter into occupation of a house in return for a weekly sum payable. Although the agreement between the parties expressly stated that a tenancy was not intended the Court of Appeal held that there was nothing in the circumstances of the occupation to negative the finding of a tenancy. The assistant's occupation was neither required by his employer nor necessary to enable him to perform his job more effectively. In *Crane v. Morris*[67] the Court of Appeal seemed to suggest that a requirement to live in the occupied premises was not necessary to constitute a service occupancy. Lord Denning M.R. held that a service occupancy could arise even where the occupier was only permitted to live in the premises for the convenience of his work.[68] However, in the more recent case of *Norris v. Checksfield*[69] the Court of Appeal seemed to reaffirm the need for a requirement to occupy. Woolf L.J. stated:

> "an employee can be a licensee, although his occupation of the premises is not *necessary* for the purposes of the employment, if he is genuinely *required* to occupy the premises for the *better performance* of his duties. In my judgement this . . . accurately reflects the law."[70]

A mechanic was allowed into occupation of a bungalow close to the depot where he worked on condition that he would apply for a PSV licence to be able to drive his employer's coaches. However, he had not informed his employer when he moved in that he was in fact disqualified from driving. The Court of Appeal held that although

[63] If the church could be said to occupy the building it would enjoy exemption from rate as a charity.
[64] See also: *Reed v. Cattermole* [1937] 1 K.B. 613.
[65] [1953] 1 Q.B. 211.
[66] [1952] 1 T.L.R. 1386.
[67] [1965] 3 All E.R. 77.
[68] See *Torbett v. Faulkner* [1952] 2 T.L.R. 660.
[69] [1991] 1 W.L.R. 1241.
[70] *ibid.* at 1244. He approved the judgments of the House of Lords in *Glasgow Corp. v. Johnstone* [1965] A.C. 609.

his presence in the bungalow was not strictly required in relation to his employment as a mechanic, the occupancy had been granted with the expectation that he would qualify as a coach driver, which would require his presence in the premises to enable him to assist with emergencies more effectively. That expectation provided "a sufficient factual nexus between the commencement of the occupation of the premises and the employment which would benefit from that occupation."[71] In these circumstances he was a service occupier and a mere license.

(iii) Family relationships: Where occupation is allowed on the basis of family ties it may be found that there was no intention to create a legal relationship and that therefore no tenancy is created. For example, in *Cobb v. Lane*[72] a sister owned a house in which she allowed her brother to live for more than thirteen years without paying rent. The Court of Appeal affirmed the decision of the judge at first instance that there had been no intention to grant a lease and that the brother was in occupation as a mere licensee. However, the mere existence of a family relationship does not necessarily preclude the finding that the creation of a legal relationship was intended. In *Nunn v. Dalrymple*[73] a man entered into an agreement with his parents-in-law that they should renovate a lodge on an estate that his father owned. On completing the renovation they gave up their tenancy of a council house and moved into the lodge, paying rent. The Court of Appeal held that since they enjoyed exclusive occupation of the lodge they were entitled to a tenancy, and that in the circumstances the presence of a family relationship did not negative that conclusion. A significant factor seems to have been that they did not need to move house and that they had given up their secure tenancy of a council house.

(iv) Friendship: Just as occupation on the basis of family relationships may prevent the finding of a tenancy, occupation granted on the basis of friendship may have the same result. In *Booker v. Palmer*[74] the owner of a cottage allowed evacuees who had been bombed out of their home to occupy it at the request of a friend. The Court of Appeal held that in these circumstances there was no intention to create legal relations. In *Heslop v. Burns*[75] Edward Timms purchased a cottage for Mr and Mrs Burns to live in in 1951 after developing a romantic attraction to Mrs Burns and becoming concerned over their poor living conditions when they were expecting a child. He subsequently became the god-daughter of the child and paid for her education. They remained in accommodation provided for him until after his death in 1970. At no point did they pay any rent. They claimed that their occupancy was in the nature of a tenancy.[76] The Court of Appeal held that there was a mere licence because there was no intention to create legal relations at all. As Stamp L.J. observed, "The home was not to be the [Burns'] castle but the house in which he allowed them to

[71] *ibid.* at 1245.
[72] [1952] 1 T.L.R. 1037.
[73] (1990) 59 P. & C.R. 231.
[74] [1942] 2 All E.R. 674.
[75] [1974] 3 All E.R. 406.
[76] A tenancy at will.

live."[77] In *Rhodes v Dalby*[78] Goff J. held that there was no tenancy created where a farmer allowed a teacher to live in a bungalow on his farm for two years on the basis of what was described as a "gentleman's agreement."

(v) Charity and generosity: Closely related to the preceding category, if an occupancy is granted on the basis of charitable or other motives of kindness or generosity this may indicate that no tenancy was intended. For example in *Marcroft Wagons Ltd v. Smith*[79] a daughter lived with her mother who was the statutory tenant of a house. On the mother's death the daughter asked the landlord to transfer the tenancy to herself, but the landlord refused. He did, however, allow her to remain in occupation in return for the payment of a rent. The Court of Appeal held that she was not entitled to a tenancy but was instead a mere licensee. Evershed M.R. took the view that it would be wrong to give landlords a disincentive to acting out of "ordinary human instincts of kindliness and courtesy" because of the fear that they would be stuck with tenants they could no longer removed if they allowed persons to remain in occupation for short periods in such circumstances.

(vi) Occupation of premises prior to completion of sale: Traditionally a person allowed into occupation of premises which he had agreed to purchase but before the transfer was completed was regarded as a tenant at will.[80] However, in *Street v. Mountford*[81] Lord Templeman suggested that in such cases there was no intention to create a tenancy.[82] However, this approach has not been universally applied. In *Javad v. Mohammed Aqil*[83] the defendant was allowed into occupation of business premises owned by the plaintiff in anticipation of their being able ultimately to agree the terms of a lease. The Court of Appeal held that the defendant was a tenant at will. This case may not be determinative since there was no contract between the parties and the issue before the court was not whether there was a tenancy or a licence but a tenancy at will or a periodic tenancy. In *Essex Plan Ltd v. Broadminster*[84] the plaintiff occupied premises of the defendant under a licence agreement which granted them an option to call for a long lease. After the licence had expired they remained in occupation. Hoffman J. held that irrespective of whether the agreement had granted the plaintiff's exclusive possession it had not created a tenancy. He stated the principle:

> "contracts for the sale of land commonly provide for the purchaser to be allowed into occupation as a licensee pending completion on terms that he is to pay all outgoings together with interest on the purchase money and is to keep the premises in good repair. The purchaser's possession is ancillary and referable to his interest in the land created by his contractual right to a conveyance and Lord Templeman acknowledges that such a relationship, although exhibiting the ordinary badges of a tenancy, does not create one."

[77] *ibid.* at 411.
[78] [1971] 2 All E.R. 1144.
[79] [1951] 2 K.B. 497.
[80] *Doe d Tomes v. Chamberlaine* (1839) 5 M. & W. 14.
[81] [1985] A.C. 809.
[82] See also: *Errington v. Errington* [1952] 1 K.B. 290; *Hyde v. Pearce* [1982] 1 W.L.R. 560.
[83] [1991] 1 W.L.R. 1007.
[84] [1988] 56 P. & C.R. 353.

3 Period which is certain

(a) Introduction to the requirement

The second requirement for a valid lease identified by Lord Templeman in *Street v. Mountford*[85] was a certain period of time. This means that if there is any uncertainty as to the commencement and duration of a lease it will fail. These are long established requirements. As Lush L.J. observed in *Marshall v. Berridge*[86]: "There must be a certain beginning and a certain ending, otherwise it is not a perfect lease, and a contract for a lease must . . . contain those elements."

(b) Certainty as to the commencement of a lease

(i) Agreement for a lease with no certain start date: Where an agreement contains no clear and certain date for the tenancy to commence there will be no valid creation of a lease. In *Harvey v. Pratt*[87] the parties made a written agreement for the lease of a garage which included the length of the term and details of the rent but did not give the date for commencement of the tenancy. The intended tenant had never gone into occupation and the Court of Appeal held that in the absence of a commencement date there was no valid contract for the lease.

(ii) Agreement for a lease with an uncertain start date: An agreement for the creation of a lease commencing on the occurrence of an uncertain event will not be invalid, and will be enforceable on the occurrence of the specified event. In *Brilliant v. Michaels*[88] Evershed J. held that a contract for a lease of a flat entered in 1943 and which did not include the date of commencement but was instead to take effect when the flat became vacant was not unenforceable when the tenant had actually taken possession on the flat becoming vacant. He stated the principle:

> "a contract for a lease is enforceable notwithstanding that the commencement of the term may be expressed by reference to the happening of a contingency which is at the time uncertain provided that, at the time that the contract is sought to be enforced, the event has occurred and the contingency has happened."[89]

Similarly, in *Swift v. Macbean*[90] an agreement for a lease made in August 1939 to run from the outbreak of any hostilities between Britain and another power was held valid when the war had broken out and the tenants taken possession.

(iii) Reversionary leases: Where an agreement is entered for the creation of a lease from a specified future date the lease is described as reversionary. For example, in *Mann, Crossman & Paulin Ltd v Registrar of the Land Registry*[91] a deed was executed by the lessor of a pub in 1917 granting a lease to run for 30 years from 1946. This was held to create an already vested proprietary interest in favour of the tenant which

[85] [1985] A.C. 809.
[86] (1881) 19 Ch.D. 233 at 245.
[87] [1965] 1 W.L.R. 1025.
[88] [1945] 1 All E.R. 121.
[89] *ibid*, at 128.
[90] [1942] 1 K.B. 375.
[91] [1918] 1 Ch. 202.

could be registered. However, the position was reformed by the Law of Property Act 1925 which renders void the creation of leases which will take effect more than 21 years after the date of the instrument creating them.[92] Contracts to create such void reversionary leases are themselves rendered void.

(c) Certainty as to the maximum duration of a lease

(i) A traditional common law requirement: The requirement that a lease will be invalid unless it has a certain maximum duration and clear end point is long established at common law.[93] Obviously this requirement is intended to prevent the possibility of a lease which might last forever, since such an interest in land would make a nonsense of the fee simple estate out of which the leasehold interest is carved. In most cases leases have a clearly defined length, as for example in a lease for 99 years. However, the difficulties have arisen in relation to leases whose length is defined in relation to the happening of an event rather than by specified period. In *Lace v. Chantler*[94] a tenant of a house granted a sub-lease to the defendant during World War Two which was expressed to be "for the duration of the war." The Court of Appeal held that this did not create a good leasehold interest because the term was uncertain. Lord Greene M.R. stated:

> "A term created by a leasehold tenancy agreement must be expressed either with certainty and specifically or by reference to something which can, at the time when the lease takes effect, be looked to as a certain ascertainment of what the term is meant to be. In the present case, when this tenancy agreement took effect, the term was completely uncertain. It was impossible to say how long the tenancy would last."

The court felt unable to follow the example of Rowlatt J. in *Great Northern Railway Co. v. Arnold*[95] who in a similar case during the First World War had construed such an agreement as a lease for 999 years determinable on the cessation of the war. Although the Court of Appeal did not feel such a result should be construed it does demonstrate the ease with which the purported difficulties of an uncertain term can be avoided. In the event the decision in *Lace v. Chantler* had the effect of rendering many war-time leases invalid and led to the passage of remedial legislation in the form of the War-Time Leases Act 1944.

(ii) An attempted re-interpretation of the requirement: Although the requirement of a certain duration was well established the Court of Appeal attempted a radical re-interpretation of what it meant in *Ashburn Anstalt v. Arnold*.[96] The occupier of a shop which was part of a complex which was being redeveloped was permitted to remain in occupation of his unit rent free until given a quarter's notice to give up possession by the owner. The Court of Appeal held that *Lace v. Chantler* was distinguishable as it

[92] s.149(3).
[93] See: *Say v. Smith* (1563) Plowd. 269.
[94] [1944] K.B. 368.
[95] (1916) 33 T.L.R. 114.
[96] [1989] Ch. 1.

was the event ending the lease which was uncertain and not the period of the lease itself. As Fox L.J. explained:

> "In *Lace v. Chantler* the duration of the war could not be predicated and there was no provision for either party to bring the tenancy to an end before the war ended, and that event itself might be very hard to pinpoint."

In contrast on the facts at issue the event which would bring the tenancy to an end, namely the giving of a quarter's notice, was sufficiently certain. Fox L.J. therefore explained this new approach to the requirement of certainty:

> "The result . . . is that the arrangement could be brought to an end by both parties in circumstances which are free from uncertainty in the sense that there would be no doubt whether the determining event had occurred. The vice of uncertainty in relation to the duration of the term is that the parties do not know where they stand."[97]

In consequence a valid tenancy was found.

(iii) A re-assertion of the traditional requirement: Despite the attempts of the Court of Appeal to introduce a more liberal interpretation of the requirement in *Ashburn Anstalt v. Arnold* in *Prudential Assurance Co Ltd v. London Residuary Body*[98] the House of Lords firmly re-asserted the traditional approach and overruled the innovative interpretation of *Lace v. Chantler*. The case concerned an agreement entered into in 1930 between the London County Council and the owner of a strip of land which fronted a highway. The owner sold the land to the Council and in return leased it back at a rent of £30 per annum. Their agreement stated that the tenancy should "continue until the . . . land is required by the council" for the purpose of widening the highway. The plaintiff and defendants were the successors in title to the original council and owner. The central question was whether the agreement was effective to create a lease on its terms. Lord Templeman held that *Ashburn Anstalt v. Arnold* had been wrongly decided and that if it was correct it would "make it unnecessary for a lease to be of a certain duration."[99] Lord Templeman pointed out that the argument that only the event which would bring the lease to an end must be certain was fallacious:

> "A lease can be made for five years subject to the tenant's right to determine if the war ends before the expiry of five years. A lease can be made from year to year subject to a fetter on the right of the landlord to determine the lease before the expiry of five years unless the war ends. Both leases are valid because they create a determinable certain term of five years. A lease might purport to be made for the duration of the war subject to the tenant's right to determine before the end of the war. A lease might be made from year to year subject to a fetter on the right of the landlord to determine the lease before the war ends. Both leases would be invalid because each purported to create an uncertain term. A

[97] *ibid.* at 12.
[98] [1992] 2 A.C. 386.
[99] *ibid.* at 395.

> term must either be certain or uncertain. It cannot be partly certain because the tenant can determine it at any time and partly uncertain because the landlord cannot determine it for an uncertain period. If the landlord does not grant and the tenant does not take a certain term the grant does not create a lease."[1]

The re-assertion of the requirement, although orthodox, was a matter of some regret to the House of Lords. The consequence was that the original lease was ineffective to create a lease. However, the fact that rent had been paid and accepted by the owners of the land was sufficient to generate an implied yearly periodic tenancy of the land. The nature of periodic tenancies is explained more fully below, but the consequence of this for the parties in *Prudential Assurance v. London Residuary Body*[2] was that the owners of the land had the right to terminate the Prudential's tenancy by giving six months notice. Lord Browne-Wilkinson pointed out that this led to a result wholly contrary to what the parties had intended when they contracted in 1930. The agreement had intended to ensure that the owners of the premises enjoyed a permanent road frontage for their premises, and that the only circumstances in which this could be lost was if the Council decided to widen the road, thus bringing the road closer to the premises. Instead the owners of the premises were left with unguaranteed frontage and the council with the freehold to a strip of land that they could not in practice use for any other purpose. In the light of this Lord Browne-Wilkinson questioned the appropriateness of the present rule, but felt that the security of existing property interests militated against a judicial change:

> "This bizarre outcome results from the application of an ancient and technical rule of law which requires the maximum duration of a term of years to be ascertainable from the outset. No one has produced any satisfactory rationale for the genesis of that rule. No one has been able to point to any useful purpose that it serves at the present day. If, by overruling the existing authorities, this House were able to change the law for the future only I would have urged your Lordships to do so. But for this house to depart from a rule relating to land law which has been established for many centuries might upset long established titles. I must therefore confine myself to expressing the hope that the Law Commission might look at the subject to see whether there is in fact any good reason now for maintaining a rule which operates to defeat contractually agreed arrangements between the parties."

(iv) The requirement applied to periodic tenancies: The requirement that the term of a lease must be of a fixed certain duration is especially difficult to apply in the context of periodic tenancies. The conceptual relationship between this requirement and periodic tenancies will be considered below, when the nature and operation of periodic tenancies is examined.[3]

[1] *ibid.*
[2] [1992] 2 A.C. 386.
[3] See below p. 98.

(v) Drafting leases which comply with the requirement: Although in both *Lace v. Chantler*[4] and *Prudential Assurance Co Ltd v. London Residuary Body*[5] the respective agreements were held ineffective to create valid leases, the difficulties could have been avoided by relatively simple drafting devices. There is no difficulty providing that a lease is to be determinable by one or both of the parties upon the happening of a particular event, and therefore to draft such leases with reference to a fixed maximum term coupled with a right to determine would satisfy the requirements. A lease for 99 years subject to the tenant's or landlord's right to determine "if the war ends" would have created a valid lease in *Lace v. Chantler*. Similarly, a lease for 999 years subject to the landlord's right to determine "when the land was required for a road widening scheme" would have created a valid lease in *Prudential Assurance Co. Ltd v. London Residuary Body*.
(vi) Statutory solution to common examples of uncertain terms: In a number of cases where parties might accidentally create a lease for an uncertain term statute has intervened to ensure that a valid lease is created. By Law of Property Act 1925, s.149(6) a lease granted for the period of a person's life will take effect as a lease for 90 years determinable on the death of that person.[6] Under the same section a lease granted to a person until marriage also takes effect as a 90 year lease determinable on marriage. A lease which is perpetually renewable, and therefore potentially capable of permanent endurance, takes effect as lease for 2000 years determinable only by the lessee.[7]
(vii) A single continuous term? It seems that it a single continuous term is not a necessity for a valid lease provided that the overall term is certain. In *Cottage Holiday Associates Ltd v. Customs and Excise Commissioners*[8] the question was whether leases of time-share cottages were leases for a period exceeding 21 years. The leases granted the right to occupy a cottage for one week a year for 80 years. Woolf J. held that the effect of these agreements was to create leases of discontinuous periods less than 21 years in duration, since a distinction was to be drawn between the duration of the lease creating the interest and the duration of the interest itself.[9]

4 Payment of rent

(a) Meaning of rent

One of the main functions of leases is to enable landowners to profit from land which they do not intend to put to use themselves. Rent is the consideration which is paid to the landlord in return for the tenancy. Rent only includes payments which are made in return for the use of the land,[10] and would not include any money which the tenant was required by the lease to expend on repair to the property. Rent will usually take the

[4] [1944] K.B. 368.
[5] [1992] 2 A.C. 386.
[6] Provided that the lease was granted "at a rent, or in consideration of a fine."
[7] Law of Property Act 1925, s.145, Sched. 15, para. 1; see: *Re Greenwood's Agreement* [1950] 1 All E.R. 436; *Re Hopkins Lease* [1972] 1 All E.R. 248.
[8] [1983] Q.B. 735.
[9] See also: *Smallwood v. Sheppards* [1895] 2 Q.B. 627.
[10] *Bostock v. Bryant* (1990) 61 P. & C.R. 23.

form of a money payment, but could also comprise benefits in kind, such as the performance of services for the landlord.

(b) Rent a necessity?

In *Street v. Mountford*[11] Lord Templeman seemed to suggest that the payment of rent was an essential criteria for the existence of a lease, since his repeated refrain through the judgment was that a tenancy consists of "exclusive possession, for a term, at a rent." However, in *Ashburn Anstalt v Arnold*[12] the Court of Appeal held that a tenancy could arise where exclusive possession was granted even though no rent was payable. Fox L.J. concluded that Lord Templeman had not intended to suggest that rent was essential: "We are unable to read Lord Templeman's speech . . . as laying down a principle of "no rent, no lease".[13] There were two main reasons why the Court of Appeal was able to reach this conclusion. Firstly, to hold that a rent was essential would be inconsistent with section 205(1)(xxvii) of the Law of Property Act 1925, which defines a "term of years absolute" as a "term of years (taking effect either in possession or in reversion *whether or not at a rent*)." Second, it would be inconsistent with the judgment of Windeyer J. in the Australian case of *Radaich v. Smith*,[14] which Lord Templeman had expressly approved, and which made no reference to a rent. Although many of the elements of the Court of Appeal's decision in *Ashburn Anstalt v. Arnold*[15] have been overruled in subsequent cases, this rejection of the requirement of a rent as an integral feature of a tenancy has been followed and remains good law.[16]

(c) Absence of a rent may indicate that no tenancy was intended

Although a rent is not a necessary requirement of a lease it may prove an important relevant factor in determining if there was an intention on the part of the parties to grant exclusive possession of land. In *Colchester Council v. Smith*[17] a man had occupied agricultural land under an agreement with the Council in 1967 allowing him to remain in occupation for the rest of that year without charge and at his own risk. Ferris J. held that this agreement was a licence and not a tenancy, even though he in fact enjoyed exclusive use of the land. The absence of rent was highly relevant to this conclusion:

> "Although in this case the council did, in my judgement, grant exclusive possession to Mr Tillson it did not do so at a rent and only in a limited sense can it be said to have done so for a term. In my view the rejection of Mr Tillson's implied offer to pay a reasonable rent, the expression of the transaction in terms of non-objection to continued occupation as distinct from the grant, the

[11] [1985] A.C. 809.
[12] [1989] Ch. 1.
[13] *ibid.* at 9.
[14] (1959) 101 C.L.R. 209.
[15] [1989] Ch. 1.
[16] *Birrell v. Carey* (1989) 58 P. & C.R. 184; *Prudential Assurance Co. Ltd v. London Residuary Body* (1992) 63 P. & C.R. 386, C.A.; *Canadian Imperial Bank of Commerce v. Bello* (1992) 64 P. & C.R. 48; *Skipton Building Society v. Clayton* (1993) 66 P. & C.R. 223.
[17] [1991] Ch. 448.

insistence that Mr Tillson must occupy at his own risk and must give up possession at short notice if the land were required for other purposes, all point towards this being an exceptional transaction, not intended to give rise to legal obligations on either side."[18]

THE CREATION AND LEGAL QUALITY OF FIXED TERM LEASES

1 Mechanisms of creation

(a) Granting a lease

The means by which tenancy of land is created is by the grant of a lease. A lease is technically a conveyance[19] which transfers the appropriate estate in the land to the tenant, leaving the owner holding the freehold reversion. The precise form that a lease is required to take will depend upon the duration of the tenancy it is intended to create. Provided that the appropriate formalities are observed the grant of a lease will create a legal leasehold interest in the land.

(b) Contracting to grant a lease

Rather than granting a lease a landowner might merely enter into a contract to grant a lease. This may be deliberate on his part. Alternatively, the requisite formalities for the creation of a lease by deed may not have been complied with, rendering the attempt to grant the lease void, but they have reached an agreement which constitutes a valid contract for the creation of the lease. In such cases, because of the operation of the maxim that "equity treats as done that which ought to be done" the contract to create a lease is effective to create a genuine leasehold interest which is equitable in character.

(c) Appropriate formalities

Whether a lease is legal or equitable will generally depend on whether the parties have observed the appropriate formalities for deeds and contracts concerning interests in land. For transactions taking place after September 26, 1989 the formality requirements are found in Law of Property (Miscellaneous Provisions) Act 1989.[20]

(i) Formalities for deeds: An instrument will only be valid as a deed if it makes clear on its face that it is intended to be a deed and is signed by the person creating it in the presence of a witness who attests the signature.[21]

(ii) Formalities for contracts for the disposition of an interest in land: A contract will only be valid if made in writing and incorporating all the terms which the parties have expressly agreed. The document incorporating the terms must be signed by or on behalf of each party to the contract.[22]

[18] *ibid.* at 485.

[19] Law of Property Act, s.205(1)(ii) states that a "Conveyance" includes a lease.

[20] See above, p. 53.

[21] s.1. Alternatively, it may be signed at the direction of the person creating the instrument in the presence of two witnesses who attest the signature.

[22] Law of Property (Miscellaneous Provisions) Act 1989, s.2.

2 Creation of leases for a term of less than three years

(a) Necessary formalities

Law of Property Act 1925, s.54(2) provides that a lease for a period less than three years can be created orally without the need for further formalities if it takes effect "in possession . . . at the best rent which can be reasonably obtained without taking a fine." The section will only apply if a lease is for a definite period less than three years and in *Kushner v. Law Society*[23] it was held that it did not apply to a lease for 14 years, even though it might have been terminated within the three year period by the tenant. Section 54(2) also has no application to the grant of a lease, whether orally or in writing but not by deed, which does not entitle the tenant to immediate possession of the land. In *Long v. Tower Hamlets B.C.*[24] the council wrote to the plaintiff's confirming that they would grant a quarterly tenancy of a shop at a rent of £55. The letter was written on September 4, and stated that the tenancy would commence on September 29. James Munby Q.C. held that since the effect of the letter was to grant a reversionary lease which would only entitle the tenant to possession in the future it was wholly outside of the scope of section 54(2), and that since it had not been granted by deed had not given rise to a legal lease.

(b) Character of the leasehold interest

A lease granted orally for a period of less than three years will constitute a legal term of years absolute.[25]

3 Creation of leases for a term exceeding three years

(a) Necessary formalities

In relation to leases for a period exceeding three years the statutory exception does not apply and therefore Law of Property Act 1925, s.52 must be complied with. This section states:

> "All conveyances of land or of any interest therein are void for the purpose of conveying or creating a legal estate unless made by deed."

A lease for more than three years can, therefore, only be created by deed.

(b) Character of the leasehold interest

A lease for more than three years which is granted by deed will also create a legal term of years absolute.

[23] [1952] 1 K.B. 264.
[24] [1996] 2 All E.R. 683.
[25] Law of Property Act 1925, s.1(1)(b).

4 Contracts to create a lease for more than three years

(a) The concept of an equitable lease

Where parties have entered a contract to grant a lease for a term of more than three years, but no deed has been executed to create a legal lease, an equitable lease may arise on the basis of the contract. The rationale underlying the creation of an equitable lease in this way is that a contract to create an interest in land is specifically enforceable and that equity treats as done that which ought to be done. Therefore when a landowner agrees to grant a lease and fails to do so, since the intended tenant could seek the aid of equity to force the landlord to grant the promised lease, equity treats the contract as generating an already existing estate in the land.[26] This lease is equitable rather than legal in character, but consists of the same terms or covenants that were agreed in the contract.[27] The principle was recognised in *Parker v. Taswell*[28] but the classic case where an equitable lease was held to have been created is *Walsh v. Lonsdale*.[29] The theory was well summarised by Stamp L.J. in *Warmington v. Miller*[30]:

> "The equitable interests which the intended lessee has under an agreement for a lease do not exist in vacuo, but arise because the intended lessee has an equitable right to specific performance of the agreement. In such a situation that which is agreed to be and ought to be done is treated as having been done and carrying with it in equity the attendant rights."

(b) Equitable leases in practice

In *Walsh v. Lonsdale* the defendant agreed to grant the plaintiff a lease of a cotton mill for seven years, at a rent of 30s a year for each loom run, in 1879. The rent was stipulated to be payable in advance. No deed was ever executed and the plaintiff entered into possession of the mill and ran 560 looms. The plaintiff paid his rent in arrears. In 1882 the defendant exercised the remedy of distress, claiming rent which was outstanding if the plaintiff was obliged to pay in advance. In these circumstances the Court of Appeal held that the plaintiff enjoyed an equitable lease of the mill on the same terms as the contract, *i.e.* at the agreed rent which was payable in advance. The exercise of the remedy of distress was therefore legitimate and the plaintiff's claim for damages for illegal distress was rejected. Jessel M.R. stated the principles under which an equitable lease was found to exist:

> "There is an agreement for a lease under which possession has been given . . . [The tenant] holds, therefore, under the same terms in equity as if a lease had been granted, it being a case in which both parties admit that relief is capable of

[26] This doctrine operates in relation to contracts to create other interests in land besides leases, for example in *Mason v. Clarke* [1955] A.C. 778 an agreement to grant a profit a prendre was held to create an equitable profit despite the absence of a deed.

[27] *Rochester Post Services Ltd v. Dartford BC* (1991) 63 P. & C.R. 88.

[28] (1858) 2 De. G. & J. 559.

[29] (1882) 21 Ch.D. 9.

[30] [1973] Q.B. 877 at 887.

being given by specific performance. That being so, he cannot complain of the exercise by the landlord of the same rights as the landlord would have had if a lease had been granted."[31]

A more recent example where the principles were applied is *Rochester Poster Services Ltd v. Dartford Borough Council*.[32] In 1980 Forrest Amusements granted Rochester poster Services the right to erect poster panels on the perimeter of their premises in return for a rent of £2800 per annum. The agreement was for 12 years initially. As there was no deed there was no creation of a legal lease. However, it was held that the contract operated to create an equitable lease since it was specifically enforceable. Rochesters was therefore entitled to receive compensation from the council when they compulsorily purchased the land because they were in lawful possession under an equitable lease.

(c) Essential conditions for the existence of an equitable lease

(i) A valid contract for a lease: An equitable lease will only arise if there was a valid contract for the grant of a lease. As has been noted above, after September 26, 1989 such a contract must be made in writing which incorporates all the terms the parties have expressly agreed and is signed by or on behalf of them. In the case of contracts entered before the Law of Property (Miscellaneous Provisions) Act 1989 came into effect, such contracts had merely to be evidenced in writing.[33] However, the doctrine of part performance was also operative, so that a tenant who entered into possession on the basis of a purely oral agreement would enjoy an equitable lease even though there was no written evidence of the contract.[34] After September 26, 1989 a contract which does not comply with the new formalities' requirements will be ineffective even if there was part performance. The scope of operation of *Walsh v. Lonsdale*[35] and the equitable lease is therefore much reduced.

(ii) Availability of specific performance: Even if there is a valid contract for the creation of a lease an equitable lease will only come into existence if specific performance of that contract is available. Since specific performance is an equitable remedy it is not available as of right, and there are a number of factors which may prevent the award of an order for specific performance and which therefore prevent the existence of the equitable lease. Specific performance is not available in favour of a volunteer. It will also be unavailable if the party seeking it is in breach of the covenants agreed in the contract. In *Coatsworth v. Johnson*[36] a tenant had entered possession of agricultural land under an agreement for a lease for 21 years. The contract contained a number of covenants including an obligation to cultivate the land in a good and husband-like manner. As the tenant was in breach of this covenant the Court of Appeal held that specific performance would have been unavailable to him and that there was therefore no equitable lease. The court will also refuse to grant specific performance of a persons contract when to do so would necessitate him breaching a

[31] *ibid.* at 14–15.
[32] (1991) 63 P. & C.R. 88.
[33] Law of Property Act 1925, s.40.
[34] See for example, *Mason v. Clarke* [1955] A.C. 778; [1974] 2 All E.R. 977.
[35] (1882) 21 Ch.D. 9.
[36] (1886) 55 L.J.Q.B. 220; [1886-1890] All E.R. 547.

contract with a third person. In *Warmington v. Miller*[37] a tenant's lease contained an express term prohibiting from granting a sub-lease. In breach of this term the defendant granted the plaintiff an oral sub-lease of the premises, following which the plaintiff took possession. The Court of Appeal held that the plaintiff enjoyed no equitable lease in these circumstances since specific performance of the contract would not have been available.[38]

(d) Primacy of an equitable lease

In many circumstances where there is a contract for a lease but no deed, and where the tenant has taken possession of the land and paid a periodic rent to the landlord, his interest could be analysed in two ways. First, as has been seen, he would be entitled to an equitable lease on the same terms as agreed in the contract. Secondly, the common law would regard the payment of periodic rent as giving rise to an implied periodic tenancy, which would generate a legal interest in the land. Given that both these conclusions can be construed from the same facts the question arises as to how the tenant's interest should be characterised. This was the central issue in *Walsh v. Lonsdale*.[39] The landlord claimed that his distress was justified under the terms of the contract for a lease requiring rent to be paid in advance. The tenant claimed that his interest was in the form of a periodic tenancy under which the rent would be payable in arrears, thus rendering the distress illegal. The Court of Appeal held that following the Judicature Acts, which enacted that in cases of conflict equity was to prevail over the common law, the interest of the tenant was in the form of an equitable lease and not a legal periodic tenancy. As Jessel M.R. stated:

> "There is agreement for a lease under which possession has been given. Now since the Judicature Act the possession is held under the agreement. There are not two estates as there were formerly, one estate at common law by reason of the payment of the rent from year to year, and an estate in equity under the agreement. There is only one Court and the equity rules prevail in it. The tenant holds under an agreement for a lease."[40]

5 Leases granted by the court as a remedy to satisfy an equity raised by way of proprietary estoppel

Although leases are generally created only by the express acts of the parties a leasehold interest may be awarded to a person by the court as one of the range of potential remedies to satisfy an equity raised by way of proprietary estoppel. Tenancies

[37] [1973] Q.B. 877.
[38] Following *Willmott v. Barber* (1880) 15 Ch.D. 96.
[39] (1882) 21 Ch.D. 9.
[40] *ibid.* at 14.

were awarded by the Court in *Siew Soon Wah v. Yong Tong Hong*[41] and *Andrews v. Colonial Mutual Life Assurance Society Ltd.*[42] The principles of proprietary estoppel are examined in detail in Chapter 13.

FIXED TERM LEASES AND REGISTRATION OF TITLE

1 Leasehold interests as registrable interests

As has been noted earlier, the system of land registration is based upon the existence of registered titles of estates in land against which other interest can then be protected by means of an entry on the register of the estate which they affect. Although all leases are capable of constituting a legal estate in land[43] not every lease is likewise a registrable interest. In essence a distinction is drawn between leases on the basis of their legal character and their duration. Only those leases which are legal are capable of registration[44] and a line is drawn at a duration of at least 21 years, so that leases for a shorter period will not be registrable as individual titles. It would obviously prove inefficient if every lease, no matter how short term, had to be registered as a separate title at the Land Registry. Where a legal lease for more than 21 years is created of registered land a "notice" will be entered on the registered title of the estate from which the lease was carved out.[45]

2 First registration of leasehold interests

(a) First registration on creation

By Law of Property Act 1925, s.123(1) a grant of a term of years absolute of more than 21 years is a "qualifying conveyance" and must be registered within two months of the grant. If the lease is not registered then the grant is void and does not create a legal estate. However, by section 123A(5)(b) the unregistered grant takes effect "as if it were a contract to grant or create that estate . . . for valuable consideration (whether or not it was so made or satisfies any of the formal requirements of such a contract)" so that an equitable lease is created on the terms of the grant.

(b) First registration on assignment

For the sake of completeness it should be noticed that where a lease has been created in the past at a time when registration was not required and is subsequently transferred by assignment to a new tenant, the lease must be registered within two months if it has more than twenty-one years to run from the date of delivery of the assignment,

[41] [1973] A.C. 836.
[42] [1982] 2 N.Z.L.R. 556.
[43] Law of Property Act 1925, s.1(b).
[44] Land Registration Act 1925, s.2(1).
[45] See, Land Registration Act 1925, s.48.

because the assignment is a "qualifying conveyance" under Law of Property Act 1925, s.123(1)(c).[46] Again, if the assigned leasehold estate is not subsequently registered, the assignment is void, but by, section 123(5)(a) it will revert to the transferor/assignor who will hold it on trust for the transferee/assignee.

3 Quality of title awarded by the Land Registrar

(a) The need to demonstrate good title

When an application is made to register a leasehold interest it is the task of the Land Registrar to determine whether the person seeking registration in fact enjoys the interest that he claims. This is especially important since the effect of registration may be conclusive to override any defects in the title claimed.[47] In the case of leasehold interests this process is particularly complex because the Land Registrar is concerned to examine whether the tenant has a valid lease of the land and also whether the landlord had a valid title to the land which entitled him to grant the lease. Whether the tenant is able to demonstrate both his own good title and that of his landlord will determine the quality of title which the registrar is willing to award. This quality of title will appear in the Proprietorship Register of the estate when it is registered.

(b) Qualities of title awarded to leasehold interests when registered

The provisions governing the qualities of title that may be awarded on a first registration of a leasehold estate are found in Land Registration Act 1925, s.8. There are three potential grades of title which the registrar can award.

(i) **Absolute title:** Where the freehold of land is already registered the tenant will be registered with absolute leasehold title if he can demonstrate that his lease was validly granted. If the land subject to the lease is presently unregistered he will have to demonstrate the validity of both his lease and the freehold title of his landlord. Where the tenant's interest is by way of a sub-lease he will have to demonstrate the validity of the intermediate leasehold interest.[48] By Land Registration Act 1925, s.9 first registration with absolute title has the effect of vesting the person registered as proprietor with the possession of the leasehold interest described, together with all the implied or expressed rights and privileges and appurtenances attached to the interest.[49]

(ii) **Good leasehold title:** It is often difficult for a tenant to prove the validity of his landlord's title because he is not entitled to call for and investigate it.[50] However, provided he is able to prove that his own leasehold estate was validly granted he will be registered with good leasehold title. This has the same effect as registration with an absolute title except that it "shall not affect or prejudice the enforcement of any estate,

[46] Land Registration Act 1925, s.123(1).
[47] See: *Re 139 High Street Deptford ex p. British Transport Commission* [1951] Ch. 884.
[48] Of the leasehold title of his immediate landlord if the interest is a sub-tenancy.
[49] The proprietor also takes subject to: (a) all the express and implied covenants obligations and liabilities incident to the registered land; (b) incumbrances and other interests appearing on the register; (c) overriding interests; (d) where he takes the estate as a trustee but is not beneficially entitled himself, to minor interests of which he has notice.
[50] Law of Property Act 1925, s.44(4).

right or interest affecting or in derogation of the title of the lessor to grant the lease."[51]

(iii) Possessory title: If a tenant cannot establish his leasehold interest but relies on a period of adverse possession, he will be registered as enjoying only possessory title. In such a case his registration will be subject to all other estates, rights and interests in the land which were subsisting or capable of arising at the time of his registration.[52] However, after registration with possessory title for 12 years or more he is entitled to be registered as enjoying a good leasehold title.[53]

PERIODIC TENANCIES

1 Defining the periodic tenancy

A fixed term lease is clearly the grant of a tenancy for a specified period of time. The tenant will enjoy that interest until the lease comes to an end naturally through the passage of time, unless its terms permit an earlier termination or either of the parties is entitled to terminate because of the others' breach of covenant. A periodic tenancy has no fixed maximum duration at its inception. The essential nature of a periodic tenancy was stated by Nicholls L.J. in *Javad v. Mohammed Aqil*[54]:

> "A periodic tenancy . . . is one which continues from period to period indefinitely, until determined by proper notice. For example, from year to year, quarter to quarter, month to month, or week to week."

2 Creating a periodic tenancy

(a) *Express periodic tenancies*

A periodic tenancy may be expressly created by the parties. The parties are free to stipulate whatever term they choose, for example to create a tenancy from "week to week", "month to month" or "year to year."

(b) *Implied periodic tenancies*

(i) General requirements of an implied periodic tenancy: A periodic tenancy may also come into existence by implication. Whenever a person enjoys the exclusive occupation of premises and pays rent in consideration thereof, he will be found to have a periodic tenancy of the land. The general principles were stated by Nicholls L.J. in *Javad v. Mohammed Aqil*[55]:

[51] Land Registration Act 1925, s.10.
[52] Land Registration Act 1925, s.11.
[53] Land Registration Act 1925, s.77(2).
[54] [1991] 1 W.L.R. 1007, at 1009.
[55] [1991] 1 W.L.R. 1007, at 1012.

"A tenancy, or lease is an interest in land . . . [it] springs from a consensual arrangement between two parties . . . As with other consensually-based arrangements, parties frequently proceed with an arrangement whereby one person takes possession of another's land for payment without having agreed or directed their minds to one or more fundamental aspects of their transaction. In such cases the law, where appropriate, has to step in and fill the gaps in a way which is sensible and reasonable. The law will imply, from what was agreed and all the surrounding circumstances, the terms the parties are to be taken to have intended to apply. Thus if one party permits another to go into possession of his land on the payment of a rent of so much per week or month, failing more the inference sensibly and reasonably to be drawn is that the parties intended that there should be a weekly or monthly tenancy."

(ii) Exclusive possession: Since exclusive possession is an essential prerequisite to a lease there can be no periodic tenancy unless the person occupying the land enjoys it.
(iii) The relevant term: Where a periodic tenancy is implied the length of the term is not expressly agreed between the parties. Older cases seem to suggest that whenever rent is payable in reference to a year or a proportion of a year then a yearly tenancy is created. However more recent cases, for example *Javad v. Mohammed Aqil*,[56] suggest that the correct principle is that the length of the term is determined by the period with reference to which the rent payable is calculated.[57] For example, if the rent is £100 per month then there will be an implied monthly periodic tenancy. If the rent is £1200 per year then the tenancy will be yearly. It does not matter how the rent is actually paid, so if the £100 per month were collected in weekly instalments by the landlord this would not create a weekly tenancy. In *Ladies Hosiery and Underwear Ltd v. Parker*[58] Maugham J. held that a payment of £2 per week gave rise at most to a weekly and not a yearly tenancy.
(iv) Factors negativing an intention to create a tenancy: The mere fact that a person has entered into the occupation of premises and paid rent does not incontrovertibly generate an implied periodic tenancy. The facts of the occupancy may indicate that no tenancy was intended, as has already been seen in the context of fixed term leases. As Russell L.J. observed in *Lewis v. MTC (Cars) Ltd*[59]:

"It is quite plain that if you find one person in occupation paying sums by way of rent quarterly or half yearly to another person, ordinarily speaking it is a right conclusion that there is a relationship between them of contractual landlord and tenant; but, of course, the circumstances may show that there is no justification for such an inference."

In *Javad v. Mohammed Aquil*[60] the owner of business premises allowed the defendant into occupation on the payment of £2,500, said to represent three months rent, in

[56] [1991] 1 W.L.R. 1007.
[57] *Martin v. Smith* (1874) L.R. 9 Ex. 50; *Adams v. Cairns* (1901) 85 L.T. 10.
[58] [1930] 1 Ch. 304.
[59] [1975] 1 W.L.R. 457 at 462.
[60] [1991] 1 W.L.R. 1007; see also *Sopwith v. Stutchbury* (1983) 17 H.L.R. 50.

anticipation of the parties being able to agree the terms of a lease. Two further payments of quarterly rent were made. When negotiations eventually broke down the defendant claimed that he was a tenant under an implied periodic tenancy. The Court of Appeal upheld a finding that in these circumstances no periodic tenancy was intended but merely a tenancy at will,[61] as there was nothing more than a permissive occupation while negotiations proceeded.

(v) Implied periodic tenancy where an express lease has failed: An implied periodic tenancy will often arise if a person has entered into exclusive possession of premises and paid rent to the owner on the basis of a lease which was subsequently found to be invalid. For example, in *Prudential Assurance Co. Ltd v. London Residuary Body*[62] it was held that a lease was invalid because it did not specific a maximum duration. However, the House of Lords found that since the tenants had taken possession and paid a yearly rent they enjoyed an implied periodic tenancy.

(vi) Implied periodic tenancy where there is an equitable lease: As has been noted above, where a person is in occupation on the basis of a specifically enforceable contract for a lease they are entitled to an equitable lease on the basis of the contract. It is clear from *Walsh v. Lonsdale*[63] that where the facts would support the finding of either an equitable lease or an implied periodic tenancy the equitable lease will take primacy and govern the relationship between the landlord and tenant.

(vii) Implied periodic tenancy where a lease has expired: An implied periodic tenancy may also commonly arise where a tenant initially occupied premises under a fixed term lease which has expired. If he is allowed to remain in possession paying rent to the landlord even after the lease has expired he will enjoy a period tenancy.

(c) Legal quality of the periodic tenancy

Since the length of the period is invariably less than three years the Law of Property Act 1925, s.54(2) applies and a valid legal lease is created despite the absence of any formalities.

(d) Problems relating to the duration of a periodic tenancy

(i) A fixed maximum duration? In *Prudential Assurance Co. Ltd v. London Residuary Body*[64] the House of Lords re-asserted the requirement that a lease must have a fixed maximum duration. However, this requirement is not easily applied to periodic tenancies, since of their very nature the period is continually renewed unless and until appropriate notice is given to bring the tenancy to an end. It is therefore uncertain at the beginning of the tenancy how long it will last in total, since it is uncertain when, or if, notice will be given. This problem was addressed by the Court of Appeal in *Re Midland Railway Co's Agreement*[65] where Russell L.J. stated:

> "If you have an ordinary case of a periodic tenancy (for example, a yearly tenancy) it is plain that in one sense at least it is uncertain at the outset what will

[61] See also: *Cardiothoracic Institute v. Shrewdcrest Ltd* [1986] 1 W.L.R. 368.
[62] [1992] 2 A.C. 386.
[63] (1882) 21 Ch.D. 9.
[64] [1992] 2 A.C. 386.
[65] [1971] Ch. 725.

> be the maximum duration of the term created, which term grows year by year as a single term springing from the original grant. It cannot be predicated that in no circumstances will it exceed, for example, 50 years; there is no previously ascertained maximum duration for the term; its duration will depend upon the time that will elapse before either party gives notice of determination. The simple statement of the law that the maximum duration of a term must be certainly known in advance of its taking effect cannot therefore have direct reference to periodic tenancies."[66]

Although this approach has the merit of simplicity, more recent cases have tended to attempt to accommodate periodic tenancies with the requirement of a certain term rather than declare that they are an exception. The approach of Russell L.J. was expressly rejected by Lord Templeman in *Prudential Assurance Co Ltd v. London Residuary Body*[67] where he stated:

> "I consider that the principle in *Lace v. Chantler* reaffirming 500 years of judicial acceptance of the requirement that a term must be certain applies to all leases and tenancy agreements. A tenancy from year to year is saved from being uncertain because each party has power by notice to determine at the end of the year. The term continues until determined as if both parties made a new agreement at the end of each year for a new term for the ensuing year."

The justification for the validity of periodic tenancies seems therefore to be that each period is itself certain. This leaves the difficulty of attempting to reconcile the certainty of the individual periods with the fact that the entire period of occupation under a periodic tenancy is viewed by English law as a single period. In *Hammersmith LBC v. Monk*[68] Lord Bridge seemed to take the view that although retrospectively the period possessed is viewed as a single term, the continuation of the tenancy at the end of each term depends upon the will of the parties and that prospectively it should continue no further than they have impliedly agreed, namely one term. Therefore each period is in itself certain, but once commenced is agglomerated into the single continuous period comprised of any earlier periods. As he explained "the law regards a tenancy from year to year which has continued for a number of years, considered retrospectively, as a single term."[69] Despite the complexity of this distinction in comparison to the practical realism of Russell L.J. the effect is the same, namely that a periodic tenancy does not fall foul of the requirement that a lease must have a certain maximum duration.

(ii) Limiting the right to determine: A further associated problem is whether a periodic tenancy can be created where the landlord has agreed not to determine the tenancy except in specified circumstances. In *Re Midland Railway Co's Agreement*[70] the Court of Appeal upheld as valid a periodic tenancy which contained a clause that the

[66] *ibid.* at 732.
[67] [1992] 2 A.C. 386.
[68] [1992] 1 A.C. 478.
[69] *ibid.* at 490.
[70] [1971] Ch. 725.

landlords could not terminate the tenancy until they required the land for their purposes. This approach was extended by the decision of the Court of Appeal in *Ashburn Anstalt v. Arnold*,[71] but both authorities were overruled by the House of Lords in *Prudential Assurance Co Ltd v. London Residuary Body*,[72] where Lord Templeman considered that there were inconsistent with the rule that a lease must be for a fixed maximum duration. He concluded that: "A grant for an uncertain term which takes the form of a yearly tenancy which cannot be determined by the landlord does not create a lease."[73] A periodic tenancy of the land in question from year to year which could not be determined by the landlord except when it was needed for road-widening would therefore be invalid.

(e) Termination of a periodic tenancy

A periodic tenancy, whether express or implied, will continue until proper notice is given to terminate. With the exception of tenancies from year to year, notice of one period must be given to terminate. For example, a monthly tenancy can only be determined by a month's notice. However, in the case of yearly tenancies six months' notice is sufficient. The precise mechanics of notice to determine will be examine below in the context of the determination of leasehold interests.

TENANCIES AT WILL

1 Nature of a tenancy at will

The central characteristic of a tenancy at will was identified by Nicholls L.J. in *Javad v. Mohammed Aqil*[74]:

> "a tenancy at will exists where the tenancy is on terms that either party may determine it at any time."

Therefore, although the tenant enjoys exclusive occupation[75] of the land he enjoys no security. He does not have an estate in the land which he can transfer to others, and to this extent his relationship with his landlord is personal rather than proprietary, and akin to a licence. Unlike a licensee, however, he is able to maintain an action in trespass against strangers.[76] A tenancy at will may be created expressly or impliedly. Common situations where such a tenancy may arise are when a purchaser of property goes into possession before completion, or a tenant takes possession of premises in anticipation of negotiations for a lease, as was the case in *Javad v. Mohammed Aqil*.

71 [1989] Ch. 1.
72 [1992] 2 A.C. 386.
73 *ibid.* at 395.
74 [1991] 1 W.L.R. 1007, at 1009.
75 *Goldsack v. Shore* [1950] 1 K.B. 708.
76 *Heslop v. Burns* [1974] 1 W.L.R. 1241.

2 Termination of a tenancy at will

A tenancy at will may be determined by either the tenant or the landlord, but no notice to quit is required. A mere demand for possession is sufficient.[77] The death of either party automatically determines the tenancy.

LEASEHOLD COVENANTS

1 Introduction to leasehold covenants

Having examined the essential nature of leasehold interests in land, the forms of tenancy and the means by which they can be created, it is the purpose of this section to examine the substantive content of leases. The terms of a lease, determining the rights and obligations of the parties, are known as the covenants of the lease. The covenants of a lease may either be expressly included by the parties in their agreement, but many of the most important covenants are either implied by law or imposed by statute. The precise covenants in any lease will vary depending upon the terms of the parties' agreement and it is the purpose of this section to consider only the most common and most significant of such covenants.

2 Covenants of the landlord

(a) Covenant to provide quiet enjoyment

(i) An implied covenant in every lease: Whenever a tenancy is granted there is an implied covenant that the landlord will provide the tenant with quiet possession of the premises let.

(ii) Obligations of the covenant: The essence of the covenant to provide quiet enjoyment is that the landlord will not interfere with the tenant's possession of the land. The nature of the obligation was explained by Lord Alverstone C.J. in *Budd-Scott v. Daniell*[78]:

> "when one person agrees to give possession of his house for a time to another that ought to carry with it an agreement that he, the landlord, and those claiming through him, will not dispossess the tenant during that time. Therefore, a covenant or contract was to be implied that the landlord and those claiming under him would not disturb the possession of the tenant."

In *McCall v. Abelesz*[79] Lord Denning M.R. identified the obligation as extending to "any conduct of the landlord or his agents which interferes with the tenant's freedom of action in exercising his rights as tenant." In *Kenny v. Preen*[80] Pearson L.J. pointed

[77] *Doe d Price v. Price* (1832) 9 Bing 356.
[78] [1902] 2 K.B. 351.
[79] [1976] Q.B. 585, at 594.
[80] [1963] 1 Q.B. 499.

out that the covenant meant that the tenant was entitled to have the full benefit of his tenancy and not merely to derive some pleasure from it.

(iii) Examples of breach of the covenant by acts of the landlord: It is clear that acts of the landlord or his agents which interfere with the tenants possession will amount to a breach of the covenant to provide quiet enjoyment. In *Lavender v. Betts*[81] a landlord was in breach when he removed the doors and windows of the rented premises. In *Perera v. Vandiyar*[82] the disconnection of the gas and electricity supplies were held to constitute a breach, as was the removal of the central heating in *Mallay and Lunt v. Alexander*.[83] In *Owen v. Gadd*[84] a landlord was held to be in breach where he erected scaffolding outside a shop occupied by the tenant, preventing customers access to the window. Although some earlier cases suggested that a breach would only be committed if the landlord physically interfered with the land[85] it is now clear that such physical interference is not essential. In *Kenny v. Preen*[86] a landlord let two rooms of a flat to an elderly widow. After serving a notice to quit he intimidated her in a variety of ways, including writing letters threatening to evict her from the rooms and put her property in the street, repeatedly knocking at the door and shouting threats. Pearson L.J. held that this was a breach of the covenant despite the absence of physical interference since it amounted to an "invasion of her rights as tenant to remain in possession undisturbed."[87] In *McCall v. Abelesz*[88] Lord Denning M.R. held that the covenant is not confined to direct physical interference but extends to "any acts calculated to interfere with the peace or comfort of the tenant or his family."[89]

(iv) Landlord's liability for the acts of others: The landlord will be liable for the acts of his agents and also for those of other persons claiming their title from him. For example, if a house has been converted into a number of self-contained flats the landlord will be liable if the tenant of one flat's quiet enjoyment is disturbed by the tenant from another. In *Sanderson v. Berwick-upon-Tweed Corporation*[90] a landlord was held liable for breach of covenant where the tenant of one of his farms caused damage, by his use of drains, to a neighbouring farm which was also occupied by another of his tenants. However, the landlord will only be liable for the unlawful acts of those claiming title from him. Landlords are not liable for interference caused by a person claiming a superior title[91] or claiming under a predecessor in title to the landlord.[92]

(v) Remedies for breach of the covenant to provide quiet enjoyment: A number of remedies are available to a tenant where a landlord is in breach of his covenant to provide quiet enjoyment. He may seek and injunction to prevent the landlord committing threatened or continuing present breaches, as for example in *Kenny v. Preen*.[93] Where a breach has been committed the tenant may also seek damages to compensate

[81] [1942] 2 All E.R. 72.
[82] [1953] 1 W.L.R. 672.
[83] (1982) C.L.Y. 1747.
[84] [1956] 2 Q.B. 99.
[85] See: *Browne v. Fletcher* [1911] 1 Ch. 219; *Owen v. Gadd* [1956] 2 Q.B. 99.
[86] [1963] 1 Q.B. 499.
[87] He also held that there was sufficient physical interference if this was a necessary criteria.
[88] [1976] Q.B. 585.
[89] See also *McMillan v. Singh* (1985) 17 H.L.R. 120.
[90] (1884) 13 Q.B.D. 547.
[91] *Jones v. Lavington* [1903] 1 K.B. 253.
[92] *Celsteel Ltd v. Alton House Holdings Ltd (No. 2)* [1987] 1 W.L.R. 291.
[93] [1963] 1 Q.B. 499.

him for the disturbance of his possession. However, in *Branchett v Beaney*[94] the Court of Appeal held that such damages should not compensate the tenant for mental distress or injured feelings arising from the breach, on the basis that the covenant was not a contract to provide "pleasure, relaxation, peace of mind or freedom from molestation"[95] but merely to "enjoy" the use of the land which Pearson L.J. had expressly stated in *Kenny v. Preen*[96] did not include the right to derive pleasure from it. However, it is clear that if the defendants breach of covenant involves a trespass to the land the tenant will be able to maintain an action in tort, and that the court can award compensation for mental distress and injured feelings, especially when awarded as aggravated or exemplary damages.[97] In *Branchett v. Beaney*[98] the Court of Appeal upheld an award of £3,250 exemplary damages for trespass which was also a breach of the covenant.

(vi) Breach of covenant also a criminal offence: Action by a landlord which constitutes a breach of the covenant to provide quiet enjoyment may also amount to the offence of harassment, which is defined by section 1(3) of the Protection from Eviction Act 1977:

> "[the offence of harassment] If any person with intent to cause the residential occupier of any premises —
> (a) to give up the occupation of the premises or any part thereof; or.
> (b) to refrain from exercising any right or pursuing any remedy in respect of the premises or part thereof;
>
> does acts likely to interfere with the peace or comfort of the residential occupier or members of his household, or persistently withdraws or withholds services reasonably required for the occupation of the premises as a residence, he shall be guilty of an offence."

(b) Covenant not to derogate from the grant

(i) An implied covenant in every lease: Whenever a landlord grants a lease of his property he will be taken to have covenanted not to act in a way which would derogate from the tenancy he granted.

(ii) Meaning of the covenant: The obligation on a landlord not to derogate from his grant is closely related, although not synonymous, with the covenant to provide quiet enjoyment. It means that the landlord cannot subsequently behave in a manner which would reduce the usability of the land by the tenant given the purpose for which the tenancy was granted. Often difficulties will arise where the landlord has let part of his land and retained the rest. As Parker J. explained in *Browne v. Flower*[99]:

> ". . . if the grant or demise be made for a particular purpose, the grantor or lessor comes under an obligation not to use the land retained by him in such a way as to render the land granted or demised unfit or materially less fit for the particular purpose for which the grant or demise was made."

[94] [1992] 3 All E.R. 910.
[95] See: *Watts v. Morrow* [1991] 1 W.L.R. 1421.
[96] [1963] 1 Q.B. 499.
[97] *Cassell & Co Ltd v. Broome* [1972] A.C. 1027; *Drane v. Evangelou* [1978] 1 W.L.R. 455; *Guppy's (Bridport) Ltd v. Brookling* (1983) 14 H.L.R. 1.
[98] [1992] 3 All E.R. 910.
[99] [1911] 1 Ch. 219, 226.

The rational for this limitation on the landlord's freedom of use of his own retained land is simply a "rule of common honesty"[1] that "a grantor having given a thing with one hand is not to take away the means of enjoying it with the other."[2]

(iii) Breach of the covenant: In *Aldin v. Latimer Clark Muirhead & Co.*[3] a landlord was held to be in breach where he had let premises to a tenant who was a timber merchant and then built on land he had retained in a way which would interfere with the access of air to the tenant's sheds used for drying timber. In *Grosvenor Hotel Co v. Hamilton*[4] a landlord was in breach where he caused vibrations to the land leased by his use of powerful engines to pump water from the adjacent land he had retained. In *Browne v. Flower*[5] the Court of Appeal held that there was no breach where an iron staircase was erected on the outside of a block of flats because it did not render other flats materially unfit for the purposes of residential flats. It seems that there will be no breach of covenant where a landlord lets neighbouring premises to others who will be in competition with the original tenant. In *Port v. Griffith*[6] there was no derogation from grant where a landlord had let a shop to the plaintiff with an express covenant that it was to be used for "the sale of wool and general trimmings" and then let an adjoining shop for the business of a tailor and the sale of dressmaking trimmings. In *Romulus Trading Co Ltd v. Comet Properties Ltd*[7] Garland J. held that there was no breach of the covenant where a landlord had let one unit in his buildings to the plaintiffs who intended to use it for their banking business and as a safe deposit centre, and then leased another unit in the same building to a rival bank which also intended to use it to provide the public with safe deposit facilities. If a tenant wishes to ensure that his landlord does not let neighbouring or close premises to business rivals it seems that he will have to insist on an express covenant to that effect in the lease.

(iv) Landlord's knowledge of the purpose of the tenancy: A landlord will only be liable for breach of covenant if he was aware of the purpose for which the tenant intended to use the land. In *Harmer v Jumbil (Nigeria) Tin Areas*[8] Younger L.J. stated that in all cases the obligation must "be such as, in view of the surrounding circumstances, was within the reasonable contemplation of the parties at the time when the transaction was entered into, and was at that time within the grantor's power to fulfil." The landlord had granted the tenant a lease in 1911 for the purpose of an explosives' magazine. He was held to be in breach of covenant when in 1919 he granted a lease of adjoining land permitting the working of minerals which involved opening shafts and building within a distance from the tenant's magazine prohibited by his operating licence. In *Johnston & Sons Ltd v. Holland*[9] it was held that a landlord's duty not to derogate from grant did not extend to cover his use of land which he had acquired after the lease had been granted, so that the erection of a large hoarding concealing an advertisement which the tenant displayed on the flank wall of the premises he rented was no breach because his landlord had not owned that land at the date of the lease.

[1] *Harmer v. Jumbil (Nigeria) Tin Areas Ltd* [1921] 1 Ch. 200, at 225 *per* Younger L.J.
[2] *Birmingham, Dudley and District Banking Co v. Ross* (1888) 38 Ch.D. 295, at 313 *per* Bowen L.J.
[3] [1894] 2 Ch. 437.
[4] [1894] 2 Q.B. 836.
[5] [1911] 1 Ch. 219.
[6] [1938] 1 All E.R. 295.
[7] [1996] 9648 E.G. 157.
[8] [1921] 1 Ch. 200.
[9] [1988] 1 E.G.L.R. 264.

(v) Remedies for breach of covenant: A tenant may seek an injunction to restrain any breach[10] and damages to compensate for any loss suffered as a consequence of the breach. In *Grosvenor Hotel Company v. Hamilton*[11] such damages were held to include the cost of the plaintiff moving his business to alternative premises.

(c) Covenants to repair

(i) Obligations implied by the common law: In *Smith v. Marrable*[12] it was held that a landlord impliedly undertakes that furnished premises[13] are fit for human habitation. This obligation was held to be breached where the premises were infested with bugs. In the event of breach the tenant is entitled to quit the premises immediately without notice. The obligation only applies to the condition of the premises at the commencement of the tenancy and in *Sarson v. Roberts*[14] the Court of Appeal held that there was no implied covenant that premises continue to be habitable throughout the term.

(ii) Obligations implied by express covenants of the lease: In *Barrett v. Lounova*[15] the Court of Appeal construed a lease so as to imply a covenant of the landlord to repair the exterior of the premises in order to give "business efficacy" to the agreement. The lease contained an express term that the tenant was to repair the interior but there were no express terms concerning the exterior, which had fallen into serious disrepair. Kerr L.J. stated the circumstances which called for the implication of a covenant:

> "It is obvious . . . that sooner or later the covenant imposed by the tenant in respect of the inside can no longer be complied with unless the outside has been kept in repair . . . In my view it is therefore necessary, as a matter of business efficacy to make this agreement workable, that an obligation to keep the outside in repair must be imposed on someone."

He held that the only solution which made business sense was to imply that the landlord was under an obligation to repair.

(iii) Obligations to keep common areas in good repair implied by necessity: In *Liverpool City Council v. Irwin*[16] the House of Lords held that the council landlord of a block of flats was under an obligation to maintain the staircases and common areas of access in reasonable repair and usability. The tenants occupied under a document described as "conditions of tenancy" which contained no provisions relating to the landlord's obligations. Lord Wilberforce held that the appropriate test for the implication of an obligation to repair was that of necessity[17]:

> "Such an obligation should be read into the contract as the nature of the contract itself implicitly requires, no more, no less: a test in other words, of necessity. The relationship accepted by the corporation is that of landlord and tenant: the

[10] As was granted in *Harmer v. Jumbil (Nigeria) Tin Areas Ltd* [1921] 1 Ch. 200.
[11] [1894] 2 Q.B. 836.
[12] (1843) 11 M & W 5.
[13] Unfurnished premises are excluded from the scope of the implied covenant: *Hart v. Windsor* (1843) 12 M. & W. 68; *Lane v. Cox* [1897] 1 Q.B. 415.
[14] [1895] 2 Q.B. 395.
[15] [1990] 1 Q.B. 348.
[16] [1977] A.C. 239.
[17] *ibid.* at 254.

tenant accepts obligations accordingly, in relation inter alia to the stairs, the lifts and the chutes. All these are not just facilities, or conveniences provided at discretion: they are essentials of the tenancy without which life in the dwellings, as a tenant, is not possible. To leave the landlord free of contractual obligation as regards these matters, and subject only to administrative or political pressure, is, in my opinion, inconsistent totally with the nature of this relationship. The subject matter of the lease (high rise blocks) and the relationship created by the tenancy demand, of their nature, some contractual obligation on the landlord."

However, the House of Lords held that an absolute obligation was inappropriate and therefore implied a covenant to maintain reasonable repair and usability, including taking reasonable care to keep the lifts working and staircases lit. A repairing obligation of necessity was also implied in *King v. Northhamptonshire District Council*[18] where a tenant of a house was wheelchair bound and needed to use the rear access to the property by means of a path in poor repair. The Court of Appeal held that there was an implied obligation to maintain the rear access.[19]

(iv) Statutorily implied term of fitness for human habitation: The Landlord and Tenant Act 1985, s.8 implies a condition into every lease of a house for human habitation at a low rent that it is fit for human habitation at the commencement of the tenancy and an undertaking that the landlord will keep it fit during the tenancy. These obligations are only implied if the rent does not exceed £80 in London or £52 elsewhere,[20] and if the house is not let for a term of more than three years upon terms that the tenant puts the premises into a condition reasonably fit for human habitation.[21] The protection afforded by section 8 is therefore relatively narrow.

(v) Statutorily implied covenant to repair: A more significant covenant is implied by Landlord and Tenant Act 1985, s.11. This section applies to leases of dwelling houses granted after October 24, 1964 for a term of less than seven years.[22] Section 11(1) implies the following obligations:

(a) to keep in repair the structure and exterior of the dwelling-house (including drains, gutters and external pipes),

(b) to keep in repair and proper working order the installations in the dwelling-house for the supply of water, gas and electricity and for sanitation (including basins, sinks, baths and sanitary conveniences, but not other fixture fittings and appliances for making use of the supply of water, gas or electricity), and

(c) to keep in repair and proper working order the installations in the dwelling-house for space heating and water heating.

By section 4 any express covenant by the tenant to repair the property in these respects is of no effect. One common question which has arisen is whether particular parts of a dwelling-house are to be regarded as the "structure and exterior". In *Re Irwin's Estate*[23]

[18] (1992) 24 H.L.R. 284.
[19] Compare *Duke of Westminster v. Guild* [1985] Q.B. 688.
[20] s.1(4).
[21] s.1(5).
[22] s.13.
[23] [1990] 24 H.L.R. 1.

it was held that window frames and sashes were within the scope of the covenant,[24] but that a garage and yard separate from the dwelling-house were not. In *Hussein v. Mehlman*[25] wallplaster was held to be part of the structure. It has also been held that the covenant relates only to physical defects in the premises. In *Quick v. Taff-Ely Borough Council*[26] windows caused severed condensation. However, it was held that there was no breach of the covenant since they were not in a state of disrepair but merely inadequate for their task and no physical damage had been caused by the condensation. In contrast in *Stent v. Monmouth District Council*[27] it was held that there was a breach of covenant when water had come into a house under the front door which had itself been physically damaged by the water.

(vi) Express covenants: Obviously a lease may contain whatever express covenants in relation to repair which are agreed by the parties.

(vii) Remedies for breach of covenant: Where a landlord is in breach of his repairing obligations, whether express, implied or statutory, a number of remedies are available to the tenant. The tenant will be entitled to damages for breach of covenant assessed as the difference between the value of the premises to the tenant in their condition of disrepair and what their value would have been if the covenants had been fulfilled.[28] The tenant may also be able to obtain an order for specific performance.[29] If the tenant undertakes the repairs himself he enjoys a common law right to recoupment of the reasonable costs from future rent, provided that he gave the landlord notice of the need to repair.[30] If the landlord sues for non-payment of rent and the tenant cross-claims for damages for breach of a repairing covenant, including any consequential damage, the tenant has an equitable right to set-off his claim against the landlord's.[31]

(viii) Other potential liability of a landlord for property in a state of disrepair: As well as the covenant to repair a landlord may be subject to a number of other common law and statutory liabilities if the property is not kept in repair. Following the long established authority of *Cavalier v. Pope*[32] a landlord is not liable in tort for negligence for premises which are defective at the commencement of a tenancy, except if he was also the builder.[33] A landlord may also be liable for damage caused as a result of his failure to repair under the defective Premises Act 1972. By section 4(1) a landlord who is under an obligation to maintain or repair the premises owes a duty of care to all persons who might reasonably be expected to be effected by defects to "see that they are reasonably safe from personal injury or from damage to their property caused by a relevant defect." By section 4(4) the landlord will attract liability under, section 4(1) even if the tenancy contains no repairing obligations if the tenancy "expressly or impliedly gives the landlord the right to enter the premises to carry out any description of maintenance or repair of the premises."

[24] See also: *Boswell v. Crucible Steel of America* [1925] 1 K.B. 119.
[25] [1992] 32 E.G. 59.
[26] [1986] Q.B. 809.
[27] (1987) 19 H.L.R. 269.
[28] See: *Calabar Properties Ltd v. Sticher* [1984] 1 W.L.R. 287.
[29] *Jeune v. Queens Cross Properties Ltd* [1974] Ch. 97; *Francis v. Cowcliffe* (1977) 33 P. & C.R. 368.
[30] See: *Lee-Parker v. Izzet* [1971] 1 W.L.R. 1688.
[31] *British Anzani (Felixstowe) Ltd v. International Marine Management (UK) Ltd* [1979] 2 All E.R. 1063.
[32] [1906] A.C. 428; *McNerny v. London Borough of Lambeth* (1988) 21 H.L.R. 188.
[33] *Rimmer v. Liverpool City Council* [1985] Q.B. 1.

3 Covenants of the tenant

(a) Covenant not to disclaim the landlord's title

(i) An implied covenant in every lease: There is an implied covenant in every lease that the tenant will not do anything which might prejudice the title of the landlord.[34]
(ii) Meaning of disclaimer: The essence of the obligation is that the tenant must not do anything which evinces an intention to no longer be bound by the relationship of landlord and tenant.
(iii) Breach of covenant: The tenant will be in breach of this covenant only where a disclaimer is "clear and unambiguous." This was so held by Thomas Morison Q.C. in *Clarke Ltd v. Dupre Ltd*[35] by analogy with the doctrine of repudiation of contract. A tenant sued his landlord for damages where he had extended the premises let into a courtyard to which the landlord claimed title by adverse possession. As part of his pleadings the tenant alleged that the courtyard was owned by a third party and the landlord claimed that this was a breach of the covenant entitling him to forfeit the lease. It was held that denying the title to the courtyard was only a partial disclaimer and that this did not constitute a sufficiently clear and unambiguous repudiation of the relationship of landlord and tenant of the whole premises let.

(b) Covenant not to commit waste

(i) Meaning of waste: The concept of waste refers to any physical alteration of the land which is the result either of action or inaction on the part of the tenant. For example, in *Mancetter Ltd v. Garmanson Ltd*[36] it was held that a tenant who removed an extractor fan which he had installed, leaving a hole in the wall, was liable for waste. Waste may take two forms. Waste caused by the actions of the tenant is described as voluntary waste. Waste which is cause by inaction, in other words the failure to prevent waste caused by external or natural factors, is described as permissive waste.
(ii) Liability for voluntary waste: All tenants are liable for waste they voluntarily inflict on the land.
(iii) Liability for permissive waste: A tenant under a fixed term lease will incur liability for permissive waste unless expressly agreed otherwise.[37] A tenant under a yearly periodic tenancy is only liable for permissive waste which arises if he fails to keep the premises wind and water tight.[38] In *Haskell v. Marlow*[39] it was held that a tenant under a yearly tenancy was not liable for the effect of "reasonable wear and tear" on the property. Tenants under other periodic tenancies are not subject to these minimal requirements and are only liable for voluntary waste.[40]

[34] *W. G. Clarke (Properties) Ltd v. Dupre Properties Ltd* [1992] Ch. 297 , 303, approving *Hill and Redman's Law of Landlord and Tenant*, (18th ed, 1991), Vol. 1, para. 2181.
[35] [1992] Ch. 297.
[36] [1986] Q.B. 1212.
[37] *Yellowly v. Gower* (1855) 11 Ex.D. 274.
[38] *Auworth v. Johnson* (1832) 5 C. & P. 239; *Leach v. Thomas* (1835) 7 C. & P. 327; *Wedd v. Porter* [1916] 2 K.B. 91.
[39] [1928] 2 K.B. 45.
[40] See: *Warren v. Keen* [1954] 1 Q.B. 15.

(c) Covenant to use the property in a "tenantlike manner"

(i) An implied covenant in every lease: Although there is no general implied covenant to repair every tenant is under a limited obligation to use the premises in a tenantlike manner.[41]
(ii) Scope of the duty: Denning L.J. attempted to give some shape to the duty to use the premises in a tenantlike manner in *Warren v. Keen*[42]:

> "But what does to use the premises in a tenantlike "manner" mean? It can, I think, best be shown by some illustrations. The tenant must take proper care of the place. He must, if he is going away for the winter, turn off the water and empty the boiler. He must clean the chimneys, when necessary, and also the windows. He must mend the electric light when it fuses. He must unstop the sink when it is blocked by his waste. In short, he must do the little jobs about the place which a reasonable tenant would do."

(d) Covenant to repair

(i) Implied covenants to repair: As has already been seen there is no implied covenant for a tenant to repair the premises subject to the tenancy, and such covenants as are implied concerning his care of the demised premises are minimalistic in the obligations they impose.
(ii) Express covenants to repair: The parties are free to incorporate whatever express repairing provisions they agree, with the exception that the obligations imposed on landlords by the Landlord and Tenant Act 1985, s.11 cannot be excluded. Tenants obligations to repair are far more likely in longer term leases. If the express covenant excluded liability for damage caused by "fair wear and tear", this only includes normal and reasonable use.[43]

(e) Covenant to pay rent

Since rent is not a necessary requirement of a lease there is no general implied covenant to pay it. However, in the majority of cases the payment of rent will be provided for by means of an express covenant. In the case of longer leases this will often include a provision for periodic rent review.

(f) Covenant not to assign

The tenant under a lease enjoys a right in the property which is capable of being transferred by him. The process by which such a transfer is effected is called assignment. A lease may contain an express covenant against assignment by the tenant. The operation of such covenants is discussed in detail below where assignment is fully considered.[44]

[41] *Horsefall v. Mather Holt* (1815) N.P. 7; *Marsden v. Edward Heyes Ltd* [1927] 2 K.B. 1; *Warren v Keen* [1954] 1 Q.B. 15.
[42] [1954] 1 Q.B. 15, at 20.
[43] *Haskell v. Marlow* [1928] 2 K.B. 45.
[44] See p. 120.

4 Remedies of the landlord on tenant's breach of covenant

(a) Remedial options

When a tenant commits a breach of covenant, whether express or implied, four potential remedies may be available to the landlord:
(i) Forfeiture of the lease: Forfeiture entitles the landlord to terminate the tenancy before the expiry of the agreed term. It is the most powerful of the remedies available to him and therefore its availability and exercise are carefully circumscribed by the law.
(ii) Distress: Distress is in effect a self-help remedy available to the landlord where the tenant has failed to pay his rent. It entitles the landlord to seize goods on the premises let and sell them to recover the arrears of rent.
(iii) Damages: The contractual remedy of damages for breach of covenant is also available to the landlord wherever the tenant is in breach.
(iv) Action for arrears of rent: The landlord also has a right to bring an action for the recovery of up to six years arrears of rent.

(b) Forfeiture of the lease

(i) Availability of forfeiture: Not every breach of a covenant entitles the landlord to forfeit the lease and the ordinary remedy is simply one of damages. However, forfeiture will be available in three circumstances. First, a landlord enjoys an implied right to forfeit if the tenant disclaims his title.[45] Secondly, the landlord will enjoy a right to forfeit if an obligation of the lease is formulated as a condition.[46] Thirdly, the landlord will be entitled to forfeit for breach of covenant if the lease contains an express forfeiture clause. In most professionally drawn leases the obligations of the lease are drafted as conditions and the lease will contain a general forfeiture clause.
(ii) Effect of breach of covenant where forfeiture is available: Even if the tenant commits a breach which would entitle the landlord to forfeit the lease forfeiture is not automatic. The breach merely renders the lease voidable by the landlord.
(iii) Means of forfeiture — exercise of the right of re-entry: Where forfeiture is available the landlord forfeits the lease by means of exercising his right of re-entry, which simply means that he re-takes possession of the land. Re-entry may involve physical entry of the premises, but service of possession proceedings is equivalent.[47] Forfeiture is effective from the moment of re-entry and the tenant is thereafter a trespasser.[48]
(iv) Re-entry and residential leases: In the contexts of residential leases the Protection from Eviction Act 1977, s.2 provides that:

> "Where any premises are let as a dwelling on a lease which is subject to a right of re-entry or forfeiture it shall not be lawful to enforce that right otherwise than by proceedings in the court while any person is lawfully residing in the premises or part of them."

[45] *Clarke Ltd v. Dupre Ltd* [1992] Ch. 297.
[46] *Doe d Lockwood v. Clarke* (1807) 8 East 185.
[47] *Bilson v. Residential Apartments Ltd* [1992] 1 A.C. 494.
[48] *Canas Property Co Ltd v. KL Televison Services Ltd* [1970] 2 Q.B. 433.

A landlord who re-enters other than by such proceedings commits a criminal offence.[49] As has already been noted in the context of the landlord's covenant to provide quiet enjoyment above, section 1(3) also create an offence of harassment. The Housing Act 1988, s.27 provides that a tenant will be entitled to damages[50] from a landlord who unlawfully deprives him of his occupation, whether by wrongful eviction or harassment.

(v) Re-entry and non-residential leases: As the provisions of the Protection from Eviction Act do not apply, there is nothing to prevent a peaceable physical re-entry of non-residential property. However, under Criminal Law Act 1977, s.6(1) it is an offence to use or threaten violence without lawful authority for the purposes of securing entry into any premises where, to the knowledge of the entrant, there is someone present who is opposed to entry. This means that most cases of peaceful re-entry of business premises will have to take place outside of working hours. In *Billson v. Residential Apartments Ltd*[51] the landlord of unoccupied residential premises re-entered at 6am and changed the locks. However, the House of Lords expressed a dislike of even peaceable re-entry and expressed a preference for the issue of a writ and a reduction of any incentives for landlords pursuing what Lord Templeman described as "the dubious and dangerous method of determining the lease by re-entering the premises."[52] Even where re-entry may be available the landlord will have to comply the statutory requirement to serve notice on the tenant as required by section 146(1) of the Law of Property Act 1925 considered below.

(vi) Forfeiture for non-payment of rent: A landlord seeking to forfeit for non-payment of rent must first make a formal demand for rent to the tenant. However, no such formal demand is required if the lease expressly exempts the landlord from such a requirement or if the tenant is more than six months in arrears and there are insufficient goods on the premises to satisfy the arrears by means of a distress.[53] If possession is sought through proceedings in the High Court and the tenant is more than six months in arrears[54] the proceedings will be stayed if the tenant[55] pays the arrears and landlord's costs before the date of judgment.[56] If possession is sought in the County Court the proceedings will be stayed if the tenant pays the arrears and landlord's costs not later than five days before the date of the trial.[57]

(vii) Forfeiture for breach of covenants other than the covenant to pay rent: The procedure for forfeiture for other covenants is governed by Law of Property Act 1925, s.146 which provides:

> "A right of re-entry of forfeiture under any proviso or stipulation in a lease for a breach of any covenant or condition in the lease shall not be enforceable, by action or otherwise, unless and until the lessor serves on the lessee a notice —

[49] s.1(2).
[50] See: *Tagro v. Cafane* [1991] 1 W.L.R. 378.
[51] [1992] 1 A.C. 494.
[52] *ibid.* at 525.
[53] Common Law Procedure Act 1852, s.210. Goods are regarded as unavailable for distress if the premises are locked.
[54] *Standard Pattern Co. Ltd v. Ivey* [1962] Ch. 432.
[55] Payment by a third party will not entitle the tenant to a stay of the proceedings: *Matthews v. Dobbins* [1963] 1 W.L.R. 227.
[56] Common Law Procedure Act 1855, s.212.
[57] County Courts Act 1984, s.138(2).

(a) specifying the particular breach complained of; and
(b) if the breach is capable of remedy, requiring the lessee to remedy the breach; and
(c) in any case, requiring the lessee to make compensation on money for the breach;

and the lessee fails, within a reasonable time thereafter, to remedy the breach, if it is capable of remedy, and to make reasonable compensation in money, to the satisfaction of the lessor, for the breach."

The notice required by section 146(1) must be served on the "lessee," which term is given the extended meaning of "an original or derivative under-lessee, and the persons deriving title under a lessee; also a grantee under any such grant as aforesaid and the persons deriving title from him."[58] Where the lease has been assigned service of a notice on the original tenant will be insufficient.[59] The element of the notice offering the tenant the chance to remedy breaches of covenant or provide adequate financial compensation were said by Slade L.J. in *Expert Clothing Service & Sales Ltd v. Highgate House Ltd*[60] to give tenants "one last chance" to comply with their obligations. The tenant is entitled to a reasonable time to comply with the notice. What is reasonable will obviously depend upon the nature and remediability of the breach.[61] The need to offer a "reasonable period" to remedy any breach is only required if the breach is remediable. In general positive covenants, requiring the tenant to do something such as repair or maintain the premises, are capable of remedy.[62] In regard to negative covenants *Scala House and District Property Co. Ltd v. Forbes*[63] suggested that breaches can never be remedied since the breach cannot be undone,[64] for example a breach of a covenant not to assign, sub-let or alter the premises. As Bingham L.J. remarked in *Bass Ltd v. Morton Ltd*[65] the traditional view was that:

"A covenant to do something can be substantially performed even if late. A covenant not to do something, once broken, is broken for ever. As Lady Macbeth, referring to her breach of the sixth (negative) commandment observed: 'what's done is done'."

However, more recent decisions suggest a more flexible approach differentiating between breaches which are "once for all" and cannot be undone and where the breach is of a continuing nature which can be stopped and any harm the landlord has suffered effectively remedied. In *Expert Clothing Service & Sales Ltd v. Hillgate House Ltd*[66] Slade L.J. indicated that the ultimate question for the court was whether

[58] s.146(5)(b).
[59] *Fuller v. Judy Properties Ltd* (1991) 64 P. & C.R. 176.
[60] [1986] Ch. 340.
[61] In *Billson v. Residential Apartments Ltd* [1992] 1 A.C. 494 a 14 day period was held sufficient where the tenants had no intention of remedying the breach. In *Horsey Estates v. Steiger* [1899] 2 Q.B. 79 two days was insufficient where there was an irremediable breach.
[62] See *Expert Clothing Service and Sales Ltd v. Hillgate House Ltd* [1986] Ch. 340 where it was held that a covenant to reconstruct premises was capable of remedy by performance and compensation.
[63] [1974] Q.B. 575.
[64] See also: *Rugby School (Governors) v. Tannahill* [1934] 1 K.B. 695.
[65] [1988] Ch. 493.
[66] [1986] Ch. 340, at 358.

compliance with a section 146 notice, coupled with the payment of any appropriate monetary compensation, would "have effectively remedied the harm which the lessors had suffered or were likely to suffer from the breach." In *Bass Ltd v. Morton Ltd*[67] Bingham L.J. indicated that a breach was only irremediable if the landlord could show "continuing damage" to himself once the breach had ceased and appropriate compensation been paid. Applying these tests, a breach of a covenant not to use a premises for immoral purposes as in *Rugby School (Governors) v. Tannanhill*[68] would be irremediable,[69] since the harm caused to the landlord's reputation could not be remedied. As O'Connor L.J. commented in *Expert Clothing Service & Sales v. Hillgate House Ltd*[70]:

> "To stop what is forbidden by a negative covenant may or may not remedy the breach even if accompanied by compensation in money. Thus to remove the window boxes and pay for the repair of any damage done will remedy the breach, but to stop using the house as a brothel will not, because the taint lingers on and will not dissipate within a reasonable time."

Thus use of premises for illegal purposes will generally constitute an irremediable breach, as for example in *Van Haarlam v. Kasner*[71] where a tenant had used a flat for spying in breach of the Official Secrets Act 1911.

(viii) Forfeiture for breach of a covenant to pay a service charge: In many long leases the tenant is requires to pay a service charge as well as a rent. The Housing Act 1996 has introduced provisions to protect tenants from forfeiture for non-payment of service charges because of the tendency of some landlords to exploit the levying of service charges as a way of terminating leases. The problem is particularly acute where the tenant contests the amount of the service charge levied. Section 81 of the Housing Act 1996 provides that a landlord cannot exercise a right of re-entry or forfeiture for non-payment of a service charge unless the amount of the service charge is agreed or admitted by the tenant, or has been the subject of determination by a court or tribunal. This does not prevent the landlord from serving a section 146 notice on a tenant for non-payment, but section 82 of the Housing Act 1996 provides that such a notice must inform the tenant of his rights under section 81.

(ix) Breach of a covenant to repair — additional protection for the tenant under the Leasehold Property Repairs Act 1938: Where a tenant is in breach of his covenant to repair he can claim the additional protection afforded by the Leasehold Property Repairs Act 1938. This act applies to leases for a period of more than seven years with a term of at least three years to run. In the event of a breach the landlord must serve a section 146 notice on the tenant informing him that he has a 28 day period in which to serve a counter-notice on him claiming the protection of the Act. When such a counter-notice has been served the landlord requires leave of the court before enforcing the covenant. In *Associated British Ports v. CH Bailey Plc*[72] Lord Templeman

[67] [1988] Ch. 493, at 541.
[68] [1934] 1 K.B. 695.
[69] See also *Dunraven Securities Ltd v. Holloway* (1982) 264 E.G. 709, where there was an irremediable breach of covenant when premises were used as a sex shop in Soho.
[70] [1986] Ch. 340, at 362.
[71] (1992) 64 P. & C.R. 214.
[72] [1990] 1 All E.R. 929.

explained that this leave will generally be granted if "the immediate remedying of a breach of the repairing covenant is required in order to save the landlord from substantial loss of damage which the landlord would otherwise sustain."[73]

(x) Relief against forfeiture for non-payment of rent: Even where a landlord is entitled to forfeit a lease because of the tenant's breach of covenant to pay rent the tenant may be able to obtain relief against forfeiture. Where a landlord has been granted possession by the High Court, and the tenant was more than six months in arrears,[74] Common Law Procedure Act 1852, s.210 allows the tenant to claim relief if he pays the rent due and landlord's costs within six months of the execution of the judgment. Where possession has been ordered by the County Court the tenant may prevent the execution of the order by paying the arrears and costs within a period specified by the court.[75] If the landlord has recovered possession the tenant may apply for relief within six months and the court has the discretion to grant such order as it thinks fit. The tenant may also apply to the county court for relief within six months of a peaceful re-entry.[76] Outside these statutory provisions there is a general equitable jurisdiction to grant relief where the tenant has paid all the arrears and costs.[77]

(xi) Relief against forfeiture for breach of other covenants: Law of Property Act 1925, s.146(2) provides a wide-ranging general jurisdiction to the court to grant a tenant relief from forfeiture for breach of covenant other than that to pay rent:

> "Where a lessor is proceeding, by action or otherwise, to enforce such a right of re-entry or forfeiture, the lessee may, in the lessor's action, if any, or in any action brought by himself, apply to the court for relief; and the court may grant or refuse relief, as the court, having regard to the proceedings and conduct of the parties . . . and to all the other circumstances, thinks fit; and in case of relief may grant it on such terms, if any, as to costs, expenses, damages, compensation, penalty or otherwise, including the granting of an injunction to restrain any like breach in the future, as the court, in the circumstances of each case, thinks fit."

In the case of forfeiture by court proceedings the tenant's right to apply for relief is only lost when the landlord has entered into possession of the premises. However, in the case of peaceable re-entry the House of Lords held in *Billson v. Residential Apartments*[78] that the tenant can apply for relief even after the landlord has taken possession. Generally the courts will not grant relief for an irremediable breach, where a third parties' rights have intervened, for example by a re-letting of the premises after re-entry,[79] or where the breach involves immoral or illegal conduct.[80] Relief will usually be granted in the case of trivial breaches. Unlike the general equitable jurisdiction to grant relief, the jurisdiction under section 146(2) includes potential relief where the

[73] See also: *Sedac Investments v. Tanner* [1982] 3 All E.R. 646; *Hamilton v. Martell Securities* [1984] 1 All E.R. 665.

[74] *Billson v. Residential Apartments Ltd* [1992] 1 A.C. 494.

[75] County Counts Act 1984, s.138. The period must not be less than four weeks.

[76] County Courts Act 1984, s.139(2).

[77] *Howard v. Fanshawe* [1895] 2 Ch. 581; *Lovelock v. Margo* [1963] 2 Q.B. 786.

[78] [1992] 1 A.C. 494.

[79] *Fuller v. Judy Properties Ltd* (1991) 64 P. & C.R. 176.

[80] *Hoffman v. Fineberg* [1949] Ch. 245; *Borthwick-Norton v. Romney Warwick Estates Ltd* [1950] 1 All E.R. 798; *GMS Syndicate Ltd v. Gary Elliott Ltd* [1982] Ch. 1.

tenant committed a wilful breach of covenant.[81] It remains unclear whether in the light of section 146 the general equitable jurisdiction has survived and is available for breaches other than non-payment of rent.[82]

(xii) Relief from forfeiture on behalf of a sub-tenant: The forfeit of a lease has the effect that any sub-leases are automatically extinguished.[83] Law of Property Act 1925, s.146(4) therefore allows such persons to apply independently for relief from forfeiture of the head lease. The court is granted jurisdiction to:

> "make and order vesting, for the whole term of the lease or any less term, the property comprised in the lease or any part thereof in any person entitled as under-lessee to any estate or interest in such property upon such conditions as to execution of any deed or other document, payment of rent, costs, expenses, damages, compensation, giving security, or otherwise, as the court in the circumstances of each case may think fit, but in no case shall such under-lessee be entitled to require a lease to be granted to him for any longer term than he had under his original sub-lease."

This entitles the court to grant the sub-tenant a direct lease from the landlord when the original tenant's head lease is forfeited.

(xiii) Relief from forfeiture on behalf of a mortgagee of a leasehold interest: The right to seek relief against forfeiture under Law of Property Act 1925, s.146(4) also extends to a mortgagee of a leasehold interest.[84] The statutory jurisdiction is not available if the landlord has obtained possession by proceedings[85] although in *Abbey National Building Society v. Maybeech Ltd*[86] Nicholls J. held that the equitable jurisdiction was still available in such circumstances.

(xiv) Waiver of breach: A landlord will not be entitled to forfeit a lease for breach of covenant if he has expressly or impliedly waived the breach. The general principles of waiver were explained by Parker J. in *Matthews v. Smallwood*[87]:

> "Waiver of a right of re-entry can only occur where the lessor, with knowledge of the facts upon which his right to re-entry arises, does some unequivocal act recognising the continued existence of the lease. It is not enough that he should do the act which recognizes, or appears to recognize, the continued existence of the lease, unless, at the time when the act is done, he has knowledge of the facts under which, or from which, his right of entry arose."

[81] *Billson v. Residential Apartments Ltd* [1992] 1 A.C. 494; *WG Clark (Properties) Ltd v. Dupre Properties Ltd* [1992] Ch. 297.

[82] *Official Custodian of Charities v. Parkway Estates Developments Ltd* [1985] Ch. 151; *Billson v. Residential Apartments Ltd* [1992] 1 A.C. 494; [1991] CLJ 401 (Bridge); [1991] Conv. 380 (Goulding); [1992] Conv. 32 (Smith).

[83] *Great Western Railway Co. v. Smith* (1876) 2 Ch.D. 235; *GMS Syndicate Ltd v. Gary Elliott Ltd* [1982] Ch. 1.

[84] Since the mortgage may take effect by way of a long lease, thus creating a sub-tenancy, or in the case of a charge by way of legal mortgage the mortgagee has a sub-term by virtue of, Law of Property Act 1925, s.87(1): See *Grand Junction Co. Ltd v. Bates* [1954] 2 Q.B. 160.

[85] *Rogers v. Rice* [1892] 2 Ch. 170; *Abbey National Building Society v. Maybeech Ltd* [1985] Ch. 190.

[86] [1985] Ch. 190.

[87] [1910] 1 Ch. 777, at 786.

These principles were adopted by the House of Lords in *Kammins Ballrooms Co. v. Zenith Investments*.[88] The most common form of waiver will be if the landlord continues to accept rent from the tenant,[89] which indicates an intention to continue the lease despite the breach. As Buckley LJ stated in *Central Estates (Belgravia) Ltd v. Woolgar (No. 2)*[90]:

> "If [the landlord] chooses to do something such as demanding or receiving rent which can only be done consistently with the existence of a certain state of affairs, *viz*, the continuance of the lease or tenancy in operation, he cannot thereafter be heard to say that that state of affairs did not then exist."

There is no need for the landlord to intend to waive the breach.[91] In *Matthews v. Smallwood* Parker J. indicated that since the issue whether an act constitutes a waiver is a matter of law, the landlord is not entitled to treat the tenancy as continuing and receive rent without prejudice to his right to re-enter, a position re-iterated by later cases.[92] A mere demand for rent will also be sufficient.[93] If rent is in arrears a landlord cannot accept money and avoid waiver by stipulating that the money is not accepted as rent.[94] In the case of acts other than the continued receipt of rent Slade LJ stated in *Expert Clothing Ltd v. Hillgate House*[95] that the court is "free to look at *all* the circumstances of the case" to determine whether an act was so unequivocal as to amount to an election. Examples of conduct which may amount to an election include an agreement by the landlord to grant a new tenancy on the normal determination of the existing lease,[96] and an offer by the landlord to vary a lease or to purchase the tenants interest.[97] A landlord who exercises his remedy of distress for failure to pay rent will also be unable to seek forfeiture. Although in *Expert Clothing Ltd v. Hillgate House* it was recognised that the proffering of a mere negotiating document may amount to a waiver, the Court of Appeal held that on the facts the sending of a draft deed of variation did not, since it was not unequivocal in the light of the surrounding circumstances, including the service of a section 146 notice seeking possession 14 days beforehand manifesting a clear intention to forfeit. Central to the doctrine of waiver is the idea that the landlord will only be taken to have waived a breach if he had knowledge that it had taken place. This does not require actual knowledge and constructive knowledge will suffice. The landlord will also be affixed with the knowledge of his agent or employee.[98] In *Matthews v. Smallwood*[99] it was held that there was no waiver when a landlord continued to accept rent after a tenant had committed a breach of his covenant not to sub-let the premises by granting a

[88] [1971] A.C. 850.
[89] *Segal Securities Ltd v. Thoseby* [1963] 1 Q.B. 887.
[90] [1972] 1 W.L.R. 1048, at 1054.
[91] *Cornillie v. Saha* [1996] 28 H.L.R. 561.
[92] *Segal Securities Ltd v. Thoseby* [1963] 1 Q.B. 887; *Central Estates (Belgravia) Ltd v. Woolgar (No. 2)* [1972] 1 W.L.R. 1048; *Expert Clothing Service & Sales Ltd v. Hillgate House Ltd* [1986] Ch. 340.
[93] *David Blackstone Ltd v. Burnetts (West End) Ltd* [1973] 1 W.L.R. 1487.
[94] *Croft v. Lumley* (1858) 6 H.L. Cas. 672; *Davenport v. The Queen* (1877) 3 Ch. App Cas 115 .
[95] [1986] Ch. 340, at 360.
[96] *Ward v. Day* (1863) 5 B. & S. 359.
[97] *Bader Properties Ltd v. Linley Property Investments Ltd* (1967) 19 P. & C.R. 620.
[98] *Metropolitan Properties Co. Ltd v. Cordery* (1979) 39 P. & C.R. 10.
[99] [1910] 1 Ch. 777.

mortgage, since the landlord did not have any knowledge that the mortgage had been granted. In *Chrisdell Ltd v. Johnson*[1] the Court of Appeal held that a landlord's mere suspicion of a breach was insufficient knowledge to hold that there was a waiver where he had received representations from the tenant that there had been no breach but was insufficiently confident that they were untrue to take proceedings for re-entry. In *Van Haarlam v. Kasner*[2] widespread media coverage of a tenant's illegal and immoral conduct was held sufficient knowledge.[3] The principles of waiver were applied in the recent case of *Cornillie v. Saha*.[4] In February 1993 Mr Cornillie purchased the freehold reversion of a block of flats, Flat 18 of which was leased to Mr and Mrs Saha on terms which included a covenant against sub-letting. In October 1993 Mr Cornillie served a section 146 notice. The county court judge held that this did not amount to a waiver because Mr Cornillie did not at that stage know the identity of all the occupiers of flat 18 and whether they enjoyed tenancies or mere licences, although he did know that one of them had a tenancy. However, the Court of Appeal reversed this decision and held that Mr Cornillie had waived his right to forfeit. His wife had known from early February that flat 18 had been divided into six rooms and these had been sub-let in breach of covenant. Aldous L.J. concluded that it was irrelevant that he did not know the identity of all the occupiers and that the "near certainty" that they all occupied on the same terms was sufficient to inform him of the fact of the breach. A waiver will only be effective in relation to the breach to which it relates as provided in section 148(1) of the Law of Property Act 1925. A waiver cannot therefore protect a tenant against future similar breaches.[5] In the case of a continuing breach the landlord can withdraw the waiver and seek forfeiture.[6] If in such a case the landlord has already served the requisite section 146 notice he does not need to serve another.[7] The effect of waiver is only to prevent the landlord seeking to forfeit the lease. He will still be entitled to claim damages from the tenant.[8]

(c) Distress

(i) The remedy of distress: Distress is an ancient common law remedy available to a landlord when his tenant is in arrears of rent. It allows the landlord to seize and sell goods found on the premises which are let to recover the rent arrears. Its exercise does not require the sanction of the court and it is therefore a form of self-help remedy. However, a number of statutory and common law restrictions restrict the availability and exercise of distress.

(ii) When the remedy is available: Distress is only available to a landlord as a remedy for a tenant's failure to pay rent and not for breach of other covenants. It is only available where the rent is in arrears, namely the day after it is due.[9] As a result of the Limitation Act 1980 the remedy will be unavailable for rent more than six years in

[1] (1987) 54 P. & C.R. 257.
[2] (1992) 64 P. & C.R. 214.
[3] But contrast *Official Custodian for Charities v. Parway Estates Developments Ltd* [1985] Ch. 151.
[4] [1996] 28 H.L.R. 561.
[5] *Billson v. Residential Apartments* [1992] 1 A.C. 494.
[6] *Greenwich LBC v. Discreet Selling Estates Ltd* (1990) 61 P. & C.R. 405.
[7] *Penton v. Barnett* [1898] 1 Q.B. 276; *Farimani v. Gates* (1984) 271 EG 887.
[8] *Stephens v. Junior Army and Navy Stores Ltd* [1914] 2 Ch. 516; *Greenwich LBC v. Discreet Selling Estates Ltd* (1990) 61 P. & C.R. 405.
[9] *Duppa v. Mayo* (1669) 1 Wms Saund 275; *Re Aspinall* [1961] 1 Ch 526.

arrears.[10] If distress is exercised where rent is not due the distress will be unlawful, as was the case in *Walsh v. Lonsdale*.[11]

(iii) Leave of the court required: In some instances distress cannot be exercised by the landlord without the leave of the court. The most important situation where leave is required is if the tenant is a Rent Act tenant.

(iv) Exercise of distress: Distress may be exercised by the landlord personally, or by a certified bailiff. Distress cannot be exercised between sunset and sunrise[12] and access cannot be gained forcibly to the premises. The landlord cannot break down an outer door[13] or enter via a closed window.[14] He may, however, enter by means of an unlocked door[15] or open window.[16] Once he has gained entry he is entitled to break down internal doors and partitions.[17]

(v) Goods which can be seized: At common law the landlord is entitled to seize any goods physically found on the land. However, this general right is subject to the exception that some goods and categories of goods are regarded as privileged and are not available for distress. Some goods enjoy absolute privilege and are exempt from seizure. These include perishable goods,[18] things in actual use by the tenant at the time he seeks to distrain,[19] clothes and bedding of the tenant and his family to a value of £100,[20] tools of the tenants trade to the value of £150 and money which is not in a closed purse or bag.[21] Other goods enjoy a qualified privilege and may not be seized unless without them there would be insufficient goods to recover the rent arrears. This category includes the tools and implements of a man's trade,[22] animals which are used to plough the land[23] and animals on the land which belong to a third party which the tenant is feeding commercially.[24] Goods belonging to third parties which are on the land may also enjoy an absolute privilege. The goods of undertenants and lodgers are privileged under the Law of Distress Amendment Act 1908.

(vi) Sale of seized goods: Once distress has been levied the landlord must give the tenant notice, informing him of the reason for the distress, the proposed date of sale of the goods and of where goods have been removed to.[25] The goods may be sold at least five days after the tenant has been given such notice. The landlord must obtain the best price possible and he cannot purchase the goods himself.

[10] s.19. In the case of agricultural land only one years rent may be recovered: Agricultural Holdings Act 1986, s.16.
[11] (1882) 21 Ch.D. 9.
[12] *Aldenburgh v. Peaple* (1834) C. & P. 212; *Tutton v. Drake* (1860) 29 L.J. Ex. 271.
[13] *Semayne's Case* (1605) 5 Co. Rep 91a; *American Concentrated Must Corp v. Hendry* (1893) 62 L.J.Q.B. 388; Cassidy v. Foley [1904] 2 I.R. 427.
[14] *Nash v. Lucas* (1867) L.R. 2 Q.B. 590.
[15] *Ryan v. Shilock* (1851) 7 Exch. 72; *Southam v. Smout* [1964] 1 Q.B. 308.
[16] *Crabtree v. Robinson* (1885) 15 Q.B.D. 312; *Long v. Clarke* [1894] 1 Q.B. 119.
[17] *Browning v. Dann* (1735) Buller's NP (7th ed.) 81c.
[18] *Morely v. Pincombe* (1848) 2 Exch. 101.
[19] *Pitt v. Shew* (1821) 4 B. & Ald. 206.
[20] Law of Distress Amendment Act 1888, s.4; Protection from Execution (Prescribed Value) Order 1980/26.
[21] *East India Co. v. Skinner* (1695) 1 Botts P.L. 259.
[22] *Nargett v. Nias* (1859) 1 E. & E. 439.
[23] *Simpson v. Hartropp* (1744) Willes 512.
[24] Agricultural Holdings Act 1986, s.18.
[25] Distress for Rent Act 1689, s.1; Distress for Rent Act 1737, s.9.

(vii) Abolition of distress?: The Law Commission has examined distress a number of times.[26] Its abolition was recommended by the Payne Committee in 1969[27] and by the Law Commission in 1991[28] on the grounds that it is "riddled with inconsistencies, uncertainties, anomalies and archaisms." However, it was recognised that abolition was only practical if a more rapid court procedure was introduced for the recovery of arrears of rent.

(d) Damages for breach of covenant

(i) Availability of damages: The landlord will be entitled to recover damages wherever the tenant is in breach of his covenants, except the covenant to pay rent.
(ii) The measure of recovery: The landlord is entitled to recover the contractual measure of damages for the loss that he has suffered. The object is to restore the landlord to the position he would have been in if the breach had not been committed.
(iii) Damages for breach of covenant to repair: The provisions of the Leasehold Property Repairs Act 1938, which have been discussed above, apply to the recovery of damages for breach[29] of repairing covenants as well as to forfeiture.[30] The Landlord and Tenant Act 1927, s.1 provides that any award of damages cannot exceed the diminution in value of the landlord's reversionary interest caused by the breach.

(e) Action for arrears of rent

By Limitation Act 1980, s.19 a landlord cannot bring an action to recover rent "after the expiration of six years from the date on which the arrears became due."

TRANSFERS OF THE TENANT'S LEASEHOLD INTERESTS AND THE LANDLORD'S FREEHOLD REVERSION

1 Principles of assignment

When a lease is validly created the landlord and the tenant both enjoy proprietary interests in the land concerned. The tenant enjoys his leasehold estate and the landlord holds the freehold reversion, in other words the full freehold fee simple estate will revert to him when the lease comes to an end. These interests are capable of being transferred to other persons by assignment. A leasehold interest in either residential or commercial property is therefore a marketable commodity, and the person to whom the lease is assigned will enjoy the same interest as was enjoyed by the original tenant.

[26] Law Commission No. 5, *Interim Report on Distress for Rent* (1966); Law Commission Working Paper No. 97, *Landlord and Tenant: Distress for Rent* (1986).
[27] *Report of the Committee on the Enforcement of Judgment Debts* (1969) Cmnd. 3909.
[28] Law Comm. No. 194: *Landlord and Tenant: Distress for Rent* (1991).
[29] s.1.
[30] [1986] Conv. 85 (Smith).

2 Assignment of the tenant's leasehold estate

(a) Tenant's right to assign

In the absence of express provisions of the lease a tenant enjoys an absolute right to assign his interest under the lease.[31] When the lease is validly assigned the assignee stands in the shoes of the assignor as tenant under the lease and the assignor retains no interest in the land.[32]

(b) Covenant against assignment

(i) Nature of covenants against assignment: The tenant's absolute right to assign his leasehold interest may be qualified by the presence of an express covenant in the lease restricting his right to assign. Such restrictions are most common in short term leases.
(ii) Types of covenant against assignment: Such covenants restricting the tenant's right to assign may either take the form of absolute or qualified covenants. In the case of an absolute covenant the tenant has no right to assign at all. Under a qualified covenant he cannot assign without the consent of the landlord.
(iii) Statutory jurisdiction over qualified covenants against assignment: In the case of qualified covenants Landlord and Tenant Act 1927, s.19(1) provides that the landlord shall not withhold his consent from an assignment "unreasonably." The Landlord and Tenant Act 1988, s.1 provides a procedure for ensuring that a tenant's written request for consent is dealt with rapidly. It imposes a duty on the landlord:.

(a) to give consent, except in a case where it is reasonable not to give consent,

(b) to serve on the tenant written notice of his decision whether or not to give consent specifying in addition:

  (i) if the consent is given subject to condition, the conditions,
  (ii) if the consent is withheld, the reasons for withholding it.

He must fulfil his duty within a reasonable time of receipt of the request. In applying the test of reasonableness to a landlord's refusal to grant consent Balcombe L.J. held in *International Drilling Fluids Ltd v. Louisville Investments (Uxbridge) Ltd*[33] that the purpose of such covenants was "to protect the lessor from having his premises used or occupied in an undesirable way, or by an undesirable tenant or his assignee." The refusal of consent may be reasonable for example because of the proposed use of the premises by the assignee,[34] the unsatisfactory nature of the assignees references[35] or of his financial position.[36] It is unclear whether the court should take into account the effects on the tenant if consent is refused.[37] In each case it is a question of fact whether

[31] *Keeves v. Dean* [1924] 1 K.B. 685; *Leith Properties v. Byrne* [1983] Q.B. 433.
[32] *Milmo v. Carreras* [1946] K.B. 306.
[33] [1986] Ch. 513.
[34] *Bates v. Donaldson* [1896] 2 Q.B. 241.
[35] *Rossi v. Hestdrive* [1985] E.G.L.R. 50.
[36] *British Bakeries (Midlands) Ltd v. Michael Testler & Co. Ltd* [1986] 1 E.G.L.R. 64.
[37] For cases which suggests that the consequences for the tenant are relevant see: *Sheppard v. Hong Kong and Shanghai Banking Corporation* (1872) 20 W.R. 459; *Houlder Brothers & Co. Ltd v. Gibbs* [1925] Ch. 575; *Leeward Securities Ltd v. Lilyheath Properties Ltd* (1983) 271 E.G. 279. For cases which suggest that the landlord's interests are alone relevant see: *Viscount Tredegar v Harwood* [1929] A.C. 72; *West Layton Ltd v. Ford* [1979] Q.B. 593; *Bromley Park Garden Estates Ltd v. Moss* [1982] 1 W.L.R. 1019.

consent has been unreasonably withheld.[38] The Landlord and Tenant (Covenants) Act 1995, s.22 allows landlords of commercial premises to include a specific clause in the lease stipulating circumstances in which they are entitled to withhold consent. Any subsequent withholding of consent in such circumstances is automatically reasonable. This provision only applies to leases commencing after 1995. The withholding of consent on racial grounds is also unlawful.[39]

(c) Formalities of assignment

Where a lease has created a legal estate in the land any transfer is a conveyance and must therefore be effected by deed.[40] This is true even of the assignment of leases for less than three years which can be created orally with no need for additional formalities. An assignment of an equitable interest in land must be effected by writing.[41] An oral assignment is of no effect at all.

(d) Assignment and registration of title

(i) Assignment of leases of unregistered land: Where a legal lease of unregistered land is assigned on sale and has more than 21 years unexpired at the date of assignment it must be registered in exactly the same way as the creation of a new leasehold interest for more than 21 years.[42]

(ii) Assignment of leases of registered land: Where a leasehold interest is assigned which is already registered the transfer of the legal estate is not effective until the assignee is registered as the new proprietor. In the meantime the assignor holds the interest on trust for the assignee in equity.

(e) Assignment in breach of covenant

An assignment in breach of covenant does not prevent the transfer of an estate in the land. However, the landlord may be entitled to forfeit the lease or seek damages from the ex-tenant in breach.[43]

3 Acquisition of a leasehold interest by adverse possession

(a) Operation of adverse possession

As has been noted in the context of freehold ownership in the previous chapter an interest in land can be obtained by means of adverse possession. This has the effect of defeating the interests of the current owner, who is no longer able to assert his title against the adverse possessor by virtue of the operation of the Limitation Act 1980. The three central requirements for acquisition of adverse possession are first, that the possessor must take factual possession of the land in question, second that he must have the appropriate intention to possess, and that he must possess for a continuous period of more than 12 years.

[38] *Bickell v. Duke of Westminster* [1977] Q.B. 517; *West Layton Ltd v. Ford* [1979] Q.B. 593.
[39] Race Relations Act 1976, s.24.
[40] Law of Property Act 1925, s.52(1). See: *Crago v. Julian* [1992] 1 W.L.R. 372.
[41] *ibid.* s.53(1)(a).
[42] Land Registration Act 1925, s.123(1).
[43] See: *Peabody Fund v. Higgins* [1983] 3 All E.R. 122.

(b) Application of adverse possession in a leasehold context

(i) Possession adverse to the tenant: Where land is subject to a lease more than one person enjoys an estate in the land. The landlord enjoys the freehold and the tenant a leasehold estate. Where a person displaces the tenant and takes physical possession of the land his possession is adverse against the interests of the tenant and not the landlord during the currency of the lease. Therefore if the adverse possessor achieves the required 12 years possession the tenant's rights are extinguished against him. The adverse possessor then stands as tenant in relation to the freehold owner.

(ii) Possession adverse to the landlord's freehold: Only when the tenancy has come to an end will adverse possession begin to run against the freeholder.[44]

(iii) Landlord's right to recover the land from a tenant who has adversely acquired the leasehold ownership: While the tenancy is continuing the landlord has no right to remove the adverse possessor from the land as he enjoys the right of exclusive possession conferred by the leasehold interest he has acquired by his adverse possession. However, once the lease has come to an end the landlord can take steps to remove the adverse possessor from the land. This may occur simply by the effluxion of time, so that the lease runs out. There is some authority that a dispossessed tenant may be able to surrender the lease to the landlord, thus bringing it to an immediate end. The problem with this suggestion, which was accepted in relation to a lease of unregistered land in *St Marylebone Property Co Ltd v. Fairweather*,[45] is that technically the dispossessed tenant retains no further interest in the land which he is entitled to surrender. It is clear that in registered land the tenant has no interest which he can surrender as adverse possession entitles the possessor to be registered as proprietor of the leasehold interest.[46]

(iv) Enforceability of the leasehold covenants between the landlord and an adverse possessor of the leasehold interest: Where an adverse possessor has thereby acquired the leasehold ownership the question arises whether the covenants of the lease are binding on him and can therefore be enforced by the landlord. As will be seen below, the law has developed mechanisms to ensure the enforceability of leasehold covenants against assignees of a tenant. In the case of a lease of unregistered land there is no direct enforceability of the covenants between the landlord and the tenant entitled by way of adverse possession. The adverse possessor is not an assignee and therefore does not enjoy "privity of estate" with the landlord.[47] The landlord may, however, forfeit the lease for breach against the dispossessed tenant which has the effect of bringing the lease to an end, and along with it any entitlement of the adverse possessor to continue in possession. In such circumstances the adverse possessor has no right to apply for relief against forfeiture of the lease.[48] In registered land the leasehold covenants would seem to be directly enforceable between the landlord and the adverse possessor since by operation of the Land Registration Act he is entitled to be registered as proprietor, in effect creating a statutory privity of estate between the parties.

[44] Limitation Act 1980 Sched. 1 para. 4.
[45] [1963] A.C. 510.
[46] *Spectrum Investments Co. v. Holmes* [1981] 1 W.L.R. 221.
[47] As there is no "assignment" the Landlord and Tenant (Covenants) Act 1995 is also inapplicable.
[48] *Tickner v. Buzzacott* [1965] Ch. 426.

4 Assignment of the landlord's freehold reversion

(a) Mechanisms for assignment of the freehold

The landlord is also capable of assigning his retained interest in the land subject to a lease by transferring the fee simple to an assignee. In order to accomplish this the appropriate formalities and requirements of registration will have to be completed in the case of registered land. If the land subject to the lease is as yet unregistered, the title will have to be registered as a first registration on the assignment, since registration is compulsory on the first "qualifying conveyance".[49]

(b) Will the lease bind the transferee of the freehold reversion?

(i) General principles: Although the landlord can transfer his freehold reversion by means of an assignment, it is not inevitable that the transferee will take the land subject to the lease. Whether the assignee will be bound will depend upon the principles of priority enshrined within the system of land registration and the rules applying to unregistered land. Although these principles will be examined in detail in Parts IV and V, the outcomes will also be summarised here for convenience.

(ii) Transfer of the freehold reversion in registered land: Where title to the land subject to the lease is registered the principles governing whether the lease will bind the transferee will depend upon the length and character of the lease involved. Legal leases for more than 21 years are protected because they are themselves registered interests with their own individual title at the Land Registry. Legal leases for less than 21 years will bind the transferee of the freehold as they rank as overriding interests under Land Registration Act 1925, s.70(1)(k). Equitable leases of any length should be protected on the register as minor interests, and if unprotected are not binding on a purchaser of the freehold.[50] However, even if they have not been protected they will rank as overriding interests within section 70(1)(g) if the tenant is in actual occupation, and therefore bind the transferee.[51]

(iii) Transfer of the freehold reversion of unregistered land: Where the land subject to the lease is unregistered a legal lease will always be binding on the transferee of the freehold because it does not need to be protected as a land charge and is governed by the rule that "legal interests bind the world". However, an equitable lease constitutes an estate contract which is a Class c(iv) land charge. If the tenant has failed to appropriately protect his interest on the register it will become void against a purchaser of a legal estate in the land, who will take free form it.[52] Where the freehold reversion of unregistered land is transferred in consequence of a sale registration of title to land is compulsory[53] and the transferee must make an application to be registered as the proprietor within two months.[54]

[49] Land Registration Act 1925, s.123(1).
[50] *ibid.* s.20(1) and 59(6).
[51] See *Strand Securities v. Casewell* [1965] Ch. 958 where a tenant was unprotected because he was not in occupation of the land.
[52] Land Charges Act 1972, s.4(6).
[53] Because the whole of England and Wales is designated an area of compulsory registration: Registration of Title Order 1989 (S.I. 1989 No. 1347).
[54] Land Registration Act 1925, s.123.

CREATION OF A SUB-LEASE

1 Tenant's right to create a sub-lease

When a tenant assigns his interest he transfers it to another person who takes over his place as tenant of the land and he retains no further interest. However, instead of assigning his interest it is open to him to create a sub-lease, by carving a tenancy out of his own leasehold estate. In such a situation he will stand as a tenant in relation to his original landlord, but will stand as landlord in relation to his sub-tenant, who will in turn stand as tenant in relation to him but stand in no relationship to the landlord of the head lease.

2 Covenant against sub-letting

A lease may contain covenants against sub-letting which are absolute or qualified, just as they may contain covenants against assignment. The statutory provisions which regulate a landlord's right to refuse consent to an assignment also govern his right to refuse consent to a sub-lease.

3 Formalities for the creation of a sub-lease

Where a sub-lease is granted by the tenant the same formalities must be complied with as if it were an ordinary head lease.

ENFORCEABILITY OF LEASEHOLD COVENANTS

1 General principles

(a) Leases as contractual and proprietary interests

It has been seen how the grant of a lease creates a proprietary interest in land in the form of a leasehold estate. It has also been seen how the precise terms of a lease are comprised of the covenants entered into between the landlord and the tenant which give rise to contractual obligations. However, contractual obligations which are entered into by two parties are not binding on third parties who are not privy to the contract. This limitation of contractual liability would cause difficulties if applied rigidly to leases since on the assignment of the lease there would be no continuing liability for breach of the covenants between the landlord and the tenant. The law has therefore developed means to ensure that the provisions of a lease are binding upon subsequent assignees of the landlord or the tenant. The principles developed by the courts were subsequently supplemented by statutory provisions in the Law of Property Act 1925. However, an entirely new statutory regime was introduced to govern the enforceability of covenants in leases granted after January 1, 1996 in the Landlord and Tenant (Covenants) Act 1995.

(b) Privity of estate

The central concept which the law has developed to ensure that covenants remain enforceable between subsequent assignees of the original landlord and tenant is that of "privity of estate". This concept was recognised as long ago as *Spencer's Case*[55] and its essence was identified by Nourse L.J. in *City of London Corp v Fell*[56]: "The contractual obligations which touch and concern the land having become imprinted on the estate, the tenancy is capable of existence as a species of property independently of the contract." What this means is that the contractual obligations which form part of the lease between the original landlord and tenant are considered as attached to the leasehold estate which exists between them, and not as merely personal obligations arising under their contract. When the estate is transferred to others, whether the assignment of the freehold reversion or of the tenancy itself, these covenants are enforceable between the transferees who stand in the same positions in relation to the estate as the original landlord and tenant. The operation of privity of estate was further explained by Lord Templeman when *City of London Corp v. Fell*[57] came before the House of Lords. He stated that the solution to the problem of enforceability of covenants between assignees of the original parties to a lease was:

> "to annex to the term and the reversion the benefit and burden of covenants which touch and concern the land. The covenants having been annexed, every legal owner of the term granted by the lease and every legal owner of the reversion from time to time holds his estate with the benefit of and subject to the covenants which touch and concern the land."

The enforceability of leasehold covenants is therefore a combination of the principles of privity of contract and privity of estate. Between the original landlord and tenant all covenants are enforceable in contract. Between successors in title to the original landlord and tenant covenants which "touch and concern" the land are enforceable on the basis of their privity of estate. The interaction between these two principles was summarised by Nourse L.J. in *City of London Corp v. Fell*[58]:

> "A lease of land, because it originates in contract, gives rise to obligations enforceable between the original landlord and the original tenant in contract. But because it also gives the tenant an estate in the land, assignable, like the reversion, to others, the obligations so far as they touch and concern the land, assume a wider influence, becoming, as it were, imprinted on the term of the reversion as the case may be, enforceable between the owners thereof for the time being as conditions of the enjoyment of their respective estates. Thus landlord and tenant stand together in one or other of two distinct legal relationships. In the first it is said that there is privity of contract between them, in the second privity of estate."

[55] (1583) 5 Co. Rep. 16a.
[56] [1993] Q.B. 589, at 604.
[57] [1994] 1 A.C. 459.
[58] [1993] Q.B. 589, at 603–4.

(c) Covenants which "touch and concern" land

(i) A limit to the scope of privity of estate: As is evident from the judicial descriptions of privity of estate it is clear that not all covenants of the original landlord and tenant are enforceable between their successors in title. Only those covenants which can be said to "touch and concern" the land are enforceable on the basis of privity of estate. The object of this requirement is to differentiate those contractual terms which are genuinely imprinted on the estate from those which are purely personal and should not be binding on the land.
(ii) A general test of "touching and concerning": It has proved difficult to provide a simple comprehensive test to determine whether a covenant is to be regarded as touching and concerning the land. In *Hua Chiao bank v. Chiaphua Ltd*[59] Lord Oliver adopted the formulations of *Cheshire and Burns Modern Law of Real Property*[60] that:

> "If the covenant has direct reference to the land, if it lays down something which is to be done or is not to be done upon the land, or, and perhaps this is the clearest way of describing the test, if it affects the landlord in his normal capacity as landlord or the tenant in his normal capacity as tenant, it may be said to touch and concern the land . . . If a simple test is desired for ascertaining into which category a covenant falls, it is suggested that the proper inquiry should be whether the covenant affects either the landlord *qua* landlord or the tenant *qua* tenant. A covenant may very well have reference to the land, but, unless it is reasonably incidental to the relation of landlord and tenant, it cannot be said to touch and concern the land so as to be capable of running therewith or with the reversion."[61]

In the subsequent case of *Swift Investments v. Combined English Stores PLC*[62] he went on to offer a number of practical considerations which would identify whether a covenant was to be found to touch and concern land:

> "Formulations of definitive tests are always dangerous, but it seems to me that, without claiming to expound an exhaustive guide, the following provides a satisfactory working test for whether, in any given case, a covenant touches and concerns the land: (1) the covenant benefits only the reversioner for the time being, and if separated from the reversion ceases to be of benefit to the covenantee; (2) the covenant affects the nature, quality, mode of user or value of the land of the reversioner; (3) the covenant is not expressed to be personal (that is to say neither being given only to a specific reversioner nor in respect of the obligations only of a specific tenant); (4) the fact that a covenant is to pay a sum of money will not prevent it from touching and concerning the land so long as the three forgoing conditions are satisfied and the covenant is connected with something to be done on, to or in relation to the land."

[59] [1987] A.C. 99, at 107.
[60] (13th ed., 1982), pp. 430-431.
[61] See also: *Congleton Corp v. Pattison* (1808) 10 East 130; *Horsey Estate Ltd v. Steiger* [1899] 2 Q.B. 79.
[62] [1989] A.C. 632, at 642.

(iii) Application of the "touch and concern" requirement: Many leasehold covenants will obviously "touch and concern" the land since they are clearly referable to the relationship between the landlord and tenant. Covenants of the tenant which clearly touch and concern the land include covenants to pay rent,[63] to keep the demised premises in repair,[64] to insure against fire,[65] not to use the premises other than as a dwelling house[66] and not to assign the tenancy without consent.[67] Similarly a landlord's covenants to provide quiet enjoyment, to supply water,[68] to repair, and not to build on adjoining land[69] would touch and concern. An option granted by the landlord to the tenant to purchase the freehold of the premises has been held not to touch and concern[70] but an option to renew the lease does touch and concern the land.[71] Covenants which involve purely personal matters between the landlord and tenant will not touch and concern the land. In *Thomas v. Hayward*[72] a covenant by the landlord of a pub not to open another within half a mile was held to be personal because it did not affect the landlord's behaviour on the land let. However, a covenant by the tenant of a pub not to do anything which would cause a suspension of a licence did touch and concern the land.[73] A covenant not to employ a named person on business premises was held to touch and concern the land[74] whereas a covenant not to employ a particular class of people on the property did not.[75] A covenant to provide personal services for the landlord would not touch and concern the land. In *Gower v. Postmaster-General*[76] a covenant by a tenant to pay the rates due on land owned by the landlord other than that which he had rented was held not to touch and concern the land. In *P & A Swift Investments v. Combined English Stores Group Plc*[77] the question arose whether a covenant to act as a surety of tenant's obligations touched and concerned the land. When the original landlord had granted an underlease of premises to a company the defendants acted as surety and guaranteed that the undertenant would pay the rent and observe all the covenants. The original landlord assigned the freehold reversion to the plaintiffs and the undertenants became insolvent and defaulted on the rent. The House of Lords held that the plaintiffs, as successors in title to the original landlords, could recover the £4,250 arrears of rent from the defendants since the surety agreement was a covenant which touched and concerned the land and was therefore enforceable by them.[78] Lord Oliver explained that since the tenant's covenant which was guaranteed by the surety touched and concerned the land the covenant of the surety must also touch and concern "if [the primary obligation] of the

[63] *Parker v. Webb* (1693) 2 Salk. 5.
[64] *Matures v. Westwood* (1598) Cro. Eliz. 599.
[65] *Vernon v. Smith* (1821) 5 B. & Ald. 1.
[66] *Wilkinson v. Rogers* (1864) 2 De G.J. & Sm. 62.
[67] *Williams v. Earle* (1868) L.R. 3 Q.B. 739.
[68] *Jourdain v. Wilson* (1821) 4 B. & Ald. 266.
[69] *Ricketts v. Enfield Church Wardens* [1909] 1 Ch. 544.
[70] *Woodall v. Clifton* [1905] 2 Ch. 257; *Griffiths v. Pelton* [1958] Ch. 205.
[71] *Phillips v. Mobil Oil Co. Ltd* [1989] 1 W.L.R. 888.
[72] (1869) L.R. 4 Exch. 311.
[73] *Fleetwood v. Hull* (1889) 23 Q.B.D. 35.
[74] *Re Hunters Lease* [1942] Ch. 124.
[75] *Mayor of Congleton v. Pattison* (1808) 10 East 130.
[76] (1887) 57 L.T. 527.
[77] [1989] A.C. 632.
[78] See also: *Coronation Street Industrial Properties Ltd v. Ignall Industries plc* [1989] 1 W.L.R. 304.

tenant touches and concerns the land that of the surety must, as it seems to me, equally do so."[79] In *Hua Chiao Commercial Bank Ltd v. Chiaphua Industries Ltd*[80] the Privy Council held that a landlord's obligation to repay a tenant's deposit paid at the beginning of a lease was purely personal and did not touch and concern the land. The original landlord and tenant entered an agreement for a five year lease. One term of their agreement was that the tenant should provide two months rent as a security deposit, returnable at the end of the term. The landlord assigned his interest to the defendant bank as part of a mortgage arrangement. At the end of the term the plaintiff tenant sought to recover the deposit from the bank since the original landlord was insolvent. Lord Oliver explained the conclusion of the Privy Council that the obligation to repay the deposit was purely personal between the contracting parties:

> "It certainly does not *per se* affect the nature quality or value of the land either during or at the end of the term. It does not *per se* affect the mode of using or enjoying that which is demised . . . Whilst it is true that the deposit is paid to the original payee because it is security for the performance of contractual obligations assumed throughout the term by the payer and because the payee is the party with whom the contract is entered into, it is, in their Lordship's view, more realistic to regard the obligation as one entered into with the landlord qua payee rather than qua landlord . . . The nature of the obligation is simply that of an obligation to repay money which has been received and it is neither necessary nor logical, simply because the conditions of repayment relate to the performance of covenants in a lease, that the transfer of the reversion should create in the transferee an additional and co-extensive obligation to pay money which he has never received and in which he never had any interest or that the assignment of the term should vest in the assignee the right to receive a sum which he has never paid."[81]

The decisions in these two cases are extremely difficult to reconcile since in *P & A Swift Investments v. Combined English Stores plc*[82] the surety covenant was held to touch and concern because it was linked to the performance of other covenants which did touch and concern, yet the obligation to repay a deposit in *Hua Chiao Commercial Bank Ltd v. Chiaphua Industries Ltd*[83] was held not to touch and concern even though its return was linked to the performance of covenants which did touch and concern. The central distinction seems to be that a right to repay money is purely personal against the recipient, whereas a guarantee of the performance of a third party's obligations is enforceable by whoever performance is owed to.[84]

[79] *ibid.* at 642.
[80] [1987] A.C. 99.
[81] *ibid.* at 112–3.
[82] [1989] A.C. 632.
[83] [1987] A.C. 99.
[84] See also: *Kumar v. Dunning* [1989] Q.B. 193.

2 Enforceability of covenants in legal leases granted prior to January 1, 1996

(a) Enforceability of covenants between the original landlord and the original tenant

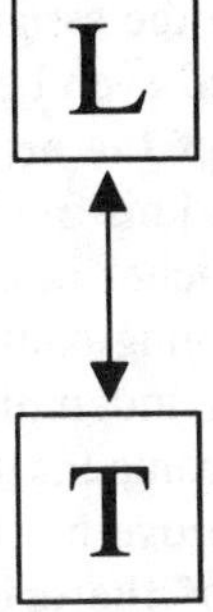

Since the original landlord and tenant are parties to the contract formed by the lease all the covenants are enforceable between them on the simple basis of their contract, whether they touch and concern the land or not.

(b) Enforceability of the covenants between the original tenant and an assignee of the original landlord

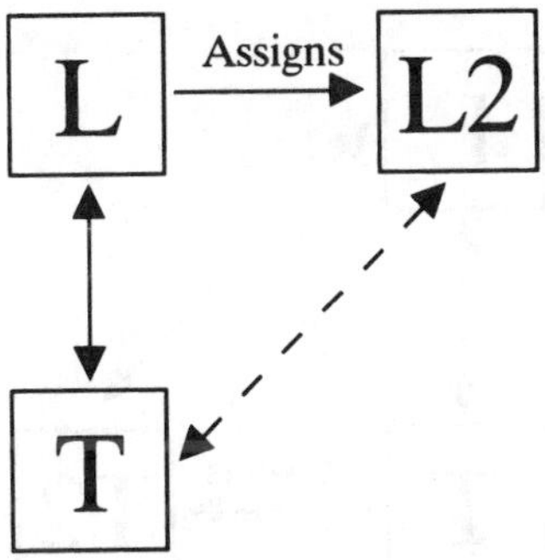

(i) Enforceability of the landlord's covenants by the tenant against the assignee of the freehold reversion: Although governed by the principles of privity of estate the enforceability of the landlord's covenants has been placed on a statutory basis by Law of Property Act 1925, s.142(1). This has the effect that the burden of the covenants entered into by the original landlord pass with the assignment of the reversion so that they are enforceable against him by the tenant. However, the statute only transfers the burden of covenants which are "with reference to the subject matter of the lease." This has been held to mean that the tenant may only enforce the leasehold covenants which "touch and concern the land" against the new landlord.[85] However, the new landlord will only be liable for breaches which occurred after the freehold reversion had been assigned to him. The tenants can only seek a remedy for previous breaches against the landlord who committed them.

[85] *Hua Chiao Commercial Bank v. Chiaphua Industries Ltd* [1987] A.C. 99.

(ii) Enforceability of the tenant's covenants by the assignee of the freehold reversion: Law of Property Act 1925, s.141(1) has the effect that the assignee of the landlord's interest enjoys the benefit of every covenant of the tenant which has "reference to the subject matter" of the lease. This again means that the new landlord can enforce covenants which "touch and concern" the land against the tenant. It has been held that the effect of the assignment transfers to the assignee the exclusive right to seek remedies for breaches of covenant which occurred even before the assignment took place.[86]
(iii) Continuing contractual liability of the original landlord to the original tenant: Where an original landlord has assigned his freehold reversion he remains liable to the original tenant in contract for any breaches of covenant, even those committed by the assignee, on the grounds of his continuing contractual liability under their contract.[87] The landlord will generally obtain an indemnity for any liability from the assignee which will enable him to recover any compensation he may have to pay to the tenant for breaches committed, but this will prove ineffective if the assignee is insolvent.
(iv) Continuing contractual liability of the original tenant to the original landlord where the freehold reversion has been assigned: Since Law of Property Act 1925, s.141(1) transfers the exclusive right to seek remedies for breach of covenants which touch and concern the land to the assignee of the landlord there is no continuing contractual liability between the original landlord and tenant.

(c) Enforceability of covenants between the original landlord and an assignee of the original tenant

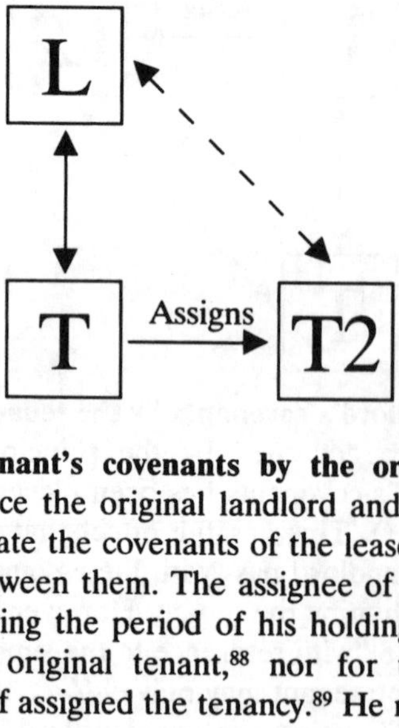

(i) Enforceability of the tenant's covenants by the original landlord against the assignee of the tenancy: Since the original landlord and the assignee of the original tenant stand in privity of estate the covenants of the lease which "touch and concern" the land are enforceable between them. The assignee of the tenancy is only liable for the breaches committed during the period of his holding the tenancy, and he is not liable for breaches of the original tenant,[88] nor for the breaches of subsequent assignees after he has himself assigned the tenancy.[89] He remains liable to the landlord

[86] *Re King* [1963] Ch. 459; *London & County (A. & D.) Ltd v. Wilfred Sportsman Ltd* [1971] Ch. 764; *Arlesford Trading Co. Ltd v. Servansingh* [1971] 1 W.L.R. 1080.
[87] *Stuart v. Joy* [1904] 1 K.B. 362.
[88] *Grescott v. Green* (1700) 1 Salk. 199; *Granada Theatres Ltd v. Freehold Investments (Leytonstone) Ltd* [1959] Ch. 592.
[89] *Onslow v. Corrie* (1817) 2 Madd. 330; *Paul v. Nurse* (1828) 8 B. & C. 486.

for breaches committed during the period when he was the tenant even when he has assigned the lease so that he no longer stands in a tenant relationship.[90]

(ii) Enforceability of the landlord's covenants by the assignee of the original tenant: Since there is privity of estate between the original landlord and an assignee of the original tenant the assignee may enforce the covenants of the lease which touch and concern the land. In *Celsteel Ltd v. Alton House Holdings Ltd (No. 2)* it was suggested both at first instance[91] and in Court of Appeal[92] that Law of Property Act 1925, s.142(1) has the effect that the original landlord remains liable to an assignee of the tenancy even where he has assigned his reversionary interest.

(iii) Continuing contractual liability of the original tenant to the landlord: Where an original tenant has assigned his tenancy he remains liable to the original landlord in contract for any breaches of covenant, even those committed by the assignee, on the grounds of his continuing contractual liability under their contract. Commonly the landlord will be able to recover any arrears of rent from an original tenant if his successors in title have failed to pay. In *Allied London Investments Ltd v. Hambro Life Assurance plc*[93] the plaintiff let premises to the defendant in 1972, and the defendant assigned his lease in 1973. In 1982 the assignees defaulted in their payments of rent and it was held that the defendant was liable to the plaintiff for the arrears. An original tenant will even be liable for an assignee's failure to pay an increased rent agreed under the terms of the lease. In *Centrovincial Estates Ltd v. Bulk Storage Ltd*[94] the original tenant had taken a lease for 21 years in 1965 at a rent of £17,000 per annum. The lease contained a provision to review the rent after 14 years and a new rent to be fixed by agreement between the parties. The tenant assigned his lease in 1978 and in 1979 the assignee agreed an increase in rent to £40,000 per annum with the landlord. the assignee subsequently defaulted on the payment of this rent and Harman J. held that the original tenant was liable to the landlord in contract for then arrears at the increased rent.[95] Similarly, in *Selous Street Properties Ltd v. Oronel Fabrics Ltd*[96] the original tenant was held liable to pay a rent which had been increased because of improvements made by the assignee. An original tenant will also be liable to the landlord for any breach of a repairing covenant by an assignee, as was held in *Thames Manufacturing Co Ltd v. Perrotts (Nichol & Peyton) Ltd.*[97] This contractual liability continues for the entire duration of the lease,[98] even if the lease is extended by the exercise of an option within it.[99] Obviously the continuation of contractual liability can impose a heavy burden on an original tenant, and breaches of covenant of a lease

[90] *J. Lyons & Co. Ltd v. Knowles* [1943] K.B. 366; *Estates Gazette Ltd v. Benjamin Restaurants Ltd* [1995] 1 All E.R. 129.

[91] [1986] 1 W.L.R. 666.

[92] [1987] 1 W.L.R. 291.

[93] (1985) 50 P. & C.R. 207.

[94] (1983) 46 P. & C.R. 393.

[95] See also: *Selous Street Properties Ltd v. Oronel Fabrics Ltd* (1984) 270 EG 643; *Gus Property Management Ltd v. Texas Homecare Ltd* [1993] 27 E.G. 130.

[96] (1984) 270 E.G. 643.

[97] (1985) 50 P. & C.R. 1.

[98] *Warnford Investments Ltd v. Duckworth* [1979] Ch. 127.

[99] *Baker v. Merckel* [1960] 1 Q.B. 657. In *City of London Corp v. Fell* [1994] 1 All E.R. 458 the House of Lords held that a tenant's contractual liability did not continue after a statutory extension of a business tenancy.

which he assigned many years before may come back to haunt him. The landlord can release him from his continuing liability but has little incentive to do so since this will reduce his own protection. The existence of continuing liability also acts as an incentive to ensure that a tenant only assigns to a person who is likely to be able to perform the covenants of the lease. A tenant may obtain some protection for himself by obtaining an indemnity from his assignee and he has a right to restitution from the assignee if he is held liable for the assignees breach.[1] In the event of a number of assignments there well be a chain of indemnities. Such indemnities are implied by statute.[2] However, they provide the tenant with no protection if the assignee is insolvent, which may be the very reason he has breached his covenants. In *RPH Ltd v. Mirror Group Newspapers and Mirror Group Holdings*[3] the plaintiffs were the original tenants of a lease which had been granted in 1970. The lease had been assigned three times to companies forming part of Robert Maxwell's business empire. First it was assigned to Mirror Group Holdings Ltd, which at the date of the action was insolvent, then to Mirror Group Newspapers, which was solvent, and finally to Maxwell Communications Corp, which had defaulted on the rent. It was held that the plaintiffs were liable to pay the £1.5 million arrears of rent to the landlord even though they had assigned the lease more than 20 years previously. Their indemnity against Mirror Group Holdings was worthless because the company was insolvent, and although Mirror Group Holdings had an indemnity against Mirror Groups Newspapers, which was solvent, the plaintiffs were not entitled to compel them to enforce their indemnity covenant because the two indemnities were distinct. The plaintiff therefore had to bear the loss without the possibility of recourse against any of the assignees. Such far reaching consequences of the continuing contractual liability between the original tenant and landlord was one of the major factors behind the reforms introduced by the Landlord and Tenant (Covenants) Act 1995, which has drastically curtailed the scope of such continuing liability in leases created after January 1, 1996. However, for leases outside of the scope of the statute the traditional rules continue to apply.

(d) Enforceability of covenants between assignees of the original landlord and assignees of the original tenant

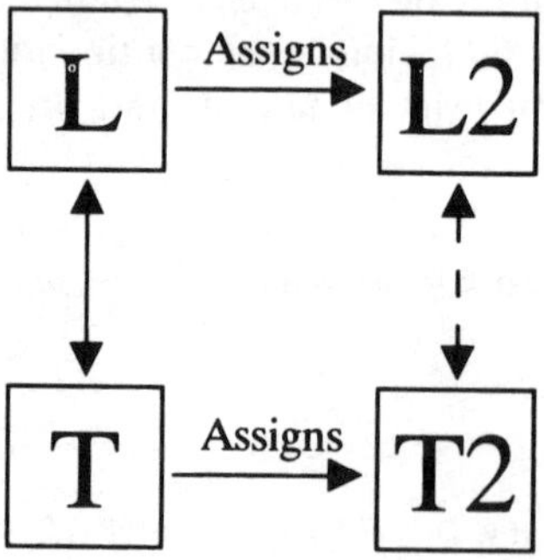

[1] On the grounds of "legal compulsion". See: *Moule v. Garrett* (1872) L.R. 7 Exch. 101; *Selous Properties Ltd v. Oronel Fabric Ltd* (1984) 270 E.G. 643; *Becton Dickinson Ltd v. Zwebner* [1989] Q.B. 208.
[2] Law of Property Act 1925, s.77(1)(c); Land Registration Act 1925, s.24(1)(b).
[3] (1993) 65 P. & C.R. 252.

(i) Mutual enforceability: Where the interests of both the original landlord and tenant have been assigned the covenants of the lease which "touch and concern" the land are enforceable between the present landlord and tenant because they enjoy privity of estate.
(ii) Liability only for breaches committed during the period they enjoyed privity of estate: An assignee of the reversion of the tenancy is only liable for the breaches that he has committed during the period of time that he stood in the position of landlord and tenant, and not for past of future breaches.
(iii) Continuing liability between assignees for breaches committed during the period they enjoyed privity of estate: Where an assignee of either the reversion or the tenancy has assigned his interest he retains the right to remedies for breach of covenant against the person who stood in relation to him as landlord or tenant at the time when the breach was committed.[4]

(e) Enforceability of leasehold covenants between an assignee of the landlord and the original tenant where the lease has also been assigned

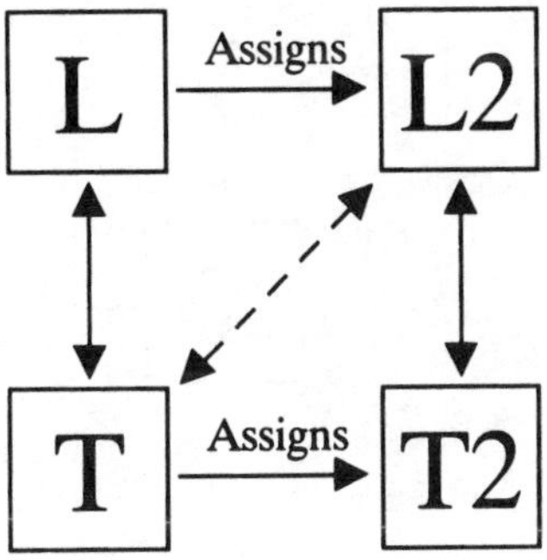

(i) Enforceability of the leasehold covenants between the assignees of the original landlord and tenant: As has been noted above it is clear that since there is privity of estate between the assignees of the landlord and tenant covenants which touch and concern the land will be enforceable between them. However, such a remedy may be of little use to the landlord if the tenant is insolvent, especially if the rent is in arrears. In such circumstances he may be able to enforce the covenants against the original tenant on the basis of his continuing liability under his contract with the original landlord.
(ii) Continuing contractual liability of the original tenant to an assignee of the landlord even where he has assigned the lease: It has been noted above that where a tenant has assigned his interest under the lease he remains liable for any breaches to the original landlord on the basis of their contract. This liability is not defeated by an assignment by the landlord of the freehold reversion. Rather, the assignee of the freehold reversion is entitled to the benefit of all the original tenant's covenants which touch and concern the land by virtue of Law of Property Act 1925, s.141. The assignee of the landlord may therefore enforce the covenants to that extent against the original tenant, even though the breach has been committed by the assignee of the lease. These principles were applied by the Court of Appeal in *Arlesford Trading Co. Ltd v.*

[4] *City and Metropolitan Properties Ltd v. Greycroft Ltd* [1987] 1 W.L.R. 1085.

Servansingh.[5] The defendant was the original tenant of a lease created in 1966. In 1969 he assigned the lease to his brother-in-law and a month later the landlord assigned the freehold to the plaintiffs. It was held that the plaintiffs could enforce the covenant to pay rent against the defendant who remained liable under his contract with the original landlord. The principle was stated by Russell L.J.:

> "an original lessee remains at all times liable under the lessee's covenants throughout the lease, and that assignment of the reversion does not automatically release him from that liability."[6]

(f) Enforceability of leasehold covenants between the head lessor and a sub-tenant

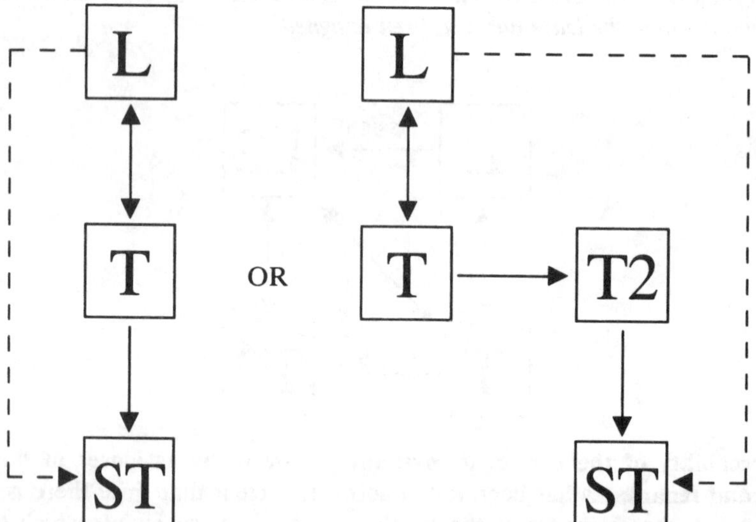

Where a tenant[7] has created a sub-tenancy there is no privity of estate between the landlord of the head lease[8] and the sub-tenant. The tenant will be liable to his landlord and the sub-tenant to the tenant who granted him his sub-lease, and the landlord will be unable to obtain direct monetary remedies against him. However, if the landlord is able to forfeit the head lease this will have the effect of destroying the sub-lease as well, although as has been noted above the sub-tenant may be entitled to relief from forfeiture. Restrictive covenants of the lease may also be enforceable against the sub-tenant by the landlord by means of an injunction, as the burden of the covenant can pass to him under the equitable doctrine of *Tulk v. Moxhay*.[9]

[5] [1971] 1 W.L.R. 1080.
[6] *ibid.* at 1082. See also: *London and County (A & D) Ltd v. William Sportsman Ltd* [1970] 3 W.L.R. 418.
[7] Whether the original tenant or an assignee of the tenancy.
[8] Whether the original landlord or an assignee of the reversion.
[9] (1848) 2 Ph. 774.

3 Covenants in equitable leases created prior to January 1, 1996

(a) Substantial application of the same principles

Where the lease concerned is equitable rather than legal, or where there has been a merely equitable assignment of a legal lease, many of the same principles continue to operate. However there is some doubt whether the doctrine of privity of estate applies to equitable leases.

(b) Applicability of privity of contract between the parties

The liability between the original parties is governed by their privity of contract and will be continuing in the same way through the duration of the lease.[10]

(c) Statutory privity of estate between the tenant and an assignee of the landlord

Where the freehold reversion has been assigned enforceability of the leasehold covenants between the tenant and the assignee of the reversioner is governed by sections 141 and 142 of the Law of Property Act 1925, which have been held to be equally applicable to equitable leases.[11]

(d) Applicability of privity of estate

Since the concept of privity of estate developed in *Spencer's Case*[12] was a creature of the common law, it has been questioned whether it should have any application to equitable leases. This is significant since although the benefit of covenants can be expressly assigned in equity the burden cannot. In *Purchase v. Litchfield Brewery*[13] a tenant of a house under an equitable lease assigned his tenancy to assignees. The court held that there was no privity of estate and that therefore the assignees were not liable to the landlord for the rent. However, even though there is no privity of estate this only prevents the landlord seeking to recover monetary remedies against the assignees. He will still be entitled to an injunction to restrain the assignee from breach of restrictive covenants of the lease, the burden of which passes in equity,[14] or to forfeit the lease by means of re-entry for breach.[15] Despite the authority of *Purchase v. Litchfield Brewery*[16] it has been argued that the failure to extend privity of estate to equitable leases is anomalous. In *Boyer v. Warbey*[17] Denning L.J. suggested that following the Judicature Acts the fusion of law and equity meant that there was no reason why the burden of leasehold covenants should not run with land in equity as well as in common law.[18] This conclusion is highly contentious since it is unlikely that

[10] *John Betts & Sons Ltd v. Price* (1924) 40 T.L.R. 589.
[11] *Rickett v. Green* [1910] 1 K.B. 253; *Weg Motors Ltd v. Hales* [1962] Ch. 49.
[12] (1583) 5 Co. Rep. 16a.
[13] [1915] 1 K.B. 184.
[14] *Tulk v. Moxhay* (1848) 2 Ph. 774.
[15] In the case of unregistered land the assignee of the equitable lease will be bound by the restrictive covenant or right of re-entry as he is not a bona fide purchaser of a legal estate and therefore protected by the doctrine of notice. In the case of registered land a restrictive covenant or right of re-entry will constitute an overriding interest under, s.70(1)(g) as the landlord is a person in receipt of the rent and profits of the land.
[16] [1915] 1 K.B. 184.
[17] [1953] 1 Q.B. 234.
[18] See also: [1978] C.L.J. 98 (Smith).

this was the intended effect of the Judicature Acts. An alternative possibility is that a new contract is implied between the landlord and the assignee when the assignee goes into possession and pays rent. If this is the case the covenants would be enforceable because of a new privity of contract between the landlord and the assignee. The possibility of such a conclusion seems to have been left open in *Purchase v. Litchfield Brewery* where the judges stressed that the assignee had neither paid rent nor taken possession. These difficulties have been eliminated in relation to leases created after January 1, 1996 because the statutory regime introduced by the Landlord and Tenant (Covenants) Act 1995 is equally applicable to legal and equitable leases.

4 Covenants in leases granted after January 1, 1996

(a) Reform of the traditional principles

The traditional rules were thoroughly examined by the Law Commission which published a Report in 1988.[19] The Commission recognised two central principles which it felt should underlie the law relating to the enforceability of leasehold covenants:

> "First a landlord or tenant of property should not continue to enjoy rights nor be under any obligation arising from a lease once he has parted with all interest in the property.
>
> Secondly, all terms of the lease should be regarded as a single bargain for letting the property. When the interest of one of the parties changes hands the successor should fully take his predecessor's place as landlord or tenant, without distinguishing between different categories of covenant."[20]

The implementation of these cardinal principles would radically alter two foundations of the existing law. First, it would put an end to the continuing contractual liability of the original tenant to the original landlord or his assignees after the lease had been assigned. Secondly, it would mean the abolition of the limitation to enforceability on the grounds of privity of estate to covenants which "touch and concern" the land. The Law Commission proposed that such reforms should be enacted to apply to both existing and new leases. However, this recommendation was not followed and instead a more limited reform was introduced by means of a private member's Bill in the Landlord and Tenant (Covenants) Act 1995. This Act radically reforms the rules of privity of estate and of continuing contractual liability, but it does not apply to all leases. In consequence the traditional rules and the statutory framework continue to operate side-by-side, thus complicating this field.

(b) Scope of the Landlord and Tenant (Covenants) Act 1996

(i) Application to "new tenancies": By section 1(1) the provisions of the Act which introduce a statutory framework for the enforceability of leasehold covenants apply only to "new tenancies".

[19] Law Commission Report No. 174, *Landlord and Tenant: Privity of Contract and Estate* (1988).
[20] para. 4.1.

(ii) Tenancies created after January 1, 1996: By section 1(3) a new tenancy is defined as a tenancy "granted on or after the date on which this Act comes into force." Since the Act came into force on January 1, 1996 it will, subject to the exceptions outlined below, apply to all tenancies created since that date.
(iii) Tenancies created after January 1, 1996 pursuant to an earlier agreement or court order: Tenancies which are created after January 1, 1996 in pursuance of a prior agreement or court order are excluded from the scope of the Act by sections 1(3)(a) and 1(3)(b). Such tenancies will continue to be governed by the traditional rules.
(iv) Tenancies created after 1st January 1996 pursuant to an earlier option: A tenancy granted after January 1, 1996 in pursuance of an option which had been granted before that date is excluded from the scope of the Act by section 1(6) as it is regarded as a tenancy created in pursuance of a prior agreement.
(v) Variation of tenancies by deemed surrender and regrant: Where the terms of a lease are varied by the parties and the law regards the variation as a deemed surrender and regrant of the tenancy there is in effect a fresh tenancy. This fresh tenancy falls within the scope of the Act under section 1(5). Following *Friends Provident Life Office v. British Railways Board*[21] such a surrender and re-grant is only likely to be deemed where the variation involves an increase in the property comprising the lease or the term extended.
(vi) Application to equitable leases: Unlike the preceding law the provisions of the Landlord and Tenant (Covenants) Act 1995 are equally applicable to legal and equitable leases, since by section 28(1) a "tenancy" is defined to include "an agreement for a tenancy."

(c) Transmission of the benefit and burden of covenants

(i) Statutory privity of estate: Section 3 of the Landlord and Tenant (Covenants) Act 1996 introduces a statutory framework governing the transmission and enforceability of the benefit and burden of leasehold covenants between assignees of the original landlord and tenant of a lease. This places the traditional rules of privity of estate on a statutory footing. The limited statutory provisions in sections 141 and section 142 of the Law of Property Act 1925 are also superseded. Covenants are categorised as either "landlord covenants," which are covenants "falling to be complied with by the landlord of the premises demised by the tenancy," or "tenant covenants" which are covenants "falling to be complied with by the tenant of premises demised by the tenancy."[22]
(ii) Annexation of leasehold covenants to the demised premises: Section 3(1) provides that:

> "The benefit and burden of all landlord and tenant covenants of a tenancy —
>
> (a) shall be annexed and incident to the whole, and to each and every part, of the premises demised by the tenancy and of the reversion in them, and.
>
> (b) shall in accordance with this section pass on an assignment of the whole or any part of those premises or of the reversion in them."

[21] [1995] 48 E.G. 106.
[22] s.28(1).

(iii) Transmission of covenants on assignment by the tenant: Section 3(2) has the effect that where a tenant assigns his tenancy the assignee becomes bound by the tenant covenants and becomes entitled to the benefit of the landlord covenants of the tenancy. The only exceptions are that the assignee will not be burdened by any covenants which did not burden the assignor immediately before the assignment,[23] nor by any covenants which affect any of the premises which are not assigned to him.[24] Similarly he does not enjoy the benefit of any covenants of the landlord which relate to premises not assigned to him.[25]

(iv) Transmission of covenants on assignment by the landlord: The same principles are mirrored in the event of the assignment of the freehold reversion by the landlord. The assignee of the landlord is bound by the landlord covenants and becomes entitled to the benefit of the tenant covenants. The assignee is similarly not bound by covenants which did not bind the assignor immediately before the assignment[26] and those which relate to part of the premises which have not been assigned to him.[27] Nor does he enjoy the benefit of covenants which do not relate to the land which has been assigned to him.[28]

(v) Elimination of the restriction that only covenants which "touch and concern" the land are transmissible: The most significant difference between this statutory scheme for the transmissibility of the benefit and burden of leasehold covenants to the assignees of the lease or the freehold reversion and the traditional rules of privity of estate is that the benefit and burden of covenants which do not touch and concern the land are also transmitted. The "touching and concerning" requirement is therefore completely eliminated.

(vi) No transmissibility of "personal" covenants: Although the Act eliminates the "touching and concerning" requirement this does not mean that covenants which are truly intended to be personal between a landlord and tenant will be binding upon subsequent assignees of their interests. By section 3(6)(a) the rules of transmissibility do not apply to make a covenant enforceable "in the case of a covenant which (in whatever terms) is expressed to be personal to any person" against any other person. This means that such personal covenants must be expressly identified and such a characterisation will be not implied from the mere nature of the obligation a covenant imposes.

(d) Limitation of the continuing liability of the tenant on the assignment of his tenancy

(i) Release from tenant covenants on assignment: As has been noticed in the case of leases outside of the scope of the Landlord and Tenant (Covenants) Act 1995 the contractual liability of the original tenant to the landlord and his assignees continues even when he has assigned his tenancy. This continuing liability has now been removed by section 5 of the Act. This section provides that where the tenant assigns the whole of the premises demised to him he is "released from the tenant covenants of the tenancy"[29] and "ceases to be entitled to the benefit of the landlord covenants of the

[23] s.3(2)(a)(i).
[24] s.3(1)(a)(ii).
[25] s.3(2)(b).
[26] s.3(3)(a)(i).
[27] s.3(3)(a)(ii).
[28] s.3(3)(b).
[29] s.5(2)(a).

tenancy."[30] An assignment of only part of the demised premises has the same effect to the extent that the tenant and landlord covenants "fall to be complied with in relation to [the assigned] part of the demise premises."[31]

(ii) Effect of release on the liability of the tenant: Since the tenant is released from his covenants on assignment of the tenancy there will be no inherent liability for defaults committed by his assignees. The original tenant in such a case as *RPH Ltd v. Mirror Group Newspapers and Mirror Group Holdings*[32] would no longer be liable for rent to the landlord where an assignee had defaulted. Similarly an original tenant would not be liable for an assignee's breaches or repairing covenants, as was the case in *Thames Manufacturing Co Ltd v. Perrotts (Nichol & Peyton) Ltd*.[33] However, section 24(1) has the effect that the tenant remains liable to his landlord for any "liability of his arising from a breach of the covenant occurring before the release".

(iii) Effect of release of the tenant on a third party guarantor: Where a third party has provided a guarantee of the tenant's performance of his covenants under the lease the release of the tenant from his covenants has the effect of releasing the guarantor to exactly the same extent.[34] Thus the guarantor will not be liable for breaches committed by the assignee, but will retain liability for any breaches committed by the tenant during his tenancy.

(iv) Tenant's continuing rights against a landlord in breach after release: Although release from the tenant's covenants on assignment carries with it the corresponding cessation of entitlement of the tenant to the benefit of the landlord covenants, section 24(4) makes clear that "this does not affect any rights of his arising from a breach of the covenant occurring before he ceases to be so entitled." This means that he can maintain an action against the landlord for breaches of covenant which were committed while he was the tenant.

(e) Obtaining an authorised guarantee agreement from an assigning tenant

(i) Reduction in protection of the landlord: Although the statutory cancellation of a tenant's liability on assignment of his lease prevents the unacceptable consequences of continuing contractual liability, it necessarily has a corresponding effect of reducing the protection afforded to the landlord. The possibility of continuing liability acts as a powerful incentive to a tenant to ensure that any assignment is only made to a tenant who is likely to be capable of meeting the obligations under the lease. For example, a tenant might think twice before assigning his interest to a company in danger of insolvency. In order to provide the landlord with some continuing protection and to provide tenants with a continuing incentive to make careful assignment decisions the Landlord and Tenant (Covenants) Act 1995 introduces a statutory system of guarantees, whereby a tenant who assigns his lease can be required by the landlord to execute a guarantee that the assignee will perform his obligations. In the event of default the landlord will have recourse against the assigning tenant not on the basis of any continuing contractual liability, but under the specific guarantee.

[30] s.5(2)(b).
[31] s.5(3).
[32] (1993) 65 P. & C.R. 252.
[33] (1985) 50 P. & C.R. 1.
[34] s.24(2).

(ii) Circumstances where an authorised guarantee agreement can be required: A valid authorised guarantee agreement can only be created in the circumstances outlined in, section 16(3), namely if:

(a) by virtue of a covenant against assignment (whether absolute or qualified) the assignment cannot be effected without the consent of the landlord under the tenancy or some other person;

(b) any such consent is given subject to a condition (lawfully imposed) that the tenant is to enter into an agreement guaranteeing the performance of the covenant by the assignee; and

(c) the agreement is entered into by the tenant in pursuance of that condition.

An authorised guarantee agreement can never therefore be imposed when the lease does not contain a covenant against assignment. Since the landlord cannot unreasonably withhold consent for an assignment,[35] this means that the landlord's imposition of an authorised guarantee agreement as a condition of his consent must also be reasonable. In the case of a commercial lease[36] where the execution of an authorised guarantee agreement is expressly stated to be a condition of the grant of consent to assign, the Landlord and Tenant (Covenants) Act 1995 has amended Landlord and Tenant Act 1927, s.19 so that the requirement of such a guarantee as a condition of consent cannot be regarded as unreasonable.[37]

(iii) Enforceability of an authorised guarantee agreement against the direct assignee only: It is clear that an authorised guarantee agreement can only validly extend to a guarantee of the obligations of the immediate assignee of the lease from the tenant executing it, and not to those of subsequent assignees. Section 16(4) provides:

> "An agreement is not an authorised guarantee agreement to the extent that it purports —
>
> (a) to impose on the tenant any requirement to guarantee in any way the performance of the relevant covenant by any person other than the assignee; or.
>
> (b) to impose on the tenant any liability . . . in relation to any time after the assignee is released from that covenant by virtue of this Act."

In other words, as soon as the assignee is no longer directly bound to the landlord by the tenant covenants in the lease the former tenant who assigned his interest to him is no longer liable under the guarantee if the covenants are broken.

(iv) Authorised guarantee agreement does not extend to variations of the lease occurring after the assignment: As was noted above one of the harsh consequences of the continuing contractual liability of a tenant was that he would be liable for breach of covenants even when they had been varied long after he had assigned his interest. In the case of covenants for rent this could mean that he would be liable to pay an

[35] Landlord and Tenant Act 1927, s.19.
[36] *i.e.* non-residential leases:, s.19(1C) of the Landlord and Tenant Act 1927.
[37] s.19(1A).

increased rent rather than the rent specified in the original lease, as in *Centrovincial Estates Ltd v. Bulk Storage Ltd*.[38] Landlord and Tenant (Covenants) Act 1995 introduces some limitations to the scope of a guarantor's liability under an authorised guarantee agreement where the terms of the lease are varied subsequently to the assignment. The general principle is that the former tenant is not liable for any amount "referable to any relevant variation of the tenant covenants."[39] Covenants are "relevant covenants" under, section 18(4) if:

(a) the landlord has, at the time of the variation, and absolute right to refuse to allow it; or

(b) the landlord would have had such a right if the variation had been sought by the former tenant immediately before the assignment by him but, between the time of the assignment and the time of the variation, the tenant covenants of the tenancy have been so varied as to deprive the landlord of such a right.

This complex provision has the following effect. First, the former tenant will remain liable for increased liability where this is a consequence of the covenants of the lease itself, since such an increase will not constitute a "relevant variation." Most significantly this means that a former tenant will continue to be liable for rent increased under a rent review term in the lease after assignment. Secondly, the tenant will be freed from liability under his agreement where a variation amounts to an express or implied surrender or regrant of the lease. This will include a variation by way of an increase in the term of the lease or of the extent of the demised property. Thirdly, he will not be liable under his agreement for any increased liability arising as a result of variations of the terms of the lease.

(f) Limitation of the continuing liability of the landlord on the assignment of his reversion

(i) No automatic release of the landlord covenants on assignment: Unlike the tenant, who is automatically released from his covenants on assignment by section 5, a landlord who assigns his freehold reversion is only free from liability if he is actively released from his landlord covenants. Under section 8 the tenant alone is entitled to grant such a release.

(ii) Release where granted: The effect of release is set out in section 6(2) of the Act which provides that:

> "If the landlord assigns the reversion in the whole of the premises of which he is the landlord —
>
> (a) he may apply to be released from the landlord covenants of the tenancy in accordance with section 8; and
>
> (b) if he is so released from all of those covenants, he ceases to be entitled to the benefit of the tenant covenants of the tenancy as from the assignment."

[38] (1983) 46 P. & C.R. 393.
[39] s.18(2).

Section 6(3) provides for similar consequences where the landlord has assigned "part only of the premises of which he is the landlord" in which case he may be released for his landlord covenants and lose the benefit of the tenant's covenants "to the extent that they fall to be complied with" in relation to the part of the premises assigned. By section 8(3) any release from the landlord covenants is to be regarded as occurring at the date of assignment, even when the actual release was granted at a later date.

(iii) Application for a release: Where a landlord seeks to be released from his landlord covenants on assignment of the freehold reversion by serving notice of the assignment on the tenant, section 8(1) provides that:

> ". . . an application for the release of a covenant to any extent is made by serving on the tenant, either before or within the period of four weeks beginning with the date of the assignment in question, a notice informing him of —
> (a) the proposed assignment or (as the case may be) the fact that the assignment has taken place, and
> (b) the request for the covenant to be released.

(iv) Release granted by tenant's counter-notice: By section 8(2)(c) the landlord will be released from his covenants if the tenant serves a notice in writing on him consenting to the release, to the extent mentioned in the notice.

(v) Release because of the tenant's failure to respond to the landlord's notice: By section 8(2)(a) a landlord will be released from his covenants if he has requested release and the tenant does not "within the period of four weeks beginning with the day on which the notice is served, serve on the landlord..a notice in writing objecting to the release."

(vi) Tenant's objection to release: The landlord will not be released from his covenants if the tenant serves a counter notice on him objecting to the release.

(vii) Landlord's application to the court for a declaration that release is reasonable: If the tenant serves a counter notice on the landlord objecting to release the landlord is entitled under section 8(2)(b) to make an application to the county court,[40] and if appropriate the court may make a declaration that "it is reasonable for the covenant to be so released." The effect of such a declaration will be to release the landlord from his covenants.

(viii) Extension of provisions regulating release from landlord covenants to "former landlords": These provisions which govern the release of a landlord's covenants are also applicable in favour of a "former landlord" who had previously assigned his reversion but who "remains bound by a landlord covenant of the tenancy."[41] He will remain bound because, for whatever reason, he was not released from his landlord covenants when the tenancy was previously assigned. He is entitled to apply to the current tenant for release whenever the current landlord assign the reversion. Whether he is released from his covenants is determined by the same provisions in section 8 as govern the release of the current assigning landlord.

[40] Which has exclusive jurisdiction:, s.8(4)(c).
[41] s.7(1).

(ix) Effect of release on the liability of a landlord: Where a landlord has been released from his covenant he will attract no liability for the acts of his assignee. However, by section 24(1) this release will not effect any liability to the tenant for breaches of covenant committed before the release.
(x) Landlord's continuing rights against a tenant in breach after release: Although the release of a landlord from his landlord covenants has the effect that he ceases from that moment to be entitled to the benefit of the tenant's covenants, section 24(4) makes clear that this "does not affect any rights of his arising from a breach of covenant occurring before he cease to be so entitled." In other words the tenant will remain liable to him for breaches of covenant committed while he was the landlord.

TERMINATION OF LEASES

1 Consequences of termination

When a lease is terminated the leasehold interest of the tenant comes to an end, he no longer has any estate in the land, and the freehold owner will be entitled to immediate possession of the land. If the ex-tenant remains in occupation without permission his possession of the land will be adverse to the freehold owner. The freehold owner must use appropriate legal procedure to remove such a squatting ex-tenant.[42]

2 Termination by expiry

In the case of a fixed term lease the lease will automatically terminate at the end of the specified term without the need for the landlord to serve notice on the tenant. It should be noted that many residential leases are converted on expiry by statute into periodic tenancies[43] and business tenants generally have the right to request a new lease.[44]

3 Termination by notice

(a) Termination of fixed leases by notice

A fixed term lease is only determinable by notice if such a possibility is expressly provided for in the terms of the lease. For example, a lease for life, which by statute becomes a lease for 90 years determinable on the death of the original lessee, is determinable by "one month's notice in writing" from the lessor.[45] Long term leases may include a "break clause" allowing the parties to terminate it before the expiry of the full term by appropriate notice.[46]

[42] Protection from Eviction Act 1977, s.3(1).
[43] See: Rent Act 1977; Housing Acts 1985 and 1988.
[44] Landlord and Tenant Act 1954.
[45] Law of Property Act 1925, s.149(6).
[46] *Industrial Properties (Barton Hill) Ltd v. Associated Electrical Industries Ltd* [1977] Q.B. 580.

(b) Termination of periodic tenancies

(i) Determinability a defining characteristic of periodic tenancies: As has been noted above the very essence of a periodic tenancy is that the period continues until it is determined by proper notice given by either the landlord or the tenant.[47]

(ii) No limitations on the ability to determine: It has also been seen that the House of Lords held in *Prudential Assurance Co v. London Residuary Body*[48] that no limits can be imposed as to when h the parties are entitled to determine a periodic tenancy.[49] Such limitations would mean that the tenancy contravened the rule that a lease must be for a fixed maximum duration.

(iii) Length of notice which must be given: In the absence of express contrary provisions[50] the common law position is that the tenancy can only be determined by giving notice of the duration of one whole period, with the exception of a yearly periodic tenancy which can be determined by six months notice.[51] Therefore, a weekly periodic tenancy can be determined by a week's notice, a monthly tenancy by a month's and a quarterly tenancy by a quarter's notice. However, in the case of dwelling houses statute intervenes to require a period of at least four weeks notice to quit.[52]

(iv) Time at which notice should be given: The mere giving of a sufficient length of notice will not alone bring a periodic tenancy to an end. The notice must be given at the appropriate time since the tenancy can only end at the end of a relevant period. Notice of the relevant period must be given in such a way that the notice period itself expires at the end of a completed period of the tenancy.[53] This is known as the "corresponding date" rule. What it means in practice is that notice must be served on the tenant either on the anniversary of the period, or the day preceding that anniversary. For example, in the case of a monthly tenancy which commenced on the 1st of the month notice will only be effective to terminate the tenancy at the end of a month if it is given on the 1st of that month or the last day of the preceding month. If the notice is not given at the appropriate time it will not terminate the tenancy and the tenancy will continue into the following period. For example if the landlord served notice on the tenant on the 20th of a month this would be ineffective to terminate the tenancy at the end of the next month since the notice period would not have corresponded with the end of a period of the lease.[54] In the case of yearly periodic tenancies notice must be give at least given six months before the end of the particular period. In the case of a yearly tenancy beginning on a quarter day[55] this means notice of at least two quarters must be given. In the case of a yearly tenancy beginning on any other day it means notice of at least 182 days.[56]

[47] *Javad v. Mohammed Aqil* [1991] 1 W.L.R. 1007; *Prudential Assurance v. London Residuary Body* [1992] 2 A.C. 386.

[48] [1992] 2 A.C. 386.

[49] Contra *Re Midland Railway Co's Agreement* [1971] Ch. 725; *Ashburn Anstalt v. Arnold* [1989] Ch. 1.

[50] *Re Threlfall* (1880) 16 Ch.D. 274; *Queen's Club Gardens Estates Ltd v. Bignell* [1924] 1 KB 117; *Lemon v. Lardeur* [1946] K.B. 613. See *Land Settlement Association Ltd v. Carr* [1944] K.B. 657 where a periodic tenancy for 364 days was expressly stated to be determinable by three calendar months notice.

[51] *Prudential Assurance Co. v. London Residuary Body* [1992] 2 A.C. 386.

[52] Protection from Eviction Act 1977, s.5(1)(b).

[53] *Lemon v. Lardeur* [1946] K.B. 613; *Queen's Club Garden Estates Ltd v. Bignell* [1924] 1 KB 117; *Bathavon RDC v. Carlile* [1958] 1 Q.B. 461.

[54] See *Lemon v. Lardeur* [1946] K.B. 613.

[55] Lady day (March 25); Midsummer Day (June 24); Michaelmas (September 29); Christmas (December 25).

[56] *Sidebottom v. Holland* [1895] 1 Q.B. 378.

(v) Effectiveness of notice to terminate by joint tenants: Problems have arisen in the context of periodic tenancies where either the freehold or the lease are held by two or more persons as joint tenants. In such circumstances an important issue is whether notice given by one of the joint tenants without the concurrence of the others is effective to terminate the tenancy. This question was considered at length by the House of Lords in *Hammersmith and Fulham LBC v. Monk*[57] where, on grounds of principle, it was held that notice served by any joint tenant was effective to terminate the tenancy, irrespective of the intentions of the others that it should continue. Mr and Mrs Monk enjoyed a joint tenancy of a council flat determinable on four weeks notice. They fell out and Mrs Monk left the flat. The council agreed to re-house her if she terminated the tenancy by appropriate notice and she duly gave notice without Mr Monk's knowledge. The House of Lords held that this was effective to determine the periodic tenancy on the basis that the tenancy could only continue with the consent of all parties. As Lord Bridge explained:

> "in any ordinary agreement for an initial term which is to continue for successive terms unless determined by notice, the obvious inference is that the agreement is intended to continue beyond the initial term only if and so long as all parties to the agreement are willing that it should do so . . . Thus the application of ordinary contractual principles leads me to expect that a periodic tenancy granted to two or more joint tenants must be terminable at common law by an appropriate notice to quit given by any one of them whether or not the others are prepared to concur."

This principle only applies because a continuing intention is assumed until notice is served, and the serving of notice is a negative dealing with the tenancy. As Lord Bridge stated:

> "The action of giving notice to determine a periodic tenancy is in form positive; but . . . the substance of the matter is that it is by his omission to give notice of termination that each party signifies the necessary positive assent to the extension of the term for a further period."[58]

In contrast all positive dealings with a joint tenancy require the concurrence of all joint tenants. Such positive dealings include the exercise of an option to renew, the exercise of a break clause in the lease, making a disclaimer or applying for relief from forfeiture. Therefore, in *Houslow LBC v. Pilling*[59] it was held that a purported exercise of a break clause in a lease by a since joint tenant giving notice was ineffective to terminate the lease.

(c) Termination of tenancies at will

As has been noted, a tenancy at will may be determined by either party at any time. It is also brought to an end automatically if either party performs acts inconsistent with the continuation of the tenancy.

[57] [1992] 1 A.C. 478; [1992] C.L.J. 218 (Tee); [1992] Conv. 279; (1992) 109 L.Q.R. 375 (Dewar).
[58] *ibid.* at 490–491.
[59] [1993] 1 W.L.R. 1242; [1994] C.L.J. 227 (Tee).

4 Termination by surrender

(a) *Meaning of surrender*

Since a tenancy is an interest in land carved out of the landlord's freehold ownership[60] the return of the tenancy to the landlord will have the consequence of bringing the leasehold interest to an end and leaving the landlord with the unencumbered freehold. This process of returning the tenancy to the landlord is known as surrender.

(b) *Express surrender of a tenancy*

A tenancy may be surrendered expressly to the landlord. Such a surrender is a conveyance of an interest in land and under Law of Property Act 1925, s.52(1) it must be effected by a deed.

(c) *Surrender by operation of law*

In some circumstances a tenant will be taken to have impliedly surrendered his interest to the landlord, which takes effect as a surrender by operation of law and is exempt from any formalities requirement by Law of Property Act 1925, s.52(1)(c). Most commonly the tenant will be taken to have surrendered his interest if he gives up possession of the land subject to the tenancy. The principle stated in *Hill and Redman's Law of Landlord and Tenant* was accepted by the Court of Appeal in *Hoggett v. Hogget*,[61] namely "delivery of possession by the tenant to the landlord and his acceptance of possession effect a surrender by operation of law." However, it was held that in the circumstances there had been no effective surrender. Mr Hoggett enjoyed a weekly periodic tenancy of a house which he occupied with his wife and son. After arguments and violence the wife left home. Her husband brought a Miss Willis to share the house with him. He then purported to surrender the tenancy to the landlord and asked him to accept Miss Willis as a tenant, which he did, providing her with a rent book. Two days later he left the house. The Court of Appeal held that this purported surrender was a sham. There had been no delivery of possession to the landlord as the intention had been for Mr Hoggett to continue to occupy. He had left his furniture in the premises, along with his dog and motor car, and had never returned his rent book to the landlord. In contrast the most common circumstances which would give rise to an implied surrender would be if the tenant left possession of the land and returned the key to the landlord.[62] A tenant's acceptance of a new status from the landlord inconsistent with the continuation of a tenancy will also effect an implied surrender, as in *Foster v. Robinson*[63] where a tenant accepted a licence for life of the premises.

5 Termination by merger

If the tenant acquires the landlord's freehold reversion this will have the immediate effect of bringing the lease to an end, as will the acquisition of both the interests of the landlord and tenant by a third party.

[60] Or in the case of a sub-tenancy out of the superior landlord leasehold estate.
[61] (1980) 39 P. & C.R. 121.
[62] *ES Schwab & Co. Ltd v. McCarthy* (1976) 31 P. & C.R. 196.
[63] [1951] 1 K.B. 149.

6 Termination by disclaimer

As has been noted above, every lease contains an implied covenant that the tenant will not disclaim the landlord's title to the land he leases. Breach of this covenant entitles the landlord to forfeit the lease.[64] The Insolvency Act 1986, s.315 permits a trustee in bankruptcy to disclaim the tenant's lease if its is "unsaleable or not readily saleable, or is such that it may give rise to a liability to pay money or perform any other onerous act."

7 Termination by forfeiture

As has been noted above, where the tenant is in breach of other covenants of the lease the landlord may be entitled to forfeit it, which has the effect of bringing the tenant's interest to an end.

8 Termination by repudiation

In contract where one party commits a breach of a fundamental condition the other party is entitled to treat the breach as a repudiation of the contract and to sue for damages. Historically, English law has held that the doctrine of repudiation does not apply to leases[65] on the grounds that they are not to be assimilated with other contracts. However in *Hussein v. Mehlman*[66] Stephen Sedley Q.C. held that the concept of repudiatory breach should be applied to leases, pointing to various decisions where the courts had tended to assimilate contract and leases, especially the extension of frustration to them.[67] He therefore held that there was a repudiatory breach when a tenant was in breach of his covenant to keep the demised premises in repair, as a result of which they were uninhabitable, and the tenant had made clear that he would not effect the repairs. He also indicated that the extension of the doctrine of repudiation to leases may have implications for cases where a tenant was in arrears of rent:

> "if the obligation to pay rent is as fundamental as the obligation to keep the house habitable, it will follow that a default in rent payments is a repudiatory act on the tenant's part. That this may follow is not, however, a reason for going back on what appears to me to be the inexorable effect of binding authority. It will, however, have effect subject only to all the statutory provisions which now hedge the right to recover possession, but also, I would think, to the provisions contained in the contract of letting itself in relation to forfeiture."

[64] *Wisbech St Mary Parish Council v. Lilley* [1956] 1 W.L.R. 121; *Warner v. Sampson* [1959] 1 Q.B. 297; *WG Clark (Properties) Ltd v. Dupre Properties Ltd* [1992] Ch. 297.
[65] *Total Oil Great Britain Ltd v. Thompson Garages (Biggin Hill) Ltd* [1972] 1 Q.B. 318.
[66] [1992] 2 E.G.L.R. 87; [1993] C.L.J. 212; [1993] Conv. 71.
[67] *United Scientific Holdings Ltd v. Burnley Borough Council* [1978] A.C. 904.

9 Termination by frustration

Traditionally the doctrine of frustration applied only to suspend or discharge individual terms of a lease affected by supervening impossibility of performance.[68] However, in *National Carriers Ltd v. Panalpina (Northern) Ltd*[69] the House of Lords held by a majority of three that frustration could discharge a lease as a whole. This does not mean that frustration of leases will be widespread. The defendants were the tenants of a warehouse leased from the plaintiffs under a 10 year fixed term lease. After five years the closure of the access road by a local authority would prevent them using the warehouse for 20 months. The House of Lords held that this interruption, which would last only a relatively short period of the duration of the tenancy and leave a further three years remaining after access was restored, did not "approach the gravity of a frustration event."[70]

COMMONHOLD: AN ALTERNATIVE TO LEASEHOLD OWNERSHIP

1 Leasehold utilised because freehold ownership incapable of achieving the enforceability of positive covenants affecting land

The leasehold estate in land has long proved the only viable means in English law of facilitating the ownership of property where there are a number of units which are dependent upon each other, in particular for the ownership of flats. Although there is no theoretical difficulty with the grant of a freehold title to a flat a major practical problem is caused by the fact that in English law it is impossible for the burden of a positive obligation to pass with the title of the land to which it relates. The reasons for this inadequacy will be examined in detail in Chapter 10, but in the context of flats it has the consequence that it is impossible to ensure that one flat will be permanently able to require support from another. For example, if a house is divided into two independent flats, one on the ground floor and the other on the upper floor, the upper flat is obviously dependent on the structural support provided by the lower flat. If the two flats were to be owned as freeholds the owner of the upper flat would not be able to ensure that owner of the lower flat permanently provided the necessary support, and did not exercise his right as a freeholder to allow the land to deteriorate, and ultimately for the structures on it to collapse. It would be possible to extract an agreement from an owner of the lower flat to continue to maintain the structure of the flat, thus providing support, and such an agreement could be enforced in contract. However, if the owner were to sell the flat the transferee of the title would not be bound by the agreement, and it could not be enforced against him. Similar problems would arise if there were units of land which shared common parts or facilities, or required the provision of services. If the title were freehold such positive obligations as a requirement to contribute to the upkeep, or to the costs of the provision of such

[68] *Cricklewood Property and Investment Trust Ltd v. Leighton's Investment Trust Ltd* [1945] A.C. 221.
[69] [1981] A.C. 675.
[70] *ibid.* at 697 *per* Lord Wilberforce.

services, would not be capable of binding successors in title. Leasehold arrangements enable such positive obligations to be met because they can be stipulated as terms of the lease which, as has been seen, are capable of passing with the title by virtue of the doctrine of privity of estate. Freehold ownership is thus incapable of meeting the needs of land ownership where there are mutually dependent units. For this reason it has been suggested that an entirely new form of ownership should be introduced which is a hybrid of elements of leasehold and freehold, namely commonhold. This is modelled on "strata titles" or condominium schemes which have been adopted elsewhere, for example in Australia.

2 The nature of commonhold

The introduction of commonhold ownership was recommended by a working party of the Law Commission in 1987,[71] and in 1990 the Lord Chancellor's department issued a consultation paper proposing draft legislation to implement it.[72] The essence of commonhold is that the owners of units of interdependent buildings enjoy the freehold of their individual units. They also own and run a "commonhold association," which is a corporation which would own and manage any common parts and other facilities. The commonhold association would enjoy a charge against each unit in respect of any arrears of service charge from the owners. The detailed obligations of the unit owners would be laid down in the "commonhold regulations" which would provide for such issues as the use and enjoyment of the common services and facilities, and the obligations of the unit owners to maintain their units. The commonhold regulations would be enforceable against the unit owners and by this means positive obligations would pass with the title to the land, since a person who acquired a unit would become a member of the commonhold association and be subject to the regulations irrespective of their character, whether positive or negative.

3 Potential scope of commonhold ownership

The consultation paper expected that the most obvious situation in which a commonhold would be appropriate is a block of flats which at present are held on a long-leasehold basis. However, commonhold would not be limited to residential or horizontally divided land but could also be applied to commercial and mixed, use developments, housing or industrial estates, and shopping precincts.

4 Advantages of commonhold

The prime advantages of commonhold as a means of ownership of land were stated in the consultation paper:

[71] *Commonhold: Freehold Flats and Freehold Ownership of Other Interdependent Buildings* (1987) Cm. 179.
[72] *Commonhold - A Consultation Paper* (1990) Cm. 1345; see [1991] Conv. 70 & 170.

> "The adoption of the commonhold scheme would lead to savings in the time and complexity of conveyancing by reducing to an absolute minimum the need for conveyancers to consider the rules applicable to essentially similar arrangements, and by ensuring that departures from the standard rules were quickly identifiable. Most importantly, it would institutionalise arrangements for the democratic management by and for the benefit of the freehold unit owners within a commonhold, through a "commonhold association" (a corporate body controlled exclusively by them.)"[73]

As of the present time, however, commonhold ownership has yet to be introduced by legislation.

[73] *ibid.* at para 1.2.

Chapter 6

Equitable Ownership of Land

The Nature of Equitable Ownership of Land

1 Introduction to the trust

In the proceeding chapters the two most important estates which constitute the ownership of land have been examined, namely the freehold (fee simple) and leasehold estates. Although it has been noted that a contract for a lease will give rise to an equitable lease in general these estates take effect at law. However, in Chapter 3 it was explained how the Courts of Chancery developed the concept of the trust whereby the owner of a legal estate in land is compelled to hold it not for his own benefit but for the benefit of others, who are known as the beneficiaries. Trusts play a central part in the ownership of land in England, and as will be explained in this chapter the scheme adopted for land holding under the property legislation of 1925 has the effect that a substantial majority of private land will be held on some form of trust.

2 Trusts of land

Although personal property is equally capable of forming the subject matter of a trust as land, trusts of land are especially significant and are subject to special statutory regimes. Under the Law of Property Act 1925 all forms of shared concurrent ownership of land took effect under a special form of trust known as a "trust for sale." Successive interests in land, where there is some form of life-estate, or other estates which cannot take effect at law as a consequence of section 1(1) of the Law of Property Act 1925 such as the determinable fee simple, took effect either under an express trust for sale or under the provisions of the Settled Land Act 1925 as a "strict settlement" of the land. However, following sustained criticism of this dual system over many years, and especially of the appropriateness of the trust for sale as a vehicle for land holding, a single unitary statutory "trust of land" was introduced by the Trusts of Land and Appointment of Trustees Act 1996.

3 Function of the trustees of land

The trustees of a trust generally enjoy the full legal ownership of the estate in the land to which the trust relates.[1] Either a freehold or leasehold estate may be subject to a

[1] An equitable trust interest may itself form the subject matter of a trust, which is known as a sub-trust.

trust. By virtue of this ownership a trustee possesses the same powers of management and disposition over the property as would be held by an absolute owner unencumbered by the trust. This is confirmed by section 6(1) of the Trusts of Land and Appointment of Trustees Act 1996 which provides that:

> "For the purposes of exercising their functions as trustees, the trustees of land have in relation to the land subject to the trust all the powers of an absolute owner."

The trust does not essentially effect the trustee's capacity to deal with the land. As Lord Browne Wilkinson pointed out in *Hammersmith LBC v. Monk*[2]: "The fact that a trustee acts in breach of trust does not mean that he has no capacity to do the act he wrongly did." However, the terms of the trust impose obligations upon him as to how he should deal with the property, and often more importantly how he should refrain from dealing with it. For example, in most cases it is clear that the trustees should not sell the land to a friend at a substantial undervalue in order to defeat the interests of the beneficiaries. If the trustees breach their obligations and deal with the property in a manner inconsistent with the terms of the trust the beneficiaries will be entitled to remedies against them for breach of trust.

4 Nature of the Beneficiaries' Interest Under a Trust

(a) *Proprietary ownership or a personal obligation?*

Where an estate in land is held on trust the beneficiaries enjoy rights to the trust property which are best considered as a form of ownership. It is clear from *Saunders v. Vautier*[3] that the beneficiaries of a trust can demand that the trustees transfer the full legal title to them if they unanimously ask for it to be transferred.[4] The interests of the beneficiaries behind the trust can be dealt with in many of the ways that are indicative of a proprietary right. For example, the beneficiary can transfer his equitable interest to another person, whether by sale or as a gift, provided that he observes the necessary formalities for the transfer.[5] When he dies his beneficial interest can be validly disposed of by will, or pass under the rules of intestate succession. However, most significantly his beneficial interests in the land are capable of enduring a change of ownership of the legal title. This capacity to endure changes of ownership was identified as a defining characteristic of property rights by Lord Wilberforce in *National Provincial Bank Ltd v. Ainsworth*.[6] An example of the enduring character of beneficial interests can be seen in *Kingsnorth Finance Co. Ltd v. Tizard*,[7] where a husband held land on trust for himself and his wife in equal shares. After they had separated the wife no longer lived at the house but she visited daily. The husband mortgaged the house without her consent. It was held that her equitable beneficial

[2] [1992] 1 A.C. 478, at 493.
[3] (1841) 4 Beav. 115.
[4] In order to do this they must all be of age and legally competent.
[5] Law of Property Act 1925, s.53(1)(c).
[6] [1965] A.C. 1175.
[7] [1986] 1 W.L.R. 783.

interest was binding on the mortgage company, because they had acquired the land with notice of the existence of her interest. It should be noted that the doctrine of notice was applicable in the case only because the land was unregistered. However, the corollary is that if the bank had not had notice of her equitable interest then it would have taken free from it since the doctrine of notice has the effect that equitable interests are not binding against a bona fide purchaser for value of a legal estate without notice. This qualification, which means that the potential durability of an equitable beneficial interest is not absolute, has been the cause of much debate whether a trust interest is to be regarded as a genuine property right *in rem*. Maitland argued that equity had never regarded the beneficiary of a trust as the "owner" since the trust merely entitled him to enforce a personal obligation against the trustee to carry out the terms of the trust. He explained that: "[the trustee] is the owner, the full owner, of the thing, while the [beneficiary] has no rights in the thing . . ."[8] Some support for this analysis can be gleaned from recent cases in the field of private international law. In *Webb v. Webb*[9] a claim by a father that his son held a holiday home in France on trust for him was held not to be founded on a right *in rem* for the purposes of Article 16(1) of the Convention on Jurisdiction and the Enforcement of Judgements in Civil and Commercial Matters 1968. In *Re Hayward, dec'd*[10] Rattee J. held that a claim to be entered as owner of a half-share of a Spanish villa by a trustee in bankruptcy was to be characterised as a claim *in rem*. However, both these cases concerned questions of the jurisdiction of English courts in relation to issues concerning property abroad, and the characterisation of such claims for the purposes of private international law should not be determinative of the jurisprudential question whether beneficial interests under a trust are to be regarded as proprietary or not since concepts are often pragmatically given a different meaning for the purposes of private international law than they bear in domestic law. The whole character of beneficial interests behind trusts and the ability of the beneficiaries to transfer them is suggestive of a real property right, albeit one qualified to some extent by the principles of bona fide purchase. Even Maitland himself eventually came to the conclusion that more than a mere personal obligation was involved:

> ". . . I believe that for the ordinary thought of Englishmen "equitable ownership" is just ownership pure and simple, though it is subject to a peculiar, technical and not very intelligible rule in favour of *bona fide* purchasers . . . so many people are bound to respect these rights that practically they are almost as valuable as if they were *dominium*."[11]

It should be noted that not even legal ownership is absolute in its nature so that third parties may defeat the interests of the legal owner. As has been seen, a person may effectively defeat the interests of the owner of an estate of land, whether freehold or leasehold, by means of adverse possession. Similarly, in the case of money the legal owner loses his ownership the moment that it becomes mixed with other money so that

[8] Maitland, *Equity*, p.17.
[9] [1994] Q.B. 696.
[10] [1996] 3 W.L.R. 673.
[11] Collected Papers, Vol. III, p.349.

it is no longer identifiable.[12] These examples illustrate that if the defining characteristic of a property right is that it is absolutely indefatigable. then there is no such thing as a proprietary right in English law. The better approach is that taken by Lord Browne-Wilkinson in *Tinsley v. Milligan*[13] who assimilated the proprietary character of legal and beneficial ownership: "Although for historical reasons legal estate and equitable estates have differing incidents, the person owning either type of estate has a right in property, a right in rem not merely a right in personam."

(b) A right of occupation of the land

One question which has arisen in the context of trusts of land is whether the beneficiaries enjoy a right to occupy the land in consequence of their equitable entitlement. Such a right of occupation would be indicative of a proprietary interest in the land itself. Historically, this question was complicated because of the uncertain impact of the doctrine of conversion. Since the majority of land held on trust was held under a "trust for sale", the key characteristic of which was the duty of the trustees to sell the land, an application of the doctrine of conversion would have the effect of treating the beneficiaries interests as only arising in any potential proceeds of sale of the land and not in the land itself.[14] However, given the reality that most trusts of land have the practical object of enabling the beneficiaries to live in the property the courts moved away from the full implications of the doctrine of conversion and have regarded the beneficiaries as enjoying rights in the land itself and not merely the proceeds of sale. In *Williams & Glynn's Bank Ltd v. Boland*[15] Lord Wilberforce considered that ". . . to describe the interests of spouses in a house jointly bought to be lived in as a matrimonial home as merely an interest in the proceeds of sale . . . is just a little unreal." In *City of London Building Society v. Flegg*[16] the House of Lords held that the beneficiary of a trust for sale had the right to occupy the land. Both of these conclusions have now been placed on a statutory basis by the Trusts of Land and Appointment of Trustees Act 1996. Section 3 abolishes the doctrine of conversion completely and section 12(1) provides that, subject to limited exceptions:

> "a beneficiary who is beneficially entitled to an interest in possession in land subject to a trust of land is entitled by reason of his interest to occupy the land at any time."

CREATION OF EQUITABLE OWNERSHIP OF LAND

1 Means of creating trusts of land

Since trusts are created by the imposition of obligation on the legal owner of property the creation of a trust of land only occurs when the legal owner is made effectively

[12] See: *Taylor v. Plumer* (1815) 3 M. & S. 562; *Agip (Africa) Ltd v. Jackson* [1990] Ch. 265.
[13] [1993] 3 All E.R. 65 at 86.
[14] *Irani Finance Ltd v. Singh* [1971] Ch. 59.
[15] [1981] A.C. 487 at 507.
[16] [1988] A.C. 54.

subject to obligations in favour of the intended beneficiaries of the trust. This process of the imposition of the trust obligation, which has the effect of generating the beneficiaries equitable ownership of the land, may take place either by the express act of the legal owner or by implication of law.

(a) Express creation of trusts of land

A trust of land may be created by the express intention of the legal owner of land either declaring himself to be a trustee of it in favour of the beneficiaries or by transferring the legal title to the person who is to act as the trustee. In either case the necessary formalities for the creation of the trust must be observed.

(b) Creation of trusts of land by implication of law

However, the express intention of the legal owner of land is not always necessary for the creation of a trust. The law is willing to imply trusts from the circumstances in which land has been acquired, and those who have contributed in some way to its acquisition may be entitled to a share of the equitable ownership by means of a trust even though they are not the legal owners. A trust may even be imposed on the land in the hands of a legal owner who expressly states that there should be no trust. The law is willing to imply or impose a trust in two superficially similar but essentially different situations. First, where a person has contributed to the purchase price of land he may be entitled to a share of the equitable ownership directly proportional to the extent of his contribution by way of a resulting trust. Secondly, where the understanding between two people was that they were to share the ownership of land but the land is owned at law by only one of them, the other may be entitled to a share of the equitable ownership equivalent to what they were mutually intended to have by way of a constructive trust. Although the technical rules relating to each type of implied trust have been specified in detail by the courts, the general principle is that resulting trusts protect the position of persons who contribute to the purchase price of land whereas constructive trusts protect the interests of persons where there was a common intention that they were intended to have a share of the property which has not been fulfilled by the legal owner.

2 Creation of express trusts of land

(a) Declaration of trust by the legal owner

(i) Mechanism of declaration: A trust of land will be created where the legal owner declares himself to be a trustee of the land he owns for the benefit of the beneficiary or beneficiaries. In such a situation the person declaring the trust remains the legal owner of the property and there is therefore no need to effect a transfer of it, but the nature of his ownership is qualified by the immediate creation of the trust. He no longer holds the property as an absolute owner but as a trustee. All that is needed to declare a trust is a "present irrevocable declaration of trust"[17] and it is clear that there is no need to use technical language.[18] As Scarman L.J. stated in *Paul v. Constance*[19] "there must be clear evidence from what is said or done of an intention to create a trust."

[17] *Re Cozens* [1913] 2 Ch. 478 at 486 *per* Neville J.
[18] *Richards v. Delbridge* (1874) L.R. 18 Eq. 11; *Re Kayford* [1975] 1 W.L.R. 279.
[19] [1977] 1 W.L.R. 527.

(ii) Necessary formalities: The most important limitation to the creation of express trusts is the formalities' requirement imposed by Law of Property Act 1925, s.53(1)(b). This section provides that "a declaration of a trust respecting any land or any interest therein must be manifested and provided by some writing signed by some person who is able to declare such trust or by his will." This does not require that the actual declaration be made in writing. A purely oral statement of an immediate intention to hold on trust will be effective provided that it is evidenced by some written documentation containing all the material terms of the trust[20] signed by the legal owner. This writing need not be contemporaneous with the declaration of the trust.[21] Failure to evidence the declaration in writing does not render the trust void but merely unenforceable.[22]

(b) Creation of a trust by transfer of the legal title to trustees

(i) Mechanism of creation: Alternatively, the owner of land may create a trust over it by transferring it to a person who is intended to hold it as trustee for the beneficiaries of the trust. In such a case the legal title to the property changes hands, from the person creating the trust who initially owned the land absolutely for himself, who is known as the settlor, to the trustee. The beneficiaries only gain equitable interests in the land at the moment when the legal title is transferred into the hands of the trustee. Until an effective transfer to the trustee is made the trust is said to be unconstituted and the beneficiaries have no interest in the land.

(ii) When is an effective transfer made? Since the trust is only created when the settlor effectively transfers the land to the trustee the question arises as to what he must do to effect a transfer. In the case of unregistered land a transfer of the legal title to freehold or leasehold land is made by means of a conveyance by deed. The position is more complicated in the case of a freehold or leasehold estate for more than 21 years in registered land, since these interests are registrable and a transfer can only be effected by means of the registration of the transferee as the new proprietor of the estate at the land registry. Since the act of a third party is required to effect a transfer of title to the trustee the courts have developed a principle that the trust is to be treated as constituted from the moment that the settlor has done everything that he needs to do to effect a transfer and the only acts remaining are those of third parties. This principle was established in *Re Rose*[23] in the context of a transfer of shares, but was applied to registered land in *Mascall v. Mascall*.[24] A father wanted to transfer land which was registered to his son and completed the land registry transfer form. He then handed the form to his son, who was required to complete it and sent it to the land registrar who would effect a transfer of the title. The Court of Appeal held that since the father had done all that he was required to do when he had handed the completed form to the son the transfer of the land was to be treated as effective from that moment and the father could not change his mind. Although the case involved a transfer of absolute title the principle would be equally applicable to a transfer on

[20] *Smith v. Matthews* (1861) 3 De G.F. & J. 139; *Rochefoucauld v. Boustead* [1897] 1 Ch. 196.
[21] *Forster v. Hale* (1798) 3 Ves. 696; *Rochefoucauld v. Boustead* [1897] 1 Ch. 196.
[22] *Gardener v. Rowe* (1828) 5 Russ 258; *Gissing v. Gissing* [1969] 2 Ch. 85; *Cowcher v. Cowcher* [1972] 1 W.L.R. 425; *Midland Bank plc v. Dobson* [1986] 1 F.L.R. 171.
[23] [1952] Ch. 499.
[24] (1984) 50 P. & C.R. 119.

trust. If the son had been intended to take the land on trust the beneficiaries would have been entitled to equitable interests in the land from the moment that the father handed the completed form to him.

(iii) Necessary formalities: Where a trust of land is created by a transfer of the title to trustees, the formalities required by section 53(1)(b) must be complied with. In the absence of written evidence that the transferee was intended to take the property as a trustee and not for himself absolutely he will be able to deny the trust which is unenforceable against him.

(c) Enforcement of an express trust of land even where the necessary formalities have not been observed

Although the clear effect of the statute is that express trusts of land are unenforceable in the absence of the requisite formalities, equity has developed the principle that the legal owner should not be entitled to use the statute as an instrument of fraud by denying the trust merely on the ground of the absence of writing. In *Rochefaucauld v. Boustead*[25] land in Ceylon was transferred to the defendant with the intention that it was to be held on trust for the Comtesse de la Rochefaucauld. The defendant subsequently mortgaged the land and the Comtesse sought a declaration that the defendant had acquired the land as a trustee. He claimed that the trust was unenforceable because of the absence of writing.[26] The Court of Appeal held that the existence of the trust could be proved by oral evidence since to allow the defendant to rely on the lack of writing would be to permit him to commit a fraud against the Comtesse. The principle was explained by Lindley L.J.:[27]

> ". . . the Statute of Frauds does not prevent the proof of a fraud; and that it is a fraud on the part of a person to whom land is conveyed as a trustee, and who knows it was so conveyed, to deny the trust and claim the land himself. Consequently, notwithstanding the statute, it is competent for a person claiming land conveyed to another to prove by parol evidence that it was so conveyed upon trust for the claimant, and that the grantee, knowing the facts, is denying the trust and relying upon the form and conveyance and the statute, in order to keep the land himself."

The application of what has become known as the rule in *Rochefaucauld v. Boustead* has the clear merit of preventing injustice between the parties, but it also runs contrary to the wording of the statute and has the danger of rendering the requirement of writing virtually irrelevant. In more recent cases such as *Bannister v. Bannister*[28] an attempt has been made to explain the principle as resting on the doctrine of constructive trusts, so that in the absence of writing the court imposes a constructive trust on the land in the hands of the transferee who knew that he was intended to take it only as a trustee. This analysis has the advantage that it does not offend against the statute because the Law of Property Act 1925, s.53(2) states that section 53(1)(b) has

[25] [1897] 1 Ch. 196.
[26] Under what was then, Statute of Frauds, s.7.
[27] *ibid.* at 206.
[28] [1948] 2 All E.R. 133. See also: *Neale v. Willis* (1968) 19 P. & C.R. 836; *Re Densham* [1975] 1 W.L.R. 1519.

no application to the creation of constructive trusts. However, a mere shift of semantics should not hide the reality, which is that the court is in effect upholding and enforcing a trust obligation where the statutory requirement has not been met. The Court of Appeal in *Rochefaucauld v. Boustead*[29] were clear that they were enforcing an express trust despite the absence of writing.

(d) Grants of interests taking effect under a trust void for reasons of perpetuity

(i) Future interests must take effect behind a trust: Following the legislation of 1925, and especially the Law of Property Act 1925, s.1(1) which provides that only the fee simple absolute in possession and term of years absolute are capable of existing as legal estates, all successive and future interests created after 1925 must take effect behind a trust. Future interests in land are interests which do not vest in an owner at the moment that they are granted, but are dependent upon some future contingency. For example, if a testator leaves land to "my first grandchild to be called to the Bar" this does not create a gift which is vested in anyone at the date of the testator's death. Similarly, if the owner of land was to transfer it to "my son for life, remainder to my first grandchild to be called to the Bar" the grant would not vest in its entirety at the date of the transfer. Either gift would only become vested when the contingency occurred, namely that a grandchild was called to the Bar.[30]

(ii) The rule against perpetuities: Where a gift is contingent it will only be valid if it does not offend the rule against perpetuities. This long established rule (now modified by Statute) operates to render a grant of a future contingent interest void if it is possible that it will not vest within the recognised perpetuity period. The rule is designed to prevent uncertainty as to the ownership of land, and also to prevent an owner of land predetermining its ownership beyond his death for an unacceptably long time. For example, if the owner of land were permitted to leave it to his son for life, remainder to his eldest grandson for life, remainder to his eldest great-grandson for life, remainder to his great-great grandson for life, this would have the effect of dictating the ownership of the land for four generations, and preventing the land from being sold. Although this might facilitate an intention to keep the land within the family, it is not economically efficient that the land cannot be sold to a person who would derive a greater utility from it. The grant is likely to infringe the rule against perpetuities.[31] An exhaustive treatment of the rule is outside of the scope of this book and a more detailed consideration can be found elsewhere.[32]

(iii) The perpetuity period: At common law the perpetuity period is defined as the period of a "life or lives in being at the date of the grant plus a further period of 21 years." A central question arises as to which life is to act as the "measuring life" of a contingent gift. The measuring life must be in existence at the date that the grant is made, either on the death of the testator if it is made by will, or at the time that an inter vivos grant is made. The grant may itself specify a "measuring life," and it is not

[29] [1897] 1 Ch. 196.

[30] Obviously the gift would not be contingent if there were a grandchild who had been called to the Bar, since it would be vested in that grandchild.

[31] It is difficult to envisage circumstances where the rule would apply to resulting or constructive trusts.

[32] See: Cheshire and Burn, *Modern Law of Real Property*, (15th ed., 1994) pp.275–333; Gray, *Elements of Land Law*, (2nd ed., 1993), pp.645–672; Riddall, *Introduction to Land Law*, (5th ed., 1993).

necessary that the measuring life has any interest in the gift at all. It has been common to utilise a "royal lives clause" which nominates the life of the longest surviving lineal descendant of the monarch who is alive at the date of the grant. For example in *Re Villar*[33] a testator's gift to "such of my descendants as are living 20 years after the death of the last survivor of the lineal descendants of Queen Victoria living at my death" was valid as it did not offend the perpetuity period. However, it must be possible to ascertain without difficulty the date of death of the nominated life.[34] Often the relevant life will be that of the grantee or other persons expressly or impliedly mentioned in the grant and alive at the date that it takes effect. For example, if a testator leaves land to "my first grandchild to be called to the Bar" the testator's own children and grandchildren living at the date of his death will be "lives in being" for the purposes of the rule against perpetuities, but not any grandchildren born subsequent to his death.

(iii) Application of the common law rule against perpetuities: At common law a grant of a contingent interest would be void *ab intio* if there was any possibility at all that the gift could vest outside of the perpetuity period. It was irrelevant that the events that would have to happen to lead to such a result were wholly unlikely or improbable. For example, if a testator left land by will to "Albert for life, remainder to the first of Albert's sons to be called to the Bar," and at the date of the death of the testator Albert was alive and had no children, his life would be the only measuring life of the gift. Since it would be possible that Albert might yet have a child who could be called to the bar more than twenty-one years after his (*i.e.* Albert's) death, the grant of the remainder interest would be void on grounds of perpetuity. If instead the grant was made to "Albert for life, remainder to the first of his sons to reach the age of eighteen" the contingent grant of the remainder interest would be valid. It is impossible that Albert could have a son who would not reach the relevant age within the perpetuity period, *i.e.* within 21 years of his own death. The extent to which the common law rule renders grants void despite ludicrously improbable events is well illustrated by *Ward v. Van Der Leoff*[35] where a testator left property to his wife for life, terminable if she remarried anyone but a British subject, remainder to all or any of the children or child of his brothers and sisters who should be living at the death or remarriage of his wife who attained the age of 21. The House of Lords held that this gift was void for perpetuity since it was possible that a future born child of his brothers or sisters might attain the age of 21 outside of the perpetuity period. This was because his parents, or a surviving parent, might have another child after his death, which could itself have a child attaining the age of 21 more than 21 years after the death of everyone else named in his will who was living at his death, *i.e.* his brothers and sisters and their children. Such an eventuality would require both an immense family tragedy, and a miracle of Biblical proportions since his parents were 66 years old at the date of the will and his father had died since his death. However, Viscount Cave held that evidence of the inability of his mother to have further children was inadmissible.[36] In *Re Gaite's Will Trusts*[37] Roxburgh J. only avoided the absurdity of finding that a 65 year old widow could become a grandmother within five years by having a new-born child

[33] [1929] 1 Ch. 243.
[34] See: *Re Moore* [1901] 1 Ch. 936; *Re Warren's Will Trusts* (1961) 105 Sol. Jo. 511.
[35] [1924] A.C. 653.
[36] See also: *Jee v. Audley* (1787) 1 Cox. Eq. Cas. 324.
[37] [1949] 1 All E.R. 459.

who subsequently married and itself gave birth by holding that such a grandchild would be illegitimate.[38]

(iv) gift to a class: Where property is left to be divided proportionately between the members of a class it would be logical to assume that the grant would fail if there was any possibility that there might be members of the class arising outside of the perpetuity period. For example, if a testator left property to "Albert for life, remainder to all his children who attain the age of 25" it would be possible for a child to attain that age beyond the perpetuity period. However the rule in *Andrews v. Partington*[39] provides that a class is treated as closed if one member is already qualified when the gift takes effect, and the class will only be open thereafter to the potential qualifiers in existence at that date. If Albert has a child who is over the specified age at the date of the testator's death the class is closed and only Albert's children also alive at that date can qualify. Any subsequently born child is not treated as a member of the class. Thus there would be no possibility of the interest vesting outside of the perpetuity period.

(v) Gifts rendered void for perpetuity because of an excessive age qualification: In cases where a grant would be void for perpetuity because a beneficiary is required to attain an age greater than 21, thus meaning that vesting could potentially occur outside the perpetuity period, Law of Property Act 1925, s.163 provides that the age of 21 shall be substituted. This provision only applies to instruments executed after 1925 and before July 14, 1964.

(vi) Application of the perpetuity rules to gifts taking effect after July 16, 1964: The application of the rule against perpetuities to gifts taking effect after July 16, 1964 has been substantially modified by the Perpetuities and Accumulations Act 1964, which has rendered the common law rule obsolete. The most important effect of the Act is to introduce a "wait and see" approach, so that a gift is not rendered void merely because there is a theoretical possibility that it *might* vest outside of the perpetuity period. Instead section 3(1) allows the gift to remain valid until it is established that vesting *must* occur outside of the perpetuity period. The relevant perpetuity period during which the court will "wait and see" if the gift vests can either be specified in the instrument as a period of up to eighty years,[40] or will comprise one of the statutory lives in being identified in section 3(5), plus 21 years. These lives include the life of the person making the disposition, the persons in whose favour the disposition was made, and in certain circumstances the parents and grandparents of the designated beneficiaries. Where a contingent grant is made to a class and at the end of the "wait and see" period there are potential members of the class, either alive or unborn, who would render the grant void, section 4(4) operates so that they are "deemed for all purposes of the disposition to be excluded from the class." This operates in a similar way to the class closing rule at common law. Section 4(1) provides that where a grant would be void because it requires an age of attainment exceeding 21 years, then the age specified will be substituted by the age, not less than 21, which would have prevented the grant being void. The Act also eliminates the problem of improbable possibilities inherent in the common law rule by enacting presumptions that a woman can only have a child between the ages of 12-55 and a man at 14 or above.[41]

[38] Since a five years old is too young to marry: Age of Marriage Act 1929, s.1(1).
[39] (1791) 3 Bro. C.C. 401.
[40] s.1(1).
[41] s.2(1).

(vii) Future of the rule against perpetuities: A number of significant criticisms have been raised in relation to the rule against perpetuities as it presently operates, including its complexity, uncertainty, inconsistency, interference with commercial transactions, harshness, lack of adaptability and expense. It has been recently examined by the Law Commission, which has recommended either abolition or reform.[42] The arguments in favour of abolition seem strongest, especially that the rule has no purpose to serve in a society where there are very few landed estates and family dynasties and that strong tax-disincentives operate so as to discourage donors from attempting to prevent the alienability of land for long periods after their death. The Law Commission stated:

> "One view, therefore, is that the desire to tie up property for excessively long periods was a social evil of a bygone age, and that nowadays the absence of a rule against perpetuities would have no harmful effect in terms of rendering property inalienable or allowing dead hand control to be exerted to an unacceptable extent."[43]

3 Creation of Resulting Trusts of Land

(a) General principles of resulting trusts

(i) Rationale for resulting trusts: Resulting trusts are trusts which arise without the expressed intention of the parties. In essence they are found where a person has received the legal title to property in circumstances where he cannot be regarded as having received the full equitable ownership. They derive from the general principle stated by Megarry J. in *Re Sick and Funeral Society of St John's Sunday School, Golcar*[44] that "any property a man does not effectually dispose of remains his own."

(ii) Classification of resulting trusts: For the sake of convenience two categories of resulting trust have been identified: automatic and presumed resulting trusts.[45] However, it should be noted that the legitimacy of this classification was called into question by the recent decision of the House of Lords in *Westdeutsche Landesbank Girocentrale v. Islington London Borough Council*[46] where Lord Browne-Wilkinson emphasised that both categories were depended upon the intentions of the original owner of the property.

(iii) Automatic resulting trusts: An automatic resulting trust will generally arise where the settlor of property has transferred it to the intended trustee but the trust has either failed for some reason[47] or the settlor has failed to identify the beneficiaries of the trust.[48] In such cases the holder of the legal title cannot retain the property for himself absolutely, so he is compelled to hold it on a resulting trust for the settlor. In this way

[42] Law Commission Consultation Paper No. 133.
[43] para. 5.20.
[44] [1973] Ch. 51 at 59.
[45] *Re Vandervell's Trusts (No. 2)* [1974] Ch. 269.
[46] [1996] 2 All E.R. 961.
[47] For examples see: *Re Ames Settlement* [1946] Ch. 217; *Re Chocrane* [1955] Ch. 309; *Re Astor's Settlement Trusts* [1952] Ch. 534.
[48] As in *Vandervell v. IRC* [1967] 2 A.C. 291.

the settlor retains his ownership of the property in equity, even though he has transferred the legal title. The most likely scenario in which such an automatic resulting trust would arise in land is if the settlor transferred the land to a person clearly on trust but without specifying who was to be beneficially entitled. In such a case the trustee would hold the land on resulting trust for him.

(iv) Presumed resulting trusts: Of far greater significance to the equitable ownership of land are the principles of presumed resulting trusts. These arise on the basis of a series of rebuttable presumptions concerning the intentions of an owner of property who transfers it into the name of someone else, or of a person who contributes to the purchase price of property purchased in someone else's name. In both cases it is presumed that the person who has provided the essential material input to the transaction, whether the property or the money, cannot have intended to have lost all his interests in his wealth without making plain that such was his intention. In the absence of contrary intention he will be taken to have retained his interest by way of a resulting trust in either the property transferred or purchased. The basis of the operation of resulting trusts is therefore a rebuttable presumption that the owner of property does not intend to make a gift of it. However, in some circumstances, because of the nature of the relationship between the transferee or purchaser and the recipient of the property, there is a counter-presumption that a gift was intended and that there is no resulting trust. This counter-presumption is known as the presumption of advancement.

(b) A presumption of resulting trust where there has been a voluntary conveyance of land

(i) A presumption against gifts of land? Where property is transferred by its owner to a third party and there is no presumption of advancement a resulting trust will be presumed, so that the third party holds the transferred property on trust for its original owner. Although this presumption against a gift clearly applies in the case of a transfer of personal property[49] there is some controversy whether it applies in the case of a voluntary transfer of land. The difficulties arise from the impact of the Law of Property Act 1925, s.60(3) which Lord Browne-Wilkinson indicated in *Tinsley v. Milligan*[50] had arguably altered the position of resulting trusts of land. The section provides that: "In a voluntary conveyance a resulting trust for the grantor shall not be implied merely by reason that the property is not expressed to be conveyed for the use or benefit of the grantee." Prior to the enactment of this section it was necessary to declare expressly in a voluntary conveyance of land that the land was granted "unto and to the use of" the grantee, otherwise the transfer would not be effective to transfer the land. It seems that the impact of section 60(3) is not that there can never be a presumption of a resulting trust of land where there is a voluntary conveyance, but rather that the mere absence of an express statement that an effective transfer of the absolute title was intended in the conveyance will not alone give rise to a resulting trust. Section 60(3) was therefore only intended to reform conveyancing practice and eliminate unnecessary complications rather than to abrogate the presumption of resulting trusts in

[49] See: *Re Vindogradoff* [1935] W.N. 68; *Thavorn v. Bank of Credit and Commerce International SA* [1985] 1 Lloyd's Rep 259.
[50] [1993] 3 All E.R. 65.

relation to voluntary conveyances of land altogether. This approach is supported by the practice of the courts which have continued to find resulting trusts of land in the context of voluntary conveyances. For example, in *Hodgson v. Marks*[51] the Court of Appeal held that there was a resulting trust where an old lady has transferred the title to her house to her lodger, intending that he should look after her affairs, without an express declaration that he was to take the land as trustee for her.

(c) A presumption of resulting trust where a person has contributed to the purchase price of land

(i) The presumption that a contribution to the purchase price generates an interest by way of a constructive trust: As with the presumption against gifts the presumption that a contribution to the purchase price of property will generate an interest in the equitable ownership in favour of the contributor by way of a resulting trust arises in relation to all types of property.[52] The general principle was identified by Eyre C.B. in *Dyer v. Dyer*[53]:

> "the trust of a legal estate . . . whether taken in the names of the purchasers and others jointly, or in the names of others without that of the purchaser; whether in one name or several; whether jointly or successive, results to the man who advances the purchase-money."

(ii) Application of the presumption to the purchase of land: it is clear that a contribution to the purchase price of land will gain for the contributor a share of the equitable ownership by way of a resulting trust. As Lord Reid stated in *Pettitt v. Pettitt*[54] ". . . in the absence of evidence to the contrary effect a contributor to the purchase-price will acquire a beneficial interest in the property." This was reiterated by Lord Pearson in *Gissing v. Gissing*[55] where the issue was whether a wife was entitled to a share of the matrimonial home which had been purchased in the sole name of her husband:

> "If [she] did make contributions of a substantial amount towards the purchase of the house, there would be a resulting trust in her favour. That would be the presumption as to the intention of the parties at the time or times when she made and he accepted the contributions. The presumption is a rebuttable presumption: it can be rebutted by evidence showing some other intention."[56]

These cases demonstrate that a contribution to the purchase price of land will give rise to a resulting trust of the land. However, the central question remains as to what precisely will constitute a contribution to the purchase price for the purpose of generating a resulting trust.

[51] [1971] Ch. 892.
[52] See *Fowkes v. Pascoe* (1875) 10 Ch. App. 343 for an example of the presumption arising in the context of personal property.
[53] (1788) 2 Cox. Eq. Cas 92 at 93.
[54] [1970] A.C. 777 at 794.
[55] [1971] A.C. 886.
[56] *ibid.* at 794.

(iii) What will constitute a contribution to the purchase price? The most straightforward contribution which will give rise to a resulting trust in favour of the contributor is a direct contribution to the purchase price of the land. For example, in *Tinsley v. Milligan*[57] a lesbian couple purchased a house which they intended to run as a lodging house. It was purchased in the name of Tinsley, who was registered as the sole legal owner. The purchase price of £29,000 was raised by way of a mortgage of £24,000 with the remainder raised from the sale of a car which was jointly owned by them. Since half of this money could be considered to be Milligan's she had effectively contributed half of the purchase price and it was held that she was entitled to a half share of the property by way of a resulting trust. Although such a direct contribution to the purchase price will certainly give rise to a resulting trust other less direct contributions have also been held sufficient provided that they are referable to the purchase price of the property. Where land is purchased by means of a mortgage a person who has contributed to the mortgage repayments may be regarded as having contributed to the purchase price and will acquire an interest by way of a resulting trust. This possibility was examined by Bagnall J. in *Cowcher v. Cowcher*[58] where he considered the consequences of a conveyance of a house to A for £24,000 where A had provided £8,000 of his own money and the remainder was provided by way of a mortgage taken out in the name of B:

> "... suppose that at the time A says that as between himself and B he, A, will be responsible for half the mortgage repayments ... Though as between A and B and the vendor A has provided £8,000 and B £16,000, as between A and B themselves A has provided £8,000 and made himself liable for the repayment of half the £16,000 mortgage namely a further £8,000, a total of £16,000; the resulting trust will therefore be as to two-thirds for A and one-third for B."

He concluded that a wife who had made some mortgage repayments was entitled to a share of the house by way of a resulting trust. In *Tinsley v. Milligan*[59] it has already been noted that the majority of the purchase price was raised by way of a mortgage. This was repaid with money from a bank account in the sole name of Milligan, but since it contained the proceeds of their business and was treated by them as their joint property this did not make any difference to the finding that they had contributed equally to the purchase price of the house. Where one party has enabled another to purchase land at an undervalue or reduced price because they qualify for some discount then the amount of the discount will be regarded as a contribution to the purchase price. In *Marsh v. Von Sternberg*[60] Bush J. held that a discount gained on the purchaser of a long lease because one of the parties was a sitting tenant was to be assessed as a contribution to the purchase price for the purposes of determining their respective interests under a resulting trust. Similarly, in *Springette v. Defoe*[61] a discount of 41 per cent of the market value of a council flat obtained because the plaintiff had been a tenant for more than 11 years was regarded as a contribution to the purchase

[57] [1993] 3 All E.R. 65.
[58] [1972] 1 W.L.R. 425.
[59] [1993] 3 All E.R. 65.
[60] [1986] 1 F.L.R. 526.
[61] [1992] 2 F.L.R. 388.

price by the Court of Appeal. In *Midland Bank v. Cooke*[62] a house was purchased in the sole name of a husband in 1971 for £8,500. the purchase price consisted of a mortgage of £6,450 and the balance provided by the husband's savings and a wedding gift of £1,100 given to them by his parents. The Court of Appeal held that since the gift was to regarded as made to them jointly, the wife had contributed half of the amount of the gift, namely £550, to the purchase price and to that extent was entitled to a share of the equitable ownership by way of a resulting trust. However, it seems that money contributions which cannot be related to the purchase price of the land will not be sufficient to give rise to a resulting trust. In *Burns v. Burns*[63] Mr and Mrs Burns began living together as man and wife in 1961. In 1963 a house was purchased in the sole name of Mr Burns, who financed the purchase by way of a mortgage. Mrs Burns later worked and used part of her earnings to pay the rates, telephone bills and to buy various items of furniture for the house. When they separated in 1980 she claimed that she was entitled to a share of the house by reason of these contributions. The Court of Appeal held that in these circumstances she had not made any direct contribution to the purchase price and that she was not therefore entitled to any interest by way of a resulting trust. It should, however, be noted that the fact that contributions are ineffective to generate a resulting trust does not mean that it is inevitable that the contributor has no equitable interest in the land, since they may give rise to a constructive trust which operates by applying different principles.

(iv) Quantification of the extent of the equitable interest under a resulting trust: Where a person is entitled to a share of the equitable ownership of property by way of a resulting trust the quantification of their share is a matter of pure arithmetic. The court possesses no discretion and the share will be the equivalent of the exact proportion of the purchase price that was contributed. For example, in *Tinsley v. Milligan*[64] Milligan was held entitled to a half share in the house because she had contributed exactly a half of the deposit that had been paid and half of the mortgage repayments. In *Midland Bank v. Cooke*[65] the Court of Appeal held that Mrs Cooke would have been entitled to a 6.74 per cent share of the equitable ownership of the house by way of a resulting trust since this was the exact correspondence between her contribution of £550 and the purchase price of the property. In the event it was held that she was entitled to a half share of the house by way of a constructive trust, which emphasises the essential distinct nature of the two concepts. In the case of a resulting trust the court is merely giving effect to any contribution that has been made and the contributor will only be entitled to an equitable interest equivalent to their contribution, no more and no less. However, it is recognised that in some contexts it may be difficult for the Court to assess the extent of a contribution with exact precision, especially where the contribution was made by way of assistance with mortgage repayments. In such cases the court is prepared to adopt a practical approach, as was recognised by Lord Reid in *Gissing v. Gissing*[66]:

> ". . . where [the contributor] does not make direct payments towards the purchase it is less easy to evaluate her share. If her payments are direct she gets a

[62] [1995] 4 All E.R. 562.
[63] [1984] Ch. 317.
[64] [1993] 3 All E.R. 65.
[65] [1995] 4 All E.R. 562.
[66] [1971] A.C. 886 at 987.

> share proportionate to what she has paid. otherwise there must be a more rough and ready evaluation. I agree that this does not mean that she would as a rule get a half share . . . There will be many others where a fair estimate might be a tenth or a quarter or something even more than a half."

(v) Reliance on a presumption of resulting trust where the underlying transaction was effected to pursue an illegal purpose: One question which has arisen recently is whether a person can rely on a presumption of resulting trust to claim an equitable interest in property when the property was acquired in the pursuance of an illegal purpose. It is a maxim of equity that "he who comes to equity must come with clean hands," meaning that equity will not step in to assist a persons whose conduct is illegal. In *Tinsley v. Milligan*[67] there was no doubt that under the principles of presumed resulting trusts Milligan would be prima facie entitled to a half-share of the house that had been purchased, but the House of Lords had to determine whether she should be entitled to assert her entitlement in circumstances where the house had been conveyed into the sole name of Tinsley to enable her to continue to claim housing benefit, thus defrauding the Department of Social Security. Two members of the House of Lords held that the maxim should be applied strictly, so that Milligan could not maintain a claim to a half-share of the house against Tinsley. However, the majority took the view that a person should be entitled to assert their equitable proprietary interest provided that they did not have to rely on their illegal conduct to do so. Since the presumption of an automatic resulting trust arises from the mere fact of contribution it can be established without the need to demonstrate the purpose of the transaction. Milligan was not therefore prevented from claiming her half-interest in the house. The principle was explained by Lord Browne-Wilkinson[68]:

> "the time has come to decide clearly that the rule is the same whether a plaintiff founds himself on legal or equitable title: he is entitled to recover if he is not forced to plead or rely on the illegality, even if it emerges that the title on which he relied was acquired in the course of carrying through an illegal transaction."

As will be seen, the problems are more complex in cases were the presumption of advancement applies and a plaintiff seeks to rebut the presumption on grounds which reveal an illegal purpose.

(d) Rebuttal of the presumption of a resulting trust

(i) Possibility of rebuttal: The conclusion that a person who has contributed to the purchase price of property intended to obtain a share of the ownership thereby is only a presumption and as such is capable of rebuttal by evidence that a gift was intended. As Lord Diplock observed in *Pettitt v. Pettitt*[69] the presumptions are "no more than a consensus of judicial opinion disclosed by reported cases as to the most likely inference of fact to be drawn in the absence of any evidence to the contrary." Where the presumption of a resulting trust is rebutted the person who enjoys the legal title of the

[67] [1993] 3 All E.R. 65.
[68] *ibid.* at 91.
[69] [1970] A.C. 777 at 823.

property will be absolutely entitled to it and the contributor will enjoy no interests in it by way of a trust.

(ii) Evidence which will rebut the presumption: Any evidence that the transferee or contributor to the purchase price of the property was not intending to retain ownership for himself will be effective to rebut the presumption of a resulting trust. Evidence that a gift was intended will clearly rebut the presumption. This can be seen in the context of personal property in *Fowkes v. Pascoe*[70] and *Re Young*[71] and the principles are the same in relation to land. Evidence that a contribution was made by way of a loan will also rebut a presumption of resulting trust since a lender enjoys only a contractual obligation for the repayment of the money lent and not an interest in property acquired with it. For example, in *Re Sharpe (A Bankrupt)*[72] Mr and Mrs Sharpe lived in a maisonette with their 82-year old aunt, Mrs Johnson. The property had been purchased in the name of Mr Sharpe for £17,000. Of this Mrs Johnson had provided £12,000 and the remainder was raised by way of a mortgage. Subsequently the Sharpe's became bankrupt and Mrs Johnson claimed to be entitled to an interest in the property under a resulting trust. However, Browne-Wilkinson J. held that the money had been advanced by her by way of a loan which it had been intended Sharpe would repay, and that this intention rebutted the presumption of a resulting trust.

(iii) Degree of evidence required to rebut the presumption of a resulting trust: The weight of evidence required to rebut a presumption of a resulting trust will vary with the nature of the circumstances in which property was transferred or a contribution made. In *Fowkes v. Pascoe*[73] the Court of Appeal suggested that if a man invested in shares in the name of himself and his solicitor there would be a very strong inference that a trust was intended because people do not usually make gifts to their professional advisers. In contrast, the presumption of a resulting trust arising between a wife and her husband, which is somewhat anomalous because there is no presumption of advancement despite the nature of the relationship, is extremely weak and can be rebutted by slender evidence that a gift was intended. As Lord Upjohn remarked in *Pettitt v. Pettitt*[74]:

> "If a wife puts property in her husband's name it may be that in the absence of all other evidence he is a trustee for her, but in practice there will in almost every case be some explanation (however slight) of this (today) rather unusual course. If a wife puts property into their joint names I would myself think that a joint tenancy was intended for I can see no other reason for it."[75]

(e) A counter presumption of advancement

(i) When the presumption of advancement arises: As has been seen in cases where there is a voluntary transfer of property or a contribution to the purchase price there is

[70] (1875) 10 Ch. App 343.
[71] (1889) 28 Ch.D. 705.
[72] [1980] 1 W.L.R. 219.
[73] (1875) 10 Ch. App. 343.
[74] [1970] A.C. 777 at 815.
[75] See also: *Knightly v. Knightly* (1981) 11 Fam. Law 122.

a presumption of a resulting trust in favour of the transferor or the contributor. However, in limited circumstances there is a counter-presumption that a gift was intended. This presumption is known as the presumption of advancement, and when such a presumption applies the transferor or contributor is presumed to have made a gift and not to have retained any interest in the property. As with the presumption of a resulting trust this presumption of advancement can also be rebutted by evidence that no gift was intended. A presumption of advancement will only arise between parties who are in a relationship which historically was regarded as giving rise to a duty by the one party to provide for the other's support. To this extent the contexts in which the presumption arise are reflective of Victorian concepts of family responsibility, and today there are anomalies which are purely anachronistic. There is a clear presumption of advancement between a father and child[76] and between a child and a person standing in *loco parentis* to that child.[77] For example, in *Warren v. Gurney*[78] it was held that a presumption of advancement applies where a father had purchased a house in the name of his daughter prior to her wedding. Similarly in *Webb v. Webb*[79] there was a presumption of advancement where a father purchased an apartment in Antibes in the name of his son. However there is no presumption of advancement between a mother and child[80] or in the context of other family relationships,[81] and therefore in such cases a presumption of resulting trust will continue to apply, although obviously the nature of the relationship may mean that it is relatively easy to rebut. A presumption of advancement will also apply between a husband and wife, reflecting a traditional understanding that the husband would provide for his wife's material needs.[82] The continuing application of the presumption between a husband and wife was affirmed by the House of Lords in *Pettitt v. Pettitt*[83] although it was recognised that it had lost its force due to the increasing economic independence of wives. By analogy the presumption also applies between a man and his fiancé,[84] though not between a man and his mistress.[85] However, there is no presumption of advancement between a wife and her husband[86] or between cohabiting couples.[87]

[76] See: *Re Roberts* [1946] Ch. 1; *B. v. B.* (1975) 65 D.L.R. (3d) 460.
[77] *Hepworth v. Hepworth* (1870) L.R. 11 Eq. 10; *Bennet v. Bennet* (1879) 10 Ch.D. 474; *Re Orme* (1883) 50 L.T. 51; *Shephard v. Cartwright* [1955] A.C. 431; *Re Paradise Motor Co. Ltd* [1968] 1 W.L.R. 1125.
[78] [1944] 2 All E.R. 472.
[79] [1992] 1 All E.R. 17.
[80] *Re de Visme* (1863) 2 de G.J. & Sm. 17; *Bennet v. Bennet* (1879) 10 Ch.D. 474;.
[81] *Noack v. Noack* [1959] V.R. 137 (sister); *Gorog v. Kiss* (1977) 78 D.L.R. (3d) 690 (sister); *Knight v. Biss* [1954] N.Z.L.R. 55 (son-in-law); *Dury v. Cury* (1675) 75 S.S. 205 (nephew); *Russell v. Scott* (1936) 55 C.L.R. 440 (nephew).
[82] *Re Eykyn's Trusts* (1877) 6 Ch.D. 115; *Silver v. Silver* [1958] 1 All E.R. 523; *Heavey v. Heavey* [1971] 111 I.L.T.R. 1; *M v. M* [1980] 114 I.L.T.R. 46; *Doohan v. Nelson* [1973] 2 N.S.W.L.R. 320; *Napier v. Public Trustee (Western Australia)* (1980) 32 A.L.R. 153.
[83] [1970] A.C. 777.
[84] *Moate v. Moate* [1948] 2 All E.R. 486; *Tinker v. Tinker* [1970] P 136; *Mossop v. Mossop* [1988] 2 All E.R. 202.
[85] *Diwell v. Farnes* [1959] 1 W.L.R. 624.
[86] *Re Curtis* (1885) 52 L.T. 244; *Mercier v. Mercier* [1903] 2 Ch. 98; *Pearson v. Pearson* (1965) *The Times*, November 30; *Pettitt v. Pettitt* [1970] A.C. 777; *Heseltine v. Heseltine* [1971] 1 W.L.R. 342; *Northern Bank v. Henry* [1981] L.R. 1; *Allied Irish Banks Ltd v. McWilliams* [1982] N.I. 156.
[87] *Rider v. Kidder* (1805) 10 Ves. 360; *Soar v. Foster* (1858) 4 K. & J. 152; *Allen v. Snyder* [1977] 2 N.S.W.L.R. 685; *Calverly v. Green* (1984) 56 A.L.R. 483.

(ii) Rebutting the presumption of advancement: When a presumption of advancement arises it may be rebutted by evidence demonstrating that no gift was intended by the transferor or contributor. For example, in *Warren v. Gurney*[88] the father who had purchased the house for his daughter had retained the title deeds until his death. The Court of Appeal held that this rebutted the presumption of advancement because the father would have been expected to hand the deeds over to her if he had intended a gift. In *McGrath v. Wallace*[89] a house had been acquired by a father and son in the sole name of the son for their joint occupancy. The purchase price had been raised partly by the sale of the father's previous house and partly by means of a mortgage. The Court of Appeal held that the presumption of advancement was rebutted by evidence, including a declaration of trust which had never been signed, demonstrating that they intended to share the beneficial ownership in the proportions represented by the proceeds of sale and the mortgage. The mere fact that any rents and profits derived from land are returned to the contributor is not necessarily conclusive to rebut the presumption of advancement. In *Stamp Duties Comrs v. Byrnes*[90] a father purchased property in Australia in the names of his sons, and they paid over to him the rents they received from the properties and he paid the cost of rates and repairs. The Privy Council held that the presumption of advancement was not rebutted because it was natural for the sons to feel some delicacy about taking the profits from the land during their father's lifetime.

(iii) Admissibility of evidence to rebut a presumption of advancement: Since it would be very easy for a person who has made a gift of property to change their mind and seek to have it set aside on the grounds that no advancement was intended the Court has introduced a rule that a person may only rely on evidence of his acts and declarations which were contemporaneous with the transaction to rebut the presumption. Evidence of subsequent acts and declarations will only be admissible against a party and not in their favour.[91]

(iv) Rebuttal of a presumption of advancement by evidence of an illegal purpose: It is a basic rule that the court will not allow a person to rely on evidence of his own illegal conduct to rebut a presumption of advancement. It has been seen in *Tinsley v. Milligan*[92] that a party claiming share of the beneficial ownership of land by way of a presumption of resulting trust does not need to rely on his illegal conduct in order to establish his interest because the presumption arises from the mere fact of his contribution, irrespective of his reasons for making it. However, where a person seeks to claim an interest in land by way of a resulting trust where a prior presumption of advancement arises he may be required to rely on his illegality in order to rebut that counter-presumption and establish his interest. For example, in *Gascoigne v. Gascoigne*[93] a husband took a lease of land in the name of his wife in order to defeat his creditors. The Court of Appeal held that he could not rely on this reason to demonstrate that no gift was intended. The same principles applied in *Tinker v. Tinker*[94] where a husband purchased a house in the name of his wife to prevent it being

[88] [1944] 2 All E.R. 472.
[89] (1995) *The Times*, April 13.
[90] [1911] A.C. 386.
[91] *Shepherd v. Cartwright* [1955] A.C. 431.
[92] [1993] 3 All E.R. 65.
[93] [1918] 1 K.B. 223.
[94] [1970] P. 136.

seized by creditors if his business failed.[95] Lord Denning M.R. held that he could not rebut the presumption of advancement:

> ". . . he cannot say that the house is his own and, at one and the same time, say that it is his wife's. As against the wife, he wants to say that it belongs to him. As against his creditors, that it belongs to her. That simply will not do. Either it was conveyed to her for her own use absolutely; or it was conveyed to her as a trustee for her husband. It must be one or the other. The presumption is that it was conveyed to her for her own use; and he does not rebut that presumption by saying that he only did it to defeat his creditors. . . ."[96]

However, in the recent case *Tribe v. Tribe*[97] the Court of Appeal adopted the approach that a person could still rebut a presumption of advancement even where they had transferred the property in pursuance of an illegal purpose, provided that the purpose had not yet been carried into effect. A father owned 459 of 500 shares in a private company. He transferred these into the name of his son because of fears that he would become liable for the cost of repairs to two premises occupied by the company. In the event the father was never required to meet the cost of the repairs and he demanded that his son return the shares to him. The son refused and the father sought a declaration that he had been holding them on resulting trust for him. The Court of Appeal held that in the circumstances the presumption of advancement which applied between father and son could be rebutted by evidence of the purpose of the transaction since the illegal objective of enabling the father to avoid his creditors was never carried into effect. The principle was explained by Nourse L.J.:

> "Certainly the transaction was carried into effect by the execution and registration of the transfer. But . . . that is immaterial. It is the purpose which has to be carried into effect and that would only have happened if and when a creditor or creditors of the [father] had been deceived by the transaction. . . . Nor is it any objection to the [father's] right to recover the shares that he did not demand their return until after the danger had passed and it was no longer necessary to conceal the transfer from his creditors. All that matters is that no deception was practised on them."[98]

(f) The practical importance of resulting trusts

(i) A means of obtaining a share of the equitable ownership of land: It has been seen that the presumption of a resulting trust is an important means by which a contributor to the purchase price of property can gain a share of the equitable ownership. However, often those seeking such an interest have only contributed a very small percentage of the purchase price. This is not always the case, as in *Tinsley v. Milligan*[99] where the parties had contributed equally to the purchase price. But a more normal

[95] See also: *Re Emery's Investment Trusts* [1959] Ch. 410; [1962] 1 All E.R. 494.
[96] *ibid.* at 141.
[97] [1995] 4 All E.R. 236.
[98] *ibid.* at 248.
[99] [1993] 3 All E.R. 65.

reality is that seen in *Midland Bank v. Cooke*[1] where the wife had contributed only a very small proportion of the purchase price. Whether this matters to the claimant will depend upon the purpose for which they are seeking an equitable interest in the land. If they are merely seeking to demonstrate that they have some interest in the land, which will be binding upon some third party other than the legal owner who is claiming that they have no interest in the land, then the exact proportion of their equitable entitlement will be irrelevant as between them and the third party. For example, if a person is seeking to assert that they have an equitable interest in the land which is binding on a mortgage company which has lent money to the legal owner, it may only be necessary for the claimant to show that they have some beneficial interest and the precise quantification of that interest is less important. This was the issue in *Williams & Glynn's Bank v. Boland*[2] where a matrimonial home was owned in the sole name of a husband but the wife had contributed a substantial sum of her own money to the purchase price. The husband later mortgaged the house to the bank and the issue was whether the bank took its mortgage subject to any equitable interest of the wife. There was no question that the wife enjoyed an interest by way of a resulting trust arising from her contribution, but the extent of that interest was largely irrelevant to the issue in point, which was whether her actual occupation of the land converted her equitable interest into an overriding interest under Land Registration Act 1925, s.70(1)(g) which would bind the mortgage company. Similarly in *Abbey National Building Society v. Cann*[3] it was clear that the claimant enjoyed an interest in the equitable ownership of a house because of her contribution to the purchase price by way of a reduction to which she was entitled as a sitting tenant under a protected tenancy, but the extent of that interest was irrelevant to the question whether it was binding on a subsequent mortgage lender. However, if a person is claiming an entitlement against the legal owner of the land, it is much more likely that they will want to establish that they enjoy a substantial interest in it. If they have only contributed a small proportion of the purchase price this will not be possible by means of a resulting trust, but where it can be established that there was a common intention between the claimant and the legal owner that the claimant was to enjoy an interest in the land then the claimant may be entitled to a constructive trust to give effect to that common intention, even where the practical effect is that they are thereby entitled to a much greater percentage of the equitable ownership of the land than would have been justified by their contribution alone. This is evident from the facts of *Midland Bank v. Cooke*[4] where as has already been noted, a wife contributed 6.74 per cent of the purchase price of her matrimonial home which was registered in the sole name of her husband, who had also contributed to the purchase price and made the mortgage contributions alone throughout. The Court of Appeal held that since on the facts it was possible to infer a common intention that the husband and wife were to share the ownership of the house equally, her interest was not limited to the strict amount resulting from her cash contribution to the purchase price but she was entitled to a half-interest in the equitable ownership by way of a constructive trust. This means that in practice where there is a relatively small

[1] [1995] 4 All E.R. 562.
[2] [1981] A.C. 487.
[3] [1991] 1 A.C. 56.
[4] [1995] 4 All E.R. 562.

financial contribution the party seeking a share of the equitable ownership of the property will prefer to demonstrate entitlement by way of a constructive trust.

(ii) Nature of the co-ownership arising under a resulting trust: Where a person is entitled to a proportion of the equitable ownership of land by way of a resulting trust one question which arises is as to the nature of their relationship with the persons who are entitled to the remainder of that ownership. English law recognises two forms of co-ownership of the equitable interest of land, namely a joint tenancy and a tenancy in common. These concepts will be examined in more detail in the following chapter, but at this stage it is sufficient to know that where parties are joint tenants they are not treated as enjoying distinct and separate shares in the land which they can deal with individually. Most importantly the principle of survivorship operates between joint tenants so that when one joint tenant dies his interest in the land passes automatically to the other joint tenants and he cannot leave his notional share in the land to anyone else by means of a will.[5] Where a person is entitled to a share of the equitable ownership as a tenant in common they are regarded as holding that share distinctly from the interests of the other co-owners and the principle of survivorship does not apply to it. Where parties have contributed to the purchase price of land unequally, so that their entitlements are also unequal, they will be taken to hold their respective shares as tenant in common. However, where their contributions are identical, there appears to be no reason why they should not be joint tenants.

(iii) Reform of resulting trusts: Although a well established aspect of the law of trusts, and enjoying particular prominence in relation to land, the doctrine of resulting trusts has been criticised on the grounds that it contains many anomalies and anachronisms, especially in relation to the presumptions of advancement. The area was reviewed by the Law Commission in 1988.[6] The possibility of a generalised concept of community of property between husband and wife was rejected on the grounds that it would prevent the independent ownership and management of property during marriage. However, a revision of the presumptions operating was proposed so that they would correspond more closely to their likely intentions:[7]

> (i) Where money is spent to buy property, or property or money is transferred by one spouse to the other, for their joint use or benefit the property acquired or money transferred should be jointly owned.
>
> (ii) Where money or property is transferred by one spouse to the other for any other purpose, it should be owned by that other.

In both cases, the general rule should give way to a contrary intention on the part of the paying or transferring spouse, provided that the contrary intention is known to that other spouse.

This proposal has the effect of eliminating the anomaly that the presumption of advancement applies only between a husband and his wife and not between a wife and her husband.

[5] Nor will it pass to his heirs under the rules of intestacy if he dies without making a will.
[6] "Family Law: Matrimonial Property" Law Com. No. 175 (1988).
[7] Para. 4.1.

4 Constructive Trusts of Land

(a) Historical background to constructive trusts of land

(i) Traditional concepts of family property: Central to an understanding of the operation of the principles under which the courts may find that a constructive trust of land has arisen is an appreciation of how the principles have developed to facilitate changes in society, and in particular the role of women within the realm of property ownership. The paradigm of land ownership during the earlier half of this century was that most women were married, did not go to work and looked after their children, and the matrimonial home was owned in the sole name of their husband who was at work and provided money both to purchase the property, whether out-right or by means of a mortgage, and for the needs of the family. With a extremely small divorce rate there was little need for women to assert any form of ownership in the matrimonial home since they were assured of living in it throughout their lives. Generations of women owned no land. The post-war social changes rendered this traditional paradigm obsolete and increasingly women who were not legally entitled to the ownership of their matrimonial homes sought to assert some form of proprietary entitlement. If the parties were to divorce it was essential that the wife could demonstrate that she was entitled to a share of the equitable ownership of the house since the court possessed no jurisdiction to divided the matrimonial property between the parties on divorce. In the absence of an express declaration of trust the wife could claim that she was entitled to a share by way of a resulting trust if she had contributed to the purchase price, but as has been noted in many cases any such financial contribution would have been relatively insignificant in comparison with the husband's contribution since he would generally be the main income earner and the wife would have little money of her own to contribute. In this context the courts began to develop the concept of the constructive trust, whereby a person could gain an interest in the equitable ownership of property not merely on the basis of a financial contribution but in fulfilment of some common intention between themselves and the legal owner that they should be entitled to a share of the ownership.

(ii) Development of the principles of constructive trusts of land: The seminal authority on the development of the principles of constructive trusts of land was the decision of the House of Lords in *Gissing v. Gissing*.[8] The facts reveal the changing emphasis from the traditional paradigm outlined above and the more modern realities of property ownership in families. The parties were husband and wife who had married in 1935 when they were in their early twenties. They were both in work, the wife as secretary for a firm of printers. The house which was the subject of the proceedings was purchased in 1951 for £2,695 and conveyed into the sole name of the husband . Of this, the husband was lent £500 by the managing director of the printing firm, £2,150 was raised by way of a mortgage, and he provided the balance of £45 from his own money. The wife then spent £220 of her money laying a lawn and providing furniture for the house. The wife continued to work and used her earnings to purchase clothes for herself and her child as well as adding to the housekeeping allowance provided by her husband. He paid all the instalments on the loan and the mortgage as well as the

[8] [1971] A.C. 881.

other outgoings of the home. In 1960, after 25 years of marriage he left to live with a younger woman. She remained in the matrimonial home and was granted a divorce in 1966. She sought a declaration that she was beneficially entitled to the house. The House of Lords held that in these circumstances the husband was absolutely entitled to the house and that the wife had no interest in it by way of a trust. The central reason for this denial of any entitlement was that there was no conduct from which it could be inferred that the parties had a common intention that the wife was to be entitled to a share of the house. The general principles upon which such a trust would be inferred were stated by Lord Diplock[9]:

> "A resulting, implied or constructive trust . . . is created by a transaction between the trustee and the [beneficiary] in connection with the acquisition by the trustee of a legal estate in the land, whenever the trustee has so conducted himself that it would be inequitable to allow him to deny to the [beneficiary] a beneficial interest in the land acquired. And he will be held so to have conducted himself if by his words or conduct he has induced the [beneficiary] to act to his own detriment in the reasonable belief that by so acting he was acquiring a beneficial interest in the land."

This analysis of the circumstances under which a constructive trust may be established requires two central ingredients. First, that the legal owner of the land had in some way induced the claimant to believe that they would be entitled to a share of the ownership. This inducement could take either the form of an express agreement or of a inference from the parties' conduct that an interest in the property was intended by them. Secondly, that the person claiming an interest must have acted to her detriment in some way by contributing to the purchase price of the land. Where these two factors were present the court would not allow the legal owner to enjoy the absolute ownership of the land free from the contributor's interests. As Lord Diplock explained:

> "I take it to be clear that if the court is satisfied that it was the common intention of both spouses that the contributing wife should have a share in the beneficial interest and that her contributions were made upon this understanding, the court in the exercise of its equitable jurisdiction would not permit the husband in whom the legal estate was vested and who had accepted the benefit of the contributions to take the whole beneficial interest merely because at the time the wife made her contributions there had been no express agreement as to how her share in it was to be quantified."[10]

In the event Mrs Gissing was held not to have any interest because her contributions were not of such a type as would entitle the court to infer that there was a common intention between her and her husband that she was to be entitled to a share of the ownership of the house. As Lord Diplock explained[11]:

[9] *ibid.* at 905.
[10] *ibid.* at 908.
[11] *ibid.* at 911.

"On what is the wife's claim based? In 1951 when the house was purchased she spent about £190 on buying furniture and a cooker and refrigerator for it. She also paid £30 for improving the lawn. As furniture and household durables are depreciating assets whereas houses have turned out to be appreciating assets it may be that she would have been wise to have devoted her savings to acquiring an interest in the freehold; but this may not have been so apparent in 1951 as it has now become. The court is not entitled to infer a common intention to this effect from the mere fact that she provided chattels for joint use in the new matrimonial home; and there is nothing else in the conduct of the parties at the time of the purchase or thereafter which supports such an inference. There is no suggestion that the wife's efforts or her earnings made it possible for the husband to raise the initial loan or the mortgage or that her relieving her husband from the expense of buying clothing for herself and for their son was undertaken in order to enable him the better to meet the mortgage instalments or to repay the loan. The picture presented by the evidence is one of husband and wife retaining their separate proprietary interests in the property whether real or personal purchased with their separate savings and is inconsistent with any common intention at the time of the purchase of the matrimonial home that the wife, who neither then nor thereafter contributed anything to its purchase price or assumed any liability for it, should nevertheless be entitled to a beneficial interest in it."

The essence of the constructive trust as adopted in *Gissing v. Gissing* is that the court merely fulfils the intention of the parties that they should share the ownership of the land. As Glass J.A. explained in the Australian case *Allen v. Snyder*[12]:

"... when it is called a constructive trust, it should not be forgotten that the courts are giving effect to an arrangement based upon the actual intentions of the parties, not a rearrangement in accordance with considerations of justice, independent of their intentions and founded upon their respective behaviour in relation to the matrimonial home."

However, in reality the circumstances in which such a trust arise are those where the parties have given little or no thought to their intentions, as issues such as the ownership of property have been assumed or misunderstood, or indeed one party has misrepresented his intentions to the other and taken advantage of the other's trusting nature or naiveté. In such cases the emphasis on the "actual intentions" of the parties is, to say the least, artificial, and the development of the doctrine of constructive trusts has been characterised by an ongoing tension between the desire to ensure that just results are achieved and the continued stress on the need to enforce the real intentions of the parties.

(iii) Application of the *Gissing v. Gissing* criteria: Although *Gissing v. Gissing* recognised the possibility of a constructive trust the application of the principles was extremely traditional and represented a strict property based approach which was more concerned with the nature of the parties' contributions as determinative of their significance rather than to the nature of the parties' relationship. Under this approach

[12] [1977] 2 N.S.W.L.R. 685 at 693.

contributions to family life which could not be related to ownership of the house, such as child-rearing or the performance of the usual domestic tasks that partners ordinarily have to do around the home, would not be sufficient to gain an interest in the property. Some judges preferred a less rigorous and limiting approach to the determination of constructive trust interests and Lord Denning in particular was responsible for attempting to introduced a radically different approach by giving the court a wide discretion to determine on the facts of any given case whether a person should be entitled to an interest by way of a constructive trust, so that the chief criterion was that of "justice" and not the type of contribution which had been made.

(iv) Development of the "new model" constructive trust: Lord Denning advocated the adoption of what he described as a "new model" constructive trust which would give the court a wide discretion to award claimants' interests in property by way of constructive trusts so that the constructive trust became a discretionary equitable remedy in much the same way as it is used in the United States. Ironically he claimed authority for this development from the judgment of the House of Lords in *Gissing v. Gissing*. However, his use of citations was somewhat selective and he was prone to quote only those sentiments of the judges which indicated the inequitability of allowing the legal owner to enjoy an unencumbered legal title and not those where they attempted to lay down criteria for judging whether in the circumstances it would be inequitable. In *Hussey v. Palmer*[13] he explained the principles under which such a trust could be imposed:

> ". . . it is a trust imposed whenever justice and good conscience require it. It is a liberal process, founded on large principles of equity, to be applied in cases where the defendant cannot conscientiously keep the property for himself alone, but ought to allow another to have the property or a share in it. The trust may arise at the outset when the property is acquired, or later on, as the circumstances may require. It is an equitable remedy by which a court can enable an aggrieved party to obtain restitution."

A classic example of a case where Lord Denning found that justice demanded the imposition of a constructive trust was *Eves v. Eves*.[14] Janet Eves, who was nineteen, moved in with Stuart Eves and changed her name by deed poll. They intended to marry after his divorce and moved into a house which was purchased in his name only. He told Janet that the house could not be put in their joint names because she was not yet twenty-one, which was untrue, but that he intended to put it in their joint names in the future. She contributed no money to the purchase price, but did a great deal of work to improve the condition of the house, which had been very dirty and dilapidated. This included decorating and breaking up concrete in the front garden. Lord Denning considered that "she did much more than many wives would do." After a couple of years Stuart met another woman and decided to sell the house. The Court of Appeal held that in these circumstances Janet should be entitled to a share of the equitable ownership by way of a constructive trust. Lord Denning M.R. explained the basis upon which such a trust would be imposed[15]:

[13] [1972] 3 All E.R. 744 at 747.
[14] [1975] 1 W.L.R. 1338.
[15] *ibid.* at 1342.

> "it seems to me that this conduct by Mr Eves amounted to a recognition by him that, in all fairness, she was entitled to a share in the house equivalent in some way to a declaration of trust; not for a particular share, but for such share as was fair in view of all she had done and was doing. By so doing he gained her confidence. She trusted him. She did not make any financial contribution but she contributed in many other ways. She did much work in the house and garden. She looked after him and cared for the children. It is clear that her contribution was such that if she had been a wife she would have had a good claim to have a share in it on a divorce . . . In view of his conduct, it would, I think, be most inequitable for him to deny her any share in the house. The law will impute or impose a constructive trust by which he was to hold it on trust for them both."

Having concluded that it was appropriate to impose a constructive trust the question of the extent of the interest which Janet had acquired remained to be determined. Although the assurances of Stuart that he would ultimately place the house in their joint names suggested an equal sharing Lord Denning seemed to take the approach that it was for the court to determine in its discretion the appropriate share: "But what should be the shares? I think one half would be too much. I suggest it should be one quarter of the equity."[16] The decision in *Eves v. Eves* illustrates the central aspects of the "new model" constructive trust and how it differs from the approach adopted by the House of Lords in *Gissing v. Gissing*. First, it places greater emphasis on the totality of the parties' conduct and relationship and not merely on activities which can be related to the purchase price of the land. Secondly, the question whether a constructive trust should be imposed and the extent of any interest granted thereby is a matter for the court's discretion. Both of these elements introduce a degree of uncertainty into the process of determination whether a trust affecting the ownership of land has arisen, and for this reason the "new model" constructive trust proved unacceptable to property lawyers.

(v) Rejection of the "new model" constructive trust: Although some applications of Lord Denning's "new model" constructive trust may be regarded as achieving practical justice between the parties, and the outcomes have been regarded as correct by later cases, the concept of the "new model" constructive trust has been categorically rejected on the grounds of its uncertainty and inconsistency with the earlier House of Lords' authorities. In *Grant v. Edwards*[17] Nourse L.J. said that the basis of Lord Denning's decision in *Eves v. Eves* had been "at variance with the principles stated in *Gissing v. Gissing*." However, the major factor influencing this rejection was the concern of conveyancers that rights in property must be certain in relation to their existence, creation and extent. If this is not the case then there is a great danger that persons will be uncertain of their rights and entitlements, and in particular that third parties either with or acquiring rights in land cannot be certain that their interests will not be prejudicially affected by the later imposition of equitable rights by means of a constructive trust because the Court feels such an imposition is just. Placing such a discretion in the hands of the court would lead inevitably to inconsistency of result and an impossibility of predicting whether a property right would be granted or not.

[16] *ibid.* at 1342.
[17] [1986] Ch. 638 at 647.

Underlying this rejection was the feeling that property rights should not depend upon the individual moral feelings of a judge, which will inherently be subjective and unpredictable, but on more clearly defined criteria. These fears were well articulated by Bagnall J. in *Cowcher v. Cowcher*[18] who considered the advantages of applying the more legalistic approach to constructive trusts adopted by the House of Lords in *Pettitt v. Pettitt*[19] and *Gissing v. Gissing*[20]:

> "In any individual case the application of these propositions may produce a result which appears unfair. So be it; in my view, that is not an injustice. I am convinced that in determining rights, particularly property rights, the only justice that can be attained by mortals, who are fallible and are not omniscient, is justice according to law; the justice flows from the application of sure and settled principles to proved or admitted facts. So in the field of equity the length of the chancellor's foot has been measured or is capable of measurement. This does not mean that equity is past the age of child bearing: simply that its progeny must be legitimate — by precedent out of principle. It is well that this should be so; otherwise no lawyer could safely advise on his client's title and every quarrel would lead to a law suit."

This concept of justice was also echoed by Dillon L.J. in *Springette v. Defoe*[21] who insisted that "the court does not as yet sit under a palm tree, to exercise a general discretion to do what the man in the street, on a general overview of the case, might regard as fair." The "new model" constructive trust was also rejected by commonwealth jurisdictions, for example in Australia in *Allen v. Snyder*[22] and *Muschinski v. Dodds*.[23] In New Zealand Mahon J. described the "new model" constructive trust in *Carly v. Farrelly*[24] as a "supposed rule of equity which is not only vague in its outline but which must disqualify itself from acceptance as a valid principle of jurisprudence by its total uncertainty of application and result."

(vi) Re-statement of the principles under which constructive trusts will arise in England: Having rejected the "new model" constructive trust the House of Lords attempted to re-state the principle under which a constructive trust of land will arise in the leading case *Lloyd's Bank v. Rosset*.[25] The House of Lords effectively re-affirmed the approach that had been taken in *Gissing v. Gissing* that a constructive trust arises because of the parties' intentions that they should share the ownership of the land. Since such shared ownership cannot be given effect at law in relation to the legal title a constructive trust arises in equity and the legal owner is required to hold the land on trusts which give effect to the intention to share. The court is merely forcing the parties to give effect to their own intentions that there should be a sharing of the ownership of the land. The central question therefore becomes one of identifying when

[18] [1972] 1 W.L.R. 425 at 430.
[19] [1970] A.C. 777.
[20] [1971] A.C. 886.
[21] [1992] 2 F.L.R. 388 at 393.
[22] [1977] 2 N.S.W.L.R. 685.
[23] (1985) 160 N.Z.L.R. 356.
[24] [1975] 1 N.Z.L.R. 356.
[25] [1991] 1 A.C. 107.

the parties can be said to have intended that they should share the ownership of the land. This essential requirement is termed the need to establish a "common intention" between the parties. Although the parties may sometimes have made a clear indication of their intentions in relation to the ownership of the property, which will not have been appropriately acted upon by means of an express declaration of trust by the legal owner, often there is no evidence that the parties have ever expressly agreed as to the ownership. The question then becomes whether an intention to share the land can be inferred from the conduct of the parties, and the main issue in *Lloyd's Bank v. Rosset*[26] was as to the type of conduct from which an inference can be drawn. The House of Lords held that only a financial contribution would be sufficient. *Lloyd's Bank v. Rosset*[27] therefore reduces any relevance of the nature of the parties' relationship as a factor determining whether there was a constructive trust, and also leaves limited significance to non-financial contributions to family life. The central deficiency of the decision is that the House of Lords has seemingly diminished the importance of such contributions at a time when society seems to be increasingly concerned to value the non-financial contributions of women in particular so that they are not discriminated against in the context of the ownership of shared property.

(vii) Modern significance of the constructive trust: Despite the rejection of the "new model" constructive trust and the re-assertion of strict criteria in *Lloyd's Bank v. Rosset* it is somewhat ironic that the need for a mechanism whereby the court can apportion the ownership of land justly between a husband and wife has been provided by statute. Under the Matrimonial Causes Act 1973 the court has the power to make orders adjusting the property rights of the parties on divorce. This effectively amounts to a discretion similar to that envisaged by Lord Denning in the context of his "new model" constructive trust. However, it may still be necessary for a husband or wife to invoke the principles of constructive trusts if, rather than seeking to stake a claim to a share of the value of property owned at law by the other party to the marriage on divorce, a husband or wife is seeking to claim an equitable interest in land which they hope will take priority over the interests of a third party, frequently a mortgage company. For example, in *Lloyd's Bank v. Rosset* the wife was seeking to claim an interest in the matrimonial home, to which she had made no financial contribution, by way of a constructive trust so that she would have an interest binding on the bank to whom her husband had granted a mortgage. If she had been able to establish this interest she may have been able to prevent the Bank from repossessing the house when the husband was no longer able to pay the mortgage instalments. Similarly, in *Midland Bank v. Cooke*[28] Mrs Cooke was attempting to assert a share of the equitable ownership of her matrimonial home which would bind the bank who had been granted a mortgage to secure the husband's business overdraft. However, although constructive trusts may still be relevant between married couples the most significant context in which they will determine proprietary rights is in cases of cohabitation, whether heterosexual or homosexual. In such cases the parties may never have agreed upon the ownership of any house they occupy and it is all too easy for a more legally aware partner to ensure that they remain the legal owner as an insurance that it will continue

[26] [1991] 1 A.C. 107.
[27] [1991] 1 A.C. 107.
[28] [1995] 4 All E.R. 562.

to belong to them if the relationship breaks down. The social context in which constructive trusts tends to be sought was recognised by the Court of Appeal in *Midland Bank v. Cooke* where Waite L.J. commented[29]:

> "Equity has traditionally been a system which matches established principle to the demands of social change. The mass diffusion of home ownership has been one of the most striking social changes of our time. The present case is typical of hundreds, perhaps thousands, of others. When people, especially young people, agree to share their lives in joint homes they do so on a basis of mutual trust and in the expectation that their relationship will endure. Despite the efforts that have been made by many responsible bodies to counsel prospective cohabitants as to the risks of taking shared interests in property without legal advice, it is unrealistic to expect that advice to be followed on a universal scale. For a couple embarking on a serious relationship, discussion of the terms to apply at parting is almost a contradiction of the shared hope which brought them together. There will inevitably be numerous couples, married or unmarried, who have no discussion about ownership and who, perhaps advisedly, make no agreement about it."

In such cases the other party will only be able to seek a share of the ownership by way of a resulting or constructive trust, and if their financial contribution is relatively small as a proportion of the purchase price then their only realistic prospect of securing a substantial benefit is by way of a constructive trust imposed on the basis of a common intention that they were to share the ownership of the land. Since there is no equivalent discretion to that of the court in the case of married couples to apportion property between cohabitees when their relationship breaks down, the principles of constructive trusts will often be the only way that a party who was not the legal owner can maintain a claim. This was exactly the situation in which Janet Eves found herself and her position would be no different today. It remains to be seen whether the principles enunciated in *Lloyd's Bank v. Rosset* would continue to ensure her a share of the ownership of the house she had cohabited.

(viii) Commonwealth approaches to constructive trusts: Virtually all common law jurisdictions have had to grapple with the fundamental problem how to determine whether a person has acquired an interest in the ownership of land informally. Although such jurisdictions tended to reject the "new model" constructive trust as too uncertain they have evolved principles which are generally more liberal than the restrictive approach adopted by the House of Lords in *Lloyd's Bank v. Rosset*. They tend to be more generous in the significance accorded to non-financial contributions and the nature of the relationship between the parties.

(ix) Relationship between constructive trusts and proprietary estoppel: Although English law has adopted a restrictive concept of the constructive trust it must be noted that a constructive trust is not the only means by which a person can obtain an interest in land informally. The closely related doctrine of proprietary estoppel also enables a person to obtain an interest in land. There are three key differences between the operation of the two concepts. First, whereas constructive trusts are awarded because

[29] *ibid.* at 575.

of a supposed common intention between the parties, an interest by way of proprietary estoppel will arise wherever a person has acted to their detriment in reliance upon an representation they received that they would enjoy an interest in the land. Secondly, whereas under a constructive trust the court has no remedial discretion but merely recognised that the claimant is entitled to a share of the equitable ownership of the land, in the case of proprietary estoppel once a party has demonstrated that they are entitled to some remedy because the requirements have been met, the precise remedy that they are awarded is a matter for the court to determine in its discretion taking into account all the circumstances. In some cases the court has felt that it is appropriate to award the claimant the full fee simple ownership of the land concerned. In other cases a lesser interest, such as a right to occupy, has been granted. The court has also awarded merely monetary compensation. Thirdly, whereas a constructive trust arises at the moment when the common intention is acted upon which means that it may bind third parties acquiring interests in the land after that time but before the court has recognised the entitlement, any interest by way of proprietary estoppel only arises after it has been awarded by the court. It may therefore be the case that inadequacies in the English law relating to constructive trusts are illusory since a remedy may yet be available under the principles of proprietary estoppel. For example, although non-financial contributions may not be sufficient to infer a common intention to share the ownership of the property they may give rise to an estoppel equity if they have been made on the basis of some assurance from the landowner, and it will be open to the court to determine how as a matter of justice that equity should be satisfied.

(b) Establishing a constructive trust: Lloyd's Bank v. Rosset

(i) Mrs Rosset's claim: Mr and Mrs Rosset had married in 1972. In 1982 Mr Rosset became entitled to a substantial sum of money under a trust fund established by his grandmother in Switzerland. They decided to purchase a house which was in a semi-derelict condition and to renovate it. The house was purchased for £57,000 and title was registered in the sole name of Mr Rosset. The purchase was made in his sole name at the insistence of the trustees advancing the money to him. The cost of the renovations work was also provided solely by Mr Rosset. Mrs Rosset helped with the renovation by decorating the bedrooms of the property and preparing other rooms for decoration. She had also supervised and encouraged the builders who were employed to work on the house. Unknown to Mrs Rosset Mr Rosset in fact mortgaged the house to the Bank to secure his overdraft up to £15,000. After marital difficulties Mr Rosset left his wife and children in occupation of the house and on failing to repay his loan the Bank demanded possession and sale of the house to enforce their security. Mrs Rosset claimed that she was entitled to a share of the ownership of the house by way of a constructive trust which would be binding on the Bank as an overriding interest under Land Registration Act 1925, s.70(1)(g). The House of Lords was therefore asked to determine whether Mrs Rosset enjoyed a share of the equitable ownership of the house and it concluded that no trust had arisen.

(ii) The requirement of a common intention: The central reason why the House of Lords held that Mrs Rosset was not entitled to a constructive trust was that she was unable to demonstrate that there had been a common intention between herself and her husband that she was to enjoy a share of the ownership of the house. Lord Bridge, delivering the judgment of the House, draw a sharp distinction between two circumstances in which a common intention could be established, namely where there was evidence of an express intention which was articulated between the parties that they were to share the ownership, and where there was no evidence of an express intention but an intention to share could nevertheless be inferred from the conduct of the parties. He criticised the judge at first instance, who had reached the conclusion that there was such an intention, on the grounds of his failure to keep these two categories distinct:

> "I cannot help thinking that the judge in the instant case would not have fallen into error if he had kept clearly in mind the distinction between the effect of evidence on the one hand which was capable of establishing an express agreement or an express representation that Mrs Rosset was to have an interest in the property and evidence on the other hand of conduct alone as a basis for an inference of the necessary common intention."[30]

The approach to constructive trusts adopted by the House of Lords therefore means that essentially different criteria may apply depending upon whether a case involves an express or implied common intention.

(iii) Establishing an express common intention: The first category of circumstance in which a constructive trust may arise is where there was an express common intention between the parties that they were to share the ownership of the land. The establishment of such an express intention is a matter of evidence of what the parties said to each other at the time that the property was purchased and thereafter. Such an intention cannot be inferred from the nature of the parties' expectations arising from their relationship, or from their conduct alone. In *Lloyd's Bank v. Rosset* Lord Bridge stated what a party must demonstrate in order to establish an express common intention:

> "The first and fundamental question which must always be resolved is whether . . . there has at any time prior to the acquisition, or exceptionally at any later date, been any agreement, arrangement or understanding reached between them that the property is to be shared beneficially. The finding of an agreement or arrangement to share in this sense can only, I think, be based on evidence of express discussions between the partners, however imperfectly remembered and however imprecise their terms may have been."[31]

On the evidence that was presented he concluded that no such common intention could be established. Lord Bridge explained that in the light of the known circumstances of the purchase a particularly heavy evidential burden would have to have been satisfied by Mrs Rosset that she was intended to be a joint owner of the house:

> "Spouses living in amity do not normally think it necessary to formulate or define their respective interests in property in any precise way. The expectation of

[30] [1991] 1 A.C. 107 at 134.
[31] *ibid.* at 132.

> parties to every happy marriage is that they will share the practical benefits of occupying the matrimonial home whoever owns it. But this is something quite distinct from sharing the beneficial interest in the property asset which the matrimonial home represents . . . Since Mr Rosset was providing the whole purchase price of the property and the whole cost of its renovation, Mrs Rosset would, I think, in any event have encountered formidable difficulty in establishing her claim to joint beneficial ownership. The claim as pleaded and as presented in evidence was, by necessary implication to an equal share in the equity. But to sustain this it was necessary to show that it was Mr Rosset's intention to make an immediate gift to his wife of half the value of a property acquired for £57,000 and improved at a further cost of some £15,000. What made it doubly difficult for Mrs Rosset to establish her case was the circumstance, which was never in dispute, that Mr Rosset's uncle, who was trustee of his Swiss inheritance, would not release the funds for the purchase of the property except on terms that it was to be acquired in Mr Rosset's sole name. If Mr and Mrs Rosset had ever thought about it, they must have realised that the creation of a trust giving Mrs Rosset a half share, or indeed any other substantial share, in the beneficial ownership, of the property would have been nothing less than a subterfuge to circumvent the stipulation which the Swiss trustee insisted on as a condition of releasing the funds to enable the property to be acquired. In these circumstances, it would have required very cogent evidence to establish that it was the Rosset's common intention to defeat the evident purpose of the Swiss trustee's restriction by acquiring the property in Mr Rosset's name alone but to treat it nevertheless as beneficially owned by both spouses."[32]

Lord Bridge therefore emphasised that to establish that the parties had "entered into an agreement, made an arrangement, reached an understanding or formed a common intention that the beneficial interest in the property would be jointly owned," expressions he felt were synonymous, required very clear evidence. However, although the Rossets had failed to satisfy this evidential burden he noted cases where he considered that the burden would have been satisfied. He suggested that *Eves v Eves*[33] and *Grant v. Edwards*[34] were "outstanding examples"[35] of cases where there had been an express common intention. In *Eves v. Eves* Stuart had told Janet when they set up home together that the only reason why the house had not been put in their joint names was that she was too young. In *Grant v. Edwards* a man who set up home with a woman told her that he was purchasing the house they shared in his name alone as to put her on the title would prejudice her divorce proceedings. However, although superficially these assurances could be taken as evidence of an ultimate intention that the land should be co-owned when the supposed impediment was overcome, it is somewhat artificial to represent these statements as reflecting a real intention on the part of the legal owner of the property. In both cases the explanation given to the co-habiting woman was merely an excuse by the man to ensure that he was protected as

[32] [1991] 1 A.C. 107 at 128.
[33] [1975] 1 W.L.R. 1338.
[34] [1986] Ch. 638.
[35] [1991] 1 A.C. 107 at 133.

the owner of the property if the relationship failed. There was never any intention that the woman should enjoy a share of the beneficial ownership. In fact the real intention was that she should never enjoy such an interest. This points to the artificiality of the imposition of a constructive trust as a fulfilment of the expressed common intention of the parties. It seems rather that what is important is that the legal owner gave the other person the impression that they intended the ownership of the land to be shared, and that having created that impression they cannot claim the defence of their "real" intentions. In this sense the express intention is extremely close to the concept of an express representation in cases of proprietary estoppel where a landowner deliberately misleads a person as to their entitlement in the land. This overlap between the two concepts seems to have been recognised by Lord Bridge since he failed to distinguish them rigorously and suggested that in both *Eves v. Eves* and *Grant v. Edwards* the court had "rightly held" that the female partner was entitled to "a constructive trust or proprietary estoppel." However, as has been noted there are important conceptual distinctions between the doctrines of constructive trusts and proprietary estoppel, including the form of the remedy that is available and the time at which any interest in the land is taken to arise. Although the same facts may support both a claim to a constructive trust and an estoppel equity, it is important the principles should not be muddled.

(iv) Giving effect to an express common intention by means of a constructive trust: The mere fact of an express common intention is not alone sufficient to entitle a person to an interest by way of a constructive trust. An owner of property is perfectly entitled to make unenforceable promises about what he will do with it and then fail to carry them into effect. For example, if a man promises to make a gift and then fails to do so the intended donor cannot claim entitlement to the property. A constructive trust is only enforced because it would be inequitable in the circumstances for the legal owner to retain the absolute ownership of the land, in effect failing to abide by the expressed or agreed intentions. This will only be the case if the party claiming the interest has acted to their detriment in some way which on the basis of the common intention. A constructive trust will therefore only arise if their was an express common intention and the person seeking the interest has acted to their detriment. This raises the question as to what conduct will constitute sufficient detriment to establish the entitlement to a constructive trust. It is clear from *Lloyd's Bank v. Rosset*[36] that the level of conduct which will constitute detriment is significantly lower from that which is required in order to infer that there was a common intention in the first place. As Lord Bridge commented in relation to *Eves v. Eves* and *Grant v. Edwards*:

> "The subsequent conduct of the female partners in each case, which the court rightly held sufficient to give rise to a constructive trust . . . fell far short of such conduct as would by itself have supported the claim in the absence of an express representation by the male partner that she was to have such an interest."

The standard of conduct required to establish detriment to give effect to an express common intention is relatively low. As Lord Bridge stated:

[36] [1991] 1 A.C. 107.

> "Once a finding [of an express common intention] is made it will only be necessary for the partner asserting a claim to a beneficial interest against the partner entitled to the legal estate to show that he or she acted to his or her detriment or significantly altered his position in reliance on the agreement in order to give rise to a constructive trust . . ."[37]

The affirmation of *Eves v. Eves* on this basis suggests that the conduct need not involve significant financial contributions to constitute detriment, but that non-financial activity such as Janet's decoration and building work are themselves sufficient. The position of detriment was more fully considered by the Court of Appeal in *Grant v. Edwards*, which also received the House of Lord's approval. Lidia Grant moved in with George Edwards in circumstances where there was an express common intention that she would be entitled to a share of the house. George paid the mortgage but Lidia made financial contributions to the housekeeping expenses and to the bringing up of their children. Nourse L.J. took the view that this could be regarded as making an indirect financial contribution to the mortgage instalments, because it enabled George to pay them out of his wages. However, Browne-Wilkinson V.-C. took a more liberal and expansive view:

> "Once it has been shown that there was a common intention that the claimant should have an interest in the house, any act done by her to her detriment relating to the joint lives of the parties is, in my judgement, sufficient detriment to qualify. The acts do not have to be referable to the house . . . In many case of the present sort, it is impossible to say whether or not the claimant would have done the acts relied on as a detriment even if she thought she had no interest in the house. Setting up house together, having a baby, making payments to general housekeeping expenses (not strictly necessary to enable the mortgage to be paid) may all be referable to the mutual love and affection of the parties and not specifically referable to the claimant's belief that she has an interest in the home."

Given that Lord Bridge spoke in terms of a "substantial change of position" as sufficient detriment it seems that Browne-Wilkinson's views should be preferred and that any conduct of the claimant should be taken into account when determining if there was detriment, not merely conduct referable to the property. However, although all varieties of conduct will be taken into account in assessing detriment a threshold must be exceeded so that conduct which is only "de minimis" will not amount to a "substantial change of position." On this basis Lord Bridge considered that even if there had been an express common intention Mrs Rosset's contributions to the work of renovating the house would have been insufficient to support a claim to a constructive trust.

(v) Quantifying the extent of the equitable interest arising under a constructive trust where there was an express common intention: In principle, where a constructive trust arises because of an express common intention between the parties' the claimant should be entitled to a share of the equitable ownership equivalent to that which it was

[37] *ibid.* at 132.

mutually intended they should enjoy. In this respect the decision of the Court of Appeal in *Eves v. Eves*,[38] a supposed paradigm of a constructive trust imposed because of an express common intention, is anomalous. All the indications were that the intention was that Janet should be named as a joint owner of the legal title, but it was held that she was only entitled to a quarter share of the equitable interest. Brightman L.J. expressed some doubts about this and seemed to prefer the view that she should be entitled to a half-share. In *Grant v. Edwards*[39] Browne-Wilkinson L.J. suggested that this anomaly could be explained by analogy with the law of proprietary estoppel, and it reflects Lord Denning's rejected concepts of the "new model" constructive trust.

(vi) Inferring a common intention from the parties' conduct: The absence of an express common intention between the parties' does not inevitably mean that there can be no constructive trust. As has already been noted the most difficult situations arise where the parties have given no direct consideration to their respective proprietary entitlements and have acted on the basis of assumptions and pre-conceptions derived from the nature of their relationship, which only become apparent when some difficulties arise between them. The courts have always been reluctant to infer merely from the facts that parties are in a relationship, whether marriage or of a quasi-matrimonial nature, that this inevitable involves an assumption that any land occupied should be jointly owned. Ownership of property is such a significantly more important entitlement than mere occupation that something beyond the ordinary course of human relationships has been expected. In *Pettitt v. Pettitt*[40] Lord Diplock stressed that a common intention of joint ownership is not to be inferred from the mere fact that the parties have done what spouses or partners would ordinarily do:

> "It is common enough nowadays for husbands and wives to decorate and to make improvements in the family home themselves, with no other intention than to indulge in what is now a popular hobby, and to make the home pleasanter for their common use and enjoyment. If the husband likes to occupy his leisure by laying a new lawn in the garden or building a fitted wardrobe in the bedroom while the wife does the shopping, cooks the family dinner or bathes the children, I, for my part, find it quite impossible to impute to them as reasonable husband and wife any common intention that these domestic activities or any of them are to have any effect upon the existing proprietary rights in the family home on which they are undertaken."

Although these sentiments may reflect a more traditional concept of the family and of family roles than is current today, the basic proposition remains valid that only exceptional conduct by a party will give rise to an inference of a common intention. In *Lloyd's Bank v. Rosset*[41] the House of Lords took the view that only substantial financial contributions to the purchase price of the property could be regarded as sufficient to raise an inference of a common intention. Lord Bridge explained:

> "In sharp contrast [with the case where there is an express common intention] is the very different one where there is no evidence to support a finding of an

[38] [1975] 1 W.L.R. 1338.
[39] [1986] Ch. 638 at 657–658.
[40] [1970] A.C. 777 at 826.
[41] [1991] 1 A.C. 132–3.

agreement or arrangement to share, however reasonable it might have been for the parties to reach such an arrangement if they had applied their minds to the question, and where the court must rely entirely on the conduct of the parties both as the basis from which to infer a common intention to share the property beneficially and as the conduct relied on to give rise to a constructive trust. In this situation direct contributions to the purchase price by the partner who is not the legal owner, whether initially or by payment of the mortgage instalments, will readily justify the inference necessary to the creation of a constructive trust. But, as I read the authorities, it is at least extremely doubtful whether anything less will do."

Thus it seems that non-financial contributions to a partnership, such as providing child care and looking after the house will alone be insufficient to give rise to a constructive trust. Contribution to house-keeping expenses which enabled the mortgage to be paid would be sufficient as a direct contribution to the purchase price. The House of Lords held that Mrs Rosset's conduct in decorating the house and supervising the work of the renovating builders was incapable of founding such an inference. As Lord Bridge commented, "on any view the monetary value of Mrs Rosset' work expressed as a contribution to a property acquired at a cost exceeding £70,000 must have been so trifling as to be almost de minimis." It also seems that there is no difficulty inferring a common intention from the parties' conduct even when there is evidence that the parties had had no intentions as to the ownership of the property. In *Midland Bank plc v. Cooke*[42] the evidence presented at trial by a husband and wife demonstrated that at the time that the matrimonial home was purchased in the husband's name there had been no discussions as to how the property should be owned beneficially. Counsel for the bank argued that since the parties had testified on oath that they had made no agreement then there was no scope for equity to make one for them. Waite L.J., giving the judgment of the court, dismissed this argument as counter to the very system of equity[43]:

> "It would be anomalous . . . to create a range of home-buyers who were beyond the pale of equity's assistance in formulating a fair presumed basis for sharing of beneficial title, simply because they had been honest enough to admit that they never gave ownership a thought or reached any agreement about it."

(vii) Distinguishing a constructive trust arising as a consequence of an inferred common intention from a resulting trust: Given that the decision of the House of Lords in *Lloyd's Bank v. Rosset* has effectively eliminated the possibility of finding a constructive trust in the absence of an express common intention if there was no direct financial contribution to the purchase of the property the question arises as to whether there is any substantive difference between a constructive trust where a common intention was inferred from a contribution to the purchase price and a resulting trust. Again, despite the superficial similarity of the two principles, both of which confer a beneficial interest in the land informally as a consequence of financial contribution, the

[42] [1995] 4 All E.R. 562.
[43] *ibid.* at 575.

two concepts are distinct. This is evident at the level of the quantification of the extent of the share of the equitable ownership which will be gained. Under a resulting trust the share is determined mathematically as proportion of the purchase price contributed. In the case of a constructive trust it is the inferred common intention which is given effect, and the share arising under the constructive trust may be far in excess of the relative proportion of the price contributed. This was recognised by Lord Bridge, who commented[44]:

> "It is significant to note that the shares to which the female partners in *Eves v. Eves* and *Grant v. Edwards* were held entitled were one quarter and one half respectively. In no sense could these shares have been regarded as proportionate to what the judge in the instant case described as the "qualifying contribution" in terms of the indirect contributions to the acquisition or enhancement of the value of the properties made by the female partners."

As has already been noted above this distinction is also evident in the case of *Midland Bank v. Cooke*[45] where a contribution to the purchase price would have entitled a wife to a 6.74 per cent share in the equitable ownership by way of a resulting trust but it was held that she was entitled to a half-share by way of a constructive trust.

(viii) Relevance of non-financial factors in determining the extent of an inferred common intention where some financial contribution has been made: Although *Lloyd's Bank v. Rosset*[46] seems to suggest that non-financial contributions can never be the basis of the inference of a common intention to share the ownership of land, this does not mean that they are irrelevant in determining what precisely the parties are believed to have intended when an intention to share the ownership to some extent can be inferred from financial contributions which were also made. This suggests that the need for a financial contribution operates as a trigger to establish a common intention to share the beneficial ownership, allowing the court to take account of such factors as the nature of their relationship when inferring the precise way that the land was to be shared between them. This approach was adopted by the Court of Appeal in *Midland Bank v. Cooke*.[47] As has already been noted the circumstances of the case were that Mrs Cooke had contributed 6.74 per cent of the purchase price of the matrimonial home in the form of her half-share of a wedding gift of £1,100 which Mr Cooke's parents had made to them jointly when they married. However, she argued that she was entitled to more than a mere 6.74 per cent share of the equitable ownership by way of a resulting trust, and claimed entitlement to a half share by way of a constructive trust arising from their common intention that they were to share the house equally. The evidence clearly failed to establish that there was an express common intention to share the ownership and on the principles of *Lloyd's Bank v. Rosset* this meant that Mrs Cooke would have to establish an inferred common intention that she was to be entitled to half the ownership of the house. The Court of Appeal held that her financial contribution was sufficient to infer the necessary

[44] *ibid.* at 133.
[45] [1995] 4 All E.R. 562.
[46] [1991] 1 A.C. 107.
[47] [1995] 4 All E.R. 562.

common intention, but went on to conclude that in assessing the extent of the interest she had been intended to enjoy all the circumstances should be taken into account. As Waite L.J. explained[48]:

> "The general principle to be derived from *Gissing v. Gissing* and *Grant v. Edwards* can in my judgment be summarised in this way. When the court is proceeding, in cases like the present where the partner without legal title has successfully asserted an equitable interest through direct contribution, to determine (in the absence of express evidence of intention) what proportions the parties must be assumed to have intended for their beneficial ownership, the duty of the judge is to undertake a survey of the whole course of dealing between the parties relevant to their ownership and occupation of the property and their sharing its burdens and advantages. That scrutiny will not confine itself to a limited range of acts of direct contribution of the sort that are needed to found a beneficial interest in the first place. It will take into consideration all conduct which throws light on the question what shares were intended. Only if that search proves inconclusive does the court fall back on the maxim that 'equality is equity'."

Having examined all the evidence of the parties' relationship the court concluded that their intention should be presumed to have been one to share the property equally. Waite L.J. pointed especially to the fact that she had looked after their children and maintained the property, contributed to household bills from her own salary and consented to a second mortgage of the house to guarantee her husband's business debts. He concluded:

> "One could hardly have a clearer example of a couple who had agreed to share everything equally: the profits of his business while it prospered, and the risks of indebtedness suffered through its failure; the upbringing of their children; the rewards of her own career as a teacher; and most relevantly, a home into which he put his savings and to which she was to give over the years the benefit of the maintenance and improvement contribution. When to all this there is added the fact (still an important one) that this was a couple who had chosen to introduce into their relationship the additional commitments which marriage involves, the conclusion becomes inescapable that their presumed intention was to share the beneficial interest in the property in equal shares."

(c) Criticism of the common intention constructive trust

Although in *Lloyd's Bank v. Rosset*[49] the House of Lords has clearly stated that a constructive trust will only arise where there is either an express or inferred common intention that the equitable ownership of land was to be shared, the principles identified can be subjected to a number of serious criticisms.

[48] *ibid.* at 574.
[49] [1991] 1 A.C. 107.

(i) The identification of common intention is artificial:[50] The very essence of the approach adopted in *Lloyd's Bank v. Rosset*, inherited from the earlier House of Lords' decision in *Gissing v. Gissing*,[51] that a constructive trust derives from the parties' intentions is highly artificial. This is true whether the intention is supposed to be express or implied. Lord Bridge described the cases of *Eves v. Eves*[52] and *Grant v. Edwards*[53] as "outstanding" examples where there had been an express common intention. However the reality of these cases is that there was no common intention at all as to sharing the ownership of the property. In each case the male partner had no intention of placing the house in joint names and provided a convenient excuse to their partners explaining why it would not be possible to do so. It may well be that they had misrepresented their intentions to their partners and given the impression that they intended to share the ownership of the house, but this can hardly be described as a "common" intention. A constructive trust was imposed in each case not because the man wanted his partner to enjoy a share of the ownership, but because she had acted to her detriment in circumstances where she believed that this was his intention. The true rationale for the imposition of the trust was therefore more akin to the principles of proprietary estoppel, where the key element is not a common intention, but a representation which was acted upon to the claimant's detriment. Where there is no express common intention the process of inferring an intention is even less authentic. The court is engaged in a process of creative assessment of the parties' desires and to suggest that the court is fulfilling what they would have wanted is entirely false. The artificiality is disclosed by the conflicting statements of the Court of Appeal in *Midland Bank v. Cooke*.[54] At different points in the judgment Waite L.J. describes the parties as having "never given ownership a thought" and yet finds that "their presumed intention was to share the beneficial ownership in the property in equal shares." This emphasis on the "presumption" of their intention makes clear what is really happening. The court is involved in a process of inventing a "common intention" in order to justify a conclusion that a person is entitled to a share of the equitable ownership. What has caused most difficulty is the question what factors should be taken into account in determining when a person should be entitled to such an interest and the extent to which non-financial contributions to the partnership of the parties should be sufficient to give rise to ownership of the land. Although this debate has occurred under the rubric of the supposed "common intention" the court could have imposed exactly the same limitation, in other words that in the absence of any relevant financial contributions a party cannot be entitled to a share of the equitable interest in the absence of an express declaration of trust, as a matter of policy. This would have been a more honest approach, which avoided the inherent uncertainty of the "new model" constructive trust and also the mystique of the language of common intention.

(ii) A financial contribution is essential to founding a claim to a constructive trust where there is no express common intention: The practical effect of the decision in *Lloyd's Bank v. Rosset* is that a person who has made no financial contribution at all to the purchase or upkeep of land will be unable to claim entitlement to a share of the

[50] See: (1993) 109 L.Q.R. 263 (S. Gardener).
[51] [1971] A.C. 886.
[52] [1975] 1 W.L.R. 1383.
[53] [1986] Ch. 638.
[54] [1995] 4 All E.R. 562.

equitable ownership unless they can establish an express common intention on the evidence. For example, a woman who moves in with a man, who does not work but who looks after the house and garden, who does a substantial amount of renovation work with materials provided by her partner, and who bears and brings up their children over many years, will be unable to establish a constructive trust. Even though everything about their relationship may suggest an intention to share this will not be sufficient if they never articulated that intention and the hurdle of the financial contribution cannot be overcome. In contrast it is clear that once the financial hurdle is overcome the court is free to examine all the details of the parties' relationship to indicate the extent of the share of ownership the court is prepared to presume was intended. It is this inconsistency of approach between a case where there is no financial contribution such as *Rosset* itself and where there is a relatively insignificant financial contribution such as in *Midland Bank v. Cooke* which calls into question the logic and fairness of the principles developed. It might be thought that in a modern age where the relative contributions of parties to relationships are not judged by society in purely economic and monetary terms, that non-financial contribution should be placed on a par with financial contributions for the purpose of a presumption of a common intention from which a constructive trust can be derived. However, before the approach of English law is too quickly dismissed it should be noted that non-financial contributions may be sufficient to establish an entitlement by way of the complimentary and parallel principles of proprietary estoppel.

(d) Commonwealth approaches to constructive trusts of land

Whilst English law has adopted a relatively restrictive approach to constructive trusts of land, similar difficulties of determining when an interest in a share of the ownership of land should arise informally have been addressed by other commonwealth jurisdictions. Generally they have adopted more flexible approaches, but essentially they have had to grapple with the same problems, namely: the relevance of the parties' intentions; the extent to which non-financial contributions should give rise to an interest in the land; and the extent to which any equitable interest in the land arise by right or from an exercise of the court's discretion.

(i) Canada: The Canadian courts have moved furthest from the traditional intention based constructive trust and have developed the concept of the constructive trust as a means of effecting restitution by reversing an unjust enrichment. In order to establish a constructive trust a person is required to demonstrate that the legal owner of the land had been enriched in a way which meant that they had experienced a corresponding deprivation.[55] For example in *Sorochan v. Sorochan*[56] it was held that there was an enrichment and deprivation where a man and woman lived together for 42 years jointly working a farm which was owned at law by the man. He was held to have enjoyed the benefit of her years of labour in the farm and home. Similarly in *Peter v. Beblow*[57] a man was held to have been enriched when the woman he lived with had acted as a house-keeper, home-maker and step-mother. Once enrichment is established the claimant will be entitled to a constructive trust in the absence of any "juristic reason

[55] See: *Pettkus v. Becker* (1980) 117 D.L.R. (3d) 257.
[56] (1986) 29 D.L.R. (4th) 1.
[57] (1993) 101 D.L.R. (4th) 621.

for the enrichment." This means that there must be no reason why the claimant would have conferred the enrichment without a reasonable expectation of retaining the benefit of it. The Canadian approach is different to that adopted in England in three major respects. First, it adopts a more positive attitude towards non-financial contributions to family life, such as house-keeping and child-rearing, which can constitute an enrichment calling for restitution but would not support the finding an inferred common intention under the principles of *Lloyd's Bank v. Rosset*. Secondly, once it is established that there is an enrichment which calls for restitution the appropriate remedy is a matter for the court's discretion. The court may award a constructive trust, as for example in *Sorochan v. Sorochan* where it was felt that a third share of the farm was appropriate, or alternatively a lesser remedy such as monetary compensation. Thirdly, if a constructive trust interest is awarded it does not necessarily affect other third party rights in the land since it does arise until granted by the court.

(ii) Australia: The Australian courts initially adopted the common intention constructive trust[58] but now justify the imposition of constructive trusts on the grounds of "unconscionability." The essence of a constructive trust imposed under this principle was explained by Deane J. in *Muschinski v. Dodds*[59] as a "remedial institution which equity imposes regardless of actual or presumed intention . . . to preclude the retention or assertion of beneficial ownership to property to the extent that such retention or assertion would be contrary to equitable principle." The main advantage of this approach over the English approach is that it abandons the need to find any intention, reducing the degree of artificiality in rationalising the imposition of a trust. For example, in *Baumgartner v. Baumgartner*[60] the majority of the High Court held that a trust should be imposed in favour of a woman who had lived with a man even where there was no common intention because the pooling of their financial resources meant that it would be unconscionable for him to claim that the house was his sole property. Again, because the constructive trust is imposed by the court rather than arising from the parties' intentions it is open to the court to determine if it should take effect retrospectively or only from the date of the judgment.

(iii) New Zealand: The New Zealand courts also began by adopting the common intention approach[61] but have more recently justified the imposition of constructive trusts on the basis of the fulfilment of the parties' "reasonable expectations". In *Gillies v. Keogh*[62] Cooke P. regarded supposed common intentions as fictitious, and held instead that the parties reasonable expectations should be construed from their conduct. Relevant factors in determining a reasonable expectation might include the length of the parties' relationship and the value of their contributions, whether financial or non-financial. The court is therefore involved in the process of objectively deciding whether conduct like that of the parties should give rise to a reasonable expectation of a share of the ownership of the land. If the legal owner has made clear that the other party would not obtain an interest in the land then the court will not find that conduct was based on a reasonable expectation since it was done in the full knowledge that no ownership was intended to be gained thereby. For this reason, the

[58] *Allen v. Snyder* [1977] 2 N.S.W.L.R. 685; *Baumgartner v. Baumgartner* (1987) 164 C.L.R. 137.
[59] (1985) 160 C.L.R. 583.
[60] (1987) 164 C.L.R. 137.
[61] *Hayward v. Giordani* [1983] N.Z.L.R. 140.
[62] [1991] 2 N.Z.L.R. 327.

Court of Appeal held that a man who had moved in with a woman who subsequently purchased a house in her sole name and who indicated throughout the relationship that she regarded it as hers, did not have a reasonable expectation that by contributing to household expenses and improvements he would gain a share of the ownership.

(iv) Summary: Although these four jurisdictions have reached such varied solutions to the problem of the creation of informal trust interests in land, it should be noted that they are all attempting to wrestle with the same difficulties. None have been attracted by the idea of a wide discretion of the court to impose a trust on the basis of simple justice and have sought to establish criteria by which a situation where a constructive trust is justified can be differentiated from one where it is not, whether by the demonstration of a "common intention", an "enrichment" or an "expectation." In the application of all these criteria the parties' thinking remains relevant, and it may simply be that the commonwealth approaches have avoided the artificial language of a real or presumed "common intention" with terminology that confronts the reality that the court is objectively assessing whether any share of the ownership of the land should arise in the circumstances rather than disguising it as an attempt to identify whether the parties subjectively wanted such an interest to arise. For this reason in *Gillies v. Keogh*[63] Cooke P. suggested that it may make little difference which analysis is adopted:

> "Normally it makes no practical difference in the results whether one talks of constructive trust, unjust enrichment, imputed common intention or estoppel. In deciding whether any of these are established it is necessary to take into account the same factors."

The main difference between the English and Commonwealth approaches is not so much as to the circumstances in which a constructive trust can arise, but as to the nature of the remedy. The English concept is of an institutional constructive trust, in the sense that the equitable trust interest arises in favour of the beneficiaries as of right from the facts. The claimant's beneficial entitlement arises at the very moment in time that there was a common intention, so that the court is merely recognising the existence of the interest not awarding it as a remedy. In consequence the beneficial interest may affect the rights of third parties acquired subsequent to the creation of the constructive trust but prior to the date of the court's judgment recognising its existence. In contrast the commonwealth cases adopt a more remedial approach so that the award of a share of the equitable ownership is only one of a range of potential remedies which may be awarded by the court and the court has the discretion to determine whether a beneficial interest, if awarded, should take precedence over other third party rights in the land. To this extent these approaches to the constructive trust are a synthesis of the English principles of constructive trusts and proprietary estoppel. Although at present these doctrines are theoretically distinct and difference requirement must be met for each there is increasing evidence of an awareness of substantial overlap both in theory and practice by the courts, and it is conceivable that in future the whole of English law in this area will develop in a manner more consistent with the commonwealth approaches.

[63] [1991] 2 N.Z.L.R. 327.

ASSIGNMENT OF THE BENEFICIARIES EQUITABLE INTERESTS

1 The beneficiaries' right to deal with their equitable ownership

Where a person is entitled to a beneficial interest under a trust, whether it has arisen under an express, resulting or constructive trust, they have an interest in the land which they are able to deal with as they choose. For example they may use it as security to raise a loan by way of a mortgage. Alternatively, they have the ability to transfer their entitlement to someone else by way of an assignment. For example, if Brian holds land on trust for Charlotte and David, David is able to transfer his equitable interest in the land subject to the trust to Elizabeth. This process has exactly the same effect as a transfer of a legal estate in the land, so that Elizabeth will take David's place and Brian will henceforth hold the land on trust for Charlotte and Elizabeth. Similarly, if Brian held land on trust for Charlotte for life, with remainder to David, Charlotte could transfer her equitable life interest to Elizabeth. In such a case Elizabeth would enjoy the rights of Charlotte in the land as her substitute, so that the interest would continue until the death of Charlotte. Such an interest is known as an interest *pur autre vie* since it is coterminous with the life of someone other than the person who enjoys the interest. Alternatively, David could transfer his remainder interest to Elizabeth, so that on the death of Charlotte she became entitled to the unencumbered freehold interest in the land.

2 Formalities necessary for assignment

(a) Assignment by appropriately signed writing

A beneficial interest under a trust can only be effectively transferred if the appropriate formalities for an assignment are observed. Section 53(1)(c) of the Law of Property Act 1925 provides that:

> "a disposition of an equitable interest or trust subsisting at the time of the disposition, must be in writing signed by the person disposing of the same, or by his agent thereunto lawfully authorised in writing or by will."

If the assignment is not made by appropriately signed writing any purported transfer will be void and of no effect. For example, if David merely states orally that he is transferring his equitable interest to Elizabeth this will have no effect and David will remain the beneficiary of the trust.

(b) A specifically enforceable contract to assign?

Where there is a trust of personal property and a beneficiary enters into a purely oral contract to assign their interest, it has been held that the interest passes from the assignor to the assignee by means of a constructive trust if the contract was specifically enforceable.[64] However, such a result is impossible in relation to a trust of land

[64] See: *Oughtred v. IRC* [1960] A.C. 206; *Re Holt's Settlement* [1969] 1 Ch. 100; *Neville v. Wilson* [1996] 3 All E.R. 171.

because the contract to assign would have to comply with the formalities' requirements for contracts for the sale or disposition of an interest in land. By Law of Property (Miscellaneous Provisions) Act 1925, s.2 such contracts must be "made in writing" which is signed "by or on behalf of each party to the contract." Inevitably such a contract would itself satisfy the requirement of Law of Property Act 1925, s.53(1)(c) for a valid assignment.

PRIORITY AND EQUITABLE OWNERSHIP

1 Balancing the rights of beneficiaries against the rights of third parties acquiring a legal estate of the land held on trust

Where land is held on trust the legal interest from which the equitable ownership behind the trust is carved out is held by the trustees.[65] By virtue of this the trustees are capable of transferring the legal interest in the land to third parties, even though this might be in breach of trust. For example, if Tim and Tina hold the leasehold interest in a house on trust for Una and Violet, they could transfer the legal lease to William. In such circumstances the central question is whether Una and Violet's beneficial interests in the land would be binding on William, or whether he has taken the land free from their equitable interests so that their continued occupation would be inconsistent with his ownership. This question is of prime interest to Una and Violet irrespective of any remedies that they may have against Tim and Tina for breach of trust. Traditionally the problem of priorities was governed by the doctrine of notice, so that William would take the land subject to Una and Violet's equitable interests if he had purchased the land with knowledge, either actual, constructive or imputed, of its existence. However, the system governing priorities introduced in the reforms of 1925 also had as a prime objective facilitating dealings with the legal title to land, and introduced a mechanism by which purchasers such as William could ensure that they would take the land free from the equitable trusts interests of beneficiaries, whether they knew about them of not. This mechanism is called overreaching, and where issues of priority arise in relation to equitable trusts interests the question of first importance is whether they have been overreached.

2 Overreaching of equitable ownership

(a) The essence of overreaching

The essence of the mechanism of overreaching is that where a legal estate in land subject to equitable trusts interests is sold, the trust interests are preserved but the subject matter of the trust experiences a substitution. Whereas before a sale of the legal estate in the land the beneficiaries enjoyed their interests in the land, after the sale they are deemed to no longer enjoy any interests in the land itself because all their

[65] With the exception of a strict settlement where the legal title is held by the tenant for life: see Chap. 9, below.

entitlement is transferred to the purchase money which was realised by the sale. For example, if Una and Violet enjoyed equal beneficial interests in a leasehold property held on trust by Tim and Tina, and the trustees sold the legal estate to William, Una and Violet would no longer enjoy any entitlements to the land itself and William would be the unencumbered legal owner thereof. However, their equitable interests would continue to subsist over the purchase money that William had paid. Tom and Tina would hold that money on trust for them equally. Similarly, if their original interests in the land had been unequal, so that Una was entitled to a third interest and Violet to a two-thirds interest, then those identical interests would be preserved in the purchase money. By means of such overreaching the twin objectives of protection of the beneficiaries' interests and efficient dealing with the legal title of land are achieved.

(b) Requirements for overreaching

Overreaching does not occur in every situation where a third party acquires the legal title of land held on trust from the trustees. Section 2 of the Law of Property Act 1925, as amended by the Trusts of Land and Appointment of Trustees Act 1996, lays down a number of criteria which must be satisfied.

(i) Interests capable of being overreached: By section 2(1)(ii) only those interests which are "capable of being overreached" can be overreached. Section 3 lists certain equitable interests which are incapable of being overreached and the net effect of this provision is that equitable trusts interests can be overreached.

(ii) Purchaser of a legal estate in the land: Section 2(1) makes clear that overreaching can only operate where there is a conveyance of a legal estate in the land to a purchaser. This will also include a legal mortgagee of the land.

(iii) Payment of the purchase moneys to two trustees: Although the Court of Appeal held in *State Bank of India v. Sood*[66] that overreaching can take place even when a conveyance of an appropriate legal estate in the land does not give rise to any capital moneys, if a conveyance does give rise to such capital money overreaching will only occur if it is applied in accordance with the statutory requirements. Section 2(1)(ii) provides that overreaching will only take place if: ". . . the requirements of section 27 of this Act respecting the payment of capital money arising on such a conveyance are complied with." Section 27 requires that proceeds of sale be paid to two trustees, or to a trust corporation. This is the most important limitation to the operation of overreaching and is intended to provide the beneficiaries with some protection, on the basis that whereas it would be easy for a sole trustee to act in fraud of the beneficiaries it is less likely, though not impossible, that two trustees will agree to act against the interests of the beneficiaries. Where a third party seeks to acquire a legal estate in land they can only be sure that they will take it free from any trust interests affecting it if they pay over their purchase money to at least two trustees. In other circumstances they should be more careful to ensure for themselves that there are no trust interests which might adversely affect them, since they will not enjoy the automatic protection of overreaching.

(iv) Notice irrelevant: Section 2(1) specifically states that overreaching takes place in favour of a purchaser "whether or not he has notice" of the relevant trust interests. Where the purchaser pays two trustees it is entirely irrelevant that he was fully aware

[66] [1997] 1 All E.R. 169.

that there were beneficiaries with equitable interests in the land, and he will take free from them.

(c) Effect of overreaching

Where overreaching of a beneficiaries' interests has occurred, they no longer retain any interests in the land at all. The purchaser of the legal estate will take the land absolutely free from it and the beneficiaries' rights and remedies will lie only against the trustees who had held the land on trust for them. In the context of registered land it is irrelevant whether the beneficiaries had protected their interests as minor interests on the register and in *City of London Building Society v. Flegg*[67] the House of Lords made clear that if the rights of a beneficiary were overreached they were no longer capable of forming the subject matter of an overriding interest under Land Registration Act 1925, s.70(1)(g), so that even the interests of a beneficiary in occupation of the land would be defeated if overreached.[68]

3 Priority of equitable ownership which has not been overreached

(a) Overreaching has not taken place

Although overreaching is such a powerful mechanism for the defeat of equitable beneficial interests in land, it will only occur if the relevant statutory criteria are met. The most common circumstances in which overreaching will not have taken place is when the land is held on trust by a sole trustee, and as a consequence the purchaser of a legal estate has not paid over the purchase money to two trustees for sale. This has been particularly common where a trust of a matrimonial or family home has arisen by means of a constructive or resulting trust, and the legal title is held by a man alone and his wife or partner is entitled to a share of the equitable ownership. In such cases issues of priority are resolved according to the ordinary rules relevant to the type of land which is in issue. These are discussed more fully at the end of the book, but for convenience are summarised here.

(b) Priority where equitable ownership of registered land has not been overreached

(i) Protection of beneficial interests as minor interests: Where a person is entitled to a share of the equitable ownership of land behind a trust their interest ranks as a minor interest and should be appropriately protected against the title to which it relates. In the event that it is not protected then sections 20(1) and 59(6) of the Land Registration Act 1925 have the effect that someone who acquires a legal estate in the land for valuable consideration will take the land free from it. The operation of the rules governing minor interests are considered in detail in Chapter 15 below.

(ii) Beneficial interests can also rank as overriding interests: Even where a beneficial interest in the equitable ownership of land has not been appropriately protected as a minor interest it may rank as an overriding interest and therefore bind a person acquiring a legal estate in the land despite the absence of protection. This possibility arises because Land Registration Act 1925, s.70(1)(g) provides that the "rights of every

[67] [1988] A.C. 54.
[68] See also: *State Bank of India v. Sood* [1997] 1 All E.R. 169.

person in actual occupation of the land or in receipt of the rents and profits thereof" are overriding interests and will bind a third party acquiring a legal estate in the land unless an appropriate enquiry was made of the beneficiary in occupation and the existence of their beneficial interest was not disclosed. In *Williams and Glynn's Bank v. Boland*[69] the House of Lords importantly held that a wife's beneficial interest in her matrimonial home was capable of binding a bank who had taken a mortgage from her husband, who was the sole legal owner, as an overriding interest even though it had not been protected as a minor interest. The rights of beneficiaries in occupation of the land will therefore enjoy priority unless they have been overreached.[70]

(c) Priority where equitable ownership of unregistered land has not been overreached

Where unregistered land is held on trust and a third party acquires a legal estate in circumstances in which they have not been overreached, the issue of priority will be determined by the doctrine of notice. If the third party had notice, either actual, constructive or imputed, of the existence of the beneficiary's interest then he will take the land subject to it. Only if he had no notice will he take the land free from the beneficial interest which has not been overreached. The operation of these principles can be seen in *Kingsnorth Finance Company v. Tizard*[71] where it was held that a bank which had taken a mortgage over a matrimonial home, legal title to which was owned solely by the husband, took subject to the wife's beneficial interest in circumstances where they were affixed with constructive notice because they had failed to make an adequate inspection for third party rights of the land.

[69] [1981] A.C. 487.
[70] *City of London Building Society v. Flegg* [1988] A.C. 54.
[71] [1986] 1 W.L.R. 783.

Chapter 7

Co-ownership

Introduction to Co-ownership

1 The meaning of co-ownership

Although there are many situations where a person is the sole owner of land and no other individual has any ownership rights in it, a more complex form of ownership is often required. For example, where a couple who are either married or living together purchase a house in which to live it is unlikely that they intend that only one of them will be the owner of the house. Instead they intend to share the ownership so that they are both owners of it at the same time. Such rights are described as concurrent since they exist at the same time. In English land law all forms of concurrent sharing of land ownership can only take place behind a trust of the land. As has been seen in the previous chapter a trust is in essence a relationship which involves a separation of the legal title to the land which is held by the trustees, from the equitable, or beneficial, interest which is enjoyed by the beneficiaries. Although it is possible for the ownership of the legal title to be shared between a number of persons, so that there will be multiple trustees, the reality of co-ownership takes place in relation to the beneficial interest, since the beneficiaries are the true owners of the land. The purpose of this chapter is to examine the means by which co-ownership may be effected, and in particular the forms of co-ownership which are possible and the relationship between the trustees of the legal title and the beneficiaries, and between the co-owning beneficiaries themselves.

2 Forms of Co-ownership

English law recognises two forms of co-ownership, a joint tenancy and a tenancy in common.[1] Although both of these forms of co-ownership facilitate sharing of the

[1] Two other forms of co-ownership which were recognised in English land law are now virtually irrelevant. Tenancy by entireties was effectively abolished by the Law of Property Act 1925 which converted all such existing tenancies into conventional joint tenancies. Coparcenary, a form of joint tenancy without the operation of the principle of survivorship, is almost extinct since it will only arise where land subject to a fee tail is inherited by female heirs.

ownership of land they are essentially different in terms of the conception of the nature of the rights that are conferred on the co-owners.

(a) Joint tenancy

(i) Nature of a joint tenancy: Where co-ownership exists in the form of a joint tenancy all the co-owners are regarded as being wholly entitled to the whole of the property that is co-owned. In the case of land this means that each of the joint tenants is regarded as simultaneously owning the whole of the land concerned and that they cannot be regarded as holding specific shares of the property. For example, if Kate and Martin are the joint tenant of a cottage it is not appropriate to regard them as each owning a half-share of it. Whether they have contributed equally to the purchase price of the cottage or not, if they have expressly taken the land as joint tenant they are each as much entitled to the whole of the cottage as the other. If the question was to be asked "who owns the cottage?" the appropriate answer would be that Kate owns the whole of the cottage and that Martin also owns the whole of the cottage at one and the same time. Expressed negatively there is no part of the cottage that they do not each completely own. The essence of a joint tenancy was expressed by Lord Browne-Wilkinson in *Hammersmith L.B.C. v. Monk*[2] where he stated that: "In property law, a transfer of land to two or more persons jointly operates so as to make them, vis-à-vis the outside world, one single owner."

(ii) The four unities: A joint tenancy will only exist if what are described as the four unities are present.[3] If any of the essential unities are absent the parties cannot properly be said to be wholly entitled to the whole of the land. *Unity of possession* means simply that the co-owners must be entitled to possess the whole of the co-owned land, and that no joint tenant is entitled to exclude the others from possession of any part thereof.[4] Returning to the example of Kate and Martin introduced above, there would be no unity of possession, and therefore no joint tenancy, if Kate was entitled to exclude Martin from the first floor of the cottage and Martin was entitled to exclude Kate from the lounge. Although unity of possession may subsequently be qualified by the intervention of the court, often because of a breakdown of the relationship between the co-owners, it is an essential prerequisite at the outset of co-ownership by joint tenants. *Unity of interest* requires that the joint tenants must have identical interests in the land. For example, if Kate was the freehold owner of the land and Martin was entitled to a 99-year lease they could not be joint tenants. Similarly if Martin was the freehold owner but Kate was only entitled to a life interest. *Unity of title* means that the joint tenants must derive their identical interests in the land by an identical means, through the same act or document — for example, if they have derived title by the same act of adverse possessions from a single conveyance. *Unity of time* requires that the interests of the joint tenants must have been acquired by them at the same time.

(iii) Survivorship: The most important practical difference between a joint tenancy and a tenancy in common is that the principle of survivorship operates between co-owners who are joint-tenants. The essence of survivorship is that when one of the joint

[2] [1992] 1 A.C. 478 at 492.

[3] *AG Securities v. Vaughan* [1990] 1 A.C. 417.

[4] See: *Wiseman v. Simpson* [1988] 1 W.L.R. 35 at 42 *per* Ralph Gibson LJ; *Meyer v. Riddick* (1990) 60 P. & C.R. 50.

tenant dies any interest he enjoyed over the land under the joint tenancy automatically passes to the remaining joint tenants. This is a logical consequence of the fact that all the joint tenants are regarded as being wholly entitled to the whole of the land. In a sense when one of the joint tenants dies the extent of the interest of the others in relation to the land remains unchanged. They are entitled to no more than they were entitled to before the death of the joint tenant, namely the whole of the land. The main impact of the principle of survivorship is that a joint tenant who dies is incapable of disposing of his interest in the land by means of a will. Nor, if he dies intestate, will those entitled under the rules of intestacy succeed to his interest. For example, if Kate was to die leaving a will stating that she wanted her sister Naomi to inherit her interest in the cottage co-owned with Martin as joint tenants, Naomi would gain no interest in the cottage since survivorship would operate between Kate and Martin and he would be left as the sole owner of the cottage. One potential problem with the operation of survivorship has been anticipated by statute, namely how to determine the order of death where joint tenants have died in circumstances where it is impossible to tell which has died first. For example, if Martin and Kate were to be killed instantly in a car crash, would the cottage pass under the will of Kate or Martin as the survivor? Section 184 of the Law of Property Act 1925 adopts the somewhat arbitrary solution that where "two or more persons have died in circumstances rendering it uncertain which of them survived the other or others" it shall be presumed that the elder died first and the younger survived them. Thus if Kate were six months younger than Martin she would be deemed to have survived him and the cottage would pass to the beneficiaries indicated in her will or to her heirs at law if she died intestate.

(iv) Severance: Where property is co-owned by means of a joint tenancy a tenant can effectively separate his interest from that of the other joint tenants by means of severance. Severance has the effect that his interest in the land is transformed from entitlement to the whole of the land to a notional share of the ownership. For example if Martin decided to sever the joint tenancy he enjoyed of the cottage with Kate, his interest would be transformed into a half share of the land as a tenant in common. Inevitably as the only other joint tenant Kate's interest would also become a half share as a tenant in common by process of elimination. However, if there are more than two joint tenants only the person whose severs his interest will become a tenant in common and the others will remain joint tenants. For example, if Martin and Kate had purchased the cottage along with his parents, Olive and Peter, as joint tenants and Martin subsequently severed his interest, he would become a tenant in common of a quarter share of the cottage and Kate, Olive and Peter would remain joint tenants of the remaining three-quarters. Once a joint tenant has severed their interest the principle of survivorship no longer operates in relation to their own interest as a tenant in common, nor do they retain any right to benefit from the operation of the right of survivorship between the remaining joint tenants. Therefore, if Olive and Peter were killed in a plane crash Kate would take their interests by way of survivorship and she would be entitled to three-quarters interest as a tenant in common and Martin would still only be entitled to the quarter share he previously severed.

(b) Tenancy in common

(i) Entitled to shares in the land: Unlike a joint tenancy a person who enjoys an interest in property as a tenant in common is not regarded as enjoying the ownership of the entirety of it. Instead they are regarded as enjoying a notional share of the ownership which is owned by them and by them alone. As has been noted if Martin and Karen were joint tenants of the cottage they would be entitled to a half share each. It should be noted that there is no requirement that the shares of the tenants in common must be equal in proportion.

(ii) Shares are undivided: Although tenants in common can be regarded as owning separate shares in the land this does not mean that the land can be divided physically between them in proportion to their shares. The shares exist only in relation to the metaphysically abstract ownership of the land and not in the physical land itself. For example, Martin and Kate as tenants in common of half shares in the cottage cannot then divide the property in two, so that Kate can claim the lounge, bathroom and back bedroom exclusively and Martin the dining room, kitchen and front bedroom. It would not be possible for Kate to maintain an action of trespass against Martin if he were to attempt to make use of the bathroom! The undivided nature of the shares and inability to physically demarcate the land follows from the fact that *unity of possession* remains a necessary requirement of a tenancy in common, thus entitling the tenants in common to possession of every part of the land. This entitlement to universal possession applies irrespective of the size of the share owned. For example, a tenant in common with a tenth share of land is as much entitled to possession of the whole of the land as the tenant in common owning the remaining nine tenths.

(iii) No survivorship: As has been noted the principle of survivorship has no application between persons who are tenants in common. Their respective shares will not pass automatically to the other tenants on death and can instead be effectively disposed of by will or in the event of intestacy will pass to the persons thereon entitled.

Co-ownership of the Legal Title of Land

1 When co-ownership of the legal title arises

Co-ownership of the legal title of land will arise if a legal estate in land, whether freehold or leasehold, is acquired by more than one person. This will occur if the land is conveyed into the name of more than one person, or if it is acquired by more than one person as adverse possessors.

2 Form of co-ownership of the legal title to land

Historically, the legal title to land could be co-owned both in the form of a joint tenancy or a tenancy in common. The availability of multiple forms of co-ownership of the legal title, coupled with the possibility of an unlimited number of legal owners, caused severe problems in conveyancing practice. If the legal title was owned only by joint tenants it would only be necessary to investigate the title of one of the joint tenants, since the presence of the four unities would mean that the titles of the other joint tenant could then be relied on as well. However, since the four unities would not necessarily be present between tenants in common it would be necessary to investigate the quality of title of each and every one of them, which could prove a long and laborious process. In order to eliminate such problems and to introduce a more straightforward system of ownership the property legislation of 1925 provides that the legal title of land can only ever be held by co-owners as joint tenants. Section 1(6) of the Law of Property Act 1925 provides that: "A legal estate in land is not capable of subsisting or of being created in an undivided share in land. . . ."[5]

3 Severance of a joint tenancy of the legal title?

It follows logically from this policy that where a valid joint tenancy of the legal title of land has been created the joint tenants cannot sever their interests to give rise to a tenancy in common. Such a possibility is expressly prevented by Law of Property Act 1925, s.36(2) which provides that: "No severance of a joint tenancy of the legal estate, so as to create a tenancy in common of land, shall be permissible, whether by operation of law or otherwise . . ." This does not, however, prevent a joint tenant of the legal title releasing his interest to the other joint tenants and dropping out of the legal ownership of the land.

4 A maximum number of co-owners of the legal title

As well as preventing a tenancy in common of the legal title of land the legislation of 1925 removed a further obstacle to efficient conveyancing by limiting the number of persons who may hold the legal ownership as joint tenants. Section 34(2) of the Trustee Act 1925 provides that where the legal title to land is conveyed to more than four persons as joint tenants "the four first named (who are able and willing to act) shall alone be the trustees."[6] Therefore if land was transferred to Albert, Brian, Charlotte, David, Erica and Fatima only Albert, Brian, Charlotte and David would take the legal title. Although Erica and Fatima could be appointed a trustee as a replacement for the others if a vacancy was to occur, they will not automatically succeed to a position of trusteeship if such a vacancy does arise, for example by the death of one of the trustees. It is important to note that although there can only be a maximum of four joint tenants of the legal title there is no limit to the number of persons who can share entitlement to the equitable interest.

5 Joint tenants of the legal title as trustees for the beneficial owners of the land

Whenever there is a multiple ownership of the legal title to land it is inevitable that there will be a trust and that the joint tenants of the legal title will be holding the land as trustees for the benefit of the beneficiaries. As such they enjoy the powers conferred on trustees of land as well as the obligations arising thereby. The nature of the trustees' powers and duties will be considered below in the context of the relationship between the trustees and beneficiaries of a trust of land.[7]

[5] See also, s.34(1) of the Law of Property Act 1925.
[6] See also, s.34(2) of the Law of Property Act 1925.
[7] See pp. 236 *et seq.*

Joint Tenancy or Tenancy in Common in Equity

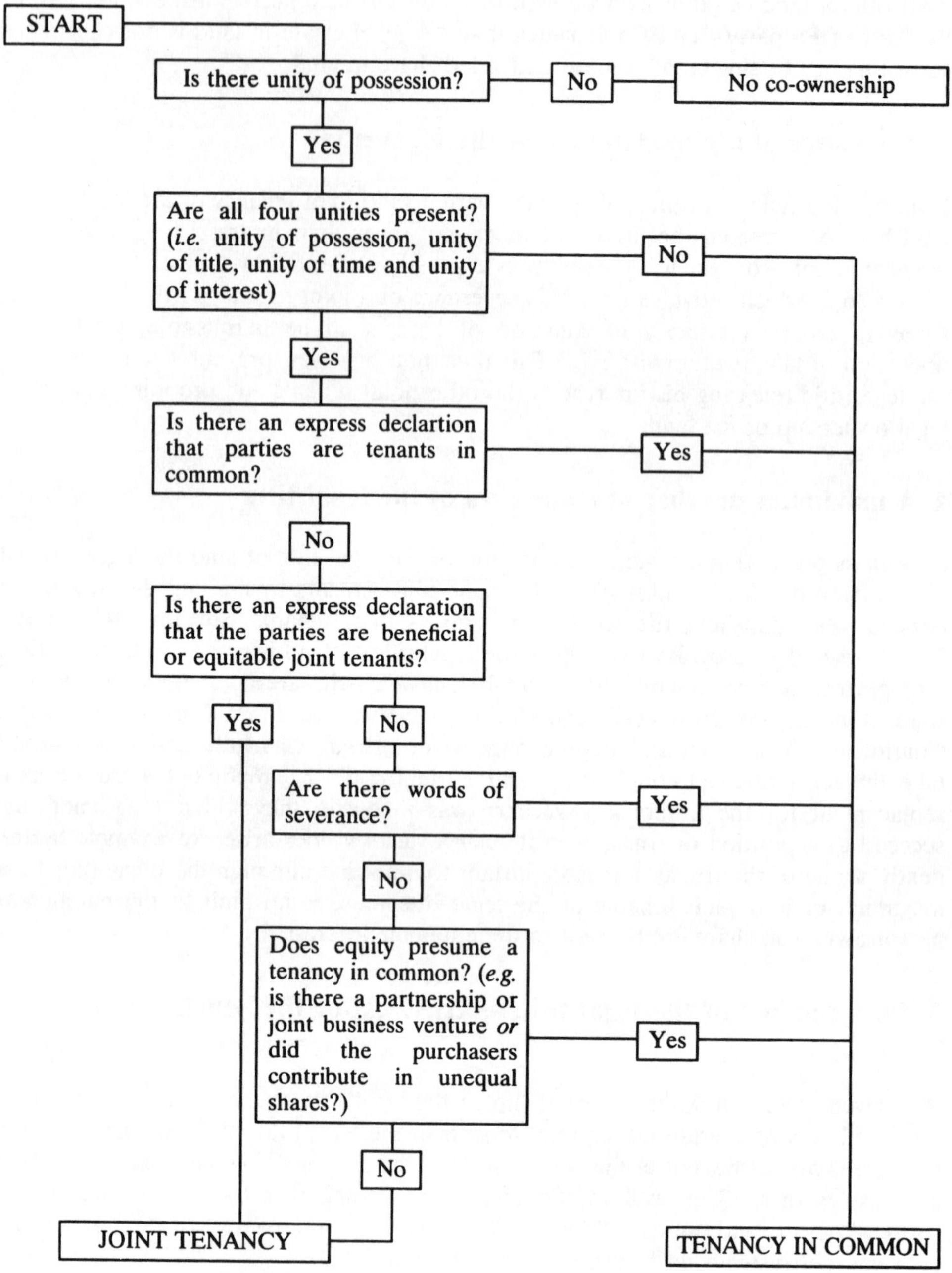

CO-OWNERSHIP IN EQUITY

1 Determining the nature of the beneficial interests of a trust of land

Irrespective of whether the legal title of land is held by a sole trustee or by a number of trustees as joint tenants it is necessary to identify who is entitled to the beneficial interest in the land so held. Three important questions have to be addressed. First, who are the beneficiaries of the trust? Secondly, whether the beneficiaries enjoy their interests as joint tenants or as tenants in common. Thirdly, if they are tenants in common, what is the extent of their respective shares in the land. Although the general principles which address these questions are straightforward, complex arrangements are possible, so that there may at one and the same time be some beneficiaries who enjoy their interests as joint tenants and others who are tenants in common. As a starting point it is necessary to distinguish between trusts which have been expressly created by the parties and those which arise informally, whether as resulting or constructive trusts.

2 Co-ownership under an express trust

(a) *Absolute freedom to define the beneficial entitlements of the co-owners*

Where a trust of land is created expressly by the party or parties competent to create it, it is open to them to define the extent of the entitlement of the beneficiaries, both in regard to whether they are to be joint tenants or tenants in common, and if they are tenants in common the proportions of their shares. Such an express stipulation of the nature of the parties' interests will take priority over any implication which could be drawn from the facts as to the nature of their co-ownership. This was confirmed by the Court of Appeal in *Goodman v. Gallant*[8] where it held that an express declaration of the beneficial interest in land was exhaustive and conclusive of the position and left no room for the doctrines of resulting or constructive trusts to be invoked. As has been noted in the previous chapter a declaration of a trust of land will only be enforceable if the necessary formalities have been observed, namely that the declaration is evidenced in writing.[9]

(b) *Declaration of a trust of land by the existing legal owner*

A trust of land may be created by the person who is already the legal owner. For example, if Kate is the sole legal owner of a cottage and then decides that when Martin moves in with her she wants him to enjoy a share of the ownership she can declare a trust of the cottage in their joint favour. If she declares that they are to enjoy the cottage jointly then the consequence will be that she will hold the legal title for them as joint tenants of the beneficial interest. Only if she makes clear in her declaration that they are to enjoy specific shares of the ownership will such a declaration be construed as giving rise to an express tenancy in common. For example, if she were to declare

[8] [1986] 1 All E.R. 311.
[9] Law of Property Act 1925, s.53(1)(b).

that Martin was to enjoy a half-share in the cottage this will give rise to a tenancy in common with Kate holding the legal title on trust from them as tenants in common, each enjoying a half-share of the equitable ownership of the cottage. If an express trust is declared of unequal shares in the land it is inevitable that the beneficiaries must hold their interests as tenants in common since such an arrangement cannot be given effect by a joint tenancy. For example, if Kate declared that she held the cottage on trust for herself and Martin in shares of a third and two-thirds respectively, this would create a tenancy in common.

(b) Conveyance of the land to the legal title holders as trustees

Alternatively a trust of the land may be created by a transfer of the legal title to a new owner or owners, often on the sale of the land. For example, if Martin and Kate were purchasing the cottage from Ian, then the conveyance may expressly state the terms under which the land is to be held. The conveyance may state that the land is transferred to Kate and Martin "on trust for themselves as joint tenants" or alternatively "on trust for themselves in equal shares". The first example would create an express joint tenancy of the beneficial interest, the second a tenancy in common.

3 Co-ownership where there is no express declaration of the beneficial entitlements

(a) Lack of an express stipulation

Although parties creating a trust of land are free to define their respective beneficial entitlements as they wish, they may have failed to do so. In such cases the law will have to presume or imply the nature of their beneficial entitlements from their conduct. This will also clearly be necessary where a trust of land is created by means of a constructive or resulting trust.

(b) Conveyance of the land into the names of more than one person

(i) A general presumption that there is to be a joint tenancy: Where land is conveyed into the name of more than one person, and there is no express declaration of how the equitable ownership is shared, the general presumption is that the legal owners will hold the property on trust for themselves as joint tenants. As has been noted above, if the land is conveyed into the name of more than four persons, only the first four named can take the legal title and the remainder will enjoy interests only as joint tenants of the beneficial interest.

(ii) Special circumstances where the presumption of a joint tenancy will be displaced by a tenancy in common: Although a joint tenancy of the beneficial interest will generally be presumed where the legal title to land is conveyed to more than one owner, in some circumstances the law is prepared to displace that conclusion in favour of a tenancy in common because the nature of the relationship between the co-owners militates against finding that they intended the principle of survivorship to operate between themselves. This was recognised by the Privy Council in *Malayan Credit Ltd v. Jack Chia-MPH Ltd*[10] where Lord Brightman stated that the circumstances in which

[10] [1986] A.C. 549.

joint tenants at law will be presumed to hold their beneficial entitlements as tenants in common are not strictly circumscribed by the law and that equity may infer a tenancy in common wherever appropriate.[11] If the parties acquire land jointly as commercial partners they will hold the legal title as joint tenants but will hold the beneficial interest as tenants in common of equal shares.[12] In *Malayan Credit Ltd v. Jack Chia-MPH Ltd*[13] the Privy Council held that a tenancy in common was to be inferred where a tenancy of business premises had been taken by a number of persons jointly at law to enable them to pursue their separate business purposes. Mortgagees who lend money on a joint legal mortgage are also inferred to hold their interests as tenants in common in equity[14] although they are joint tenants at law.[15] Another very significant circumstance where a tenancy in common will be preferred to a joint tenancy in the absence of an express declaration is where the legal owners have contributed to the purchase price of the land in unequal proportions. A tenancy in common in equity is the only means of giving effect to the relative disparity of their contributions. This was a further reason for finding that there was a tenancy in common of the lease in *Malayan Credit Ltd v. Jack Chia-MPH Ltd*.[16] The plaintiff and the defendant had agreed between themselves prior to the grant of the lease how they would apportion the space available, and roughly this meant the defendant occupying 62 per cent of the floor area and the plaintiff the remaining 38 per cent. They divided their liability for the rent and service charge in unequal shares in accordance with the areas they occupied. The Privy Council held that this was a feature of their relationship which pointed unequivocally to a tenancy in common. A similar conclusion was reached in relation to residential property in *Walker v. Hall*[17] where a house had been purchased in the joint names of a man and his mistress. The Court of Appeal held that as the woman had contributed a quarter of the purchase price the property was held by them as trustees of the legal title in unequal shares as tenants in common of a quarter and three-quarters of the beneficial interest respectively.

(iii) Conveyance of the land into the names of more than one person as tenants in common: Slightly different difficulties arise if land is conveyed at law into the names of more than one person as tenants in common, since as has been noted above, the legal title cannot be held by co-owners other than in the form of a joint tenancy. The consequence is that the persons named in the conveyance, or if there are more than four the first four who are willing and able to act as trustees, will take the legal title as joint tenants and they will hold the land on trust for the persons named in the conveyance as tenants in common in equity.

(c) Co-ownership through resulting and constructive trusts of land

(i) Context of informal trusts: As has been seen in the previous chapter there are many cases where a trust of land will be imposed on the legal owner or owners by means of a resulting or constructive trust. Most commonly this has been so in cases of

[11] *ibid.* at 560.
[12] *Lake v. Craddock* (1732) 3 P.WMs 158.
[13] [1986] A.C. 549.
[14] *Re Jackson* (1887) 34 Ch.D. 732.
[15] Law of Property Act 1925, s.111.
[16] [1986] A.C. 549.
[17] [1984] 5 F.L.R. 126.

co-habitation of residential property where only one of the co-habitees is the legal owner of the land. If the other can establish that she is entitled to a share of the equitable ownership then the question will arise as to whether the equitable ownership is shared as joint tenants or tenants in common.

(ii) Co-ownership under a resulting trust: A person will be entitled to a resulting trust interest in land if they have contributed directly to its purchase price. The extent of their interest is determined by means of an exact mathematical equivalence with the proportion of their contribution.[18] Only in circumstances where the contributions of the parties are exactly equal could a joint tenancy of the beneficial interest arise, and in cases where the contributions, and therefore respective shares of ownership, are unequal the parties must hold their interests as tenants in common.[19]

(iii) Co-ownership under a constructive trust: A constructive trust arises because of a person's financial contribution to the purchase price of property, but on the basis of a common intention with the legal owner that they were to be entitled to a share of the equitable ownership.[20] Only if the court finds that the common intention was that the parties were to share the property equally will it be possible to find that there was a joint tenancy of the beneficial interest. However since the finding is usually that a party was entitled to a specific "share" of the ownership equity will generally prefer to find that the parties were tenants in common. For example in *Midland Bank v. Cooke*[21] the Court of Appeal held that in circumstances where there was a common intention that a husband and wife were to share the ownership of a house the wife was entitled to an "equal share"[22] of the beneficial interest. Where a constructive trust gives rise to unequal shares of the beneficial interest, as in *Eves v. Eves*[23] where a co-habiting girlfriend was held to be entitled to a third interest in the quasi-matrimonial home, the interest can only be given effect through a tenancy in common.

SEVERANCE OF A JOINT TENANCY OF THE EQUITABLE OWNERSHIP OF LAND

1 The consequences of severance

It has been seen how co-ownership of the beneficial interest in land can be effected behind a trust either as a joint tenancy or a tenancy in common. Where there is a joint tenancy the co-owners are wholly entitled to the whole and the principle of survivorship operates between them. Severance is the process by which a joint tenant is enabled to separate his notional share of the ownership of the land from that of the other joint tenants, so that in relation to his share he ceases to be a joint tenant but becomes a tenant in common. As Dillon L.J. stated in *Harris v. Goddard*[24]:

[18] See: *Huntingford v. Hobbs* [1993] 1 F.L.R. 737; *Midland Bank plc v. Cooke* [1995] 4 All E.R. 562.
[19] As in *Bull v. Bull* [1955] 1 Q.B. 234.
[20] *Lloyd's Bank v. Rossett* [1991] 1 A.C. 107.
[21] [1995] 4 All E.R. 562.
[22] *ibid.* at 576.
[23] [1975] 1 W.L.R. 1338.
[24] [1983] 1 W.L.R. 203 at 210.

> "Severance . . . is the process of separating off the share of a joint tenant, so that the concurrent ownership will continue but the right of survivorship will no longer apply. The parties will hold separate shares as tenants in common."

As this statement indicates, one of the consequences of severance is that survivorship no longer operates in relation to the share of the tenant in common, and the tenant in common no longer enjoys the possibility of survivorship as regards the interests of the remaining joint tenants, if any. Where a joint tenancy is severed the party severing will be entitled to a share of the beneficial ownership equivalent to an equal share with all the joint tenants.[25] This will be the case even where the initial contributions of the joint tenants to the purchase price of the property were unequal.[26] For example, if there are two joint tenants and one severs they will become tenants in common of half-shares. If one of six joint tenants were to sever his share he would become a tenant in common of a sixth share of the beneficial interest and the others would continue as joint tenants of the remaining five-sixths. These principles were stated by Russell L.J. in *Bedson v. Bedson*[27]:

> "On severance the beneficial joint tenancy becomes a beneficial tenancy in common in undivided shares and the right of survivorship no longer obtains. If there be two beneficial joint tenants, severance produces a beneficial tenancy in common in two equal shares. If there be three beneficial joint tenants and only one severs, he is entitled to a one-third undivided share and there is no longer survivorship between him and the other two, though the other two may remain *inter se* beneficial joint tenants of the other two-thirds."

Although the general rule is that a joint tenant severing his interest will be entitled to an equal share as a tenant in common the parties may agree a different arrangement between themselves, so that an unequal share is severed.[28]

2 Means by which joint tenants may effect severance

(a) A variety of means of severance

Four means are recognised by which a joint tenant may effect severance of his interest. On the facts of many cases there may be an overlap between the different methods and one or more may be pleaded as alternative justifications for establishing that severance has taken place.

(i) Statutory severance: The Law of Property Act 1925, s.36(2) provides a statutory procedure by which a joint tenant may sever his interest merely by giving a written notice of his intention to sever to the other joint tenants.

[25] See: *Goodman v. Gallant* [1986] 1 All E.R. 311.

[26] *Goodman v. Gallant* [1986] Fam. 106. Such a situation would only arise if the beneficial interests of the contributors had been determined by an express declaration that they were to be joint tenants. In the absence of such a declaration they would be tenants in common of shares in proportion to their contributions under a resulting trust.

[27] [1965] 2 Q.B. 666.

[28] *Barton v. Morris* [1985] 1 W.L.R. 1257.

(ii) Common law severance: The statutory mechanism of severance was enacted as an addition to the three methods recognised by the common law. These were identified in *Williams v. Hensman*[29] by Page-Wood V.-C.:

> "A joint tenancy may be severed in three ways: in the first place, an act of any one of the persons interested operating upon his own share may create a severance as to that share. . . . Secondly, a joint tenancy may be severed by mutual agreement. And, in the third place, there may be a severance by any course of dealing sufficient to intimate that the interests of all were mutually treated as consisting a tenancy in common."[30]

(iii) A general limitation to the right to sever?: In *Bedson v. Bedson*[31] Lord Denning M.R. suggested that it was a general rule that where husband and wife are the beneficial joint tenants of land in the physical possession of at least one of them, the joint tenancy cannot be severed.[32] Russell L.J. dissented and stated:

> "I am unable to accept the legal proposition of Lord Denning M.R. that when husband and wife are joint tenants of the legal estate in the matrimonial home and also beneficial joint tenants in respect of it, neither can, so long as one is in possession, sell his or her beneficial interest therein or otherwise sever the beneficial joint tenancy. The proposition is, I think, without the slightest foundation in law or in equity."[33]

This rejection of the supposed limitation has been approved by all subsequent cases[34] and it seems that there is no inherent limitation on the right of joint tenants to sever their interests.

(b) Severance by written notice

(i) A statutory means of severance: Section 36(2) of the Law of Property Act 1925 provides that:

> "where a legal estate . . . is vested in joint tenants beneficially, and any tenant desires to sever the joint tenancy in equity, he shall give to the other joint tenants a notice in writing of such desire or do such other acts or things as would, in the case of a personal estate, have been effectual to sever the tenancy in equity. . . ."

This section introduced a new[35] statutory mechanism for effecting severance whilst retaining the traditional common law means of severance which will be examined

[29] (1861) 1 J. & H. 546.
[30] *ibid.* at 557.
[31] [1965] 2 Q.B. 666.
[32] *ibid.* at 683.
[33] *ibid.* at 690.
[34] *Re Draper's Conveyance* [1969] 1 Ch. 486; *Cowcher v. Cowcher* [1972] 1 W.L.R. 425; *Harris v. Goddard* [1983] 1 W.L.R. 203.
[35] Despite the view of Lord Denning M.R. in *Burgess v. Rawnsley* [1975] Ch. 429 that the statute merely enacted the position at common law, the overwhelming judicial and academic opinion is that it introduced a new means of severance: *Re Drapers Conveyance* [1969] 1 Ch. 486; *Neilson-Jones v. Fedden* [1975] Ch. 222; [1975] C.L.J. 28 (Prichard); [1976] C.L.J. 20 (Hayton). Although the statute clearly permits severance by written notice of a joint tenancy of land, it is unclear whether this method of severance is available in relation to a joint tenancy of personal property.

below. It has been argued that the wording of the section only permits severance by written notice where the legal and equitable ownership of land are held identically, *i.e.* by the same persons as joint tenants of both the legal and equitable title.[36] However, judicial pronouncements by the Court of Appeal in *Burgess v. Rawnsley*[37] favour a wider interpretation that severance by written notice is available irrespective of whether or not the legal and equitable titles are identically held.

(ii) A unilateral intention to sever will be sufficient: From the perspective of a joint tenant wishing to sever his share the main procedural advantage of severance by written notice is that he can act unilaterally without the need to obtain the consent, or even having to consult, his fellow joint tenants.

(iii) A written notice to sever: Severance under section 36(2) requires the giving of "written notice" to the other joint tenants. There is no specified form that such a notice must take. In *Re Draper's Conveyance*[38] Plowman J. held that the written notice did not need to be signed by the joint tenant as "there is no requirement in the subsection of a signature."

(iv) Can the documents commencing legal proceedings constitute written notice for the purposes of section 36(2)?: One question which has caused some controversy is whether the service of documents commencing legal proceedings claiming entitlement to a share of the ownership of land can constitute written notice for the purposes of section 36(2) and therefore effect a severance of a joint tenancy. The central obstacle to holding that such documents can constitute written notice is the concern that proceedings need not be pursued once started. The issue arose in *Re Draper's Conveyance*,[39] where a husband and wife were the joint tenants of their matrimonial home under an express declaration of trust. They divorced in 1965 and in 1966 the wife started proceedings seeking an order[40] that the house be sold and the proceeds be divided according to their respective interests in it. The husband subsequently died intestate before the house had been sold. Plowman J. held that the joint tenancy had been severed by the issuing of the summons and accompanying affidavit of the wife because these documents constituted written notice that "clearly evinced an intention on the part of the wife that she wished the property to be sold and the proceeds distributed, a half to her and a half to the husband,"[41] which intention was inconsistent with the continuation of a joint tenancy. He therefore held that the joint tenancy had been severed before the death of the husband, and that survivorship did not operate in favour of his ex-wife. In *Neilson-Jones v. Fedden*[42] Walton J, relying on the earlier case *Re Wilks*,[43] doubted whether a mere summons and supporting affidavit could be taken to constitute written notice for the purpose of section 36(2) on the grounds that the mere issuing of proceedings is not irrevocable:

> "I am also troubled about the suggestion that the mere issue of the originating summons, coupled with the affidavit in support, could amount to a notice in

[36] [1976] C.L.J. 20 (Hayton).
[37] [1975] Ch. 429.
[38] [1969] 1 Ch. 486.
[39] *ibid.*
[40] Under the Married Women's Property Act 1882, s.17.
[41] [1969] 1 Ch. 486 at 492.
[42] [1975] Ch. 222.
[43] [1891] 3 Ch. 59.

> writing. . . . [I]t appears to me that section 36(2) contemplates an irrevocable notice, and that the issue of proceedings is the very reverse of an irrevocable act. If the proceedings are, indeed, to constitute a severance, it must, I think, follow as a consequence that they themselves become irrevocable, and this I find difficult to appreciate."[44]

However, his doubts were rejected by the Court of Appeal in *Harris v. Goddard*[45] which held that *Re Draper's Conveyance*[46] had been correctly decided in so far as Plowman J. had held that effective written notice had been given under section 36(2).[47] In *Burgess v. Rawnsley*[48] Sir John Pennycuick had stated:

> "I do not see why the commencement of legal proceedings by writ or originating summons or the swearing of an affidavit in those proceedings, should not in appropriate circumstances constitute notice in writing within the meaning of s.36(2). The fact that the plaintiff is not obliged to prosecute the proceedings is I think irrelevant in regard to notice."

(v) Intention to sever: The mere fact that a written notice mentioning the possibility of severance has been given to the other joint tenants will not automatically effect severance. The crucial factor is the presence of an intention to sever. In *Gore and Snell v. Carpenter*[49] a husband and wife were the beneficial joint tenants of two houses. They decided to divorce and the husband's solicitor was asked to draw up a separation agreement. The draft agreement included a clause severing the joint tenancy of the matrimonial home. The draft proposals were accepted in principal but no agreement was reached because some financial details remained to be settled. The husband was advised to serve a severance notice on his wife but refused to do so because he thought his wife might construe such action as hostile and detrimental to the negotiation of the divorce. He died a month after the divorce papers were served. In these circumstances Blackett-Ord J. held that the service of the draft separation agreement had not effected a severance of the joint tenancy because the necessary intention to sever was lacking:

> "It is, in my judgment, a question of intention . . . It is argued for the executors that the proposed separation agreement put forward . . . amounted to [a s.36(2)] notice. It will be recalled that the [proposed agreement] expressly refers to severance, but that was only part of the deed and the deed was never accepted. It was put forward . . . not in isolation but as part of a package of proposals, and was not intended in my judgement and therefore did not take effect as a notice under s.36(2)."[50]

The wife therefore enjoyed the entire beneficial interest in the houses by way of survivorship.

[44] *ibid.* at 236.
[45] [1983] 1 W.L.R. 203.
[46] [1969] 1 Ch. 486.
[47] Dillon L.J. stated that although *Re Wilks* [1891] 3 Ch. 59 may have been rightly decided in its time, it would be decided differently today because of, s.36: [1983] 1 W.L.R. 1203 at 1210.
[48] [1975] Ch. 429 at 447.
[49] [1990] 60 P. & C.R. 456. See also: *McDowell v. Hirschfield Lipson & Rumney and Smith* [1992] 2 F.L.R. 126.
[50] *ibid.* at 462.

(vi) Intention to sever immediately: A notice will only be effective to sever if the intention is that it should effect an immediate severance, not that there should be a severance some time in the future. For this reason it was held that there was no severance in *Harris v. Goddard*[51] although the facts are superficially similar to those in *Re Draper's Conveyance*.[52] A husband and wife were the joint tenants in equity under an express trust of their matrimonial home. In 1979 the wife left her husband and sought a divorce. Her petition for divorce sought that "such order may be made" in relation to the matrimonial home as "may be just," including transferring the property, settlement of the property or variation of the existing trust interests. Three days before the hearing of the petition was due the husband was injured in a car crash, and he died a month later. His executors claimed that the joint tenancy had been severed so that survivorship did not operate in favour of the wife. Then Court of Appeal held that the divorce petition did not evidence an intention to effect an immediate transformation in the nature of the parties' beneficial interests in the house, and that therefore the joint tenancy had not been severed. Slade L.J. explained why petition was considered ineffective to sever:

> "I am unable to accept [the] submission that a notice in writing which shows no more than a desire to bring the existing interest to an end is a good notice. It must be a desire to sever which is intended to have the statutory consequence. Paragraph 3 of the prayer of the petition does no more than invite the Court to consider at some future time whether to exercise its jurisdiction under section 24 of the [Matrimonial Causes Act 1973] and if it does, to do so in one or more of three different ways. Orders under section 24(1)(a) and (b) could bring co-ownership to an end by ways other than by severance. It follows, in my judgement, that paragraph 3 of the prayer of the petition did not operate as a notice in writing to sever the joint tenancy in equity."[53]

Since there had been no severance of the joint tenancy the wife was entitled to the entire beneficial ownership as a consequence of the operation of survivorship on the death of her ex-husband.

(vii) Notice given to the other joint tenants: Section 36(2) requires that the joint tenant intending to sever his interest must "give" the notice to the other joint tenants. Most cases examined have involved only two joint tenants. However, where there are more than two the notice will only be effective if it is given to all of the others. Service to some, or even to the majority, will not be effective to sever.

(viii) Giving notice by post: Where the notice is given by post, it has been held to be effective even if not received. In *Re 88 Berkeley Road*[54] two single women, Miss Goodwin and Miss Eldridge, were the beneficial joint tenants of a house. A month before Miss Eldridge was married Miss Goodwin sent a notice of severance by recorded delivery to the correct address. The notice had asked for acknowledgement of receipt of the notice, but no receipt was received. Since the ladies were living in the

[51] [1983] 1 W.L.R. 1203.
[52] [1969] 1 Ch. 486.
[53] [1983] 1 W.L.R. 1203 at 1209.
[54] [1971] Ch. 648.

same house the post office records showed that the letter had been received and signed for by Miss Goodwin herself on behalf of Miss Eldridge who was away at the time. Miss Goodwin died soon after and her executors claimed that the joint tenancy had been severed. Plowman J. held that although the evidence supported Miss Eldridge's claim that she had never received the notice by statute the posting alone was sufficient to constitute giving notice for the purposes of section 36(2). This was because Law of Property Act 1925, s.196(4) provides that a notice under the act is deemed to have been served if "it is sent by post in a registered letter" and the letter is not returned to the post office undelivered. Plowman J. refused to distinguish "giving" notice under section 36(2) from "serving" notice under section 196(4) and held that Miss Goodwin had severed her interest and at the time of her death had been a tenant in common of a half-share of the beneficial ownership.

(c) Severance by unilateral conduct

(i) A means of unilateral severance: The first of the three common law methods of severance identified in *Williams v. Hensman*[55] was that a joint tenancy will be severed by "an act of any one of the persons interested operating upon his own share." This means of severance involves a degree of abstract inconsistency since the essence of a joint tenancy is that the joint tenants do not have individual shares in the land as such, hence it is somewhat inaccurate to speak about a tenant acting in relation to "his own share". In reality what is meant is that the joint tenant does some act which demonstrates that he is intending to treat his interest in the land as consisting of a specific share and which is therefore inconsistent with the continuation of a joint tenancy. As in the case of statutory severance by written notice this means of severance is capable of being exercised unilaterally by the joint tenant seeking to sever his share and does not require the consent or participation of the other joint tenants. A number of well recognised categories of conduct by a joint tenant in relation to his interest in the land have been held to have the effect of severing his share.

(ii) Joint tenant transfers his share to a third party: One of the clearest unilateral acts a joint tenant can perform with severing effect is to transfer his interest in the land to a third party. Such a transfer is technically termed "alienation." In *Bedson v. Bedson*[56] Russell L.J. stated generally that if a husband and wife were joint tenants "either husband or wife could . . . *at any time* by voluntary assignment or sale or mortgage of his or her beneficial interests have created a tenancy in common in undivided shares."[57] For example, if there are two joint tenants of land and one sells his interests to a third party the joint tenancy will be severed and the remaining original tenant and the new co-owner will stand as tenants in common of half-shares of the beneficial interest. If there are more than two joint tenants and one alienates his interests this will not have the effect of terminating the joint tenancy completely. The third party acquiring the interest of the alienating tenant will stand as a tenant in common of the relevant share acquired in relation to the remaining co-owners, but as between themselves those co-owners continue to hold their interests as joint tenants.[58]

[55] (1861) 1 J. & H. 546.
[56] [1965] 2 Q.B. 666.
[57] *ibid.* at 690.
[58] See: *Bedson v. Bedson* [1965] 2 Q.B. 666 at 689, referred to above at p. 209.

It is to be noted that where a joint tenant who alienates his interest is also a joint tenant of the legal title and a trustee, the alienation takes effect only in equity and has no impact on the ownership of the legal title. He will remain a joint tenant[59] of the legal title even though he has no continuing beneficial interest in the land. Severance will only occur if the transfer of the joint tenant's interest was completed and his share alienated. In the Australian case *Corin v. Patton*[60] it was held that there was no severance where a joint tenant had executed a transfer of the land because she had not done everything that was necessary for the transferee to be registered and the transfer was incomplete.[61]

(iii) Joint tenant transfers his interest to one of his fellow joint tenants: A transfer of a joint tenant's share in the land not to a third party but to someone who is already also a joint tenant will inevitably have the effect of severing the share transferred. This follows from the fact that the transfer is intended to increase the extent of the interest of the acquiring joint tenant, and this cannot be given effect by means of a joint tenancy. For example, if Philip, Quentin, Rowena and Stephanie are joint tenants of the beneficial interest in land and Philip sells his interest to Stephanie, the consequence will be that his share is severed so that Stephanie becomes a tenant in common of a quarter share and remains joint tenant along with Quentin and Rowena of the remaining three-quarter share.

(iv) Joint tenant mortgages his interest in the land: In *Bedson v. Bedson*[62] Russell L.J. stated that "a mortgage or charge of his interest by a beneficial joint tenant operates as a severance."[63] If a joint tenant mortgages his interest he will become entitled to an equal share of the beneficial interest as a tenant in common.[64] This provides one of the few means by which a joint tenant can sever his interest entirely secretly whilst retaining ownership. Virtually all other means of severance will be evident to the other joint tenants, since they require mutual conduct or written notification of intention.

(v) Joint tenant enters into a contract to transfer or mortgage his interest: Even where the transaction has not yet been carried into effect severance will be effected if a joint tenant enters into a specifically enforceable contract to alienate his share or to grant a mortgage.[65] This is a further application of the well established maxim that equity treats as done that which ought to be done.

(vi) Joint tenant fraudulently transfers or mortgages the entire interest in the land: If a joint tenant purports to deal not merely with his own interest in the land but with the entire interest under the joint tenancy by transferring or mortgaging it, and thereby acts fraudulently against the interests of the other joint tenants, this will have the effect of severing his share. In consequence his interest in the land will be bound by the fraudulent transaction but the interests of the other joint tenants will be left unaffected. For example, in *First National Securities Ltd v. Hegerty*[66] a husband and wife

[59] Or even the sole legal owner if there are no other trustees.
[60] (1990) 169 C.L.R. 540.
[61] Under the Australian Torrens system the certificate of land registration must be made available by the transferor for registration of the transferee. In *Corin v. Patton* the certificate was held by the mortgagee of the land and the transferor never authorised the mortgagee to hand the certificate to the transferee.
[62] [1965] 2 Q.B. 666.
[63] *ibid.* at 690.
[64] *First National Securities Ltd v. Hegerty* [1985] Q.B. 850; See also *Bedson v. Bedson* [1965] 2 Q.B. 666 at 690, cited above at p. 209.
[65] *Caldwell v. Fellows* (1870) L.R. 9 Eq. 410; *Re Hewett* [1894] 1 Ch. 362.
[66] [1985] Q.B. 850.

were the beneficial joint tenants of a house which was intended to be their retirement home. However, the husband left and subsequently executed a legal mortgage of the property by forging his wife's signature on the application and charge. The Court of Appeal confirmed the holding of Bingham J. that "this disposition by the husband was a sufficient act of alienation to sever the beneficial joint tenancy and convert the husband and wife into tenants in common."[67] Similarly in *Ahmed v. Kendrick*[68] Mr and Mrs Ahmed were the beneficial joint tenants of a house which Mr Ahmed sold and transferred to Kendrick by forging his wife's signature on the contract and transfer. The Court of Appeal again affirmed that the effect of this fraudulent transaction was to sever the joint tenancy so that Mr and Mrs Ahmed became tenants in common of half-shares in the house and that Kendrick was only entitled to assert his entitlement against the half-share of Mr Ahmed.[69]

(vii) Joint tenant is adjudicated bankrupt: When a person is adjudicated bankrupt by the court all property owned by the bankrupt vests automatically in his trustee in bankruptcy.[70] Although this is not technically an act of the tenant it is a form of involuntary alienation of his interest which has the effect of severing any interest in land which he may enjoy as a joint tenant. The crucial moment is that of adjudication of bankruptcy by the court. In *Re Dennis*[71] a husband and wife were the beneficial joint tenants of two houses. In September 1982 the husband committed an act of bankruptcy[72] and in December a bankruptcy petition was presented. His wife died in February and he was adjudicated bankrupt in November 1983. Nicholls V.-C. held that the effect of the relevant statute was not to vest the bankrupt's property retrospectively in the trustee but only when the adjudication order is made. Therefore at the date of the wife's death the joint tenancy had not been severed and survivorship operated so that at the date of adjudication the trustee in bankruptcy became entitled to the whole of both houses. The reverse of this situation arose in *Re Palmer*[73] where a husband, who was the joint tenant of a house with his wife, had died a debtor which led his executor to seek an insolvency administration order. The Court of Appeal held that such an administration order vested the property of the deceased in the trustee at the moment of his death, and that since at that moment there had been no severance the principle of survivorship operated and the wife was entitled to ownership of the house.

(viii) Charging order imposed on the interest of a joint tenant: The interest of a joint tenant will also be severed if a charge is imposed upon it by law. Such charges may arise, for example, under the Charging Orders Act 1979. In *Bedson v. Bedson*[74] Russell L.J. suggested that a charge imposed in favour of the Law Society to recover unpaid contributions to legal aid where the proceedings have recovered or preserved a beneficial interest for the claimant, will effect severance.

(ix) Commencement of proceedings by one joint tenant against others: In *Re Draper's Conveyance*,[75] which was considered above in the context of severance by written

[67] *ibid.* at 854.
[68] (1988) 56 P. & C.R. 120.
[69] As the wife had acquiesced in Kendrick discharging the mortgage over the property the Court of Appeal also held that in determining the respective entitlements of Mrs Ahmed and Kendrick in the house Kendrick should be given credit for the money paid to discharge in priority to any interest she might have.
[70] Insolvency Act 1986, ss.283 and 306.
[71] [1993] Ch. 72.
[72] By failing to comply with a bankruptcy notice.
[73] [1994] Ch. 316.
[74] [1965] 2 Q.B. 666.
[75] [1969] 1 Ch. 486.

notice, [76] Plowman J. suggested that his conclusion that a wife had severed her joint tenancy of the matrimonial home could be supported on the grounds that her service of a summons, together with a supporting affidavit commencing litigation asserting her right to half-share of the beneficial interest, was itself an act by a joint tenant sufficient to sever her interest under the common law principles identified in *Williams v. Hensman*,[77] irrespective of whether the documents constituted written notice for the purposes of Law of Property Act 1925, s.36(2). Subsequent cases have questioned whether the mere commencement of litigation is alone sufficient an act by a joint tenant to effect severance. Walton J. expressed doubt in *Neilson-Jones v. Fedden*[78] citing the earlier case *Re Wilks*[79] where Stirling J. had held that a beneficiary who was the joint tenant of a trust had not severed his interest merely by starting proceedings for payment of his share of the fund. The central criticism is that commencement of litigation is not a sufficiently irrevocable act since proceedings once started can be discontinued. However, in *Harris v. Goddard*[80] the Court of Appeal took the view that any danger of discontinuance is insufficient to invalidate the conclusion that the commencement of litigation amounts to unilateral conduct by a joint tenant which will sever his interest. Lawton L.J. commented:

> "I do not share the doubts about the correctness of [the] judgment on this point which Walton J. expressed in *Neilson-Jones v. Fedden* relying on in *Re Wilks*. The fact that the wife in *Re Draper's Conveyance* could have withdrawn the summons is a factor which could have been taken into account in deciding whether what was done was effectual to sever the joint tenancy in equity. The weight of that factor would have depended upon all the other circumstances and was in that case clearly negligible."[81]

(x) Joint tenant declares his intention to sever?: There has been some question whether a mere unilateral declaration by a joint tenant that he intends to sever his share is an act sufficient to effect severance under the first method identified in *Williams v. Hensman*.[82] In *Hawkesley v. May*[83] Havers J. stated that "the first method indicated, namely an act of any one of the persons interested operating upon his own share, obviously includes a declaration of intention to sever by one party." This was cited with approval by Plowman J. in *Re Draper's Conveyance*[84] but criticised by Walton J. as lacking any support in the authorities. However *Hawkesley v. May*[85] was approved by Lord Denning M.R. in *Burgess v Rawnsely*[86] and in both that case and *Harris v. Goddard*[87] the Court of Appeal rejected the criticisms Walton J. had levelled against *In*

[76] See p. 211.
[77] (1861) 1 J. & H. 546.
[78] [1975] Ch. 222.
[79] [1891] 3 Ch. 59.
[80] [1983] 1 W.L.R. 1206.
[81] *ibid.* at 1210.
[82] (1861) J. & H. 546.
[83] [1956] 1 Q.B. 304.
[84] [1969] 1 Ch. 486.
[85] [1956] 1 Q.B. 304.
[86] [1975] Ch. 429.
[87] [1983] 1 W.L.R. 203.

re Draper's Conveyance[88] in *Nielson-Jones v. Fedden*.[89] It is unclear whether these cases support the conclusion that a mere oral statement of intention is effective to sever, or whether they merely uphold the finding that severance had occurred in *Re Draper's Conveyance*,[90] a conclusion which could be justified perfectly adequately on the grounds that a written notice had been given. It seems as a matter of principle that a mere unilateral declaration of intention to sever, unaccompanied by any action, should not be sufficient to sever a joint tenancy. Otherwise severance would be too easy, and there would be little point in having a statutory mechanism of written notice if all a joint tenant needed to do was to express his intention orally. Rejection of mere unilateral declaration of intention as a means of severance is also supported by the Australian High Court in *Corin v. Patton*.[91] Mason C.J. and McHugh J. indicated that severance by unilateral intention was theoretically impossible, because severance can only be brought about by the destruction of one of the four-unities:

> "Unilateral action cannot destroy the unity of time, of possession or of interest unless the unity of title is also destroyed, and it can only destroy the unity of title if the title of the party acting unilaterally is transferred or otherwise dealt with or affected in a way which results in a change in the legal and equitable estates in the relevant property. A statement of intention, without more, does not affect the unity of title."[92]

They also pointed to two practical objections to finding that unilateral declaration would be sufficient to sever. First, that uncertainty would follow as "it would become more difficult to identify precisely the ownership of interests in land which had been the subject of statements said to amount to declarations of intention". Secondly, that "there would then be no point in maintaining as a separate means of severance the making of mutual agreement between the joint tenants."

(xi) Joint tenant transfers his share to himself?: Since a severance will occur if a joint tenant alienates his interest to a third party or one of his fellow co-owners, the question has arisen as to whether a joint tenant can convert his interest into a joint tenancy by alienating his interest to himself. Following dicta of Lord Denning in *Rye v. Rye*[93] it seems highly unlikely that such a transaction would effect severance.

(xii) Joint tenant disposes of his interest by will?: The mere fact that a joint tenant has bequeathed his interest by will does not effect a severance *inter vivos* of the joint tenancy. When he dies survivorship operates so that he has no interest in the land which is capable of passing under his will.[94]

(d) Severance by mutual agreement

(i) A means of severance which requires the participation of all the joint tenants: Unlike the two means of severance which have been examined so far, severance under

[88] [1969] 1 Ch. 486.
[89] [1975] Ch. 222.
[90] [1969] 1 Ch. 486.
[91] (1990) 169 C.L.R. 540.
[92] *ibid.* at 548.
[93] [1962] A.C. 496 at 514.
[94] *Moyse v. Gyles* (1700) 2 Vern. 385.

this second head of *Williams v. Hensman*[95] cannot be exercised unilaterally by a joint tenant wishing to sever his share. Severance will only occur if all the joint tenants are agreed that it should.

(ii) An agreement does not require an enforceable contract: For severance to occur by reason of the joint tenants' mutual agreement it is not necessary that they must have entered into an enforceable contract *inter se*. The operation of this means of severance was explained by Sir John Pennycuick in *Burgess v. Rawnsley*[96]:

> "[counsel] contended that in order that rule 2 should apply, the agreement must be specifically enforceable. I do not see any sufficient reason for importing this qualification. The significance of an agreement is not that it binds the parties; but that it serves as an indication of a common intention to sever, something which it was indisputably within their power to do. It will; be observed that Page Wood V.-C. in his rule 2 makes no mention of specific enforceability."

(iii) An agreement must have been reached: The essential requirement for severance by mutual agreement is that the joint tenants in fact reached an appropriate agreement in relation to the beneficial ownership of the land. Inconclusive negotiations and discussions may be sufficient to effect severance under the third head, namely mutual conduct, but there it is often a fine line which divides a finding of an agreement from a finding that negotiations were inconclusive. The difficulties are well illustrated by *Burgess v. Rawnsley*.[97] A house was purchased in the joint names of Mr Honick and Mrs Rawnsley, who had met at a religious rally in Trafalgar Square. He intended to marry her at the time that the purchase took place, but she had no intention of marrying him and intended that she would occupy a flat on the upper storey of the house and he would occupy the lower storey. The conveyance expressly declared that they were to be joint tenants of the beneficial interest. Mr Honick paid for the property but Mrs Rawnsley gave him more than the entire purchase price in return for her interest. A year later Mr Honick sought to purchase Mrs Rawnsely's share in the property because it was clear that she would not marry him. He came to what he thought was an oral agreement with her to purchase her share for £750 and his solicitor wrote to her asking that she confirm her willingness to sell on those terms. The next day she went to the solicitors and said she was not willing to sell and that she wanted £1000. A few days later Mr Honick told his solicitor to leave things as they were. Three years later he died, and during the intervening time he had lived in the house alone, and paid all outgoings. His daughter, Mrs Burgess claimed a half-share in the house on the grounds that her father had severed his interest and that survivorship had not operated in favour of Mrs Rawnsley. The county court judge held as a fact that the parties had reached an agreement for the sale of Mrs Rawnsley's share for £750. Since the agreement was purely oral it would not have been enforceable.[98] The majority of the Court of Appeal held that severance had occurred because they were unwilling to upset the finding of fact that an agreement had been reached.[99] However,

[95] (1861) 1 J. & H. 546.
[96] [1975] Ch. 429.
[97] *ibid.*
[98] Law of Property Act 1925, s.40.
[99] Sir John Pennycuick stated at 446 that: "I do not think this court would be justified in holding that the judge's finding was so contrary to the weight of evidence that it should be set aside."

they expressed doubt whether this finding was truly justifiable on the evidence. Browne L.J. stated that he was "bound to say that the evidence about any such agreement seems to me to have been most unsatisfactory."[1] Lord Denning M.R. also concluded that severance had occurred on the basis of the agreement[2] but in his judgment was more concerned to demonstrate that severance could be supported even if there were no agreement on the basis that the course of dealing of the parties "clearly evinced an intention by both parties that the property should henceforth be held in common and not jointly."[3] His comments in this respect will be examined below. What is clear from the decision of the Court of Appeal is that if an agreement is established as a fact, then it will have a severing effect.

(iv) The agreement need not be express: It is also clear from the judgments of the Court of Appeal in *Burgess v. Rawnsley*[4] that an agreement need not have been concluded expressly but can be implied from the circumstances of their dealings. Browne L.J. stated that "an agreement to sever can be inferred from a course of dealing . . . and there would in such a case *ex hypothesi* be no express agreement but only an inferred, tacit agreement."[5]

(v) The agreement must relate to the ownership of the land: There is no requirement that the agreement must specifically refer to severance. In *Burgess v. Rawnsley*[6] Sir John Pennycuick indicated that "Rule 2 applies equally . . . whether the agreement between the two joint tenants is expressly to sever or is to deal with the property in a manner which involves severance."[7] However, the decision of Walton J. in *Neilsen-Jones v. Fedden*[8] suggests that a mutual agreement will only sever a joint tenancy if it relates to the actual ownership of the land and how it is held by the parties. The plaintiff and her ex-husband were the beneficial joint tenants of the matrimonial home. When the marriage broke down the house was too large for him to live in alone, and they reached an agreement, recorded in a written memorandum, that he should be entitled to sell the house at his discretion and use the proceeds to provide a new home where the children could come and visit. Before the house was sold he died. Walton J. held that the agreement they had reached did not sever their joint tenancy as it was concerned with the use of the land, or the proceeds of sale, and not the ownership:

> "can the memorandum be read as a severance of their joint beneficial interests: an agreement to the effect that each of them thereafter is to be solely entitled to his and her respective one half share in such proceeds? With the best will in the world I find myself wholly unable to give the memorandum such a construction. . . . It appears to me that the memorandum is dealing solely with the use by Mr Todd of the whole of the proceeds of sale, and that, qua ownership, use is wholly ambiguous: hence it cannot be implied from the fact the Mr Todd was to have the use of the whole of the money either that the title thereto was assigned to

[1] [1975] Ch. 429 at 442.
[2] *ibid.* at 440.
[3] *ibid.*
[4] *ibid.*
[5] *ibid.* at 444, citing *Wilson v. Bell* (1843) 5 Ir.Eq.R. 501 and *Re Wilks* [1891] 3 Ch. 59.
[6] *ibid.*
[7] *ibid.* at 446.
[8] [1975] Ch. 222.

> him or that he was entitled to have his own half absolutely, and Mrs Todd her own half share absolutely."[9]

(vi) The agreement need not have been acted upon: Severance will occur provided that agreement was reached and is not dependent upon the agreement having been carried into effect. This is clear from the facts of *Burgess v. Rawnsley*[10] itself.

(e) Severance by mutual conduct

(i) Rationale for severance by mutual conduct: The essence of the third method of severance identified by Page Wood V.-C. in *Williams v. Hensman*[11] is that all the joint tenants have acted in such a way as to demonstrate that they intend to regard themselves as enjoying differentiated and specific shares in the land. It is said that it must be possible to infer from their conduct that they had a "common intention" to sever. In practice, if joint tenants treat themselves as if they were tenants in common the law will regard the joint tenancy as having been severed, even though there was no express act of severance.

(ii) A mutual course of dealing: A unilateral act of a joint tenant will not be sufficient to effect severance under this head and will only be effective to sever if it falls within the first head examined above, namely if it is an act which operates on the joint tenants own share. For this reason Page Wood V.-C. stressed that a mere unilateral expression of intention to sever was not to be regarded as a "course of dealing" for the purposes of this third head of severance:

> "When severance depends on an inference of this kind without any express act of severance, it will not suffice to rely on an intention, with respect to the particular share, declared only behind the backs of the other persons interested. You must find in this class of cases a course of dealing by which the shares of all the parties to the contest have been affected."[12]

A number of categories of mutual conduct have come to be regarded as possessing potentially severing effect.

(iii) Joint tenants have held long term assumptions about their ownership of the land: Where joint tenants have held long term assumptions about their ownership of the land which are inconsistent with the continuance of a joint tenancy this will be a sufficient course of conduct to effect a severance in fact. This was recognised by Blackett-Ord J. in *Gore and Snell v. Carpenter*[13] where he stated: "A course of dealing is where over the years the parties have dealt with their interests in the property on the footing that they are interests in common and are not as joint."[14] However, having recognised that in principle such a course of dealing could effect severance he held none had in fact been established. A husband and wife were the joint tenants of two houses. In the course of separation negotiations it was suggested that one house

[9] *ibid.* at 229.
[10] *ibid.*
[11] (1861) 1 J. & H. 546.
[12] *ibid.* at 557.
[13] (1990) 60 P. & C.R. 456.
[14] *ibid.* at 462.

should be transferred into the wife's name and although she agreed in principle there were further financial arrangements to be settled. No final agreement was ever reached and the wife continued to live in the house, which remained jointly owned, until the husband committed suicide some time later. Blackett-Ord J. held that this did not amount to a course of dealing sufficient to effect severance:

> "For severance to be effected by a course of dealings all the joint tenants must be concerned in such a course and in the present case there is no evidence that [the wife] was committing herself to accepting a tenancy in common prior to the property division which would have been made in the divorce proceedings."

Since there was no severance the entire ownership of the house vested in the wife by survivorship and did not form part of the husband's estate.

(iv) Joint tenants have executed mutual wills: Although it has been seen that the unilateral act of a joint tenant purporting to dispose of his interest in land by will does not have the effect of severing his share *inter vivos*, the execution of mutual wills by all the joint tenants leaving their interests to agreed legatees will constitute a sufficient "course of dealing" to fall under the third head of *Williams v. Hensman.* In *In the Estate of Heys*[15] a husband and wife were the joint tenants of a leasehold property. In 1907 they executed wills in identical terms leaving the property to each other if they predeceased and to the defendants in the event that they died second. Sir Samuel Evans, President of the Court of Probate, held that the execution of these mutual wills severed their joint tenancy of the leasehold so that from that time onwards they were holding as tenants in common. In consequence, on the death of the husband his half-share in the property passed to his wife under his will rather than by way of survivorship, and was bound by a trust in favour of the beneficiaries named in the mutual wills.[16]

(v) Joint tenants have been involved in inconclusive negotiations with regard to the ownership of the land: The most controversial issue to arise under this third head of severance is whether inconclusive negotiations between the joint tenants in regard to their ownership of the land are a sufficient course of conduct to effect severance. The possibility was raised by Lord Denning M.R. in *Burgess v. Rawnsley*.[17] Although, as has been noted above, the majority of the Court of Appeal held that severance had occurred because Mrs Rawnsley had reached an oral agreement to sell her share of the co-owned house to Mr Honick, Lord Denning M.R. was prepared to find that "even if there was not any firm agreement" between the parties their negotiations amounted to a "course of dealing" which had evidenced a sufficient intention to sever. He stated a general principle that:

> "a 'course of dealing' need not amount to an agreement, expressed or implied, for severance. It is sufficient if there is a course of dealing in which one party makes clear to the other that he desires that their shares should no longer be held jointly but be held in common."[18]

[15] [1914] P. 192.
[16] See also: *Re Wilford's Estate* (1879) 11 Ch.D. 267; *Gould v. Kemp* 2 My. & K. 304.
[17] [1975] Ch. 429.
[18] *ibid.* at 439.

The difficulty with this approach is that it seems to suggest that a mere unilateral statement of intention, provided that it is communicated to the other joint tenants, is sufficient to sever. It is clear that the other members of the Court of Appeal rejected the argument that a mere unilateral declaration of intention is sufficient, even if communicated,[19] but it is less clear whether the proposition that inconclusive negotiations would be a sufficient course of dealing was rejected. Browne L.J. doubted that the evidence would establish a sufficient course of dealing but refused to express a final opinion whether negotiation could ever be sufficient. Sir John Pennycuick seemed to anticipate that negotiations could have a severing effect, but not on the particular facts:

> "I do not doubt myself that where one tenant negotiates with another for some rearrangement of interest, it may be possible to infer from the particular facts a common intention to sever even though the negotiations break down. Whether such an inference can be drawn must I think depend upon the particular facts. In the present case the negotiations between Mr Honick and Mrs Rawnsley, if they can be properly described as negotiations at all, fall, it seems to me, far short of warranting an inference. One could not ascribe to joint tenants an intention to sever merely because one offers to buy out the other for £X and the other makes a counter offer of £Y."[20]

The evidence of later cases suggests that it is extremely difficulty to establish a clear mutual intention to sever from inconclusive negotiations. In *McDowell v. Hirschfield Lipson & Rumney and Smith*[21] it was submitted that inconclusive negotiations on the separation of a husband and wife and correspondence between their respective solicitors concerning the suggested sale of the matrimonial home were a sufficient course of dealing to effect severance. Eric Stockdale J. dismissed this submission finding that there was no course of dealing from which to justify a finding of a common intention to sever. He pointed out the crucial difficulty that in many such cases where negotiations have broken down severance is not at that stage inevitable for the parties.[22] Similarly, in *Gore and Snell v. Carpenter*[23] Blackett-Ord J. held that a common intention to sever could not be inferred from abortive negotiations because at that stage the wife had not been prepared to commit herself to a tenancy in common.
(vi) Joint tenants have physically divided their possession of the land: It might be thought that physical division of the land could constitute a course of dealing which manifests an intention to sever a joint tenancy. However, it should be born in mind that unity of possession is a requirement of both joint tenancies and tenancies in common, and in *Greenfield v. Greenfield*[24] Fox J. held that physical division of land was not automatically inconsistent with the continuance of a joint tenancy and therefore insufficient as a course of dealing from which to infer an intention to sever. Two brothers were the joint tenants of a house which they had purchased as joint tenants in 1947 and converted into two separate maisonettes in 1962, in which they lived with

[19] *ibid.* at 444 per Browne L.J.; at 448 per Sir John Pennycuick.
[20] *ibid.* at 447.
[21] [1992] 2 F.L.R. 126.
[22] *ibid.* at 131.
[23] (1990) 60 P. & C.R. 456.
[24] (1979) 38 P. & C.R. 570.

their respective wives. When one brother died in 1975 his wife claimed to be entitled to ownership of their maisonette under his will, but since there had been no severance it passed to the other brother by way of survivorship. Fox J. held that the long period of divided use did not indicate an intention on the part of the brothers to sever the joint tenancy:

> "The onus of establishing severance must be on the plaintiff. It seems to me that on the facts [she] comes nowhere near discharging that onus. Neither side made clear any intention of ending the joint tenancy. The defendant had no intention of ending it and never thought that he or [his brother] had ended it. The defendant's understanding was that [his brother] was of exactly the same mind. Indeed their mutual intention in 1962 was to continue the joint tenancy. And so they agreed. The mere existence of the separate maisonettes and of their separate occupation is not inconsistent with the continuation of a joint tenancy. The two can perfectly well exist together. The matter must be considered in the light of the evidence of the actual intentions of the parties."[25]

(vii) Joint tenants use their land for a business partnership? In *Barton v. Morris*[26] a man and woman purchased a farmhouse which they intended to run as a guest house. She provided the majority of the initial deposit, but the property was conveyed into their names as joint tenants in law and equity. The woman subsequently kept the accounts of their business which differentiated between their respective capital contributions to the property. She was subsequently killed in a riding accident and the administratrix of her estate claimed that the joint tenancy had been severed by this course of dealing. The Court of Appeal held that the inclusion of the property in the account was not a course of dealing which reflected an intention that the joint tenancy should be severed, but rather the intention that the financial dealings of the parties should be accurately recorded, and for tax considerations. The property therefore passed absolutely to the man by survivorship.

3 Forfeiture: severance by operation of law

(a) *Rationale of forfeiture*

Forfeiture occurs in order to prevent a person retaining property received as a consequence of unlawfully killing the previous owner. It has application where a person would receive property under the will of someone they unlawfully killed[27] or on their intestacy.[28] It has potential application to situations where there is a joint tenancy because if one joint tenant kills another he stands to gain thereby through the operation of survivorship. Rather than allow him to benefit the law regards the unlawful killing as a severing event, thus preventing its operation in the killer's favour. Since the legal title in land can only be held as a joint tenancy survivorship is allowed

[25] *ibid.* at 578.
[26] [1985] 2 All E.R. 1032.
[27] See: *Re Sigsworth* [1935] Ch. 89; *Re Callaway* [1956] Ch. 559; *Re Peacock* [1957] Ch. 310.
[28] *Re Crippen* [1911] P. 108.

to operate in relation to the legal title if the killer is a trustee, but severance operates in relation to the equitable ownership so that the killer cannot derive any real benefit from his actions.

(b) Scope of forfeiture

Forfeiture will occur in the event of murder, but it remains unclear whether it will apply in all cases of manslaughter. Some cases suggest that it is inapplicable in cases of involuntary manslaughter[29] but the courts have generally shown reluctance to draw a distinction between voluntary and involuntary manslaughter.[30] In *Gray v. Barr*[31] Geoffery Lane J. suggested at first instance that forfeiture would apply if a person was "guilty of deliberate, intentional and unlawful violence of threats of violence," a test approved by Vinelott J. in *Re K (deceased)*.[32] The forfeiture rule will apply even where there has been no criminal conviction if the unlawful killing can be established in the civil court where the burden of proof is the balance of probabilities.[33]

(c) Jurisdiction to grant relief from forfeiture

Although forfeiture prima facie operates in cases of unlawful killing section 2(1) of the Forfeiture Act 1982 grants the court a jurisdiction to "make an order . . . modifying the effect of that rule" in cases other than murder. To exercise the jurisdiction the court must be satisfied that "having regard to the conduct of the offender and of the deceased and to such other circumstances as appear to the court to be material, the justice of the case requires the effect of the rule to be modified in that case."[34] Relief from forfeiture was granted by Vinelott J. in *Re K (deceased)*[35] because the wife who had killed her husband had suffered grave violence at his hands. As a consequence of the court's order she was not prevented from taking his interests in their jointly owned matrimonial home by survivorship.

(d) Effect of forfeiture where there is a joint tenancy

The exact effects of severance by operation of law through forfeiture will depend upon the nature of the joint tenancy in question.

(i) Operation of forfeiture where there were only two joint tenants: Where land was held by two persons as joint tenants and one unlawfully killed the other the effect of the killing is to sever the joint tenancy. The consequence is that the killer will retain his half-share of the land but will not receive the interest of his victim by survivorship. Instead, his victim's half share will pass under to whoever is entitled under his will, or by the rules of intestacy. The operation of these principles are well illustrated in *Re K (deceased)*.[36] Husband and wife were the joint tenants at law and in equity of their matrimonial home. The wife subsequently shot the husband accidentally after threatening him with a loaded shotgun. Vinelott J. held that in these circumstances the

[29] See: *Tinline v. White Cross Insurance Association Ltd* [1921] 3 K.B. 327; *James v. British General Insurance Co. Ltd* [1927] 2 K.B. 311.
[30] See: *Re Giles* [1972] Ch. 544.
[31] [1971] 2 Q.B. 554.
[32] [1985] Ch. 85.
[33] *Gray v. Barr* [1971] 2 Q.B. 554. See also *Re Sigsworth* [1935] Ch. 89 where forfeiture was applied when there was no criminal conviction because of the defendant's suicide.
[34] s.2(2).
[35] [1985] Ch. 85; affd. [1986] Ch. 180.
[36] *ibid.*

forfeiture rule would prima facie apply so that although the wife held the entire legal title the joint tenancy had been severed in equity so that there was a tenancy in common and that her husband's half-share passed to whoever was entitled on his death.[37] In the event this result was only avoided because he felt able to grant relief from the effects of forfeiture.

(ii) Operation of forfeiture where there were more than two joint tenants and one has killed another: Where land is owned by more than two joint tenants and one is killed by another the operation of the forfeiture rule is less clear cut. For example, if Carolyn, Daniel, Ellen and Frank are the joint tenants in law and in equity of a house and Carolyn murders Daniel the expected result would be that this would have the effect of severing Daniel's beneficial interest in the land so that a quarter share would devolve to those entitled on his death, and that Carolyn, Ellen and Frank would continue as joint tenants of the remaining three-quarters. However, this solution deprives the innocent joint tenants, namely Ellen and Frank, of benefiting from the death of Daniel by way of the principle of survivorship. To overcome this problem an Australian court held[38] that the interests of the unlawfully killed joint tenant should be held on a constructive trust for the innocent joint tenants. If this approach were to be followed, Ellen and Frank would be joint tenants of a quarter share of the beneficial interest, representing Daniel's interest, and Ellen, Frank and Carolyn would be the joint tenants of the remaining three quarters interest. There are no English cases which decide how such problems should be resolved and neither approach is ideal from the perspective of achieving justice between the surviving parties.

Mutual Rights of Equitable Co-owners of Land

1 Right to occupation and use of the land

(a) A consequence of unity of possession

(i) The right of occupation at common law: It has already been noted that one essential element of both a joint tenancy and a tenancy in common is that the co-owners enjoy unity of possession of the co-owned land. This means that they are both entitled to occupy every part of the land and they cannot exclude each other from any part of it. This follows even if the parties are tenants in common, since their notional shares of the ownership of the land are not translated into a correspondingly proportionate right of occupation. The mutual right of occupation was recognised by the Court of Appeal in *Bull v. Bull*[39] where a house was held by a man as trustee for himself and his mother as tenants in common. The Court of Appeal held that he was not entitled to evict her. Lord Denning M.R. explained:

> "when there are two equitable tenants in common, until the place is sold, each of them is entitled concurrently with the other to the possession of the land and to

[37] See also: *Schobelt v. Barber* (1966) 60 D.L.R. (2d) 519; *Re Pechar* [1969] N.Z.L.R. 574.
[38] *Rasmanis v. Jurewitsch* (1970) 70 S.R. (NSW) 407 (Court of Appeal of New South Wales).
[39] [1955] 1 Q.B. 234.

> the use and enjoyment of it in a proper manner; and neither of them is entitled to turn the other out."[40]

Despite this general right, it seems that in some circumstances the nature of the relationship of the original co-owners will prevent a successor in title who has acquired the share of one of them from exercising the right to occupation with the others. In *Chhokar v. Chhokar*[41] Mr and Mrs Chhokar were the tenants in common in equity of their matrimonial home, the legal title to which was held by Mr Chhokar alone. After leaving his wife he sold the land to his friend Mr Parmar, who was fully aware of his wife's interest, and the sale was deliberately completed while Mrs Chhokar was in hospital. The effect of this transaction was that Parmar held the legal title to the house on trust for himself and Mrs Chhokar as equitable tenants in common of half-shares since he had taken the land subject to Mrs Chhokar's interest which was binding on him as an overriding interest under Land Registration Act 1925, s.70(1)(g). Subsequently Mr and Mrs Chhokar were reconciled and he moved back into the matrimonial home. The Court of Appeal assumed that in these circumstances Parmar had no right to occupation of the land, even though he was the owner of a half-share by way of a tenancy in common, on the grounds that he stood in the shoes of Mr Chhokar as his successor in title, and that the right of occupation was dependant on the married status of the original co-owners. Cumming-Bruce L.J. explained:

> "[counsel for Parmar] submits that he has a right in law to occupy the property. but he goes on in the next breath to concede that it is a right that cannot be exercised because he succeeded to the rights of the husband in the matrimonial home. Mr Parmar is a married man himself and no court would allow him to try to occupy the matrimonial home in common with Mrs Chhokar (and for all I know Mrs Parmar might have something to say about it too, if he tried to do so). But for this purpose he stands in the shoes of [Mr Chhokar]. . . ."[42]

This suggests that wherever the original co-owners entered into occupation of the land on the basis of an intimate relationship between themselves a successor in title will not be entitled to assert his right to occupy by virtue of his status as a co-owner alone.
(ii) A statutory right of occupation: It should also be noted that under section 12 of the Trusts of Land and Appointment of Trustees Act 1996 the beneficiaries of a trust of land have a statutory right to occupation of the land. This includes co-owners, who enjoy their rights behind a trust. Under section 13 the trustees have limited powers to exclude or restrict the occupation rights of the beneficiaries. The effect of these provisions are considered in detail below.

(b) One co-owner cannot trespass against another

Since all the co-owners of land have rights to possession of the whole land, one co-owner cannot commit an act of trespass against another. In *Jacobs v. Seward*[43] one

[40] *ibid.* at 238.
[41] [1984] F.L.R. 313.
[42] *ibid.* at 332.
[43] (1872) L.R. 5 H.L. 464.

tenant in common of land had cut hay in a field which was co-owned. The House of Lords held that a tenant in common could not maintain an action in trespass against a fellow tenant in common unless there had been an actual ouster of the tenant claimed to have trespassed from the land. The argument that the placing of a lock on the gate to the field was a sufficient ouster was rejected, since the supposedly trespassing tenant had never been refused access to the field and there was no evidence of anything passing between the parties which demonstrated that the lock had been placed with the intention of excluding the co-tenant. Lord Hatherley L.C. concluded that:

> "so far as trespass is concerned, it appears to me to be idle talk of trespass as a consequence of a man making hay upon his own field — for it is his own — or a moiety of it at least, and no definite portion of it is mapped out as his moiety."[44]

(c) Payment of rent between co-owners

(i) The context of occupational rent between co-owners: Although all the co-owners are theoretically equally entitled to occupation of the land it is inevitable that in some circumstances such shared occupation will be impossible. Such problems arise if the relationship of co-owners of residential property breaks down. In *Bull v. Bull*[45] Lord Denning M.R. took the view that the solution to the inability of the co-owners to share the land was that it should be sold and the proceeds divided appropriately between the parties. However, as will be seen below, in many more recent cases where the co-owner's relationship has disintegrated the courts have refused to order a sale of the land, with the effect that one co-owner remains in occupation of the land and the other is excluded. Where a co-owner does not enjoy the benefit of occupation of the land the question arises whether he is entitled to receive compensating payments of rent from the co-owners who are enjoying occupation. The traditional understanding is that since co-owners are equally entitled to occupy the land those that are not in occupation have no right to receive rent from those who are merely exercising their rights as co-owners. In *Henderson v. Eason*[46] Parke B. stated:

> "There are obviously many cases in which a tenant in common may occupy and enjoy the land...and have all the benefit to be derived from it, and yet it would be most unjust to make him pay anything. For instance, if a dwelling house, or barn, or room, is solely occupied by one tenant in common without ousting the other...it would be most inequitable to hold that he thereby, by the simple act of occupation or use, without any agreement, should be liable to pay a rent or anything in the nature of compensation to his cotenants for that occupation or use to which to the full extent to which he enjoyed it he had a perfect right."

(ii) No rent where a co-owner chooses not to occupy: Where a co-owner does not enjoy occupation by his own voluntary choice not to exercise his right, he is not entitled to receive a rent from the co-owners in occupation. This was recognised in *Dennis v. McDonald*[47] where Purchas J. stated:

[44] *ibid.* at 473.
[45] [1955] 1 Q.B. 234.
[46] (1851) 17 Q.B. 701.
[47] [1982] 3 F.L.R. 398.

> "Only in cases where the tenants in common not in occupation were in a position to enjoy their rights to occupy but chose not to do so voluntarily, and were not excluded by any relevant factor, would the tenant in common in occupation be entitled to do so free of liability to pay an occupation rent."[48]

(iii) Rent payable where a co-owner was excluded: It follows that were one co-owner is excluded from enjoyment of the co-owned land those co-owners who continue to enjoy occupation will be required to pay a compensating rent to those deprived of their right. In *Dennis v. McDonald* Purchas J. examined the authorities[49] and summarised the approach of the Chancery Courts:

> "the Court of Chancery . . . would always be ready to enquire into the position as between co-owners being tenants in common, either at law or in equity, to see whether a tenant in common in occupation of the premises was doing so to the exclusion of one or more of the other tenants in common, for whatever purpose or by whatever means. If this was found to be the case, then if in order to do equity between the parties an occupation rent should be paid, this would be declared and the appropriate enquiry ordered."[50]

A man and woman had lived together as husband and wife for a number of years in a house which they owned as tenants in common in equity and occupied with their five children. The woman left the property as a result of the man's violence towards her. Purchas J. held that as she had been excluded from the family home she was entitled to receive a compensating payment from the man, who had remained in occupation. In contrast in *Jones v. Jones*[51] a father purchased a house which was held on trust for himself and his son as tenants in common of three-quarters and a quarter share respectively. The purpose was to provide the son with somewhere to live. On the father's death his share passed to his wife, the son's step-mother, who wanted the house sold and who was not in occupation of it. Having refused to order a sale of the house Lord Denning M.R. held that in the absence of any ouster from the property there was no obligation for the son to pay an occupation rent.[52] The payment of a rent has often been imposed as a condition when the court has refused to order the sale of co-owned property[53] so that one of the co-owners can remain living in it. For example, in *Harvey v. Harvey*[54] a husband and wife were the equitable tenants in common of their matrimonial home in shares of a third and two-thirds respectively. The husband had left his wife and she remained in the house with three of their children. The Court of Appeal held that any sale should be postponed[55] during the lifetime of the wife or

[48] *ibid.* at 405.
[49] *M'Mahon v. Burchell* (1846) 2 Ph. 127; *Henderson v. Eason* (1851) 17 Q.B. 701; *Hill v. Hickin* [1897] 2 Ch. 579; *Jones v. Jones* [1977] 1 W.L.R. 438.
[50] *ibid.* at 404.
[51] [1977] 1 W.L.R. 438.
[52] Roskill L.J. held that there was no obligation to pay rent on the basis that the son's entitlement was by way of proprietary estoppel and that there was no justification for imposing a rent as a condition of satisfying the estoppel equity.
[53] See below, p. 247.
[54] (1982) 3 F.L.R. 141.
[55] Even though it was held on trust for sale.

until her remarriage, voluntary removal from the premises or becoming dependant on another man. However it imposed the condition that, after the mortgage was repaid, or the youngest child attained the age of 18, she was to pay an occupational rent for her continued occupancy. In *Bedson v. Bedson*[56] the court awarded an occupational rent where one co-owner remained in occupation of the matrimonial home while divorce proceedings were pending. Where the co-owned property has been purchased by means of a mortgage the requirement that a co-owner who remains in occupation makes the mortgage repayments, thus freeing a co-owner who has been excluded, also amounts to the payment of a form of compensation for non-occupation.[57]

(iv) Is an occupational rent fair?: Given that the court is willing in some circumstances to require a co-owner in occupation to pay an occupational rent to those excluded, in *Chhokar v. Chhokar*[58] the Court of Appeal suggested that the appropriate a test to determine if rent should be required was whether it would be "fair" in the circumstances. As has been noted above, in the unusual circumstances of the case Mrs Chhokar and Mr Parmar were the tenants in common of Mrs Chhokar's matrimonial home. Ewbank J. held that as Mrs Chhokar had enjoyed the sole occupation of the property for three and a half years Mr Parmar should receive a rent of £8 per week. However, the Court of Appeal rejected the submission that Mr Parmar was entitled to rent simply because he could not enjoy occupation, and deleted any requirement to pay from the judge's order. Cumming-Bruce L.J. stated that:

> "I have been unable to find anything in the authorities which should lead the court to hold that it would be fair, which I regard as the test, to require [Mrs Chhokar] to pay occupation rent to Parmar by way of payment for her occupation of the matrimonial home."[59]

Central to this conclusion seems to have been the fact that Mr Parmar in some sense stood in the shoes of the husband whose share he had purchased, and that the husband himself had not been excluded by the wife as she had taken him back and they were sharing occupation of the house.

(v) A wider jurisdiction to award an occupational rent?: In *Re Pavlou (A Bankrupt)*[60] a husband and wife were the beneficial joint tenants of a house which they had purchased in 1973. In 1983 the husband left and the wife remained in sole occupation, paying the mortgage and making improvements to the property. Millet J. held that on the evidence before him he could not determine whether an occupational rent should have been payable by the wife in respect of her sole occupation and set off against her mortgage interest payment when dividing the proceeds of sale. However, he suggested a rather broader approach to the question of rent which did not necessarily require exclusion:

> "I take the law to be to the following effect. First, a court of equity will order an inquiry and payment of occupational rent, not only in the case where a co-owner

[56] [1965] 2 Q.B. 666.
[57] *Re Evers Trust* [1980] 1 W.L.R. 1327.
[58] [1984] F.L.R. 313.
[59] *ibid.* at 332.
[60] [1993] 1 W.L.R. 1046.

in occupation has ousted the other, but in any other case in which it is necessary in order to do equity between the parties that an occupational rent should be paid. The fact that there has not been an ouster or forceful exclusion therefore is far from conclusive. Secondly, where it is a matrimonial home and the marriage has broken down, the party who leaves the property will, in most cases, be regarded as excluded from the family home, so that an occupation rent should be paid by the co-owner who remains. But that is not a rule of law; that is merely a statement of the prima facie conclusion to be drawn from the facts. The true position is that if a tenant in common leaves the property voluntarily, but would be welcome back and would be in a position to enjoy his or her right to occupy, it would normally not be fair or equitable on the remaining tenant in common to charge him or her with an occupation rent which he or she never expected to pay."[61]

He felt that there was insufficient evidence to determine whether the husband would have been welcomed back into occupation between 1983 when he left and 1986 when his wife petitioned for divorce, but that after the petition a rent was prima facie payable.

(vi) Assessment of the occupational rent: Where the court decides that the imposition of an occupational rent on a co-owner in sole occupation is appropriate the question arises as to how it should be assessed. In *Dennis v. McDonald*[62] Purchas J. held that the man in sole occupation should pay his ex-partner a rent equivalent to half the fair rent which would have been assessed as payable by a rent officer for a letting of the whole premises unfurnished to a protected tenant for the period of the occupation, giving credit for any sums expended which improved the capital value of the property but not for the costs of ordinary repair and maintenance. The Court of Appeal rejected this approach on the grounds that it did not compensate the excluded co-owner for non-occupation but punished the occupier by regarding him as "illicitly enjoying and therefore accountable for the one half of what he would have had to pay for the property if he entered the property market as a willing tenant and found a willing landlord ready to let it to him." Sir John Arnold P. explained that he considered this inappropriate:

> "I am bound to say that in the circumstances of the case, that that is somewhat unrealistic. He occupies this property not because he has been able to negotiate in the market and obtain it but because he is a tenant in common. He occupies it in respect of, and by right of, his beneficial interest. He is not, therefore, subject to the vagaries of the market and starts off with a right of occupation. Something would have to be allowed in some way for that. Moreover, it is difficult to see what justification there is for charging a person in his position with such extra payment as a tenant would have to make by reason of the scarcity of relevant accommodation in the market."[63]

The Court of Appeal therefore concluded that he should have to pay a "fair rent" as would be assessed under the Rent Act but eliminating the element for scarcity.[64]

[61] *ibid.* at 1050.
[62] [1982] F.L.R. 408.
[63] *ibid.* at 413.
[64] Assessment was ordered under, s.70(1) & (2) of the Rent Act 1977 without regard to any other provisions of the Act.

However, it was stressed that the preferable solution was that the parties negotiate to determine an acceptable rent between themselves. Since the fundamental basis of rent assessment was compensation for non-occupation, rather than restitution of the benefit of sole-occupation to the co-owner remaining, the Court of Appeal further held that the man was not entitled to any set off against rent because more of the parties' children were living with him than with her. Sir John Arnold P explained why such considerations were irrelevant to the assessment of the rent:

> "the nature of the payment, and the amount of the payment, should be regulated by reference to the circumstance that the payer is housed in the property of which he is a trustee to the exclusion of the payee, who is equally a beneficiary, and that the purpose to which the payer puts the property has nothing to do with the case."[65]

In *Harvey v. Harvey*[66] the Court of Appeal held that an occupational rent should be determined at a "reasonable, market figure."

(vii) Cost of repairs allowed against the payment of occupational rent: In *Dennis v. McDonald* the Court of Appeal also ordered an inquiry as to the costs or value of any improvements which the sole-occupier had made to the land and that he should be entitled to set-off half this amount against rent due.[67]

(viii) Statutory power of trustees to impose rent: Under Trusts of Land and Appointment of Trustees Act 1996, s.13 the trustees of land are entitled to impose conditions upon a co-owner who remains in occupation of co-owned land where the occupancy of other co-owners has been excluded or restricted by an exercise of their powers under section 12. The conditions which may be imposed specifically include requiring the beneficiary in occupation to "make payments by way of compensation to the beneficiary whose entitlement has been excluded or restricted."[68] This provision is discussed further below.

2 Right to share in the economic exploitation of the land

(a) Profits received from someone who is not a co-owner

Land is an economically valuable commodity which can be exploited so as to produce a profit for its owners. Obvious examples of such economic exploitation include leasing the land so as to produce an income in the form of rent, mining the land or farming the land. Where any profit is generated from a stranger's use or exploitation of the co-owned land the co-owners are entitled to a share proportionate to the extent of their interest. In *Henderson v. Eason*[69] Parke B held that a co-owner was obliged to account[70] for any profits he had received from third parties in excess of his legitimate entitlement:

[65] [1982] F.L.R. 408 at 412.
[66] [1982] 3 F.L.R. 141.
[67] See also: *Re Pavlou* [1993] 1 W.L.R. 1046.
[68] s.13(6)(a).
[69] (1851) 17 Q.B. 701.
[70] The co-owner liable to account is not, however, a fiduciary: *Kennedy v. De Trafford* [1897] A.C. 180.

"where the tenant in common receives money or something else, where another person gives or pays it, which the cotenants are entitled to simply by reason of their being tenants in common, and in proportion to their interests as such, and of which one receives and keeps more than his just share according to that proportion."

These principles were applied in *Bernard v. Josephs*[71] where a husband and wife were the tenants in common of half shares in their matrimonial home. After the break down of their marriage the wife left and the husband remained in occupation. He let part of the house to tenants. The Court of Appeal held that in assessing the price at which the husband should be allowed to purchase the wife's share she should be entitled to the credit of half the rent he had received.

(b) Profits generated by a co-owner from his own use of the land

(i) No duty to account for profit which is the just product of his work: Where one co-owner has made a profit for himself by use of the land, for example by farming it or siting his production facility on it, he will not be accountable for the profit he made to the extent that it can be regarded as the legitimate product of his own investment, whether of labour or capital. As Parke B. stated in *Henderson v. Eason*[72]:

"Again, there are many cases where profits are made, and are actually taken, by one co-tenant, and yet it is impossible to say that he has received more than comes to his just share. For instance, one tenant employs his capital and industry in cultivating the whole of a piece of land, the subject of the tenancy, in a mode in which the money and labour expended greatly exceed the value of the rent or compensation for the mere occupation of the land; in raising hops, for example, which is a very hazardous adventure. He takes the whole of the crops: and is he to be accountable for any of the profits in such a case, when it is clear that, if the speculation had been a losing one altogether, he could not have called for a moiety of the losses, as he would have been enabled to do had it been cultivated by the mutual agreement of the cotenants? The risk of the cultivation, and the profits and loss, are his own; and with respect to all the produce of the land, the fructus industriales, which are raised by the capital and industry of the occupier, and would not exist without it. In taking all that produce he cannot be said to receive more than his just share and proportion to which he is entitled as a tenant in common. He receives in truth the return for his own labour and capital, to which his co-tenant had no right."

(ii) Duty to account where a co-owners profits are not merely the product of his own work: In *Henderson v. Eason* Parke B. anticipated that a co-tenant will not always be entitled to retain the entire profit generated by his use of the land as he cannot retain more than his just share and proportion. He will generally be liable to account if he has exploited the land itself, diminishing its capital value, for example by mineral extraction or quarrying. In *Job v. Potton*[73] a mine was owned by a number of tenants in

[71] [1982] Ch. 391.
[72] (1851) 17 Q.B. 710.
[73] (1875) 20 L.R. Eq. 84.

common, one of whom enjoyed a two-thirds share of the ownership. He extracted coal and one question was the extent to which he was required to account for the value of the coal extracted to his fellow tenants. Sir James Bacon V.-C. presupposed that the tenant was entitled to extract the coal but that "he must not appropriate to himself more than his share." He held that he was liable to account to his fellow tenants for a third of the value of the coal that had been mined and brought to the surface, subject to a deduction of "the cost of the severance and the cost of bringing it to the pit's mouth." By means of this balance the co-tenants to whom he was obliged to account would not receive a windfall benefit of his work and investment, and he would not take more than his just share. In *Jacobs v. Seward*[74] the House of Lords held that a tenant in common who had harvested hay from a co-owned field was not liable in tort to his fellow tenants. However, it was assumed that if they had brought an action for account they would have been entitled to a share of the profits subject to allowance of the expense of making the hay.

3 Right to a contribution towards repairs and improvements

(a) No right to contribution without agreement, request or fulfilment of a common obligation

Land, and especially buildings, will always require a degree of maintenance to prevent them falling into disrepair, which will inevitably diminish its value. If one co-owner pays for the cost of repairs or provides improvements to the land is he entitled to proportionate contributions from his fellow tenants? In *Leigh v. Dickson*[75] the Court of Appeal held that a tenant in common who pays for necessary repairs to the co-owned land is not entitled to a proportionate contribution to the cost from his co-owners unless there was an agreement that they would contribute. Brett M.R. explained why there was no right of contribution where one tenant in common had spent £80 on substantial repairs and improvement to the co-owned property:

> "The cost of the repairs was a voluntary payment by the defendant, partly for the benefit of himself and partly for the benefit of his co-owner; but the co-owner cannot reject the benefit of the repairs, and if she is held to be liable for a proportionate share of the cost, the defendant will get the advantage of the repairs without allowing his co-owner any liberty to decide whether she will refuse or adopt them. . . . If the law were otherwise, a part-owner might be compelled to incur expense against his will: a house might be situated in a decaying borough, and it might be thought by one co-owner that it would be better not to repair it. The refusal of a tenant in common to bear any part of the cost of repair may be unreasonable; nevertheless, the law allows him to refuse and no action will lie against him."[76]

Consequently a co-owner will only be entitled to a contribution to the cost of repairs which he has incurred if there was an express or implied agreement that his co-tenants

[74] (1872) 5 L.R. App. Cas. 464.
[75] (1884) 15 Q.B.D. 60.
[76] *ibid.* at 65–66.

would contribute,[77] or an express or implied request[78] that the work be done. In *Leigh v. Dickson* Cotton L.J. also suggested that there would be a right to contribution if a co-owner had funded repairs in fulfilment of an obligation to repair that he and his co-tenants jointly owed to a third party, since "when two persons are under a common obligation, one of them can recover from the other the amount expended in discharge or fulfilment of the common obligation." For example, if a lease containing a repairing covenant was held by two persons as tenants in common and one of them paid for the costs of necessary repairs, he would be entitled to receive a contribution from his co-tenant proportionate to his interest.

(b) An equitable lien to recoup the benefit of expenditure on repairs or improvements

Although a co-owner will not be entitled to a contribution towards the costs of repairs or improvements it seems that he will be entitled to an equitable lien over the property which has been benefited by the repairs or improvements he funded, which must be satisfied from the proceeds of sale when the land is sold.[79] This possibility was recognised by Cotton L.J. in *Leigh v. Dickson*[80]:

> "Therefore, no remedy exists for money expended in repairs by one tenant in common, so long as the property is enjoyed in common.; but in a suit for a partition it is usual to have an inquiry as to those expenses of which nothing could be recovered so long as the parties enjoyed their property in common; when it is desired to put an end to that state of things, it is then necessary to consider what has been expended in improvements or repairs; and whether the property is divided or sold by decree of the Court, one party cannot take the increase in value without making an allowance for what has been expended in order to obtain that increase in value; in fact, the execution of the repairs and improvements is adopted and sanctioned by accepting the increased value. There is, therefore, a mode by which money expended by one tenant in common for repairs can be recovered. . . ."

It is somewhat unclear from these comments whether the nature of the recovery by way of an equitable lien is of the costs of the repairs or improvements or of any increase in the value to the land flowing from such improvements. The cost of repairs may far exceed any increase in value, or work which one co-owner considers an improvement may be of such bad taste as to actually reduce the market value of the land. In *Gross v. French*[81] where improvements to a house had been carried out at the expense of the legal owner, who was a bare trustee, the Court of Appeal held that he was entitled to an equitable lien over the land for the amount by which the value of the house had been enhanced by the work.[82] Walton J. had rejected the submission that

[77] See: *Bernard v. Josephs* [1983] 4 F.L.R. 178; *Harwood v. Harwood* [1991] 2 F.L.R. 274.
[78] *Leigh v. Dickson* (1884) 15 Q.B.D. 60 at 67 per Cotton L.J.
[79] In *Bernard v. Josephs* [1982] Ch. 391 the Court of Appeal held that only in exceptional circumstances would it be inferred that a co-owners funding of repairs or improvements was intended to alter the extent of the beneficial interests in the property.
[80] *ibid.* at 67.
[81] (1975) 238 E.G. 39.
[82] See also: *Re Cook's Mortgage* [1896] 1 Ch. 923.

the trustee should be entitled to a lien for the total expenditure he had incurred and not merely the enhancement value, and the Court of Appeal upheld this on the basis that his claim was analogous to that of a joint owner when the co-owned land is partitioned or sold. The entitlement of a co-owner to receive the value of improvements and repairs to land when it is sold is itself an equitable interest in the land which is capable of binding successors in title.[83]

(c) Equitable lien subject to other counterclaims

Any equitable lien to which a co-owner may be entitled to recover enhancements to the value of the land flowing from repairs or improvements he funded will be subject to any counterclaims of his fellow co-owners. The lien will be subject to an occupational rent if he has enjoyed sole occupation of the land, and to an account of any profits he has made by the economic exploitation of it.[84]

THE STATUTORY FRAMEWORK GOVERNING TRUSTS OF LAND

1 Special treatment for trusts of land

(a) Trusts as the main vehicle of land holding

In the preceding section it has been seen that all forms of co-ownership must take place behind a trust of the land, irrespective of whether the co-owners are joint tenants or tenants in common of the beneficial interest. The consequence of this is that a hugely significant proportion of land will be held on some type of trust, especially given that today the majority of homes that are owned by their occupants will be owned jointly rather than by the male partner alone. Trusts are therefore the major vehicle for land-holding in English land law. Given their significance legislation has intervened to provide a framework for their operation, proscribing the nature of the trustee's rights and duties, rather than allowing them to be regulated by the general equitable principles governing the operation of trusts.

(b) "Trusts for sale": the framework for trusts of land introduced by the property legislation of 1925

(i) Two parallel trust regimes: Under the property legislation of 1925 trusts of land could essentially take two forms, either a strict settlement under the Settled Land Act 1925 or a trust for sale arising under the Law of Property Act 1925. In general strict settlements provided a means of facilitating the creation and operation of successive interests in land, for example life-interests, although it should be noted that such interests could also be created behind a trust in the form of an express trust for sale. Trusts facilitating concurrent interests in land, in other words co-ownership of the legal and equitable title, took the form of trusts for sale. The powers and duties of the trustees of a trust for sale, as well as the beneficiaries rights, were defined by statute.

[83] *Williams v. Williams* (1899-1900) 81 L.T. (NS) 163.
[84] *ibid.*

(ii) Essence of a trust for sale: The defining characteristic of the trust for sale, from which it derives it name, is that the trustees who hold the land and therefore enjoy the powers of management and disposition over it, are placed under an overriding duty to sell the land.[85] This means that their prime obligation is to arrange for the land to be sold, thereby converting the asset from an estate in land to a sum of money representing its value. This arrangement seems strange since the majority of trusts of land have as their prime object the retention of the land for occupation by the beneficiaries. For example, if a husband and wife are the legal and equitable joint owners of their matrimonial home their intention is generally to live in it and to keep hold of it. The trust for sale introduces an inherent inconsistency between their duties as trustees of the land, namely to sell it, and their intentions as beneficiaries to retain it for occupation. This tension inherent in the trust for sale was resolved by the fact that in most cases the trustees also enjoyed a power to postpone sale of the land.[86] If the trustees validly exercised their power to postpone sale this would displace the duty to sell and they would retain the land. However, since trustees are required to act unanimously the power to postpone sale could only be validly exercised if all the trustees were agreed that the land should be retained and not sold. As soon as one or more of the trustees refused to exercise the power to postpone the duty to sell would revive and could not be displaced. In such a situation the land would have to be sold. The operation of the trust for sale is well illustrated by *Re Mayo*[87] where land was held[88] by three trustees, one of whom wanted the land sold immediately and the others who wished to retain it. Simmonds J. held that in the absence of a valid exercise of the power to postpone sale the trustees were under a duty to sell and he granted an order to enforce a sale by directing the trustees to take "all necessary steps for the sale of the property."[89] *Re Mayo* epitomises a strict approach to the enforcement of the duty to sell and it will be seen that in later cases the courts developed an entire jurisprudence of circumstances in which they would refuse to order a sale even though trustees were not unanimously exercising the power to postpone sale.

(iii) Trust for sale as the near universal basis of co-ownership: Under the 1925 regime trusts for sale could arise in one of two ways. First, a trust for sale could be created expressly, by conveying the legal title to land to a trustee of trustees subject to an express duty to sell the land. Since the trust for sale was foundational to the 1925 legislation it became standard conveyancing practice to create express trusts for sale. However, the Law of Property Act 1925 also provided for a number of situations where a trust of land would be implied to take the form of a trust for sale with the trustees under a concomitant duty to sell. By section 36(1) a trust for sale would be implied in all situations where there was a joint tenancy of the legal ownership of the land, whether the beneficial interests behind the trust were in the form of a joint tenancy, a tenancy in common,[90] or even if there was no co-ownership but a single

[85] s.205(1)(xxix) of the Law of Property Act 1925 defined a trust for sale as "an immediate binding trust for sale . . . with or without a power to postpone sale."

[86] By, Law of Property Act 1925, s.25(1) a power to postpone sale was implied into every trust for sale "unless a contrary intention appears."

[87] [1943] Ch. 302.

[88] The particular trust was a trust for sale arising by statute under, Settled Land Act 1925, s.36, but the principles are identical for all such trusts.

[89] *ibid.* at 304.

[90] As for example in *City of London Building Society v. Flegg* [1988] A.C. 54.

beneficiary.[91] In *Bull v. Bull*[92] the Court of Appeal construed the statutory provisions so that a trust for sale would be implied even where there was no joint tenancy of the legal title of land, because there was a sole trustee, and a tenancy in common of the beneficial interest, despite the fact that such a situation was not apparently within the strict terms of section 36(1). A house was purchased by a mother and her son, with the son providing the majority of the purchase price, and the legal title was transferred into his name alone. The consequence of this arrangement was that he was a sole trustee holding the land on resulting trust for himself and his mother as tenants in common of shares of the beneficial interest proportional to their contributions. Denning L.J. concluded that this trust was an implied trust for sale, reasoning that since Settled Land Act 1925, s.36(4)stated that tenancies in common "shall only take effect behind a trust for sale" the legislation must have intended a trust for sale to be implied in such circumstances. The effect of this decision was to ensure that the regime of the trust for sale was given virtually universal coverage in cases of co-ownership of land behind a trust. The only potential lacuna in the regime was a bare trust of the land, since the interpretative trickery of *Bull v. Bull* would not work where there was no co-ownership of either the legal title or the beneficial interest. Therefore, although it would be consistent with the general policy of the legislative framework to find that such a trust was a trust for sale, a bare trust where a sole trustee is holding the land on trust for a sole beneficiary would only be under a duty to sell if expressly imposed.

(c) "Trusts of land": reform and the introduction of a new statutory framework

(i) Background to reform: The twin regimes of trusts introduced by the property legislation of 1925 had long been subject to criticism. In particular the trust for sale was criticised on the grounds of its inconsistency with the reality of the owners' intentions in the vast majority of cases of co-ownership, which is that the land be retained for occupation not that it be sold. In 1989 the Law Commission recommended reform[93] and its proposals have been largely implemented by the Trusts of Land and Appointment of Trustees Act 1996.

(ii) A unified framework of trusts of land: Whereas the 1925 legislation introduced twin regimes for trusts of land, differentiating between successive and concurrent interests, one prime objective of the Trusts of Land and Appointment of Trustees Act 1996 is to introduce a single regime. It is no longer possible to create a strict settlement under the Settled Land Act 1925, although existing settlements will remain valid and governed by the old regime. Instead all trusts which include land as part of their trust property, whether the nature of the beneficiaries rights are successive or concurrent, will fall under the new statutory rubric of a "trust of land." This follows from section 1(a) which provides that: "Trust of land" means . . . any trust of property which consists of or includes land."[94] It is irrelevant how such a trust was created, since by section 1(2)(a) the statutory regime applies to "any description of trust (whether

[91] *Wilson v. Wilson* [1969] 3 All E.R. 945.
[92] [1955] 1 Q.B. 234.
[93] Law Com. Report No. 181, *Transfer of Land: Trusts of Land* (1989).
[94] With the exception of land which is already settled land and land to which the University and Colleges Estates Act 1925 applies:, s.1(3).

express, implied, resulting or constructive)." Logically, the "trustees of land" are defined as the "trustees of a trust of land."[95]

(iii) All existing trusts for sale become trusts of land: Section 1(2)(a) also provides that a "trust of land" includes a "trust for sale and a bare trust," and section 1(2)(b) makes clear that all existing trusts for sale are brought within the new regime as a trust of land "includes a trust created, or arising, before the commencement of this Act." The consequence of these provisions is that every trust consisting of interests in land will be brought within the statutory framework of the Trusts of Land and Appointment of Trustees Act 1996. There are no lacunas to be filled which would require such interpretative creativity as was evident in *Bull v Bull*.[96]

(iv) A comprehensive statutory framework for trusts of land: The statute introduces a comprehensive framework which governs all aspects of the relationships involved in a trust of land. It defines the various powers and duties of the trustees who own the legal title and the various rights and entitlements of the beneficiaries. It also provides a dispute resolution mechanism for situations where those relationships have broken down and there is no unanimity as to what should be done with the land.

(v) No implied duty to sell the land: One key difference between the new trust of land and the "trust for sale" which it replaces in the context of co-ownership is that no duty is imposed on the trustees to sell the land. This does not prevent a settlor expressly imposing such a duty, but in the absence of an express duty to sell there will be no inbuilt bias as to what the trustees should do with he land if they are not unanimous. Rather than the mandatory duty to sell automatically coming into effect when the power to postpone sale is not exercised, there will be no overriding obligation dictating the action that they should take. Where a trust is created incorporating an express duty to sell, section 4 of the new act makes clear that the trust is still a "trust of land" falling within the statutory framework, and provides that a power to postpone sale will be implied even if there is a provision to the contrary in the disposition creating the trust.

2 Powers and duties of the trustees of a "trust of land"

(a) Powers and duties of trustees under a trust for sale

Where land was held under a trust for sale under the 1925 statutory machinery, it has been noted that the trustees were under a mandatory duty to sell the land but enjoyed an implied power permitting them to postpone sale.[97] By section 28 Law of Property Act 1925 the trustees were granted the same powers of management and disposition over the land held on trust for sale as were enjoyed by a tenant for life and trustees of land held on a strict settlement under the Settled Land Act 1925. This entitled them to sell the land,[98] and to grant third parties subsidiary interests in it, for example leases[99]

[95] s.1(1)(b).
[96] [1955] 1 Q.B. 234.
[97] Law of Property Act 1925, s.25(1).
[98] Settled Land Act 1925, s.38.
[99] *ibid.* s.41.

or mortgages.[1] Most significantly these powers conferred on the trustees the right to re-invest the proceeds of sale of land held on trust for sale in other land, which is important because under the general law relating to trusts the trustees do not possess the power to invest in land. Under Law of Property Act 1925, s.26(3) the trustees of a trust for sale were also under a duty to consult the beneficiaries of the trust in relation to dealings with the land, but they were not obliged to put the beneficiaries wishes into practice. The trustees also had a limited ability to delegate their powers in relation to the grant and acceptance of surrender of leases of the land held on trust for sale to the beneficiaries under Law of Property Act, s.29(1) and by Trustee Act 1925, s.25(1) the trustees could delegate any of their powers and duties, including the power of sale, for not more than 12 months by means of a power of attorney.

(b) Trustees of land enjoy the powers of an absolute owner in relation to the land

(i) The general principle: Section 6(1) of the Trust of Land and Appointment of Trustees Act 1996 provides that: "For the purposes of exercising their functions as trustees, the trustees of land have in relation to the land subject to the trust all the powers of an absolute owner." This general principle means that the trustees are capable of dealing with the land in any way that an absolute owner who is not a trustee is entitled to deal with it for himself. This contrasts with the position of the trustee under a trust for sale who did not enjoy such freedom but could only deal with the land in the manners specified in the Settled Land Act 1925. Clearly this general principle entitles the trustees to sell, mortgage or lease the land. As is inherent from the fact that the relationship is a trust relationship the trustees are not entitled to exercise their powers for their own benefit. Section 6(5) provides that in exercising the powers conferred by the section "trustees shall have regard to the rights of the beneficiaries."

(ii) No duty to sell: Although section 6(1) clearly confers on a trustee of land the power to sell the land it does not impose on him a duty to sell. An absolute owner enjoys the discretion whether to sell or to retain his land.

(iii) Power to purchase land: Section 6(3) makes expressly clear that the trustee's powers to act as an absolute owner of land include the "power to purchase a legal estate in any land in England or Wales." This power may be exercised by way of investment, for the land to be occupied by any of the beneficiaries[2] or for any other reason.[3]

(iii) Express qualification of the trustee's general powers: Although prima facie the trustees of a trust of land enjoy the same powers as an absolute owner section 8 permits the settlor creating the trust to expressly restrict or qualify the trustees' powers. This allows the settlor, for example, to impose an express duty to sell, although as has been noted not to exclude a power to postpone sale. [4] This may even extend to the removal of a power to sell so that the land must be retained.

(iv) Imposition of requisite consents: The trustees' right to deal with the property in the manner of an absolute owner can also be qualified by the express requirement of consents to the exercise of any power. This does not affect the intrinsic right of the

[1] *ibid.* s.71.
[2] Avoiding the implications of *Re Power* [1947] Ch. 547.
[3] s.6(4).
[4] s.4(1).

trustees to act but section 8(2) provides that such powers "may not be exercised" without obtaining the appropriate consents.

(v) Trustees' right to terminate their trusteeship by conveyance of the land to the beneficiaries: The well established rule in *Saunders v. Vautier*[5] entitles the beneficiaries of a trust to demand that the trustees transfer the legal title to them if they are all agreed, of age and legally competent. By this means the beneficiaries may bring the trust to an end. Section 6(2) entitles the trustees to bring their trusteeship to an end by forcing a transfer of the legal title to the beneficiaries. This right only arises if the beneficiaries of the trust of land are of full age and legally competent. If the trustees do convey the land to the beneficiaries the effect will be that they cease to have the onerous duties of trusteeship. If there is a sole beneficiary of the trust of land that person will become the absolute owners. If there are co-owners of the beneficial interests those persons[6] will become the legal owners and therefore the trustees of land holding the land on a "trust of land" for themselves.

(vi) Trustees' actions subject to general restrictions: Section 6(6) provides that the trustees' rights to deal with the land as absolute owners "shall not be exercised in contravention of, or of any order made in pursuance of, any other enactment or any rule of law or equity." The precise impact of this obscure subsection is unclear, although a literal interpretation would suggest that any exercise of the trustees' powers which falls foul of it will be regarded as void and not simply as a breach of trust.

(c) trustees' right to delegate their powers in relation to the land

(i) A general right to delegate: Section 9(1) confers on the trustees of land the general right to delegate any of their powers by power of attorney to "any beneficiary or beneficiaries of full age and beneficially entitled to an interest in possession in land subject to the trust." This far exceeds the powers of delegation enjoyed by the trustees of a trust for sale, and includes the right to delegate the power of sale. The right to delegate cannot be excluded by the settlor.

(ii) Only joint delegation of the trustees' powers: Section 9 only entitles the trustees to delegate their powers jointly as a body. The provision does not permit one trustee to delegate his power to the other trustees, nor to delegate his powers as trustees to the beneficiaries. Such an individual delegation is still possible under Trustee Act 1925, s.25.

(iii) Liability of trustees where they have delegated their powers: By section 9(8) the trustees enjoy protection from liability for the defaults of the beneficiaries to whom they have delegated their powers. They will only attract liability if they "did not exercise reasonable care in deciding to delegate the function to the beneficiary or beneficiaries."[7]

(iv) Revocation of delegation: Where trustees have jointly delegated their functions section 9(3) provides that the delegation can be revoked by "any one or more of them" at any time. A delegation is also revoked automatically if a new trustee is appointed[8] or

[5] [1841] 4 Beav. 115.
[6] Note that there can still only be a maximum of four trustees of land.
[7] Compare the problems associated with a similar provisions in ss.23(1) and 30 of the Trustee Act 1925, as interpreted in *Re Vickery* [1931] Ch. 572.
[8] s.9(3).

when a person to whom a delegation was solely made ceases to be beneficially entitled under the trust.[9]

(d) Trustees' duty to consult the beneficiaries of the trust

(i) A general obligation to consult: With some small changes the duty of consultation of the trustees of a trust for sale under Law of Property Act 1925, s.26(3) have been re-enacted so as to apply to the trustees of land. Section 11(1) provides that:

> The trustees of land shall in the exercise of any function relating to land subject to the trust —
>
> (a) so far as practicable, consult the beneficiaries of full age and beneficially entitled to an interest in possession in the land, and
> (b) so far as consistent with the general interest of the trust, give effect to the wishes of those beneficiaries, or (in case of dispute) of the majority (according to the value of their combined interests).

This general requirement of consultation is subject to limited exceptions[10] and may be expressly excluded by the disposition creating the trust.[11] Where a trust of land was created prior to the commencement of the Act the trustees are under no duty to consult the beneficiaries unless the duty was expressly incorporated into the trust by a deed executed by the settlor, or such of the persons who created the trust who are still alive and of full capacity.[12] Trustees do not need to consult when exercising their right under section 6(2) to convey the legal title to the beneficiaries of the trust.
(ii) No absolute duty: The duty imposed by section 11 is not absolute. The trustees are not required to take unreasonable steps to attempt to consult them, and nor are they obliged to give effect to their wishes where consultations have taken place. Although the phrase "so far as is consistent with the general interest of the trust" seems vague, it has been taken from Law of Property Act 1925, s.26(3) and has not been the cause of litigation or dispute.

(e) Trustees' power to exclude beneficiaries from occupation of the land

(i) Beneficiaries enjoy a prima facie right to occupy the co-owned land: As will be explained more fully below the co-owners of land, whether they are tenants in common or joint tenants enjoy the right to occupy the land and cannot exclude each other from possession. This right is confirmed by section 12 of the Act. However, it is *inevitable* that sometimes the co-owners' relationship will deteriorate to such an extent that it is impossible for them to continue to share possession of the land.
(ii) Trustees' power to exclude or restrict a beneficiaries' right of occupation: By section 13(1) the trustees are granted the power to "exclude or restrict" the entitlement of any one or more beneficiaries of a trust of land who are concurrently

[9] s.9(4)(a). Where a delegation was made to a number of beneficiaries jointly and one subsequently loses his entitlement under the trust the power is revoked in as far as it relates to him.
[10] Under, s.11(2)(a) it does not apply to trusts creating or arising under wills made before the commencement of the Act.
[11] s.11(2)(a).
[12] s.11(3).

entitled to occupation under section 12. They may not, however, exclude all the beneficiaries from occupation. The trustees must not exclude or restrict the occupation rights of any beneficiary unreasonably.[13]

(iii) Consent or approval required to an exercise of the power in a manner which will cause a beneficiary presently in occupation of the land to cease occupation: Although section 13(1) grants the trustees a wide power to exclude or restrict the occupation rights of the beneficiaries of the trust, the exercise of this power is effectively circumscribed by section 13(7) which provides that:

> "The powers conferred on the trustees by this section may not be exercised —
>
> (a) so as to prevent any person who is in occupation of land (whether or not by reason of entitlement under section 12) from continuing to occupy the land, or
>
> (b) in a manner likely to result in any such person ceasing to occupy the land,
>
> unless he consents or the court has given approval."

This means that a trustee can never force a beneficiary to cease occupation by exercise of this power and withdrawing his right to occupy without that beneficiary's consent or the approval of the court. Since the very situations in which it is likely to be necessary to force a co-owner to cease occupation, such as the breakdown of a relationship, are those where it is unlikely that the beneficiary will consent to such measures the practical effect of section 13(7) is that most cases of exclusion will have to be determined by the court.

(iv) Imposition of reasonable conditions: The trustees may impose reasonable conditions on any beneficiary "in relation to his occupation of land." Section 13(5) expressly permits the trustee to impose a condition on a beneficiary to "pay any outgoings or expenses in respect of the land." Section 13(6) permits the trustees to impose conditions where a beneficiary's rights of occupation have been excluded or restricted to receive compensation from those remaining in occupation.

(v) Factors to be taken into account by the trustees in exercising their powers to restrict or exclude: Section 13 not only grants the trustees of land the power to exclude or restricts the occupation rights of beneficiaries but also specifies the factors which they must consider when contemplating the exercise of their power. These are listed in extremely general terms in section 13(4):

> "The matters to which trustees are to have regard in exercising the powers conferred by this section include —
>
> (a) the intentions of the person or persons (if any) who created the trust,
>
> (b) the purposes for which the land is held, and
>
> (c) the circumstances and wishes of each of the beneficiaries who is . . . entitled to occupy the land under s.12."

The central difficulty with this section is the such concepts as the "purposes for which the land is held" may not be immediately evident if not expressly stated in the instrument creating a trust.

[13] s.13(2).

3 Rights of the beneficiaries of a trust of land

(a) *Right to an interest in the land itself*

(i) The rights of the beneficiaries of a trust for sale: Where land was held by trustees on a trust for sale there was some question whether the beneficiaries were to be regarded as enjoying any interest in the land itself because of the potential application of the doctrine of conversion. Since the prime duty of the trustees in such a case was to sell the land, equity would anticipate the inevitability of such a sale because of the maxim that "equity treats as done that which ought to be done" with the result that the beneficiaries' interests existed only in relation to the purchase money which would be realised on sale.[14] Their interests were therefore in money and not in the land. However, with an increasing recognition that the central purpose of most trusts for sale was occupation of land by the beneficiaries the courts backed away from the logical consequences of a full-blown application of the doctrine of conversion. In *Williams and Glynn's Bank v. Boland*[15] the House of Lords regarded it as unrealistic to regard the beneficial interests of a wife who was an equitable tenant in common of the matrimonial home she occupied with her husband as enjoying an interest only in the proceeds of sale of the land.[16] Her interest was held to be sufficiently a right in land to form the subject matter of an overriding interest under Land Registration Act 1925, s.70(1)(g).[17]

(ii) Abolition of the doctrine of conversion: Although the doctrine of conversion was increasingly marginalised and disregarded for the purpose of determination of the rights of a beneficiary under a trust for sale of land, Trusts of Land and Appointment of Trustees Act 1996, s.3 abolishes it altogether and trust interests are to be treated as existing in the property which comprises the trust property, whether money or land. Section 3(1) provides:

> "Where land is held by trustees subject to a trust for sale, the land is not to be regarded as personal property; and where personal property is subject to a trust for sale in order that the trustees may acquire land, the personal property is not to be regarded as land."

Since the overall effect of the Act is that land will no longer be held with a duty to sell unless expressly imposed by the settlor in most cases the doctrine of conversion would have no application at all. Section 3(1) makes clear that it has no application even in those rare instances where the trustees remain under an express duty to sell.

(b) *Right to occupy the land*

(i) Beneficiaries' rights to occupation under a trust for sale: As the traditional doctrine of conversion suggested that the beneficiaries of a trust for sale enjoyed no actual rights in the land the concomitant effect of this was that they enjoyed no rights

[14] See: *Cooper v. Critchley* [1955] Ch. 431; *Irani Finance Ltd v. Singh* [1971] Ch. 59 at 80 *per* Cross L.J.; *Cedar Holdings Ltd v. Green* [1981] Ch. 129.
[15] [1981] A.C. 487.
[16] See also the judgment of the Court of Appeal which was approved: [1979] Ch. 312.
[17] See below, Chap. 16.

to occupation of the land.[18] Their only right was to receive an appropriate share of the proceeds on sale. However, over time the courts again backed away from the full logical implications of conversion and concluded that beneficiaries behind a trust for sale did enjoy rights of occupation. In *Bull v. Bull*[19] Denning L.J. held that a mother who was an equitable tenant in common of a house which her son held on trust for sale was entitled to "possession of the land and to the use and enjoyment of it in a proper manner," on the grounds that these rights had been enjoyed by legal tenants in common.[20] This conclusion that an equitable tenant in common was entitled to occupation was expressly approved by the House of Lords in *Williams & Glynn's Bank Ltd v. Boland*.[21] Most significantly, in *City of London Building Society v. Flegg*[22] Lord Oliver stated that: "The beneficiary's possession or occupation is no more than a method of enjoying in specie the rent and profits pending sale in which he is entitled to share. It derives from and is . . . fathered by the interests under the trust for sale."[23] His analysis reconciled both the essential nature of the trust for sale and the practical reality that the majority of such trusts had as their object the occupation of the land by the beneficiaries by making their right of occupation a present foretaste of their future entitlement to the proceeds of sale.

(ii) A statutory right to occupy: As with the abolition of the doctrine of conversion the Trusts of Land and Appointment of Trustees Act 1996 sweeps away the uncertainty which surrounded the right of a beneficiary to occupy land under a trust for sale. Section 12(1) provides for a general right of occupation for the beneficiary of a trust of land:

> "A beneficiary who is beneficially entitled to an interest in possession in the land subject to a trust of land is entitled by reason of his interest to occupy the land at any time if at that time:
>
> (a) the purposes of the trust include making the land available for his occupation (or for occupations of beneficiaries of a class of which he is a member or of beneficiaries in general), or
>
> (b) the land is held by the trustees so as to be available.

(iii) Beneficiary must have an "interest in possession": The statutory right to occupy under section 12(1) only arises in favour of a beneficiary under a trust of land who is entitled to an interest "in possession." This means that only a person who enjoys a present and immediate right to possession of the land is entitled to occupy, and excludes a person whose interest is only in remainder or reversion. Most importantly it means that the person entitled to the remainder interest where a life interest has been granted has no right to occupation while the life tenant is alive. Where a trust of land facilitates co-ownership the co-owners are concurrently entitled to possession and therefore all enjoy rights of occupation under section 12.

[18] *Re Bagot's Settlement* [1894] 1 Ch. 177; *Re Earl of Stamford and Warrington* [1925] Ch. 162.
[19] [1955] 1 Q.B. 234.
[20] *Jacobs v. Seward* (1872) L.R. 5 H.L. 464; *In re Warren* [1932] 1 Ch. 42. See also: *Barclay v. Barclay* [1970] 2 Q.B. 677 .
[21] [1981] A.C. 487 at 510 *per* Lord Scarman.
[22] [1988] A.C. 54.
[23] *ibid.* at 83.

(iv) Beneficiary only entitled to occupy if this is a purpose of the trust: Section 12(a) has the effect that a beneficiary will only enjoy a statutory right of occupation if one of the purposes of the trust was to make the land available for his occupation. In the absence of express indications in a trust deed it is unclear how the purposes of a trust are to be defined. No doubt in many cases where there is co-ownership, whether on the basis of an express, constructive or resulting trust, it will be self evident that the purpose of the trust was to enable the co-owners to occupy the land, just as it was self-evidently the purpose of the trust in *City of London Building Society v. Flegg*[24] that Mr and Mrs Maxwell-Browne were to share occupation of the house which had been purchased specifically to enable them to live with their daughter and son-in-law, Mr and Mrs Flegg. However, it seems likely that there would be no statutory right of occupation if the facts were similar to those in *Barclay v. Barclay*.[25] A man had died leaving his bungalow to be sold and divided in equal shares amongst his sons and daughter-in-laws. One son continued to live in the bungalow and claimed that he was entitled to occupy as an equitable tenant in common. The Court of Appeal held that the bungalow should be sold and the proceeds divided. Lord Denning M.R. stated that this was because *Bull v. Bull*[26] could be clearly distinguished:

> "In *Bull v. Bull* the prime object was that the house should be occupied by them both. So they were tenants in common of the house itself. In the present case, the prime object of the testator was that the bungalow should be sold and the proceeds divided. So the beneficiaries were not tenants in common of the bungalow, but only of the proceeds after it was sold."

Although the analysis of the tenants rights would be different under the framework of the new trust of land, it seems unlikely that the "purpose" of the trust should be differently assessed under section 12(1)(a).

(v) The land must be "available" for occupation: There is similarly no statutory right of occupation unless the land is held by the trustees so as to be "available" for occupation. This means that a beneficiary's rights of occupation will come to an end if the trustees decide to sell the land.

(vi) The land must be "suitable" for occupation: The exact scope of this restriction is unclear. It may be obvious that a mine held on trust is not suitable for the beneficiary's occupation, but it is less clear whether the statutory right of occupation would be excluded if the beneficiary were a drug-debauched heir to a stately home, or the co-owner of a farm incapable of running it. However, in by far the majority of co-ownership cases there will be no difficulties of the suitability of residential property for occupation by the co-owners.

(vii) Exclusion or restriction of the right to occupation: As has been noted above under section 13 of the Act the trustees enjoy the power to exclude or restrict the right of occupation of some, but not all, of the beneficiaries. Most significantly the trustees cannot exercise their powers so that a person presently in occupation of the land will be prevented from continuing to occupy,[27] or made likely to cease occupation,[28]

[24] [1988] A.C. 54.
[25] [1970] 2 Q.B. 677.
[26] [1955] 1 Q.B. 234.
[27] s.13(7)(a).
[28] s.13(7)(b).

without the consent of that person unless the exercise of the power is approved by the court.

(c) Right to be consulted by the trustees

The corollary of the trustees' duty to consult with the beneficiaries' of a trust of land over the exercise of their functions under section 11 of the Act is that the beneficiaries have a right to be consulted. As was noted above this is not an absolute right and the trustees do not have to act according to their wishes.

4 Resolving disputes in relation to the co-owned land

(a) Context of disputes

It is inevitable that where a number of persons are simultaneously interested in land they will not always agree as to what should be done with it. A number of different scenarios of dispute may be noted:

(i) Disputes among the trustees: If land is held on trust by more than one trustee then it is possible that there will be disputes between the trustees as to how they should exercise their powers. Since the exercise of their powers requires the trustees to act unanimously this may result in a stalemate situation in which they cannot agree upon any cause of action. For example, some of the trustees may want to sell the land and others not.

(ii) Disputes between the trustees and the beneficiaries: Alternatively there may be a dispute between the trustee or trustees and the beneficiaries of the trust. For example, none of the trustees may want to sell the land but some of the co-owners want it sold. Obviously in the case of residential co-ownership some of the co-owners may also be the trustees of the land.

(iii) Disputes among the co-owners: Disputes may also arise amongst those who are the beneficial co-owners of the land.

(b) Dispute resolution under trusts for sale

(i) Disputes whether to sell: The main dispute which arose in the context of trusts for sale was whether the land should be sold. As has already been noted a trust for sale imposes an immediate duty to sell on the trustees. Therefore, if the trustees are in disagreement they cannot exercise their power to postpone sale, since this requires unanimity, and the overriding duty to sell revives and dictates the course they must take. The central difficulty was not therefore as to the action which should be taken, which was inherent in the terms of the trust, but how to effect a sale if one of the trustees was recalcitrant and unwilling to act.

(ii) Power of the court to compel sale: By Law of Property Act 1925, s.30 the court was granted the power to compel trustees for sale to exercise their powers:

> "If the trustees for sale refuse to sell or to exercise any of [their powers], or any requisite consent cannot be obtained, any person interested may apply to the court for a vesting or other order for giving effect to the proposed transaction or for an order directing the trustees for sale to give effect thereto, and the court may make such order as it thinks fit."

It seems clear that section 30 was intended to provide a mechanism for the enforcement of the duty to sell where trustees were in dispute. Although it spoke of the discretion of the court to make "any order" this was not originally interpreted as permitting the court to make no order that a refusing trustee should sell and thereby postpone sale and override the immediate duty to sell inherent in the trust for sale. Simmonds J. adopted this orthodox approach in *Re Mayo*[29] where he held that the court could not exercise the discretion other than to direct sale of the land.

(iii) A jurisdiction to postpone sale: However, later cases re-interpreted Law of Property Act 1925, s.30 as conferring a discretion on the court which was sufficiently wide to entitle it to effectively postpone a sale, allowing the land to be retained, by refusing to order a trustee to sell. In *Re Buchanan-Wollaston's Conveyance*[30] Sir Wilfred Greene M.R. concluded that when exercising the discretion under section 30 the court must: "look into all the circumstances and consider whether or not, at the particular moment and in the particular circumstances when the application is made to it, it is right and proper that such an order shall be made."[31] In *Jones v. Challenger*[32] Devlin L.J. adopted a generalised approach to the exercise of the jurisdiction which considered the "prime object" of the trust and suggested that sale need not be ordered "where the trust itself or the circumstances in which it was made show that there was a secondary or collateral object besides that of sale."[33]

(iv) The development of a jurisprudence of collateral objects: Given the willingness of the courts to refuse to order sale in circumstances where there was a collateral object behind the trust there developed an entire jurisprudence, or catalogue, or such objects which would be sufficient to displace the duty to sell. Collateral objects might be found where the trustees had expressly agreed amongst themselves that the land was not to be sold unless they acted unanimously[34] or where the land had been purchased to provide a family home for the children of the trustees.[35] Since the cases relating to collateral objects are not rendered irrelevant by the new framework of the Trusts of Land and Appointment of Trustees Act 1996 they are discussed more fully below in the context of the factors which must be considered by the court in exercising its new statutory discretion to make orders relating to the exercise of the trustees' functions.

(b) Resolution of disputes arising in relation to a trust of land

(i) A general power to make orders: Section 14 of the Trusts of Land and Appointment of Trustees Act 1996 grants the court a wide jurisdiction to make orders relating to the trust of land. Section 14(2) provides that:

> "On an application for an order under this section the court may make any such order —
>
> (a) relating to the exercise by the trustees of any of their functions (including an order relieving them of any obligation to obtain the

[29] [1943] Ch. 302.
[30] [1939] 1 Ch. 738. Note that *In Re Buchanan-Wollaston's Conveyance* was not cited in *Re Mayo.*
[31] *ibid.* at 747.
[32] [1961] 1 Q.B. 176.
[33] *ibid.* at 181.
[34] See: *Re Buchanan-Wollaston's Conveyance* [1939] Ch. 217.
[35] See: *Williams v. Williams* [1976] Ch. 278.

consent of, or to consult, any person in connection with the exercise of any of their functions), or

(b) Declaring the nature or extent of a person's interests in property subject to the trust,

as the court thinks fit.

(ii) Persons who may apply for an order: Section 14(1) provides that: "Any person who is a trustee of land or has an interest in property subject to a trust of land may make an application to the court for an order under this section." This follows the pattern of Law of Property Act 1925, s.30 which is now repealed.

(iii) A wider scope of jurisdiction: Section 14 gives the court a wider scope of jurisdiction than was granted it by Law of Property Act 1925, s.30. This reflects the policy of the Law Commission report that the "courts should be able to intervene in any dispute relating to a trust of land."[36] Section 14(2)(a) is sufficiently wide to enable the court to authorise the trustees to carry out their functions in a manner which would otherwise constitute a breach a trust, something which was not possible under section 30. Section 14(2)(b) also extends the jurisdiction by expressly granting the court the power to determine the nature and extent of a claimant's interests in the land. However, by far the most likely scenario which will call for the courts' intervention is the situation where co-owners cannot agree what should be done with the land and some wish it to be sold and others that it should be retained.

(iv) No jurisdiction to appoint or remove trustees: Despite the width of the jurisdiction granted section 14(3) expressly stipulates that the court "may not under this section make any order as to the appointment or removal of trustees."

(c) Factors which the court must consider in exercising its jurisdiction under section 14 of the Trust of Land and Appointment of Trustees Act

(i) A statutory catalogue of relevant factors: It has been noted that a body of case law was developed in relation to the exercise of the jurisdiction under Law of Property Act 1925, s.30 as to circumstances in which the court should refuse to order sale of the land. These generally involved the identification of the purposes of the trust.[37] Section 15(1) of the Trusts of Land and Appointment of Trustees Act 1925 places on a statutory footing a number of factors which the court should take into account when determining how to exercise its jurisdiction so that the approach developed under the old section 30 would be consolidated and rationalised[38]:

> "The matters to which the court is to have regard in determining an application for an order under section 14 include —
>
> (a) the intentions of the person or persons (if any) who created the trust,
> (b) the purposes for which the property subject to the trust is held,
> (c) the welfare of any minor who occupies or might reasonably be expected to occupy any land subject to the trust as his home, and

[36] Law Com. No. 181, para. 12.6.
[37] *Re Buchanan-Wollaston's Conveyance* [1939] Ch. 738.
[38] Law Com. No. 181, para. 12.9.

(d) the interests of any secured creditor of any beneficiary."

Since these factors are similar to those which have been considered relevant by the courts in relation to the exercise of their jurisdiction under section 30 the relevant caselaw is not rendered obsolete by the new section 15(1) but remains the best guide as to how the court would be likely to exercise its new powers. The catalogue in section 15(1) has no application to applications for an order by a trustee of a bankrupt where section 335A of the Insolvency Act applies.[39]

(ii) The intentions of the persons creating the trust: Although section 15(1)(a) requires the court to have regard to the intentions of the persons creating the trust of land this will only be possible if their intentions are discernible. In some cases their intentions may have been stated in the instrument creating the trust, but where there is no such statement of intentions the courts may be able to infer an intention from the circumstances of the trust. There is clearly some overlap between an inference of intention and the assessment of the purpose of a trust.

(iii) The purpose of the trust: Under section 30 the prime duty to sell could be displaced by the finding of a collateral object or purpose of the trust. Although in the case of a trust of land there is no duty to sell the identification of the "purpose" of the trust will still be necessary as it is a matter which must be considered by the court when granting an order under section 14. Cases suggest a number of means by which a purpose of the trust may be identified. The co-owners of land may reach an agreement external to the instrument creating the trust indicating the purpose for which the land is held. In *Re Buchanan-Wollaston's Conveyance*[40] a section of sea front land was conveyed to four people as joint tenants. They executed a deed stating that the land had been purchased so that it would not be used in a manner which would cause a depreciation in the value of their own adjacent properties, and agreeing not to deal with the land unless they were unanimously agreed or by majority vote. The Court of Appeal held that a sale should not be ordered against the terms of the co-owners' mutual covenant. Where land was purchased to provide a home for the co-owners the courts have found that this was the purpose of the trust. For example, in *Jones v. Challenger*[41] the court of Appeal held that a house purchased as a matrimonial home was held on trust for the purpose of occupation by the spouses. However, the cases also suggest that the courts will have regard to whether the purposes of the trust are continuing or whether they have come to an end. In *Jones v. Challenger* the husband and wife had divorced and the husband had moved out of the family home. The Court of Appeal therefore held that purpose was not longer "alive" but had been "dissolved"[42] and granted an order for sale. In *Rawlings v. Rawlings*[43] it was held that the purpose of the trust had failed where a wife left her husband even though there was no divorce. In *Jones (A. E.) v. Jones (F. W.)*[44] a father and son were the equitable joint tenants of a house which had been purchased largely by the father for his son to live in. When the father died his step-mother, who had inherited the father's interest, sought

[39] s.15(4).
[40] [1939] Ch. 738.
[41] [1961] 1 Q.B. 176.
[42] *ibid.* at 183 *per* Devlin L.J.
[43] [1964] P. 398.
[44] [1977] 1 W.L.R. 438.

to have the house sold. The Court of Appeal held that no order for sale would be granted since this would defeat the purposes of the trust, which were that the son was to be able to live in the house for life.

(iv) The welfare of minors: Where land was purchased with the object of providing a home for the co-owners to share, it has been seen that the courts tended to regard the purposes as at an end if the parties' relationship ended. However, in *Rawlings v. Rawlings*[45] Salmon L.J. suggested that the position might be different if the co-owners had children still in need of a home:

> "If there were young children the position would be different. One of the purposes of the trust would no doubt have been to provide a home for them, and whilst that purpose still existed a sale would generally not be ordered. But when those children are grown up and the marriage is dead, the purposes of the trust have failed."[46]

This approach was adopted by the Court of Appeal in *Williams (J. W.) v. Williams (M.A.)*[47] where a house was owned jointly by a husband and wife who had four children. They divorced and the wife remained in the house with the children, the youngest of whom was 12. Lord Denning M.R. held that the primary purpose of the trust was to provide "a home in which the family is to be brought up,"[48] and refused to order sale unless "it were shown that alternative accommodation could be provided at a cheaper rate, and some capital released." In *Dennis v. McDonald*[49] the court refused to order sale where a house was owned by husband and wife as tenants in common and the wife had left leaving the husband in occupation with three of their children. In some cases the courts have considered postponing an order for sale to protect the interests of children. In *Re Evers Trust*[50] a man and woman owned a house as joint tenants. When their relationship ended the man left and sought an order for sale. The first instance judge held that an order should be postponed until the couple's child was 16.[51] The Court of Appeal upheld his decision not to grant an immediate order of sale on the grounds that the underlying purpose of the trust was to provide a home for the couple and their children, but held that the postponement was inappropriate because the parties' circumstances might change so that sale at that date was not appropriate. The courts are required to give consideration to the interests of children requiring a home under section 15. However, this does not mean that their needs will automatically prevail. The court will have to balance their interest against those of others interested in the land. Different weight may be given to the interests of minors where the dispute is between the co-owners *inter se*, especially when a relationship has ended, and where there is a conflict between the interests of any minors and a creditor of the co-owners who is seeking to enforce their security.

[45] [1964] P. 398.
[46] *ibid.* at 419.
[47] [1976] Ch. 278.
[48] *ibid.* at 285.
[49] [1982] Fam. 398.
[50] [1980] 1 W.L.R. 1327.
[51] Compare *Bernard v. Josephs* [1982] Ch. 391 where an order for sale was postponed for four months to enable the occupying partner to buy-out the share of the other co-owner.

(v) The interests of creditors of the beneficiaries: Where there are secured creditors who have an interest in the co-owned property the court must balance their interests against those of the co-owners and any minors when making an order under section 14. The central question is whether, following cases decided under Law of Property Act 1925, s.30 the court will only prefer the interests of persons other than the creditor if there are "exceptional circumstances." *Re Holliday (A Bankrupt)*[52] suggested that in some circumstances the interests of children might be given priority over those of a creditor. A husband and wife were the co-owners of their matrimonial home. The husband left and his wife and three children continued to occupy the house. He subsequently became bankrupt and his trustee in bankruptcy sought an order for sale of the house. The Court of Appeal exercised its discretion by refusing to grant an order. Goff L.J. stated the principles under which the court should determine its proper response:

> "we have to decide having regard to all the circumstances, including the fact that there are young children, and that the debtor was made bankrupt on his own petition, whose voice, that of the trustee seeking to realise the debtor's share for the benefit of his creditors or that of the wife seeking to preserve a home for herself and her children, ought in equity to prevail."[53]

The Court concluded that in all the circumstances the voice of the wife ought to prevail and that the sale of the house should be deferred for five years. However, in all other cases where a trustee in bankruptcy has demanded sale the courts have held that sale should be ordered.[54] In *Re Citro (A Bankrupt)*[55] the Court of Appeal adopted a strict approach and indicated that in all but the most exceptional cases the rights of the creditor should prevail. Nourse L.J. summarised the position:

> "Where a spouse who has a beneficial interest in the matrimonial home has become bankrupt under debts which cannot be paid without the realisation of that interest, the voice of the creditors will usually prevail over the voice of the other spouse and a sale of the property ordered within a short period. The voice of the other spouse will only prevail in exceptional circumstances...What then are exceptional circumstances? As the cases show, it is not uncommon for a wife with young children to be faced with eviction in circumstances where the realisation of her beneficial interest will not produce enough to buy a comparable home in the same neighbourhood, or indeed elsewhere. And, if she has to move elsewhere, there may be problems over schooling and so forth. Such circumstances, while engendering a natural sympathy in all who hear of them, cannot be described as exceptional. They are the melancholy consequences of debt and improvidence with which every civilised society has been familiar."[56]

[52] [1981] Ch. 405.
[53] *ibid.* at 420.
[54] *Re Solomon (A Bankrupt)* [1967] Ch. 573; *Boydell v. Re Gillespie* (1970) 216 E.G. 1505; *Re Turner (A Bankrupt)* [1974] 1 W.L.R. 1556; *Bailey (A Bankrupt)* [1977] 1 W.L.R. 278; *Re Lowrie (A Bankrupt)* [1981] 3 All E.R. 353; *Re Gorman (A Bankrupt)* [1990] 1 W.L.R. 616.
[55] [1991] Ch. 142.
[56] *ibid.* at 157.

These cases concerned orders for sale sought by a trustee in bankruptcy of one of the co-owners, a situation which now falls outside of the scope of Trusts of Land and Appointment of Trustees Act 1996, s.15[57] and is governed by Insolvency Act 1986, s.335A. However, it remains an important question whether the court will take a similarly strict approach where a creditor, such as a mortgagee, rather than a trustee in bankruptcy is seeking an order for sale. In *Lloyds Bank plc v. Byrne & Byrne*[58] a husband, who was the joint tenant with his wife, had secured a debt of £25,000 of a company of which he was a director, on their matrimonial home. The bank obtained a charging order on the house when the debt was not repaid, and subsequently sought an order for sale under section 30. The Court of Appeal ordered sale following the approach adopted in *Re Citro (A Bankrupt)*.[59] Purchas L.J. held that no distinction was to be drawn between the position of a chargee of the land and a trustee in bankruptcy of one of the co-owners and that therefore in the absence of exceptional circumstances the order for sale would be granted. In *Abbey National plc v. Moss*[60] Hirst L.J. held that the same principle should apply where a mortgagee was seeking an order for sale, since a mortgagee was in "an almost identical position" to the bank in *Lloyds Bank plc v. Byrne & Byrne*. Since there were no exceptional circumstances he concluded that the court should order sale. However, the majority of the Court of Appeal held that *Re Citro (A Bankrupt)* should not automatically apply in the case of an application by a mortgagee. Mrs Moss transferred the title of her matrimonial home into the joint names of herself and her daughter on the death of her husband, with the object of simplifying the transfer of the property to the daughter on her death. The daughter subsequently mortgaged the house by forging her mother's signature on the relevant application. The daughter left the country and the mortgagees commenced proceedings for repossession and sale. Peter Gibson L.J., with whom Ralph Gibson L.J. agreed, held that the correct principle to be drawn from *Re Citro* was not that sale would be ordered in the absence of exceptional circumstances wherever a debt was due, but that since bankruptcy vested the share of the bankrupt co-owner in the trustee this terminated the parties' co-ownership which was the foundation of the collateral purpose of the trust, namely that to provide them a home. Where there was no such termination of the parties' co-ownership the collateral purpose would continue to subsist, and the court could refuse to order sale. Considering the facts he concluded that it would be grossly inequitable to order sale since Mrs Morris would lose the home to which she was deeply attached when the purpose of the trust was that she remain until death, and that the mortgagees should have ensured that the mortgage had been properly executed by all the parties. It remains unclear whether in exercising its powers under Trusts of Land and Appointment of Trustees Act 1996, s.14 the court will take the view that the interests of secured creditors must prevail, even over those of other beneficiaries or minors, unless there are exceptional circumstances.

(d) Applications under section 14 made by a trustee in bankruptcy

(i) Inapplicability of section 15 matters to be taken into consideration: As has been noted section 15(3) provides that the section 15 does not apply where a trustee of a

[57] s.15(3).
[58] [1991] 23 H.L.R. 472.
[59] [1991] Ch. 142.
[60] [1994] 26 H.L.R. 249.

bankrupt is seeking an order under section 14. Such a situation is governed by Insolvency Act 1986, s.335A.

(ii) Court with jurisdiction to determine an application by a trustee in bankruptcy: Where a trustee in bankruptcy makes an application for an order for sale under section 14 of the Trusts of Land and Trustees Act 1996 section 335A of the Insolvency Act provides that the application must be made to the "court having jurisdiction in relation to the bankruptcy."

(iii) Factors to be taken into account in determining whether to order sale: Section 335A(2) provides a catalogue of factors which the court should take have regard to in determining whether to order sale:

> "On such an application the court shall make such order as it thinks just and reasonable having regard to —
>
> (a) the interests of the bankrupt's creditors;
> (b) where an application is made in respect of land which includes a dwelling house which is or has been the home of the bankrupt or the bankrupt's spouse or former spouse —
>   (i) the conduct of the spouse or former spouse so far as contributing to the bankruptcy,
>   (ii) the needs and financial resources of the spouse or former spouse, and
>   (iii) the need of any children; and
> (c) all the circumstances of the case other than the needs of the bankrupt.

These provisions allow for the considerations of circumstances which could not be regarded as truly exceptional, so that they offer a wider jurisdiction to refuse sale than was stated to be available in *Re Citro (A Bankrupt)*.

(iv) Automatic priority of the bankrupt's creditors: Section 335A(3) has the effect that where a trustee in bankruptcy makes an application for sale a year after the bankrupt's property vested in him the court "shall assume, unless the circumstances are exceptional,[61] that the interests of the bankrupt's creditors outweigh all other considerations."

[61] See: *Re Citro (A Bankrupt)* [1991] Ch. 142.

Chapter 8

Successive Ownership and Limited Interests in Land

Introduction to Successive and Limited Interests

1 Successive interests contrasted with concurrent interests

In the previous chapter it has been seen how it is possible for two or more persons to enjoy simultaneous rights of ownership in land by means of co-ownership as joint tenants or tenants in common. Such co-owners enjoy concurrent interests in the land, since they hold their respective entitlements at the same time. For this reason all the co-owners are entitled to occupy and enjoy the use of the land and none can claim a right of occupation to the exclusion of the others. In contrast, persons may enjoy interests in land which do not entitle them to simultaneous enjoyment of their rights. Instead, the rights of some persons are delayed in time until the rights of others have been exhausted. The classic example where parties enjoy successive interests is the life interest. If Grant enjoys a life interest of Victoria Manor, and Phil the remainder interest, they both enjoy simultaneous rights in the land but their interests are not concurrent. As the life tenant, Grant will be entitled to enjoy the benefit of the land, perhaps by living in the Manor or receiving any rents or profits which are generated from it, during his lifetime. He is entitled to transfer his life interest to someone else. He cannot transfer or create any rights in the land which will endure beyond his death. When he dies Phil will become entitled to the full and unencumbered freehold ownership of the Manor. However, during the lifetime of Grant he has no rights to the use and enjoyment of the land itself. He has no entitlement to live in the Manor, or to enjoy any share of the income it might generate, while Grant is alive. During the lifetime of Grant his interest is only in the remainder of the land, and he therefore has no immediate right to possession. This remainder interest is also transferable, so that if he assigns it to Lorraine, on the death of Grant she will become the owner of the Manor.

2 The regime for successive interests in land

(a) Strict settlements or express trusts for sale

Just as concurrent ownership can only take place behind a trust, so successive interests must take effect in equity behind the legal title, as only freehold and leasehold ownership are estates capable of existing at law.[1] Whereas under the scheme introduced by the 1925 legislation co-ownership was effected through the medium of an express or implied trust for sale, successive interests could take effect either behind an express trust for sale or by means of a strict settlement arising under the Settled Land Act 1925. Section 1(i) of the Settled Land Act 1925 provided that any interest "limited in trust for any persons by way of succession" would create a settlement for the purposes of the Act. It should be noted that wherever successive interests in land were created other than behind an express trust for sale a strict settlement would arise, so that in many cases land became settled land without the express intention of the person creating the successive interests. In some cases this meant that an owner of land would deal with it in such a way as to create a settlement by accident.

(b) Trusts of land

Following the recommendations of the Law Commission[2] the dual system of trusts for sale and strict settlements embodied in the 1925 legislation has been replaced by a single unitary "trust of land" under the Trusts of Land and Appointment of Trustees Act 1996. However, this does not mean that strict settlements are rendered redundant. Unlike the position in relation to trusts for sale, which are converted by the Act into trusts of land and brought within the new regime, strict settlements which were validly created before January 1, 1997, when the Act came into force, remain as such and are still governed by the Settled Land Act 1925. However, section 2(1) of the new Act provides that:

> "No settlement created after the commencement of this Act is a settlement for the purposes of the Settled Land Act 1925; and no settlement shall be deemed to be made under that Act after that commencement."

Therefore all successive interests in land created after January 1, 1997 will take effect behind a statutory trust of land.

3 Other limited interests in land

Life interests were not the only interests to take effect under a strict settlement of land. Other limited interests in land which could not exist as a legal estate also took effect in equity behind a settlement. By section 1(ii)(a) of the Settled Land Act 1925 the grant of an entailed interest in land gave rise to a strict settlement, irrespective of whether the entail was capable of being barred or defeated. By section 1(ii)(c) the grant of a determinable interest, whether of a fee simple or a leasehold interest, would have created a strict settlement. Under section 1(ii)(c) any grant of a freehold or leasehold interest subject to a condition which would lead to a gift over of the land if broken took effect behind a settlement, as did the grant of a freehold or leasehold of land to which a person would only become entitled if a specified condition was fulfilled. Under section 1(ii)(d) the grant of a freehold or leasehold in land to an infant

[1] Law of Property Act 1925, s.1.
[2] Law Commission No. 181 (1989).

gave rise to a settlement because a minor is incapable of holding a legal estate. Thus if Grant had died before January 1, 1997 leaving Victoria Manor by will to his infant daughter Courtney, the land would have been held on a strict settlement. As a consequence of the Trusts of Land and Appointment of Trustees Act 1997 all such limited interests created after January 1, 1997 will take effect under a trust of land.

4 Accidental creation of strict settlements

One of the central difficulties associated with the 1925 regime was that strict settlements would often arise accidentally. The breadth of circumstances which would constitute a settlement under Settled land Act 1925, s.1(1) and the fact that a settlement arose whenever one of the interests in land specified in section 1(1)(i)–(v) was created, led to the inevitable result that a strict settlement may have arisen without the settlor ever having intended to subject his land in that way. This was especially likely where a testator had drawn up a home made will leaving his house to his spouse for life. A professionally drafted will, or declaration of trust, would generally have preferred an express trust for sale.

5 Key features of the strict settlement

(a) Location of the legal title

One of the most important features of a strict settlement was that, unlike conventional trusts where the legal title is vested in the trustees, the legal title to the land was vested in the person presently entitled to possession. Such a person was termed the "tenant for life" of the settlement, and was defined by Settled Land Act 1925, s.19(1) as "the person of full age who is for the time being beneficially entitled under a settlement to possession of settled land for his life is for the purposes of this Act the tenant for life of that land and the tenant for life under that settlement." In the example which has been used above, if Grant enjoys a life interest in Victoria Manor created prior to January 1, 1997 he will be the tenant for life. To say that the tenant for life is the person presently entitled to possession of the land does not mean that they have to enjoy the physical occupation of it. It is a way of expressing that they are entitled to the immediate enjoyment of their rights and interests in the land, whether that be by actual possession or the receipt of any rents and profits that the land generates. Where two or more persons are entitled to possession of the land as joint tenants, for example if Phil and Kath were concurrently entitled to life interests of Victoria Manor "they together constitute the tenant for life."[3] If the settled land was registered Land Registration Act 1925, s.86(1) provided that it was to be registered "in the name of the tenant for life." Where there was no person meeting the statutory definition of a tenant for life the Settled Land Act 1925 provided a list of persons who were to enjoy the powers of the tenant for life in relation to the land[4] and in the absence of any such persons the trustees of the settlement were to enjoy those powers,[5] as for example in

[3] s.19(2).
[4] s.20(1)(i)-(x).
[5] s.26.

the case of a trust for the benefit of an infant.[6] Such persons were termed the "statutory owners." Therefore only as a last resort would the trustees of a strict settlement hold the legal title and the powers normally enjoyed by trustees of land.

(b) Management of the land by the tenant for life

Not only did the tenant for life hold the legal title of the land subject to the settlement, but he also enjoyed all the powers of management over it which are usually held and exercised by the trustees of a conventional trust. Most importantly he held the power to sell or exchange the land,[7] and to grant subsidiary interests such as leases of mortgages.[8] This meant that where there was a life interest there was no guarantee that the land would be retained and pass to the remainder beneficiary. If Victoria Manor was held on a settlement for Grant for life, remainder to Phil, Grant as the tenant for life would have the right to sell the Manor to Lorraine so that she could become the absolute freehold owner. Grant would then have to apply the proceeds of the sale in accordance with the provisions of the Settled Land Act.

(c) Identity and role of the trustees of the settlement

It should already be evident that the trustees of a strict settlement enjoy a very different role to that of trustees of a conventional trust, or under a traditional trust for sale of land. Section 30(1)(i) of the Settled Land Act 1925 provides that the trustees of the settlement are any persons expressly granted the power of sale over the land by the person creating the settlement, or whose consent is required before the exercise of such a power. If no one enjoys a power of sale, or consent to sale, section 30(1)(ii) provides that the trustees of the settlement will be those who are expressly declared to be the trustees in the instrument creating the settlement. If there is no-one within the statutory categories set out in section 30(1)(i)–(iv) the beneficiaries of the settlement are entitled to appoint trustees of the settlement by deed.[9] The trustees do not control or manage the land subject to the settlement and their chief role is rather to supervise the activities of the tenant for life so that the property subject to the settlement is conserved and not dissipated. The trustees are entitled to be informed if the tenant for life intends to exercise certain of his powers, including selling or mortgaging the land.[10] In the case of some transactions, for example the sale of the "principal mansion house" of a settlement, their consent is required.[11] Most importantly, where any transaction occurs which results in the realisation of the value of assets of the settlement in money, such "capital money" must be paid over to the trustees of the settlement and not to the tenant for life.[12] If such capital moneys are not paid to the trustees then the transaction is void. Overreaching of the beneficial interest behind a settlement can also only occur if the capital moneys are paid to at least two trustees of the settlement.[13]

[6] *ibid.*
[7] s.38.
[8] ss.41 and 71.
[9] s.30(1)(v).
[10] s.101.
[11] Alternatively the tenant for life may obtain an order of the court.
[12] s.18.
[13] s.2(3) of the Law of Property Act 1925.

SUCCESSIVE AND LIMITED INTERESTS TAKING EFFECT BEHIND A TRUST OF LAND

1 A new single system?

(a) Demise of the strict settlement

As has already been noted the trusts of Land and Appointment of Trustees Act 1996 has effectively brought about the beginning of the demise of the strict settlement as a means of land-holding, since it prevents the creation of new strict settlements. Existing settlements continue as such but it is inevitable that over the years their numbers will dwindle as they terminate.

(b) Trust of land not an entirely novel means of effecting successive interests in land

Although the Trusts of Land and Appointment of Trustees Act 1996 purports to introduce a new single system replacing the dual trust for sale-strict settlement dichotomy introduced under the legislation of 1925 this is not entirely accurate. It was always possible to give effect to successive interests behind a trust for sale prior to the new legislation, since Settled Land Act 1925, s.3 provided that land "held upon trust for sale" was not to be regarded as settled land. Therefore, if before January 1, 1997 Simon had declared himself to be holding Victoria Manor on trust for sale for Grant for life with remainder to Phil, this would not have created a strict settlement. As a result the legal title to the land would have remained with the trustees rather than the tenant for life. This meant that the tenant for life had much less control over the property than was the case in a strict settlement, unless he was also one of the trustees. It was also possible for the trustees to delegate some of their powers to the beneficiary with a life interest.[14] It has also been seen that the essence of a trust for sale was that the trustees were under a duty to sell the land which could only be displaced if they exercised their power to postpone sale unanimously. The beneficiary with a life interest could enjoy some measure of protection if any sale was made subject to his consent and there was always the possibility of the court refusing to order a sale under Law of Property Act 1925, s.30. The Trust of Land and Appointment of Trustees Act 1925 basically requires that all successive interests in land created after January 1, 1997 exist behind a modified version of the trust for sale. Since the Act only converts pre-existing implied trusts for sale into trusts of land any express trusts for sale behind which successive interests arise created before January 1, 1996 will continue to take effect as trusts of land with the trustees subject to a duty to sell.

(c) Examination of the new trust of land

In the previous chapter many of the key features of the new trust of land have already been examined in the context of co-ownership. In this chapter some of the same details of the system will be repeated, although the emphasis will be upon how a trust of land may be utilised to give effect to successive or limited interests in land.

[14] Law of Property Act 1925, s.29 now repealed.

2 Creation of a trust of land

(a) Any trust where land is included amongst the trust property

Section 1(1)(a) of the Trusts of Land and Appointment of Trustees Act 1925 provides that a trust of land means "any trust of property which consists of or includes land." A trust of land will arise irrespective of whether the trust was created expressly, or by an implied, constructive or resulting trust.

(b) Any interest in the land which must take effect behind a trust

A trust of land will arise irrespective of the type of equitable interest which arises behind it. All the interests which formerly gave rise to a settlement under Settled Land Act 1925, s.1 will now take effect behind a trust of land. Therefore any successive interests, determinable interests or trusts for the benefit of minors will give rise to a trust of land. Only in very limited circumstances will a trust created after January 1, 1997 give rise to a strict settlement.

3 Position of the trustees of a trust of land

(a) Trustees of land vested with the legal title

Where a trust of land arises the legal title is vested in the trustees. This is the central difference between the trust of land and a strict settlement, since it has been seen that under a strict settlement the legal title must be vested in the tenant for life or the statutory owner. The trustees of a trust of land have more than the mere role of supervising the tenant for life and the exercise of his powers, and receiving and properly applying the capital moneys that arise from any disposition he makes of a legal estate in the land.

(b) Trustees have all the powers of management and disposition over the land

As a consequence of their position as holders of the legal title the trustees of a trust of land enjoy all the powers of management and disposition over the land. Section 6(1) Trusts of Land and Appointment of Trustees Act 1996 provides that "[f]or the purpose of exercising their function as trustees, the trustees of land have in relation to the land subject to the trust all the powers of an absolute owner." This means that they have the complete freedom to do what they choose with the land. This contrasts with the position of a tenant for life under a settlement who was only entitled to deal with the land in accordance with the powers granted him by the Settled Land Act. The new system effectively widens the scope of dealings which can be entered. For example, under the Settled Land Act 1925 the tenant for life had no power to purchase land with the assistance of a mortgage, but the trustees of a trust of land would enjoy this power. By section 6(3) the trustees are given the power to purchase a legal estate in any land in England or Wales, and by section 6(5) they are required to "have regard to the rights of the beneficiaries" in exercising their powers.

(c) Exercise of trustees' powers subject to consents

Although the trustees of a trust of land are given the general power to deal with the land as if they were the absolute owner, their ability to exercise their powers may be made subject to the requirement that they gain the consent of persons nominated for that purpose in the instrument creating the trust. For example, in the case of a life interest the settlor may make the trustee's power of sale of the land subject to the consent of certain persons, perhaps of the life tenant or of other family members. Section 10 Trusts of Land and Appointment of Trustees Act 1996 has the effect that if the disposition creating the trust requires the consent of more than two persons to the exercise of any power by the trustees a purchaser of the land is protected if the consent of "any two of them" was obtained. Although in such circumstances the purchaser would be protected, a trustee who has failed to obtain all the specified consents will have committed a breach of trust.

(d) Requirement to consent with the beneficiaries before exercising powers

As well as the potential imposition of specific consents by the trust instrument Trusts of Land and Appointment of Trustees Act 1925, s.11 places the trustees under a duty to consult with the beneficiaries of the trust when they exercise any of their functions. This is not an absolute duty, as section 11(1)(a) provides that they must "so far as is practicable, consult the beneficiaries of full age and beneficially entitled to an interest in possession in the land." Where there are successive interests in the land this means that there is only a need to consult with the present life tenant and not the remaindermen. For example if trustees hold Victoria Manor on trust for Grant for life, remainder to Phil, and they intend to sell the land, they would be required to consult with Grant but not Phil, as he would not be entitled to an interest in possession. Where the trustees are obliged to consult they are required "so far as consistent with the general interest of the trust" to give effect to their wishes, or the wishes of the majority.

(e) Delegation of their powers to the beneficiaries of the trust

(i) A general power to delegate: From the perspective of the creation of successive interests in land the most important aspect of the new trust of land machinery is that the trustees are capable of delegating their powers to the beneficiaries of the trust. Section 9(1) provides that:

> The trustees of land may, by power of attorney, delegate to any beneficiary or beneficiaries of full age and beneficially entitled to an interest in possession in land subject to the trust *any of their functions as trustees which relates to the land.*

The statutory power to delegate only applies to a delegation of the powers of the trustees as a body, and not to the individual powers of any of the trustees alone.

(ii) Able to render a beneficiary in the same position as a tenant for life under a settlement: The right of the trustees to delegate their functions enables them to place the beneficiary of a trust of a successive or limited interest in land in the position they would have been in as a tenant for life under a strict settlement. If the trustee's delegate all their powers to the beneficiary then he will be able to dispose of legal estates in the land. The only difference is that any conveyance will have to be made by the trustees, who retain the legal title. However, the central distinction between the trust of land and the strict settlement is that, unlike the tenant for life, the beneficiary has no right to have the trustees' powers delegated to him and it is entirely within the trustees' discretion to decide whether to make a delegation. For example, if Victoria Manor is held on trust for Grant for life with remainder to Phil, Grant will only be entitled to exercise the powers of the trustees if they decide to delegate them to him. He cannot insist on such a delegation. To this extent the beneficiary will not enjoy the same degree of autonomy over what should be done with the land subject to the trust as would the tenant for life of a settlement. Even where a delegation has been made the position of the beneficiary is somewhat insecure since section 9(3) provides that it can be revoked "by any one or more" of the trustees and it is automatically revoked if a new trustee is appointed.

(iii) Automatic termination of delegation if the beneficiary ceases to be entitled to an interest in possession: Where the trustees have delegated their powers to the beneficiaries section 9(4) provides that the delegation will automatically revoke if the beneficiary "ceases to be a person beneficially entitled to an interest in possession" in the land. For example, if Victoria Mansion was held on trust for Grant for life, remainder to Phil for life, remainder to Lorraine, and the trustees had delegated their powers to Grant, the delegation would be automatically revoked if he were to surrender his interest to Phil since he would not longer enjoy any interest in possession of the land.

(iv) Automatic termination of delegation if a trustee becomes mentally incapable: A delegation will also be automatically revoked if one of the trustees who has granted it loses his mental capacity, because delegation cannot be made by an enduring power of attorney.[15]

(v) Beneficiaries cannot be trustees for the purposes of the receipt of capital moneys: Section 9(7) makes clear that a delegation of the trustee's powers to the beneficiary cannot include the power to give a good receipt for any capital moneys arising as a result of a disposition of the land. This means that overreaching of the beneficial interests behind the trust cannot occur unless payment is made to at least two trustees of land.

(vi) Protection from liability for breach of trust where they have delegated their functions: If the trustees have delegated their functions to the beneficiaries section 9(8) protects them from potential liability arising by the beneficiaries' misuse. It provides that the trustees are only libel for acts or defaults of the beneficiaries "if and only if the trustees did not exercise reasonable care in deciding to delegate the function to the beneficiary or beneficiaries."

(f) Power to convey the land to the beneficiaries if they are absolutely entitled

If the beneficiaries of a trust of land are of age and capacity and absolutely entitled to the land the trustees enjoy the right to convey the legal title to them under section 6(2), thus relieving themselves of the responsibility of trusteeship. For example, if Victoria Manor is held by trustees for Grant for life, remainder to Phil, when Grant dies the trustees will be entitled to transfer the legal title to Phil even if he does not demand it. In such a case the beneficiary is under a duty to do "whatever is necessary" to secure that the land vests in them.[16]

[15] s.9(6).

[16] s.6(2)(a) and (b).

4 Position of the beneficiaries of the trust of land

(a) Beneficiaries with an interest in possession entitled to occupy

(i) A general right to occupation: By Trusts of Land and Appointment of Trustees Act 1996, s.12(1):

> "A beneficiary who is beneficially entitled to an interest in possession in the land subject to a trust of land is entitled by reason of his interest to occupy the land at any time if at that time —
>
> (a) the purposes of the trust include making the land available for his occupation (or for the occupation of beneficiaries of a class of which he is a member or of the beneficiaries in general), or
>
> (b) the land is held by the trustees so as to be so available.

(ii) The right to occupy in relation to successive interests in land: Although it has been seen that section 12 places the rights of concurrent owners of land to occupation on a statutory footing, a right which was somewhat unclear under the old trust for sale,[17] it also ensures that the equivalent of the tenant for life of a strict settlement is entitled to occupy the land. For example, if Victoria Manor is held on trust for Grant for life, remainder to Phil, Grant will enjoy the right to occupy under section 12 because he is entitled to an interest in possession.

(iii) Qualifications to the right to occupy: Section 12(2) provides that a beneficiary with a right in possession does not enjoy a right to occupation if the land "is either unavailable or unsuitable for occupation by him." In some cases the operation of this limitation may be obvious. For example, if a factory site rather than Victoria Manor was held on trust for Grant for life it is unlikely that he would enjoy a right to occupy it residentially. However, it is unclear whether personal characteristics of the beneficiary would prevent them enjoying a right to occupy. If Grant were an alcoholic, drug addict or member of a religious cult would this render Victoria Manor "unsuitable for occupation by *him*"?

(iv) Restriction of the right to occupy: If there are two or more beneficiaries who are jointly entitled to occupy the land the trustees of the settlement may under section 13(1) "exclude or restrict the entitlement of any one or more (but not all) of them." This provision is not so relevant to situations of successive interests where there is more likely to be a sole person entitled to an interest in possession. However, if Victoria Manor were held by Grant and Phil jointly for life they would hold their interests concurrently and the trustees might be required to exercise their jurisdiction under section 13. The power to limit or exclude is rendered virtually nugatory by section 13(7) which prevents the trustees acting so as to cause a person to cease occupation unless he consents or an order of the court is obtained.

(b) Powers of the trustees may be delegated to the beneficiaries

(i) Possibility of delegation: As has already been explained the trustees possess the discretion to be able to delegate the exercise of some or all of their functions to the beneficiaries, but the beneficiaries do not have a right to have the functions delegated.

[17] See above p. 242.

(ii) Duties of the beneficiaries where trustees functions have been delegated: Where any of the functions of the trustees have been delegated to the beneficiaries section 9(7) provides that they are "in relation to the exercise of the functions, in the same position as trustees (with the same duties and liabilities)." They are therefore fiduciaries and will attract liability for breach of trust if they do not exercise appropriate care in the exercise of such delegated functions.

5 The role of the court

(a) A wide supervisory jurisdiction

Given the number of parties who may have interests in land which is held subject to successive interests under a trust of land, disputes will periodically occur. For example, if Victoria Manor is held by trustees on trust for Grant for life, with remainder to Phil, Grant may want to see the house let to Lorraine, an up and coming pop star who is willing to pay an above market rent because of its location, in order to maximise his income, whereas Phil does not want the house let because he suspects that Grant is suffering from cancer and is likely to die soon and he wants to ensure that he can live in the house immediately. Alternatively, the trustees may be concerned about the costs of repairs to the houses that will soon be needed and would prefer that it be sold and a smaller more manageable property acquired, whereas Grant is wanting to start a business using the house as an up-market conference centre. To deal with any such difficulties concerning the trust the court is given a very wide jurisdiction to intervene under Trusts of Land and Appointment of Trustees Act 1996, s.14. Section 14(2) entitles the court to make orders:

(a) relating to the exercise by the trustees of any of their functions (including an order relieving them of any obligation to obtain the consent of or to consult, any person in connection with the exercise of any of their function, or

(b) declaring the extent of a person's interest in property subject to the trust

(b) Persons who may seek the intervention of the court

Section 14(1) provides that:

> "Any person who is a trustee of land or has an interest in property subject to a trust of land may make an application to the court for an order under this section."

In the case of a trust of land facilitating successive interests all the relevant parties may seek the court's intervention, namely the trustees, the beneficiaries with interests in possession, any beneficiaries with subsequent limited interests, and those entitled to the remainder interest.

(c) General discretion of the court

When such an application is made the court has the discretion to make such order as it "thinks fit."[18]

(d) Factors which the court must consider

Although section 14(2) grants the court a general discretion to make whatever order it considers appropriate, section 15 outlines a number of factors which the court is required to take into account in determining an appropriate order. The relevance of these factors to disputes between co-owners of the land, where the most likely issue is whether the land should be sold, have been examined in the previous chapter. However, they may be relevant in a slightly different way to questions which concern land held subject to successive interests.

(i) The settlor's intentions and the purpose of the trust: Section 15(1)(a) and (b) require the court to take regard of the "intentions of the person or persons (if any) who created the trust" and "the purposes for which the property subject to the trust is held." If, for example, a testator had established a trust of Victoria Mansion for his son Grant for life with remainder to his grandson Phil, because he knew that Grant was a drug addict who only wanted to sell the house and he wanted to ensure that it remained in the family, this would be a factor, although not necessarily determinative, if there was a proposed sale of the house to which Phil objected and sought the intervention of the court.

(ii) Occupation interests of minors: Section 15(1)(c) requires the court to have regard to "the welfare of any minor who occupies or might reasonably be expected to occupy any land subject to the trust as his home." This might mean that the court would have to consider the interests of the children of a beneficiary in possession, even if they themselves were not entitled to any beneficial interests in the land. For example, if Victoria Mansion was held on trust for Grant for life with remainder to Phil, the welfare of Grant's children who have been living in the house would be a relevant factor to consider if there was some dispute whether the house should be sold to enable the money to be more profitably invested.

(iii) Interests of creditors: Under section 15(1)(c) the interests of any secured creditors of a beneficiary are to be taken into account.

(iv) Interests of beneficiaries entitled to occupy: Where the trustees are seeking to exercise their powers under section 13 to exclude or restrict the right of beneficiaries with interests in possession and the intervention of the court is sought, section 15(2) provides that the court must have regard to the "circumstances and wishes of each of the beneficiaries of full age" who has a statutory right to occupy the land under section 12. If Victoria Manor is held on trust for Grant and Phil jointly for life, and Phil returns after a number of years in prison overseas for sexual abuse of children, the court would have to consider the circumstances and wishes of both Grant, who might have a family with small children living in the house, and Phil, who has nowhere else to live, in deciding whether the trustees should exclude his right to share occupation.

(v) Interests of beneficiaries with rights in possession: The court is also required to have a general regard under section 15(3) to "the circumstances and wishes of the any

[18] s.14(2).

beneficiaries of full age and entitled to an interest in possession in the property subject to the trust or (in case of dispute) of the majority (according to the value of their combined interests)." In the case of successive interests this will mean the rights of the persons entitled to present enjoyment of the land, so the life tenants rather than the remainder beneficiaries. For example, if Grant, Phil and Lorraine are the joint life tenants of Victoria Manor, and Grant wishes the land to be sold and the money re-invested in a smaller property with the balance in a share portfolio, but Phil and Lorraine want the house retained, the court is required to have regard to the majority view.

(vi) Balance between competing factors: Section 15 provides nothing more than a requirement that certain factors must be taken into account by the court and does not provide a definitive guide by which it can be predicted how disputes should be resolved. Often the various factors will point in the direction of different orders. For example, the intention and purpose of the trust may have been that specific land was retained for the family, whereas the interests of minors in occupation may point to the purchase of a more suitable property. In such cases it is simply a matter for the court to determine the appropriate order having taken into account all the competing factors.

6 Third parties acquiring interests in the land subject to a trust of land

(a) Third parties acquiring the interests of the beneficiaries

As in the case of a strict settlement the beneficiaries under a trust of land are free to deal with their own equitable interests, For example, if Victoria Manor is held on trust for Grant for life he is perfectly able to assign his life interest to Lorraine. Whereas in the case of a strict settlement Grant would have retained the powers of a tenant for life in relation to the land, the powers would remain with the trustees so that unless Grant was also a trustee he would enjoy no continuing rights in the land. If the trustees had delegated any of their powers to him then the effect of his assignment of his interest would be to automatically terminate the delegation since by section 9(4) he would have ceased to be a person beneficially entitled to an interest in possession under the trust.

(b) Third parties acquiring a legal estate in the land

(i) Dealing with trustees who have not delegated their powers: Since the trustees retain the rights of management over the land they are entitled to transfer rights to third parties. For example, if trustees hold Victoria Manor on trust for Grant for life, remainder to Phil they are entitled to transfer a freehold estate to Lorraine, or to grant her a legal lease.

(ii) Dealing with beneficiaries to whom the trustees have delegated their powers: If the trustees have delegated their powers, or relevant powers, to a beneficiary or beneficiaries entitled to an interest in possession, then a third party can deal with such beneficiary. For example, if the trustees had delegated all their powers in relation to Victoria Manor to Grant, he would be able to transfer the freehold interest to Lorraine or to grant her a legal lease. Under section 9(2), where the trustees have purported to delegate their powers to any person it will be presumed in favour of any third party who deals with them in good faith that the delegation was valid, unless the third party "has knowledge at the time of the transaction" that the trustees were not entitled to make the delegation to him.

(iii) Will a third party acquire an interest in the land free from the existing beneficial interests? By far the most significant question will be whether a third party who acquires a legal estate in the land, whether by dealing with the trustees or a delegate, take his interest free from those of the beneficiaries. For example, if Lorraine purchases the freehold of Victoria Manor from the trustees, will she take the land free from Grant's life interest and Phil's remainder? Similarly, if the trustees had delegated their power of sale to Grant, would she take free from Phil's remainder interest? As in the case of a strict settlement the central question will be whether the third party is entitled to the protection of overreaching. Provided the statutory requirements are satisfied, namely that the conveyance is made by the trustees of land[19] and the proceeds of sale are paid over to two trustees for sale,[20] then the interests of the beneficiaries will be overreached and converted from interests in the land to interests in the purchase moneys in the hands of the trustees, and the purchaser will take the land free from the interests of the beneficiaries. If overreaching has not occurred the question of priority will be answered differently depending on whether land is registered or unregistered. In the case of registered land, the purchaser will take free from beneficial interests which have not been protected as minor interests on the register, unless the beneficiaries are also in actual occupation of the land in which case their rights will also constitute overriding interests under Land Registration Act 1925, s.70(1)(g). In the case of unregistered land the purchaser will take free of the beneficiaries' interests unless he had notice of their existence.[21]

CONTINUING STRICT SETTLEMENTS

1 When is land subject to a strict settlement?

(a) No new settlements after January 1, 1997

Following the enactment of the trusts of Land and Appointment of Trustees Act 1996 no new strict settlements can be created after the January 1, 1997. However existing settlements at that date will continue, and the relationships between the parties, including the powers and duties of the trustees and tenant for life respectively, will continue to be governed by the Settled Land Act 1925. In some sense settled land is rather like unregistered land: of constantly diminishing significance but far from completely irrelevant.

(b) Settlements created before January 1, 1997 where the legal title has been vested in the tenant for life

Settlements established before January 1, 1997 will continue to exist as such. In order to create such a settlement the Settled Land Act 1925 required the execution of two

[19] s.2(1)(ii) of the Law of Property Act 1925.
[20] s.27 of the Law of Property Act 1925.
[21] *Kingsnorth Finance Co. Ltd v. Tizzard* [1986] 1 W.L.R. 783.

instruments. For the creation of a settlement *inter vivos* Settled Land Act, s.4(1) provided:

> "Every settlement of a legal estate in land inter vivos shall, save as in this Act otherwise provided, be effected by two deeds, namely a vesting deed and a trust instrument and if effected in any other way shall not operate to transfer or create a legal estate."

The trust instrument was the document in which the creator of the settlement specified the interests of the beneficiaries and appointed the trustees of the settlement.[22] The vesting deed was the means by which the legal title to the land was conveyed to the tenant for life.[23] Where the tenant for life was already the legal owner of the land the vesting deed was merely required to declare "that the land is vested in him for that estate."[24] Therefore, if Peggy was the freehold owner of Victoria Manor and wanted Grant to enjoy a life interest with remainder to Phil, she would have had to execute both a trust instrument, and a vesting deed in favour of Grant. Section 5(1) of the Settled Land Act 1925 provided that a vesting deed should contain a number of statements:

(a) a description, either specific or general, of the settled land;

(b) a statement that the settled land is vested in the person or persons to whom it is conveyed or in whom it is declared to be vested upon the trusts from time to time affecting the settled land;

(c) the names of the persons who are the trustees of the settlement;

(d) any additional or larger powers conferred by the trust instrument relating to the settled land which by virtue of this Act operate and are exercisable as if conferred by this Act on a tenant for life;

(e) the name of any person for the time being entitled under the trust instrument to appoint new trustees of the settlement.

Failure to include all these details did not invalidate the vesting deed. Where a settlement was created by will rather than inter vivos the "two deed" requirement was maintained, but by Settled Land Act 1925, s.6(a) the will was regarded as a trust instrument for the purposes of the Act. Since the legal title to a testator's property vests in his personal representative on death, section 6(b) provided that:

> "the personal representatives of the testator shall hold the settled land on trust, if and when required so to do, to convey it to the person who, under the will, or by virtue of this Act, is the tenant for life or statutory owner, and, if more than one, as joint tenants."

[22] s.4(3).
[23] s.4(2).
[24] s.4(2).

(c) Settlements declared before January 1, 1997 but without the execution of a vesting instrument

It is perfectly possible for a settlement of land to arise as a result of a declaration prior to January 1, 1997 even if there has been no execution of the necessary vesting deed prior to that date. For example, if Peggy declared a trust of Victoria Manor for Grant for life, remainder to Phil, on December 31, 1996 this would give rise to a strict settlement, as would a gift by will leaving Victoria Manor to Grant for life if the testator died on that date. However, although the instrument has created a strict settlement as yet the legal owner has not executed an appropriate vesting instrument in favour of the tenant for life or statutory owner. In such circumstances the Settled Land Act 1925 paralyses any dealings with the legal title of the land. Section 13 provides:

> "Where a tenant for life or statutory owner has become entitled to have a principal vesting deed or a vesting assent executed in his favour, then until a vesting instrument is executed . . . *any purported disposition thereof inter vivos by any person,* other than a personal representative . . . *shall not take effect* except in favour of a purchaser of a legal estate [without notice of such tenant for life or statutory owner having become so entitled as aforesaid] but, save as aforesaid, *shall operate only as a contract for valuable consideration to carry out the transaction after the requisite vesting instrument has been executed* or made, and a purchaser of a legal estate shall not be concerned with such disposition unless the contract is registered as a land charge."

This section means that any third party who acquires a legal estate in the settled land from the legal owner before an appropriate vesting instrument has been executed will not obtain that interest in the land if they had notice of the existence of the settlement. Instead the purported disposition of the legal estate in their favour will be deemed to constitute an enforceable contract for the disposition of that interest, which they will be able to enforce after an appropriate vesting instrument has been executed. For example, if Peggy declared a settlement of Divine Mansion for Grant for life, remainder to Phil in November 1996, but has not yet executed a vesting instrument in favour of Grant as the tenant for life, and subsequently transferred the legal title to Lorraine, this will be ineffective to pass the legal title unless she had no notice of the existence of the settlement. If she knew of the settlement she will be entitled to enforce a contract for the transfer as against Grant when the land is vested in him as tenant for life. Such a contract can be protected as a Class C(iv) land charge in unregistered land and as a minor interest if the land is registered.

(d) Possible creation of settlements by a constructive trust recognised after January 1, 1997

Although Trusts of Land and Appointment of Trustees Act 1996, s.2 prevents the creation of settlements by events occurring after the January 1, 1997 it is perhaps possible that a settlement could arise in the absence of an express declaration before that date under a constructive trust flowing from events occurring before it. For example, if Grant was the legal owner of a house and he conveyed it to his brother Phil in November 1996, subject to an oral or written agreement that he was to be allowed to live in it rent free for as long as he wanted, Grant could be entitled to a determinable life interest in the house. Although the parties may not be in dispute for some time, and that there would therefore be no dispute as to the nature of his interest, if Phil subsequently gave Grant notice to quit, or sold the house to Lorraine, the nature of Grant's entitlements would fall to be considered. Since English law adopts an institutional concept of the constructive trust, which arises on the occurrence of the necessary events rather than a remedial trust which only arises from the time that it is judicially granted, Grant's interest would technically have arisen before the commencement of the new system when he acted to his detriment by conveying the house to Phil on the basis of their common intention that he was to enjoy a life interest. He could be regarded as a tenant for life under a strict settlement of the land. For this reason the possibility of discovering accidental strict settlements may not be at an end for some time. The possibility of a settlement arising by way of a constructive trust was raised in *Bannister v. Bannister*[25] where the Court of Appeal held that a person who was entitled to a determinable life interest in land by way of a constructive trust became a life tenant for the purposes of the Settled Land Act. The defendant was the legal owner of two cottages. She entered an oral agreement with the plaintiff, her brother-in-law, that she would sell the cottages to him, and he agreed that she could live rent free in one of them for the rest of her life. On the basis of this oral agreement she transferred the legal title to the cottage to him. He subsequently gave her notice to quit occupation of the cottage, and in an action for possession she claimed that he held the cottage on trust for her for life. The Court of Appeal held that the oral agreement was to the effect that the defendant was to enjoy a life interest of the cottage, determinable if she ceased to occupy it. Since a mere oral declaration is ineffective to create a trust of land[26] the court held that the life interest arose by way of a constructive trust. The court therefore granted a declaration in her favour that:

> "the plaintiff holds [the cottage] in trust during the life of the defendant to permit the defendant to occupy the same for so long as she may desire to do so and subject thereto in trust for the plaintiff. A trust in this form has the effect of making the beneficiary a tenant for life within the meaning of the settled Land Act 1925, and, consequently, there is very little practical difference between such a trust and a trust for life *simpliciter*."[27]

Two practical objections may be made to this approach. First the Settled Land Act 1925 required a settlement to be created by means of two documents, a trust instrument and a vesting deed. In a case where a trust interest arises informally neither of these instruments is present, although presumably the imposition of the constructive trust by law takes the place of the trust instrument and the plaintiff could have demanded that the defendant execute a vesting deed in her favour. However this would have the somewhat unusual consequence that as a tenant for life the defendant would have been entitled to have the legal title reconveyed to her, when she herself conveyed it to the plaintiff on the basis of their oral agreement. Although *Bannister v.*

[25] [1948] 2 All E.R. 133.
[26] Law of Property Act 1925, s.53(1)(b).
[27] [1948] 2 All E.R. 133 at 137, *per* Scott L.J.

Bannister[28] accepted the possibility of the accidental creation of a settlement by means of a constructive trust in *Binions v. Evans*[29] Lord Denning M.R. construed the Settled Land Act in such a way as to avoid this consequence. Mr Evans lived in a cottage on the Tredegar estate. On his death his widow stayed in the cottage and paid no rent or rates. Three years later the estate entered an agreement with her allowing her to stay in the cottage for the rest of her life. Lord Denning M.R. held that despite the authority of *Bannister v. Bannister* Mrs Evans was not a tenant for life under a settlement of the cottage. He stated that Settled Land Act 1925, s.1(1) only applied where there was an express limitation of the land by way of succession, and he concluded that the agreement neither expressly limited any trust of the land nor was there any succession since there was no indication of one beneficial interest succeeding another. Instead he held that Mrs Evans was entitled to an equitable licence to occupy the premises for life. He outlined the principle objections to finding that there was a settlement:

> "A tenant for life under [the Settled Land Act 1925] has power to sell the property and to lease it (and to treat himself or herself as the owner of it) . . . No one would expect the defendant here to be able to sell the property or lease it. It would be so entirely contrary to the true intent of the parties that it cannot be right."[30]

However, the majority of the Court of Appeal, Megaw and Stephenson L.JJ. held that *Bannister v. Bannister* should be followed and that Mrs Evans was entitled to a determinable life interest taking effect under a settlement of the land. Subsequent cases have failed to solve the dilemma whether accidental settlements should arise in such cases. The greater development of the concept of proprietary estoppel, where the award of a licence for life is one means of satisfying an estoppel equity, provided one means of avoiding accidental settlements.[31] In the more recent case *Ungurian v. Lesnoff*[32] Vinelott J. held that where a person was entitled to reside in a property for life on the basis of a constructive trust they were entitled to a life interest and there was a settlement of the land. He rejected the approach Lord Denning M.R. had taken in *Bannister v. Bannister* and explained why a settlement would necessarily arise:

> "Although, of course, every judgment of Lord Denning is entitled to the greatest respect, I do not find the reasons he gives for the conclusion that the defendant in *Binions v. Evans* was not a tenant for life persuasive. A person with a right to reside in an estate during his or her life, or for a period determinable on any earlier event, has a life or a determinable interest as the case may be . . . The estate is necessarily limited in trust for persons by way of succession. That is of course so whether the trust is express or arises by operation of law. Of course, the power of sale given to a tenant for life by the Settled Land Act 1925 may

[28] *ibid.*
[29] [1972] Ch. 359.
[30] *ibid.* at 366.
[31] *Foster v. Robinson* [1951] 1 K.B. 149; *Inwards v. Baker* [1965] 2 Q.B. 29; *Ivory v. Palmer* (1976) 237 E.G. 411; *Greasley v. Cooke* [1980] 1 W.L.R. 1306.
[32] [1990] Ch. 206.

> override and defeat the intentions of the settlor or of the parties to a transaction which gives rise to a constructive trust or settlement. The 1925 legislation was designed to ensure that land was not taken out of commerce, and to that extent often defeats the intention of a settlor or testator who would prefer that the land should remain in his family."[33]

Given the weight of these authorities it certainly seems possible that a settlement may be recognised as having been brought into existence by conduct occurring prior to January 1, 1997.

2 Powers of the tenant for life under a strict settlement

(a) *Tenant for life vested with the legal title*

When a strict settlement has been validly created and the appropriate vesting deed executed the tenant for life is vested with the full legal ownership of the land. He does not, however, enjoy the unencumbered rights of an absolute owner to deal with the land as he wishes, and the scope of his powers are defined by the Settled Land Act 1925.

(b) *Powers granted to the tenant for life by the Settled Land Act*

(i) Power to sell or exchange the land: By section 38 the tenant for life who has the legal title vested in him is entitled to sell, or exchange, the settled land, or any part of it, or any easement, right or privilege in the land, provided that the sale is made "for best consideration money that can reasonably be obtained."[34]
(ii) Power to grant leases of the land: By section 41 the tenant for life has the power to grant leases of the settled land for periods of up to 50 years, or longer in the cases of such leases as a mining or forestry lease. Again the lease must be for the "best rent that can reasonably be obtained."[35]
(iii) Power to grant other subsidiary rights over the land: Section 41 also entitles the tenant for life to grant such subsidiary rights as easements, rights or privileges of any kind over the land.
(iv) Power to raise money by way of a mortgage of the land: Section 71 grants the tenant for life power to raise money by way of a mortgage of the settled land provided that the money is required for one of the narrow range of purposes specified.
(v) Power to effect improvements out of the capital value of the property held under the settlement: Under section 83 the tenant for life is granted the power to effect improvements to the settled land out of the capital moneys held under the settlement.

(c) *Extension of the statutory powers enjoyed by a tenant for life*

Although the powers conferred on the tenant for life by the Settled Land Act 1925 cannot be excluded,[36] section 109 provides that the settlor who created the settlement can confer any additional powers on the tenants for life.

[33] *ibid.* at 226.
[34] s.39(1).
[35] s.42(1)(ii).
[36] s.106.

(d) Exercise of the powers of the tenant for life

(i) Powers held in a fiduciary capacity: The tenant for life enjoys his powers in relation to the settled land in a fiduciary capacity. This means that he cannot exercise them solely for his own benefit. Section 107(1) provides that:

> "A tenant for life or statutory owner shall, in exercising any power under this Act, have regard to the interests of all parties entitled under the settlement, and shall, in relation to the exercise thereof by him, be deemed to be in the position and to have the duties and liabilities of a trustee for those parties."

(ii) Powers cannot be assigned: Section 104(1) provides that the powers of the tenant for life are incapable of assignment and that if he does assign his interest he retains his powers and they are exercisable by him notwithstanding the assignment. Where the tenant for life has assigned his interests he may continue to exercise his powers without gaining the consent of the assignee.[37] Any contract that the tenant for life enters that he will not exercise some or all of his powers is void.[38]

(iii) Requirement to inform the trustees of the settlement of proposed dealings with the land: Where the tenant for life proposes to exercise certain of his powers he is required to give notice of his intention to the trustees of the settlement first. Section 101(1) of the Settled Land Act 1925 provides that he must give notice by registered letter to the trustees and to the solicitor for the trustees if he intends to "make a sale, exchange, lease, mortgage, or charge or to grant an option" in relation to the land. The notice must be given "not less than one month" before the proposed transaction is completed. By section 101(2) the notice need not be specific but may be "notice of a general intention" to make a transaction of the types covered by the section. By section 101(3) the tenant for life must make any information or particulars available to the trustees if they reasonably require it. The requirement of notice may be waived by the trustees, either in relation to a specific transaction or generally, and they may accept less than a month's notice.[39] Failure by the tenant for life to give appropriate notice does not affect the position of the third party with whom they transact concerning the land, provided that such a person was dealing in good faith, and the lack of notice does not invalidate the transaction.[40]

(iv) Exercise of powers requiring the consent of the trustees of the settlement: In some cases the tenant must do more than simply give notice to the trustees of the settlement before exercising his powers and he must obtain their consent. Under section 58 the tenant for life must obtain the consent in writing of the trustees before compromising any claim relating to the settled land,[41] and before releasing, waiving or modifying any restrictive covenant or easement affecting other land for the benefit of the settled land.[42]

[37] s.104(4).
[38] s.104(2).
[39] s.101(4).
[40] s.101(5).
[41] s.58(1).
[42] s.58(2).

(v) Exercise of powers requiring either the consent of the trustees or an order of the court: By section 65 the tenant for life cannot dispose of the principal mansion house comprising the settled land, whether by sale or lease, without the consent of the trustees of the settlement or an order of the court. Similarly, under section 66 he cannot cut and sell timber on the land which is ripe for cutting without consent or a court order.[43]
(vi) Exercise of powers requiring an order of the court: Under section 57(2) the tenant for life cannot sell or lease an area of the land greater than that specified[44] for the purpose of providing housing or allotments for the working classes for less than the best price or rent that could be reasonably obtained, without an order of the court. By section 67(3) heirlooms included in the settlement cannot be sold by the tenant for life without an order for the court. Under section 46 the tenant for life may only make mining or building leases longer than the terms specified in section 41[45] where there is a court order.
(v) Trustees may apply to the court concerning a proposed exercise of the powers of the tenant for life: When the trustees receive notice of a proposed transaction by the tenant for life concerning the settled land they are entitled to apply to the court under section 93 which provides that:

> If a question arises or a doubt is entertained —
>
> (a) respecting the exercise or intended exercise of any of the powers conferred by this Act . . .
>
> the tenant for life or statutory owner, *or the trustees of the settlement*, or any other person interested under the settlement, may apply to the court for its decision or directions thereon, or for the sanction of the court to any conditional contract, and the court may make such order or give such directions respecting the matter as the court thinks fit.

However, the trustees are not under any duty to seek the intervention of the court where a tenant for life proposes to exercise his powers and section 97(a) provides specifically that the trustees are not liable "for giving any consent, or for not making, bringing, taking or doing any such application, action, proceeding, or thing, as they might make, bring, take or do."
(iv) Capital moneys must be paid to the trustees of the settlement: Where the tenant for life exercises his powers in relation to the land and any capital moneys are payable to the trustees of the settlement. This requirement is discussed below.

3 Rights and powers of the trustees of the settlement

(a) General function in relation to the settlement

Unlike the trustees of conventional trusts the trustees of a settlement are not invested with the legal title of the land, which is instead enjoyed by the tenant for life, or

[43] If he is impeachable for waste in respect of timber.
[44] In urban areas specified as two acres in any one parish in urban districts and ten acres in rural districts.
[45] 999 years for building leases and 100 years for mining leases.

statutory owner as the case may be. The trustees do not therefore enjoy the day to day management and control of the property subject to the settlement and their role is rather one of overriding supervision. Their central role was characterised by Vaisey J. in *Re Boston's Will Trusts*[46] as ensuring that the trust property is conserved by the tenant for life. This is achieved by the requirements of the Settled Land Act concerning the payment of capital moneys realised by any transactions dealing with the settled property which are entered by the tenant for life. These have the effect that a third party will only gain the benefit of such a transaction if the capital moneys are paid to the trustees and such payment should prevent them being misappropriated or misapplied. The trustees also have to be informed of any dealing undertaken by the tenant for life and their written consent is required for some transactions.

(b) Trustees must be informed of intended transactions by the tenant for life

As has been noted above in the context of the powers of the tenant for life by section 101 the trustees must be informed if the tenant for life is intending to "make a sale, exchange, lease, mortgage or charge or to grant an option" of or over the settled property. The requirement of a month's written notice before the transaction, or contract for the transaction, is entered enables the trustee to apply to the court under section 93 if they have any question or doubts about the proposed exercise of the power.

(c) Trustees consent must be obtained to exercise of certain powers

As has been noted above, the provision of an excessive area of land by the tenant for life for the provision of dwellings or allotments for the working classes, the sale of heirlooms and the grant of mining or building leases longer than the statutory maximum require the consent of the trustees of the settlement. Sale of the "principal mansion house" and the cutting of ripe timber require either the consent of the trustees or of an order of the court.

(d) Trustees receipt of capital moneys

(i) The definition of capital moneys: Where property is held under a settlement the exercise of the tenant for life will often result in the realisation of its value in money. It is important to distinguish whether such realised value is to be regarded as the capital or the income of the settlement, since this will determine the entitlements of the beneficiaries. The tenant for life who enjoys a life interest will be entitled to any income, whereas capital forms part of the remainder interest and should not be dissipated by the tenant for life. The Settled Land Act provides that the receipts from certain transactions are to be treated as capital money.[47] Most importantly the proceeds of sale of land or heirlooms[48] forming part of the settlement comprise capital money. Where the tenant for life leases the land and receives a fine in return it is deemed to be capital money,[49] as is the consideration paid for the grant of an option to purchase or take a lease.[50] Three-quarters of the rent of a mining lease[51] and three-

[46] [1956] Ch. 395 at 405.
[47] The following examples are not exhaustive of what may constitute capital moneys for the purposes of the Settled Land Act 1925. See also ss.52, 54(4), 55(2), 56(4), 57(3), and 61(1).
[48] s.67(2).
[49] s.42(4).
[50] s.51(5).
[51] s.47: note that only a quarter of the rent will constitute capital if the tenant is not impeachable for waste.

quarters of the money from the sale of timber[52] which is cut from the land are treated as capital money if the tenant for life is impeachable for waste. Money raised by way of a mortgage of the land[53] and received as compensation for a breach of covenant by a lessee or grantee of the tenant for life[54] are also capital money.

(ii) Requirement that capital moneys be paid over to the trustees of the settlement: When the tenant for life proposes to effect a transaction in exercise of his powers which will realise money which is capital money for the purpose of the Act section 18(1) provides that:

> "Where land is the subject of a vesting instrument and the trustees of the settlement have not been discharged under this Act, then —
>
> (a) *any disposition by the tenant for life or statutory owner of the land*, other than a disposition authorised by this Act or any other statute, or made in pursuance of any additional or larger powers mentioned in the vesting instrument, *shall be void,* except for the purpose of conveying or creating such equitable interests as he has power, in right of his equitable interests and powers under the trust instrument, to convey or create; and
>
> (b) if any capital money is payable in respect of a transaction, a conveyance to a purchaser of the land shall only take effect under this Act if the capital money is paid to or by the direction of the trustees of the settlement or into court; and
>
> (c) notwithstanding anything to the contrary in the vesting instrument, or the trust instrument, *capital money shall not*, except where the trustee is a trust corporation, *be paid to or by the direction of fewer persons than two as trustees of the settlement.*

As the added italics demonstrate, the comprehensive effect of this section is that unless the capital moneys are paid over to, or at the direction of, at least two trustees any dealings of the tenant for life in relation to the legal interest he holds in the land are void and ineffective to transfer any legal title to the person with whom he has transacted. This operates as a safeguard to the interests of all the beneficiaries of the settlement from fraud by the tenant for life.

(iii) Problems where a third party is unaware that he is dealing with a tenant for life: If a third party acquires land which is settled and fails to pay over the capital moneys to the trustees of the settlement, but instead pays the tenant for life, there is some question as to whether the transaction is effective. Although section 18(1)(a) suggests that the failure to pay over to the trustees renders any disposition void section 110(1) provides that:

> "On a sale, exchange, lease, mortgage , charge or other disposition, *a purchaser dealing in good faith* with a tenant for life or statutory owner shall, as against all parties entitled under the settlement, *be conclusively taken* to have given the best

[52] s.66(2).
[53] s.71(1).
[54] s.80(1).

price, consideration, or rent, as the case may require, that could reasonably be obtained by the tenant for life or statutory owner, and *to have complied with all the requirements of this Act*."

The question has arisen whether the italicised phrases of this section have the effect that a purchaser acting in good faith is even deemed to have satisfied the requirement under section 18 that the purchase moneys must have been paid over to the trustees of the settlement. If so, a disposition to a purchaser who has acted in good faith without knowledge that he was dealing with a tenant for life will be effective and not rendered void by section 18. In *Weston v. Henshaw*[55] Dankwerts J. held that section 110(1) only applied in favour of a purchaser who knew that he was dealing with a tenant for life and did not protect a third party who had acted under the misapprehension that he was transacting with an unencumbered legal owner. The case concerned unregistered settled land which was mortgaged by the tenant for life. The mortgagee had not paid the capital moneys arising to the trustees of the settlement as he was unaware that the land was subject to a settlement. The tenant for life had been able to pass himself off as the unencumbered legal owner using some earlier title deeds which had conveyed the land to him in fee simple before the settlement had been created. On his death the fraud was discovered and the beneficiary claimed that section 18(1)(a) rendered the mortgage void. Danckwerts J. rejected the argument that the innocent mortgagee was protected by s110(1) stating: "I am satisfied . . . that that sub-section applies only to a person who is dealing with the tenant for life or statutory owner as such, whom he knows to be a limited owner, and with regard to whom he might be under a duty."[56] The mortgage was therefore void. He recognised that this result was in some measure unsatisfactory, since the case was "one of those unfortunate cases where an obvious fraud has been perpetrated by a person now deceased, with the result that one or other of two innocent persons must be deprived of what each of them naturally thought himself to be entitled to."[57] The right of the beneficiary was ultimately preferred to the right of the innocent third party. However, in *Re Morgan's Lease*[58] Ungoed-Thomas J. took a different approach to the scope of application of section 110(1). The case concerned the question whether the lessees of land subject to a settlement should be deemed to have paid the best rent that could reasonably be expected under section 110(1). He referred to the comments of Dankwerts J. and noted that the judgment did not set out the reasoning which led to his conclusion as to the scope of section 110, nor had the earlier authority *Mogridge v. Clapp*[59] been brought to the judge's attention. In that case the Court of Appeal had treated it "as self-evident that a person dealing with a life tenant without knowing that he was a life tenant would be entitled to rely on section 110 of the settled Land Act 1925."[60] He therefore concluded that the section was available in favour of a person who was unaware that he was dealing with a life-tenant:

"There is, in the section, no express provision limiting its benefit to a purchaser who knows that the person with whom he is dealing is a tenant for life. On its

[55] [1950] Ch. 510.
[56] *ibid.* at 519.
[57] *ibid.* at 515.
[58] [1972] Ch. 1.
[59] [1892] 3 Ch. 382.
[60] [1972] Ch. 1 at 9.

> face it reads as free of limitation and as applicable to a person without such knowledge as to a person who has it. There is a limitation, namely that the purchaser must act in good faith; but that limitation reads as applicable to as purchaser with such knowledge as without . . . Thus my conclusion is that section 110 applies whether or not the purchaser knows that the other party to the transaction is a tenant for life."[61]

As a matter of statutory interpretation it seems that this view should be preferred, particularly when it is realised that the implication of the approach taken in *Weston v. Henshaw*[62] is to create the only circumstances in which the bona fide purchaser of a legal estate in unregistered land takes subject to an equitable interest which falls outside of the limited system of registration of land charges.[63] Grey advocates an attempted reconciliation on the basis that section 110(1) has no application is situations where the life tenant enters a disposition which is ultra vires the Settled Land Act 1925, so that the fraud in *Weston v. Henshaw* was unauthorised as the Act does not permit the tenant for life to use old title deeds.

(e) Trustees application of capital moneys which have been received in accordance with section 18

The reason for requiring the trustees of the settlement to receive or direct the receipt of capital moneys consequential upon any dealings with the title to the land by the tenant for life is to ensure that they are then properly applied. Where the capital moneys have been raised for any special authorised object, for example improvements to the settled land, they must be used for that purpose.[64] Otherwise they are available for investment and section 73 of the Settled Land Act provides that they "shall, when received, be invested or otherwise applied wholly in one, or partly in one, or partly in another or others" of the modes specified in detail in section 73(1)(i)–(xxi). This includes investments authorised under the Trustee Investment Act 1961[65] and importantly the purchase of freehold land or a leasehold interest with 60 years of the term unexpired at the date of purchase.[66] In the absence of an express provision in the trust instrument capital money arising from the sale of settled land in England and Wales cannot be applied to the purchase of land out of England and Wales.[67]

4 Termination of the settlement

(a) Duration of the settlement

Section 3 of the Settled Land Act 1925 provides:

> "Land [which has been subject to a settlement which is a settlement for the purposes of this Act] shall be deemed for the purposes of this Act to remain and

[61] *ibid.* at 9.
[62] [1950] Ch. 510.
[63] See: (1971) 87 L.Q.R. 338; (D. W. Elliott); (1973) 36 M.L.R. 28 (R. H. Maudsley); [1985] Conv. 377 (R. Warrington); (1991) 107 L.Q.R. 596 (J. Hill).
[64] s.73(1).
[65] s.73(1)(i) since the proceeds are "trust money.".
[66] s.73(1)(xi) & (xii).
[67] s.73(2).

be settled land, and the settlement shall be deemed to be subsisting settlement for the purposes of this Act so long as —

(a) any limitation, charge or power of charging under the settlement subsists or is capable of being exercised; OR
(b) the person who, if of full age, would be entitled as beneficial owner to have that land vested in him for a legal estate is an infant."

(b) Disqualification of the current life tenant

Section 7(4) of the Settled Land Act makes provision for the situation if the current life-tenant of a settlement ceases to have the statutory powers of a tenant for life "by reason of forfeiture, surrender or otherwise." In such a case "he shall be bound forthwith to convey the settled land to the person who under the trust instrument, or by virtue of [the Settled Land Act 1925] becomes the tenant for life" as his replacement. In the event that there is no replacement the settlement will be brought to an end, and he will be required to convey the legal title to the person entitled absolutely to the land. For example, if Victoria Manor is held on trust for Grant for life, remainder to Phil, and Grant surrenders his life-interest to Phil, Grant will have to convey the title to him.

(c) Effect of death of the tenant for life

When the tenant for life of the settlement dies the consequences will differ depending upon whether the settlement continues or whether the settlement comes to an end because the person entitled on his death is entitled absolutely and is not an infant.
(i) Where the settlement continues: Section 7(1) of the Settled Land Act 1925 provides that:

> "If, on the death of a tenant for life or statutory owner . . . the land remains settled land, his personal representatives shall hold the settled land on trust, if and when required so to do, to convey it to the person who under the trust settlement or by virtue of the act becomes the tenant for life or statutory owner, and, if more than one, as joint tenants."

The "personal representatives" of the deceased life tenant who take the legal title to the land are not necessarily those who are his personal representatives in relation to the rest of his estate. By Administration of Estates Act 1925, s.22(1) the tenant for life may either appoint "special executors" in regard to the settled land expressly or alternatively, in the absence of an express appointment, the trustees of the settlement at the date of his death will become the special executors and hold the property on trust for the next tenant for life. By Settled Land Act, s.7(1) the special executors must, when required, convey the legal title to the new tenant for life. It is clear from section 2(2)(a) of the Trusts of Land and Appointment of Trustees Act 1925 that a settlement created before January 1, 1997 will continue as a strict settlement where a life tenant dies and a new life tenant succeeds him.
(ii) Where the settlement ends: If the death of the life tenant has the effect that "any person of full age becomes absolutely entitled to the settled land . . . free from all limitations, powers and charges taking effect under the settlement" under Settled Land

Act 1925, s.7(5) such a person may require the trustees of the settlement, or whoever the legal title to the land is vested in, "to convey the land to him." Thus if Victoria Manor is settled on trust for Grant for life, remainder to Phil in fee simple, on the death of Grant the legal title will pass to his special executors and Phil will be entitled to require them to transfer the legal title to him.

(d) Termination during the lifetime of the tenant for life

(i) Termination if the tenant for life becomes absolutely entitled to the settled land: If, during the course of the settlement, the tenant for life becomes absolutely entitled to the property subject to the settlement there is no need to convey the legal title to him since he will hold it already. For example, if Victoria Manor is held on trust for Grant for life, remainder to Phil, Grant will become absolutely entitled if he acquires Phil's remainder interest for himself. However by Settled Land Act 1925, s.17(1) the trustees of the settlement are "bound to execute, at the cost of the trust estate, a deed declaring that they are discharged from the trust so far as regards that land." Where such a deed of discharge contains no statement to the contrary a purchaser of a legal estate in the land is entitled to assume that the land has ceased to be settled land and that it is not subject to any trust for sale.[68]
(ii) Termination because there is no longer any relevant property subject to the settlement: Although settlements created before January 1, 1997 continue as strict settlements, Trust of Land and Appointment of Trustees Act 1996, s.2(4) provides that:

> "Where at any time after the commencement of this Act there is in the case of any settlement which is a settlement for the purposes of the Settled Land Act 1925 no relevant property which is or is deemed to be subject to the settlement, the settlement, the settlement permanently ceases at that time to be a settlement for the purposes of that Act."

"Relevant property" is defined to mean land and heirlooms.[69] This means that if all the land subject to a settlement is sold, and no heirlooms are held, then the purchase of new land with the capital moneys will give rise to a trust of land under the new regime and not to the revival of a settlement.

5 Overreaching of beneficial interests under a settlement

(a) The function of overreaching

Where land is held subject to a strict settlement the legal title is held by the tenant for life, and the beneficiaries of the settlement enjoy their interests in the equity. If a third party seeks to acquire the settled land they will wish to ensure that they can take legal title free from the interests of any of the beneficiaries of the settlement. Overreaching provides a mechanism by which they can be sure that they will acquire the land unencumbered by any such third party trust rights by converting the trust interests of

[68] s.17(3).
[69] See:, Settled Land Act 1925, s.67(1).

the beneficiaries in the land itself into identical interests in the purchase moneys which are paid over for the land.

(b) Essential preconditions to the overreaching of equitable interests in settled land

(i) Compliance with statutory conditions: Overreaching will only occur if the conditions set out in Law of Property Act 1925, s.2(1)(i) are met. This section provides:

> "A conveyance to a purchaser of a legal estate in land shall overreach any equitable interest or power affecting that estate, whether or not he has notice thereof, if —
>
> (i) the conveyance is made under the powers conferred by the Settled Land Act 1925, or any additional powers conferred by a settlement, and the equitable interest or power is capable of being overreached thereby, and the statutory requirements respecting the payment of capital money arising under the settlement are complied with."

(ii) The conveyance was made under an exercise of the settlement powers: Overreaching can only occur if the conveyance of the relevant legal estate of the land subject to the settlement was made as a consequence of the exercise of the powers conferred by the settlement, either by the Act or through an express extension of those powers. If the conveyance was not a consequence of the exercise of such powers then overreaching cannot take place. For example, a conveyance by an erstwhile tenant for life in circumstances where the settlement has come to an end, will not be capable of overreaching the equitable trust interests which exist behind what has become a bare trust of the legal title. For example, if Grant was the tenant for life of Victoria Manor and Phil was entitled to the remainder interests and Grant surrendered his life interest to Phil, the effect would be that the settlement was brought to an end. Until Grant conveyed the legal title to Phil he would hold it for him as a bare trustee. If Grant were to convey the legal title to Lorraine this could not overreach Phil's equitable interest since the conveyance would not have been made in consequence of any exercise of the powers conferred by the settlement, which had ceased to exist.

(iii) The equitable interest is capable of being overreached: Where land is not settled overreaching does not operate against all equitable interests in land but is largely reserved to trust interests, since the majority of other varieties of equitable interests are exempted from the effects of overreaching by Law of Property Act 1925, s.2(3). However, section 3 only applies in the case of overreaching under a trust of land. In the case of settled land not only are the equitable interests of the beneficiaries of the settlement overreached,[70] but section 72(3) of the Settled Land Act 1925 provides that annuities affecting the settled land and a limited owner's charge or general equitable charge are capable of being overreached even if they have been properly protected as land charges.

(iv) Payment of the capital moneys to at least two trustees of the settlement: The most important requirement which must be satisfied before overreaching can take place is that the purchase moneys must be paid over according to the statutory requirements. It

[70] See:, Settled Land Act 1925, s.72(2).

has already been seen that by Settled Land Act 1925, s.18 the capital moneys realised from a transaction must either be paid to or at the direction of at least two trustees of the settlement, or into court.[71] It has also been noted that failure to follow these requirements may have the effect not merely of preventing the overreaching of trust interests behind the settlement, but also of rendering the disposition of the legal estate void.

[71] s.18(1)(b) and (c).

Part III

Subsidiary Interests in Land

Chapter 9

EASEMENTS

INTRODUCTION TO EASEMENTS

1 General nature of easements

Whereas such interests as leases allow the owner of land to enable another person to enjoy the benefit of the possession and use of it in its entirety, an easement is a right which entitles a third party to exercise much more limited rights over land without constituting a form of ownership. One of the simplest and most common such rights is a right of way. If, for example, Hamish and Isabelle own neighbouring terraced houses, and Hamish wants to build a garage at the end of his back garden, but it would be impossible for his car to gain access to it other than using a track which runs across Isabelle's land, she could grant him an easement entitling him to enjoy the right of access and passage. An easement is not the only means by which such a right could have been facilitated. She could granted Hamish a mere licence to use the track, which would prevent him trespassing when he does so. However an easement is not merely a personal right but is a right annexed to land so that the benefit and burden are enjoyed by whoever owns the land to which it relates for the time being. If Isabelle was to grant Hamish a right of way it would not be his right alone, but a right annexed to the house he presently owns, so that if he was to sell the house to Jock, he would also be entitled to exercise the right of way as the new owner. Similarly if Isabelle were to sell her house he would still be entitled to exercise it against the new owner, provided that as a matter of priority the land had been acquired subject to the easement.

2 Means of creation of easements

There are a number of means by which easements may be created. In the example of Hamish and Isabel it was assumed that the easement was expressly granted. However, in some circumstances an easement may be found to have been granted by implication from the parties conduct. Easements may also be acquired by operation of statute and through long usage in a manner reminiscent to the principles of adverse possession.

3 Legal quality of easements

It has been seen from section 1(2)(a) of the Law of Property Act 1925 that an easement is an interest in land capable of enjoying legal status, provided that its duration is equivalent either to a fee simple estate or a term of years absolute. Whether an easement which meets these criteria is in fact legal will depend on the manner in which it was created.

4 Issues of priority relating to easements

Where land is subject to a valid easement and the title is transferred, the transferee will take the land subject to the easement unless he can establish that he enjoys priority over it. The rules of priority relating to the burden of easements are different depending on whether the land to which it relates is registered or unregistered, and in each case on whether the easement was legal or equitable.

ESSENTIAL CHARACTERISTICS OF EASEMENTS

1 No complete catalogue of easements

It is impossible to draw up a complete catalogue of the rights which the law is prepared to recognise as easements, because new easements might come to be recognised with changing social circumstances and concepts of land usage. As Lord St Leonards observed in *Dyce v. Lady James Hay*[1] with some prescience:

> "The category of servitudes and easements must alter and expand with the changes that take place in the circumstances of mankind."

The law has been ready to recognise new easements which confer a positive benefit on the owner of the land holding the right, for example the right to use land as communal gardens,[2] for aircraft movements[3] or for car parking.[4] However, there has been a much greater reluctance to recognise new negative rights, which entitle the holder to prevent the owner of the burdened land from doing something on it, as easements because they would unduly restrict a person's right to enjoy his own land. For example, in *Phipps v. Pears*[5] the Court of Appeal held it would not recognise an easement of protection from the weather, so that a landowner was not liable to the damage resulting to his neighbours house when he demolished his own, thus exposing its flank wall to the elements.

2 Easements distinguished from profits *à prendre*

One important distinction which should be drawn is between easements and another category of analogous property rights termed profits *à prendre*. The key characteristic

[1] (1852) 1 Macq. 305.
[2] *Re Ellenborough Park* [1956] Ch. 131.
[3] *Dowty Boulton Paul Ltd v. Wolverhampton Corporation* (No. 2) [1976] Ch. 13.
[4] *London & Blenheim Estates Ltd v. Ladbroke Retail Parks Ltd* [1992] 1 W.L.R. 1278.
[5] [1965] 1 Q.B. 76.

of a profit is that it entitles the owner to take some material benefit from land owned by another, by appropriating something from the land, or produced by the land, that belonged to the owner. For example, a right to take crops from land, to pasture cattle, or to take game would all constitute profits. The right to take water does not because water on land is not regarded as belonging to the landowner. In contrast an easement does not entitle the holder to take anything from the land at all, but merely to make use of it in some way. An easement may therefore be described as a privilege without a profit.[6] Profits a prendre are considered in greater detail below.[7]

3 The positive characteristics of easements

(a) Re Ellenborough Park

The leading authority which sets out the essential characteristics which must be present before a privilege over land can constitute an easement is the decision of the Court of Appeal in *Re Ellenborough Park.*[8] The central question was whether a right of the owners of freehold property to make use of neighbouring land as a park for leisure purposes was capable of existing as an easement. In answering this question in the affirmative Evershed M.R. adopted a fourfold test to determine whether a right could be recognised as an easement:

> "(1) there must be a dominant and a servient tenement: (2) an easement must 'accommodate' the dominant tenement; (3) dominant and servient owners must be different persons, and (4) a right over land cannot amount to an easement, unless it is capable of forming the subject-matter of a grant."[9]

Not all of these characteristics are equally significant and the technical language conceals what are often relatively straightforward propositions.

(b) "A dominant and a servient tenement": the need for land benefited and land burdened by the right

It has already been noted that an easement is a right annexed to particular land, which the owner thereof is entitled to exercise over other land. This requirement is expressed in the language that there must be a dominant and servient tenement. The dominant tenement is the piece of land which enjoys the benefit of the easement, and the servient tenement is the land burdened by it. In the example used above, Hamish's house would be the dominant tenement since the right of way was a privilege attached to it, and Isabelle's the servient tenement. This requirement thus ensures that easements are rights which are only associated with the ownership of particular land.[10] The grant of a privilege over land by the owner to a person without any reference to

[6] See: *Hewlins v. Shippam* (1826) 5 B. & C. 221.
[7] See pp. 321 *et seq.*
[8] [1956] Ch. 131.
[9] *ibid.* at 163, adopting the criteria formulated in Cheshire's *Modern Law of Real Property,* (7th ed., pp.456 *et seq.*
[10] See: *Ackroyd v. Smith* (1850) 10 C.B. 164; *Todrick v. Western National Omnibus Co* [1934] Ch. 561; *Alfred F. Beckett Ltd v. Lyons* [1967] Ch. 449.

land they own will be a mere licence and not an easement. For example, if Isabelle owned a country estate and granted Hamish, who lived in London, a right to come and walk there at weekends, this would not create an easement but confer a personal permission. In *Re Ellenborough Park*[11] this requirement was clearly met, because the freehold properties neighbouring the park were the dominant tenements and the park itself was the servient tenement. In *Alfred F. Beckett Ltd v. Lyons*[12] the Court of Appeal held an alleged right for all the inhabitants of the County Palatine of Durham to collect sea-washed coal from a stretch of foreshore was incapable of existing as an easement because there was no dominant tenement. Winn L.J. stated the principle that:

> ". . . no person can possess an easement otherwise than in respect of and in amplification of his enjoyment of some estate or interest in a piece of land."[13]

(c) A right "accommodating" the dominant tenement: an easement must benefit the land of the servient owner

(i) Meaning of the requirement: Behind the mystique of the language of rights "accommodating" the dominant tenement lies by far the most important limitations to the nature of the privileges over land which are capable of existing as easements. The essence of the requirement is that the right must in some way benefit the land itself, therefore increasing the utility of the servient tenement, and not merely providing a personal advantage to the owner. In *Re Ellenborough Park*, Evershed M.R. adopted the following formulation of the meaning of the requirement as accurately representing the law:

> "A right enjoyed by one over the land of another does not possess the status of an easement unless it accommodates and serves the dominant tenement, and is reasonably necessary for the better enjoyment of that tenement, for if it has no necessary connexion therewith, although it confers an advantage upon the owner and renders his ownership of the land more valuable, it is not an easement at all, but a mere contractual right personal to and enforceable between the two contracting parties."[14]

(ii) Early narrow application of the requirement: Some of the earlier cases took a very narrow and restrictive approach to the application of the requirement that the right must accommodate the dominant tenement. For example, in *Ackroyd v. Smith*[15] the owner of land granted the owners and occupiers of neighbouring land, and "all persons having occasion to resort thereto," a right to pass and repass along a road across his land for all purposes. Creswell J. held that this right was not capable of existing as an easement as it was a right unconnected with the servient land. He stated:

> "It would be a novel incident annexed to land, that the owner and occupier should, for purposes unconnected with that land and merely because he is the owner and occupier, have a right of road over other land."[16]

[11] [1956] Ch. 131.
[12] [1967] Ch. 449.
[13] *ibid.* at 483.
[14] *ibid.* at 170.
[15] (1850) 10 C.B. 164.
[16] *ibid.* at 188.

The objection seems to have been that the scope of the right was so wide that it was not exclusively limited to use for the benefit of the land but could be utilised even when there was no benefit to the land as such but only personal benefit to the user. However, in *Todrick v. Western National Omnibus Company Ltd*[17] Romer L.J. doubted whether as a matter of construction the grant should have been interpreted as a right of way for all purposes, whether or not connected with the land in question, and considered that the right should have been held to be an easement.[18] The Court of Appeal held that a right of way was capable of accommodating land over which it merely passed even though it did not terminate there. In *Re Ellenborough Park*, Evershed M.R. considered that a right of way was not disqualified from enjoying status as an easement merely because it might be used by some persons who had no connection with the dominant land at all, for example if they decided to take a short cut across the servient land.

(iii) "Accommodation" requires more than merely enhancement of the economic value of land: The mere fact that a privilege is annexed to the dominant land with the effect of thereby enhancing its value is not itself conclusive of the question whether the right "accommodates" the dominant land. This was stated by Evershed M.R. in *Re Ellenborough Park*[19]:

> "It is clear that the right did, in some degree, enhance the value of the property, and this consideration cannot be dismissed as wholly irrelevant. It is, of course, a point to be noted; but . . . it is in no way decisive of the problem; it is not sufficient to show that the right increased the value of the property conveyed unless it is also shown that it was connected with the normal enjoyment of that property."

(iv) Accommodation requires a sufficient geographical nexus between the dominant and servient land: A right will only be regarded as accommodating the dominant land to which it is annexed if that dominant land enjoys a sufficient geographical nexus with the servient land so that it can be said to benefit the land as such. In *Todrick v. Western National Omnibus Co.*[20] the Court of Appeal rejected a claimed principle that there must be contiguity between the dominant and servient tenements, but if they are separated by too much distance the right will be regarded as for the personal benefit of the owner of the dominant land and not for the land itself. For example, in *Bailey v. Stephens*[21] Byles J. stated that it was impossible to have a right of way over land in Kent appurtenant to land in Northumberland.[22] In *Re Ellenborough Park*[23] one issue was whether the right to use the park could constitute an easement when some of the houses entitled were close, but not in fact fronting it. Evershed M.R. held the fact that these house were not adjacent to the servient land did not mean that the right was not accommodated:

[17] [1934] Ch. 561.
[18] See also: *Thorpe v. Brumfitt* (1873) 8 Ch. App. 650.
[19] [1956] Ch. 131, 173.
[20] [1934] Ch. 561.
[21] (1863) 2 H. & C. 121.
[22] Comments which were approved by the Court of Appeal in *Todrick v. Western National Omnibus Company Ltd* [1934] Ch. 190.
[23] [1956] Ch. 131, 173.

> "We think that the extension of the right of enjoyment to these few houses does not negative the presence of the necessary "nexus" between the subject-matter enjoyed and the premises to which the enjoyment is expressed to belong."[24]

(v) Accommodation in the context of business use of land: Particular problems have arisen as to whether rights which enable the owner of the dominant tenement to carry out his business are capable of accommodating the dominant land and therefore existing as easements. In *Hill v. Tupper*[25] the plaintiff had leased land adjoining a canal, and in the lease he was granted the exclusive right to put pleasure boats into the water and use the canal for that purpose. The defendant, landlord of an inn also adjacent to the canal, placed boats on it and the plaintiff claimed that this amounted to an interference with his right, which he alleged was an easement. The Court held that his right was not an easement but a mere license. Pollock C.B. stated that his right was "unconnected with the use and enjoyment of the land," and it has sometimes been thought that this indicates that rights which bring a commercial advantage to the owner of the dominant land cannot be regarded as accommodating it. However, this approach is clearly too narrow, and in *Re Ellenborough Park*[26] Evershed M.R. considered that the true rational for the decision in *Hill v Tupper* was that the particular right claimed had no connection with the land:

> "It is clear that what the plaintiff was trying to do was to set up, under the guise of an easement, a monopoly which had no normal connexion with the ordinary use of his land, but which was merely an independent business enterprise. So far from the right claimed sub-serving or accommodating the land, the land was but a convenient incident to the exercise of the right."

Where a right does have sufficient connection with the use of the dominant land for business purposes, it will be regarded as accommodating the dominant land. For example, in *Moody v Steggles*[27] Fry J. held that the right of the owners of a pub to affix a sign-board to the wall of the neighbouring house was an easement. He stated:

> "It is said that the easement in question relates, not to the tenement, but to the business of the occupant of the tenement, and that therefore I cannot tie the easement to the house. It appears to me that that argument is of too refined a nature to prevail, and for this reason, that the house can only be used by an occupant, and that the occupant only uses the house for the business which he pursues, and therefore in some manner (direct or indirect) an easement is more or less connected with the mode in which the occupant of the house uses it."[28]

Similarly in *Copeland v. Greenhalf*[29] Upjohn J. held that he would have no difficulty in principle in finding that a right to deposit trade goods on neighbouring land was an

[24] *ibid.* at 175.
[25] (1863) 2 H. & C. 121.
[26] [1956] Ch. 131, 173.
[27] (1879) 12 Ch.D. 261.
[28] *ibid.* at 266. He cited *Wood v. Hewett* 8 Q.B. 913; *Lancaster v. Eve* 5 C.B. (N.S.) 717 and *Hoare v. Metropolitan Board of Works* Law Rep. 9 Q.B. 296 as examples where an easement had been held to exist where it could only possibly be of benefit to the land because of the business of the particular occupant.
[29] [1952] Ch. 488.

easement capable of accommodating the dominant tenement, even though he held that the particular right claimed in the case was too extensive to constitute an easement. In *Wong v. Beaumont Property Trust Ltd*[30] the Court of Appeal held that there was an easement entitling the tenants of premises used as a Chinese restaurant to erect a ventilation duct fixed to the wall of land owned by the landlord, which was only necessary because of the nature of the business pursued, and in *Woodhosue & Co. Ltd v. Kirkland Ltd*[31] Plowman J. held that a means of access utilised for a long period by a business and its customers and suppliers had become an easement since it was for "their reasonable business purposes." However, although it is clear that rights are capable of existing as easement when they benefit commercial activities conducted on the dominant land, there will be no easement if the benefits are not exclusively to the business of the owner of occupier of the dominant land. In *Clapman v. Edwards*[32] a tenant of a petrol station enjoy the right in his lease to use the walls of the adjoining premises for advertising purposes. Bennett J. held that since the right was not limited to entitling the tenant to advertise his own business it was not capable of existing as an easement:

> "If it were to enable the grantee, as I hold it does, to advertise anything he chooses upon the flank walls in question, there is no connection between the dominant tenement and the servient tenement in the flank walls in respect of such a user."

(vi) Accommodation and recreational or leisure use of land: As in the case of business rights, some older authorities suggest that rights to use land for recreational or leisure purposes are not capable of existing as easements because they do not accommodate the dominant land. In *Mounsey v. Ismay*[33] the court held that the claimed right of the freemen and citizens of Carlisle to hold an annual horse race on land belonging to the plaintiff was not capable of existing as an easement. Although this could be explained on the grounds that there was no dominant tenement, Martin B. held that the right did not confer a benefit in the character of an easement:

> " . . . we are of opinion that to bring the right within the term 'easement' . . . it must be a right of utility and benefit, and not one of mere recreation and amusement."[34]

In *International Tea Stores Company v. Hobbs*[35] Farwell J. considered that the right of a tenant to use his landlord's park and gardens for his enjoyment was not capable of existing as an easement because it was a *jus spatiandi* and not a right of way leading to any particular place. He applied the same reasoning in *Attorney-General v. Antrobus*[36] where it was held that access to Stonehenge was not a public right of way because such

[30] [1965] 1 Q.B. 173.
[31] [1970] 1 W.L.R. 1185.
[32] [1938] 2 All E.R. 507.
[33] (1865) 3 H. & C. 486.
[34] *ibid.* at 498.
[35] [1903] 2 Ch. 165.
[36] [1905] 2 Ch. 188.

a *jus spatiandi* was not known to English law as a right capable of forming the subject matter of an easement by prescription or grant. Irish authorities also held that use of a walk "not . . . for the purpose of reaching any definite place, but as a place of recreation, to walk, to saunter, to lounge, to chat, to meet their friends" was not a public right of way, and by analogy would have been incapable of existing as an easement.[37] However, following *Re Ellenborough Park*[38] it is now clear that a right to make use of land even for recreational or leisure activities is capable of constituting an easement provided the use has sufficient connection with the dominant tenement to which it relates. The case concerned the question whether a right of the owners of houses fronting or extremely close to the allegedly servient land, which was to be maintained as an ornamental pleasure park, to make use of it for recreation purpose was an easement. Evershed M.R. explained why the court concluded that it was with the help of an analogy:

> "A much closer analogy, as it seems to us, is the case of a man selling the freehold of part of his house and granting to the purchaser . . . the right, appurtenant to such part, to use the garden in common with the vendor and his assigns. In such a case the test of connexion, or accommodation, would be amply satisfied; for just as the use of a garden undoubtedly enhances, and is connected with the use and enjoyment of the house to which it belongs, so also would the right granted, in the case supposed, be closely connected with the use and enjoyment of the part of the premises sold. Such, we think, is in substance the position in the present case. The park became a communal garden for the benefit and enjoyment of those whose houses adjoined it or were in its close proximity. Its flower beds, lawns and walks were calculated to afford all the amenities which it is the purpose of the garden of a house to provide; and, apart from the fact that these amenities extended to a number of holders, instead of being confined to one . . . we can see no difference in principle between Ellenborough park and a garden in the ordinary signification of that word. It is the collective garden of the neighbouring house, to whose use it was dedicated by the owners of the estate and as such amply satisfied, in our judgement, the requirement of connexion with the dominant tenements to which it is appurtenant."[39]

The Court felt that the fact that the park could be used for such purposes as taking exercise and rest, or taking out small children, meant that the right to use it was of sufficient utility or benefit to the land and not for *mere* recreation or amusement.[40] However, as with rights bringing business advantage this does not mean that every recreational or leisure right will necessarily accommodate the dominant tenement. The Court of Appeal accepted that if the owner of particular land was to enjoy the right to visit a Zoological Gardens free of charge, or to attend Lord's Cricket Ground without payment, these rights could not constitute easements because there would not be sufficient nexus between the enjoyment of the right and the use of the house. Evershed

[37] *Abercromby v. Fermoy Town Commissioners* [1900] 1 I.R. 302.
[38] [1956] Ch. 131, 173.
[39] *ibid.* at 174–175.
[40] *ibid.* at 179.

M.R. also indicated that a right to use land to play games may lack sufficient utility to accommodate the dominant tenement.[41]

(d) "Dominant and servient owners must be different persons": there must be diversity of ownership

(i) Meaning of the requirement: Since an easement is a right exercised by virtue of the ownership of land over land belonging to another, it is impossible for an easement to exist if there is no diversity of ownership and the dominant and servient tenements are both owned by the same person. For example, if Hamish is the freehold owner of neighbouring terraced houses it is impossible to speak of him as enjoying a right of way across the land of one to have access to the garage of the other. He is perfectly entitled to do as he wishes on land which he owns.[42] However, an easement may arise where there is diversity of the types of ownership of land. If Hamish is the freehold owner of the houses but grants Isabelle a lease of one whilst retaining the other, she will enjoy exclusive possession of that land. If Hamish wishes to enjoy access across it he cannot do so by virtue of his freehold ownership alone. However, since there is diversity of ownership, as he is the owner of the dominant tenement but Isabel is the leasehold owner of the servient tenement, he can ensure that the lease grants him a right of way which will constitute an easement. Similarly, a tenant would be able to enjoy an easement over land retained by her landlord.[43] A trustee is also able to enjoy an easement over other land of which he is the beneficial owner behind a trust.[44]
(ii) Quasi-easements where there is no diversity of ownership: Although rights exercised over land owned and possessed by the same person cannot be easements because there is no diversity of ownership between the dominant and servient tenement, they are not entirely irrelevant to the law relating to easements. They are regarded as quasi-easements, and in the event of transactions which result in a division of the ownership of the land they may be automatically converted into full easements benefiting the part of the land which on division becomes the dominant land and burdening the part which becomes the servient tenement.

(e) "Right capable of forming the subject matter of a grant": it must have been possible to create expressly by deed

(i) Meaning of the requirement: Although an easement may in fact come into existence by a wide variety of means, the fourth requirement of in *Re Ellenborough Park*[45] stipulates that a right will only exist as an easement if it could have been expressly granted by deed. It must be shown that the right could have been granted by a person capable of making such a grant; that it was enjoyed by a person capable of being the grantee of such a grant; and that the right granted was sufficiently certain.
(ii) Need of a capable grantor: A right will only be capable of existence as an easement if there was a person owning the allegedly servient tenement who would have possessed the legal capacity to make a valid express grant to that effect. For example, if a grant by the servient owner would not have created an easement because such

[41] *ibid.* at 179, commenting on the judgement of Martin B. in *Mounsey v. Ismay*
[42] *Bolton v. Bolton* (1879) 11 Ch.D. 968; *Metropolitan Railway Co v. Fowler* [1892] 1 Q.B. 165.
[43] *Borman v. Griffiths* [1930] 1 Ch. 493.
[44] *Ecclesiastical Commissioners for England v. Kino* (1884) 14 Ch.D. 213.
[45] [1956] Ch. 131, 173.

action would have been *ultra vires* such a right would be incapable of existing as a valid easement. In *Mulliner v. Midland Railway Company*[46] it was held that a railway company could not grant a right of way under the arch of a bridge built on land it owned as by Act of Parliament it was only entitled to alienate land which was "superfluous." An identical right could not therefore have come into existence by long use. Similarly in *Paine & Co. Ltd v. St Neots Gas & Coke Co.*[47] the Court of Appeal held no easement to use water drawn from common land could have come into existence because the proprietors of the common had no capacity to grant such an easement. Likewise a tenant of land would have no capacity to grant an easement binding the freehold reversion of his landlord,[48] and in *Quicke v. Chapman*[49] it was held that a licensee of land had insufficient capacity to grant a right to light over it.

(iii) Need of a capable grantee: A right can only be an easement if it is enjoyed by some person or persons who would have been capable of receiving the benefit thereof under an express grant. This requirement will not be met if a right is claimed by a company which did not possess the capacity to accept an easement granted to it.[50] Nor will there be a capable grantee if the right is claimed by a vague, fluctuating group of people, such as the inhabitants of a particular village. However, rights granted to such groups may take the form of customary rights.[51] Such rights have included the right to pass over land to church,[52] drying of fishing nets on private land[53] and taking water from a spring.[54]

(iv) The right claimed must be sufficiently definite: A right will only be an easement if it allows those entitled to the benefit thereof to exercise rights of a sufficiently definite character. This requirement is intended to exclude rights which Evershed M.R. described in *Re Ellenborough Park*[55] as "too vague and wide." The court considered that a right to wander at will over all or every part of another persons land, which had been described by Farwell J. as a *jus spatiandi* in cases referred to above, would be too wide to constitute an easement and could only exist as a personal licence. However, it held that right conferred to use the specific park in question was "both well defined and commonly understood."[56] The more general a right is claimed to be, the less likely that it will be held to constitute an easement. A right to light through a defined window may be an easement[57] whereas a general right to light is not. A right to passage of air through a rock shaft was held to be an easement in *Bass v. Gregory*,[58] as was a right to air through defined ventilation apertures in *Cable v. Bryant*.[59] However, in *Chastey v. Ackland*[60] the Court of Appeal held that an alleged right to ventilation by

[46] (1879) 11 Ch.D. 611.
[47] [1939] 3 All E.R. 812.
[48] See: *Derry v. Sanders* [1919] 1 K.B. 223.
[49] [1903] 1 Ch. 659.
[50] *National Guaranteed Manure Co. Ltd v. Donald* (1859) 4 H. & N. 8.
[51] *Gateward's Case* (1607) 6 Co. Rep. 59b; *Race v. Ward* (1855) 4 E. & B. 702.
[52] *Brockelbank v. Thompson* [1903] 2 Ch. 344.
[53] *Mercer v. Denne* [1905] 2 Ch. 538.
[54] *Weekley v. Wildman* (1698) 1 Ld. Raym. 405.
[55] [1956] Ch. 131, 173.
[56] *ibid.* at 176.
[57] *Easton v. Isted* [1903] 1 Ch. 405; *Levet v. Gas Light & Coke Co.* [1919] 1 Ch. 24.
[58] (1890) 25 Q.B.D. 481.
[59] [1908] 1 Ch. 259.
[60] [1895] 2 Ch. 389.

the general flow of air, which had been obstructed by the defendant's low building thus preventing the smell from a public urinal being carried away, was not capable of existing as an easement. Nor are such general and intangible rights as a right to privacy,[61] or the right to a view,[62] easements.

4 Characteristics disqualifying a right from status as an easement

Even thought the four positive criteria identified in *Re Ellenborough Park* may be present, the presence of some negative characteristics may disqualify a right from being an easement.

(a) Exercise of the right amounts to enjoying possession of the servient land

(i) Possession inconsistent with an easement: Since the very nature of an easement is that the owner of the dominant land enjoys limited rights of user over the servient land, any right the exercise of which would amount to the dominant owner enjoying possession of the servient land, either exclusively or jointly with the owner, will be regarded as granting an excessive entitlement. It is not that such rights cannot be granted, since a right to possession could be given by lease or licence, but they cannot be conferred as easements.

(ii) Exercise of the right prevents the servient owner from exercising the same right at the same time: A right will not be regarded as conferring an excessive user merely because if the dominant owner chooses to exercise it that will have the inevitable consequence that the servient owner cannot use his land in the same way contemporaneously with him. In *Miller v. Emcer Products*[63] a tenant was granted a right by his landlord to use toilets on an upper floor of their building, which was occupied by third parties. The Court of Appeal rejected the argument that right could not exist as an easement because it involved an excessive user. Romer L.J. stated:

> "In my judgment the right had all the requisite characteristics of an easement . . . It is true that during the times when the dominant owner exercised the right, the owner of the servient tenement would be excluded, but this in greater or lesser degree is a common feature of many easements (for example, rights of way) and does not amount to an ouster of the servient owner's rights as [would be] incompatible with a legal easement."[64]

(iii) Rights of storage: Some case have concluded that the grant of a right of storage on the servient land was excessive. In *Copeland v. Greenhalf*[65] the defendant claimed that he had acquired an easement to leave vehicles awaiting repair in the course of his business on a strip of adjoining land belonging to the plaintiff's by long usage. Upjohn J. held that in the circumstances the right claimed was incapable of existing as an easement:

[61] *Browne v. Flower* [1911] 1 Ch. 219.
[62] *William Aldred's Case* (1610) 9 Co. Rep. 57b.
[63] [1956] Ch. 304.
[64] *ibid.* at 316.
[65] [1952] Ch. 488.

> "I think that the right claimed goes wholly outside any normal idea of an easement . . . This claim really amounts to a claim to a joint user of the land by the defendant. Practically, the defendant is claiming the whole beneficial user of the strip of land on the south-east side of the track there; he can leave as many or as few lorries there as he likes for as long as he likes; he may enter on it by himself, his servants and agents to do repair work thereon. In my judgement, that is not a claim which can be established as an easement. It is virtually a claim to possession of the servient tenement, if necessary to the exclusion of the owner; or, at any rate, to a joint user . . . It seems to me that to succeed, this claim must amount to a successful claim of possession by reason of long adverse possession."[66]

It should be noted, however, that Upjohn J. expressly limited his remarks to the creation of an easement by prescription, and did not apply them to the creation of such rights by express grant. In *Grigsby v. Melville*[67] Brightman J. also held that a right of storage in a cellar under the servient land which could only be accessed via the dominant land was incapable of being an easement since it would amount to an exclusive right of user. Whether a right of storage is in fact excessive is a matter of degree, and in *Wright v. Macadam*[68] the Court of Appeal held that a right to store coal in a shed was an easement.[69] In *London & Blenheim Ltd v. Ladbroke Parks Ltd*[70] Judge Paul Baker Q.C. distinguished this case from *Copeland v. Greenhalf* on the grounds that "a small coal shed in a large property is one thing. The exclusive use of a large part of the allegedly servient tenement is another."

(iv) Car parking: An analogous area where the degree of user raises a question whether a right is in the nature of an easement is where the owner of the dominant land is granted a right to park. In *Newman v. Jones*[71] Megarry V.-C. held that a right of tenants of flats to park a car in a defined area nearby was capable of existing as an easement, and a general right to park on defined land was held to be an easement in *Bilkus v. London Borough of Redbridge.*[72] Again it is a matter of degree, as was indicated by Judge Paul Baker Q.C. in *London & Blenheim Ltd v. Ladbroke Parks Ltd*[73]:

> "If the right granted in relation to the area over which it is to be exercisable is such that it would leave the servient owner without any reasonable use of his land, whether for parking or anything else, it could not be an easement though it might be some larger or different grant."

A right granting a person the exclusive right to park their car in a particular space is unlikely to be capable of being an easement.

[66] *ibid.* at 498.
[67] [1972] 1 W.L.R. 1355.
[68] [1949] 2 K.B. 744.
[69] See also: *Att.-Gen. of Southern Nigeria v. John Holt (Liverpool) Ltd* [1915] A.C. 599.
[70] [1992] 1 W.L.R. 1278.
[71] March 22, 1982 (unreported).
[72] (1968) 207 EG 803.
[73] [1992] 1 W.L.R. 1278.

(b) Right requires the servient owner to take positive action

(i) The general rule: Any right which requires the owner of the servient tenement to take positive action, and particularly the expenditure of money, goes beyond what is characteristic of an easement and amounts to the imposition of obligations upon him. In *Regis Property Co. Ltd v. Redman*[74] the Court of Appeal therefore held that the obligation of a landlord to supply the premises of his tenant with constant hot water and central heating was not capable of exiting as an easement as it involved the performance of services, which is essentially a matter of personal contract as distinct from a right. In *Duke of Westminster v. Guild*[75] a tenant enjoyed an easement in the form of a right of drainage via a drain running through the landlord's land which had become blocked. The Court of Appeal held that although such an easement carried with it the right of the tenant to enter the landlord's property to repair the drain, the landlord was not, as the owner of the servient tenement, under any obligation to execute any repairs necessary to ensure the enjoyment of the easement by the dominant land. The general rule also applies to easements of support, as was explained by Greene M.R. in *Bond v. Nottingham Corporation*[76]:

> "The owner of the servient land is under no obligation to repair that part of his building which provides support for his neighbour. He can let it fall into decay. If it does so, and support is removed, the owner of the dominant land has no cause for complaint. On the other hand, the owner of the dominant land is not bound to sit by and watch the gradual deterioration of the support constituted by his neighbour's building. He is entitled to enter and take the necessary steps to ensure that the support continues by effecting repairs, and so forth, to the part of the building which gives the support. But what the owner of the servient land is not entitled to do, is by an act of his own, to remove the support without providing an equivalent."

(ii) Limited exceptions: Despite this general rule several limited exceptions have been recognised. A right to have the servient land fenced, or a fence or wall kept in repair, has been held to be an easement, and by its very nature imposes an obligation on the servient landowner to take positive action.[77] It also seems that an easement may carry with it positive obligations binding the servient landowner if this is inevitably required in the circumstances. *Liverpool City Council v. Irwin*[78] concerned the liabilities of a council which was the landlord of a tower block, the flats of which were rented to tenants but the council had retained the common parts. The tenants enjoyed easements to use the stairs, the lifts and the rubbish chutes. The House of Lords held that in the particular circumstances these easements also imposed an obligation on the landlords to maintain the common parts of the building in a reasonable manner. Lord Wilberforce explained:

[74] [1956] 2 Q.B. 613.
[75] [1985] Q.B. 688.
[76] [1940] Ch. 429, 438–439.
[77] *Crow v. Wood* [1971] 1 Q.B. 77. See also: *Jones v. Price* [1965] 2 Q.B. 618; *Egerton v. Harding* [1975] Q.B. 62.
[78] [1977] A.C. 239.

> "I accept, of course, the argument that a mere grant of an easement does not carry with it any obligation on the part of the servient owner to maintain the subject matter. The dominant owner must spend the necessary money, for example in repairing a driveway leading to his house. And the same principles may apply where a landlord lets an upper floor with access by a staircase.; responsibility for maintenance may well rest on the tenant. But there is a difference between that case and the case where there is an essential means of access, retained in the landlord's occupation, to units in a building of multi-occupation, for unless the obligation to maintain is, in a defined manner, placed upon the tenants, individually or collectively, the nature of the contract, and the circumstances, require that it be placed on the landlord."[79]

CREATION OF EASEMENTS

1 Creation of legal easements

(a) General

To enjoy legal status an easement must both be created in the appropriate manner and be for a period equivalent to either a fee simple absolute or a term of years.[80]

(b) Express grant by deed

(i) Grant of easement by the owner of the servient land: A grant of an easement will occur when either there was a prior diversity of ownership of the dominant and servient tenements and the owner of the dominant tenement grants an easement to the owner of the servient tenement, or where the land was previously owned in its entirety by the owner of the now servient tenement and when he transferred the dominant tenement he granted the transferee an easement over the land he retained. For example, if Hamish owns two neighbouring houses and sells one to Isabel, he can in the conveyance grant her a right of way across his garden.
(ii) Requirement of a deed: An express grant will only create a legal easement if it was made by a deed complying with the requirements of section 1 of the Law of Property (Miscellaneous Provisions) Act 1989. This requirement will be met if the grant is incorporated in a conveyance transferring title to the dominant land to its owner.
(iii) Failure to grant by deed: If an easement is expressly granted but not by deed the purported grant will only create a mere licence.[81] However if there is a valid contract to grant the easement this will give rise to a equitable easement.
(iv) A requirement of registration where title is registered: Where the land concerned is registered, sections 19(2) and 22(2) of the Land Registration Act 1925 define easements as "registered dispositions" the creation of which must be completed by entry in the proprietorship register of the title of the land to which they relate. This would suggest that even the express grant of an easement over registered land by deed

[79] *ibid.* at 256.
[80] Law of Property Act 1925, s.1(2)(a).
[81] *Wood v. Leadbitter* (1845) 13 M. & W. 838.

is ineffective to create a legal easement until registration occurs. However this requirement seems to have been almost entirely ignored and easements which have been granted by deed in registered land are treated as enjoying overriding status under section 70(1)(a) of the Land Registration Act 1925 which has rendered the need to register otiose.

(c) Implied grant by deed

(i) Basis on which easements are implied: Where the owner of land conveys part of it to another person he is under a duty not to derogate from his grant of the land. The law is therefore willing to imply that the transferor granted easements to the transferee which are necessary for the proper use of the transferred land; which the parties had a common intention should be granted; or which were exercised by the transferor over his land before he transferred it and are necessary to the reasonable enjoyment of the land granted. Because the grant of such easements is implied into the deed they take effect as legal easements.

(ii) Easements implied by necessity: A grant of land[82] will be implied[83] to include a grant of any easements which were necessary for the use of the land by the grantee. The most common situation in which such an easement will be implied into a grant is where there would be no means of access to the land granted unless there was a right of way over the land of the grantor. In such cases the land granted will become a dominant tenement and an easement will be implied over the land retained by the grantor. The requirement of necessity is construed strictly, so that an easement will not be implied against the grantor merely because this would provide a more convenient access to the land granted. As Stirling J. stated in *Union Lighterage Company v. London Graving Dock Company*[84]:

> "In my opinion, an easement of necessity . . . means an easement without which the property retained cannot be used at all, and not merely necessary to the reasonable enjoyment of the property."

Therefore if the land granted already enjoys a right of access, so that it is not "landlocked," no easement will be implied over the grantees land no matter how inconvenient the existing access is.[85] However an easement of necessity will be implied even if the grantee enjoys access to the land if that access is either unlawful,[86] or not enjoyed "as of right." For example, in *Barry v. Hasseldine*[87] the grantee purchased land that was completely surrounded by the land of the grantor, or land owned by strangers over which he had no right of way. He in fact exercised access over a disused airfield with the permission of its owner. Danckewerts J. held that since he enjoyed no legal

[82] An easement of necessity will only arise where there is a grant of land: *Proctor v. Hodgson* (1855) 10 Ex. 824; *Wilkes v. Greenway* (1890) 6 T.L.R. 449; *Nickerson v. Barraclough* [1981] Ch. 426.

[83] Despite some arguments that the rationale for the creation of easements of necessity was public policy, in *Nickerson v. Barraclough* [1981] Ch. 426 the Court of Appeal rejected these and reaffirmed that the easement is implied from the circumstances into the grant of land.

[84] [1902] 2 Ch. 557, 573.

[85] *Titchmarsh v. Royston Water Co Ltd* (1899) 81 LT 673; *MRA Engineering Ltd v. Trimster Co. Ltd* (1987) 56 P. & C.R. 1; *Manjang v. Drammeh* (1990) 61 P. & C.R. 194.

[86] *Hansford v. Jago* [1921] 1 Ch. 322.

[87] [1952] Ch. 832.

right to access to the land granted an easement of necessity should be implied over the grantor's land. Where such an easement of necessity is implied the route is determined by the grantor who retains the servient land.[88] As the easement of necessity is implied into the grant of the land at the date that the grant is made it does not terminate if an alternative means of access becomes available in the future. However, the extent of the easement is determined by what would be necessary for the use of the dominant land at the date of the grant, and its scope is not increased merely because of a change of use in the future.[89] Although easements of necessity have generally concerned rights of way other rights have been held to be implied by necessity. In *Wong v. Beaumont Property Trust Ltd*[90] the Court of Appeal held that the tenant of three cellars which he used as a Chinese restaurant was entitled to an easement of necessity to erect a ventilation duct on the outside of the landlord's building. However, it is questionable whether this case should genuinely be regarded as an example of an easement of necessity as a ventilation shaft was not required by the land as such but only as a consequence of the use to which it was put. The creation of such an easement would have been better explained by finding a common intention of the landlord and the tenant.

(iii) Easements implied by the common intention of the grantor and grantee of the land: Even where an easement is not strictly necessary for the use of the land it may be implied into the grant if it can be shown that the grantor and grantee of the land enjoyed a common intention that the right should be granted. In *Pwllbach Colliery Company Ltd v. Woodman*[91] Lord Parker identified two circumstances in which such an easement will be implied. First, an implication arises "because the right in question is necessary for the enjoyment of some other right expressly granted." For example, if the grantor has expressly granted the grantee a right to draw water from a spring on his land this necessarily involves the right of going to the spring for that purpose. Secondly, and more importantly, he stated that easements may be implied from the circumstances in which a grant of land was made:

> "The law will readily imply the grant . . . of such easements as may be necessary to give effect to the common intention of the parties to a grant of real property, with reference to the manner or purposes for which the land was granted."

He further held that such a common intention will only be found if "the parties should intend that the subject of the grant . . . should be used in some definite and particular manner." These principles were applied by the Court of Appeal in *Stafford v. Lee*[92] where a deed of gift of woodland mentioned the fact that it fronted a private road which was the only practicable means of access. Some years later the owners of the land wanted to build a house and claimed that they were entitled to a right of way over the road by foot or vehicles for all purposes associated with a residential dwelling. The owners of the servient land claimed that the right of way was limited to use for all purposes necessary for the reasonable enjoyment of the land as woodland. The Court

[88] *Brown v. Alabaster* (1887) 37 Ch. 490.
[89] Corporation of London v. Riggs (1880) 12 Ch.D. 798.
[90] [1965] 1 Q.B. 173.
[91] [1915] A.C. 634, 646–647.
[92] (1993) 65 P. & C.R. 172.

held that since the original deed granting the land was accompanied by a plan which indicated that the parties intended it to be used for the construction of a dwelling, the parties had enjoyed a common intention to use the land for that definite and particular purpose and that an appropriate right of way had been impliedly granted. It has already been noted that the recognition of an easement in *Wong v. Beaumont Property Trust Ltd*[93] would be better explained on the grounds of a common intention of the landlord and tenant that the land be used as a restaurant.

(iv) Easements implied into the grant from quasi-easements previously enjoyed by the grantor: Where the owner of land grants part of it and retains the rest, or divides his land by simultaneous transfers, any rights which he exercised over his land in the character of easements prior to the division are termed quasi-easements. The rule in *Wheeldon v. Burrows*[94] has the effect that such quasi-easements may be implied into the grant of the land so that the grantee enjoys the same rights in relation to his land as were previously exercised by the owner himself. The rule was stated by Thesiger LJ:

> "On the grant by the owner of a tenement of part of that tenement as it is then used and enjoyed, there will pass to the grantee all those continuous and apparent easements (by which, of course, I mean quasi-easements), or, in other words, all those easements which are necessary for the reasonable enjoyment of the property granted and which have been and are at the time of the grant used by the owner of the entirety for the benefit of the part granted."

It is clear from this statement that not every quasi-easement exercised by the owner over his land will be implied into the grant. First, they must have been exercised by him "continuously and apparently", which means that they must have left some permanent mark on the land. In *Borman v. Griffiths*[95] it was therefore held that a quasi-easement exercised over a plainly visible road worn track would pass under the rule. However, in *Ward v. Kirkland*[96] Ungoed-Thomas J. held that a quasi-easement to go onto the grantor's land for the purpose of repairing a wall was not "continuous and apparent" because there was no feature on the allegedly servient land which would have been obvious on inspection as indicating the exercise of the quasi-easement. He explained the meaning of the requirement:

> "The words 'continuous and apparent' seem to be directed to there being on the servient tenement a feature which would be seen on inspection and which is neither transitory nor intermittent; for example, drains, paths, as contrasted with the bowsprits of ships overhanging a piece of land."[97]

Secondly, the quasi-easement must have been necessary for reasonable enjoyment of the land. This does not require strict necessity, so that access exercised by the grantor as a quasi-easement may be implied into the grant even though it is merely more convenient than other means of access to the land.[98] In *Wheeler v. JJ Saunders Ltd*[99] the

[93] [1965] 1 Q.B. 173.
[94] (1879) 12 Ch.D. 31.
[95] [1930] 1 Ch. 493.
[96] [1967] Ch. 194.
[97] *ibid.* at 225.
[98] *Borman v. Griffiths* [1930] 1 Ch. 493; *Castagliola v. English* (1969) 210 E.G. 1425.
[99] [1995] 2 All E.R. 697.

majority of the Court of Appeal held that a means of access was not reasonably necessary for the enjoyment of the land and that there was therefore no implied easement. The plaintiffs had purchased a farmhouse which had previously been in common ownership with the adjacent land owned by the defendants. There were two possible means of access to the farmhouse, one of which involved crossing part of the defendant's land. Staughton and May L.JJ. held that this second means of access was not necessary for the reasonable enjoyment of the farmhouse because the other entrance would do just as well. The mere fact that the other entrance was ten centimetres narrower was insufficient to produce the appropriate necessity. A quasi-easement will not be implied into the grant under the rule if it is excluded by the contrary agreement of the parties,[1] nor where the terms of the conveyance make clear that it was not intended to be exercised. For example, in *Wheeler v. JJ Saunders Ltd* the conveyance of the farmhouse contained a clause that the plaintiffs were to erect a fence along the southern boundary of their land, where they claimed they were entitled to a right of way through the operation of the rule in *Wheeldon v. Burrows*. Peter Gibson L.J. held that the fencing obligation defeated the implication of the right of way because it did not anticipate the incorporation of a gate which would have enabled access to be maintained. The other members of the Court of Appeal did not express any concluded opinion on that issue having already found that no easement could be implied into the grant. The importance of the rule in *Wheeldon v. Burrows* has been much diminished by the operation of section 62 of the Law of Property Act 1925, which is examined below and operates even in favour of rights in the nature of easements which were not exercised continuously and apparently.[2] However the rule is wider in two important respects. First, it operates even where there was no conveyance of a legal estate of land but merely a contract to convey.[3] Secondly, it operates where there was no prior diversity of occupation between the dominant and servient tenements, a condition which is an essential prerequisite to the operation of section 62.

(d) Express reservation by deed

(i) Reservation of an easement by the owner of the dominant land: Reservation occurs where rather than retaining the servient land on division of his property, the transferor retains the dominant tenement and wishes to be able to exercise rights in the character of easements over the servient land which he previously also owned. Rather than requiring the transferee to grant him the intended easements he can reserve such rights to himself in the conveyance, and the transferee will take the land as a servient tenement subject to those easements. For example, if Hamish owns two neighbouring houses and wishes to sell one to Isabelle, but he also wants to ensure that he is entitled to continue to use a path that runs across the garden of that house, he can reserve to himself a right of way to use the path when he transfers ownership of the house to her.
(ii) Words of reservation: An easement will only be reserved if the transferor of the servient tenement includes appropriate words of reservation in the conveyance or transfer. No special form of words are required as long as it is clear that the transferor

[1] *Borman v. Griffiths* [1930] 1 Ch. 493; *Squarey v. Harris-Smith* (1981) 42 P. & C.R. 118.
[2] For this reason the right to repair the wall in *Ward v. Kirkland* [1967] Ch. 194 was held to have become an easement by operation of, s.62 even though it had not been exercised continuously and apparently.
[3] *Borman v. Griffiths* [1930] 1 Ch. 493; *Horn v. Hiscock* (1972) 223 E.G. 1437.

intends to enjoy an easement over the land transferred. For example, a conveyance "subject to a right of way" has been held to create an easement by reservation.[4]

(iii) Reservation operates by way of regrant: Historically the reservation of an easement was considered as operating by way of a regrant by the transferee of the servient tenement, so that the reservation was only effective if the transferee also executed the conveyance. This requirement was removed by section 65 of the Law of Property Act 1925 so that a reservation is effective where only the transferor executes the conveyance of the land subject to it. Somewhat anomalously, however, the courts[5] have continued to regard the reservation as operating by a regrant so that as a rule of construction an express reservation will be construed against the transferee of the servient tenement and in favour of the transferor retaining the dominant land.[6]

(e) Implied reservation by deed

(i) A reluctance to imply the reservation of easements into a grant: Although it has been seen that the law will imply the grant of easements into a deed on behalf of the grantee, there is a much greater reluctance to imply that a grantor has reversed easements to himself. This is because a grantor is expected to act in his own interests and deeds are construed in favour of the grantee.[7] The principle was stated by Thesiger L.J. in *Wheeldon v. Burrows*[8]:

> ". . . if the grantor intends to reserve any right over the tenement granted, it is his duty to reserve it expressly in that grant."

In that case the grantee had conveyed land adjacent to a workshop which had windows overlooking, and enjoying light from, the land sold. The purchaser of the land subsequently built so as to obstruct the windows. The Court of Appeal held that as the grantee had not expressly reserved a right to light in the conveyance it would not be implied and the owner of the allegedly servient land was entitled to build and obstruct the windows.[9] However, Theseiger L.J. recognised that there were some very limited exceptions to the general rule that the reservation of easements will not be implied into a grant.

(ii) Implied reservation of easements of necessity: Where the effect of a grant would be to completely landlock land retained by the grantee a reservation of a right of way may be implied into the grant.[10]

(iii) Implied reservation by common intention: As easement may also be found to have been impliedly reserved if it can be shown that the parties enjoyed a common intention that the grantee should be so entitled.[11] Since this is an exception to the general rule that a grantor must expressly reserve any right he wishes to retain over the land, a heavy

[4] *Pitt v. Buxton* (1969) 21 P. & C.R. 127; *Pallister v. Clark* (1975) 30 P. & C.R. 84; *Wiles v. Banks* (1983) 50 P. & C.R. 80.

[5] With the exception of *Cordell v. Second Clanfield Properties Ltd* [1969] 2 Ch. 9.

[6] *Johnstone v. Holdway* [1963] 1 Q.B. 601; *St. Edmundsbury and Ipswich Diocesan Board of Finance v. Clark (No. 2)* [1975] 1 W.L.R. 468.

[7] *Neill v. Duke of Devonshire* [1882] 8 App. Cas. 135.

[8] (1879) 12 Ch.D. 31, 49.

[9] See also: *Ray v. Hazeldine* [1904] 2 Ch. 17.

[10] See: *MRA Engineering Ltd v. Trimster Co. Ltd* (1988) 56 P. & C.R. 1.

[11] See: *Pwllbach Colliery Co. Ltd v. Woodman* [1915] A.C. 643 at 646–647, *per* Lord Parker.

evidential burden must be discharged before such a reservation will be implied. In *In Webb's Lease*[12] Evershed M.R. held that a grantor who claims such a reservation must be able "at least to prove affirmatively that such a reservation was clearly intended by him and his grantee at the time of the grant." The Court of Appeal held that a grantor had failed to discharge that burden when he claimed an implied reservation of an easement to maintain advertisements on the outside wall of the premises granted, and that the mere fact that the grantee was aware of the presence of the adverts at the date of the grant was insufficient to establish the necessary common intention.

(f) Creation by operation of statute: section 62 of the Law of Property Act 1925

(i) Statutory creation of easements by section 62: Section 62 of the Law of Property Act 1925 in essence provides that where land is conveyed the conveyance automatically carries with it the rights and privileges which are annexed to it, so that these do not need to be laboriously detailed in the conveyance. Sections 62(1) &(2) provide:

> (1) A conveyance of land shall be deemed to include and shall by virtue of this Act operate to convey, with the land, all buildings, erections, fixtures, commons, hedges, ditches, fences, ways, waters, watercourses, liberties, privileges, easements, rights and advantages whatsoever, appertaining or reputed to appertain to the land, or any part thereof, or, at the time of conveyance, demised, occupied, or enjoyed with, or reputed or know as part and parcel of or appurtenant to the land or any part thereof.
>
> (2) A conveyance of land, having houses or other buildings thereon, shall be deemed to include and shall by virtue of this Act operate to convey, with the land, house or other buildings, all outhouses, erections, fixtures, cellars, areas, courts, courtyards, cisterns, sewers, gutters, drains, ways, passages, lights, watercourses, liberties, privileges, easements, rights and advantages whatsoever, appertaining or reputed to appertain to the land, houses, or other buildings conveyed, or any of them, or any part thereof, or, at the time of conveyance, demised, occupied, or enjoyed with, or reputed or know as part and parcel of or appurtenant to, the land, houses, or other buildings conveyed, or any part thereof.

Clearly this section has the effect that land which is conveyed carries with it the benefit of pre-existing easements,[13] but it has also been interpreted more widely so that rights enjoyed by the land conveyed over the land retained which were not formerly legal easements are converted into legal easements, and the conveyed land becomes a dominant tenement. Such easements are most likely to arise where a right in the nature of an easement was being exercised over the land retained by virtue of a mere licence. When the land is conveyed that right is converted into a full legal easement. For example, in *Wright v. Macadam*[14] a tenant of a top floor flat was permitted to use a shed in the garden of the property to store coal. A new tenancy was granted making no mention of the shed. The landlord subsequently demanded payment of an additional

[12] [1951] Ch. 808, 820.
[13] *Graham v. Philcox* [1984] Q.B. 747.
[14] [1949] 2 K.B. 744.

rent for its use. The Court of Appeal held that the licence had been converted into a legal right by the grant of the new tenancy, which was a conveyance under section 62, and that the use of the shed as a matter of right meant that rent could not be charged. Jenkins L.J. accepted that the principle that:

> "a 'right' permissive at the date of the grant may become a legal right upon the grant by the force of the general words in [section 62 of the Law of Property Act 1925]."[15]

Similarly, in *International Teas Stores Company v. Hobbs*[16] the tenant of a house had enjoyed a licence to cross the yard of the landlord's neighbouring property. When he purchased the freehold from the landlord Farwell J. held that the licence was converted into a legal right of way enjoyed on the same term as the licence, namely for the purposes of their business, between the appropriate hours and not by horse drawn carts.[17] Section 62 would also have the effect of converting pre-existing equitable easements that were enjoyed by the land conveyed into legal easements.

(ii) Section 62 only operates where there was a conveyance of the land: Rights are only converted by section 62 into legal easements if there was a conveyance of the land. A "conveyance" is given an extended meaning in section 205(1)(ii) of the Law of Property Act 1925 to include:

> a mortgage, charge, lease, assent, vesting declaration, vesting instrument, disclaimer, release and every other assurance of property or of an interest therein, by any instrument, except a will.

There is no "conveyance" where an oral lease of land is granted,[18] or an equitable lease is created.[19]

(ii) Section 62 only operates in favour of rights being exercised at the date of the conveyance: Only rights in use at the date of the conveyance will be converted into legal easements. As Megarry V.-C. stated in *Penn v. Wilkins*[20]:

> "Section 62 was apt for conveying existing rights, but it did not resurrect mere memories of past rights."

(iii) Section 62 only operates where there was a prior diversity of occupation between the land conveyed and the servient tenement: Although in *Long v. Gowlett*[21] Sargant J. seemed to suggest that section 62 could operate even though there was no prior diversity of occupation between the land conveyed and the servient tenement over which it would be enjoyed if it had been exercised continuously and apparently prior to the conveyance, the House of Lords held in *Sovmots Ltd v. Secretary of State for the*

[15] Citing *Lewis v. Meredith* [1913] 1 Ch. 571 *per* Neville J.
[16] [1903] 2 Ch. 165.
[17] See also: *Goldberg v. Edwards* [1950] Ch. 247.
[18] *Rye v. Rye* [1962] 2 A.C. 496.
[19] *Re Ray* [1896] 1 Ch. 468; *Borman v. Griffiths* [1930] 1 Ch. 493.
[20] (1974) 236 E.G. 203.
[21] [1923] 2 Ch. 177.

Environment[22] that diversity of occupation was a necessary pre-requisitie of the operation of section 62. As Lord Edmund-Davies succinctly stated:

> "But the section cannot operate unless there has been some diversity of ownership or occupation of the quasi-dominant and quasi-servient tenements prior to the conveyance."[23]

Lord Wilberforce explained that this was a necessary consequence of the theory by which section 62 operates:

> "The reason is that when land is under one ownership one cannot speak in any intelligible sense of rights, or privileges, or easements being exercised over one part for the benefit of another. Whatever the owner does, he does as owner and, until a separation occurs, of ownership or at least of occupation, the condition for the existence of the rights, etc., does not exist."[24]

This requirement is most likely to be satisfied where the allegedly dominant land was subject to a tenancy, and the landlord has subsequently conveyed the freehold reversion or granted a new lease to the tenant, or where part of the land was occupied by a licensee who has been granted a tenancy or purchased the freehold.
(iv) Section 62 will not operate to convert a right into an easement unless it satisfies all the characteristics required of an easement: Section 62 will only operate to convert into legal easements such rights over the servient land as would have been capable of being expressly created as easements. If the right lacks any of the essential characteristics of an easement, as examined above, section 62 will not operate to cure the defect. As Lord Denning M.R. observed in *Phipps v. Pears*[25]:

> ". . . in order for section 62 to apply, the right or advantage must be one which is known to the law, in this sense, that is it capable of being granted at law so as to be binding on all successors in title."

For this reason he held that whereas a right to use a coal shed or a right of way could be created as legal rights by operation of section 62, a right to protection from the weather, or a right to a fine view, could not, because they are not rights known to law. Similarly section 62 will not operate in favour of a right which the owner of the allegedly servient land would not have been entitled to grant expressly,[26] nor of rights which were intended by the parties to be merely temporary.[27]
(v) Section 62 will not operate if it is expressly excluded in the conveyance of the land: A right will not be converted into an easement by operation of section 62 if the

[22] [1979] A.C. 144.
[23] *ibid.* at 176.
[24] *ibid.* at 169. See also: *Bolton v. Bolton* (1879) 11 Ch.D. 968; *Squarey v. Harris-Smith* (1981) 42 P. & C.R. 118.
[25] [1965] 1 Q.B. 76, 84.
[26] *Quicke v. Chapman* [1903] 1 Ch. 659.
[27] *Birmingham and Dudley District Banking Co. v. Ross* (1888) 238 Ch.D. 295; *Green v. Ashco Horticulturalist Ltd* [1966] 2 All E.R. 232.

conveyance expressly excludes its operation. This follows from section 62(4) which provides:

> This section applies only if and as far as a contrary intention is not expressed in the conveyance, and has effect subject to the terms of the conveyance and to the provisions contained therein.

(g) Acquisition by long user: prescription

(i) Essence of acquisition by prescription: It has been seen how by means of adverse possession a person can acquire the legal ownership of land, whether leasehold or freehold. Prescription similarly enables the owner of land to acquire an easement over other land merely by usage over a sufficient period of time. In *Mills v. Silver*[28] Dillon L.J. explained why an easement can be created by prescription:

> "a prescriptive right arises where there has been user as of right in which the servient owner has, with the requisite degree of knowledge . . . acquiesced."

(ii) Theoretical justifications for the acquisition of an easement by prescription: Unlike the doctrine of adverse possession, the acquisition of an easement by prescription is not rooted in the concept that long use entitles the user to the right exercised, but operates on the basis of a fiction that the user was at some point in time granted the relevant right. At common law an easement could be acquired by prescription if it was shown that it had been enjoyed from time immemorial, which is taken by the common law to mean A.D. 1189. Long user gives rise to a presumption that the right claimed has been enjoyed from time immemorial,[29] but this can be rebutted by the owner of the allegedly servient land demonstrating that this was not the case, for example if the right could not have been enjoyed before that date.[30] Since the owner of the allegedly servient land will often be able to demonstrate that a claimed easement could not have existed since 1189 the courts introduced the doctrine of a "lost modern grant," under which evidence of twenty year's use generates a fiction that the right claimed had been expressly granted after 1189 but that the grant has been lost.[31] This fiction is irrebutable, so that twenty years' use will give rise to a legal easement even if it can be shown that no grant was ever made,[32] although there will be no easement if it can be shown that such a grant could never have been made. An easement may be acquired by prescription under the doctrine of a lost modern grant even on the basis of a past period of twenty years use which has since been interrupted or discontinued.[33]

(iii) Statutory acquisition of easements by long user: In addition to acquisition of easements by prescription on the basis of use since time immemorial and lost modern grant the Prescription Act 1832 provides an alternative means of establishing entitlement to an easement by long use. In the case of rights other than the right to

[28] [1991] Ch. 271.
[29] *Bryant v. Foot* (1867) L.R. 2 Q.B. 161.
[30] *Hulbert v. Dale* [1909] 2 Ch. 570.
[31] See: *Dalton v. Angus & Co.* (1881) 6 App. Cas. 740.
[32] *Tehidy Minerals Ltd v. Norman* [1971] 2 Q.B. 528.
[33] *Mills v. Silver* [1991] Ch. 271.

light, section 2 has the effect that user as of right for twenty uninterrupted[34] years immediately preceding an action disputing the existence of the right[35] cannot be defeated by mere evidence that user in fact began after time immemorial. However, twenty years user will be ineffective to create such an easement if it can be shown that it was enjoyed by the agreement or consent of the owner of the servient land, even if merely oral. Uninterrupted user for a forty years period will render a right "absolute and indefeasible" even if it was enjoyed with the consent or agreement of the servient owner, unless that agreement or consent was given in writing.[36] By section 4 of the act no physical obstruction of a right will be regarded as having interrupted user unless the claimant submitted or acquiesced in the obstruction for a year after he had notice of it and of the person responsible for it.[37] In relation to rights of light, section 3 provides that 20 years uninterrupted user is "deemed absolute and indefeasible" unless it was enjoyed by written consent or agreement.

(iv) User must have been open: Long user, even of the requisite period, will be incapable of creating an easement unless it was exercised openly and peacefully. In *Union Lighterage Co. v London Graving Dock Co.*[38] Romer L.J. stated that an easement was only acquired when:

> "the enjoyment has been open — that is to say, of such a character that an ordinary owner of the land, diligent in the protection of his interests, would have, or must be taken to have, a reasonable opportunity of becoming aware of that enjoyment."

For this reason the Court of Appeal held that no easement was acquired when a dock had been fixed to a wharf for more than 20 years by means of underground rods which were invisible to the owner of the servient land. Similarly, in *Liverpool Corporation v. H. Coghill and Son Ltd*[39] no easement was acquired where the owner of the allegedly dominant land had discharged waste irregularly at night into a sewer for more than 20 years.

(v) User must have been peaceable: No easement will be acquired by prescription if the user was forcible against the servient land, for example if the allegedly servient owner continually protested against the use.[40]

(vi) User must have been without permission: Long user will only be effective to acquire an easement, other than a right to light, if it was exercised as of right[41] without the permission of the servient landlowner, since otherwise the user would derive from an express or implied licence. In *Gardner v. Hodgson's Kingston Brewery Co. Ltd*[42] permission was implied where the user for 60 years of a right of way had made a periodic payment to the owner of the allegedly servient land. Permission which has lapsed will not prevent the acquisition of an easement if the use continued for the

[34] See: *Hyman v. van den Bergh* [1907] 2 Ch. 516.
[35] *Reilly v. Orange* [1955] 2 Q.B. 112.
[36] See: *Gardner v. Hodgson's Kingston Brewery Co. Ltd* [1903] A.C. 229.
[37] See: *Davies v. Du Paver* [1953] 1 Q.B. 184; *Dance v. Triplow* (1991) 63 P. & C.R. 1.
[38] [1902] 2 Ch. 557, 571.
[39] [1918] 1 Ch. 307.
[40] *Eaton v. Swansea Waterworks Co* (1851) 17 Q.B. 267; Dalton v. Angus & Co (1881) 6 App. Cas. 740.
[41] *Sturges v. Bridgman* (1879) 11 Ch.D. 852; *Healey v. Hawkins* [1968] 1 W.L.R. 1967.
[42] [1903] A.C. 229.

appropriate period after the lapse. Use in excess of the permission will also acquire an easement. It should be noted that the effect of the Prescription Act is that easements other than rights of light may be acquired by 40 years user even if their was permission, unless that permission was granted in writing. The mere fact that the servient owner has tolerated the exercise of a user of which he was aware, and has taken no steps to prevent it, does not mean that the user was conducted with his permission so as to prevent the acquisition of an easement. As Dillon L.J. stated in *Mills v. Silver*[43] "mere acquiescence in or toleration of the user by the servient owner cannot prevent the user being as of right for the purposes of prescription." In the case of a right to light, 20 years user without written agreement will be effective to acquire an easement by prescription even if the right was enjoyed with oral permission.[44]

(vii) User must have been lawful: No easement by prescription can be acquired if the user exercised was unlawful.[45]

(viii) User must have been exercise by the freehold owner of land: An easement can only be obtained by prescription in favour of a freehold owner of the dominant land against the freehold of the servient land. A tenant can never acquire an easement over neighbouring land owned by his landlord.[46] A tenant can gain an easement by prescription against neighbouring freehold land owned by a stranger who is not his landlord, but he acquires such a right for the benefit of the freehold of the land he leases and it endures beyond the termination of his tenancy.[47] Where user commences against a dominant tenement which is not subject to a tenancy, any easement which is acquired by prescription will bind the freehold title even if the land is subjected to a tenancy before the relevant period of user has been completed.[48] However, no easement can be acquired by prescription if the user commenced when the allegedly servient land was already subject to a tenancy.[49]

2 Creation of equitable easements

(a) Easements granted by deed which fail to meet the requirements for legal status

As has been noted the mere fact that an easement has been granted or reserved by deed is not of itself conclusive of legal stàtus. Section 1(2)(a) provides for the circumstances in which an easement is capable of existing or being created at law:

> An easement, right or privilege in or over land for an interest equivalent to an estate in fee simple absolute in possession or a term of years absolute.

This means that the easement must be granted either in perpetuity, or for a defined and specific period of time. Thus a right of way granted by Hamish to Isabel "for life"

[43] [1991] Ch. 271, 279.
[44] s.3 Prescription Act 1832. *Mallam v. Rose* [1915] 2 Ch. 222; *Plasterers' Co. v. Parish Clerks Co.* (1851) 6 Exch 630.
[45] *Neaverson v. Peterborough RDC* [1902] 1 Ch. 557; *Cargill v. Gotts* [1981] 1 W.L.R. 441; *Hanning v. Top Deck Travel Group Ltd* (1993) 68 P. & C.R. 14.
[46] *Gayford v. Moffatt* (1868) 4 Ch. App 133; *Kilgour v. Gaddes* [1904] 1 K.B. 457.
[47] *Wheaton v. Maple & Co* [1893] 3 Ch. 48; *Pugh v. Savage* [1970] 2 Q.B. 373.
[48] *Palk v. Shinner* (1852) 18 Q.B. 568.
[49] *Daniel v. North* (1809) 11 East 372; *Roberts v. James* (1903) 89 LT 282 (life tenancy).

by deed would only be capable of creating an equitable easement. However, an equitable easement will only arise if the grant or reservation was made for valuable consideration.[50]

(b) A contract to create an easement

(i) General principle: Since equity treats as done that which ought to be done a specifically enforceable contract to grant an easement will give rise to an equitable right even though the requisite formalities for a legal easement have not been satisfied. This principle will clearly operate in relation to express grants and reservations, but also extends to situations where an easement is implied under the rule in *Wheeldon v. Burrows*,[51] so that where an owner of land enters into a contract to convey part, any quasi-easements which he enjoyed continuously and apparently over the land will be implied into the contract.[52]
(ii) Contracts to grant an easement entered prior to September 27, 1989: Contracts entered into before September 27, 1989 are governed by the formalities provisions of Law of Property Act 1925, s.40. Under these provisions a purely oral contract for the creation of an easement would be effective to generate an equitable easement if it was accompanied by part performance on the part of the person enjoying the benefit of the easement.[53]
(iii) Contracts to grant an easement entered after September 27, 1989: Such contracts will only be effective to create an equitable easement if they fulfil the more stringent formalities requirements of section 2 of the Law of Property (Miscellaneous Provisions) Act 1989, which requires that they be made in writing, incorporating all the terms of the contract, signed by or on behalf of the parties. Thus a purely oral contract is incapable of creating an equitable easement, even if there is part performance, and will be construed as the grant of a mere licence over the property of the grantor.[54]

3 Creation of easements by estoppel

(i) General principle: Even where there is no grant, or contract for the grant, of an easement an owner of land will be entitled to such a right if the owner of the servient tenement is estopped from denying that he enjoys it. This is an application of the general doctrine of proprietary estoppel, examined in detail in Chapter 13 below, which allows the court to grant a proprietary right as a remedy where an "estoppel equity" has been raised.
(ii) Establishing the equity: In order to establish an equity which requires satisfaction by the court granting an easement the owner of the allegedly dominant land must show that there was a representation or assurance by the owner of the servient land that he would be entitled to exercise an easement, and that he has acted to his detriment on the basis of that assurance. For example in *Ward v. Kirkland*[55] the plaintiff owner of a

[50] *May v. Belleville* [1905] 2 Ch. 605.
[51] (1879) 13 Ch.D. 31.
[52] *Borman v. Griffith* [1930] 1 Ch. 493; *Horn v. Hiscock* (1972) 223 E.G. 1437.
[53] *McManus v. Cooke* (1887) 35 Ch.D. 681.
[54] *Wood v. Leadbitter* (1845) 13 M. & W. 838.
[55] [1967] Ch. 194.

cottage was granted permission by the owners of neighbouring land to lay drains across her land connected to a sceptic tank. The drains were installed at the plaintiff's expense. The defendant subsequently claimed the right to terminate any licence enjoyed by the plaintiff to use the drains and demanded their removal. Ungoed-Thomas J. held that since the defendant had granted permission for the drains to be installed for an indefinite period and the plaintiff had incurred expenditure on the basis of that permission, an easement to use the drains had arisen on the grounds of estoppel. In *Crabb v. Arun District Council*[56] the plaintiff owned land which he intended to sell in two plots. To achieve this it was necessary to establish a right of way onto a road for one of the intended plots, and the defendants who owned the adjoining land agreed in principle that there should be such a right of way. The defendants then fenced the boundary of their land leaving a gate at the agreed point of access. The plaintiff sold part of his land and retained the part which was intended to enjoy the right of way. The defendants subsequently removed the gate and fenced the gap, refusing to allow the plaintiff access. The Court of Appeal held that there was sufficient assurance to the plaintiff that he would be able to enjoy access, and that since he had acted to his detriment by selling part of his land without reserving a right of way over in his favour to raise an estoppel which was satisfied by the grant of an easement. Lord Denning M.R. explained:

> "The defendants actually put up the gates at point B at considerable expense. That certainly led the plaintiff to believe that he should have the right of access through point B without more ado . . . The defendants knew that the plaintiff intended to sell the two portions separately and that he would need an access point at point B as well as point A. Seeing that they knew of his intention — and they did nothing to disabuse him but rather confirmed it by erecting gates at point B — it was their conduct which led him to act as he did: and this raises an equity in favour against them. In the circumstances it seems to me inequitable that the council should insist on their strict title as they did: and to take the high-handed action of pulling down the gates without a word of warning; and to demand of the plaintiff £30,000 as the price of the easement."[57]

(iii) Satisfying the equity: Once an estoppel equity has been established, it is a matter for the court to award the appropriate remedy to "satisfy" it. In cases where the equity is established because of the denial of a right in the character of an easement the court will generally award the easement denied as the appropriate satisfaction. Although the estoppel right is described as an "equity" the court is perfectly capable of awarding a legal easement to the claimant.

SCOPE OF ENTITLEMENT CONFERRED BY AN EASEMENT

1 Scope of entitlement to rights of way

(a) Introductory

Having examined the nature of easements and the means by which they can be created, some consideration will be given to the extent of the rights which an easement

[56] [1976] Ch. 179. See also: *E. R. Ives Investment Ltd v. High* [1967] 2 Q.B. 379.
[57] *ibid.* at 189.

confers on the owner of the dominant tenement. Obviously in many cases this will be determined by the terms of the grant or reservation which will stipulate the nature of the user which the dominant owner is entitled to exercise over the servient land. Most of the principles examined arise in the context of rights of way. Any user in excess of the entitlement will amount to a trespass.

(b) Expressly created rights of way: scope of entitlement determined by the grantor's intentions

(i) Interpretation of the terms of the grant: Where a right of way has either been expressly granted or reserved the scope of the easement will be determined by construction of the terms used in the deed creating it. The principle of interpretation for such deeds was stated by Willes J. in *Williams v. James*[58]:

> "In the case of a grant the language of the instrument can be referred to, and it is of course for the court to construe that language; and in the absence of any clear indication of the intention of the parties, the maxim that a grant must be construed most strongly against the grantor must apply."

(ii) Consideration of the physical circumstances of the land at the date of the grant: The precise scope of an expressly grant easement will also be construed in the light of the nature of the land over which it was granted.[59] Sir John Pennycuick stated in *St. Edmundsbury and Ipswich Diocesan Board of Finance v. Clarke*[60]:

> "It is no doubt true that in order to construe an instrument one looks first at the instrument and no doubt one may form a preliminary impression upon such inspection. But it is not until one has considered the instrument and the surrounding circumstances in conjunction that one concludes the process of construction. Of course one may have words so unambiguous that no surrounding circumstances could affect their construction."

This principle was applied by the Court of Appeal in *White v. Richards*,[61] where part of a plot of agricultural land was conveyed with an express reservation of a right of way over a designated track to "pass and repass on foot with or without motor vehicles . . . so far as . . . may be necessary for the use and enjoyment of the retained land." It was held that the scope of this easement should be construed in the light of the physical nature of the track over which it was enjoyed, so that since it was only eight feet ten inches wide and mainly dirt it could only be exercised by vehicles with a wheelbase of less than eight feet and width of less than nine, and with a laden weight of less than ten tons. Use by 38 tons lorries, excavators and other heavy machinery was therefore excessive and damages for trespass were awarded. However, where a specific right has been expressly granted the courts will not allow the physical circumstances of the land to limit its scope. In *Keefe v. Amor*[62] a right of way was granted over a strip of land 20

[58] (1867) L.R. 2 C.P. 577, 581.
[59] See: *Todrick v. Western National Omnibus Co Ltd* [1934] Ch. 190; *Keefe v. Amor* [1965] 1 K.B. 334.
[60] [1975] 1 W.L.R. 468, affirming *Cannon v. Villiers* (1878) 8 Ch.D. 415.
[61] (1994) 68 P. & C.R. 105.
[62] [1965] 1 Q.B. 334.

feet wide which at the time of the grant had an entrance some four feet six inches wide. The Court of Appeal held that there was no excessive user when the owner of the dominant land widened the entrance and a track over the land to seven feet six inches. Russell L.J. stated:

> ". . . if the true conclusion is that the right granted embraces potentially the whole of the strip, the fact that the physical characteristics of the site (for example walls) make the exercise of the right at the time of the grant impossible over any but a limited route will not contradict or limit the scope of the grant . . . and . . . where the form of the grant shows perfectly clearly the quality of the right, and that it extends to every part of the whole area, topographical circumstances could not properly be regarded as restricting it."

(iii) Grant of a more onerous easement will include a grant of the less onerous right: Where an easement has been expressly granted or reserved it will be held to include the right to exercise less onerous uses which are logically derived from it, since the grant of the greater is deemed to include the lesser.[63] Therefore in *White v. Richards*[64] the grant of a right to "pass or repass on foot with or without motorvehicles" was also held to include the right to walk dogs and to lead a horse on foot, and to ride a pedal cycle on the grounds that it clearly included the greater right to ride a motorcycle which is a form of motorvehicle. Since a right to drive a motorvehicles includes the right to drive a horse-drawn carriage or cart,[65] it was also held to include the right to lead cows and other animals on foot, although not to drive them.

(iv) Subsequent change of use of dominant land: The scope of an expressly granted or reserved easement is not automatically limited by the use to which the dominant tenement was put at the date that the easement was granted. In *White v. Grand Hotel, Eastbourne Ltd*[66] a right of way benefiting the dominant land was expressly granted whilst it was a private dwelling house. It was subsequently converted into a hotel, with the consequence that it was more heavily used since it led to a garage for the guests. The Court of Appeal held that as there was no limitation on the scope of the easement in the words of the grant it was a general right and not limited to purely domestic use. However, a change of use may mean that even an authorised easement is used excessively.[67] In *Rosling v. Pinnegar*[68] a right of way benefiting a house was granted in 1923. In 1982 the house, which enjoyed the right of way along with the 25 residents of a hamlet, was restored and opened to the public leading to an increased use. The Court of Appeal held that since the grant was "for all purposes" the use by visitors was not unauthorised, but that the quantity of visitors interfered unreasonably with the rights of those others entitled to use it, and was thus excessive.

(c) Implied rights of way: scope of entitlement limited by the use contemplated at the time of the conveyance

Where a right of way has not been expressly granted or reserved but is found to have been implied into a conveyance or transfer of land, the scope of the right is limited to

[63] *British Railways Board v. Glass* [1965] Ch. 538.
[64] (1994) 68 P. & C.R. 105.
[65] *Ballard v. Dyson* (1808) 1 Taunt 279.
[66] [1913] 1 Ch. 113.
[67] See: *Jelbert v. Davis* [1968] 1 W.L.R. 589.
[68] [1987] 54 P. & C.R. 124.

the use which was contemplated at the date of the conveyance or transfer, which will often be determined by the actual use which was occurring at that date. In *Milner's Safe Company Ltd v. Great Northern and City Railway Co.*[69] Kekewich J. held that an implied right of way included business use because the owner conveying the land had been accustomed to using it to load and unload vans, but that it did not extend to allowing a railway company which now owned the land to use it as the main thoroughfare to and from their station. In *Corporation of London v. Riggs*[70] Jessel M.R. held that an impliedly reserved right of way to agricultural land must be limited to use for agricultural purposes, and that it did not extend to use which was necessary if the land was to be used for building purposes. Use beyond that exercised at the date of the conveyance will not be excessive if clearly contemplated by the parties. In *Stafford v. Lee*[71] an easement of necessity benefiting woodland was held to include access to a house since the conveyance indicated that it was anticipated that a residential dwelling would be constructed.

(d) Right of way acquired by prescription: scope of entitlement limited to the user which acquired the easement

In *Williams v. James*[72] Willes J. observed that "the distinction between a grant and prescription is obvious. In the case of proving a right by prescription the user of the right is the only evidence." In consequence the scope of the entitlement acquired by prescription can only be determined by that user. Mellish L.J. stated in *United Land Co. v. Great Eastern Railway Co.*[73]:

> "Where a right of way is claimed by user, then, no doubt, according to the authorities, the purpose for which the way may be used is limited by the user; for we must judge from the way in which it has been used what the purposes were for which the party claiming has gained the right."

A mere increase in the extent of use of a right acquired by prescription will not be excessive.[74] In *British Railways Board v. Glass*[75] a right of way to a caravan park was acquired by prescription. The Court of Appeal held that an increase from six caravans to 30 was not excessive use. In *Woodhouse & Co Ltd v. Kirkland Ltd*[76] Plowman J. held that there was no excessive user where a right of way used by a plumbers and their customers and suppliers was used to a greater extent when the owners of the servient land left a gate to the premises open for a longer period. However, user of a different kind, rather than mere increase in user, will be excessive. In *Williams v. James*[77] it was held that a prescriptive right to carry agricultural produce to a farm did not extend to a right to carry those items necessary when the farm was converted into a factory.

[69] [1907] 1 Ch. 208.
[70] (1880) 12 Ch.D. 798.
[71] (1965) P. & C.R. 172.
[72] (1867) L.R. 2 C.P. 577, 581.
[73] (1875) 10 Ch. App 586, 590.
[74] See: *Giles v. County Building Constructors (Hertford) Ltd* (1971) 22 P. & C.R. 978; *Cargill v. Gotts* [1981] 1 W.L.R. 441.
[75] [1965] Ch. 538.
[76] [1970] 1 W.L.R. 1185.
[77] (1867) L.R. 2 C.P. 577.

2 Scope of entitlement to rights to light

(a) Restricted to buildings

Rights to light, which are almost exclusively obtained by prescription, are not capable of existing in abstract, but rather only in relation buildings and their "windows or apertures constructed for the purpose of admitting light."[78] For this reason in *Levet v. Gas Light and Coke Co.*[79] it was held that there could be no right to light through a door.

(b) Restricted to sufficient light for comfortable enjoyment and use

Where a right to light has been acquired by prescription it does not entitle the owner of the dominant land to an absolute right to the amount of light he has been accustomed to enjoy. In *Colls v. Home and Colonial Stores*[80] Lord Lindley stated the rule that:

> ". . . generally speaking an owner of ancient lights is entitled to sufficient light according to the ordinary notions of mankind for the comfortable use and enjoyment of his house as a dwelling house, if it is a dwelling house, or for the beneficial use and occupation of the house if it is a warehouse, a shop, or other place of business."[81]

This principle was applied by Millet J. in *Carr-Saunders v. Dick McNeil Associates*[82] where the light to the second floor of a building was reduced when the owners of the servient tenement added two storeys to their building. He held that the appropriate inquiry was not as to the extent of the reduction in light but as to amount of light left, and whether this was reasonable not merely for the present use but also for other potential uses to which the dominant owner may reasonably be expected to put the premises in the future. He held that there had been actionable interference since it would mean that the space on the second floor could not longer be subdivided conveniently so that the subdivided areas would each receive an adequate amount of light.

3 Interference with exercise of easements by the owner of the servient land

(a) Wrongful interference actionable as a nuisance

(i) Substantial interference: If land is subject to an easement any wrongful interference with its exercise by the servient owner will be actionable by the dominant owner in nuisance. Interference *per se* is not actionable, but only such interference as substantially affects the use of the easement. The principles were set out by Scott J. in *Celstell v. Alton House Holdings Ltd*[83]:

[78] *Levet v. Gas Light and Coke Co* [1919] 1 Ch. 24, 27 *per* Peterson J.
[79] [1919] 1 Ch. 24.
[80] [1904] A.C. 179.
[81] *ibid.* at 208, applying *City of London Brewery v. Tennant* L.R. 9 Ch. 212.
[82] [1986] 1 W.L.R. 922.
[83] [1985] 1 W.L.R. 204, 217.

> "There emerge . . . two criteria relevant to the question whether a particular interference with a right of way is actionable. The interference will be actionable if it is substantial. And it will not be substantial if it does not interfere with the reasonable use of the right of way."

Although the case concerned interference with a right of way the principles are more generally applicable. It has already been noted how in the case of rights to light mere reduction in the quantity of light is not actionable, but only such a reduction as leaves too little light for the reasonable enjoyment of the premises. In *Keefe v. Amor*[84] Russel L.J. pointed out that what constitutes substantial interference will vary with the use to which the dominant tenement is put, so that an actionable interference will be caused by:

> "such obstacles as impeded the user of the strip for such exercise of the right granted as from time to time is reasonably required by the dominant tenement."

In assessing whether an interference is reasonable, the Court of Appeal indicated in *Saint v. Jenner*[85] that the entitlement of other users of the right of way must be considered. Stampt L.J. stated:

> " . . . it is to be observed that in deciding what is a substantial interference with the dominant owner's reasonable use of a right of way, all the circumstances must be considered, including the rights of other persons entitled to use the way."

On this basis measures to reduce the speed of cars were not unreasonable when the right of way was also used by horses.

(ii) Examples of interference which was not substantial: Most cases have concerned some kind of obstruction of rights of way. In *Clifford v. Hoare*[86] the owner of the servient tenement erected a building which encroached two feet into a roadway 40 feet wide. It was held that this did not amount to an actionable interference with a right of way over the road because the encroachment was trivial and would not interfere with reasonable use and enjoyment of it. In *Petty v. Parsons*[87] the Court of Appeal considered that the erection of a gate by the servient owner across the right of way would not be an actionable interference if the gate was kept open during business hours. In *Celsteel v. Alton House Holdings Ltd*[88] Scott L.J. held that the narrowing of a driveway leading to garages would not be actionable if the only effect was that relatively easy manoeuvring would be required to drive in and out.

(iii) Examples of substantial interference: In *Celsteel v. Alton House Holdings Ltd* the occupiers of the servient land were proposing to build a car wash which would have the effect of reducing the width of a right of way over a driveway leading to garages from nine metres to four metres. Scott J. held that since this was hardly a trivial encroachment, and that it was reasonable for the driveway to be used by large commercial vans and lorries, the interference would be substantial and therefore

[84] [1965] 1 Q.B. 334.
[85] [1973] Ch. 275, 279.
[86] (1874) L.R. C.P. 362.
[87] [1914] 2 Ch. 653.
[88] [1985] 1 W.L.R. 204, 218.

actionable. In *Saint v. Jenner*[89] the owner of the servient tenement had surfaced a cart track over which the plaintiff enjoyed a right of way, and built speed-humps to reduce the speed of cars using the track, which was also used by horse-riders. The Court of Appeal held that this alone was not an actionable interference, but subsequently large pot holes had developed by the humps and it was held that these did constitute substantial interference.

(b) Remedies where wrongful interference has occurred

Since wrongful interference constitutes the tort of nuisance the appropriate remedies are either an injunction to remove or prevent such interference, and damages to compensate for any loss that has occurred.

PASSING OF THE BENEFIT AND BURDEN OF EASEMENTS

1 Enforceability between the original owners of the dominant and servient tenements

An easement is clearly enforceable between the original owners of the dominant and servient tenements when it was granted or acquired by prescription. However, the question arises as to whether it remains exercisable when ownership of the relevant tenements has been transferred to new owners. Since an easement is a proprietary interest it is capable of binding and benefiting successors in title and the central question will be whether a transferee of the dominant tenement enjoys the benefit of the easement and whether a transferee of the servient tenement is subject to the burden thereof, or whether he has acquired his title free from the easement.

2 Benefit of easement passing to transferee of the dominant tenement

The benefit of any easements will usually pass with the title to the dominant land since by section 62 of the Law of Property Act 1925 they are deemed to be included in any conveyance unless expressly excluded. A transferee of a dominant tenement will thus almost always enjoy the benefit of any easements.

3 Burden of easement binding transferee of the servient tenement

(a) Registered land

(i) Legal easements: Despite the fact that the Land Registration Act 1925 seems to require legal easements to be completed by registration as they are "registered dispositions" this has been largely ignored and is impractical in relation to most easements which are not granted expressly. All legal easements rank as "overriding interests" within section 70(1)(a) of the Land Registration Act 1925 and are therefore

[89] [1973] Ch. 275.

automatically binding on a transferee of the servient tenement even though they do not appear on the register of title.

(ii) Equitable easements: Greater problems are caused in relation to easements which are purely equitable because they appear to be excluded from the scope of section 70(1)(a) which refers to "other easements not being equitable easements required to be protected by notice on the register." If they are not overriding interests then they would need to be protected as minor interests on the title of the servient tenement, and if not protected a purchaser of the land would take free from them.[90] However, in *Celsteel v. Alton House Holdings Ltd*[91] Scott J. interpreted this provision in such a way that equitable easements which were openly exercised and enjoyed by the dominant owner at the time of the transfer would be overriding interests binding the transferee.[92]

(b) Unregistered land

(i) Legal easements: Since legal easements are not land charges falling within the limited system of land charges registration they are binding on a transferee merely by virtue of their legal status.

(ii) Equitable easements: As in registered land more problems are posed by easements which are merely equitable in status. By section 2(5) of the Land Charges Act 1925 "an equitable easement" ranks as a Class D(iii) land charge. If not properly protected by registration a purchaser of a legal estate in the servient land would be entitled to take free from it, even if the purchaser knew of its existence.[93] However, in *E.R. Ives Investments v. High*[94] Lord Denning M.R. took a restrictive interpretation of the scope of Class D(iii) land charges and held that they only comprised easements which would have been legal if created before 1925 but which were rendered merely equitable by the reforms of the property legislation introduced in that year. Easements which would have been equitable prior to 1925 would not require registration and would be binding on all transferees of the land except a bona fide purchaser of a legal estate for value without notice of its existence. This interpretation is questionable as there is no indication in the Land Charges Act 1972 that the definition was intended to bear this limited meaning. An equitable easement arising because of a specifically enforceable contract is registrable as Class C(iv) land charge since it is an "estate contract."

(iii) Estoppel easements: An alternative analysis of *E.R. Ives Investments v. High*, supported by the majority of the Court of Appeal, is that the right claimed was in the nature of an estoppel, which is a right falling outside of the definition of land charges. Priority is therefore determined by the doctrine of notice.

EXTINGUISHMENT OF EASEMENTS

1 Release

(a) Meaning of release

The owner of the dominant land is entitled to release the servient land from the burden of the easement which he is entitled to exercise over it. Once an easement has

[90] Land Registration Act 1925, s.20.
[91] [1985] 1 W.L.R. 204.
[92] See below p. 523.
[93] Land Charges Act 1972, s.4(6).
[94] [1967] 2 Q.B. 379.

been released it cannot revive in his favour. Release is therefore similar to the surrender of a leasehold term. The dominant owner can grant a release either expressly or by implication from his conduct.

(b) Express release

(i) Effective release at common law: The dominant owner can only expressly release an easement at law by means of a deed.[95]

(ii) Effective release in equity: Even where no deed has been executed equity will refuse to allow an owner of the previously dominant land to assert his strict entitlement to an easement if he has released it informally and it would be inequitable to allow him to do so, generally because he has acquiesced in some action taken by the servient owner in the belief that the easement had been released. For example in *Waterlow v. Bacon*[96] the dominant owner of land entitled to a right to light entered into an agreement with the servient owner that he was to be allowed to increase the height of his wall if he built new and larger skylights in return. Having built the wall it was considered that it would be inequitable for the dominant owner to complain of interference with his easement.

(c) Implied release

If the dominant owner abandons his easement he will be taken to have impliedly released it so that it no longer burdens the servient land. The mere fact that the dominant owner has not used the easement is not conclusive of abandonment.[97] What is required was spelt out by Buckley L.J. in *Tehidy Minerals v. Norman*[98]:

> "Abandonment of an easement or of a profit can only, we think, be treated as having taken place where the person entitled to it has demonstrated a fixed intention never at any time thereafter to assert the right himself or to attempt to transmit it to anyone else."

For this reason the Court of Appeal held that the fact that owners of land entitled to a prescriptive easement to graze on a down had allowed an association of commoners to control the management of the grazing was not an abandonment of their individual rights. Buckley L.J. stated that although they had submitted to the control of the association for advantages of fencing and maintenance it did not follow that "if at some time in the future the arrangement should come to an end, the commoners might not wish to reassert their common rights." In *Benn v. Hardinge*[99] the Court of Appeal held that even a period of 175 years non-user was ineffective to establish abandonment when it had not been used because an alternative had been available. In

[95] *Lovell v. Smith* (1857) 3 C.B.N.S. 120.
[96] (1866) L.R. 2 Eq. 514.
[97] *Swan v. Sinclair* [1924] 1 Ch. 254.
[98] [1971] 2 Q.B. 528, 553.
[99] (1993) 66 P. & C.R. 246.

contrast an abandonment was held to have taken place in *Swan v. Sinclair*[1] where a right of way at the back of houses had not been used for 38 years and the dominant owner had acquiesced in physical alterations in the land which would prevent its use as a right of way. Similarly, in *Moore v. Rawson*[2] the owner of the dominant tenement was held to have abandoned his right to light when he demolished a building with windows and rebuilt a stables with no windows. The owner of the previously servient tenement then built a building which would have interfered with the light, but it was held that the dominant owner could not reassert his entitlement when three years later he made a window in the stable.

2 Unification of title and possession

The idea that an owner of one piece of land enjoys rights over land owned by someone else is the very essence of an easement. Therefore if ownership of the dominant and servient land is united in the same person any easements will cease to exist, since the owner will be entitled to exercise whatever rights he wishes over his own land. In effect such easements as existed prior to unification become mere quasi-easements. Such unification will only occur if a single owner acquires the freehold title to both the dominant and servient land. If the dominant owner acquires a leasehold interest in the servient land any easements will merely be suspended until the lease terminates or is assigned.[3] Where unification has occurred a subsequent re-division of the land will not revive the pre-existing easements, although any quasi-easements exercised by the unitary owner may be recreated by the rule in *Wheeldon v Burrows.*[4]

3 Easement rendered obsolete

In *Huckvale v. Aegean Hotels Ltd*[5] the Court of Appeal accepted the possibility that an easement might be extinguished by frustration if it were rendered obsolete by changes in circumstances. Slade L.J. stated:

> "I would . . . be prepared to accept in principle that . . . circumstances might have changed so drastically since the date of the original grant of an easement (for example by supervening illegality) that it would offend common sense and reality for the court to hold that an easement still subsisted. Nevertheless, I think the court could properly so hold only in a very clear case . . . [I]n the absence of evidence or proof of abandonment, the court should be slow to hold that an easement has been extinguished by frustration, unless the evidence shows clearly that because of a change in circumstances since the date of the original grant there is no practical possibility of its ever again benefiting the dominant tenement in the manner contemplated by that grant."[6]

[1] [1924] 1 Ch. 254.
[2] (1824) 3 B. & C. 332.
[3] *Thomas v. Thomas* (1835) 2 Cr.M. & R. 34; *Simper v. Foley* (1862) 2 Johns & H. 555.
[4] (1879) 12 Ch.D. 31.
[5] (1989) 58 P. & C.R. 163.
[6] *ibid.* at 173–174.

In the event, however, it was held that a right of way was not rendered completely obsolete because complimentary rights over other land owned by the servient landowner had been lost. Although it was presently of very limited practical use there was no certainty that it might not benefit the dominant land again in the future, especially if the ownership of the servient tenement changed.

PROFITS À PRENDRE

1 Nature of profits

(a) Right to appropriate from land

As has been noted above, a *profit à prendre* entitles a person not merely to exercise some limited right of user over the servient land it burdens, but to sever and appropriate something from that land. For example, the holder of the profit might be entitled to graze his cattle on the servient land or enjoy the exclusive right to kill game.

(b) No requirement of a dominant tenement

Whereas an easement will only exist if there is a dominant tenement a *profit à prendre* can be granted over the servient land to a person even if they do not own any dominant tenement. The right to profit is enjoyed by them personally, not *qua* owner of some specific land. The profit is therefore said to be capable of existing in gross.[7]

(c) Types of profit

(i) Several profits: A *profits à prendre* is described as "several" where it entitles the holder to an exclusive right to appropriate the subject of the profit from the servient land.
(ii) Profits in common: A profit is described as "in common" where the entitlement to appropriate from the servient land is enjoyed by a number of people together, which group may include the servient owner himself.

(d) Examples of profits

There are a number of well recognised profits. The common of pasture entitles the commoners to graze their cattle on the servient land. Where held in gross there was no limit to the number of cattle which could be grazed under such a common, but at common law a common of pasture appurtenant to land was restricted to the right to graze as many cattle as the dominant tenement could support through the winter,[8] a limitation removed by the Commons Registration Act 1965. The common of piscary entitles the holders to take fish from inland waters of the servient land, but if appurtenant to land is limited to a right to take as many fish as are needed for the family of the owner of the dominant tenement,[9] and not to take fish for sale. A right to fish can be enjoyed as a several profit, thus excluding the owner of the land from

[7] *Lord Chesterfield v. Harris* [1908] 2 Ch. 397, 421.
[8] *Robertson v. Hartropp* (1889) 43 Ch.D. 484.
[9] *Lord Chesterfield v. Harris* [1908] 2 Ch. 397.

fishing himself. The common of turbary entitles the commoners to cut such turf or peat as they need for fuel. It must be appurtenant to a house and not merely land.[10] The common of estovers entitles the commoners to take wood, for use as fuel or for making or repairing furniture, fencing and equipment.

2 Acquisition of profits

Profits may generally be acquired in an identical means to easements. These have been examined in detail above, and attention will be focused on areas of difference.

(a) Express grant

A profit may be granted expressly by the owner of the servient land. Such a profit will only be legal if it was granted by deed,[11] although a valid contract for a profit will give rise to an equitable profit.[12]

(b) Implied grant

Section 62 of the Law of Property Act 1925 applies equally to profits as easements.[13] However, the rule in *Wheeldon v. Burows* will not apply because profits are not enjoyed continuously and apparently.

(c) Prescription

A profit may be acquired by prescription. However the Prescription Act 1832 adopts longer period for profits before its provisions apply. Thus 30 years use will be sufficient to establish a profit by prescription if there was no permission, but where permission was granted 60 years is required unless there was written consent. The Prescription Act has no application to profits in gross. However, the doctrine of a lost modern grant applies to profits after 20 years, so that this will be sufficient if it cannot be proved that no such grant was made.

(d) Registration of profits in common

The Commons Registration Act 1969 required the registration of common land in England and Wales with county councils, and of its owners and those claiming to enjoy common rights over it. If such land was not registered before August 1970 it would be incapable of being registered thereafter, and any unregistered rights of common over such land were extinguished at that date No new rights of common are capable of arising over such land after that date, but new commons may be created of other land.

3 Extinguishment of profits

As in the case of easements a profit will be extinguished if the holder of the profit acquires the ownership of the servient land, or if he grants a release. Non-user of the

[10] *Att.-Gen. v. Reynolds* [1911] 2 K.B. 888; *Warrick v. Queen's College, Oxford* (1871) 6 Ch. App 716.
[11] *Wood v. Lleadbitter* (1845) 13 M. & W. 838; *Mason v. Clarke* [1954] 1 Q.B. 460.
[12] *Mason v. Clarke* [1955] A.C. 778.
[13] *White v. Williams* [1922] 1 K.B. 727.

profit will not itself extinguish the right, but alteration of the dominant land so that the profit can no longer benefit it will cause extinguishment, for example if agricultural land is developed. A profit could also be wholly or partially extinguished by means of approvement or inclosure.[14] A profit over common land acquired prior to August 1970 will have been extinguished if not registered under the Commons Registrations Act 1969.

4 Priority and profits

Where a profit is not held in gross but is appurtenant to dominant land the benefit of the profit will be deemed to pass with a conveyance of the land by section 62 of the Law of Property Act 1925. In registered land a *profit à prendre* ranks as an overriding interest under section 70(1)(a) of the Land Registration Act 1925 and will be binding on all transferees of the servient land. In unregistered land a profit will generally be a legal interest binding on all transferees. A contract for a profit will be an estate contract registrable as a Class C(iv) land charge.

REFORM OF EASEMENTS AND PROFITS

1 Reform of prescription

As has been seen the law relating to the acquisition of easements and profits by prescription is extremely complex, with three separate means of prescription recognised by the common law and statute. The role of prescription was examined by the Law Reform Committee in 1966, which recommended that it be abolished altogether for easements and profits.[15] A minority wished to retain a revised form of prescription for easements only, with a prescription period of 12 years.

2 Reform of easements within registered land

It has been seen how there is some confusion concerning the creation of easements in registered land as the Land Registration Act 1925 provides that they should be completed by registration. The Law Commission[16] has recommended that expressly granted easements should be so completed, and that where they have not been registered they should not rank as overriding interests within section 70(1)(a) but only as minor interests,[17] thus rendering them liable to be defeated if title is acquired by a purchaser and they have not been protected on the register. Easements created by implication or prescription would remain as overriding interests. It was also recommended that equitable easements should not be overriding interests but merely minor interests, thus reversing the interpretation of s70(1)(a) adopted in *Celsteel v. Alton House Holdings Ltd*.[18]

[14] See: Cheshire & Burn, *Modern Law of Real Property*, Butterworths, 15th ed, pp.572-575.
[15] 14th Report (1966) Cmnd. 3100.
[16] Third Report on Land Registration, Law. Com. No. 158.
[17] *ibid.* para. 2.25-2.26.
[18] [1985] 1 W.L.R. 204.

PARTY WALLS: A NEW STATUTORY REGIME

One area of recent development is the enactment of a general scheme for regulating the rights of neighbouring landowners where there is a party wall on the border of their land. Although rights in relation to such walls, for example to repair, can be conferred by easements, the Party Wall, Etc., Act 1996 provides a mechanism enabling work to be done to party walls and structures, and a means of settling disputes rapidly without the need to go to court. The system introduced by the Act is not novel, but is based on an earlier scheme operating in London.[19] Section 1 provides a mechanism for an owner who wishes to build a party wall or party fence wall on the boundary of their adjoining land. He must serve a notice on the adjoining owner a month before commencing work and describing the intended wall.[20] If consent is given he may build the wall half on the land of the two owners and sharing the costs in proportion to their respective use of the wall, but in the absence of consent he may only build the wall placed wholly on his own land and at his own expense.[21] Section 2 provides for the repair of existing party walls and entitles an owner to a number of rights such as underpinning or thickening the wall and demolishing and rebuilding a wall which is not of sufficient for any building he intends to do. Before exercising such rights the owner must serve a notice on the adjoining owner two months before the work is due to start.[22] The adjoining owner then has the option to serve a counter notice requiring the building of such things as chimney flues and copings into the wall or deeper foundations. The building owner is under a duty to compensate the adjoining owner for any loss or damage caused by work performed under the Act[23] and a building owners and his servants are entitled to enter any land during working hours to execute work pursuant to the Act.[24] Where there is a dispute section 10 provides that the parties shall either agree on the appointment of a surveyor, or each appoint a surveyor, which surveyors will then appoint a third, to resolve the dispute. Where an award has been made, the parties can appeal against it to the county court.[25]

[19] Under the London Building Acts (Amendment) Act 1939.
[20] s.1(2).
[21] s.1(3).
[22] s.3.
[23] s.7.
[24] s.8.
[25] s.10(17).

Chapter 10

COVENANTS AFFECTING FREEHOLD LAND

INTRODUCTION TO COVENANTS ENTERED BETWEEN FREEHOLD OWNERS

1 The nature of covenants

A covenant is simply an agreement entered by deed whereby the party making the covenant, the covenantor, makes a promise to the party or parties intended to enjoy the benefit of the covenant, the covenantee(s). In a sense the covenant is simply a form of contract which is enforceable at common law even if the covenantee provided the covenantor with no consideration. If the covenantor fails to keep his promise the covenantee will be able to recover damages from the covenantor to compensate for any loss he has suffered as a result of the breach. The promise made by the covenantor may take any form. If the covenant is granted in the context of land the covenantor may agree to do something on his land for the benefit of the covenantee, for example to build a wall along the boundary of his land. Since the obligation created by this covenant requires the covenantor to do something it is described as a positive covenant. Conversely, the covenantor may make a promise that he will not do some specified thing, for example that he will not play football in his garden. Since the obligation requires the covenantor to refrain from doing something the covenant is said to be negative or restrictive.

2 Problems associated with the enforceability of covenants

(a) Enforcement between the original parties to the covenant

Where parties have entered into a covenant it is clearly enforceable between them. The covenantee can seek damages from the covenantor for breach, and if equitable remedies are also available may be able to obtain a prohibitory injunction to prevent a breach or a mandatory injunction to restrain a continuing breach. The covenant is enforceable between the original parties because they enjoy privity of contract.

(b) Assignment of the benefit of a contract

At contract law it is possible for the benefit of a contract to be transferred by the promisee to a third party. This is because the benefit of a contract is regarded as a species of property, termed a chose in action. If this occurs the third party will be able to enforce the contract directly against the promisor, even though he was not originally privy to the contract. The means by which such a transfer of the benefit of a contract occurs is assignment, and the requirements for a legal assignment are found in section 136 of the Law of Property Act 1936. However, although the benefit of a contract is capable of being assigned there is no parallel mechanism for the transfer of the burden of a contract. A promisor cannot transfer his obligation to a third party so that the promisee is entitled to enforce the contract directly against the third party. The doctrine of privity prevents such a result.

(c) Covenants affecting land

(i) Limited enforceability under contract principles: Where covenants are entered by the owners of land the problems of enforceability are especially acute. For example if Bill and Ted are neighbouring landlowners and Ted entered into a covenant with Bill that he will build a boundary wall and not use his garden for playing football, clearly Bill will be able to enforce these covenants against Ted if he breaches them, either by failing to build the wall, or by playing football. However, problems of enforceability arise if Bill sells his land to Wayne and Ted his land to Garth. As matter of contract law Bill could have expressly assigned the benefit of his covenants to Wayne, but there is no means by which the burden of the covenant could have been passed by Ted to Garth. If Garth was in breach of the covenants Wayne would perhaps be entitled to seek remedies against Ted, but not against Garth.

(ii) No concept of privity of estate between freehold owners: A similar problem has already been encountered in relation to the covenants which are entered into between a landlord and a tenant forming the terms of the lease. Again such leasehold covenants are enforceable between the original landlord and tenant as they enjoy privity of contract, but the covenants, whether positive or negative in nature, are also capable of being enforced between successors in title to the original landlord and tenant because of the doctrine of privity of estate developed in *Spencer's Case*[1] and more recently placed on a statutory footing in the Landlord and Tenant (Covenants) Act 1995. However, there is no parallel doctrine operating between the successors in title to freehold owners who have granted covenants.

(iii) Possibility of transfer of the benefit and burden of covenants to successors in title: Despite the absence of any comprehensive mechanism for the transfer of the benefit and burden of covenants between freeholders the law has developed so as to enable some measure of enforceability of covenants affecting land between successors in title to the original covenantor and covenantee. If a covenant was made to benefit the land owned by the covenantee, and not with the original covenantee in a personal capacity, then at common law the benefit of that covenant will pass with the land so that successors in title will be able to enforce it against the original covenantor. Although there is no possibility at common law that the burden of the covenant will run with the land and bind successors in title to the original covenantor, equity has intervened to transform the contractual right generated by a negative covenant into a species of proprietary right capable of binding the land owned by the original covenantor. The burden of a negative covenant, but not of a positive covenant, is

[1] [1583] 5 Co.Rep. 16a.

capable of running with the land so as to potentially bind a successor in title to the original covenantor in equity, and it will be enforceable by any successor in title to the original covenantee who in equity enjoys the benefit of the covenant. Such a right is described as a restrictive covenant.

(d) Principles of enforceability of covenants affecting land

Given the development of the restrictive covenant as a proprietary interest by equity, the amalgam of the common law and equitable principles regulating the enforceability of covenants can be summarised:

(i) Enforceability of covenants between the original parties to the covenant: All covenants entered between the original parties are enforceable because there is privity of contract between the parties, whether they are positive or negative, and whether related to the land or purely personal in character..

(ii) Enforceability of covenants between successors in title to the covenantee and the original covenantor: Provided that the covenant is concerned with the land and is not purely personal the benefit of all covenants, whether positive or negative, will pass at law to successors in title of the land owned by the covenantee. The covenants will therefore be enforceable against the original covenantor, who remains subject to the burden irrespective of whether he has retained the land or transferred it.

(iii) Enforceability of restrictive covenants against successors in title of the original covenantor: Where a covenant is negative in nature the burden is capable of passing in equity with the land. A restrictive covenant will be enforceable in equity against a successor in title to the original covenantor who has acquired the land subject to the burden, by either the original covenantee, or a successor in title to the original covenantee who has acquired the land with the benefit of that covenant in equity.

ENFORCEMENT OF FREEHOLD COVENANTS BETWEEN THE ORIGINAL PARTIES TO THE COVENANT

1 Enforcement by the parties of the original covenant

As has been noted, where the owners of freehold land have entered into covenants they are enforceable by the parties thereto on the basis of their privity of contract. For example, if Ted covenants with Bill that he will: build a boundary wall; not play football in his garden; and do Bill's laundry weekly, Bill will be entitled to enforce all these covenants against him.

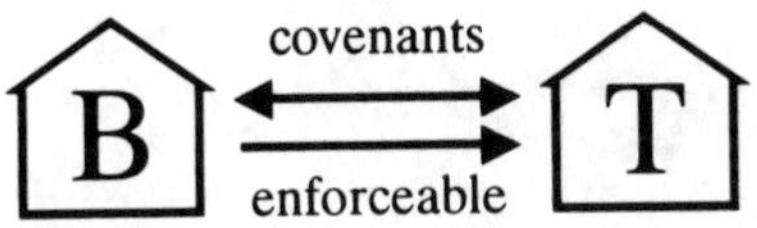

All such covenants are enforceable between the original parties to the covenant irrespective of whether they were positive or negative, personal or relating to the land.

2 Who are the parties to the original covenant?

(a) Persons named as parties in the covenant

A covenant will be enforceable by all the persons who are expressly named as covenantees in the covenant, even though they were not themselves party to it. For example, if Wayne owned other freehold land neighbouring Bill's land, and Ted covenanted "with Bill and with Wayne" that he would not use his land for industrial purposes this would entitle Wayne to enforce the covenant as an original covenantee.

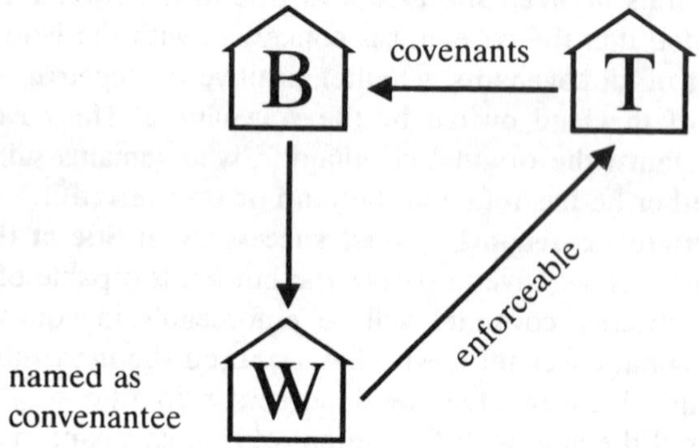

This is in contrast to the situation where a covenant is entered between two persons for the benefit of a third who is not expressly named as a covenantee. In such circumstances the third party cannot enforce the covenant because he is not a covenantee and is not therefore privy to it. For example, if Ted covenanted with Bill to build a boundary wall for all his land, and Wayne owns land neighbouring Ted which would inevitably be benefited by the performance of the covenant, Wayne will be incapable of enforcing it against Ted.

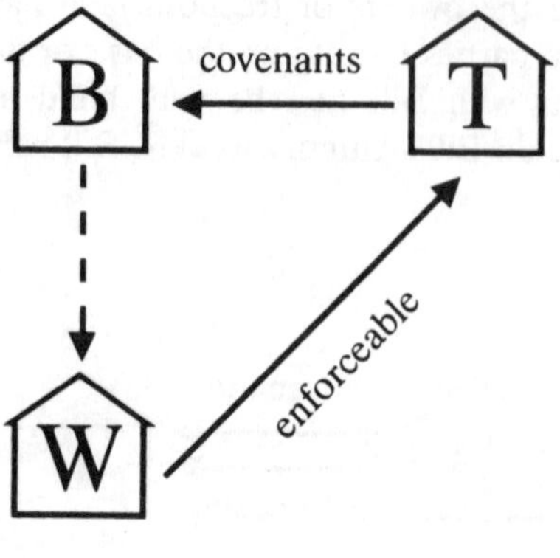

(b) Persons party to the covenant by statute: section 56(1) of the Law of Property Act 1925

(i) Operation of section 56(1): Section 56(1) of the Law of Property Act 1925 provides that:

> "A person may taken an immediate or other interest in land or other property, or the benefit of any condition, right of entry, covenant or agreement over or respecting land or other property, although he may not be named as a party to the conveyance or other instrument."

Despite some judicial comments by Lord Denning M.R. construing this section as effecting a complete abrogation of the doctrine of privity of contract,[2] it merely enables a person to be regarded as a party to a covenant even though he is not specifically named as a covenantee if there is a generic description of the covenantees. Section 56(1) applies to all covenants, whether or not related to land, but it has an important role to play in the context of covenants between freehold owners in identifying the original covenantees of such a covenant. For example, if Ted covenanted with "Bill and the owners of all the other land adjoining my land" Wayne would be regarded an original party to the covenant and would be entitled to enforce the covenant against Ted even though he was not named in the covenant.

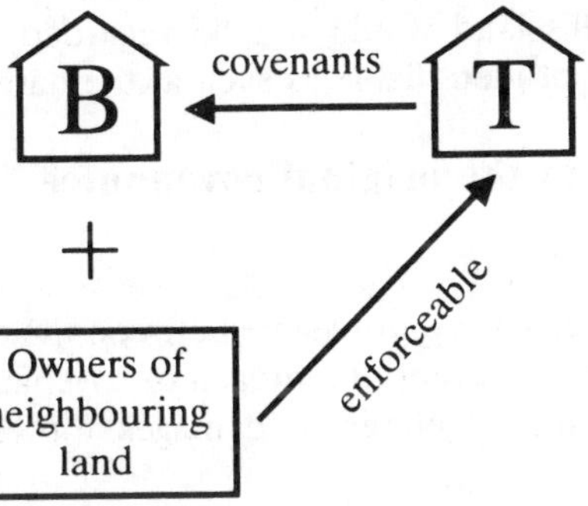

Section 56(1) operated in *Re Ecclesiastical Commissioners for England's Conveyance*.[3] In 1887 a freehold owner entered a restrictive covenant with the Ecclesiastical Commissioners and "their successors and also as a separate covenant with their assigns owners for the time being of the land adjoining or adjacent to" a house the Commissioners were conveying to him. Luxmore J. held that by section 56(1) those persons who owned land adjacent or adjoining the land conveyed, which had also previously been owned by the Commissioners, were original covenantees of the covenant even though they were not parties to it.[4] However, section 56(1) will not

[2] See: *Smiths and Snipes Hall Farm Ltd v. River Douglas Catchment Board* [1949] 2 K.B. 500, 514; *Beswick v. Beswick* [1966] Ch. 588, 556.
[3] [1936] Ch. 430.
[4] In consequence the benefit of the covenants made with them was capable of passing to their successors in title.

operate where there is no clear statement in the covenant that it is intended to be made with a person or generic group. In *White v. Bijou Mansions Ltd*[5] the purchaser of a piece of land entered into restrictive covenants in 1890 with the vendor and with "their heirs and assigns." Four years previously the vendor had sold the neighbouring land to a purchaser named Fellows. One question was whether Fellows was a party to the covenant granted in 1890. Simonds J. held that section 56 did not operate in his favour because there was no indication in the covenant that the grant was purported to be made with Fellows, but only with the vendors.[6] Although Fellows would benefit from the covenants being observed this was not the same as his being a party to them.
(ii) Limitation to the operation of s56(1): Section 56 can only operate in favour of a person who could have been a party to the covenant when it was granted.[7] For example, if Ted granted a covenant to Bill and "the owners for the time being of the land adjacent or adjoining my land" section 56(1) would only operate to establish that the owners of such land at the date of the covenant were original covenantees. Thus, if Wayne did not own any land adjoining Ted's land at the date of the covenant, but a year later purchased such land, he would not be able to claim that he was an original covenantee under section 56. He would be able to enforce the covenant against Ted if he had acquired the land with the benefit of the covenant, since the previous owner would have been an original covenantee, but not under the covenant itself. As will be seen this distinction is important because it is not the case that the benefit of all covenants granted to the owner of land will run with the freehold ownership. Similarly, if Ted granted a covenant to "Bill and his successors in title" those persons who subsequently acquired Bill's land would not be regarded as original parties to the covenant since they were not identifiable as such at the date of the covenant.

3 Remedies available to the original covenantee

(a) Compensation and specific remedies

It has been seen how a covenant is enforceable between the original covenantor and all the original covenantees. In the event of a breach of covenant, or a threatened breach, the covenantee may be entitled either to damages for breach of covenant or an injunction.

(b) Remedies where an original covenantee has parted with his land

The mere fact that an original covenantee no longer owns the land to which a covenant relates does not mean that he automatically ceases to be able to enforce the covenant against the original covenantor. Unless the covenant specifically provides that he is only entitled to enforce it so long as he remains the owner of his land as a matter of contract law the obligations created by the covenant are still owed to him and he can enforce them. For example, if Ted grants covenants in relation to his land to Bill, and Bill then sold his land to Wayne, Bill will remain entitled to enforce the covenants against Ted.

[5] [1937] Ch. 610; [1938] Ch. 351 C.A.
[6] His successor in title could not therefore enforce the covenant because he had not been entitled to the benefit when it was granted.
[7] See: *Kelsey v. Dodd* (1881) 52 L.J. Ch. 34; *Stromdale and Ball Ltd v. Burden* [1952] Ch. 223; *Lyus v. Prowsa Developments Ltd* [1982] 1 W.L.R. 1044, 1049 *per* Dillon L.J.

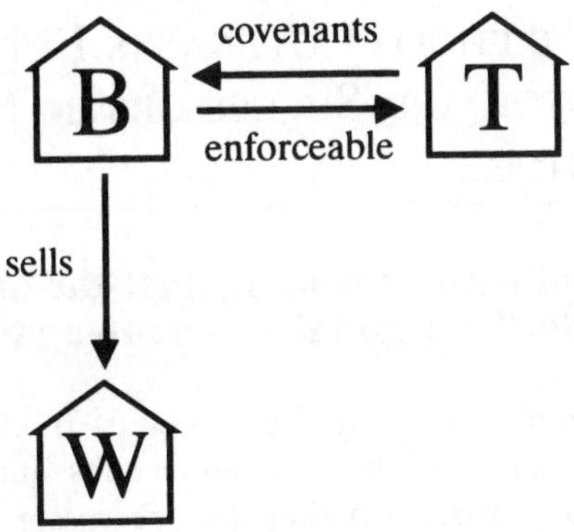

However such a liability is of little practical relevance since the covenantee will no longer be entitled to an injunction as he has no legal interest to protect and any damages would be purely nominal because he suffers no loss through the breach.[8]

4 Continuing liability of the covenantor when he has parted with his land

The mere fact that the original covenantor has transferred his land does not automatically mean that he is relieved from any continuing liability under the covenant he granted. Unless the covenant expressly provides that his liability is to cease when he no longer owns the land section 79(1) of the Law of Property Act 1925 has the effect that he remains liable for breaches committed by his successors in title. For example, if Ted covenanted with Bill that he would not use his land for industrial purposes and he subsequently sold his land to Garth, Ted would remain liable to Bill for any breach committed by Garth.

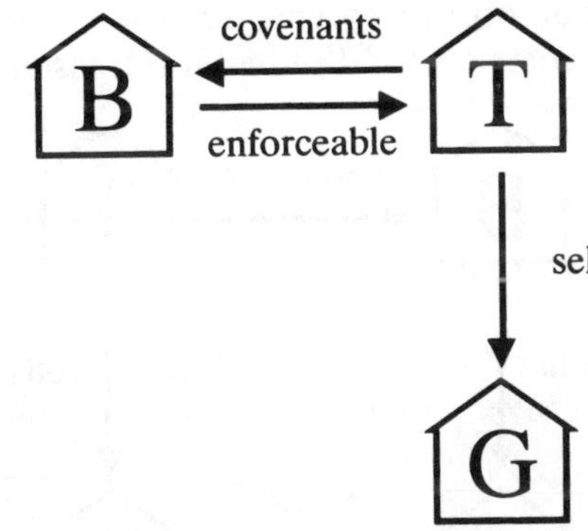

An original covenantor may protect himself to some extent from liability for breaches committed by his successors in title by ensuring that he obtains an indemnity when the land is transferred. As will be seen it is also possible that a restrictive covenant may be directly enforceable against a successor in title of the original covenantee.

[8] *Formby v. Barker* [1903] 2 Ch. 539; *London County Council v. Allen* [1914] 3 K.B. 642.

ENFORCEMENT OF FREEHOLD COVENANTS BETWEEN THE ORIGINAL COVENANTOR AND SUCCESSORS IN TITLE TO THE ORIGINAL COVENANTEE

1 Covenants capable of enforcement against the original covenantor by successors in title to the original covenantee at law

Where a covenant has been granted by the owner of freehold land in favour of a covenantee who also owns land, and the covenantee subsequently transfers his land to a third party, the question arises whether the successor in title to the original covenantee is able to enforce the covenant against the original covenantor. For example, if Ted covenants with Bill that he will: build a boundary wall around his land; not play football in his garden; and do Bill's laundry weekly, and Bill sells his land to Wayne, will Wayne be able to enforce these covenants against Ted?

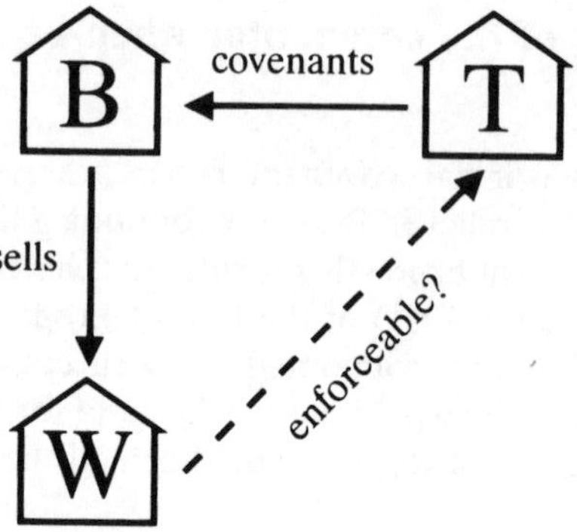

Given that the liability of an original covenantee is not terminated if he transfers his land, the same possibility arises even if Ted has also transferred his land to Garth.

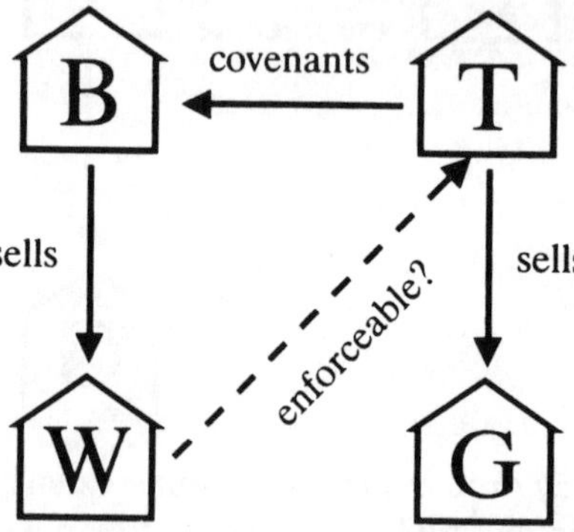

It is an entirely separate question whether in such a case the successor in title to the original covenantor is liable for his breach, and irrespective of whether he is or not, the original covenantor will be liable at law to a successor in title to the original covenantee who has taken the land with the benefit of the covenant.

2 Does a successor in title to the original covenantee enjoy the benefit of the covenant at law?

(a) Transmission of the benefit of a covenant at common law

At common law it has long been held that the benefit of a covenant is capable of passing to a successor in title to the land of the original covenantee without the need for an express assignment. This was established in *The Prior's Case*[9] in the fourteenth century. The principles were identified and applied by the Court of Appeal in *Smith and Snipes Hall Farm Ltd v. River Douglas Catchment Board*[10] where the defendants had entered into a covenant in 1938 with owners of land which was subject to flooding, including a Mrs Smith who owned land know as the Low meadows, that they would carry out works to ease the problem. Mrs Smith transferred the Low Meadows to the plaintiff's in 1940. The Court of Appeal held that as the benefit of the covenant had passed to the plaintiffs as successors in title to the original covenantee they were entitled to enforce it against the defendant original covenantors who were in breach.

(b) Requirements for the transmission of the benefit of a covenant at common law

The benefit of a covenant will only run with the land to a successor in title to the original covenantee if a number of conditions are met.
(i) The covenant touches and concerns the land: Only a covenant which touches and concerns the land will be capable of passing with the land to a successor in title of the original covenantee. As Tucker L.J. stated in *Smith and Snipes Hall Farm Ltd v. River Douglas Catchment Board*[11]:

> "It is first necessary to ascertain from the deed that the covenant is one which "touches or concerns" the land, that is, it must either affect the land as regards mode of occupation, or it must be such as *per se*, and not merely from collateral circumstances, affects the value of the land."[12]

This requirement of "touching and concerning" has already been encountered as a limitation in the context of leasehold covenants.[13] It is intended to distinguish between covenants which genuinely relate to the land itself, so that it is appropriate that they should be binding on subsequent owners, and obligations which are purely personal to the original covenantor and covenantee and which it would be inappropriate to regard as passing with the land. In *P. & A. Swift Investments v. Combined English Stores Group Plc* Lord Oliver formulated a working test for whether in any given case a covenant touches and concerns the land:

> "(1) the covenant benefits only the [freehold owner] for the time being, and if separated from the [freehold ownership] ceases to be of benefit to the covenantee; (2) the covenant affects the nature, quality mode of user or value of the

[9] (1368) Y.B. 42 Edw. 3 pl 14 fol 3A.
[10] [1949] 2 K.B. 500.
[11] *ibid.* at 506.
[12] *Derived from Congleton Corporation v. Pattison* (1808) 10 East 130, adopted by Farwell J. in *Rogers v. Hosegood* [1900] 2 Ch. 388, and approved by Lord Oliver in *P. & A. Swift Investments v. Combined English Stores Group Plc* [1989] A.C. 632.
[13] See above p. 126.

> land of the [freehold owner]; (3) the covenant is not expressed to be personal (that is to say neither given only to a specific [freehold owner] nor in respect of the obligations of a specific [other owner]; (4) the fact that a covenant is to pay a sum of money will not prevent it from touching and concerning the land so long as the three forgoing conditions are satisfied and the covenant is connected with something to be done on, or in relation to the land."[14]

Applying this test he held that the benefit of a covenant to stand as a surety of a tenant's leasehold obligations entered into with the landlord who owned the freehold reversion was a covenant which touched and concerned the land so that it was enforceable against the original covenantee by a successor in title to the freehold reversion. If a covenant touches and concerns land the benefit may pass irrespective of whether the obligation it imposes on the covenantor is positive or negative. Thus if Wayne were the successor in title to Bill, he would be able to enforce both Ted's covenant to build a boundary wall and his covenant not to play football in his garden, provided that the other requirements for the passing of the benefit were satisfied, but he would not be able to enforce the covenant to do the laundry because this does not touch and concern the land.

(ii) The original covenantee must have had a legal estate in the land benefited: The benefit of a covenant which touches and concerns the land will only be capable of passing at common law if the original covenantee enjoyed a legal estate in the land benefited by the covenant.[15]

(iii) The successor in title has acquired a legal estate in the land: The benefit of a covenant will only pass at common law to a person who acquires a legal estate in the land. In some cases it was held that the benefit of a covenant would only pass to a person who acquired an identical legal estate to that enjoyed by the original covenantee.[16] However, in *Smith and Snipes Hall Farm Ltd v. River Douglas Catchment Board*[17] the Court of Appeal held that section 78 of the Law of Property Act 1925 had the effect that the benefit of a covenant could pass to a person acquiring any legal estate in the land and not merely to a person acquiring an identical estate to that of the original covenantee. Therefore the benefit of a covenant was capable of *passing* to a person who had taken a legal lease from the freeholder who was the original covenantee.

(iv) The benefit of the covenant was intended to run with the land: The mere fact that a covenant touches and concerns land will not alone suffice to establish that the benefit passes to a successor in title of the original covenantee. In *Smith and Snipes Hall Farm Ltd v. River Douglas Catchment Board* Tucker L.J. stated that: "it must then be shown that it was the intention of the parties that the benefit thereof should run with the land."[18] In the circumstances he found that the requirement was satisfied because the deed itself "shows that its object was to improve the drainage of land liable to flooding and prevent future flooding" and that there was an "intention that the benefit of the obligation to maintain shall attach thereto into whosoever hands the land shall come."

[14] [1989] A.C. 632, 642.
[15] *Webb v. Russell* (1793) 3 T.R. 393.
[16] *Westhoughton UDC v. Wigan Coal and Iron Co Ltd* [1919] 1 Ch. 159.
[17] [1949] 2 K.B. 500.
[18] *ibid.* at 506.

However, for covenants entered into after 1925 the difficulties of establishing that a covenant was intended to run with the land have been greatly diminished by the decision of the Court of Appeal in *Federated Homes v. Mill Lodge Properties Ltd*[19] One central question raises in the case was as to the effect of section 78(1) Law of Property Act 1925, which provides that:

> "A covenant relating to any land of the covenantee shall be deemed to be made with the covenantee and his successors in title and the persons deriving title under him or them, and shall have effect as if such successors and other persons were expressed. For the purposes of this subsection in connexion with covenants restrictive of the user of land "successor's in title" shall be deemed to include the owners and occupiers for the time being of the covenantee intended to be benefited."

Brightman L.J. considered whether this section merely reduced the length of legal documents or whether it effected a statutory annexation of the benefit of covenants to land. He concluded that:

> ". . . if the condition precedent of section 78 is satisfied — that is to say, there exists a covenant which touches and concerns the land of the covenantee — that covenant runs with the land for the benefit of his successors in title, persons deriving title under him and other owners and occupiers."[20]

Thus the requirement that the benefit of a covenant must have been intended to run with the land will be satisfied by statutory annexation unless the deed expressly provides that the benefit is not intended to run with the land.

(v) The successor in title must have acquired the whole land of the original covenantee? There is some suggestion that the benefit of a covenant will not pass at law to a successor in title to the original covenantee who acquires only part of his land. In *Re Union of London and Smith's Bank Ltd's Conveyance*[21] Romer L.J. stated: "at law the benefit of a covenant could not have been assigned in pieces. It would have to be assigned as a whole or not at all." It is unclear whether this limitation has been abrogated following *Federated Homes Ltd v. Mill Lodge Properties Ltd*[22] where Brightman L.J. held that in the absence of a contrary intention the benefit of a covenant should be regarded as annexed to the whole of the land to which it relates, so that the benefit will pass to a person who acquires part of that land. The case concerned a restrictive covenant and it may be that the common law limitation still applies where the issue in equity is whether the benefit of a covenant has passed at law. However, there is no theoretical reason why the extent of annexation should differ between common law and equity.

[19] [1980] 1 W.L.R. 594.
[20] *ibid.* at 605.
[21] [1933] Ch. 611, 630.
[22] [1980] 1 W.L.R. 594. See also *Smith and Snipes Hall Farm Ltd v. River Douglas Catchment Board* [1949] 2 K.B. 500.

3 Enforcement against the original covenantor by a successor in title of the original covenantee where the benefit of the covenant has passed in equity

(a) Circumstances in which a successor in title to the original covenantee will have to rely on the equitable rules for the transmission of the benefit of a covenant

Although it has been seen that at common law the benefit of a covenant is capable of passing to successors in title to the covenantee there are some circumstances where a covenant has been granted and the common law rules will not apply to transmit the benefit of the covenant. In such cases the covenant may still be enforceable against the original covenantor in equity if the benefit of the covenant has passed by any of the recognised equitable mechanisms.

(i) Original covenantor only enjoyed an equitable interest in land: Where a covenant was granted by a covenantor who enjoyed a merely equitable interest in the land the benefit of the covenant is incapable of passing with the land of the original covenantee at common law, and only a successor in title who can show that he was entitled to the benefit of the covenant in equity will be capable of enforcing the covenant against the original covenantee. Clearly in such a case the covenant is not a covenant affecting freehold land.

(ii) Original covenantee only enjoyed an equitable interest in land: A similar consequence will follow if the original covenantee enjoyed a merely equitable interest in land. A successor in title will only be able to enforce the covenant against the original covenantor if the benefit has passed in equity.[23]

(iii) An ineffective express assignment: If the successor in title to the original covenantee claims to be entitled to the benefit of the covenant by way of an express assignment, he will have to rely on equity if the assignment does not comply with section 136 of the Law of Property Act 1925.

(iv) Where the original covenantee conveyed only part of his land to a successor in title: If it remains the case that at common law the benefit of a covenant only passes to a successor in title who acquires the whole of the land benefited, a successor in title to only part of the land of the original covenantee will have to rely on the equitable rules for the passing of benefit. In equity the benefit of a covenant is capable of passing to a successor in title to only part of the dominant tenement, who will then be able o enforce it against the original covenantee.

(b) Equitable mechanisms for passing the benefit of a covenant

The benefit of a covenant may pass in equity to a successor in title of the original covenantee by annexation, assignment or under a scheme of development. These mechanisms are examined in detail below in the context of restrictive covenants, but they are equally applicable where a successor in title seeks to enforce covenants, whether positive or negative, against the original covenantor and he cannot claim to be entitled to the benefit of the covenant at law.

[23] *Fairclough v. Marshall* (1878) 4 Ex.D 37; *Rogers v. Hosegood* [1900] 2 Ch. 388.

ENFORCEMENT OF FREEHOLD COVENANTS AGAINST SUCCESSORS IN TITLE TO THE ORIGINAL COVENANTOR AT LAW

1 Covenants incapable of enforcement against a successor in title to the original covenantor at law

In the preceding section it has been seen how the benefit of a covenant which touches and concerns land can pass with the land to which it is annexed, so that a successor in title to the original covenantee is able to enforce it against the original covenantor. Although it might be thought appropriate that a covenant which touches and concerns the land should also be capable of being enforced against a successor in title to the original covenantor this is impossible at common law because of the rule that the burden of a covenant is incapable of passing with the land. This absolute inability of the burden of a covenant to pass at common law was recognised by the Court of Appeal in *Austerberry v. Corporation of Oldham*.[24] The plaintiffs and defendants were the successors in title of the original covenantee and covenantor of a covenant which contained an obligation to keep a road in good repair. The Court held that the benefit of the covenant had not passed to the plaintiff because it did not touch and concern the land, thus rendering it unenforceable by him. However, Lindley L.J. also made clear that the burden had not passed to the defendant:

> "But it strikes me, I confess, that there is a still more formidable objection as regards the burden. Does the burden of this covenant run with the land so as to bind the defendants? . . . I am not prepared to say that any covenant which imposes a burden upon land does run with the land, unless the covenant does, upon its true construction, amount to either a grant of an easement, or a rent-charge, or some other estate or interest in the land . . . I am not aware of any other case which either shews, or appears to shew, that a burden such as this can be annexed to land by a mere covenant, such as we have got here; and in the absence of authority it appears to me that we shall be perfectly warranted in saying that the burden of this covenant does not run with the land."[25]

The inability of the burden of covenants to be annexed to land and pass at common law was re-affirmed by the House of Lords in the more recent case of *Rhone v. Stephens*,[26] where the issue was whether a covenant to maintain the condition of a roof was capable of binding a successor in title to the original covenantor. Lord Templeman explained why the House was unwilling to remove the limitation:

> "In these circumstances your lordships were invited to overrule the decision of the Court of Appeal in the *Austerberry* case. To do so would destroy the distinction between law and equity . . . it is plain from the articles, reports and papers to which we were referred that judicial legislation to overrule the

[24] (1885) 29 Ch.D. 750.
[25] *ibid.* at 781–783.
[26] [1994] 2 A.C. 310.

> *Austerberry* case would create a number of difficulties, anomalies and uncertainties and affect the rights and liabilities of people who have for over 100 years bought and sold land in the knowledge, imparted at an elementary stage to every student of the law of real property, that positive covenants, affecting freehold land are not directly enforceable except against the original covenantee."[27]

As has been noted, in the context of the passing of the benefit of a covenant, section 78 of the Law of Property Act 1925 has been construed so that the benefit of a covenant which touches and concerns land is annexed to the land in the absence of a contrary indication. Section 79(1) is a parallel provision in relation to the burden of covenants, which provides:

> "A covenant relating to any land of a covenantor or capable of being bound by him, shall, unless a contrary intention is expressed, be deemed to be made by the covenantor on behalf of himself, his successors in title and the persons deriving title under him or them, and subject as aforesaid, shall have effect as if such successors and other persons were expressed."

The House of Lords were unwilling to construe this section in a similar manner and find that it affected a statutory annexation of the burden of covenant to the land of the covenantor. Lord Templeman referred to the cases holding that section 78 effected a statutory annexation of the benefit of covenants[28] and concluded: "Without casting any doubt on those long standing decisions I do not consider that it follows that section 79 of the act of 1925 had the corresponding effect of making the burden of positive covenants run with the land."[29] Therefore, if Ted covenants with Bill that he will: build a boundary wall around his land; not play football in his garden; and do Bill's laundry weekly, and Ted sells his land to Garth, Bill will be unable to enforce any of the covenants against Garth in law since the burden is incapable of passing with the land.

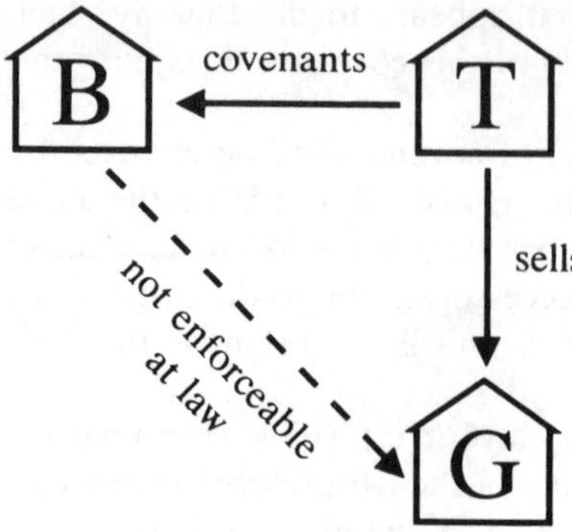

[27] *ibid.* at 321.
[28] *Smith and Snipe's Hall Farm Ltd v. River Douglas Catchment Board* [1949] 2 K.B. 500; *Williams v. Unit Construction Co. Ltd* (1955) 19 Conv. (N.S.) 262; *Federated Homes v. Mill Lodge Properties Ltd* [1980] 1 W.L.R. 594, 605–606.
[29] [1994] 2 A.C. 310, 322. See also: *Jones v. Price* [1965] 2 Q.B. 618; *Sefton v. Tophams Ltd* [1967] 1 A.C. 50.

It should be remembered that the mere fact that the covenants cannot be enforced against Garth does not mean that Bill is without remedies at all. Ted remains liable to him as the original covenantor and will be held accountable even for breaches committed by Garth. Obviously the same limitations will apply if there is a successor in title to the original covenantee who enjoys the benefit of the covenants which touch and concern the land. If Ted has transferred his land to Garth, and Bill has transferred his land to Wayne, Wayne will enjoy the benefit of the covenants which touch and concern the land. As the burden of a covenant is incapable of passing with the land at law Wayne will be unable to enforce any covenants against Garth at law, but he will be able to seek remedies against Ted as the original covenantor for any breach of the covenants which touch and concern the land.

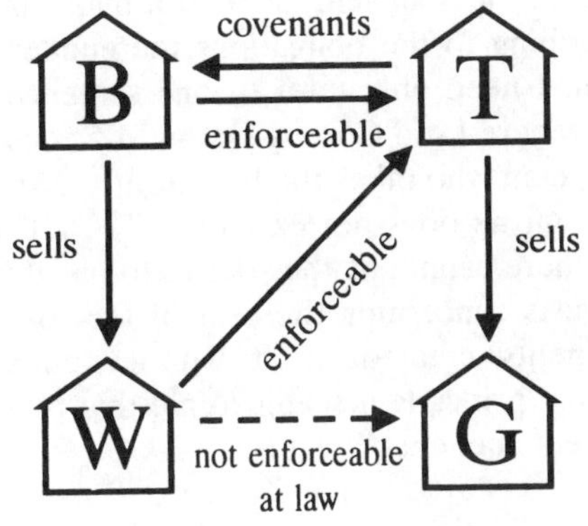

2 Circumstances in which a covenant may be enforceable against a successor in title to the original covenantor

Despite the general rule that the burden of covenants are incapable of passing at law there are some circumstances in which, either directly or indirectly, such enforceability may be achieved.

(a) Enforceability of restrictive covenants in equity

The absolute inability of the burden of a covenant to pass with land is a limitation arising under the common law. However equity has intervened so that the burden of a covenant which is negative, or restrictive, in nature is capable of binding a successor in title to the original covenantor. The principles governing the enforceability of restrictive covenants in equity are examined in detail below. The availability of such equitable enforceability means that the other methods by which covenants can be rendered enforceable against a successor in title to the original covenantor are of most importance in the context of positive covenants where there is no possibility at law or in equity of the burden passing with the land.

(b) Enforceability of positive covenants on the basis of "mutual benefit and burden"

It has been suggested that where a covenant confers both benefits and burden on the covenantor a successor in title cannot take the land with the benefit conferred without also being subject to the burden imposed. In *Halsall v. Brizell*[30] the purchasers of building plots covenanted that they would contribute to the cost of the repairs and maintenance of the sewers and roads "for the common use convenience and advantage of the owners for the time being" of the plots. Upjohn J. held that although this covenant was prima facie unenforceable against a successor in title to one of the original covenantors because the burden of a positive covenant was incapable of passing with the land, the successors in title could not take advantage of the right of way conferred in the same covenant without also being subject to the burden:

> "But it is conceded that it is ancient law that a man cannot take benefit under a deed without subscribing to the obligations thereunder. If authority is required for that proposition, I need only refer to one sentence during the argument in *Elliston v. Reacher*[31] where Lord Cozens-Hardy M.R. observed: "It is laid down in Co. Litt 230b that a man who takes the benefit of a deed is bound by a condition contained in it, though he does not execute it." . . . Therefore, it seems to me, that the defendants here cannot, if they desire to use this house, as they do, take advantage of the trusts concerning the user of the roads contained in the deed and the other benefits created by it without undertaking the obligations thereunder. Upon that principle it seems to me that they are bound by this deed, if they desire to take its benefits."[32]

However, despite the identification of a general doctrine of benefit and burden by Megarry V.-C. in *Tito v. Wadell (No. 2)*[33] the exact scope of the operation of the principle is in doubt. The cases from which it is drawn are concerned with enforceability between the original parties to a covenant and not to successors in title. In *Rhone v. Stephens*[34] Lord Templeman accepted that the decision in *Halsall v. Brizell* had been correct, but considered that the doctrine had no application where a successor in title had no real choice whether to decide to forgo the benefits conferred by the covenant which also imposed obligations upon him:

> ". . . it does not follow that any condition can be rendered enforceable by attaching it to a right nor does it follow that every burden imposed by a conveyance may be enforced by depriving the convenantor's successor in title of every benefit which he enjoyed thereunder. The conditions must be relevant to the exercise of the right. In *Halsall v. Brizell* there were reciprocal benefits and burdens enjoyed by the users of the roads and sewers. In the present case [the conveyance] imposes reciprocal benefits and burdens of support but clause 3

[30] [1957] Ch. 169.
[31] [1908] 2 Ch. 665, 669.
[32] See also: *Hopgood v. Brown* [1955] 1 W.L.R. 213; *Ives Investments Ltd v. High* [1967] 2 Q.B. 379; *Montague v. Long* (1972) 24 P. & C.R. 240.
[33] [1977] Ch. 106.
[34] [1994] 2 A.C. 310.

which imposed an obligation to repair the roof is an independent provision. In *Halsall v. Brizell* the defendant could, at least in theory, choose between enjoying the right and paying his proportion of the cost or alternatively giving up the right and saving his money. In the present case the owners . . . could not in theory or in practice be deprived of the benefit of the mutual rights of support if they failed to repair the roof."[35]

(c) Indirect enforceability of positive covenants by means of a right of re-entry

Indirect enforceability of positive covenants may be achieved if the covenantee subjects the land to a right of re-entry in the event of breach. Since the right of re-entry is a legal interest in the land it is capable of binding successors in title.[36] However, such a mechanism may not secure absolute enforceability since the court has the jurisdiction to relieve the estate owner from forfeiture in the even of breach.

(d) Indirect enforceability by means of an estate rentcharge

Although in general the Rentcharges Act 1977 prevents the creation of new rent charges, section 1(4)(a) provides that it is possible to create a new "estate rentcharge," which means a rentcharge created for the purpose of "making covenants to be performed by the owner of the land affected by the rentcharge enforceable by the rent owner for the time being of the land." A right of re-entry is then annexed to the rentcharge, with the consequence that the estate can be forfeited in the event of breach of the covenant.

(e) Statutory enforceability following enlargement of a leasehold estate into freehold ownership

It has already been noted that in the case of leasehold interests the burden of positive covenants is capable of passing with the land by means of the doctrine of privity of estate. Some statutory provisions allowing the conversion of long leases into freehold ownership would seem to have the effect that any covenants of the lease are binding on the land as if it had not been converted.[37]

ENFORCEMENT OF RESTRICTIVE COVENANTS IN EQUITY

1 Enforceability of restrictive covenants against successors in title to the original covenantor in equity

(a) Development of restrictive covenants in equity

Whereas the common law provided no general means by which the burden of a covenant was capable of passing with land, equity developed a doctrine that the burden of negative covenants was capable of passing so as to burden the land in the hands of a

[35] *ibid.* at 322–323.
[36] See: *Shiloh Spinners v. Harding* [1973] A.C. 691.
[37] Law of Property Act 1925, s.153; Leasehold Reform Act 1967, s.8(3).

successor in title to the original covenantee. This doctrine originated in *Tulk v. Moxhay*[38] where it was held that the successor in title to a piece of land in Leicester Square who had covenanted to keep it free from building development was bound to observe the covenant because he had acquired the land with notice of its existence. The judgements in *Tulk v. Moxhay* made no distinction between positive and negative covenants, and the rationale for enforcement seems simply to be founded on the fact of notice. However, subsequent cases fine-tuned both the scope of the doctrine and the justification for it.[39] The doctrine which was the culmination of this judicial development was explained by Jessel M.R. in *London and South Western Railway Co. v. Gomm*[40]:

> "The doctrine of [*Tulk v. Moxhay*] . . . appears to me to be either an extension in equity of the doctrine of *Spencer's Case* to another line of cases, or else an extension in equity of the doctrine of negative easements; . . . The covenant in *Tulk v. Moxhay* was affirmative in its terms, but was held by the court to imply a negative. Where there is a negative covenant expressed or implied . . . the court intervenes on one or other of the above grounds. This is an equitable doctrine, establishing an exception to the rules of common law which did not treat such a covenant as running with the land, and it does not matter whether it proceeds on an analogy to a covenant running with the land or an analogy to an easement."

Thus in equity it is possible for the burden of a negative covenant to pass with the land. Therefore, if Ted covenants with Bill that he will: build a boundary wall around his land; not play football in his garden; and do Bill's laundry weekly, and Ted sells his land to Garth, Bill may be able to enforce the negative covenants against Garth in equity, provided that the relevant criteria are satisfied.

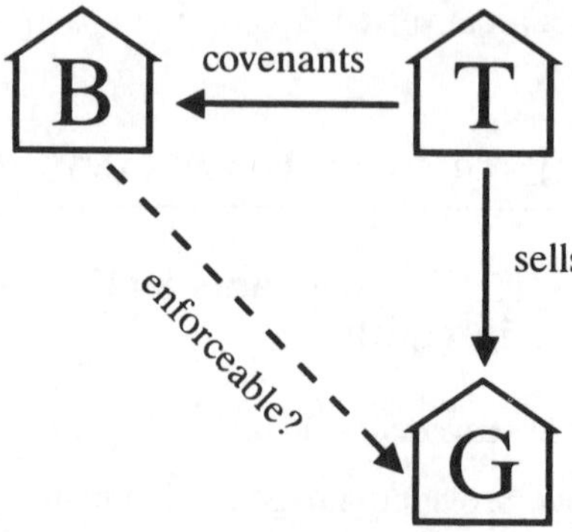

[38] (1848) 2 Ph. 774.
[39] See: *Morland v. Cook* (1868) L.R. 6 Eq. 252; *Cooke v. Chilcott* (1876) 3 Ch.D. 694; *Haywood v. Brunswick Permanent Benefit Building Society* (1881) 8 Q.B.D. 403; *London County Council v. Allen* [1914] 3 K.B. 642; (1982) 98 L.Q.R. 279 (Gardner).
[40] (1882) 20 Ch.D. 562.

Similarly a negative covenant may be enforced by a successor in title to the original covenantee against a successor in title to the original covenantor. If Ted has transferred his land to Garth, and Bill has transferred his land to Wayne, Wayne will enjoy the benefit of the covenants which touch and concern the land. He may be able to enforce the negative covenant against Garth in equity.

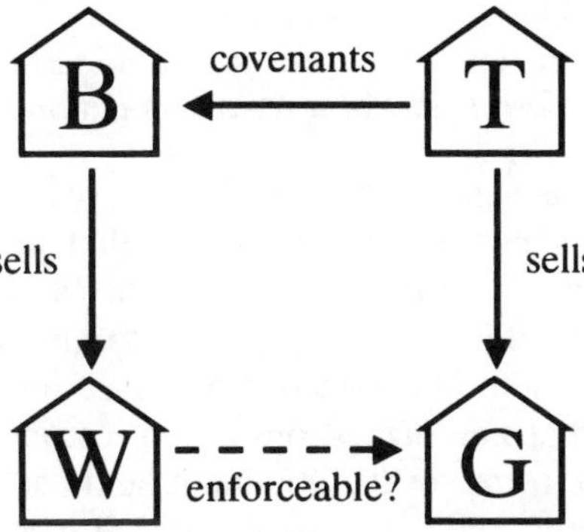

A restrictive covenant is capable not only of binding a successor in title to the freehold of the land owned by the original covenantor, but also anyone acquiring a lesser interests therein, for example a tenant under a lease[41] or a licensee.[42]

(b) Rationale for the enforcement of restrictive covenants in equity

Prior to the widespread intervention of the state to control the development of land by planning regulations restrictive covenants served an important function as a means by which private owners and developers of land could effectively ensure that land was not utilised in a manner they considered inappropriate or disadvantageous to themselves. For example, the vendor who sold part of his land for development might wish to ensure that only a single dwelling house was build on the land sold, with the prime objective of protecting the value and amenity of the land that he retained. Similarly, the developer of an area of residential housing might wish to ensure that none of the properties could be used for other than residential purposes, thus increasing the value and saleability of the properties built. The rationale for allowing the burden of such covenants to pass in equity, since they could not at common law, was that it would be unjust for a person to acquire land knowing that it was subject to such a limitation to proceed to ignore it. For example the purchaser of a house subject to a restriction that it was not to be used for business purposes might have acquired it at a far lower price than would have been payable in the absence of such a limitation. It would be unconscionable for him to take advantage of the benefit of the reduced price yet to deny the detriment of the restriction. As Lord Cottenham L.C. stated in *Tulk v. Moxhay*[43]:

> "It is said that, the covenant being one which does not run with the land, this Court cannot enforce it; but the question is, not whether the covenant runs with

[41] *Wilson v. Hart* (1866) L.R. 1 ChApp 463; *Nicoll v. Fenning* (1881) 19 Ch.D. 258.
[42] *Mander v. Falcke* [1891] 2 Ch. 554.
[43] (1848) 2 Ph. 774, 777.

the land, but whether a party shall be permitted to use the land in a manner inconsistent with the contract entered into by his vendor, and with notice of which he purchased. Of course the price would be affected by the covenant, and nothing could be more inequitable than that the original purchaser should be able to sell the property the next day for a greater price, in consideration of the assignee being allowed to escape from he liability which he had himself undertaken."

(c) Requirements for the enforceability of a restrictive covenant in equity

(i) Person entitled to the benefit of the covenant: A restrictive covenant will only be enforceable in equity by a person who can show that he is entitled to the benefit thereof. Clearly the original covenantee will be entitled to the benefit, but a successor in title will only be so entitled if the benefit passed to him when he acquired the land. The means by which the benefit of a covenant may pass in equity are generally slightly wider than at law.[44] Despite some suggestions that a restrictive covenant is enforceable irrespective of whether the owner of the dominant land has obtained the benefit of the covenant at law[45] or in equity the better view is that it can only be enforced against a successor in title to the original covenantor who has taken the servient land subject to the burden by a person who enjoys the benefit according to the equitable rules.[46]
(ii) Person subject to the burden of the covenant: A restrictive covenant can only be enforced against someone who owns the land affected subject to the burden of the covenant. In the case of successors in title to the original covenantor not only must the burden have been capable of passing with the land in equity, but the successor in title must have taken the land subject to the restrictive covenant as an equitable interest in the land according to the appropriate priority rules. These differ depending on whether the land is registered or unregistered. If the successor in title acquires the land in circumstances in which he takes free form the restrictive covenant it will be unenforceable against him.

2 Servient owner subject to the burden of the restrictive covenant in equity

(a) Covenant must be negative

(i) Recent reassertion of the limitation: Only the burden of a covenant which is negative in nature is capable of passing with land in equity. As has been seen this means that there is no possibility of the passing of the burden of positive covenants. This restriction was applied in *Rhone v. Stephens*[47] where Lord Templeman stated:

[44] See above p. 333.
[45] *Rogers v. Hosegood* [1900] 2 Ch. 388.
[46] *Re Union of London and Smith's Bank Ltd's Conveyance* [1933] Ch. 610, 630.
[47] [1994] 2 A.C. 310.

> "Equity can . . . prevent or punish the breach of a negative covenant which restricts the user of land or the exercise of other rights in connection with land. Restrictive covenants deprive an owner of a right which he could otherwise exercise. Equity cannot compel an owner to comply with a positive covenant entered into by his predecessors in title without flatly contradicting the common law rule that a person cannot be made liable upon a contract unless he was a party to it. Enforcement of a positive covenant lies in contract; a positive covenant compels an owner to exercise his rights. Enforcement of a negative covenant lies in property; a negative covenant deprives the owner of a right over property."

Therefore a covenant entered into in 1960 when a house was divided into two, whereby the owner who retained part covenanted to maintain the roof in a wind and watertight condition was unenforceable by a successor in title to the original purchaser of the part of the house which was benefited by the covenant.

(ii) A question of substance: Whether a particular obligation imposed by a covenant is positive or negative is a matter of substance rather than of form. For example, an obligation not to allow a roof to fall into disrepair is as much a positive covenant as that in *Rhone v. Stephens* despite the fact that it is phrased in a negative manner. In *Haywood v. Brunswick Permanent Benefit Building Society*[48] Cotton L.J. indicated hat a covenant to repair was positive because it could only be enforced "by making the owner put his hand into his pocket." Thus a simple test for determining if a covenant is negative or positive is whether fulfilment of the obligation would necessitate expenditure by the owner.

(b) Covenant must accommodate the dominant land

Since the equitable doctrine of restrictive covenants converts what is essentially a contractual right into a property right in the nature of a negative easement analogies can be drawn with the requirements of easements as rights in land.[49] When an equitable restrictive covenant is created the land of the original covenantee becomes a dominant tenement and the land of the original covenantor a servient tenement. The restrictive covenant is the inverse of an easement. Whereas an easement confers a right on the dominant owner to exercise some form of limited user over the servient land, a restrictive covenant entitles the dominant owner to insist that the servient owner restrains from exercising some otherwise legitimate user of his land. Although all covenants may be enforceable between the original parties in contract, only such covenants as can be said to accommodate the dominant tenement become proprietary interests capable of binding successors in title. A negative covenant can be said to be a restrictive covenant in equity which accommodates the dominant tenement if the following criteria are fulfilled:

(i) The original covenantee must have owned land to be benefited at the time the covenant was granted: A restrictive covenant will only accommodate a dominant tenement if the original covenantee was the owner of land to be benefited at the date when the covenant was granted.[50] Clearly this will be impossible if he owned no land at

[48] (1881) 9 Ch.D. 403, 409.
[49] See above Chap. 9.
[50] *Application of Fox* (1981) 2 BPR 9310.

that date. For example, in *London County Council v. Allen*[51] it was held that a covenant entered into by the owner of land that he would not build on a plot across the end of a proposed street was unenforceable against a successor in title by the council, who were the covenantees, as they did not own any land at the time that the covenant was granted. Buckley L.J. stated that the doctrine of *Tulk v. Moxhay* required the ownership of land by the covenantee as a pre-condition of enforceability of a restrictive covenant in equity against a successor in title to the covenantor:

> "The doctrine is that a covenant not running with the land, but being a negative covenant entered into by an owner of land with an adjoining owner, binds the land in equity and is enforceable against a derivative owner taking with notice. The doctrine ceases to be applicable when the person seeking to enforce the covenant against the derivative owner has no land to be protected by the negative covenant. The fact of notice is in that case irrelevant."[52]

Although a covenant granted in gross is incapable of creating a restrictive covenant, it is not a pre-requisite in equity that the covenantee must have owned the freehold of the dominant land. A restrictive covenant can be enforced in favour of the holder of the freehold reversion of land[53] or a mortgagee.[54] Once the original covenantee has parted with land he can no longer enforce a restrictive covenant in equity against the servient owner, although he may continue to enjoy purely contractual remedies. Statute has intervened so that many bodies, such as local authorities, are entitled to enforce restrictive covenants even though they do not own land benefited.

(ii) The dominant tenement enjoyed sufficient physical proximity with the servient tenement: Just as an easement will only accommodate the dominant land if there is sufficient physical proximity with the servient tenement to justify finding that the land itself is benefited, a restrictive covenant will only be created if here is sufficient proximity between the dominant and servient land. In *London County Council v. Allen* Buckley L.J. spoke of adjoining land, but contiguity is not strictly necessary. In *Kelly v. Barrett*[55] Pollock M.R. indicated that land at Clapham would be too remote to carry a right to enforce a covenant restrictive of the use of land at Hampstead.

(iii) The original parties to the covenant must have intended the burden to run with the land: A negative covenant will not generate a restrictive covenant in equity unless it can be shown that the original parties intended the burden of the covenant to run with the land. This intention may be made clear in the deed, but this is not essential as section 79(1) of the Law of Property Act 1925 has the effect that the burden of a negative covenant will be taken as intended to run with the land unless the parties indicated a contrary intention[56] in the deed. Section 79(1) is expressly limited in scope of application to covenants "relating to land" which is the direct equivalent of the familiar concept of covenants which touch and concern the land.

[51] [1914] 3 K.B. 642.
[52] *ibid.* at 654–655.
[53] *Hall v. Ewin* (1988) 37 Ch.D. 74.
[54] *Regent Oil Co. Ltd v. J. A. Gregory (Hatch End) Ltd* [1966] Ch. 402.
[55] [1924] 2 Ch. 379.
[56] See *Re Royal Victoria Pavilion, Ramsgate* [1961] Ch. 581, where Pennycuick J. held that the parties had demonstrated a counter intention.

(c) Servient tenement must have been acquired subject to the burden of the covenant

The mere fact that a covenant is a restrictive covenant capable of passing with the land in equity does not mean that a person acquiring the servient land, or an interest in the servient land, will necessarily take their interest subject to it. This will depend upon the rules of priority regulating the land in question and whether they are entitled to take free from the burden of the restrictive covenant.

(i) Servient tenement is registered land: If the servient land is registered then a restrictive covenant ranks as a minor interest.[57] If it has not been protected against the title of the servient land by entry of a notice or caution on the register, a person who purchases a legal estate of the servient land will take his interest free from the unprotected restrictive covenant,[58] and the owner of the dominant land will be incapable of enforcing it against him.

(ii) Servient tenement is unregistered land: Where the servient tenement is unregistered the applicable priority rules depend upon when the covenant was created. Restrictive covenants created after January 1, 1926 are Class D(ii) Land Charges[59] and if not properly protected on the Land Charges Register will be rendered void as against a purchaser of a legal estate in the land, irrespective of whether the purchaser had notice of the existence of the covenant.[60] In the case of restrictive covenants created before January 1, 1926 questions of priority are determined by the doctrine of notice,[61] so that a purchaser of a legal estate in the land without notice of the existence of the restrictive covenant will take their interest in the land free from it.

3 Dominant owner entitled to the benefit of the restrictive covenant

(a) Benefit enjoyed by the original covenantee

In order for a restrictive covenant to be enforceable the dominant land must be owned by someone entitled to the benefit of the covenant. Clearly the original covenantee will be entitled to the benefit of the covenant and will therefore be able to enforce a restrictive covenant against a successor in title to the original covenantor who has acquired the servient land subject to the burden of the covenant. More complex questions arise where the dominant land has also been transferred, so that the person with an interest in enforcing the restrictive covenant is a successor in title to the original covenantee.

(b) Benefit of the covenant annexed to the dominant tenement

(i) Meaning of annexation: When the benefit of a covenant is annexed to the land it is in effect attached to the dominant tenement so that it passes with the land to any successors in title without the need for an express assignment. Equitable annexation parallels the equivalent common law rules in *Smith and Snipes Hall Farm Ltd v. River*

[57] See Chap. 15 below.
[58] Land Registration Act 1925, s.20.
[59] Land Charges Act 1972, s.2(5)(ii).
[60] Land Charges Act 1972, s.4(6).
[61] See below p. 570.

Douglas Catchment Board.[62] Since annexation of the benefit of a covenant to the covenantee's land occurs when the covenant is made, there can be no such annexation if at that date the covenantee was not the owner of land capable of being benefited by the covenant. Similarly annexation can only occur of a covenant which is for the benefit of the land, so that only a covenant which satisfies the familiar requirement of touching and concerning the land is capable of being annexed to it. Ultimately annexation will only occur if the parties to the original covenant intended the benefit to be annexed to the land. Historically this intention could either be expressed in the covenant itself or implied. More recently section 78 of the Law of Property Act 1925 has been construed so that annexation is effected by statute in the absence of a counter intention by the parties. This means that in the vast majority of cases it will be relatively easy to establish annexation in equity.

(ii) Express annexation: It is ultimately a question of construction[63] whether a deed expressly annexes the benefit of a covenant to the covenantees land. An intention to annex will be found if the land to be benefited is identified in the covenant, and it is stated to be for the "benefit of the land" or for the owners of the land in their capacity as such. In *Rogers v. Hosegood*[64] a covenant was granted to covenantees who enjoyed an interest in the land benefited as mortgagees, that no more than one house would be built on the land. The deed stated that the covenant was to "enure to the benefit of the [mortgagees] their heirs, and assigns and others claiming under them to all or any of their lands adjoining or near to the premises." The Court of Appeal upheld the decision of Farwell J. that this evidenced an intention that the benefit of the covenant was annexed to the land of the covenantee. In contrast, it seems that the mere fact that a covenant is made with the covenantee and his "heirs, executors, administrators and assigns" will be insufficient to effect annexation if no mention is made of the land to be benefited.[65]

(ii) Implied annexation: *Marten v. Flight Refuelling Ltd*[66] is authority that an intention to annex can be implied from the circumstances surrounding the grant of a covenant even though there is no such intention in the deed itself. The case concerned a covenant granted by the purchaser of part of an estate that the land would be used solely for agricultural purposes, and which was expressed to be made with the covenantee and "its successors in title." Although there was no express statement that the covenant was intended to benefit the land Wilberforce J. held that "an intention to benefit may be found from surrounding or attending circumstances."[67] He considered the fact that the land had formed part of a larger estate which had been used exclusively for agricultural purposes and that the purchaser had been a tenant of the farm, as had his father before him, and concluded that the covenant was taken to benefit the land of the vendors who owned the remainder of the estate. There has been a large measure of academic criticism of the decision, which has cast doubt on whether

[62] [1949] 2 K.B. 500.
[63] See: *Chambers v. Randall* [1923] 1 Ch. 149, 155.
[64] [1900] 2 Ch. 388.
[65] *Renals v. Cowlishaw* (1878) 9 Ch.D. 125; *Reid v. Bickerstaff* [1909] 2 Ch. 305; *Ives v. Brown* [1919] 2 Ch. 314; *Sainsbury Plc v. Enfield LBC* [1989] 1 W.L.R. 591.
[66] [1962] Ch. 115.
[67] *ibid.* at 132.

it truly establishes the possibility of an implied annexation because the plaintiffs were the original covenantees.[68] In *Sainsbury Plc v. Enfield LBC*[69] Morrit J. rejected the proposition that an intention to benefit land could be inferred from the surrounding circumstances of a conveyance alone, but accepted that such circumstances might be relevant to construing the effect of a conveyance:

> "the intention must be manifested in the conveyance in which the covenant was contained when construed in the light of the surrounding circumstances, including any necessary implication in the conveyance from those surrounding circumstances."[70]

(iv) Statutory annexation by section 78(1) Law of Property Act 1925: As has been noted above in the context of the passing of the benefit of covenants at law, the position with regard to covenants entered after 1925[71] is now much simplified as a result of the interpretation of section 78(1) of the Law of Property Act 1925 adopted by the Court of Appeal in *Federated Homes v. Mill Lodge Properties*.[72] Despite repetition, for the sake of convenience this section provides:

> "A covenant relating to any land of the covenantee shall be deemed to be made with the covenantee and his successors in title and the persons deriving title under him or them, and shall have effect as if such successors and other persons were expressed.
>
> For the purposes of this subsection in connexion with covenants restrictive of the user of land "successors in title" shall be deemed to include the owners and occupiers for the time being of the land of the covenantee intended to be benefited."

Federated Homes v. Mill Lodge Properties concerned four equal sized areas of land, the red, green, pink and blue land, originally owned by a single developer. The blue land was sold to the defendant who entered into a covenant that they would not build more than 300 houses on it. The plaintiff subsequently purchased the green land and there was an express assignment of the benefit of the covenant and later acquired the red land but without any express assignment. On discovering that the defendants were proposing to build an additional 32 houses on the blue land the plaintiffs sought to enforce the covenant against them and restrain the proposed breach. The Court of Appeal held that the benefit of the covenant had passed with the green land by means of a chain of assignments, but the central question was whether the benefit had passed with the red land. Mills Q.C., sitting as a deputy High Court judge, held that it had not been annexed because there was no express annexation in the conveyance granting

[68] (1968) 84 L.Q.R. 22 (Baker); (1972) 36 Conv. 20 (Ryder). See however, (1972B) C.L.J. 151 (Wade) in support.
[69] [1989] 1 W.L.R. 590.
[70] *ibid.* at 595.
[71] Section 78(1) Law no application to covenants entered before January 1, 1996 and the its predecessor, section 58 of the Conveyancing Act 1881, contains different language which has been held not to effect automatic annexation: *J. Sainsbury Plc v. Enfield LBC* [1989] 1 W.L.R. 590.
[72] [1980] 1 W.L.R. 594.

the covenant and no such intention could be implied from the circumstances. However the Court of Appeal held that the language of the conveyance was sufficient to amount to an express annexation, but that in any even the benefit of the covenant had been annexed to the land by operation of section 78 of the Law of Property Act 1925. Brightman L.J. explained that section 78 was not merely intended to facilitate a short-cut in the drafting of conveyances, but that it has the effect that any covenant relating to land must be read as if made with the covenantor and his successors in title, and the persons deriving title under it or them, including the owners and occupiers for the time being of the covenantee's land, and that therefore such a covenant must be regarded as annexed to the land.[73] In effect section 78 implies into the language of the covenant words which would inevitably amount to an express annexation. Brightman L.J. stated that:

> "If, as the language of section 78 implies, a covenant relating to land which is restrictive of the user thereof is enforceable at the suit of (1) a successor in title of the covenantee, (2) a person deriving title under the covenantee or under his successors in title, and (3) the owner of occupier of the land intended to be benefited by the covenant, it must, in my view, follow that the covenant runs with the land, because *ex hypothesi* every successor in title to the land, every derivative proprietor of the land and every other owner and occupier has a right by statute to the covenant. in other words, if the condition precedent of section 78 is satisfied — that is to say, there exists a covenant which touches and concerns the land of the covenantee — that covenant runs with the land for the benefit of his successors in title, persons deriving title under him or them and other owners or occupiers."[74]

As Brightman L.J. noted, the operation of section 78 is limited to such covenants as are "relating to land," a requirement identical to the traditional and familiar concept of touching and concerning. A further limitation to the operation of section 78 is that its effect may be excluded by express counter intention. This was recognised in *Roake v. Chadha.*[75] The case concerned a covenant entered into in 1934 that no more than one house would be built on a plot of land which stated that "this covenant shall not enure for the benefit of any owner or subsequent purchaser of any part of the . . . estate unless the benefit of this covenant shall be expressly assigned." Judge Paul Baker Q.C. held that even where section 78 operates so that a covenant is deemed to be made with the successors in title of the covenantee, "one still has to construe the covenant as a whole to see whether the benefit of the covenant is annexed." He held that although annexation could be readily inferred in such cases as *Federated Homes v. Mill Lodge Properties* where there was no qualification to the covenant, the fact that the covenant in question expressly stated that it was not to be binding on successors in title meant that as a whole its true effect could not be to annex the covenant to the land. However, where a covenant does touch and concern, and there is no counter intention,

[73] For criticism see: (1981) 97 L.Q.R. 32; (1982) 98 L.Q.R. 202 (Newson); (1982) 2 Legal Studies 53 (Hurst); [1985] Conv. 177 (Todd).
[74] *ibid.* at 605.
[75] [1984] 1 W.L.R. 40.

the effect of section 78 as interpreted in *Federated Homes* is very wide ranging and renders many of the formerly important mechanisms for passing the benefit of covenants at law and in equity much less relevant in practice. Its impact in the context of restrictive covenants is even more wide ranging because of the inclusion of mere occupiers within its scope, so that a restrictive covenant may be enforced by a mere licensee of the dominant tenement.

(v) Ineffective annexation to the dominant tenement: It seems that a purported annexation of the benefit of a covenant will be ineffective if the dominant tenement is so large that the covenant could not possibly be of benefit to the majority of the land. This problem occurred in *Re Ballard's Conveyance*,[76] where a covenant was entered by the purchaser of the servient tenement not to erect buildings other than dwelling-houses in favour of the "Childwick Estate of Sir John Blundell Maple," which comprised some 1700 acres. Clauson J. held that although the covenant touched and concerned "some comparatively small portion of the land to which it has been sought to annex it" it failed to touch and concern the larger part of the dominant tenement. He concluded that there was no authority justifying him severing the covenant and treating it as annexed only to "such part of the land as is touched and concerned with it" and that therefore "I must hold that the attempted annexation has failed and that the covenant has not been effectively annexed to the land and does not run with it."[77] However in more recent cases the size of he dominant tenement does not seem to have presented an insuperable barrier to annexation and it is a matter of evidence in each case whether it can be established that the covenant benefited the whole of the dominant land. In *Earl of Leicester v. Wells-Next-the-Sea UDC*[78] Plowman J. held that a covenant affecting a servient tenement of 19 acres was annexed to a dominant tenement of 32,000 acres on the basis of evidence by the managing agent that the covenant afforded great benefit and protection to the estate as a whole, as well as to particular parts adjacent to the servient land.[79] Perhaps more significantly the servient owners had not attempted to counter this evidence.

(v) Problems of annexation where the dominant land is subsequently divided: One particular problem which has arisen in the context of annexation is whether the benefit of a covenant passes to a successor in title who acquires only part of the dominant land to which the benefit was annexed. For example, if Ted covenanted with Bill and Bill sold and conveyed half of his land to Wayne, would Wayne enjoy the benefit of the covenant so that he could enforce it against Ted? As has been noted above[80] there is some authority that at law the benefit of a covenant can only pass with the whole of the land benefited and not with a mere part.[81] Historically in equity it seems that if the benefit of a covenant was annexed only to the whole of the dominant tenement it would not pass to a person who acquired only part thereof.[82] In contrast in *Marquess of Zetland v. Diver*[83] the Court of Appeal held that a covenant expressly annexed to any

[76] [1937] Ch. 473.
[77] *ibid.* at 482.
[78] [1973] Ch. 110.
[79] See also: *Marten v. Flight refuelling Ltd* [1962] Ch. 115; *Wrotham Park Estate Co. Ltd v. Parkside Homes Ltd.* [1974] 1 W.L.R. 798.
[80] See above p. 335.
[81] *Re Union of London and Smith's Bank Ltd's Conveyance* [1933] Ch. 611.
[82] See: *Re Ballard's Conveyance* [1937] Ch. 473.
[83] [1939] Ch. 1.

part or parts of the dominant land would be enforceable by subsequent purchaser of a part of the dominant land. However, the Court of Appeal in *Federated Homes v. Mill Lodge Properties*[84] made clear that it is not necessary for the covenant to expressly stipulate that the benefit is to be annexed to each and every part. Brightman L.J. stated:

> "I find the idea of the annexation of a covenant to the whole of the land but not to a part of it a difficult conception fully to grasp. I can understand that a covenantee may expressly or by necessary implication retain the benefit of a covenant wholly under his own control, so that the benefit will not pass unless the covenantee chooses to assign; but I would have thought that, if the benefit of a covenant is, on a proper construction of a document, annexed to the land, prima facie it is annexed to every part thereof, unless the contrary clearly appears."[85]

This suggests that in the absence of a clear contrary intention in the covenant that it is only intended to be annexed to the dominant land as a whole, a successor in title to part of the dominant tenement will be entitled to the benefit of the covenant.

(c) Benefit of the covenant expressly assigned to the owner of the dominant tenement

(i) Continuing relevance of assignment: The introduction of statutory annexation in *Federated Homes v. Mill Lodge Properties*[86] has rendered assignment far less important as a means of passing the benefit of a covenant to successors in title of the original covenantee.[87] If, for whatever reason, the benefit of a covenant has not been annexed to the dominant land[88] it can still pass to a successor in title if there is an express assignment. An assignment differs from annexation in that it occurs when the dominant land is transferred by a person who enjoys the benefit of the land, whereas annexation is effected the moment that the covenant is granted.

(ii) Requirements of a valid express assignment: For an effective assignment of the benefit of a covenant at common law the requirements of section 136 of the Law of Property Act 1925 must be satisfied. In equity three requirements were identified by Romer L.J. in *Re Union of London and Smith's Bank Ltd's Conveyance.*[89] First, the covenant which is assigned must be capable of benefiting the dominant land. Second, the dominant land must have been "ascertainable" or "certain". Third, the assignment must have occurred contemporaneously with the transfer of the dominant land , so that it formed part of the transaction transferring the dominant land. These requirements of effective equitable assignment were applied by Upjohn J. in *Newton-Abbot Co-operative Society Ltd v. Williamson and Treadgold Ltd*[90] Bessie Mardon was the owner

[84] [1980] 1 W.L.R. 594.
[85] *ibid.* at 606.
[86] [1980] 1 W.L.R. 594.
[87] (1980) 43 M.L.R. 445 (Hayton).
[88] For example, if the original covenant provides that the benefit can only be passed by express assignment: *Marquess of Zetland v. Driver* [1937] Ch. 651.
[89] [1933] Ch. 611.
[90] [1952] Ch. 286.

of property known as Devonia, from which she carried on a business as an ironmonger. She sold land opposite to purchasers who covenanted that they would not use it for any business in competition with her ironmongers. The covenant simply referred to Mrs Mardon "of Devonia," and did not describe the land to which it related. Bessie died and Devonia devolved under her will to her son, but her executors never expressly assigned the benefit of the covenant to him. He subsequently leased Devonia to the plaintiffs, with an express assignment of the benefit of the covenant. Upjohn J. held that in these circumstances the benefit of the covenant had passed to the plaintiffs by assignment. He held that the son enjoyed the benefit of the covenant because when his mother died her executors held it on trust for him, and his entitlement was not defeated by the absence of an express assignment. He then held that the covenant had been for the benefit of the land and not for Mrs Mardon personally. Finally, he held that it did not matter that the land benefited was not defined in the deed granting the covenant, as it could be ascertained with reasonable certainty from the attendant circumstances in which the covenant was granted.

(iii) Effect of assignment: Where the benefit of a covenant is expressly assigned in equity the assignee is entitled to enforce the covenant against the covenantor, or his successors in title if it is restrictive, as long as he owns the dominant land. However, it has been argued that an express assignment does more that merely transfer the benefit of the covenant to the assignee personally. It has been claimed that a subsequent assignment by the original covenantee has the effect of annexing the benefit of the covenant to the land. Thus the assignment operates as a "delayed annexation" of the benefit of the covenant to the land, so that the benefit will pass to successors in title of the assignee without the need for further express assignments.[91] However in *Re Pinewood Estate, Farnborough*[92] Wynn-Parry J. held that in the absence of annexation or a building scheme a continuous chain of assignments was necessary to pass the benefit of a covenant to the present owner of the dominant land. In *Stillwell v. Blackman*[93] Ungoed-Thomas J. indicated that: "there is no reason either in contract or in the relevant principles of equity why an express assignment of the benefit of a covenant with the passing of land should automatically operate exclusively, as an annexation of the covenant to the land." The "delayed annexation" theory was also rejected by the first instance judge in *Federated Homes v. Mill Lodge Properties* and is inconsistent with the reasoning of the Court of Appeal.

(iv) Statutory assignment by section 62(1) of the Law of Property Act 1925? In the context of leases it has been seen how section 62 of the Law of Property Act passes the benefit of the tenant's covenants to an assignee of the freehold reversion. There has been some suggestion that this section could also operate so as to pass the benefit of freehold covenants to a transferee of the dominant land, as the section provides that:

[91] See: *Renals v. Cowlishaw* (1878) 9 Ch.D. 125; *Rogers v. Hosegood* [1900] 2 Ch. 388, 408; *Reid v. Bickerstaff* [1909] 2 Ch. 305; [1938] 6 C.L.J. 339 (Bailey); [1957] C.L.J. 146 (Wade); [1962] J.P.L. 234 (Bowles); (1968) 84 L.Q.R. 22 (Baker); [1972B] C.L.J. 157 (Wade); (1971) 87 L.Q.R. 539 (Hayton).

[92] [1958] Ch. 280.

[93] [1968] Ch. 508, 526.

"A conveyance of land shall be deemed to include and shall by virtue of this Act operate to convey, with the land, all . . . rights and advantages whatsoever . . . appertaining or reputed to appertain to the land, or to any part thereof, or at the time of the conveyance . . . enjoyed with . . . the land or any part thereof."

However such an interpretation has been rejected on the grounds that the benefit of a covenant cannot be said to "appertain" to land unless it is annexed to it.[94] This was explained by Browne-Wilkinson V.-C. in *Kumar v. Dunning*[95]:

"the main intention of section 62 was to provide a form of statutory shorthand rendering it unnecessary to include such words expressly in every conveyance. It is a matter of debate whether, in the context of the section, the words "rights . . . appertaining to the land" include rights arising under covenant as opposed to strict property rights. However, I will assume, without deciding, that rights under covenant are within the words of the section. Even on that assumption it still has to be shown that the right "appertains to the land." In my judgement, a right under a covenant cannot appertain to the land unless the benefit is in some way annexed to the land. If the benefit of a covenant passes under section 62 even if not annexed to the land, the whole modern law of restrictive covenants would have been established on an erroneous basis . . . It is established that, in the absence of annexation to the land or the existence of a building scheme, the benefit of a restrictive covenant cannot pass except by way of *express* assignment. The law so established is inconsistent with the view that a covenant, the benefit of which is not annexed to the land, can pass under the general words in section 62."

(d) Benefit of the covenant passes to the owner of the dominant tenement under a scheme of development: establishing a "local law"

(i) The need for a separate regime for schemes of development: One common situation where restrictive covenants are imposed is when the owner of land wishes to develop it and sell it as a number of separate plots, with each of the purchasers agreeing to restrict their user of their land. The objective of the scheme is straightforward, namely that the land of all of the successors in title to the developers should be subject to the restrictions, and that each owners of an individual plot should be able to enforce the restrictions against all the other owners. For example, if Bill wishes to develop his land by building three houses on separate plots, each of which is sold in turn to Ted, Wayne and Garth in successive months, he may wish to ensure that there is a restrictive covenant affecting all the houses that they be used for residential purposes only.

[94] *Roake v. Chada* [1984] 1 W.L.R. 40. Judge Paul baker Q.C. also suggested that, s.62 may only operate in relation to legal rights, and that it excludes the benefit of a restrictive covenant which is equitable.
[95] [1989] Q.B. 193, 198.

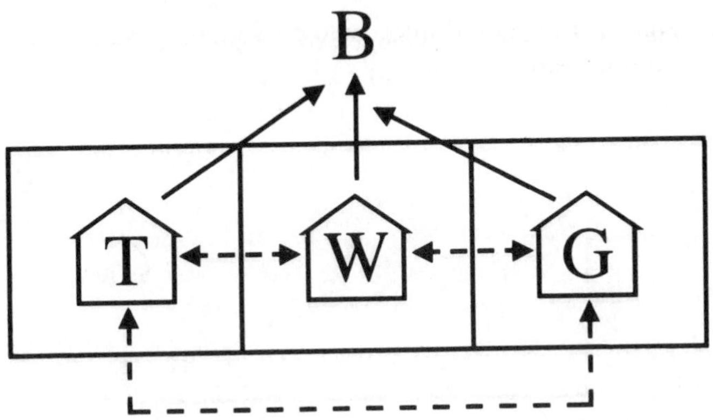

The rules relating to annexation and assignment of the benefit of restrictive covenants are incapable of achieving the objectives of reciprocity and mutual enforceability between the three house owners. When Ted purchased the first house in July and entered into the restrictive covenant with Bill, the benefit of the covenant would be annexed to the two plots remaining in Bill's ownership.

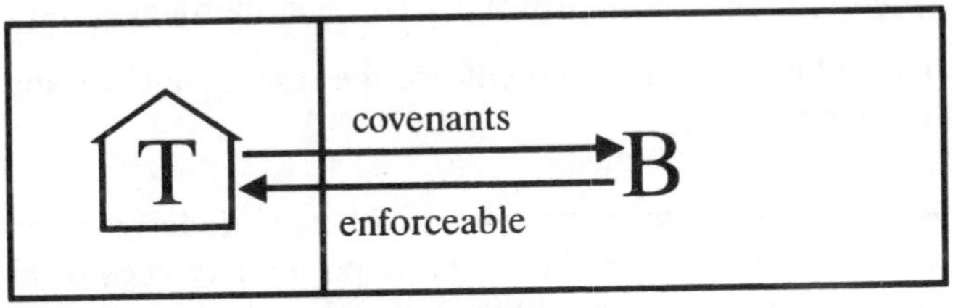

When Wayne purchased the second house from Bill in August he would take the land with the benefit of the covenant entered into by Ted, and would be able to enforce it against him if he were in breach. However, the benefit of the restrictive covenant which he himself granted to Bill would not be annexed to the land owned by Ted, meaning that Ted would not be able to enforce it against him if he was in breach.

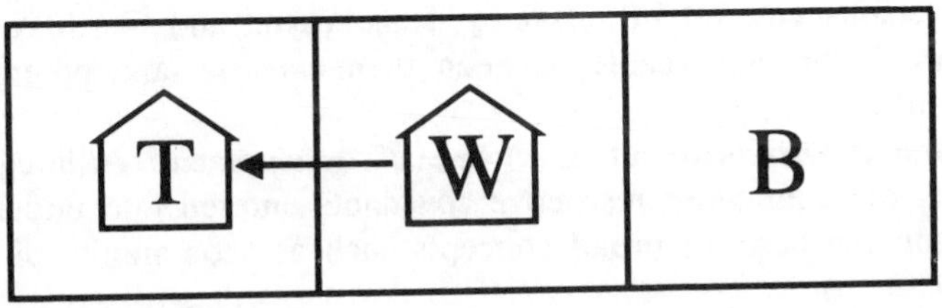

Similarly, when Garth purchased the third house in September, he would take the land with the benefit of the covenants entered into by Ted and Wayne and would be able to enforce them in the event of breach. However, there would be no land to which the benefit of the covenant he entered into could be annexed, since the covenantor, Bill, would not have retained any.

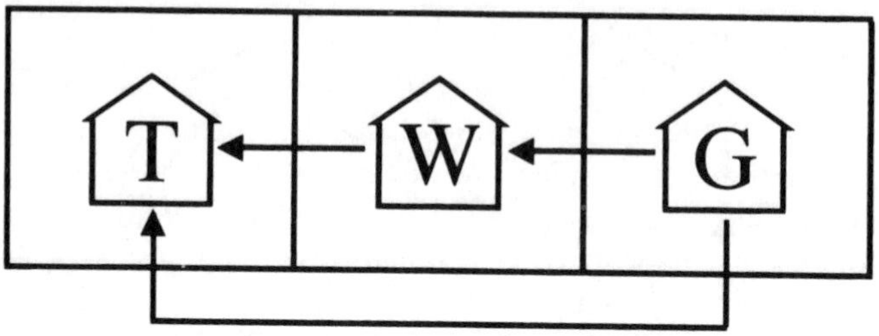

Therefore in this simple scenario the end result would be that:

(1) Garth could enforce the restrictive covenant burdening the land of Wayne.

(2) Wayne and Garth could both enforce the restrictive covenant burdening the land of Ted.

(3) Ted could not enforce the restrictive covenant burdening the land of Wayne.

(4) Neither Ted nor Wayne could enforce the restrictive covenant burdening the land of Garth.

The specifically equitable rules relating to a scheme of development enable such difficulties to be overcome and facilitate the imposition of reciprocal and mutually enforceable restrictive covenants on all the land included within the scheme.

(ii) Operation of a scheme of development: Where it is found that land is subject to a building scheme the consequence is that restrictive covenants are enforceable amongst all the purchasers of plots of land subject to the development even though they would not otherwise gain the benefit of all such covenants by the traditional rules regulating assignment and annexation. As Lord Browne-Wilkinson observed in *Emile Elias & Co. Ltd v. Pine Groves Ltd*[96] the effect of a scheme of development is to create "a local law[97] to which all owners are subject and of which all owners take the benefit." Thus, if in equity it was held that Bill's land was subject to a scheme of development the restrictive covenants entered with Bill by Ted, Wayne and Garth respectively and sequentially would be enforceable between them *inter se*, and potentially by their successors in title.

(iii) Traditional requirements of a scheme of development: Although Nineteenth Century equity cases enforced restrictive covenants entered into under a scheme of development on the basis of broad concepts such as "community of interest,"[98] in

[96] [1993] 1 W.L.R. 305.

[97] See also: *Reid v. Bickerstaff* [1909] 2 Ch. 305, 319 *per* Cozens-Hardy M.R.

[98] See: *Renals v. Cowlishaw* (1878) 9 Ch.D. 125; *Nottingham Patent Brick and Tile Co v. Butler* (1885) 15 Q.B.D. 261; *Collins v. Castle* (1887) 36 Ch.D. 243; *Spicer v. Martin* (1888) 14 App. Cas. 12.

Elliston v. Reacher[99] Parker J. adopted four criteria, subsequently approved by the Court of Appeal,[1] which had to be satisfied before land would be found to be subject to a scheme of development:

> "In order to [establish a scheme of development] it must be proved (1) that both the plaintiffs and the defendants derive title under a common vendor; (2) that previously to selling the lands to which the plaintiff's and defendants are respectively entitled the vendor laid out his estate, or a defined portion thereof (including the lands purchased by the plaintiffs and defendants respectively), for sale in lots subject to restrictions intended to be imposed on all the lots, and which, though varying in details as to particular lots, are consistent and consistent only with some general scheme of development; (3) that these restrictions were intended by the common vendor to be and were for the benefit of all the lots intended to be sold, whether or not they were also intended to be for the benefit of other land retained by the vendor; and (4) that both the plaintiffs and the defendants, or their predecessors in title, purchased their lots from the common vendor on the footing that the restrictions subject to which the purchases were made were to enure for the benefit of the other lots included in the general scheme whether or not they were also to enure for the benefit of other lands retained by the vendors."

Applying these criteria it was held that land which was laid out into plots by a building society was subject to a scheme of development, so that restrictive covenants entered into by the purchasers of some plots that they would not use the land for a hotel or public house were enforceable against their successors in title by the successors in title of others who had purchased plots from the society and therefore enjoyed the benefit of the covenants. However, the criteria appear to have presented such a barrier to establishing a scheme of development that there were only two reported cases between 1908 and 1961 where such a scheme was held to exist. In *Reid v. Bickerstaff*[2] the Court of Appeal seemed to add the additional requirement that the area subject to the scheme must be well defined. Cozens-Hardy M.R. stated:

> "What are some of the essentials of a building scheme? In my opinion there must be a defined area within which the scheme is operative. Reciprocity is the foundation of the idea of a scheme. A purchaser of one parcel cannot be subject to an implied obligation to purchasers of an undefined and unknown area. he must know both the extent of his burden and the extent of his benefit."[3]

(iv) Relaxation of the traditional requirements: Despite their long standing, a number of cases in the sixties and seventies backed away from a strict application of the requirements identified in *Elliston v. Reacher* as essential for the existence of a scheme of development, and instead concentrated on the question whether there was a

[1] [1908] 2 Ch. 365 at 384.
[2] [1908] 2 Ch. 665.
[3] [1909] 2 Ch. 305.
[4] *ibid.* at 319.

common intention to subject land to reciprocal covenants. In *Baxter v. Four Oaks Properties Ltd*[5] Cross J. held that the court was not precluded from finding a scheme of development as a matter of law merely because the common vendor did not lay out the land in plots before the first land was sold. Instead he considered that what was required was ". . . a clearly proved intention that the purchasers were to have rights *inter se* . . . "[6] In *Re Dolphin's Conveyance*[7] Stamp J. held that it was not essential that all the land subject to the scheme of development must have been sold by a common vendor. He considered that the requirements stated in *Elliston v. Reacher* evidenced a common intention that the parties should be subject to mutually enforceable reciprocal covenants but that this was not the exclusive means by which such an intention could be established. He concluded that there was a building scheme because the necessary common intention was evident in the conveyances of the land from the vendors to the purchasers. Although in *Emile Elias & Co. Ltd v. Pine Groves Ltd*[8] the Privy Council referred to *Elliston v. Reacher* as indicating "the requirements which have to be satisfied in order to establish such a building scheme" Lord Browne-Wilkinson expressly noted that there "have been certain developments in the law since that date" but that these did not bear on the case in issue. The case does not therefore re-assert the *Elliston v. Reacher* criteria and the more liberal regime continues.

(v) No building scheme unless a common intention can be established: The essential criteria for the establishment of a scheme of development is therefore that there was a common intention that the purchasers would be subject to mutual reciprocal restrictions enforceable *inter se*. If no such intention can be identified there will be no "local law." In *Lund v. Taylor*[9] the Court of Appeal held that there was no scheme of development where there was no evidence that the purchasers of plots were told that the common vendor intended to exact similar covenants from the purchasers of other plots, nor was any such intention evidenced by the conveyances themselves. More significantly, in *Emile Elias & Co. Ltd v. Pine Groves Ltd*[10] the Privy Council held that a common intention could not be established if there was a lack of uniformity of the covenants required from the purchasers of different plots. The case concerned land which was formerly part of a golf club in Trinidad sold in five parcels to four purchasers, each of whom entered into restrictive covenants. All the covenants contained a restriction on erecting more than one dwelling-house, but the covenants of lots 2 and 3 also restricted the use of any building erected as a private dwelling house. Lord Browne-Wilkinson explained that this meant that there was insufficient reciprocity to find the necessary common intention:

> "It is one of the badges of an enforceable building scheme . . . that they accept a common code of covenants. It is most improbable that a purchaser will have any intention to accept the burden of covenants affecting the land which he acquires being enforceable by other owners of the land in the scheme area unless he himself is to enjoy reciprocal rights over the lands of other such owners; the

[5] [1965] 1 Ch. 816.
[6] *ibid.* at 828.
[7] [1970] Ch. 654.
[8] [1993] 1 W.L.R. 305.
[9] (1976) 31 P. & C.R. 167.
[10] [1993] 1 W.L.R. 305.

crucial element of reciprocity would be missing. That does not mean that all lots within the scheme must be subject to identical covenants. For example, in a scheme of mixed residential and commercial development, the covenants will obviously vary according to the use intended to be made of each category of lot. But if, as in the present case, they are all of a similar nature and all intended for high class development consisting of one dwelling house on a substantial plot, a disparity in the covenants imposed is a powerful indication that there was no intention to create reciprocally enforceable rights."[11]

(vi) No building scheme unless there is a defined scheme area known to all the original purchasers: The second main requirement for the existence of a building scheme in the modern law is that there is a defined area of land subject to the common intention to impose mutually enforceable reciprocal covenants. As has been noted, this requirement was identified by the Court of Appeal in *Reid v. Bickerstaff.*[12] In *Lund v. Taylor*[13] it was claimed that a scheme of development enabled the enforcement of covenants not to erect blocks of flats on land between purchasers from a common vendor. Although the common vendor had drawn up an architects plan for the development of part of the land the Court of Appeal held that there was insufficient evidence to establish a scheme of development. Stamp L.J. explained that the individual purchasers had not been made aware that a defined area of land was intended to be subject to reciprocal covenants:

> "In the instant case there is no evidence that the Estate Plan was brought to the attention of any of the purchasers . . . There is no evidence that any proposing purchaser of a plot was told that the vendor was proposing to exact similar covenants, or indeed any covenants, from the purchasers of other plots . . . Because there was no extrinsic evidence, nor anything in his own conveyance to show a purchaser that there was a scheme relating to a defined area, or that [the vendors] intended that stipulations should be imposed in respect of each part of that area [the plaintiff] could not on the authority of *Reid v. Bickerstaff* be subject to an implied obligation to the other purchasers. On this ground alone the action must . . . fail."[14]

Similarly, in *Emile Elias & Co. Ltd v. Pine Groves Ltd*[15] the Privy Council held that there was no defined area subject to a scheme of development. Lord Browne-Wilkinson stated that the rationale for the requirement was that "to create a valid building scheme, the purchasers of all the land within the area of the scheme must also know what that area is." The general plan of the land sold by the golf club in five plots, which was attached to all the conveyances, did not show plot five. Lord Browne-Wilkinson explained that this had the consequence that the requirement of a defined area was not met:

[11] *ibid.* at 311.
[12] [1909] 2 Ch. 305.
[13] (1976) 31 P. & C.R. 167.
[14] *ibid.* at 174–176.
[15] [1993] 1 W.L.R. 305.

> "If therefore lot 5 falls to be treated as part of the designated scheme area, it has not been proved that in 1938 the purchasers of lots 1, 2 and 3 were aware of that fact. [Counsel] suggested that it would be inferred from the fact that all the purchasers were associated with the golf club and . . . were aware of lot 5 . . . Their Lordships feel unable to attach to any such inference sufficient probative force to reach an affirmative conclusion that all the purchasers of the lots in 1938 knew that lot 5 was included. If lot 5 was to be part of a scheme area giving rise to mutually enforceable obligations between all the lots, it would surely have been shown on the plan annexed to each of the conveyances. In the view of the Board, if there was any intention to create mutually enforceable rights in a scheme area, lot 5 must have been part of that area. it was sold at the same time as lots 1–4 and was subjected to the same covenants as affected lot 4 and lot 1. It is entirely incredible that there was any intention to create rights which would be mutually enforceable between the owners of lots 1, 2, 3 and 4 but not enforceable by and against the owner of lot 5. Accordingly, lot 5 being part of any scheme that could be established and it not having been shown that the purchasers of lots 1–3 were aware of that fact, the requirement of a defined scheme area known to the original purchasers cannot be satisfied."[16]

(vii) Sub-schemes within a wider scheme of development: Complex questions of enforceability arise where land subject to a scheme of developments is further subdivided, so that within the overall scheme there are areas subject to sub-schemes which might impose different covenants. The main issues are whether the covenants of the sub-scheme are mutually enforceable between the purchasers of the land comprising the sub-scheme, and whether the covenants of the head scheme are similarly enforceable by the purchasers of the land in the sub-scheme *inter se*. These questions were raised in *Brunner v. Greenslade*[17] Clearly the covenants entered by the purchasers of land subject to the sub-scheme will be enforceable inter se on the basis of the local law that the sub-scheme creates amongst them. Megarry J. rejected the view, derived from the decision of Romer J. in *Knight v. Simmonds*,[18] that the covenants of a head scheme could never bind the purchasers of land subject to a sub-scheme *inter se*. Instead he considered that the covenants of the head scheme would be enforceable between them unless they had made clear an intention that the new covenants should replace the old. This would clearly be the case if the purchasers of the sub-lots had mutually covenanted that all should be released *inter se* form the head scheme and subjected to the sub-scheme, but this was not essential to demonstrating the necessary intention.

4 Enforcement of restrictive covenants

(a) An injunction or damages in lieu

Where the equitable rules regulating the passing of the benefit and burden of restrictive covenants are satisfied, so that the servient land is subject to the covenant

[16] *ibid.* at 310–311.
[17] [1971] Ch. 993.
[18] [1896] 1 Ch. 653.

and the owner of the dominant land is entitled to the benefit thereof, remedies will be available to the dominant owner in the event of breach. If a breach has not yet occurred but the servient owner is proposing to act in breach the court may grant a prohibitory injunction to restrain the breach. Where the breach has already occurred the court may grant a mandatory injunction ordering the servient owner to remove whatever is causing it. This will be especially so if the servient owner has gone ahead and breached the covenant having been warned that his activities would constitute a breach. In *Wakeham v. Wood*[19] the owner of servient land subject to a covenant not to erect any buildings which would obscure the sea view of the dominant land was ordered to pull down a building he had erected in flagrant disregard of the dominant owner's rights, despite the fact that he had been warned by the dominant owner and his solicitor. However the court is naturally reluctant to order the wasteful destruction of buildings which have been completed, and in cases where the breach is less flagrant are more likely to award the dominant owner damages in lieu of an injunction. For example, in *Wrotham Park Estates v. Parkside Homes*[20] the servient owners built housing on land in breach of a restrictive covenant requiring them to obtain the prior approval of the dominant owner to the plans of the development. Although the dominant owners had protested at the breach and the servient owners had continued building Brightman J. refused a mandatory injunction. He stated:

> "The erection of the houses, whether one likes it or not, is a *fait accompli* and he houses are now the homes of people. I accept that this particular *fait accompli* is reversible and could be undone. But I cannot close my eyes to the fact that the houses now exist. It would, in my opinion, be an unpardonable waste of much needed houses to direct that they now be pulled down and I have never had a moments doubt during the hearing of this case that such an order ought to be refused."[21]

He accordingly awarded the dominant owners the equivalent of 5 per cent of the servient owners expected profits from the development in lieu of an injunction.

(b) Refusal of any remedy

Since equitable remedies are discretionary it is open for the court to refuse to award any remedy for breach of covenant if it so chooses. In *Chatsworth Estates Co. v Fewell*[22] Farwell J. anticipated the possibility that a court would not enforce covenant restricting the use of land to residential purposes if the entire character of the neighbourhood had been changed by the dominant owners licensing non-residential use so that "there is no longer any value left in the covenants at all." However, he concluded that in the circumstances of the case the character of the neighbourhood had not been so changed by the dominant owner licensing some of the land to be used for schools, some of the houses to be converted into flats and allowing three boarding houses and a hotel to start business. Acquiescence in a breach of covenant may also

[19] (1982) 43 P. & C.R. 40.
[20] [1974] 1 W.L.R. 798.
[21] *ibid.* at 811.
[22] [1931] 1 Ch. 224.

disentitle a dominant owner from any remedy. This was recognised by the Court of Appeal in *Shaw v. Applegate*[23] where the dominant owner took no action for three years while the servient owner used his land as an amusement arcade in breach of covenant. Buckley L.J. stated that the appropriate test was whether "the situation has become such that it would be unconscionable for the [servient owner], or the person having the right sought to be enforced, to continue to seek to enforce it." Again it was held that in the circumstances of the case the dominant owner had not acquiesced in the breach because the parties had been confused in their minds as to whether what was being done was in law a breach of the covenant. However, the failure to act meant that the appropriate remedy was not an injunction but damages in lieu.

5 Extinction of restrictive covenants

Since a restrictive covenant operates as a form of negative easement affecting land just as an easement would be extinguished by the unification of title to the dominant and servient tenements in a single owner a restrictive covenant will also be extinguished if there is no longer any distinction of ownership between the dominant and servient land.[24] However, where the title to distinct plots in a scheme of development are unified the covenants are not extinguished but merely suspended. They will therefore revive if the land is subsequently re-divided. In *Texaco Antilles Ltd v. Kernochan*[25] Lord Cross, giving the advise of the Privy Council, stated:

> "It is no doubt true that if the restrictions in question exist simply for the mutual benefit of two adjoining properties and both those properties are bought by a one man the restrictions will automatically come to an end and will not revive on a subsequent severance unless the common owner then recreates them. But their Lordships cannot see that it follows from this that if a number of people agree that the area covered by all their properties shall be subject to a "local law" the provisions of which shall be enforceable by any owner for he time being of any part against any other owner and the whole area has never at any time come into common ownership an action by one owner of a part against another owner of a part must fail if it can be shown that both parts were either at the inception of the scheme or at any time subsequently in common ownership."

The covenants will therefore revive on subsequent re-division of the land unless the parties have indicated a clear intention to the contrary.

6 Modification or discharge of restrictive covenants

(a) *Power of the Land Tribunal to modify or discharge*

Where land has been subjected to restrictive covenants in the past it is not necessarily the case that those covenants will be appropriate for the present. Section 84(1) of the

[23] [1977] 1 W.L.R. 970.
[24] In *Re Tiltwood, Sussex* [1978] Ch. 269; *Re Victoria Recreation Ground, Portslade's Application* (1979) 41 P. & C.R. 119.
[25] [1973] A.C. 609, 626.

Law of Property Act 1925 empowers the Land Tribunal "wholly or partially to discharge or modify any . . . restriction" affecting an interest in freehold land on the application of "any person interested" in the land.

(b) Grounds justifying exercise of the power to modify or discharge

Section 84 sets out a variety of grounds entitling the Land Tribunal to modify or discharge a covenant:

(i) Obsolescence[26]: Section 84(1)(a) provides that a restrictive covenant may be modified or discharged if the restriction has become obsolete because of "changes in the character of the property or the neighbourhood or other circumstances."

(ii) Impediment to reasonable user[27]: Section 84(1)(aa) provides for modification or discharge if the continued existence of the covenant "would impede some reasonable user of the land for public or private purposes." In order to exercise their jurisdiction on these grounds the Land Tribunal must be satisfied that the restriction impeding the reasonable user "does not secure to persons entitled to the benefit of it any practical benefits of substantial value or advantage to them," or that it "is contrary to public policy," and that "money will be an adequate compensation for the loss or disadvantage (if any)" which the dominant owner would suffer by a modification or variation.[28]

(iii) Holders of benefit have agreed to discharge or modification[29]: The land tribunal may exercise their power by section 84(1)(b) if those entitled to the benefit of the covenant are of age and legally competent and they have "agreed, either expressly or by implication, by their acts or omissions" to a modification or discharge.

(iv) No injury to the holders of the benefit[30]: Under section 84(1)(c) the Land Tribunal may modify or discharge a covenant if "the proposed discharge or modification will not injure the persons entitled to the benefit of the restriction."

(v) Imposition of additional limitations: When an application is sought for the modification or discharge of a restriction the Land Tribunal may add such additional limitations to the user of the land "as appear to the Lands Tribunal to be reasonable in view of the relaxation of the existing provisions."[31] Although such additional restrictions can only be imposed with the consent of the applicant, the Tribunal can "refuse to modify a restriction without some addition."

(c) Compensation where covenant modified or discharged

Where the court modifies or discharges a covenant under section 84(1) the Land Tribunal may order the payment of compensation to the person entitled to the benefit thereof to compensate for "any loss or disadvantage suffered by that person in consequence of the discharge of modification"[32] or "to make up for any effect which

[26] See: *Keith v. Texaco Ltd* (1977) 34 P. & C.R. 249; *Re Cox's Application* (1985) 51 P. & C.R. 335; *Re Quaffers Ltd's Application* (1988) 56 P. & C.R. 142.

[27] See: *Re Bass Ltd's Application* (1973) 26 P. & C.R. 156; *Gilbert v. Spoor* [1983] Ch. 27; *Stannard v. Issa* [1987] A.C. 175.

[28] s.84(1A).

[29] See: *Re Fettishaw's Application (No. 2)* (1973) 27 P. & C.R. 156; *Re Memvale's Securities Ltd's Application* (1975) 233 E.G. 689.

[30] See: *Re Forestmere Properties Ltd's Application* (1980) 41 P. & C.R. 390; *Re Livingstones' Application* (1982) 47 P. & C.R. 462.

[31] s.84(1B).

[32] s.84(1)(i).

the restriction had, at the time when it was imposed, in reducing the consideration then received for the land affected by it."[33]

REFORM OF THE LAW RELATING TO COVENANTS AFFECTING FREEHOLD LAND

1 Complexity of the present law

As has no doubt been appreciated the law relating to the enforceability of covenants affecting freehold land is extremely complex. The whole area illustrates the difficulties which arise at the interface between the law of property and the law of contractual obligations, and the difference between personal and proprietary rights. This is further complicated by distinctions developed by the historic separation between equity and the common law. This causes a fundamental distinction between positive and restrictive covenants, and whilst a number of concepts are common to both for determining whether the benefit of a covenant passes with the land, namely assignment and annexation, they are applied with subtle variations. This present complexity has led to a number of reviews of the law in this area with the objective of reform and simplification.[34] Most recently in 1984 the Law Commission proposed a complete overhaul of the law in its report *Transfer of Land: The Law of Positive and Restrictive Covenants*.[35]

2 Recommendations of the Law Commission

(a) Defects of the present law

The Law Commission identified a number of defects in the present law which it considered required reform. First, it was felt inappropriate that the burden of positive covenants could never run with the land, and that the present means for avoiding this limitation are inadequate. Paragraph 4.4 stated that "there can be no justification for the fact that a simple positive obligation — to keep trees pruned below a certain height, for example, or to maintain a boundary wall — cannot be imposed as a covenant with the land." More significantly it was pointed out how this inability would prevent the creation of freehold flat schemes because the obligation of a lower flat to be kept in good repair for the benefit of an upper flat could not be made to pass with the title. Second, it was felt that the rules concerning restrictive covenants were too complex and uncertain. In relation to complexity, paragraph 4.9 stated that:

> "the burden of a restrictive covenant does not run at all at law, but it does run in equity if certain complicated criteria are met. The benefit, by contrast, runs both

[33] s.84(1)(ii).
[34] Wilberforce Committee on Positive Covenants [1965], Cmnd. 2719; Law Com. No. 11, *Transfer of Land: Report on Restrictive Covenants* (1967); Law Commission Working Paper No. 36, *Transfer of Land: Appurtenant Rights* (1971) .
[35] Law Com. No. 127 (1984).

> at law and in equity, but according to rules which are different. These rules are, if anything, more complicated than the rules about the burden, and some of them are particularly technical and hard to grasp; as examples one may cite the rules about "annexation" and those about "building schemes."

It was felt that the decision in *Federated Homes* had engendered uncertainty by making radical and controversial changes to what the law was thought to be in the context of annexation, as had the successive cases considering the appropriate criteria for a scheme of development.

(b) Proposed reform: the creation of "land obligations"

The law Commission proposed to remedy the defects in the present law not by small piecemeal changes but by the introduction of a wholly new interest in land, the "land obligation," derived by an analogy with easements. In a sense this proposal carries the equitable developments begun in *Tulk v. Moxhay* to their logical conclusion by elevating contractual agreements by freeholders in relation to their land to the status of proprietary interests rather than purely personal obligations. The Law Commission recommended two types of "land obligation":

(i) "Neighbour obligations": "Neighbour obligations" are those intended for use where an obligation is imposed on one piece of land for the benefit of another. It was recommended that such obligation could take the form of: (a) an obligation imposing a restriction which benefits the whole or part of the dominant land on the doing of some act on the servient land; (b) an obligation requiring the carrying out on the servient land or the dominant land of works which benefit the whole or part of the dominant land; (c) an obligation requiring the provision of services for the benefit of the whole or part of the dominant land; and (d) an obligation requiring the making of payments in a specified manner (whether to a person of a specified description or otherwise) on account of expenditure which has been or is to be incurred by a person in complying with a positive obligation. Such obligations would only be capable of being "neighbour obligation" if they touched and concerned the land.

(ii) "Development obligations": Where the situation is more complex and an area of land divided into separately owned but interdependent units, whether in a building scheme or flats, the land obligation would take the form of a "development obligation." The main difference is that such obligations would be enforceable by the owners of the "development land" or by a "manager" acting on their behalf. They could also comprise a wider range of obligations than those outlined for "neighbour obligations" including an obligation "requiring the servient land to be used in a particular way which benefits the whole or part of the development land" and granting access to, and making payments to reimburse, the manager of the development land. Such land obligations would only come into existence as a legal interest if created by deed and for a duration equivalent to that of a legal easement. In other cases the land obligation would be equitable. In unregistered land they would be registrable as land charges whether legal or equitable in status. In registered land they would not have the status of overriding interests and they would be noted on the title of the servient land concerned. The benefit of land obligations would run with the land as appurtenant to the dominant tenement. The burden of land obligations which are restrictive or provide for access would be binding upon everyone who is an owner of an estate or interest in the servient land, and also an occupier.

In the case of other land obligations a smaller class of persons would be subject to the burden, namely freeholders, long leaseholders, owners of the burdened estate and mortgagees of the servient land. Obviously no person would be bound by a land obligation if they had taken their title to the land free from it because it had not been appropriately protected. Just as the Landlord and Tenant (Covenants) Act 1995 provides that the contractual liability of the original landlord and tenant will terminate when they assign their respective estates in the land, the person who creates a land obligation will no longer be liable under it when he transfers his land. These recommendations have not yet been translated into legislation.

(c) Introduction of commonhold and its implications for covenants affecting land

Subsequent to the Law Commission proposals relating to land obligations it has been suggested that English law should adopt some form of commonhold ownership of land. If such a concept is introduced it is likely that much of the scope covered by the "development obligations" would be adequately served by the commonhold structure and that therefore a simplified version of such "development obligations" could be introduced.[36]

(d) Automatic obsolescence of restrictive covenants

If the proposed system of land obligations were to be introduced, one problem would be that existing restrictive covenants would not automatically become "land obligations." The Law Commission has therefore recommended that if the scheme of "land obligations" is introduced all restrictive covenants should cease to have effect eighty years after their creation and that every covenant which is not obsolete should be replaced with an equivalent land obligation. Such a covenant would not be obsolete if at the end of the period it secures "any practical benefits of substantial value or advantage" to the owners of the dominant tenement.[37]

[36] See: *Commonhold: Freehold Flats and Freehold Ownership of Other Interdependant Buildings* (1987) Cm. 179; *Commonhold—a Consultation Paper* (1990) Cm. 1345; [1991] Conv. 170.
[37] Law Com. No. 201: *Transfer of Land: Obsolete Restrictive Covenants* (1991).

Chapter 11

MORTGAGES

THE NATURE OF MORTGAGES AND SECURITY

1 Introduction

Most people buying a house are not in the fortunate position of having enough cash to pay for the house outright. They therefore need to borrow in order to pay for it. In comparison with their earnings, the borrowings which the housebuyers will need to make are relatively large. A young couple acquiring their first home may have only a small deposit and may therefore have to borrow two or three times their joint income in order to finance the purchase of even a relatively modest property. Any lender advancing this much money will want to take precautions against the possibility that the loan is not repaid. Suppose, for instance, that the borrowers die before they have repaid the loan, or some other misfortune occurs, such as one or both of them losing their job. There are various ways in which a lender can obtain protection against such events. When a lender takes protection in this way, it is said to be taking security for the loan. Of course, there are also commercial situations where a lender will want to take security. A bank lending money to a company will want protection against the possibility of the company becoming insolvent and being unable to meet all its financial obligations. It will not always be content to join a queue for payment with all the other creditors.

2 The nature of security

A lender is said to have security for a loan where some arrangement has been made under which the lender has some rights over and above the right to sue the borrower for the money if the loan is not repaid.[1] There are two main ways in which a lender can obtain security. The first is by entering into an agreement under which, if the borrower does not repay the loan, someone else is liable to do so. This is described as personal

[1] See Sheridan, *Rights in Security* (1974) p.1.

Forms of Security

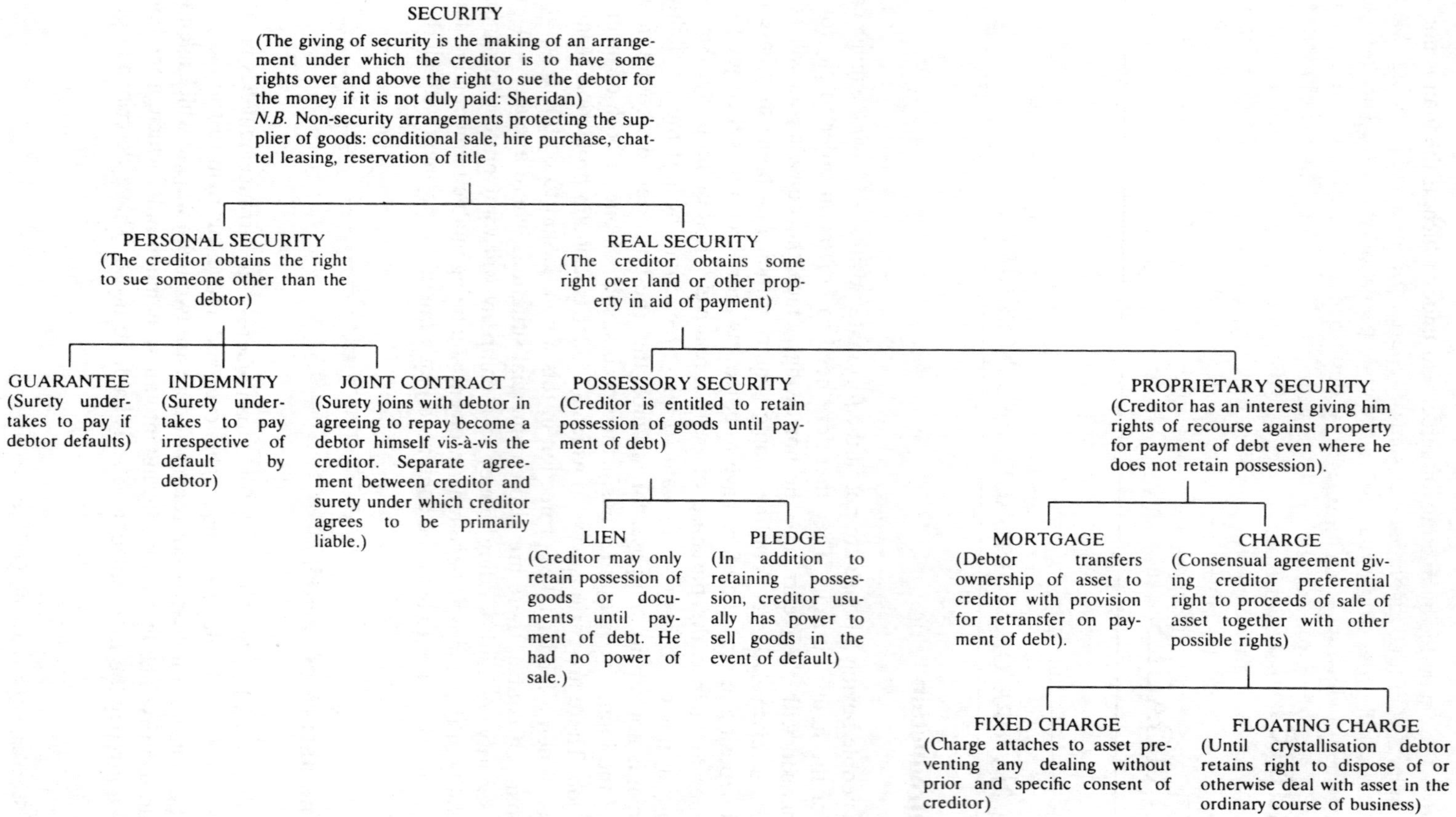
SECURITY
(The giving of security is the making of an arrangement under which the creditor is to have some rights over and above the right to sue the debtor for the money if it is not duly paid: Sheridan)
N.B. Non-security arrangements protecting the supplier of goods: conditional sale, hire purchase, chattel leasing, reservation of title
PERSONAL SECURITY
(The creditor obtains the right to sue someone other than the debtor)
REAL SECURITY
(The creditor obtains some right over land or other property in aid of payment)
GUARANTEE
(Surety undertakes to pay if debtor defaults)
INDEMNITY
(Surety undertakes to pay irrespective of default by debtor)
JOINT CONTRACT
(Surety joins with debtor in agreeing to repay become a debtor himself vis-à-vis the creditor. Separate agreement between creditor and surety under which creditor agrees to be primarily liable.)
POSSESSORY SECURITY
(Creditor is entitled to retain possession of goods until payment of debt)
PROPRIETARY SECURITY
(Creditor has an interest giving him rights of recourse against property for payment of debt even where he does not retain possession).
LIEN
(Creditor may only retain possession of goods or documents until payment of debt. He had no power of sale.)
PLEDGE
(In addition to retaining possession, creditor usually has power to sell goods in the event of default)
MORTGAGE
(Debtor transfers ownership of asset to creditor with provision for retransfer on payment of debt).
CHARGE
(Consensual agreement giving creditor preferential right to proceeds of sale of asset together with other possible rights)
FIXED CHARGE
(Charge attaches to asset preventing any dealing without prior and specific consent of creditor)
FLOATING CHARGE
(Until crystallisation debtor retains right to dispose of or otherwise deal with asset in the ordinary course of business)

security. The second is by making an agreement under which, if the loan is not repaid, the lender has limited rights against some property, for instance, by being able to sell the property in order to use the proceeds of sale to pay off the loan. This latter kind of arrangement (which includes mortgages) is described as real security, since some thing (or *res*, to use the Latin expression) is providing the security or safeguard to the lender. Within each of these two types of security, there are a number of variants. Although this book is primarily concerned with mortgages, it is worth briefly examining other forms of security because this helps to explain the context. Moreover, it is not uncommon for more than one form of security to be used in a single transaction. The diagram on page 342 sets out in schematic form the different types of personal and real security. In addition to the forms of security which are considered here, there are also other arrangements which can be used to protect suppliers of goods. These include conditional sales, hire-purchase, finance leases and retention of title arrangements. Descriptions of these arrangements can be found in most standard textbooks on commercial law, and are not considered further in this book.

3 Personal security

Personal security consists of the lender's right to sue someone else if the borrower fails to repay. As the diagram on page 342 shows, there are several ways in which the lender can acquire such rights. The person who undertakes to give security to the lender by agreeing to this liability is known as a surety.

(a) Guarantee[2]

A guarantee represents a long-stop against a failure on the part of the borrower to honour his obligation to repay. In the context of security arrangements, the term guarantee is normally confined to situations where the lender can only call upon the surety if the borrower is in default. The extent of the surety's liability rests upon the proper interpretation of the contract under which such liability was assumed.[3] For instance, where a loan is repayable in instalments, the surety might have undertaken to guarantee payment of each instalment on the date on which it falls due.[4] Alternatively, where the loan provides that on the borrower's default in paying any instalment, the whole loan is repayable, the surety's contract might oblige him to repay the whole loan,[5] and not merely the instalment. Whether the lender must pursue all its legal remedies against the borrower before making any claim against the surety will again depend upon the terms of the contract, but this is not normally a requirement.[6] Where the surety has been called upon to pay the whole or part of the loan on the borrower's default, the surety has a right to an indemnity from the borrower[7] (*i.e.* a right to be repaid by the borrower). If the surety has repaid the whole of the loan, then he is

[2] As well as being used to describe a form of personal security, the word guarantee is used in other contexts, such as to describe a specific undertaking in a sales contract as to the quality or performance of goods.
[3] Lord Reid in *Moschi v. Lep Air Services Ltd* [1972] 2 All E.R. 393 (H.L.) at 398 "Parties are free to make any agreement they like."
[4] See *Moschi v. Lep Air Services Ltd* [1973] A.C. 331.
[5] As in *Re Hawkins* [1972] Ch. 714.
[6] *Wright v. Simpson* (1802) 6 Ves.Jr. 714.
[7] *Anson v. Anson* [1953] 1 Q.B. 636.

entitled, in addition, to a transfer of any further security held by the lender.[8] Guarantees rest for their enforceability upon contract, and therefore have to be supported by consideration, except where made by deed. Consideration is obviously supplied where the lender advances money on a loan after the guarantee has been given. If the loan has already been taken out before the guarantee has been given, then the lender's continuation of the loan after obtaining the guarantee will normally constitute consideration.[9] By virtue of section 105 of the Consumer Credit Act 1974, any security relating to a regulated consumer credit agreement must be set out in a signed document in the prescribed form.[10] In other cases, section 4 of the Statute of Frauds 1677 requires that the agreement be in writing or that there be some written note of it signed by or on behalf of the surety.[11]

(b) Indemnity

The effect of an indemnity is practically indistinguishable from that of a guarantee. With an indemnity, the surety enters into an independent contract with the lender under which, rather than guaranteeing that the main borrower will discharge his obligations, he undertakes to make good any loss which the lender might incur as a result of entering into the lending transaction. The practical difference between an indemnity of this kind and a guarantee is that if for some reason the loan agreement is not enforceable against the borrower, the indemnity remains enforceable whilst a guarantee of performance would not. Since in the overwhelming majority of cases both guarantees and indemnities are called upon because of the default of the borrower to make repayments owing to a lack of means rather than because of any legal reason which prevents the loan being enforced, the difference between indemnity and guarantee is rarely of significance. In addition, both a guarantee and an indemnity may be incorporated into a single contract, and the infinite variety of special terms which can be agreed further fudges the difference. However, the difference can be significant, for the requirement of proof in writing applies to guarantees and not to indemnities. Thus a contract in which a surety says "If the borrower does not repay, I will" is a guarantee which must be proved in writing. But a contract in which the surety says, "If you lend money to the borrower, I will see that you are paid", is an indemnity and does not require written proof.[12] The principles under which a surety who has honoured a guarantee is entitled to recover the sums which he has paid from the main borrower apply equally to a surety who honours an indemnity, subject to any special agreement in the contract.

(c) Joint liability

In some instances a loan may be made to two persons contracting as joint borrowers, even though it is intended that only one of them will use the money.[13] From the

[8] Mercantile Law Amendment Act 1856, s.5; *Duncan, Fox & Co v. North and South Wales Bank* (1880) 6 App. Cas. 1.

[9] For an exception, see *Provincial Bank of Ireland Ltd v. Donnell* [1934] N.I. 33.

[10] The Act also contains other provisions applicable to sureties relating to regulated consumer credit agreements. It is possible for a surety agreement to which the Act applies to be enforced by court order notwithstanding the absence of writing (section 105(7)).

[11] For an analysis of the caselaw on this section, see Cheshire, Fifoot and Furmston's *Law of Contract* (12th ed., 1991) pp. 203–208.

[12] *Birkmyr v. Darnell* (1704) 1 Salk. 27.

[13] See, for instance *CIBC Mortgage plc v. Pitt* [1993] 4 All E.R. 433.

lender's point of view, the person providing the security is not a surety in a strict sense. The lender has exactly the same rights against the "surety" as against the main borrower. Both parties can therefore be treated as principal borrowers by the lender. Subject to any special term in the contract, the lender can therefore pursue its full remedies against any one of the borrowers. The lender can, for instance, call upon either to repay the loan in full. The lender does not have to pursue all its rights and remedies against the main borrower before seeking payment from the "surety". The lender would be within its legal rights in demanding payment from the "surety" without even asking the main borrower for payment. It would then be for the main borrower and surety to sort the matter out between themselves in accordance with whatever personal arrangement they may have had. There are some special rules which apply to joint borrowing arrangements in which only one of the "borrowers" obtains the benefits of the loan and is therefore acting, in effect, as a surety. First, there will almost certainly be a contract between the borrowers under which the main borrower is liable to indemnify the surety if the latter is called upon to pay the lender. If no contract has been made expressly between the parties, then a contract to this effect is likely to be implied on the principle that a request to meet a person's debts or liabilities implies an undertaking to provide reimbursement.[14] There is no automatic right to an indemnity where the suretyship was undertaken without the request of the main borrower,[15] although there may be circumstances in which the court will consider it just and reasonable that the surety should be indemnified for meeting the payment of the loan despite the absence of any express or implied agreement.[16] The argument in favour of conferring a right of indemnity on the surety even in the absence of an express agreement or of an agreement implied on the basis of request is that the surety has enriched the main borrower at the surety's expense. However, if the enrichment was not solicited, and in some cases, perhaps not even desired, the alternative principle which comes into play is that a benefit vountarily conferred is not recoverable.[17] There is no satisfactory explanation of how, in the grey area where these two principles meet, a decision can be made as to which is to apply. In *Owen v. Tate*[18] Scarman L.J. said that "a broad approach is needed . . . and that broad approach requires the court to look at all the circumstances of the case . . . [T]he fundamental question is . . . whether in the circumstances it was 'just and reasonable' that a right of reimbursement should arise."

A second special rule applies to joint borrowers where only one of the borrowers benefits from the loan. This applies where the lender knows that only one of the borrowers is obtaining the benefit of the loan (as where the payments are made directly by the lender to only one of the borrowers), and where the borrowers are in a relationship in which there is a manifest danger that one can exercise undue influence over the other. In these circumstances, the lender is under a specific duty to take adequate steps to ensure that the borrower acting as surety has been properly informed of the nature of the transaction and of its possible consequences, and has been given an opportunity to obtain independent advice.[19]

[14] *Re a Debtor* [1937] 1 All E.R. 1; *Toussaint v. Martinnant* (1787) 2 Term.100.
[15] *Owen v. Tate* [1976] Q.B. 402.
[16] *Brook's Wharf and Bull Wharf Ltd v. Goodman Brothers* [1937] 1 K.B. 534.
[17] See *Re National Motor Mail-Coach Co Ltd, Clinton's Claim* [1908] 2 Ch. 515 at 520.
[18] [1975] 2 All E.R. 129 at 133–134.
[19] *Barclays Bank v. O'Brien* [1993] 4 All E.R. 417 (HL). See the discussion of undue influence below.

(d) Loans for house purchase

Personal security is often sought when a person takes out a loan to buy a house. For instance, where a couple are buying a house and the income of one of them alone is considered by the lender to be insufficient to meet the monthly repayments, the lender may insist on the loan being made to the couple jointly. This means, as has been seen above, that if the repayments are not made, the lender will be able to sue either or both of the couple for the amount outstanding. Another way in which security is sought is through a mortgage indemnity policy. Banks lending for house purchase will normally require a mortgage over the property bought. As we will see later, this means that if the loan is not repaid, the bank can ultimately sell the house in order to discharge the loan. But where the loan is for a high proportion of the value of the house — such as where 95 per cent of the purchase price is raised on mortgage — there is a danger that if property prices fall, or unpaid loan interest accumulates, the value of the house will no longer be sufficient to pay off the loan. This is often described as negative equity — the borrower owes more than the house is worth. The danger for the lender is that if a borrower with negative equity defaults — that is, fails to repay the loan — the lender is not adequately protected merely by being able to sell the house. Banks and Building Societies will often therefore insist that a mortgage indemnity insurance policy is taken out to provide an indemnity to the lender in the event that the loan is not repaid in accordance with its terms and on a sale of the house, too little is received to discharge the whole of the loan. The way in which these insurance policies are drawn means that a payment is not automatically triggered if the house value falls below the amount of the mortgage, even if the borrower chooses to sell. It is only if the lender sells under the mortgage and experiences a shortfall that the insurance company is obliged to provide the indemnity payment. Even then, the insurance company can bring a personal action against the borrower to recover the sums it has paid out. Since the indemnity is provided as security for the principal obligation of the borrower to repay the loan, the insurance company, as surety, is entitled to stand in the shoes of the lender to enforce that main obligation of the borrower.

4 Real security

With real security the lender has some rights in relation to property in aid of payment of the loan. Real securities divide into those where the lender has a right to retain possession of goods until payment and those (historically more recently developed) where even though the borrower is allowed to keep the property, the lender has rights which can be enforced against the property. As the diagram on page 342 shows, these different ways of providing security can be categorised as possessory and proprietary. In the context of land law, we are principally concerned with proprietary security, but possessory security is worth a brief mention.

(a) Lien

Liens, or rights of retention, as they might more graphically be described, arise mainly in contexts other than loan. They entitle a person who is owed money (the creditor) to refuse to hand back property to the person who owns it (the debtor), until the debt has been paid. There are a number of examples of situations where such a right can arise. For example, a car repairer who has been requested to carry out car repairs can refuse to return the vehicle to its owner until the owner has paid for the repairs.[20] Except where authorised by the court or by statute, the creditor has no right to sell the goods. Similarly, a solicitor who has carried out work for a client but who has not been paid can retain any documents he holds belonging to his client until he has received payment for his professional services.[21]

(b) Pledge

A pledge (often and synonymously called a pawn) is a deposit of goods as security for meeting an obligation, usually a loan. The borrower gives goods to the lender which are then kept by the lender until the loan has been repaid. Generally under the terms of the contract, the lender is entitled to sell the goods if the loan has not been repaid within a set period of time.[22] Even where there is no express power of sale, a power to sell is implied at common law once the period for redeeming the loan has expired.[23] Most pledging transactions are now governed by the Consumer Credit Act 1974, although transactions between companies and large loans to individuals (over £15,000) are excluded by the Act.

(c) Welsh mortgages

It is not possible to make a pledge of land,[24] and it is possible that in England an attempt to pledge land would be treated as a mortgage.[25] However, some jurisdictions, including Ireland, recognise the possibility of creating what is known as a Welsh mortgage, which is in effect a form of pledge of land.[26] With this form of security, the borrower agrees that the lender may take possession of land belonging to the borrower until the loan is repaid. Instead of the borrower paying interest to the lender, the lender is entitled to retain the income or profits from the land. Unless the bargain is considered to be extortionate, or some statutory authority permits the courts to intervene,[27] the lender is able to keep the whole of the income and profits from the land, even if this exceeds what would be a reasonable return on the capital invested.[28] Similarly, if the income from the land turns out to be disappointingly poor, the lender has no right to claim more, for the right to the income from the land replaces the right to receive interest.[29] In some cases a Welsh mortgage will continue for as long as the loan remains outstanding.[30] In other cases, where the contract so provides, the lender retains the income from the land not only in lieu of interest, but also as a means of

[20] *Chase v. Westmore* (1816) 5 M. & S. 180 (a case involving the grinding of wheat where earlier cases were reviewed). *Albemarle Supply Co. Ltd v. Hind & Co* [1928] 1 K.B. 307 is a case involving taxicabs.

[21] *Re Hawkes* [1898] 2 Ch. 1; *Hughes v. Hughes* [1958] P. 224.

[22] See for instance *Franklin v. Neate* (1844) 13 M. & W. 481.

[23] *Pothonier v. Dawson* (1816) Holt N. P. 383.

[24] Sheridan, *Rights in Security* (1974) p.145.

[25] See below.

[26] Welsh mortgages are given statutory recognition in Ireland by the Statute of Limitations Act 1957 (RI), s.34. They are also recognised in certain States of the United States of America: see for instance *Humble Oil & Refining Co. v. Atwood* 150 Tex 617 (1951).

[27] For example, in *Gore v. Spotten* (1858) 7 I.Ch.R. 508 it was held that the usury laws then in force meant that any surplus rents from the land in excess of the statutory rate of interest had to be applied to repaying capital.

[28] *Yates v. Hambly* (1741) 2 Atk. 360.

[29] See *Cassidy v. Cassidy* (1889) 24 L.R. Ir. 577.

[30] *Conway v. Shrimpton* (1710) 5 Bro PC 187; compare *Hartpole v. Walsh* (1740) 5 Bro. P.C. 267.

repaying the capital on the loan. It has been held that if the lender has an express power of sale, the mortgage will take effect as a conventional modern mortgage.[31]

5 Proprietary security

Proprietary security differs from possessory security in that the lender retains a security interest in property even though the borrower is allowed to have possession of it. Proprietary security, indeed, developed expressly for the reason that in many cases the borrower will need to have the use of the assets over which the security rights are given in order to generate the income which is needed to repay the loan. Imagine, for instance, the difficulties that would arise if the only way in which an individual borrowing money from a bank to buy a house could use the house as security was by allowing the bank to have the use of it — perhaps as a home for the bank manager! What the bank really wants is not the use of the house, but some means of being able to resort to the house if the lender fails to repay the loan. In the meantime, the bank is quite happy for the borrower to live in it. Proprietary securities allow this.

(a) Mortgage

Historically, the first kind of proprietary security to be created was the mortgage, using that term in its original, narrow meaning. In return for making the loan, the lender would expect the borrower to transfer ownership to the lender of the property being used as security. Under the terms of the loan and transfer, the lender would undertake to transfer ownership back to the borrower if and when the loan was repaid or redeemed. This meant that, if the loan was not repaid, the lender would retain ownership of the property, keeping it for its own benefit or selling it. There were variants on this kind of mortgage. Although outright transfer with a right of redemption (*i.e.* a right to a retransfer on repayment of the loan) was the only means by which a mortgage could be created over goods or shares or insurance policies, an alternative for land was for the borrower to grant a long lease to the lender with a provision in the lease that it would come to an end immediately the loan was repaid. This form of mortgage of land is still possible, although a mortgage by a transfer of full ownership in land is no longer permitted in England.

(b) Charge

Although a mortgage gives the lender ownership of the property mortgaged, this is not really what the lender wants. The lender is simply looking for security. Equity recognised this, and therefore permitted the creation of what are known as charges. That is, the property which is being used to provide security is subject to the imposition of the remedies that the lender wants: it is charged to secure the repayment of the loan. Apart from this, the borrower's ownership of the property is not affected. The kind of charge which will most often be encountered by individuals is a fixed charge. This arises where a specific asset is subject to a charge. The borrower is unable to release the property from the charge without either repaying the loan or obtaining the prior specific consent of the lender. A fixed charge could be used by the buyer of a house to provide security for a

[31] *Re Cronin* [1914] I.R. 23.

Building Society loan as an alternative to creating a mortgage. Floating charges are normally only encountered where money has been lent to a trading company. A large part of a trading company's assets may be tied up in its stock-in-trade. It needs to buy goods to use in its manufacturing process, and once it has made its products it will want to sell them. It could create a fixed charge over all of its newly manufactured products, but it would then need the consent of the lender every time it wished to make a sale. The whole process would be far too cumbersome. Instead, the company enters into an agreement with the lender that all of the goods which belong to the company can be used as security for the loan, but that until some specified and identifiable event occurs, such as the company ceasing to trade in the ordinary course of business, the company has full liberty to use its stock-in-trade by selling manufactured goods and replacing them with new raw materials. Should the defined event occur, then the charge "crystallises" and fixes itself upon whetever property the company then holds. The lender is adequately protected whilst the company continues to trade normally because it is replenishing its stock of goods as rapidly as it is disposing of them.

(c) Modern mortgages and charges

A charge over land is just as effective in protecting a lender as a mortgage, and, indeed, for practical purposes is indistinguishable. It would make sense for mortgages of land to be abolished, with charges being the only recognised form of proprietary security over land. The legislature has not yet chosen to adopt this simplification. Instead, charges of land are described in the legislation by reference to mortgages. This makes the rules on the creation of mortgages unnecessarily complex and obscure.

THE CREATION OF MORTGAGES AND CHARGES

Since 1925, it is no longer possible to create a mortgage by means of an outright transfer of the whole of the borrower's[32] interest in land with a provision for redemption (the return of the land discharged from the obligation) upon repayment of the loan. A legal mortgage or charge must therefore be created in one of two ways.[33] One is by the grant of a lease with a provision for cesser on redemption. The other is by means of a charge by way of legal mortgage.

1 Grant of lease with proviso for cesser on redemption

Where a mortgage is created in this way, the borrower grants a lease for an extremely long period (such as 3,000 years) to the lender. The lease contains a provision that it will automatically come to an end once the loan is redeemed. If the borrower does not own the fee simple, any sublease granted to support a mortgage must be for a period

[32] For convenience, it is assumed that in every case where a mortgage is granted, it is the borrower's land which is used as security. This will usually be the case, although it is possible for a mortgage to be granted by someone other than the borrower, for instance where a parent mortgages his or her land to support a loan made to a son or daughter.
[33] Law of Property Act 1925, ss.85(1), 86(1).

shorter than the borrower's own leasehold interest. In order to create a legal mortgage, the arrangement must be made by deed. Because the borrower retains a legal estate in the land by means of the freehold reversion (or where the borrower is a leaseholder, by means of a short reversion on the borrower's own lease), it is possible for a further legal mortgage to be created through the grant of a further lease (or sublease), slightly longer (perhaps only by a day or two[34]) than the lease granted to the first lender. Where the owner of land attempts to grant a mortgage by way of a transfer of the whole of his freehold or leasehold estate, the Law of Property Act 1925 automatically converts the arrangement into a mortgage by way of a lease for 3,000 years in the former, and by way of a lease for 10 days less than the borrower's own lease in the latter.[35] In deciding whether a mortgage has been created, equity looks to the intent rather than to the form. What on the face appears as a sale of land with an option to repurchase could, therefore, be held to be a mortgage if the reality of the arrangement was that the land was being used as security for a loan.[36]

2 Charge by way of legal mortgage

As with the creation of any other legal right in land, charges by way of legal mortgage must be created by deed. They must also state that they are intended to take effect as a charge by way of legal mortgage.[37] There is no other requirement as to form or content. Once created in this way, a charge by way of legal mortgage operates to confer on the mortgagee (the lender) "the same protection, powers and remedies" as if the mortgage had been created by way of lease. A charge by way of legal mortgage can therefore for convenience be called a mortgage even though a pedant could argue that a charge is not strictly speaking a mortgage, since it does not involve the conveyance of title to the land, but merely the creation of rights of security. It has been held that a mortgage by way of charge can be created before the mortgagor has acquired the legal estate in the property concerned. The mortgagor will be estopped from denying the validity of the mortgage so created, and that estoppel will be fed without the need for a new grant once the mortgagor acquires the relevant legal estate.[38]

3 Mortgages of registered land

Mortgages of registered land are created by the same methods as mortgages of unregistered land, namely by lease or sublease, as appropriate to the title of the borrower, or by way of charge by way of legal mortgage. In order to complete the mortgage, however, it must be registered at the Land Registry.[39] Once registered, the charge is described as a registered charge, and the mortgagee will gain the statutory protection which is conferred on those in whose favour a disposition for valuable consideration has been registered.[40] The deed of mortgage is insufficient in itself to

[34] For example, see the provision in Law of Property Act 1925, s.85(2)(b).
[35] Law of Property Act 1925, ss.85(2), 86(2).
[36] See *Grangeside Properties Ltd v. Collingwood Securities Ltd* [1964] 1 W.L.R. 139.
[37] Law of Property Act 1925, ss.85(2), 86(2).
[38] *First National Bank plc v. Thompson* [1996] 1 All E.R. 140.
[39] Land Registration Act 1925, s.26.
[40] See Land Registration Act 1925, ss.20, 23.

vest a legal interest in the mortgagee, and, prior to registration, the mortgagee will have only an equitable, rather than a legal, mortgage.[41] This can have important consequences for the priority of the mortgage.

4 Creation of equitable mortgages

A legal mortgage can, of course, be created only by a person who holds a legal interest out of which the mortgage can be granted. If the borrower has only an equitable interest in land, then any attempt to create a legal mortgage or charge can create only an equivalent equitable mortgage. The same result follows if one of two co-owners enters into a mortgage having forged the signature of the other co-owner.[42] A failure to register a mortgage of registered land can also result in the creation of an equitable mortgage. So too can an attempt to create a mortgage where no deed is used. The use of a deed — whether the land is registered or unregistered — is an essential requirement of the creation of a legal mortgage. Equity, however, does not stand upon such formality as the common law, and recognises any specifically enforceable agreement to provide security as sufficient to create a mortgage or charge.[43] It was formerly the case that the mere deposit of the title deeds to a property in return for a loan, and with the intention of providing security, was sufficient to create an equitable mortgage.[44] That no longer applies. Since 1989[45] any contract for the grant of an interest in land must be made in writing, contain all the relevant terms, and be signed by both parties.[46] In *Bank of Kuwait v. Sahib*[47] it was held that the basis of an equitable mortgage by deposit is that there is an enforceable contract to create a mortgage. It follows, therefore, that such mortgages now require the formality of being made in writing. This applies both to registered[48] and to unregistered land.

THE RIGHTS OF THE MORTGAGOR

1 The equity of redemption

The fact that the lender under a mortgage or charge has either a lease in the land concerned for three millennia,[49] or is said to have the same protection, powers and remedies as if that had been the case, rather obscures the reality of the position. The reality is that the borrower is the owner. The lease (or deemed lease[50]) enjoyed by the

[41] Land Registration Act 1925, s.106.
[42] See *Thames Guarantee Ltd v. Campbell* [1985] Q.B. 210.
[43] *Matthews v. Goodday* (1861) 31 L.J. Ch. 282.
[44] *Russel v. Russel* (1783) 1 Bro. C.C. 269.
[45] After September 26, 1989.
[46] Law of Property (Miscellaneous Provisions) Act 1989, s.2.
[47] [1996] 3 All E.R. 215, C.A.
[48] But see Land Registration Act 1925, s.66 which is expressed in terms which appear to contemplate the deposit of a land certificate operating as a lien.
[49] This is a period longer than the period since the birth of Christ; it is three times as long as the origins of the modern English law of the ownership of land. It is therefore long enough to be virtually indistinguishable from a right to the land for ever.
[50] In *Grand Junction Co. Ltd v. Bates* [1954] 2 Q.B. 160 at 169 Upjohn J., said that a chargee of a lease by way of legal mortgage is entitled to say "I am to be put in the same position as if I had a charge by way of sub-demise".

lender confers only rights of security and not the rights which would be enjoyed by a tenant under an ordinary beneficial lease from a landowner. The borrower remains living in the property upon which the loan was secured.[51] If the property is sold, and there is an increase in value, it is the borrower who benefits. If there is any fall in value, it is the borrower who incurs the loss. This is because the borrower is entitled to the whole value of the property, subject only to repayment of the loan. All is not, therefore, what it seems. This is not the only way in which the appearance is at odds with the reality. If the property is sold under a forced sale by the lender (for instance if the borrower fails to repay the loan, or breaks some other condition of the mortgage), the lender, who has at most a long lease over the property, is able to sell the whole fee simple in the property.[52] The whole state of affairs has been described in a famous phrase as "one long suppressio veri and suggestio falsi."[53] It does no credit to the law that it has been allowed to continue without reform. It is equity which ensures that, despite the semblance of the situation, the borrower remains an effectual owner of the property. The borrower has thus been described as having an "equity" in the property, or, more fully, an "equity of redemption". This phrase describes the full bundle of the borrower's rights in the property, subject to the obligations imposed by the mortgage. This equity of redemption is capable of being bought and sold,[54] made subject to a further mortgage, given away by will, or acquired by the Crown as property without an owner.[55]

2 The right to redeem

One of the rights making up the equity of redemption, but by no means the only one, is the borrower's equitable right to redeem. That is the borrower's right to repay the loan and have the mortgage discharged from the property, even in cases where there has not been strict compliance with any time limits imposed by the mortgage deed or agreement. Redemption is the process by which, following the discharge of the loan or other obligation secured against property, the property is freed from the mortgage. The process is simple. In the case of unregistered land all that is required is that a receipt is endorsed on the mortgage deed, or is annexed to it.[56] In the case of registered land, application in the prescribed form must be made to the Land Registry.

It is in the nature of a mortgage that there must always be a right to redeem, and this will normally be an express term of the agreement. A right to redeem on the basis of an express term is described as the legal right to redeem. At common law, any such express right had to be exercised strictly in accordance with its terms. If a mortgage provided for repayment on a certain day, say, after six months, the borrower would be expected at common law to repay on that day, not earlier,[57] not later. Any delay in repayment would result in a forfeiture of the right to redeem.

[51] The right of the landlord to continue living in the property which he has let to a tenant would normally be inconsistent with the tenant having exclusive possession — an essential requirement of a valid lease.
[52] Or whatever other estate the borrower holds subject to the mortgage.
[53] "One long suppression of the truth and suggestion of untruth". Maitland, *Equity* (1936) p.182.
[54] Although the usual practice in England is to repay the loan out of the proceeds of sale in order to discharge the mortgage, it is common practice in some other countries (for instance in North America) to sell a property subject to the mortgage.
[55] *Re Sir Thomas Spencer Wells* [1933] Ch. 29.
[56] Law of Property Act 1925, s.115(1); Building Societies Act 1986, Sched. 4 para. 2.
[57] *Brown v. Cole* (1845) 14 Sim. 427; *Burrough v. Cranston* (1840) I. Eq. R. 203.

Equity considered this rule too harsh, and moderated it by permitting borrowers to repay at any stage upon reasonable notice to the lender,[58] even if the date fixed in the contract had gone past. This right was known as the equitable right to redeem. The only way in which a borrower could lose the equitable right to redeem was if, in court proceedings, the right was "foreclosed" on the application of the lender. Even then, it was possible for a foreclosure to be reopened on the application of a borrower willing to make good any financial loss to the lender. Because of equity's intervention, the date fixed for repayment in the mortgage became of little significance, and the practice grew up of providing in the mortgage agreement for repayment after three or six months even if the loan was actually intended to last much longer. This was yet another respect in which form and substance did not correspond. Some modern mortgages continue to adopt this artificiality, but there is a growing and welcome practice to describe the obligation to repay in more accurate terms.

3 Possession

The purpose of a mortgage is normally to provide security for a loan. In most cases that loan is taken out to finance the purchase of a property in which the purchaser intends to live. The way in which a mortgage is created, however, may confer the right to possession on the lender (the mortgagee) rather than on the borrower. Where a mortgage is created by way of a demise with a proviso for cesser on redemption, the lease confers on the mortgagee an automatic right to possession. A statutory charge by way of legal mortgage is treated as conferring the same powers and remedies on the chargee as a mortgage by demise "including the right to take proceedings to obtain possession from the occupiers."[59] The wording suggests that the right to possession may require a court order.[60] Since possession will almost invariably be sought by way of court order,[61] or by consent,[62] there is, though, no practical difference between a mortgage by demise and a mortgage by legal charge except for the rare possibility of a mortgagee seeking to take possession peaceably without a court order. Harman J. in *Four Maids Ltd v. Dudley Marshall Properties Ltd*[63] used colourful language to describe the position on possession:

> "The right of the mortgagee to possession in the absence of some contract has nothing to do with default on the part of the mortgagor. The mortgagee may go into possession before the ink is dry on the mortgage unless there is something in the contract, express or by implication, whereby he has contracted himself out of that right. He has the right because he has a legal term of years in the property or its statutory equivalent."

[58] By convention, this period of notice is six months (see *Cromwell Property Investment Co. Ltd v. Western & Toovey* [1934] Ch. 322), which is said to provide the lender with adequate time to find other ways of using or investing the money to be repaid.

[59] Law of Property Act 1925, s.87(1).

[60] A court order is required where an equitable mortgagee wishes to take possession: *Ladup Ltd v. Williams & Glyn's Bank plc* [1985] 1 W.L.R. 851; *Re O'Neill* [1967] N.I. 129.

[61] For residential property, this may be required as a consequence off the statutory jurisdiction to provide relief to mortgagors in certain circumstances under Administration of Justice Act 1970, s.36 (see below).

[62] For instance where a borrower in default under a mortgage posts the keys to the property through the building society's office door.

[63] [1957] Ch. 317 at 320.

In practice, mortgagees will not normally take possession of the property except where there has been default by the mortgagor, and then they will do so only as a precursor to exercising their right to sell.[64] This is because this was the intention at the time of the mortgage. In addition, a mortgagee taking possession is under an obligation to take reasonable care of the physical state of the property[65] and is under a strict duty to account for any notional benefit which could be derived from possession. For instance in *White v. City of London Brewery Co.*,[66] the defendant mortgagees (a brewing company) took possession of a public house which the plaintiff had mortgaged to them. They leased it to a tenant with a provision tying him to obtaining all his beer from the defendants. The Court of Appeal held that the defendants were liable to account, not merely for the rent which they had received, but rather for the higher rent they could have obtained if the public house had been let as a free house.

The mortgagee's right to possession is therefore another instance of the way in which mortgages are not always what they seem. Many mortgages now reflect reality by conferring a right of possession on the mortgagor, either by means of an attornment clause (*i.e.* a leaseback),[67] or more usually, by providing that the mortgagee will not seek possession unless the mortgagor is in default.[68] The courts will not lightly imply a term deferring the mortgagee's right to possession where there is no express term to this effect,[69] although they are more likely to do so in the case of an instalment mortgage than in other cases.[70] The courts may, however, defer an order for possession of residential property in certain circumstances.

4 Grant of leases

A mortgagor in possession has a statutory power to grant leases of land, normally not exceeding 50 years, binding on the mortgagee.[71] It is standard practice in leases for this power to be excluded. It is only in the most exceptional circumstances[72] that a lease entered into after the creation of a mortgage will be binding on the mortgagee where the statutory power has been excluded. Such a lease will be binding on the mortgagor, but not on the mortgagee.[73] In *Barclays Bank plc v. Zaroovabli*,[74] however, a bank taking a charge by way of legal mortgage over registered land had failed to register the charge as was required to complete it. The charge contained a prohibition on the creation of leases by the mortgagor. Despite this, the mortgagor granted a lease for six months to a tenant which developed, on expiry, into a statutory tenancy under the

[64] For a rare exception, where the mortgagee wished to take possession in order to preserve the value of the property, see *Western Bank Ltd v. Schindler* [1977] Ch.
1.
[65] *Palk v. Mortgage Services Funding plc* [1993] Ch. 330 at 338 *per* Nicholls V-C.
[66] (1889) 42 Ch.D. 237.
[67] *Peckham Mutual Building Society v. Registrar* (1980) 42 P. & C.R. 186.
[68] *Birmingham Citizens Permanent Building Society v. Caunt* [1962] Ch. 883.
[69] *Western Bank Ltd v. Schindler* [1977] Ch. 1.
[70] *Esso Petroleum v. Alstonbridge Properties Ltd* [1975] 1 W.L.R. 1474.
[71] Law of Property Act 1925, s.99.
[72] As in *Quennell v. Maltby* [1979] 1 W.L.R. 318 where a mortgage was used as a device to avoid the Rent Acts. See [1979] C.L.J. 257 (R.A. Pearce).
[73] *Britannia Building Society v. Earl* [1990] 1 W.L.R. 422; *Dudley and District Benefit Building Society v. Emerson* [1949] 2 All E.R. 252.
[74] [1997] 2 All E.R. 19.

Rent Act 1977. The Court of Appeal held that this lease was binding on the bank as an overriding interest, notwithstanding the later registration of the legal charge. The delay in registering the charge meant that it initially took effect only in equity, whilst the lease, when granted, took effect as a legal interest since it was not required to be registered to have full force and effect.[75] Under the priority rules affecting registered land, the lease, being equivalent to a registered disposition of a legal estate for valuable consideration, took priority over a mortgage operating only as a minor equitable interest unprotected by any entry on the register.[76]

SETTING ASIDE A MORTGAGE FOR UNDUE INFLUENCE

1 General

It will on occasions be possible for a mortgagor to have a mortgage set aside, or to have some of its provisions modified or declared void, because of some mitigating factor. This includes the possibility that the mortgage has been obtained through undue influence, which is considered next, or through oppressive and unconscionable conduct, or where the terms which the mortgagee has sought to impose are inconsistent with the nature of a mortgage. These are considered later.

2 Undue influence

Equity has long exercised a jurisdiction to set aside transactions which have been obtained through the abuse of a relationship of trust and confidence. The jurisdiction is not confined to setting aside mortgages. However, there has been a recent explosion in the number of reported cases applying equity's principles governing undue influence to mortgage transactions.

(a) Direct undue influence

Mortgages can be set aside on the grounds that the mortgagor's consent to the mortgage was obtained by undue influence. This can happen in a number of ways. One is where there has been the direct exercise of undue influence by the lender. If the lender, taking advantage of a special relationship of trust and confidence with the borrower, persuaded the borrower to take out a mortgage when the borrower would have been better advised not do so, then the lender will not be allowed to take advantage of the breach of the position of trust and confidence by enforcing the mortgage and evicting the borrower. The lender, in exercising undue influence, could act either personally or through an agent. A lender who employed a salesman to market mortgages would be treated as having used undue influence if the salesman preyed upon the fears of an elderly householder to persuade her to take out a mortgage to invest in the purchase of an annuity[77] without ensuring that she fully

[75] Land Registration Act 1925, s.19.
[76] See Land Registration Act 1925, s.20.
[77] Using a mortgage in this way is a means of converting the capital value of a house into income. The capital sum released by the mortgage is used to buy an annuity (a pension) of a guaranteed amount. The income which the annuity produces is used to pay the interest on the mortgage, and any surplus can be kept by the borrower. The mortgage is repaid by a sale of the property when the borrower dies. The amount of the annuity will normally be more than the amount of the interest charges, since insurance companies take account in fixing annuity rates of the life expectancy of the person purchasing the annuity, and can therefore return part of the capital sum in each of the annuity payments. The risk which the borrower takes is that rises in mortgage interest rates may absorb a large part of the annuity income, and might even exceed it.

understood the nature of the transaction and the risks involved in it. Where actual influence is exercised, it is no defence for the lender to show that in every other respect the terms of the transaction were completely fair and reasonable.

(b) Presumed undue influence

In addition to situations where actual undue influence is affirmatively proved, there are others in which undue influence can be presumed. This applies in cases where "there was a relationship of trust and confidence between the complainant and the wrongdoer of such a nature that it is fair to presume that the wrongdoer abused that relationship in procuring the complainant to enter into the impugned transaction."[78] This relationship is automatically presumed in some instances, such as solicitor and client or doctor and patient, but can also be shown to exist in other situations. Where such a relationship is found or presumed, and a transaction is to the manifest disadvantage of the complainant,[79] "there is no need [for the complainant] to produce evidence that actual undue influence was exerted in relation to the particular transaction impugned; once a confidential relationship has been proved, the burden then shifts to the wrongdoer to prove that the complainant entered into the impugned transaction freely, for example by showing that the complainant had independent advice."[80] Following these principles, if a mortgagor seeking to set aside a mortgage as against a bank showed that the bank, through an employee or other agent, had put itself into a position where the mortgagor reposed trust and confidence in the bank or its agent, it would then be for the bank to discharge the onus of disproving undue influence in relation to a mortgage which was not, on the face of things, for the the mortgagor's benefit.

(c) Undue influence exercised by a third party

Most cases of undue influence, however, do not involve the direct exercise of undue influence by the lender. Instead, they are cases where the mortgagee is prevailed upon by some other person close to them, typically a member of their family, to take out the mortgage. The issue is then whether the mortgagee is affected by the exercise of undue influence by this third party. The leading case on this point is the decision of the House of Lords in *Barclays Bank plc v. O'Brien.*[81] One matter which this case makes clear is that it will very rarely be the case that the third party, if otherwise unconnected with the mortgagee, will be treated as the mortgagee's agent. Suppose, for instance, that a husband, wanting to borrow money for his own purposes, goes to a bank which agrees to make the loan only if he gives the bank a mortgage over the family home owned jointly with his wife. Suppose also that the bank gives him the mortgage deed and asks him to take it home for his wife to sign. In doing so, is the husband acting as the bank's agent so that, if he improperly persuades his wife to sign, the bank will be

[78] *Bank of Credit and Commerce International S.A. v. Aboody* [1990] 1 Q.B. 923 at 953 as approved by Lord Browne-Wilkinson in *Barclays Bank plc v. O'Brien* [1994] 1 A.C. 180 at 189–190.
[79] A requirement identified in *National Westminster Bank plc v. Morgan* [1985] A.C. 686 which was queried by Lord Browne-Wilkinson in *CIBC v. Pitt* [1994] 1 A.C. 200 at 209 but is generally accepted still to be needed in cases of presumed undue influence: see *Dunbar Bank v. Nadeem* [1997] 2 Ch.D. 253 at 264.
[80] *Bank of Credit and Commerce International SA v. Aboody* [1990] 1 Q.B. 923 at 953 as approved by Lord Browne-Wilkinson in *Barclays Bank plc v. O'Brien* [1994] 1 A.C. 180 at 189–190.
[81] [1994] 1 A.C. 180. For commentary see [1994] Conv. 140, 421; [1994] C.L.J. 21; (1994) 110 L.Q.R. 167; (1994) 57 M.L.R. 467; [1994] Restitution Law Rev 3; (1995) 15 *Legal Studies* 35; (1995) 15 O.J.L.S. 119.

treated as having exercised undue influence in procuring the loan? Some cases before *Barclays Bank plc v. O'Brien* had suggested that this would, indeed, be the case. The House of Lords thought that this was wrong. The Law Lords view was that it would be a very rare occurrence for a husband to be treated as the lender's agent. Their opinion was that agency should be found only where it could be said to exist "in a real sense."[82]

In the view of the House of Lords in *Barclays Bank plc v. O'Brien*, the question of whether a mortgagee is affected by undue influence exercised by a third party will normally depend on the knowledge or notice of the mortgagee.[83] In some cases, although they are likely to be rare, the mortgagee may have actual knowledge of the exercise of undue influence by some third party upon the mortgagor. The impersonal nature of most modern bank transactions makes that situation unusual. In most cases, therefore, the mortgagee is likely to be affected by undue influence on the basis of constructive notice. The theory which the House of Lords adopted in *O'Brien's case* was that, where a mortgage had been obtained by undue influence, the person so induced to enter into it has a right in the nature of an equity against the wrongdoer to set the mortgage aside. On general equitable principles, that equitable right is enforceable against the mortgagee if the latter had notice, actual or constructive, of the equitable right.[84]

In *CIBC Mortgages plc v. Pitt*,[85] the House of Lords held that a bank was not treated as having constructive notice of the undue influence exercised by a husband over his wife to raise a loan supported by a mortgage of the family home since, even though the purpose of the loan was to enable the husband to make speculative investments, the bank had been informed that it was to be used by both of them. In *Barclays Bank plc v. O'Brien*, however, a mortgage over the jointly owned matrimonial home had been taken by the bank to secure the husband's business debts. The fact that the wife was obaining no direct benefit from the arrangement and that, being in a close personal relationship with the borrower, she was likely to have been influenced by him, were enough to put the bank on inquiry.

3 The importance of manifest disadvantage

The House of Lords in *Barclays Bank plc v. O'Brien*[86] suggested that the fact that a wife was acting as surety was an important factor in making the determination that a creditor was put on inquiry about the possibility of undue influence. Lord Browne-Wilkinson would have extended the same principle to heterosexual and homosexual cohabitees. Subsequent cases have taken it further. For instance, in *Massey v. Midland Bank plc*,[87] the Court of Appeal thought that there was the same possibility of an impairment of judgmental capacity where a woman acted as guarantor for the debts of

[82] See *CIBC v. Pitt* [1994] 1 A.C. 200 at 211; *Dunbar Bank v. Nadeem* [1997] 2 Ch.D. 253 at 270.
[83] This does not need to be specially pleaded: *Barclays Bank plc v. Boulter* (1997) *The Times*, April 25 C.A. It is also irrelevant whether the land is registered or unregistered.
[84] The Scottish courts require actual notice of undue influence: *Mumford v. Bank of Scotland* [1996] 1 F.L.R. 344.
[85] [1994] 1 A.C. 200.
[86] [1994] 1 A.C. 180 at 196.
[87] [1995] 1 All E.R. 929.

her lover of 14 years standing, even though she did not live with him because her parents objected to the relationship. In *Credit Lyonnais Bank Nederland v. Burch*,[88] where the Court of Appeal held that an "extravagantly improvident" unlimited guarantee by a junior employee of all of her employer's debts was in itself evidence of the abuse of a relationship of trust and confidence, Millett L.J. rejected the argument that it was always necessary to find evidence of a sexual or emotional tie before it could be presumed that there was a relationship of confidence. In his view, the existence of a sexual or emotional tie would at least make a surety transaction explicable where there was no apparent benefit to the surety.[89]

> "A wife might well consider (and be properly advised) that it was in her interest to provide a (suitably limited) guarantee of her husband's business borrowings and to charge it on her interest in the matrimonial home, even if she had no legal interest in the company which owned the business. Her livelihood and that of her family would no doubt depend on the success of the business; and a refusal to entertain the husband's importunity might put at risk the marital relationship as well as the continued prosperity of herself and her family."

From these developments it can be surmised that the important factor in putting a lender on inquiry about the possibility of undue influence is not so much the relationship between borrower and surety (of which the lender may have little or no knowledge), but the fact that the transaction is one in which the surety appears to gain no personal benefit. This establishes the manifest disadvantage which was held in *National Westminster Bank plc v. Morgan*[90] to be the identifying characteristic of the presumption of undue influence.

In a recent case the principle was extended to a case where the arrangement combined features both of personal benefit and of surety. In *Dunbar Bank plc v. Nadeem*,[91] the husband, who was already seriously in debt and in arrears with interest payments on outstanding personal loans, negotiated a loan in order to buy a new leasehold of the matrimonial home jointly with his wife. The majority of the loan was used in the purchase, but some was also used to help pay off outstanding overdue interest on the husband's personal loans. The loan was secured by way of a mortgage over the house which extended not only to the amount advanced by way of loan, but also to any other indebtedness of the husband to the bank. The wife signed the mortgage deed without having been given, or advised to seek, independent advice. The husband's financial position subsequently deteriorated badly,[92] and the bank sought to enforce its security over the matrimonial home against the wife. Robert Englehart Q.C., sitting as a deputy High Court judge, held that the unlimited nature of the mortgage in respect to the husband's debts and the fact that part of the loan had been used to reduce them meant that, even though the wife derived some benefits under the

[88] [1997] 1 All E.R. 144.
[89] [1997] 1 All E.R. 144 at 155.
[90] [1985] A.C. 686.
[91] [1997] 2 Ch.D. 253.
[92] If this appears to be a familiar story, it is in part because court cases represent the pathology of the law. If Mr Nadeem's business had prospered, there would have been no default on his loans, and hence no application by the lenders to the court.

arrangement, it was still manifestly disadvantageous to her. There was evidence to support a presumption that her husband had procured her signature on the loan through undue influence, and since the bank had not taken any steps whatever to ensure that she understood the nature of the mortgage or was independently advised, the mortgage should therefore be set aside.

4 Commercial considerations

The view that the existence of a surety relationship might be enough in itself to raise a presumption of undue influence has, however, been challenged by another recent case, *Banco Exterior Internacionale S.A. v. Thomas.*[93] A woman, recently bereaved,[94] in straightened financial circumstances, and suffering from cancer, agreed to guarantee all of a close friend's debts in return for a payment of £125 per week. She signed the mortgage in front of a solicitor appointed by the mortgagee, who saw her on her own and who explained the nature of the arrangement to her. Although the trial judge held that there was a presumption of undue influence, the Court of Appeal was less sure that this was so, since the fact that the mortgagee had been fully informed of the transaction and nevertheless agreed to it was enough to rebut any initial presumption to which the nature of a surety arrangement might give rise. Sir Richard Scott V.-C. in the Court of Appeal thought that to expect a bank to delve further (as finding that there was a presumption of undue influence in these circumstances might require) would be unacceptable for a number of reasons.[95]

> "First, the enquiries that it is suggested the bank should have made would have constituted unwarranted impertinence on the bank's part. A bank has no business enquiring into the personal relationship between those with whom it has business dealings or as to their personal motives for wanting to help one another. A bank is not to be treated as a branch of the social services agencies. Second, if these impertinent enquiries had been made, and if answers on the lines suggested had been elicited, the answers, far from suggesting undue influence, would have revealed that Mrs Dempsey might have had a very firm and clearly thought out reason for entering into the arrangement, namely, that she wanted extra income and was prepared to take a risk with her capital in order to achieve it. The critical point, however, to my mind is that the bank was engaging in a business transaction and had no reason to do more than to ensure that Mrs Dempsey knew what she was doing and wanted to do it."

Balancing the desire to protect the vulnerable against the desire to facilitate the task of lenders was also a consideration which led the House of Lords in *CIBC v. Pitt* to hold that a bank was not put on notice of the possibility of undue influence where, on the face of a transaction, the person later seeking to impugn it appeared to be benefiting. To have held that the fact that the borrowers were married was enough to raise a

[93] [1997] 1 All E.R. 46.
[94] Her "common law husband" of many years standing had died some three years before.
[95] [1997] 1 All E.R. 46 at 55–56.

presumption of undue influence would have increased the cost and difficulty of mortgage lending. Lord Browne-Wilkinson said: "It accords neither with justice nor with practical common sense . . . To establish the law in that sense would not benefit the average married couple and would discourage financial institutions from making the advance." Despite the resonance of the views expressed in *CIBC v. Pitt* and in *Banco Exterior Internacionale S.A. v. Thomas*,[96] it is submitted that the latter case should not be treated as holding that there is no presumption of undue influence in a surety case where advice has been given to the surety; it is better to treat it as holding that the initial presumption of undue influence arising from a surety relationship is rebutted where adequate steps have been taken to ensure that the surety knew and understood the nature of the transaction unless the circumstances known to the mortgagee require more.

5 Rebutting the presumption of undue influence

If the nature of the mortgage and the circumstances in which it was granted are such as to raise a real possibility that undue influence might have been exercised, the mortgagee is treated as being put on enquiry as to the existence of undue influence. This knowledge includes situations where, as with surety arrangements in which there appears to be no personal benefit to the surety, there is a presumption of undue influence. If the mortgagee then "fails to make such enquiry or take such other steps as are reasonable to verify whether such earlier right does or does not exist, he will have constructive notice of the earlier right and take subject to it."[97]

There is thus a direct obligation on a mortgagee in cases of presumed undue influence to take active steps to assure itself that there has in fact been no undue influence. The classic way of showing that there has been no undue influence is to demonstrate that the complainant was independently advised about the transaction. The purpose of this is to ensure that the nature of the transaction has been fully explained, the complainant understands it, and any consent has been given on that footing. In *Barclays Bank plc v. O'Brien*, the House of Lords said that it would not normally be necessary for a bank to insist that independent advice was obtained where it had notice of the possibility of undue influence. It would normally be sufficient to discharge the burden which such a presumption of undue influence imposed on it if the wife had been seen by a bank official separately from her husband so that the effect of the mortgage could be explained to her and so that she could be urged to seek independent advice.[98] The Law Lords added that if, in addition, a mortgagee knew of facts which made undue influence probable, rather than merely a real possibility, the mortgagee might have to go further and see that the wife did, indeed, have separate advice. Merely writing to the husband requesting that the wife take independent advice is insufficient without checking that she has taken this advice.[99] In *Banco Exterior*

[96] [1997] 1 All E.R. 46.
[97] *Barclays Bank plc v. O'Brien* [1994] 1 A.C. 180 at 196 *per* Lord Browne-Wilkinson.
[98] A bank cannot normally be expected to do more since it is not capable of itself providing independent advice. It is not independent: *Midland Bank plc v. Kidwai* (1995) *The Independent*, June 5.
[99] *Hemsley v. Brown (No. 2)* [1996] F.C.R. 107.

Internacionale S.A. v. Thomas,[1] the facts of which have been described above, the Court of Appeal thought that the bank taking the surety had fully discharged any obligation on it where it had employed a solicitor who saw the woman privately to explain the nature and effect of the mortgage before witnessing her signature. The bank did not need to ask the woman any detailed personal questions about her personal circumstances and her reasons for agreeing to act as a surety. In *Credit Lyonnais Bank Nederland v. Burch*,[2] however, a different division of the Court of Appeal concluded that more was required in a case so extreme that it "shocked the conscience of the court."[3] If so challenged, it would almost certainly have been held to have been an unconscionable bargain. The owner of a small business wished to increase his overdraft facility from £250,000 to £270,000. The bank required additional security. He therefore persuaded a junior employee, without any incentive for doing so, to mortgage her London apartment for this purpose. The security which the bank used for this purpose imposed on the complainant an unlimited liability for meeting the whole of the employer's debts to the bank. The bank, through its solicitors, wrote to the complainant advising her to obtain independent legal advice, but probably after consulting her employer, she declined to do so. In the view of the Court of Appeal, it was not enough that she had been invited to take independent legal advice. "It was at the least necessary that she should receive such advice."[4] That was because she had inadequate information about the true extent of the risks she was running, and of the existing level of the company's debts at the time she gave her guarantee. Any competent legal adviser would strongly have advised her not to enter into the transaction in the form in which it was presented to her.

6 Using an agent to provide advice

A mortgagee wishing to avoid being fixed with the consequences of a finding of presumed undue influence will normally be able to do so by appointing a solicitor to act on its behalf in obtaining the signature of the guarantor or surety. In *Banco Exterior Internacional v. Mann*,[5] Mr Mann wished to use the family home to secure borrowings for the purpose of his business. The mortgagee wrote to him saying that his wife would have to consent to the mortgage, and that she should sign in the presence of a solicitor who was required to attest that he had explained the nature and effect of the charge to her and that she appeared fully to understand. Although one member of the court thought that this was insufficient to protect the mortgagee, the majority held that it was enough. The Court held that the principle established in *Bank of Boroda v. Shah*[6] remained applicable. The bank "was entitled to assume (in the absence of clear indications to the contrary) that the solicitor who did advise was honest and competent."[7] The mortgagee was therefore permitted to rely upon the charge even

[1] [1997] 1 All E.R. 46.
[2] [1997] 1 All E.R. 144 discussed in *Barclays Bank v. O'Brien* and independent advice [1997] N.L.J. 726 (Anthony Pugh-Thomas).
[3] [1997] 1 All E.R. 144 at 152.
[4] [1997] 1 All E.R. 144 at 152 *per* Nourse L.J.
[5] [1995] 1 All E.R. 936.
[6] [1988] 3 All E.R. 24.
[7] [1995] 1 All E.R. 936 at 944 *per* Morritt L.J.

though it appeared that Mrs Mann was not separately and independently advised of the effect of the mortgage without her husband being present. Similarly in *Massey v. Midland Bank plc*,[8] a bank was held to have done all that was required of it when it advised a woman giving security over her home for her lover's debts to obtain independent legal advice and later received confirmation from a firm of solicitors that independent advice had been given to her. The firm of solicitors had, in fact, been selected by her lover, as the bank knew, and he attended the interview at which she was advised (which was not known by the bank). Nevertheless, in the view of Steyn L.J.:[9]

> "It is generally sufficient for the bank to avoid a finding of constructive notice if the bank urged the proposed surety to take independent advice from a solicitor. How far a solicitor should go in probing the matter, and in giving advice, is a matter for the solicitor's professional judgment and a matter between him and his client. The bank is not generally involved in the nature and extent of the solicitor's advice. And in my judgment there is nothing in the circumstances of the present case which required the bank to do more than urge or insist on independent advice."

The charge in *Massey v. Midland Bank plc*[10] was limited to a fixed amount. In *Credit Lyonnais Bank Nederland v. Burch*,[11] which has already been described above, "the truly astonishing feature"[12] of the case was that the surety was unlimited both in time and in amount. This was important in driving the Court of Appeal to the conclusion that the bank seeking to rely on it was required to do more than merely to urge independent advice, particularly since no such advice was taken.

7 Knowledge of the solicitor

In *Halifax Mortgage Services Ltd v. Stepsky*,[13] a husband and wife executed a mortgage of their home which was stated to be for the purchase of shares in the family business. Mr Stepsky informed his solicitor that the money would be used to pay off his debts. The lender instructed the same solicitors to act for them in the transaction. It was held that the solicitor's knowledge of the true purpose of the loan was not to be imputed to the lender because of the duty of the solicitor not to pass the information on without the consent of his client. The lender was therefore entitled to enforce the mortgage.

8 The effect of undue influence

Where a mortgage provided by way of surety has been obtained by undue influence of which the mortgagee has actual or constructive notice, the mortgage will be set aside in

[8] 1995] 1 All E.R. 929 (noted at [1995] Conv. 148). See also for other decisions to similar effect *Bank of Baroda v. Rayarel* [1995] 2 F.L.R. 376 and *Barclays Bank plc v. Thomson* (unreported, Court of Appeal, November 7, 1996).
[9] [1995] 1 All E.R. 929 at 934–935.
[10] 1995] 1 All E.R. 929.
[11] [1997] 1 All E.R. 144.
[12] [1997] 1 All E.R. 144 at 150 *per* Nourse L.J.
[13] [1995] 4 All E.R. 656.

its entirety as against the surety, even where no undue influence has been exercised over the surety as respects part of the mortgage. So, in a case where a wife had been misled into agreeing to a mortgage over the family home to secure all of the husband's debts by being told that it extended only to debts up to £15,000, when it actually covered all of his debts, the Court of Appeal held that unlike the curate's egg, which was good in parts, no part of the mortgage was enforceable against the wife.[14] It is different where the mortgagor obtains a personal benefit from the transaction. In this situation, it has been held that it would be wrong to set aside the mortgage unless the mortgagor accounts to the mortgagee for the benefits which the mortgagor has received.[15] This is surely correct in principle, since the purpose of equity's jurisdiction in undue influence is to prevent the imposition of unfair burdens on the weak and impressionable, not to confer an uncovenanted bounty on them. In *Dunbar Bank plc v. Nadeem*,[16] the husband raised a mortgage loan, in part to buy a long leasehold interest in the matrimonial home, and in part to pay off his existing business debts. Since the wife derived a benefit through her beneficial interest in the leasehold, the judge made it a condition of setting aside the mortgage that the wife refund to the bank the proportion of the mortgage which represented the cost of financing the purchase of her half share in the beneficial interest in the property.

UNCONSCIONABLE BARGAINS AND COLLATERAL ADVANTAGES

1 Equity's jurisdiction

Equity's protection of mortgagors goes beyond merely extending the right to redeem. Doctrines of equity of general application have also found special expression in relation to mortgages. One is the right to set aside unconscionable bargains. Where a contract which no properly informed legal adviser could support has been obtained from someone of weak mind, equity will not permit the bargain to stand. For instance, where a tenant and her husband prevailed upon their feeble-minded landlady (who was suffering from Parkinson's disease) to grant them a lease on terms which they knew they could not extract from her agent or anyone else, the Privy Council had no hesitation in confirming that the trial judge was right in setting the lease aside.[17] Similarly in relation to mortgages. In *Credit Lyonnais Bank Nederland v. Burch*,[18] the Court of Appeal was of the view that a mortgage granted by a junior employee of her employer's debts, unlimited in time and in amount, so "shocked the conscience of the court"[19] that if it had been challenged on that basis, it would almost certainly have been held to have been an unconscionable bargain. The mortgage transaction was so extreme that "an independent solicitor would certainly have advised her as strongly as he could that she should in no circumstances enter into the mortgage."[20]

[14] *TSB Bank plc v. Camfield* [1995] 1 All E.R. 951.
[15] *Dunbar Bank plc v. Nadeem* [1997] 2 All E.R. 253. See also *Midland Bank plc v. Greene* [1994] 2 F.L.R. 827.
[16] [1997] 2 Ch.D. 253.
[17] *Boustany v. Pigott* (1993) Lawtel document No. C1605332.
[18] [1997] 1 All E.R. 144.
[19] [1997] 1 All E.R. 144 at 152.
[20] [1997] 1 All E.R. 144 at 158 *per* Swinton Thomas L.J.

In order to show that a transaction is so harsh and oppressive that it should be set aside as unconscionable, it must be shown that "one of the parties to it has imposed the objectional terms in a morally reprehensible manner, that is, in a way which affects his conscience."[21] This latter may be evident from the very improvidence of the transaction in question.[22] It is not enough that a transaction is seriously disadvantageous or commercially misguided, since "the law in general leaves every man at liberty to make such bargains as he pleases, and to dispose of his own property as he chooses."[23] A good example of this is *Multiservice Bookbinding Ltd v. Marden.*[24] A bookbinder, seeking to raise money for the purpose of his business, agreed to make repayments which were linked to movements in the rate of exchange between the Swiss franc and the pound sterling. He also agreed to pay interest at two per cent above Minimum Lending Rate. He was accordingly agreeing to what would now be called a "double whammy", because U.K. interest rates were running at very high levels, and the pound was depreciating rapidly against the Swiss franc.[25] Over the ten-year fixed period of the loan, repayments of capital and interest amounted to nearly four times the amount borrowed. Despite this extremely high cost to the loan, Browne-Wilkinson J. refused to set the bargain aside. The parties to the loan agreement were not in unequal bargaining positions, there was no evidence of sharp practice, and the borrower had received independent advice. The property which he had bought with the loan had also increased in value threehold. The bargain which he had made was hard — even unreasonable — but it was not unconscionable.

By way of contrast, in *Cityland and Property Holdings Ltd v. Dabrah*,[26] the tenant of residential property agreed to buy the freehold from his landlord. The majority of the purchase price was to be supplied by means of payments to the landlord secured by a mortgage against the property. These payments totalled substantially more than the portion of the purchase price which they replaced, and all of the payments were due immediately on default by the buyer, without any discount for early payment. The buyer did default relatively soon after granting the mortgage. If the whole of the amount secured was then repayable, it would have amounted to a notional interest rate of 57 per cent per annum. Goff J. held that this premium was so unreasonably high that it was unfair and unconscionable. The notional interest payable should be reduced to an amount which was fair and reasonable having regard to the risks involved.

2 Extortionate credit bargains

The Consumer Credit Act 1974 gives the courts a statutory jurisdiction to reopen extortionate credit bargains. There is no financial limit to this jurisdiction in relation to mortgages, but the Act does not apply to loans by building societies or local

[21] *Multiservice Bookbinding Ltd v. Marden* [1979] Ch. 84 at 110 per Browne-Wilkinson J.

[22] *Alec Lobb (Garages) Ltd v. Total Oil GB Ltd* [1983] 1 All E.R. 944 at 961 *per* Millett J.

[23] *Brusewitz v. Brown* (1922) 42 N.Z.L.R. 1106 at 1110 *per* Sir John Salmond.

[24] [1979] Ch. 84. See [1978] C.L.J. 211 (A.J. Oakley); (1979) 42 M.L.R. 338 (W.D. Bishop and B.V. Hindley).

[25] High interest levels in the U.K. reflected the weak position of the pound. If the loan had been taken out in Swiss francs (exchange controls permitting), the borrower would have paid much lower interest rates. The lender was in effect having his cake and eating it.

[26] [1968] Ch. 166. See also *Kevans v. Joyce* [1896] 1 I.R. 442 and *Wells v. Joyce* [1905] 2 I.R. 134.

authorities. A credit bargain is considered extortionate if it "requires the debtor . . . to make payments . . . which are grossly exorbitant, or . . . otherwise grossly contravenes ordinary principles of fair dealing."[27] Factors which the court is expected to take into account include the degree of risk which the creditor (lender) is taking, and the age, experience, business capacity, state of health, and financial circumstances of the debtor (borrower).[28] In *A Ketley Ltd v. Scott*,[29] Foster J. held that an interest rate of 48 per cent was not excessive for a temporary bridging loan given to enable the defendants to take advantage of an opportunity to buy the flat in which they lived for a substantial discount. In other cases, apparently high interest rates have been upheld because the loan has been made as a matter of last resort to a borrower who has a poor record of repayments (and therefore represents a high risk).

3 Collateral advantages

Perhaps as a development at a time when usury laws restricted the rates of interest payable,[30] equity developed a set of rules prohibiting certain advantages which were seen as "collateral" to the mortgage; that is, as not being a part and parcel of the mortgage itself. The rules were associated with the theory that upon redemption of a mortgage, the mortgagor should receive a return of his property, free from all charges and claims against it.

(a) There must be a right to redeem

The first principle equity applied was that the nature of a mortgage required that the mortgagor had a real right to redem his property free from the mortgage.[31] The right to redeem could not be illusory. So, although there was (and remains) in itself no objection to a mortgage which restricts the freedom of the mortgagor to redeem for a fixed period,[32] the mortgage must be capable of redemption while the asset subject to the mortgage still has some genuine residual value. This is neatly illustrated by two contrasting cases. In *Fairclough v. Swan Brewery Co. Ltd*,[33] a publican's 172 year lease was mortgaged on terms that it could not be redeemed until six weeks before the lease expired. The Privy Council held that this contractual fetter on redemption was invalid since it made the mortgage for all practical purposes irredeemable. There would have been almost no residual value. By contrast, in *Knightsbridge Estates Trust Ltd v. Byrne*,[34] a commercial mortgage at competitive rates, made between two experienced parties negotiating at arms length, provided that the loan could not be redeemed or called in for a period of 40 years. The property was freehold, and would still have had a significant residual value at the end of the mortgage period. The borrower wished to

[27] Consumer Credit Act 1974, s.138(1).
[28] Consumer Credit Act 1974, s.138.
[29] [1980] CCLR 37.
[30] See *Jennings v. Ward* (1705) 2 Vern 520 at 521: "A man shall not have interest for his money, and a collateral advantage besides for the loan of it, or cog the equity of redemption with any by-agreement".
[31] *Cheah v. Equiticorp Finance Group Ltd* [1992] 1 A.C. 472.
[32] As in *Multiservice Bookbinding Ltd v. Marden* [1979] Ch. 84 where the mortgage was not to be repaid for ten years.
[33] [1912] A.C. 565.
[34] [1939] Ch. 441.

repay the loan only because interest rates had fallen before the contractual redemption date, and the loan could be replaced at lower cost. In the view of the Court of Appeal, there was no reason to set the mortgage aside. It could not be seen "as anything but a proper business transaction".

(b) Redemption must be free from "clogs and fetters"

Since redemption is the right to the return of the property subject to the mortgage once the obligation secured by the mortgage has been discharged,[35] equity initially took the view that, upon redemption, all obligations contained in the mortgage transaction must immediately be discharged. For instance, in *Bradley v. Carritt*[36] the owner of shares in a tea company mortgaged them to a broker and agreed that, even if the mortgage was repaid, he would continue to use the broker for selling the company's tea or pay him the commission that he would have earned had he been so employed. The House of Lords held that this was a fetter on the equity of redemption — an obligation continuing after the discharge of the mortgage — and was unenforceable. Similarly, in *Noakes and Co. Ltd v. Rice*,[37] the owner of a public house mortgaged it to a brewery. He covenanted to buy all his beer from the brewery, not only during the mortgage, but also after the mortgage was redeemed. This was held to be invalid as a restriction on the right to get back the security free from the terms of the mortgage. In both cases, had the tie agreement continued only for the duration of the mortgage, it would almost certainly have been valid,[38] unless the terms were harsh and unconscionable or in restraint of trade.[39]

(c) Options to purchase

Even where a "perfectly fair bargain" has been made between two businessmen, "each of whom was quite sensible of what they were doing" and "without any trace or suspicion of oppression, surprise or circumvention", the bargain will not be upheld if it confers, as part of a mortgage, an option on the mortgagee to purchase the property mortgaged. This was the reluctant conclusion of the House of Lords in *Samuel v. Jarrah Timber and Wood Paving Corporation Ltd.*[40] The House of Lords treated the rule as absolute. In Lord Lindley's words[41]:

> "The doctrine once a mortgage, always a mortgage, means that no contract between a mortgagor and a mortgagee made at the time of the mortgage and as part of the mortgage transaction, or, in other words, as one of the terms of the loan, can be valid if it prevents the mortgagor from getting back his property on

[35] In *Santley v. Wilde* [1899] 2 Ch. 474, the mortgage of a theatre provided for the mortgagee to receive a share of profits as well as the repayment of the loan with interest. The Court of Appeal held that the mortgage secured the performance of the obligation to share profits as well as the obligation to repay the loan, and accordingly the mortgage was not redeemed merely by the repayment of the loan with interest. The provision for a share of profits was justified by the high level of risk involved in making a loan against a theatrical business.

[36] [1903] A.C. 253.

[37] [1902] A.C. 24.

[38] [1902] A.C. 24.

[39] *Biggs v. Hoddinott* [1898] 2 Ch. 307.

[40] [1902] A.C. 323.

[41] [1902] A.C. 323 at ??.

paying off what is due on his security. Any bargain which has that effect is invalid, and is inconsistent with the transaction being a mortgage."

In that case, a mortgage of debenture stock in a company gave the mortgagee the option to purchase the stock at a fair valuation within twelve months of the date of the loan secured by the mortgage. It was held that the mortgagee was not entitled to enforce that option against the wishes of the mortgagor.

(d) Independent contractual stipulations

The courts' objection to collateral advantages does not extend to provisions which form no part of the mortgage itself, but which are part of an independent and distinct contract. For instance, in *Reeve v. Lisle*,[42] decided by the House of Lords immediately before the *Jarrah Timber case*, the mortgagor had granted the mortgagee an option to purchase the property mortgaged in an agreement signed ten or eleven days after the mortgage was made. This option was held to be enforceable since "the agreement to buy the equity of redemption was no part of the original mortgage transaction, but was entered into subsequently, and was an entirely separate transaction to which no objection could be taken."[43] A similar view was taken in *Kreglinger v. New Patagonia Meat and Cold Storage Co. Ltd.*[44] A firm of woolbrokers agreed to lend £10,000 to the respondents, who packed meat. The loan was secured by a charge on the respondents' assets. The woolbrokers agreed that, although they would not call in the loan for five years, it could be repaid at any time by the respondents. The respondents, in return, agreed to give a right of first refusal on all its sheepskins to the woolbrokers, and to pay a commission on any sold to a third party, for the full period of five years, even if the loan had already been repaid. Even though this right of pre-emption was included in the same document as the mortgage, the House of Lords upheld it. Lord Haldane said that: "The question is in my opinion not whether the two contracts were made at the same moment and evidenced by the same instrument, but whether they were in substance a single and undivided contract or two distinct contracts". The right of pre-emption was a preliminary and separable condition of the loan, freely and knowingly entered into. In *Re Petrol Filling Station, Vauxhall Bridge Road, London,*[45] Ungoed-Thomas J. applied Lord Haldane's principle in holding that a solus agreement[46] made between a garage proprietor and a petrol company was enforceable after the redemption of an associated loan, even if the loan had already been repaid.

These decisions make good commercial sense. In both *Kreglinger* and *Vauxhall Bridge*, the main purpose of the mortgagee was not to make loans. The solus agreement in each case was the commercial advantage which the mortgagee sought, and there was evidence in both cases that the loan was a "sweetener" to entice the mortgagor to enter into the agreement. To deprive agreements of this kind of their validity would inhibit perfectly reasonable business arrangements between businessmen who understand fully what they are doing.

[42] [1902] A.C. 461.
[43] *Per* Lord Lindley in *Samuel v. Jarrah Timber and Woodparing Corporation Ltd* [1902] A.C. 323.
[44] [1914] A.C. 25.
[45] (1969) 20 P. & C.R. 1.
[46] That is, an agreement to purchase supplies exclusively from a sole supplier.

THE POSITION OF THE MORTGAGEE

1 The right to payment

A mortgage provides security for the performance of an obligation, normally to repay a loan. The expectation of most mortgagees is that the mortgage will be needed only as a last resort. If the loan is not repaid, the mortgagee may bring an action for repayment on the loan contract. Even where the mortgage is enforced, this right of action normally survives. For instance, in *Palk v. Mortgage Services Funding plc*,[47] where a mortgagee was seeking to take possession of the mortgagor's house, the mortgagor was still liable to make any payments due under the loan contract. Similarly, if the mortgagee enforces a mortgage through sale, and because there is negative equity, the proceeds of sale fail to meet the amount of the loan with interest and costs, the mortgagor remains liable in contract to pay the outstanding balance. The mortgagor faced with negative equity cannot therefore escape his problem by posting the keys to the property through the lender's door and walking away.

Even where a mortgage indemnity policy has been taken out at the mortgagor's expense to cover the possibility of a sale by the mortgagee at less than the amount of the loan, the mortgagor remains liable in contract. Except where the policy expressly provides an indemnity to the mortgagor, the insurance company making good the deficiency to the mortgagee is subrogated to the mortgagee's contractual right and may therefore take over the mortgagee's cause of action.[48]

2 The right to possession

It has already been seen that, although in most cases the mortgagee has the right to possession, the mortgagee will not normally exercise that right where the borrower is not in default, and there may even be an express or implied term of the mortgage that the borrower is entitled to retain possession until in default. Because the liability of a mortgagee to account while in possession is strict, it will be rare for possession to be sought except where the mortgagee intends to sell. In *Palk v. Mortgage Services Funding plc*,[49] however, the circumstances in which a mortgagee sought possession were rather unusual. A property which had been mortgaged for a very substantial sum fell in value below the amount of the mortgage during the property recession. The mortgagors were also in arrears on their mortgage payments, and arrears were building up at an alarming rate. The mortgagees sought possession with the intention of retaining the property until the market improved. In the meantime, repayment arrears were still building up. The Court of Appeal held that it had the power, at the request of the mortgagor, to order a sale[50] even if the sale would not fully discharge the debt.

(a) Jurisdiction to postpone a possession order

In the case of mortgages of residential property, the Administration of Justice Act 1970 places statutory restrictions on the ability of the mortgagee to recover possession.

[47] [1993] Ch. 330.
[48] *Woolwich Building Society v. Brown, The Independent*, January 22, 1996.
[49] [1993] Ch. 330.
[50] Under Law of Property Act 1925, s.91.

These statutory provisions operate in addition to the court's inherent jurisdiction to grant temporary relief by staying proceedings to enable a mortgagor to assemble the funds needed to redeem the mortgage. That inherent jurisdiction is extremely limited. In *Birmingham Citizens' Permanent Building Society v. Caunt*[51] it was held that the court could merely adjourn proceedings for a short time in order to "afford the mortgagor a limited opportunity to find means to pay off the mortgagee or otherwise satisfy him if there was a reasonable prospect of either of those events occurring."[52] An adjournment of more than 28 days would not normally be possible, nor could new repayment terms be forced on an unwilling mortgagee.

The Court of Appeal has held in *Cheltenham and Gloucester plc v. Booker*[53] that, although the circumstances in which the conditions are met will be rare, the inherent jurisdiction enables it to permit mortgagors to remain in possession pending a sale by the mortgagee if the mortgagors are willing to co-operate in the sale, their presence will not depress the price, and they will give up possession on completion. In *Quennell v. Maltby*,[54] where an action for possession was brought by a mortgagee as a device to oust a tenant protected by the Rent Acts, Lord Denning said "A mortgagee will be restrained from getting possession except when it is sought bona fide and reasonably for the purpose of enforcing the security and then only subject to such conditions as the court thinks fit to impose". Whilst the case illustrates that there is a jurisdiction to decline an order for posession in appropriate circumstances, the jurisdiction is probably less broad than Lord Denning asserts.

(b) Statutory relief

(i) The statutory jurisdiction: Under the Administration of Justice Act 1970, s.36, the court may adjourn possession proceedings relating to a "dwelling-house" for such period as the court considers reasonable "if it appears to the court that in the event of its exercising the power the mortgagor is likely to be able within a reasonable period to pay any sums due under the mortgage or to remedy a default consisting of a breach of any other obligation arising under or by virtue of the mortgage". There was a problem with the drafting of this provision. In *Halifax Building Society v. Clarke* a mortgagor had defaulted in making periodical payments under an instalment mortgage. Under a common standard provision in a mortgage repayable by instalments, the whole sum borrowed was immediately repayable if the mortgagor was late in making any single repayment. It was held that the phrase "any sums due" meant the whole of the capital debt and not just the outstanding arrears. The court considered that there was no prospect of this sum being found by the mortgagor "within a reasonable period". To cover this defect, amending legislation has in effect reversed the decision in *Halifax Building Society v. Clark* by defining "any sums due under the mortgage" as those sums which "the mortgagor would have expected to pay if there had been no . . . provision for earlier payment" in the event of a breach.[55] Subsequent decisions have made it clear that the Act applies both to repayment mortgages and also to mortgages where the capital sum is payable in a single instalment, for instance through a separate

[51] [1962] Ch. 883 noted (1962) 78 L.Q.R. 171 (REM).
[52] At 891 *per* Russell L.J.
[53] *The Times*, November 20, 1996.
[54] [1979] 1 W.L.R. 318, noted [1979] C.L.J. 257.
[55] Administration of Justice Act 1973, s.8.

endowment policy,[56] and even in cases where the mortgagee is seeking possession prior to any default on the part of the mortgagor.[57] There may still, though, be some situations to which the Acts do not apply, for instance where a mortgage is used to support a bank overdraft which is repayable only on demand by the bank,[58] and where a warrant for possession has already been issued.[59]

(ii) A reasonable period: The courts initially exercised the jurisdiction under the Administration of Justice Act 1970, s.36 on the basis that the "reasonable period" over which the Act permitted the court to reschedule payments was a short period of no more than, say, one or two years.[60] In *Cheltenham and Gloucester Building Society v. Norgan,*[61] however, following dicta in some earlier cases,[62] the Court of Appeal held that the whole of the remaining period of a mortgage could be taken into account in deciding what amounted to a reasonable period. Waite L.J. said[63]: "The court should take as its starting point the full term of the mortgage and pose at the outset the question: would it be possible for the mortgagor to maintain payment off of the arrears by instalments over that period". According to Evans L.J., the factors to be taken into account in establishing a reasonable period include the ability of the mortgagor to make payments now and in the future, the likely duration of any temporary financial difficulty, the reason for the arrears, the period remaining of the original mortgage, and the adequacy of the security to support the loan and arrears over the repayment period.[64] The court must be satisfied that, over the period which it schedules for repayment, the mortgagor will be able to pay off the arrears and any other sums which fall due for payment under the mortgage.[65] The fact that the mortgagor has a cross-claim against the mortgagee is a factor which may be taken into account in deciding whether to postpone a possession order for a reasonable period, but it is not in itself sufficient to justify refusing an order for possession, even where it amounts to more than the sum owing by way of mortgage.[66]

(iii) Postponement to enable sale: The reason for mortgagees seeking possession of the mortgaged property is normally to facilitate a sale with vacant possession. The mortgagor may, however, feel that a sale conducted by an owner-occupier with the owner still in occupation is likely to realise a higher price than a forced sale under the mortgage of a repossessed property. In *Target Homes Ltd v. Clothier*[67] there was evidence from an estate agent that the property could be sold by the owner for a price sufficient to repay the loan with arrears (no repayments had been made for over 15

[56] *Bank of Scotland v. Grimes* [1985] Q.B. 1179, noted [1985] Conv. 407.
[57] *Western Bank Ltd v. Schindler* [1977] Ch. 1.
[58] *Habib Bank Ltd v. Taylor* [1982] 3 All E.R. 561.
[59] *Cheltenham and Gloucester Building Society v. Obi* (1996) 28 H.L.R. 22.
[60] *Royal Trust Co. of Canada v. Markham* [1975] 1 W.L.R. 1416; *National Westminster Bank plc v. Skelton (note)* [1993] 1 W.L.R. 72.
[61] [1996] 1 All E.R. 449.
[62] *First Middlesburgh Trading and Mortgage Co. Ltd v. Cunningham* (1974) 28 P. & C.R. 69 and *Western bank Ltd v. Schindler* [1977] Ch. 1.
[63] [1996] 1 All E.R. 449 at 458.
[64] See also *First Middlesburgh Trading and Mortgage Co. Ltd v. Cunningham* (1974) 28 P. & C.R. 69.
[65] *First National Bank plc v. Syed* [1991] 2 All E.R. 250; *Town and Country Building Society v. Julien* (1991) 24 H.L.R. 312.
[66] *Mobil Oil Co. Ltd v. Rawlinson* (1981) 43 P. & C.R. 221, noted [1982] Conv. 453; *National Westminster Bank plc v. Skelton* [1993] 1 W.L.R. 72; *Ashley Guarantee plc v. Zacaria* [1993] 1 W.L.R. 62, noted [1993] Conv. 459.
[67] [1994] 1 All E.R. 439.

months) and that an offer to purchase had already been received. Although considering that the estate agent's evidence might need to be slightly discounted, the Court of Appeal nevertheless granted a postponement of the possession order for three months to enable the mortgagor to negotiate a sale. As with the deferral of an order for possession to enable repayment by instalments, there must be a real prospect that a deferral to enable a sale to be made will not leave the lender inadequately secured and that the sale will discharge the loan.[68] As Phillips L.J. said in *Cheltenham and Gloucester plc v. Krausz*[69]:

> "It is . . . quite clear that section 36 does not empower the court to suspend possession in order to permit the mortgagor to sell the mortgaged premises where the proceeds of sale will not suffice to discharge the mortgage debt, unless of course other funds will be available to the mortgagor to make up the shortfall."

Provided that these conditions are met, the suspension of an order for possession is not necessarily confined to a period no longer than three months. In *National and Provincial Building Society v. Lloyd,*[70] the mortgagor sought a delay in an order for possession in order to subdivide the mortgaged property and sell it off in lots. The Court of Appeal held that, although the "reasonable period" for which proceedings could be deferred could be for six or nine months, or even a year,[71] the mortgagor's aspirations to sell the property for enough to cover the loan and arrears owed more to hope than to reality. It therefore declined to defer the order. The court also declined to postpone a possession order in *Bristol and West Building Society v. Ellis,*[72] although the court was prepared to contemplate deferring an order for possession for three to five years.

(c) Protection of spouses

A mortgagee seeking possession of land must serve notice on any spouse who has registered his or her rights of occupation under the Matrimonial Homes Act 1983. The spouse of the mortgagor is also entitled to any relief which is available under the statutory jurisdiction to defer an order for possession under the Administration of Justice Act 1970, s.36. There is, however, no obligation on the mortgagee to inform the spouse of any arrears under the mortgage.[73]

In the case of joint mortgagors, any proceedings must be brought against all the co-owners. Each will then have an opportunity to invoke the protection of section 36. Where one of two joint mortgagors has a defence to the possession proceedings, for instance on the basis that their agreement to the mortgage was obtained through undue influence, it is possible for possession to be ordered against the mortgagor who has no such defence. Since a mortgagee is unlikely to stand to gain any benefit from an order against one co-owner alone, though, "it is not in general right to make an order

[68] *Bristol and West Building Society v. Ellis* EGCS 74; *The Times* May 2, 1996 .
[69] [1997] 1 All E.R. 21 at 29.
[70] [1996] 1 All E.R. 630.
[71] See also *Cheltenham and Gloucester Building Society v. Johnson* (1996) 28 H.L.R. 885.
[72] *The Times* April 24, 1996.
[73] *Hastings and Thanet Building Society v. Goddard* [1970] 1 W.L.R. 1544.

requiring him to leave within the period during which the other mortgagee is in possession and entitled to be in possession. This must particularly be the case when the two mortgagors share the home as husband and wife."[74] The proper practice in most such cases would be to adjourn the proceedings with liberty to restore if the other mortgagor leaves the property or an order for possession is made against him or her.

3 Right to sell

(a) Nature of the power of sale

The right to sell is the most potent of the mortgagee's rights, for it is normally the ultimate means of enforcing the security and repaying the debt which it secures. It is for this reason that prudent lenders ensure that the amount which they advance on loan does not amount to too high a proportion of the value of the property over which security is taken.

There is a right to sell with the authority of a court order in the case of all mortgages, whether legal or equitable. A power of sale without recourse to court can be conferred by the mortgage instrument (which will need to be by deed to confer on the mortgagee the power to grant a legal estate). In addition, for mortgages made by deed (which inevitably includes all legal mortgages), there is a statutory power of sale conferred by the Law of Property Act 1925, s.101. This power of sale arises "when the mortgage money becomes due", but does not become exercisable until certain other conditions have been met. The purpose of this distinction between the power of sale arising and becoming exercisable is to protect purchasers from the mortgagee. The date on which the mortgage money becomes due can be verified from the mortgage deed. The conditions to be satisfied before the power becomes exercisable require an investigation of the mortgage account or actions of the mortgagor. These enquiries might be difficult or inconvenient for a purchaser, but will inevitably be known to the mortgagee. A mortgagee who sells before the relevant conditions have been satisfied will be liable to the mortgagor in damages.[75]

A purchaser is not required to make enquiries to see whether the power of sale has become exercisable.[76] However, if the purchaser has actual knowledge of an irregularity, he will be affected by it.[77]

(b) When the statutory power of sale arises

The statutory power arises (*i.e.* the mortgagee first becomes enabled to sell the property the subject of the mortgage) when any special restrictions contained in the mortgage deed have been satisfied and the mortgage money has become due under the mortgage. This latter condition is satisfied where the legal or contractual date for redemption has passed or where any instalment of capital is due under a repayment mortgage.[78] In the case of a term mortgage where the capital is not repayable until the

[74] *Albany Home Loans Ltd v. Massey* [1997] 2 All E.R. 609 at 613 *per* Schiemann L.J.
[75] Law of Property Act 1925, s.104(2).
[76] *Property and Bloodstock Ltd v. Emerton* [1968] Ch. 94 at 114 *per* Danckwerts L.J.
[77] Law of Property Act 1925, s.104(2). See also *Bailey v. Barnes* [1894] 1 Ch. 25 at 30 and *Lord Waring v. London and Manchester Assurance Co. Ltd* [1935 Ch. 310 at 318.
[78] *Payne v. Cardiff RDC* [1932] 1 K.B. 241 at 251 and 253.

end of the mortgage term, it is not sufficient that a payment of interest has fallen due,[79] but most such mortgages, if properly drafted, will contain an express provision under which the power of sale can be invoked.

(c) When the statutory power of sale becomes exercisable

The statutory power of sale becomes exercisable when one of three alternative conditions has been satisfied. There must either have been three months default after service of a notice requiring payment of the capital moneys due under the mortgage, or some interest due under the mortgage is in arrears and unpaid for two months after becoming due, or there has been a breach of some other provision in the mortgage.[80]

(d) Effect of sale

A sale by the mortgagee under the statutory power is effective to convey the whole of the mortgagor's estate to the purchaser, be it the whole freehold or leasehold interest, rather than merely the actual or notional leasehold interest demised to the mortgagee. The title which the purchaser receives is subject to any paramount claims, such as rights in land and mortgages having priority to the mortgagee, but it is otherwise free from any subsequent mortgages, or rights of the mortgagor and those claiming under him. So, for instance, where the mortgagor, after the date of the mortgage, has contracted to sell the land, the rights of the purchaser against the land under this contract are overreached by any sale by the mortgagee.[81] The person contracting with the mortgagor will retain contractual rights against the mortgagor, but since the mortgagor will invariably be in default, those rights may be of comparatively little value.

(e) Conduct of the sale

The mortgagee is selling in his own interest and is therefore not to be treated in the same way as a trustee exercising a power of sale under a trust instrument.[82] However, although the mortgagee "has rights of his own which he is entitled to exercise adversely to the mortgagor,"[83] he "is not entitled to conduct himself in a way which unfairly prejudices the mortgagor."[84] The mortgagee owes a duty to the mortgagor in exercising the power of sale which is capable of being categorised as a duty to take reasonable care.[85] In the case of a sale of land mortgaged to a building society, the society is under a duty "to take reasonable care to ensure that the price at which the land is sold is the best price that can reasonably be obtained."[86] Even though the duty on the mortgagee can be expressed in terms of an obligation to take reasonable care, and it has been argued that it should be treated as a duty of care in negligence,[87] that

[79] *Twentieth Century Banking Corporation Ltd v. Wilkinson* [1977] Ch. 99.
[80] Law of Property Act 1925, s.103.
[81] *Duke v. Robson* [1973] 1 W.L.R. 267. See also *Lyus v. Prowsa Developments Ltd* [1982] 1 W.L.R. 1044. In relation to rgistered land see Land Registration Act 1925, s.34(4).
[82] *Cuckmere Brick Co. Ltd v. Mutual Finance Ltd* [1971] Ch. 949.
[83] *Farrar v. Farrars Ltd* (1888) 40 Ch.D. 395 at 311 *per* Lindley L.J.
[84] *Palk v. Mortgage Services plc* [1993] 2 W.L.R. 415 at 420.
[85] *Standard Chartered Bank Ltd v. Walker* [1982] 1 W.L.R. 1410.
[86] Building Societies Act 1986 Sched 4 para. 1. *Reliance Permanent Building Society v. Harwood-Stamper* [1944] Ch. 362.
[87] See *Standard Chartered Bank Ltd v. Walker* [1982] 1 W.L.R. 1410; *American Express International Banking Corporation v. Hurley* [1985] 3 All E.R. 564.

view has not been approved by the Court of Appeal which, in *Parker-Tweedale v. Dunbar Bank plc,*[88] held that a mortgagee exercising power of sale owed no duty to persons other than the mortgagor, such as the beneficiary under a trust of which the mortgagor was trustee. Nourse L.J. said that "it is both unnecessary and confusing for the duties owed by a mortgagee to the mortgagor and the surety, if there is one, to be expressed in terms of the tort of negligence". He pointed out that the origins of the mortgagee's duty preceded the development of the modern tort of negligence.

Even if the duty on the mortgagee is not a duty in the tort of negligence, it goes well beyond a duty simply to act in good faith.[89] There are many respects in which the mortgagee owes a duty to act with reasonable prudence or to take proper account of the interests of the mortgagor, and this duty is one which is unlikely to be avoided even by a widely drafted exclusion clause.[90] For instance, it has been said that the mortgagee is under no duty to exercise any of his rights or powers under a mortgage, nor is he obliged to sell, and far less to incur any expenditure in improving the mortgaged property.[91] The mortgagee can choose when to sell, and is not obliged to wait for an improvement in the market.[92] Neither will the mortgagee be liable for postponing a sale, even if in consequence the security, which was sufficient to cover the debt at the time of default, subsequently declines in value.[93] However, the mortgagee "cannot sell hastily at a knock-down price sufficient to pay off his debt"[94] and he will be liable to the mortgagor if a property is sold without being left on the market for a reasonable time.[95] If the sale is by way of auction, the sale must be properly advertised, and potential purchasers must have a reasonable opportunity to view the property and to bid for it, at least in a case where the sale was to a company associated with the mortgagees.[96] The mortgagee must also ensure that in marketing the property, the attention of purchasers is drawn to any material information which might help to improve the price. For instance, in *Cuckmere Brick Co. Ltd v. Mutual Finance Ltd,*[97] the mortgagee was held in breach of duty for failing to mention a planning permission which would almost certainly have increased the selling price.

(f) Sale to the mortgagee

Where the mortgagee is selling the mortgaged property under the statutory power of sale, the mortgagee itself may not purchase the property, although the property may be sold to an associated copmpany.[98] However, where the sale is made by order of the court, it is possible for the mortgagee to be a purchaser.[99]

[88] [1991] Ch. 26.
[89] *Kennedy v. de Trafford* [1897] A.C. 180.
[90] See *Bishop v. Benham* [1988] 1 W.L.R. 742.
[91] *Lloyds Bank plc v. Bryant* (1996) Lawtel document No. C0003846. (Lightman J.).
[92] *Cuckmere Brick Co. Ltd v. Mutual Finance Ltd* [1971] Ch. 949.
[93] *China and South Sea Bank Ltd v. Tan Soon Gin* [1990] 1 A.C. 536.
[94] *Palk v. Mortgage Services Funding plc* [1993] 2 W.L.R. 415 at 420.
[95] *Predeth v. Castle Phillips Finance Co. Ltd* [1986] 2 E.G.L.R. 144.
[96] *Tse Kwong Lam v. Wong Chit Sen* [1983] 1 W.L.R. 1349.
[97] [1971] Ch. 949.
[98] *Tse Kwong Lam v. Wong Chit Sen* [1983] 1 W.L.R. 1349.
[99] *Palk v. Mortgage Services Funding plc* [1993] 2 W.L.R. 415.

(g) Application of proceeds of sale

The mortgagee, following a sale, holds the proceeds of sale upon trust to apply them in the way set out in section 105 of the Law of Property Act 1925. This requires that mortgages having priority to that of the mortgagee should first be paid off and that any balance should be applied successively in paying for the costs of sale, repaying the mortgagee, repaying any subsequent mortgagee, and finally, paying the remaining balance, if any, to the mortgagor. The mortgagee is not entitled to keep the whole proceeds of the sale if they exceed the amount of the loan, even where the mortgage was obtained by fraud.[1] As has already been described, if the proceeds of sale are insufficient to repay the mortgage, the mortgagor remains contractually liable for the balance.

4 Appointment of receiver

A mortgagee may appoint a receiver of mortgaged property either by order of the court or, in the case of mortgages made by deed, by virtue of Law of Property Act 1925, s.109. The statutory power arises and becomes exercisable upon the same events as apply to the power of sale arising and becoming exercisable.[2]

A receiver intercepts the rents and profits of land before they reach the mortgagor. The receiver then uses this income to pay off any outgoings on the land, then to meet liabilities under any prior mortgages, then to meet his own costs, and, finally, to pay off any interest or capital due under the mortgage of the mortgagee who appointed him.[3]

The nature of the functions of receivers mean that they are most likely to be appointed for commercial rather than residential property. They confer broadly the same benefits on a mortgagee as if the mortgagee had taken possession of the land with the advantage that a receiver is treated as the agent of the mortgagor rather than of the mortgagee. This means that the liability of the mortgagee to account is less strict than if he took possession.[4]

5 Foreclosure

Foreclosure is the process by which, formerly, the mortgagor's equity of redemption was extinguished by court order. By foreclosing or terminating the mortgagor's right to redeem, the estate vested in the mortgagee became absolute. Since with modern mortgages the mortgagee has either only a notional or actual term of years by demise or sub-demise rather than a full estate, the court order has the effect of transferring title to the mortgagee.[5] The procedure is fraught with technicality, and no longer serves any real purpose. The Law Commission has recommended that the remedy should be

[1] *Halifax Building Society v. Thomas* [1995] 4 All E.R. 673.
[2] See Law of Property Act 1925, s.101.
[3] Law of Property Act 1925, s.109.
[4] Law of Property Act 1925, s.109; *White v. Metcalf* [1903] 2 Ch. 567; *American Express International Banking Corp v. Hurley* [1985] 3 All E.R. 564.
[5] Law of Property Act 1925, ss.88 and 89; Land Registration Act 1925, s.34.

abolished. Foreclosure, alone of all the remedies available to the mortgagee, has the effect of extinguishing the mortgagor's contractual obligation to repay the loan which the mortgage secured. It is, perhaps for this reason that the mortgagee in *Palk v. Mortgage Services Funding plc*[6] chose not to seek foreclosure. Foreclosure will be unattractive to the mortgagee in most cases where there is negative equity, since the mortgagee cannot pursue the mortgagor for the deficiency. Where the mortgaged property is worth more than the loan secured, foreclosure will be unattractive to the mortgagor, since the mortgagor would receive the surplus on a sale. The mortgagor is able to apply for an order for sale in a foreclosure action,[7] and a court would be unlikely to refuse it where the property is worth more than the loan.

PRIORITY OF MORTGAGES

1 Multiplicity of rights

It is possible for the owner of land to create more than one mortgage over it, and it is not uncommon for impecunious owners to do just that. If the value of the land is insufficient to pay off all the sums borrowed, the question may therefore arise to the priority of these mortgages between themselves. In other words, if the land is sold, which mortgage must be paid off first? In addition, there may be issues as to the extent to which a mortgagee is bound by interests created before the mortgage was made, and in some cases there may be an issue as to whether a mortgagee is bound by interests created subsequent to the mortgage. These issues are largely determined in accordance with priority rules of general application, but there are some special rules which apply exclusively to mortgages.

2 Retention of documents of title and registration

A first legal mortgagee of unregistered land has the right to possession of the title deeds relating to the land.[8] This confers important protection on the mortgagee, since anyone claiming a major interest in the land subsequent to the mortgage, for instance by way of purchase or subsequent mortgage, would normally wish to inspect the deeds. A first legal mortgagee protected by deposit of title deeds by this means has priority over all interests in the land created subsequent to the mortgage. Where a mortgage of unregistered land is created without the mortgagee retaining the documents of title, the mortgagee requires to register under the Land Charges Act 1972 in order to retain priority against certain subsequent purchasers.[9] A motgagee of registered land is given priority by the entry of the charge on the register. In addition, the Land Certificate is retained by the Land Registry whilst the charge remanis on the register.[10]

[6] [1993] 2 W.L.R. 415.
[7] Law of Property Act 1925, s.91.
[8] Law of Property Act 1925, s.85.
[9] Legal mortgages not rotected by deposit of title deeds are Class C(i) land charges; equitable mortgages are Class C(iii) land charges.
[10] Land Registration Act 1925, s.65.

3 Priority over earlier inconsistent rights

Where the legal owner of land creates a mortgage or a charge by way of legal mortgage, difficult questions can arise concerning the extent to which earlier inconsistent rights are binding on the mortgagee. Some of these questions are well illustrated by *Abbey National Building Society v. Cann.*[11] Mrs Cann lived in a house which had been bought in the name of her son. The purchase price had been met, in part by a loan from the Abbey National Building Society secured by mortgage, and in part from the proceeds from the sale of the house in which Mrs Cann was previously living, and in which it was accepted that she had a beneficial interest. Mrs Cann claimed that this financial contribution gave her a beneficial interest in the newly purchased house which took priority over the Building Society mortgage. Her claim failed comprehensively.

(a) Which rights arise first?

The first question was whether Mrs Cann's rights could be said to be prior in time to those of the Building Society. It was argued on her behalf that the building society mortgage could only take effect once her son had acquired a legal estate in the house of which the mortgage could then be created. By that stage, it was said, her beneficial interest in the house in which she was previously living had already been transferred into the new house through the use of the proceeds of sale of the old one. This argument relied upon the premise that only the legal owner of property could grant a mortgage, and that, where property was purchased with the aid of mortgage finance, there was a fragment of time, a *scintilla temporis* as it had been described in previous cases,[12] after the purchaser acquired the legal estate, and before mortgagee acquired its interest by way of charge upon that legal estate. The House of Lords rejected the argument and the premise upon which it was based. As Lord Oliver said, although there was an attractive legal logic in the argument that a person cannot charge a legal estate that he does not have, "it flies in the face of reality." Lord Jauncey put it in this way[13]:

> "In my view, a purchaser who can only complete the transaction by borrowing money for the security of which he is contractually bound to grant a mortgage to the lender *eo instanti* with the execution of the conveyance in his favour cannot in reality ever be said to have acquired even for a *scintilla temporis* the unencumbered fee simple or leasehold interst in land whereby he could grant interests having priority over the mortgage . . . Since no one can grant what he does not have, it follows that such a purchaser could never grant an interest which was not subject to the limitations of his own interest."

[11] [1991] A.C. 56. Discussed by Oakley [1990] C.L.J. 397. See also Chap. 16.
[12] See *Church of England Building Society v. Piskor* [1954] Ch. 533.
[13] *Abbey National Building Society v. Cann* [1990] 1 All E.R. 1085 at 1107.

The House of Lords therefore rejected the *scintilla temporis* principle and adopted instead a line of cases[14] which had disregarded it. The Lords concluded that Mrs Cann's son never acquired an unencumbered estate in the new house "and was therefore never in a position to grant to Mrs Cann an interst in [the new house] which prevailed over that of the society. The interests that Mrs Cann took in [the new house] could only be carved out of George Cann's equity of redemption."[15]

(b) Are the earlier rights enforceable against the mortgagee?

Even though this would have been enough to defeat Mrs Cann's claim against the Building Society, there were other reasons too. Title to the house in which Mrs Cann was living was registered. The mortgagee, having a registered charge, was able to claim the protection of Land Registration Act 1925, section 23. Under this the society acquired its charge free from all earlier interests and encumbrances except those which had been protected by way of entry on the register or which overriding interests. Mrs Cann's rights were not protected by way of entry on the register. She claimed, however, that at the time the mortgage was registered, she was in actual occupation of the house, so that her rights were enforceable against the building society as overriding interests.[16] This argument again failed. The House of Lords decided that the relevant date for deciding whether Mrs Cann was in actual occupation was not the date of registration,[17] but the date upon which the mortgage took effect. That was the date of completion. If the relevant date was the date of registration, it would produce the conveyancing absurdity that, after the mortgagee had made all possible inquiries and parted with his money, the mortgagee could be bound by the rights of a newly arrived occupant coming in after the mortgage documents had all been signed and the sale completed but before the mortgage had been registered. By this stage the mortgagee would be committed and unable to back out.

This did not exhaust Mrs Cann's armoury. She said she was in actual occupation at the date of completion. The vendor himself moved out only on the date of completion, and as he left, he allowed the Canns, who were waiting outside, to move in. Mrs Cann herself was on holiday, but her carpets were laid and some of her furniture moved in some 35 minutes or so before the exact moment of completion. Not surprisingly, the House of Lords agreed with the trial judge that this was insufficient to amount to

[14] *Re Connolly Bros Ltd (No. 2)* [1912] 2 Ch. 25; *Coventry Permanent Economic Building Society v. Jones* [1951] 1 All E.R. 901 and *Security Trust Co. v. Royal Bank of Canada* [1976] A.C. 503.

[15] *Abbey National Building Society v. Cann* [1990] 1 All E.R. 1085 at 1108 *per* Lord Jauncey. In reaching this conclusion, the House of Lords appears to have disregarded the fact that, just as the purchase could not be made without the aid of the mortgage, equally it could not have been made without the aid of the financial contribution from Mrs Cann through the sale of the previous house. It ought, perhaps, to have followed that Mrs Cann's interest in the new house took effect at the very same time as both the purchase and the mortgage. If that was so, then neither the mortgage nor Mrs Cann's interest could be treated as having priority simply on the basis of being earlier in time. An additional complication is that Lord Oliver (at 1097) suggests that the building society could claim an equitable charge from the moment the contract to grant a loan had been made and the money advanced to Mr Cann's solicitors, even before the date of completion. Presumably this equitable charge would have bitten upon the interest created by Mr Cann's contract to purchase the new house. Mrs Cann's interest, by contrast, depended upon the movement of funds from the sale of the old house to the purchase of the new, which did not occur until completion. See *Smith* (1990) 106 L.Q.R. 545.

[16] See Land Registration Act 1925, s.70(1)(g).

[17] Which would be the relevant date for determining whether most or all other types of overriding interest were in existence.

actual occupation by Mrs Cann. These were no more than "preparatory steps leading to the assumption of actual residential occupation."

(c) Consent to postponement of earlier inconsistent rights

There was yet another ground on which Mrs Cann lost her claim to an interest enforceable against the building society. The Court of Appeal found that Mrs Cann knew that her son needed to raise additional money on the security of the new house. This was enough to prevent her from relying on her own rights having priority to the society. Her rights were therefore postponed to those of the building society. In this case there was an implied postponement, but the postponement of earlier inconsistent rights can also be express.

(i) Express postponement: Since the decision in *Williams and Glyn's Bank v. Boland*[18] held that the rights of people sharing occupation are binding as overriding interests on a mortgagee, it has been common practice for mortgagees to require a waiver of any prior rights from any person who is, or is proposing to, share occupation of the property with the mortgagor. A binding consent cannot be obtained from minors, but it has been held that their rights do not automatically bind the mortgagee.[19] In *Woolwich Building Society v. Dickman,*[20] the Court of Appeal held that a form signed by Rent Act protected tenants consenting to the grant of a mortgage and postponing their rights to the mortgagee would have been effective to give the mortgagee priority except for the policy objective of the Rent Acts to confer protection on tenants, which overrode any consent given to the mortgagee.

(ii) Implied postponement: Even where the mortgagee has not received express consent from a person with a prior interest to the creation of a mortgage, a consent by that person to the mortgage can in some circumstances be implied. This was first established in *Bristol and West Building Society v. Henning.*[21] An unmarried couple bought a house together intending that it should be half owned by each of them, but raising the purchase and the mortgage in the name of Mr Henning alone. Most of the purchase price was supplied by the mortgage, without which the purchase would not have been possible. Mrs Henning was aware of this. This was enough to give the building society priority. As Browne-Wilkinson L.J. said:

> "Mrs Henning knew of and supported the proposal to raise the purchase price of the villa on mortgage. In those circumstances, it is in my judgment impossible to impute to them any common intention other than that she authorised Mr Henning to raise the money by mortgage to the society. In more technical terms, it was the common intention that Mr Henning as trustee should have power to grant the mortgage to the society. Such power to mortgage must have extended to granting to the society a mortgage having priority to any beneficial interests in the property".

[18] [1980] 2 All E.R. 408.
[19] *Hypo-Mortgage Services Ltd v. Robinson* (1996), *The Times*, January 2, C.A.
[20] [1996] 3 All E.R. 254.
[21] [1985] 1 W.L.R. 778.

This decision has been followed and applied in *Paddington Building Society v. Mendelsohn*[22] and *Abbey National Building Society v. Cann*.[23] In the latter case, although it was not necessary to reach a decision on the point, the House of Lords considered that, even though Mrs Cann believed that the mortgage would cover only a small proportion of the cost of acquisition, her rights were postponed to the full extent of the very much larger loan which her son negotiated. In *Equity and Law Home Loans Ltd v. Prestridge*,[24] the Court of Appeal held that a person claiming an equitable interest in the property on a contribution basis whose claim was postponed to a first mortgagee was also postponed to a subsequent mortgagee to whom the property had been remortgaged, although her interest was postponed to the extent only of the amount of the original loan.

It is not yet clear from the decisions on the implied postponement of the rights of an equitable claimant whether they are based upon implied or imputed consent, agency, or estoppel.[25] In effect, where an interest in a property vested in a single legal proprietor is held on constructive trust as a result of common intention or proprietary estoppel, the rights of the beneficiary relate merely to the mortgagor's equity of redemption.[26] In any event, as has already been seen, where a mortgage is created contemporaneously with a purchase, a person claiming an equitable interest cannot claim that the mortgagee is bound by their interest on the basis of actual occupation, or presumably, under the equitable doctrine of notice in the case of unregistered land. Furthermore, even if a mortgage is not binding on one equitable owner of the property, for instance because one co-owner has procured a mortgage by fraud,[27] the mortgage will still be binding on the person who granted it to the extent of his or her putative beneficial interest. This will be sufficient to enable the mortgagee to proceed by way of an application for sale of the property under the Trusts of Land and Appointment of Trustees Act 1996, ss.13 and 14 and to use the mortgagor's portion of the proceeds of sale towards the discharge of the loan.[28]

4 Priority of mortgages in unregistered land

Priority in relation to mortgages of unregistered land is governed by the old legal and equitable rules as modified by the rules relating to the registration of land charges now contained in the Land Charges Act 1972.

(a) priority of a legal mortgage over subsequent interests acquired in the land

A first legal mortgage of unregistered land which is protected by the deposit of title deeds is enforceable over any subsequently created interest affecting the land, except where this is authorised by the mortgage deed (as in a mortgage which contemplates the grant of leases by the mortgagor) or where the mortgagee has specifically

[22] (1985) 50 P. & C.R. 244.
[23] [1991] A.C. 56.
[24] [1992] 1 W.L.R. 137.
[25] *Skipton Building Society v. Clayton* (1993) 66 P. & C.R. 223.
[26] See *Abbey National Building Society v. Cann* [1991] A.C. 56 at 102.
[27] As in *First National Securites Ltd v. Hegarty* [1985] Q.B. 850.
[28] See *The trustee of the property of Martin Kit Sheung Ng v. Ng* (1996) Lawtel Document No. C0005225 (Lightman J.).

authorised or adopted the transaction concerned. This is on the principle that legal rights bind the world. The only major exception to the principle that the legal rights of the first mortgagee are unassailable is where the mortgagee has deprived himself of his protection against a subsequent purchaser through fraud, misrepresentation or gross negligence, for instance by failing to take possession of all the title deeds[29] or by allowing or inducing the claimant to believe that there is no existing mortgage.[30]

(b) Priority of an equitable mortgage over subsequent interests acquired in the land

Where a first mortgage of unregistered land takes effect in equity only, the mortgagee will still have effective protection against most subsequent claims by virtue of retaining the title deeds to the property since subsequent purchasers will be put on notice of the earlier charge,[31] although this priority can be lost through the negligence or fraud of the first mortgagee.[32] In addition, the caselaw suggests that it will be rare for a subsequent legal mortgagee to be bound by an earlier equitable mortgage unless the subsequent mortgagee's failure to ascertain the existence of the earlier charge can be said to arise from gross negligence.[33]

(c) Priority of mortgages not protected by the deposit of title deeds

Where a mortgage, whether legal or equitable, is not protected by a deposit of title deeds, it will be registrable as a Class C(i) or C(iii) land charge respectively under the Land Charges Act 1972.[34] A failure to register renders the mortgage void as against a subsequent purchaser of a legal or equitable interest in the land for valuable consideration.[35]

5 Priority of mortgages in registered land

(a) Priority of registered charge

Mortgages of registered land do not take effect as legal charges unless and until they have been registered.[36] As between several registered charges, the charges take priority in accordance with the date order in which they were registered, regardless of the order in which they were created, except where the contrary is indicated on the register.[37] A registered legal charge will therefore automatically take priority over any

[29] *Walker v. Linom* [1907] 2 Ch. 104.
[30] *Perry Herrick v. Attwood* (1857) 2 De G. & J. 21.
[31] Since it was held in *United Bank of Kuwait plc v. Sahib* [1996] 3 All E.R. 215 that an equitable mortgage operates on the basis of a specifically enforceable contract to create a legal mortgage, it could be argued that equitable mortgages of a legal estate require registration as a Class C(iv) estate contract under Land Charges Act 1974. This, however, would deprive of substance the provision for registering equitable mortgages as Class C(iii) general equitable charges and cannot have been intended by the draftsman. See (1962) 26 Conv. 445 (Rowley).
[32] *Taylor v. Russell* [1892] A.C. 244.
[33] *Oliver v. Hinton* [1899] 2 Ch. 264; *Agra Bank Ltd v. Barry* (1874) L.R. 7 H.L. 135 at 150 *et seq.*
[34] s.2(4).
[35] See Land Charges Act 1972, s.4(5) and the definition of A purchaser in, s.17. There is an apparent conflict with Law of Property Act 1925, s.97, which suggests that priorities are determined by the date of registration. This would have the consequence of converting a mortgage which is void in relation to a subsequent right in accordance with the Land Charges Act into a mortgage which is inferior to it.
[36] Land Registration Act 1925, s.26(1).
[37] Land Registration Act 1925, s.29.

subsequently created registered or unregistered charge. A registered legal charge will also benefit from the protection given by Land Registration Act 1925, s.20 to registered dispositions for valuable consideration. It will have priority to all earlier rights, save those which take effect as overriding interests[38] or have been protected by entry on the register.

(b) Priority of equitable mortgages

A purported legal charge of registered land which has not been registered takes effect only as an equitable minor interest.[39] This, like an equitable charge,[40] can be protected by way of a notice.[41] Once so protected, it will, in accordance with the general principles concerning priorities in registered land, take priority over any subsequently created right. The mortgagee may, instead of protecting an equitable mortgage by notice, protect it by way of caution.[42] This does not automatically confer priority for the mortgage over all subsequent interests, but does enable the mortgagor to object to the registration of any subsequent interest, thereby conferring a large measure of protection. That protection is not, however, complete, as the facts of *Barclays Bank plc v. Zaroovabli*[43] illustrate. The registered proprietors of a property mortgaged it to the bank under a mortgage prohibited them from granting leases without the consent of the bank. The mortgage was, for some reason, not registered immediately by the bank. Prior to registration of the charge, the mortgagors created a lease for less than 21 years. Sir Richard Scott V.-C. held that this lease was binding as an overriding interest on the mortgagees when they subsequently registered their charge. The mortgagors, despite the prohibition in the mortgage, had the power under Land Registration Act 1925, s.18(1) to grant leases (even though they might be in breach of covenant in doing so),[44] and, by section 19 of the Act a lease for 21 years or less takes effect "as if it were a registered disposition immediately on being granted". It therefore benefited from section 20 of the Act under which a registered disposition for valuable consideration took priority over all other rights in the land except those protected by way of registration and overriding interests.[45] The bank had not, in this case, lodged a caution, but, following the decision in *Clark v. Chief Land Registrar*[46] there is no reason to believe that a caution would have given them any greater protection.

(c) Priority between mortgages

Where a question of priority arises between several minor interests, such as successive unregistered charges, the charges will rank in accordance with the date of their

[38] See for, instance *Skipton Building Society v. Clayton*, *The Times*, March 25, 1993, where the Court of Appeal held that the mortgagees were bound by a lease-back to the vendors of property who remained in actual occupation and therefore had an overriding interest. See also *Barclays Bank plc v. Estates and Commercial Ltd* [1997] 1 W.L.R. 415 where mortgagees who helped to support a purchase of property were held to be subject to the unpaid vendor's lien of an earlier vendor who had remained in actual occupation.
[39] Land Registration Act 1925, s.106(2).
[40] Land Registration Act 1925, s.106(1).
[41] Land Registration Act 1925, s.106(3)(a).
[42] Land Registration Act 1925, s.106(3)(c).
[43] [1997] 2 All E.R. 19.
[44] Compare *Leeds Permanent Building Society v. Fanimi* (1997) Lawtel Document No. C0005086 where a lease granted in similar circumstances was held by the Court of Appeal not to bind the mortgagee since the mortgagor was not the registered proprietor at the time of the grant of the tenancy.
[45] This is an example of a right being created in the so-called "registration gap".
[46] [1994] Ch. 370.

creation,[47] even if the subsequent mortgagee has entered a notice or caution.[48] Since there is no statutory rule governing priority between unregistered charges of registered land, and priorities are governed by general principles of equity, it is possible that the rule that the first in time prevails could be displaced on the grounds of fraud, misrepresentation or negligence as in the case of unregistered land.[49]

6 Mortgages of interests under trusts

Special rules govern the priority of mortgages of beneficial interests under a trust of land (*i.e.* mortgages granted by the beneficiaries rather than by the trustees). Instead of priority being based on the ordinary land law rules, priority depends upon the order in which the trustees have been informed of the mortgage concerned. This is known as the rule in *Dearle v. Hall*[50] which was extended to cover trusts of land by Law of Property Act 1925, s.137. The rule that mortgages rank according to the date that notice is received by the trustees is modified where a subsequent mortgagee has actual or constructive notice of an earlier mortgage. Even if he notifies the trustees first, he will not gain priority.[51]

7 Special priority rules

Notwithstanding the general rules governing the priority of mortgages, it is possible for two mortgagees to agree between themselves that their charges will rank in some other way, and such an agreement will be effective as between the parties to the arrangement.[52] In certain cases, where there are multiple mortgages over the same property, a mortgagee can gain priority by "tacking" or adding a further advance to an earlier mortgage, so conferring priority over other later charges. The right to tack applies where the prior mortgagee is under an obligation to make additional advances or where the prior mortgagee is unaware of any subsequent charge.[53] Where the same mortgagee holds mortgages over more than one parcel of land made by the same mortgagee, the mortgagee may be able to "consolidate", that is, to insist that if one mortgage is redeemed, the other must also be redeemed at the same time. The purpose of this equitable right is to prevent a mortgagee from redeeming a mortgage over a property which is worth more than the amount secured whilst leaving the other loan inadequately secured.

[47] *Barclays Bank Ltd v. Taylor* [1974] Ch. 137.
[48] *Mortgage Corporation Ltd v. Nationwide Credit Corporation Ltd* [1994] Ch. 49.
[49] See *Abigail v. Lapin* [1934] A.C. 491 at 500–510 *per* Lord Wright.
[50] (1828) 3 Russ. 1.
[51] *Re Holmes* (1885) 29 Ch.D. 786.
[52] *Cheah Theam Swee v. Equiticorp Finance Group Ltd* [1992] 1 A.C. 472.
[53] Law of Property Act 1925, s.94; Land Registration Act 1925, s.30.

Chapter 12

Licences and Occupational Rights

Introduction to Licences

1 The essences of licences

A licence is simply a permission which entitles a person to be physically present on land owned by someone else. Without a licence such presence would be actionable as a trespass. As Vaughan C.J. stated in *Thomas v. Sorrell*[1]: "A dispensation or licence properly passeth no interest, nor alters or transfers property in anything, but only makes an action lawful, which without it had been unlawful." Licences are capable of authorising a very wide variety of degrees of presence on land, from the right enjoyed by a milkman to deliver milk to the front door, to a right to occupy land which is not a lease because there is no entitlement to exclusive possession.[2]

2 Distinguishing between types of licence

(a) Express and implied licences

A licence may arise over land where it is expressly granted by the owner, who is termed the licensor. However, in some circumstances a licence will be held to have arisen by implication without any express grant.

(b) Bare and contractual licences

Where a licence is granted by the licensor without the licensee providing any consideration in return the ensuing licence is said to be a bare licence. However if a licence is granted in return for consideration it is a contractual licence.

(c) Estoppel licences

As well as licences granted expressly or impliedly the court may award a licence as one of the potential remedies for a successful proprietary estoppel claim.

[1] (1673) Vaughan 330, 351.
[2] See: *Street v. Mountford* [1895] A.C. 809.

3 Revocation of licences

Since a licence is a mere permission to do that which would otherwise be actionable as a trespass, the question arises as to the circumstances in which the permission can be withdrawn by termination of the licence. The ease with which a licence can be revoked varies depending upon its character.

4 Licences as proprietary interests in land

One of the key distinctions between a lease and a licence is that a licence is a purely personal interest enjoyed by the licensee, which is incapable of binding anyone other than the licensor. Thus if the licensor transfers the land over which the licence is enjoyed it will not be binding on the transferee who will acquire the land free from it. The licensee will be confined to remedies against the licensor if the licence was contractual. This traditional position has been reasserted by the courts in recent years despite the attempts of Lord Denning to elevate contractual licences to the status of proprietary rights in land by judicial pronunciation. In *Street v. Mountford*[3] Lord Templeman stated that: "A licence in connection with land while entitling the licensee to use the land for the purposes authorised by the licence does not create an estate in the land." However, it seems that a licence may still be capable of binding a transferee of the land subject in the very limited circumstances in which the court is willing to impose a constructive trust in favour of the licensee.

BARE LICENCES

1 Nature of a bare licence

A bare licence is a permission to use land which is granted gratuitously, in other words without the licensee providing any consideration.

2 Creation of a bare licence

(a) Express grant

A bare licence may be granted expressly by the owner of land. For example, when a person invites their friends round to watch the cup final, or allows a child living next door into their garden to recover a lost ball, a bare licence is granted entitling the guests or child to enter the land for the stated purpose.

(b) Implied licence

A bare licence may also be implied even when there is no express grant. In *Robson v. Hallett*[4] the Court of Appeal held that owners of houses impliedly license members of

[3] *ibid.*
[4] [1967] 2 Q.B. 939.

the public to approach their front door. Diplock L.J. stated the scope of this implied licence:

> "when a householder lives in a dwelling-house to which there is a garden in front and does not lock the gate of the garden, it gives an implied licence to any member of the public who has lawful reason for doing so to proceed from the gate to the front door or back door, and to inquire whether he may be admitted and to conduct his lawful business."

For this reason a police officer was not trespassing when he went to knock the door of a house to make inquiries. Similarly, an election canvasser, double-glazing salesman or Jehovah's Witness would be entitled to enter premises. In *Holden v. White*[5] the Court of Appeal held that a milkman delivering to a house enjoyed an implied licence to use a path which led to it, and in *Lambert v. Roberts*[6] Donaldson L.J. considered that the implied licence extended to all citizens who reasonable think they have legitimate business on the premises. However the implication of a licence can be rebutted. In *Robson v. Hallett*[7] Diplock L.J. indicated that there would have been no implied licence if there had been a notice on the front gate stating "No admittance to police officers." In *Cole v. Police Constable 443A*[8] it was held that members of the public have no implied licence to enter any church they wish to attend worship, but only their own parish church. Similarly, the implied licence to customers to enter business premises would not extend to investigative journalists.

3 Revocation of a bare licence

Where a person has entered land on the basis of a bare licence the licensor can withdraw the permission at any time, thus rendering the ex-licensee a trespasser if he continues his presence on the land. However, the ex-licensee is entitled to a reasonable time to leave the land. In *Robson v. Hallett*[9] a licence was revoked when the owner of the house told a police sergeant who had entered at the request of his son to leave. Diplock L.J. stated:

> "He withdrew it, and, upon its being withdrawn, the sergeant had a reasonable time to leave the premises by the most appropriate route for doing so, namely, out of the front door, down the steps and out of the gate, and, provided that he did so with reasonable expedition, he would not be a trespasser while he was doing so."

What will constitute a reasonable time will depend on the nature of the land and the purpose of the licence, so that in the case of a residential licence in a family context a much longer period would apply.[10] Somewhat surprisingly, in *Gilham v.*

[5] [1982] 1 Q.B. 679.
[6] [1981] 2 All E.R. 15, 19.
[7] [1967] 2 Q.B. 939.
[8] [1937] 1 K.B. 316.
[9] [1967] 2 Q.B. 939.
[10] See: *E & L Berg Homes Ltd v. Grey* (1980) 253 E.G. 473.

Breidenbach[11] the court held that the expression "fuck off" was to be regarded as a term of abuse rather than the withdrawal of an implied licence to enter property.

4 User in excess of the licence granted

The licensee is only entitled to use the land to the extent permitted by the licence and any excessive use will constitute a trespass. For example, permission to recover a ball from a garden would not extend to playing football there. As Scrutton L.J. said in *The Carlgarth*:[12] "when you invite a person into your house to use the staircase, you do not invite him to slide down the banisters."

5 Effect on third party transferees of the land?

A bare licence is a purely personal interest which arises between the licensor and the licensee. It is incapable of binding a third party who acquires title of the land to which it relates from the licensor.

LICENCES COUPLED WITH AN INTEREST

1 Nature of a licence coupled with an interest

(i) Licence necessary to enjoy an interest granted: When the owner of land grants a person an interest or right which will only be able to be enjoyed by them if they enter onto his land, the grant of the right or interest will be taken to confer a licence on the grantee such as is necessary for them to enjoy it. For example, in *James Jones & Sons Ltd v. Earl of Tankerville*[13] a landowner had contracted to sell timber growing on his land to a third party. Parker J. held that: "a contract or the sale of specific timber growing on the vendor's property, on the terms that such timber is cut and carried away by the purchaser certainly confers on the purchaser a licence to enter and cut the timber sold . . . ." Similarly a right to take game from land will carry with it a licence to enter the land for that purpose.[14] Such licences are therefore often created by the grant of a profit a prendre,[15] and in *Hounslow L.B.C. v. Twickenham Garden Development Ltd*[16] Megarry J. said "a licence to go on land to sever and remove trees or hay, or to remove timber or hay that have already been severed, are accepted examples of a licence coupled with an interest."[17] Such a licence will only arise if the interest to which it is coupled is properly created.

(ii) A proprietary interest?: Some cases have held that a licence will arise even where the interests granted is not a proprietary right in land. In *Vaughan v. Hampson*[18] a

[11] [1982] R.T.R. 328n.
[12] [1927] P. 93, 110.
[13] [1909] 2 Ch. 440.
[14] *Frogley v. Earl of Lovelace* (1859) John. 333.
[15] See above pp. 321 *et seq.*
[16] [1971] Ch. 233.
[17] See also: *Wood v. Manley* (1839) 11 Ad. & El. 34.
[18] (1875) 33 L.T. 15.

solicitor acting under a proxy from a creditor attended a general meeting of creditors convened by the debtor as his solicitor's office. The solicitor refused to leave the premises when asked. The Court of Exchequer held that the subsequent physical ejection of the solicitor was an assault because he enjoyed a right to be present on the grounds that he enjoyed a right coupled with a licence. In *Hurst v. Picture Theatres Ltd*[19] the Court of Appeal held that a customer who had purchased a ticket for a seat at a theatre enjoyed a licence coupled with a grant and that his ejection on the mistaken grounds that he had not paid was an assault. Buckley L.J. explained:

> "What is the grant in this case? The plaintiff in the present action paid his money to enjoy the sight of a particular spectacle. He was anxious to go into a picture theatre to see a series of views of pictures during, I suppose, an hour or a couple of hours. That which was granted to him was the right to enjoy looking at a spectacle, to attend a performance from its beginning to its end. That which was called the licence, the right to go upon the premises, was only something granted to him for the purpose of enabling him to have that which had been granted him, namely the right to see. He could not see the performance unless he went into the building. His right to go into the building was something given to him in order to enable him to have the benefit of that which had been granted to him, namely the right to hear the opera, or see the theatrical performance, or see the moving pictures as was the case here. So that here there was a licence coupled with a grant."[20]

However, in neither of these cases can it be said that the grantee enjoyed any proprietary right in the land over which he was held to have enjoyed a licence. In *Hounslow LBC v. Twickenham Garden Development Ltd*[21] Megarry J. held that if such non-proprietary rights were to give rise to licences then a contractor could enjoy a licence to continue building works:

> "If for this purpose "interest" is not confined to an interest in land or in chattels on the land, what does it extend to? If a right to attend a creditor's meeting or to see a cinema performance suffices to constitute an interest, can it be said that the right and duty to do works on land fall short of being an interest? I cannot see why it should. Yet, if this be so, it is not easy to see any fair stopping place in what amounts to an interests short of any legitimate reason for being on the land."[22]

For this reason he went on hold that *Vaughan v. Hampson*[23] was a "curiosity" and to conclude that a licence coupled with an interest could only arise if the interest were proprietary in nature, enjoyed either in the land itself or in chattels found on the land:

[19] [1915] 1 K.B. 1.
[20] *ibid.* at 7.
[21] [1971] Ch. 233.
[22] *ibid.* at 244.
[23] (1875) 33 L.T. 15.

> "First, as regards a licence coupled with an interest . . . I feel great doubt whether the word "interest" means anything more than an interests in property, though it matters not whether that property is real or personal, or legal or equitable . . . I should hesitate very long before holding that a licence was coupled with an interest unless that interest was an interest in property, and that I doubt very much whether in this case the contractor's licence is coupled with an interest."[24]

2 Creation of a licence coupled with an interest

Since the existence of the licence is derived from the interest to which it is coupled the licence will be created by the effective creation of the interest. In the case of a *profit à prendre* this will generally require a grant by deed or acquisition by prescription, but a contract for the grant of a profit creating an equitable right will also give rise to a licence.

3 Revocability of a licence coupled with an interest

The reason why the nature of interests which will give rise to a licence has engendered such discussion is because such a licence cannot be revoked as long as the interest to which it is coupled endures. This was recognised by Megarry J. in *Hounslow L.B.C. v. Twickenham Garden Development Ltd*[25] where he suggested that the fact that contractual licences had become capable of being irrevocable in their own right meant that there was no longer "need to torture the word "interest" into embracing miscellaneous collections of rights."

4 Effect of a licence coupled with an interest on third party transferees of the land

A licence coupled with a interest will be binding on a third party transferee of the land to which it relates if he acquires the land subject to the proprietary interest from which it is derived. For example, if the licensee is entitled to a profit a prendre the licence will be binding on a transferee of the servient tenement if he acquired the land subject to the burden of the profit.

CONTRACTUAL LICENCES

1 Nature of a contractual licence

As the name would suggest, a contractual licence is a licence granted either expressly or impliedly in return for valuable consideration. For example, the purchase of a ticket

[24] [1971] Ch. 233, 254.
[25] [1971] Ch. 233, 254.

to attend an event, whether a race-meeting[26] or a cinema performance,[27] will generate a contractual licence to enter the premises where the event is held. In *Ashby v. Tolhurst*[28] purchase of a 1s ticket to use a car park at Southend was held to confer a contractual licence to park. Contractual licences are also capable of providing the basis for longer term rights of occupation. University students with rooms in halls of residence, lodgers, hotel guests and residents of old peoples homes all have contractual licences since, as has been seen,[29] they do not enjoy the exclusive possession essential to the existence of a lease. It has been seen how in *AG Securities v. Vaughan*[30] four persons occupying a flat under separate agreements for a six-month term, granted at separate times, in return for the payment of a monthly rent, were contractual licensees of the owners.

2 Creation of a contractual licence

A contractual licence will only come into existence if the licensee enters into a valid contract with the licensor. The precise terms of the licence will depend upon the terms of the contract. For example, a contractual licence to attend a theatrical performance will terminate when the performance is over. A contractual licence for residential occupation may be held to contained an implied terms that the licensor will ensure that the licensee enjoys quiet possession,[31] and that the premises are fit for the purposes envisaged when the licence was granted.[32]

3 Revocability of a contractual licence

(a) Problem of revocability

One central question which has arisen in the context of contractual licences is whether they can be revoked at will by the licensee. There is no doubt that where such a revocation would amount to a breach of contract the licensee is entitled to a remedy of damages to compensate him for any loss he suffered as a result of the breach. However, if the court were to grant specific performance of the contract granting the licence this would have the effect of enabling the licensee to assert his contractual rights, rendering the licence irrevocable in practice. For example, if a customer purchases a ticket to watch a film at a multiplex cinema, can the management simply demand that he leave the premises, even though the film has not finished and he has not in any way broken the terms of his licence by wrong behaviour, or is the customer entitled to remain viewing? If the management uses force to remove him against his will this may amount to an assault if he enjoyed a continued right to remain on the premises, but not if he had become a trespasser.

[26] *Wood v. Leadbitter* (1845) 13 M & W 838.
[27] *Hurst v. Picture Theatres Ltd* [1915] 1 K.B. 1; *Clore v. Theatrical Properties Ltd and Westby & Co. Ltd* [1936] 3 All E.R. 483.
[28] [1937] 2 K.B. 242.
[29] See above p. 75.
[30] [1990] 1 A.C. 417.
[31] *Smith v. Nottinghamshire County Council*, *The Times*, November 13, 1981.
[32] *Wettern Electrical Ltd v. Welsh Development Agency* [1983] Q.B. 796.

(b) Revocable at common law

At common law a contractual licence is revocable at any time by the licensor, and the licensee's only remedy was to recover damages for breach of contract. In *Wood v. Leadbitter*[33] the plaintiff had purchased a four-day ticket for a race meeting at Doncaster. He refused to leave when requested and was removed by force. He claimed that this amounted to an assault on the grounds that he enjoyed an irrevocable licence for the duration of the races. Alderson B. held that as the plaintiff did not enjoy a licence coupled with a grant it remained revocable, and that although he might have a remedy for breach of contract against the owners of the racecourse, since there was no good reason for terminating the contract, their actions were not an assault because the revocation had rendered him a trespasser. This approach was also applied in *Thompson v. Park*[34] where the owners of two prep schools agreed that they should be amalgamated for the duration of the war, and that the defendant and his pupils could enter and use the plaintiff's premises. After a year the plaintiff demanded that the defendant and his boys leave the premises, but the defendant forcibly re-entered after the Christmas holidays. The Court of Appeal held that the defendant had committed a trespass because the licence had been effectively revoked.

(c) Potentially irrevocable in equity

(i) An injunction to prevent revocation: Whereas at common law a contractual licence remained revocable by the licensor at any time, the courts have developed the jurisdiction of equity, and in particular the availability of an injunction to restrain a breach of contract, to render a contractual licence irrevocable. This possibility was confirmed by the House of Lords in *Millenium Productions Ltd v. Winter Garden Theatre (London) Ltd.*[35] The defendants had granted the plaintiffs a licence to use their theatre for six months, with options to renew, for the production of plays, concerts or ballets. The options to renew were exercised and after several years occupation the defendants purported to revoke the licence, despite the fact that the plaintiff's were not in breach of its terms. The Court of Appeal held that in the circumstances this licence was irrevocable, because the contract granted the defendants no express power to revoke it. Lord Greene M.R. explained the basis on which a contractual licence might be found to be irrevocable:

> "The [defendants] have purported to determine the licence. If I have correctly construed the contract their doing so was a breach of contract. It may well be that, in the old days, that would only have given rise to a right to sue in damages. The licence would have stood revoked, but after the expiration of what was the appropriate period of grace the licensees would have been trespassers and could have been expelled and their right would have been to sue for damages for breach of contract . . . But the matter requires to be considered further, because the power of equity to grant an injunction to restrain a breach of contract is, of course, a power exercisable in any court. The general rule is that before equity will grant such an injunction, there must be, on the construction of the contract, a

33 (1845) 13 M. & W. 838; see also *Kerrison v. Smith* [1897] 2 Q.B. 455.
34 [1944] K.B. 408.
35 [1946] 1 All E.R. 678.

> negative clause express or implied. In the present case it seems to me that the grant of an option which, if I am right, is an irrevocable option, must imply a negative undertaking by the licensor not to revoke it. That being so, in my opinion such a contract could be enforced in equity by an injunction."[36]

In the event the House of Lords held that the contract could not be construed so as to find a term that it was irrevocable, but accepted the principle that equity would enforce a licence where there was a contractual term that it should be irrevocable. If the licensee has not yet entered into possession of the premises the same effect can be achieved by the award of the equitable remedy of specific performance. In *Verrall v. Great Yarmouth Borough Council*[37] the defendant council had agreed to allow the National Front to use a hall for its annual conference. After a change of political control the council repudiated the contract. The Court of Appeal held that the principle in *Winter Garden Theatre v. Millennium Productions Ltd* was applicable and ordered specific performance of the contract.

(ii) Is there a contractual term that the licence should be irrevocable?: The central question is therefore whether a contractual licence contains a term, either express or implied, that it is not to be revoked by the licensor. Such terms are relatively easy to find where a ticket is sold for the viewing of a particular event. As Viscount Simon commented in *Millenium Productions Ltd v. Winter Garden Theatre Ltd*:[38] "the implication of the arrangement . . . plainly is that the ticket entitles the purchaser to enter, and if he behaves himself, to remain on the premises until the end of the event which he has paid his money to see." For this reason he held that the decision in *Wood v. Leadbitter*[39] was explicable only on the grounds of the strict rules of pleading existing at the time that it was decided, and that following the fusion of law and equity it should no longer be regarded as good authority. In contrast the decision in *Hurst v. Picture Theatres Ltd*[40] was approved. Although it can be criticised in as far as it suggests that the licence concerned was coupled with an interest, the Court of Appeal noted as an alternative basis for the decision that there was an irrevocable contractual licence. Buckley L.J. stated:

> "If there be a licence with an agreement not to revoke the licence, that, if given for value, is an enforceable right. If the facts here are . . . that the licence was a licence to enter the building and see the spectacle from its commencement until its termination, then there was included in that contract a contract not to revoke the licence until the play had run to its termination."

It is much more difficult to establish that a long term occupation agreement is intended to be irrevocable in the absence of an express term. In *Millenium Productions Ltd v. Winter Garden Theatre Ltd*[41] the House of Lords held that although it was clear that the parties did not intend that the licensor should be able to make an immediate

[36] *ibid.* at 684.
[37] [1981] Q.B. 202.
[38] [1948] A.C. 173.
[39] (1845) 13 M. & W. 838.
[40] [1915] 1 K.B. 1.
[41] [1948] A.C. 173.

out of hand revocation, nor was it intended that it should be perpetual. Lord McDermott concluded that there was an implied term allowing the licensor to terminate the licence after a year by a reasonable period of notice. However it is not impossible to find that a contract for a longer term occupation does contain an implied term that it is irrevocable. In *Hounslow LBC v. Twickenham Garden Developments Ltd*[42] one question was whether builders who had entered into a contract with a council were entitled to remain in possession of the site. Megarry J. held that in the circumstances they were entitled to a contractual licence and he found that this was subject to an implied term not to revoke:

> "Now in this case the contract is one for the execution of specified works on the site during a specified period which is still running. The contract confers on each party specified rights on specified events to determine the employment of the contractor under the contract. In those circumstances, I think that there must be at least an implied negative obligation of the borough not to revoke any licence (otherwise than in accordance with the contract) while the period is still running."[43]

An irrevocable contractual licence has also been held to have been granted in family circumstances. In *Tanner v. Tanner*[44] a milkman who was unhappy with his marriage got a girl pregnant. She took his name and became known as Mrs Tanner. After the birth of twin daughters they decided to purchase a house to provide a home. It was purchased in his name and she left her rent controlled flat to move in with the children. He never lived there and after three years he demanded that she leave so that the house could be sold. The Court of Appeal held that she enjoyed a contractual licence to occupy the house which was irrevocable. Lord Denning M.R. explained:

> "It is said that they were only licensees — bare licensees — under a licence revocable at will: and that the plaintiff was entitled in law to turn her and the twins out on a moments notice. I cannot believe that this is the law . . . She herself said in evidence: "the house was supposed to be ours until the children left school." It seems to me that enables an inference to be drawn, namely, that in all the circumstances it is to be implied that she had a licence — a contractual licence — to have accommodation in the house for herself and the children as long as they were of school age and the accommodation was reasonably required. There was, it is true, no express contract to that effect, but the circumstances are such that the court should imply a contract to that effect . . . if therefore the defendant has sought an injunction restraining the plaintiff from determining the licence, it should have been granted. The order for possession ought not to have been made."[45]

[42] [1971] Ch. 233.
[43] *ibid.* at 247.
[44] [1975] 1 W.L.R. 1347.
[45] *ibid.* at 1350. See also: *Hardwick v. Johnson* [1978] 1 W.L.R. 683; *Chandler v. Kerley* [1978] 1 W.L.R. 693.

Although the decision supports the general rule that a contractual licence subject to an implied term restricting revocability will be enforced by equity it is questionable whether a contractual licence should be implied by the court in such circumstances. It is highly artificial, as there is no intention for the parties to enter into a contractual relationship, and the implication is merely an *ex post facto* rationalisation of the desire to find a remedy to do justice between the parties where an informal undertaking has not been kept.[46] Proprietary estoppel provides the appropriate basis for establishing an entitlement to occupation in such cases, not an implied contract.[47]

4 Effect of contractual licences on third party transferees of the land

(a) Contractual licences historically incapable of binding transferees of the land

The traditional common law position is that since a licence, whether contractual or not, is a purely personal interest between the licensor and the licensee it is incapable of affecting third parties who acquire the land, or an interest in it, from the licensor. This approach was applied by the House of Lords in *King v. David Allen & Sons (Billposting) Ltd.*[48] The plaintiff had been granted a contractual licence by the defendant to put up posters and advertisements on the flank wall of a cinema which a company intended to build on his land. The defendant subsequently leased his land to the company, which entered into possession and built the cinema, but then refused to allow the plaintiffs to post their bills on the wall. Lord Buckmaster LC explained why the licence was unenforceable against the company, thus leaving the plaintiff with merely a remedy against the defendant for breach of contract:

> "The matter then is left in this way. There is a contract between the [plaintiff] and the [defendant] which creates nothing but a personal obligation . . . It is difficult to see how it can be reasonably urged that anything beyond personal rights was ever contemplated by the parties. Those rights have undoubtedly been taken away by the action on the part of the company, who have been enabled to prevent the [plaintiffs] from exercising their rights owing to the lease granted by the [defendant], and he is accordingly liable in damages . . "

In *Clore v. Theatrical Properties Ltd*[49] the Court of Appeal similarly held that the grant of a contractual licence to enjoy the front of house rights of a theatre was a purely personal right and therefore only binding between the parties who enjoyed privity of contract.

(b) Irrevocable contractual licences elevated to proprietary status

(i) Precedents for the elevation of contractual rights to proprietary rights: Although contractual licences were traditionally regarded as personal rights only, there are precedents of other essentially contractual rights being elevated to the status of

[46] *Horrocks v. Forray* [1976] 1 W.L.R. 230.
[47] *Coombes v. Smith* [1986] 1 W.L.R. 808.
[48] [1916] 2 A.C. 54.
[49] [1936] 3 All E.R. 483.

proprietary interests. For example in *Tulk v. Moxhay*[50] the doctrine was developed that the burden of a restrictive covenant was an interest in land capable of passing to bind a successor in title to the original convenantor. In a series of decisions Lord Denning M.R. attempted to elevate the status of a contractual licence to a proprietary right capable of binding third party transferees of the land over which such a licence was enjoyed.

(ii) Contractual licences capable of binding a person claiming title through the licensor: In *Errington v. Errington and Woods*[51] Denning L.J. stated that the recognition by the House of Lords that a contractual licence could be irrevocable in equity should be developed a stage further so that such a licence would be capable of binding a transferee of the title of the land:

> "Law and equity have been fused for nearly 80 years, and since 1948 it has been clear that, as a result of the fusion, a licensor will not be permitted to eject a licensee in breach of a contract to allow him to remain: see *Winter Garden Theatre London v. Millennium Productions Ltd*[52] *per* Lord Greene, and in the House of Lords *per* Lord Simon; nor in breach of a promise on which the licensee has acted, even though he gave no value for it: see *Foster v. Robinson*[53] where Sir Raymond Evershed M.R. said that as a result of the oral agreement to let the man stay, he was entitled as licensee to occupy the premises without any payment of rent for the rest of his days. This infusion of equity means that contractual licences now have a force and validity of their own and cannot be revoked in breach of contract. Neither the licensor nor anyone who claims through him can disregard the contract except a purchaser for value without notice."[54]

The case concerned a house which had been purchased by a father, with the help of a mortgage, to provide a home for his son. He had promised the son and daughter-in-law that if they continued to pay the mortgage instalments he would transfer the house to them when the mortgage was discharged. On his death the father left all his property to his widow. The son left his wife, who continued to live in the house, and returned to live with his mother. She sought possession of the house, which the Court of Appeal refused on the grounds that she entitled to occupy as a contractual licence for as long as she paid the mortgage instalments. It therefore seems that a contractual licence was held enforceable against a successor in title to the original licensor, and for this reason the decision was the subject of academic[55] and judicial[56] criticism.

(iii) Contractual licences as equitable interests in land: However, in *Binions v. Evans*[57] Lord Denning M.R. followed his earlier decision as authority for the proposition that a contractual licence gives rise to an equitable interest in land. The

[50] (1848) 2 Ph. 774.
[51] [1952] 1 K.B. 290.
[52] [1946] 1 All E.R. 678; [1948] A.C. 173.
[53] [1951] 1 K.B. 149.
[54] *ibid.* at 298–299.
[55] (1952) 68 L.Q.R. 337 (Wade); (1953) 69 L.Q.R. 466 (Hargreaves); *cf* (1953) 16 M.L.R. 1.
[56] *National Provincial Bank Ltd v. Hastings Car Mart Ltd* [1964] Ch. 665, *per* Russell L.J.; *National Provincial Bank Ltd v. Ainsworth* [1965] A.C. 1175; *Re Solomon* [1967] Ch. 573, *per* Goff J.
[57] [1972] Ch. 359.

defendant's husband had been employed by the Tredegar Estate and lived rent free in a cottage which it owned. On his death she was allowed to remain in the cottage and they entered an agreement that she was to reside in the cottage "as tenant at will . . . rent free for the remainder of her life", in return for which she agreed to keep the cottage in good repair and to manage the garden. The cottage was subsequently sold by the estate to the plaintiffs, who purchased the land at a reduced price because of a term in the contract of sale by which they agreed to take the land subject to the plaintiff's interest. The plaintiffs then gave the defendant notice to quit the cottage. The Court of Appeal held that she was entitled to remain in occupation of the cottage, but for a variety of reasons. Megaw and Stephenson L.JJ. held that she was entitled to a life interest taking effect under the Settled Land Act 1925. Neither felt it necessary to consider whether a contractual licence was a proprietary right capable of binding third party successors to the licensor's title. Lord Denning M.R. however held that her right was in the nature of a contractual licence and that it bound the plaintiff's because they had acquired the cottage, title to which was unregistered, with notice of its existence. He stated:

> "What is the status of such a licence as this? There are a number of cases in the books in which a similar right has been given. They show that a right to occupy for life, arising by contract, gives to the occupier an equitable interest in the land; just as it does when it arises under a settlement . . . .The courts of equity will not allow the landlord to turn the occupier out in breach of contract; see *Foster v. Robinson*[58]; nor will they allow a purchaser to turn her out if he bought with knowledge of her right — *Errington v. Errington and Woods*."[59–60]

He also considered that, in the event that the contractual licence did not give rise to an immediate equitable proprietary interest, a constructive trust of her right to occupy would be imposed on the plaintiff purchasers because they had agreed to take the land expressly subject to her interest and it would be inequitable to turn her out. Subsequent cases followed the judgement of Lord Denning M.R. and held that occupational rights under an irrevocable contractual licence were capable of binding successors in title, as for example in *Re Sharpe (A bankrupt)*[61] where Browne-Wilkinson J. held that a contractual licence enjoyed by an aunt to occupy a house owned by her nephew was binding on his trustee in bankruptcy.[62]

(c) Irrevocable contractual licences are purely personal rights: a re-assertion of the traditional orthodoxy

The law relating to the status of contractual licences was examined in detail by the Court of Appeal in *Ashburn Anstalt v. Arnold.*[63] After a thorough review of the history of the law in this area the Court categorically rejected the proposition that a

[58] [1951] 1 K.B. 149.
[59] [1952] 1 K.B. 290.
[60] [1972] Ch. 359, 367.
[61] [1980] 1 W.L.R. 219.
[62] See also: *DHN Food Distributors Ltd v. Tower Hamlets London Borough Council* [1976] 1 W.L.R. 852.
[63] [1989] Ch. 1. See: [1988] CLJ 353 (Oakley); [1988] Conv. 201 (Thompson); (1988) 104 L.Q.R. 175 (Sparkes); (1988) 51 M.L.R. 226 (Hill).

contractual licence was in and of itself a proprietary interest in land capable of binding successors in title to the licensor. The Court reviewed all the authorities prior to *Errington v. Errington and Woods,*[64] and in particular the House of Lords decisions in *Edwards v. Barrington*[65] and *King v. David Allen*[66] and concluded that: "Down to this point we do not think that there is any serious doubt as to the law. A mere contractual licence to occupy land is not binding on a purchaser of he land even though he has notice of the licence."[67] The Court then reviewed the authorities where it had been suggested that a contractual licence was in and of itself capable of existing as a proprietary interest, and considered that they were inconsistent with those earlier House of Lords authorities:

> "It must, we think, be very doubtful whether this court's decision in *Errington v. Errington and Woods*[68] is consistent with its earlier decisions in *Daly v. Edwards*[69]; *Frank Warr & Co. v London County Council*[70] and *Clore v. Theatrical Properties Ltd.*[71] That decision cannot be said to be in conflict with any later decision of the House of Lords, because the House expressly left the effect of a contractual licence open in the *Hastings Car Mart* case. But there must be very real doubts whether *Errington* can be reconciled with the earlier decisions of the House of Lords in *Edwards v. Barrington*[72] and *King v. David Allen and Sons (Billposting) Ltd*[73]. It would seem that we must follow those cases or choose between the two lines of authority. It is not, however, necessary to consider those alternative courses in detail, since in our judgement the House of Lords cases, whether or not as a matter of strict precedent they conclude this question, state the correct principle which we should follow . . . Before the *Errington* case the law appears to have been clear and well understood. It rested on an important and intelligible distinction between contractual obligations which gave rise to no estate or interest in the land and proprietary right which, by definition, did. The far-reaching statement of principle in *Errington* was not supported by authority, not necessary for the decision of the case and per incuriam in the sense that it was made without reference to authorities which, if they would not have compelled, would surely have persuaded the court to adopt a different ratio."[74]

(d) Present status of contractual licences

(i) Incapable of existing as proprietary rights in and of themselves: Despite the force and detailed reasoning of the Court of Appeal in *Ashburn Anstalt v. Arnold*[75] and the

[64] [1952] 1 K.B. 290.
[65] (1901) 85 L.T. 650.
[66] [1916] 2 A.C. 54.
[67] [1989] Ch. 1, 15.
[68] [1952] 1 K.B. 290.
[69] 83 L.T. 548.
[70] [1904] 1 K.B. 713.
[71] [1936] 3 All E.R. 483.
[72] (1901) 85 L.T. 650.
[73] [1916] 2 A.C. 54.
[74] [1989] Ch. 1, 21–22.
[75] [1989] Ch. 1.

clear renunciation of the *Errington* doctrine that an irrevocable contractual licence is a property right capable of binding third parties, the decision does not finally settle the matter. Since the Court of Appeal held that the defendant was entitled to a lease rather than a contractual licence the comments relating to such licences are strictly *obiter* to the decision and do not form part of the ratio of the case. The Court of Appeal also accepted the possibility that the law might develop in the future. However, subsequent cases have treated it as repudiating the claimed proprietary status of contractual licences,[76] for example in *Camden L.B.C. v. Shortlife Community Housing*[77] Millet J. stated that the Court of Appeal had "finally repudiated the heretical view that a contractual licence creates an interest in land capable of binding third parties."

(ii) A contractual licence given effect against a third party by means of an independent constructive trust: Although *Ashburn Anstalt v. Arnold* effectively means that contractual licences are not to be regarded as proprietary interests in land it does not follow that there are no circumstances in which a successor in title to a licensor can possibly be required to take his interest subject to a pre-existing contractual licence. The Court of Appeal accepted that if the circumstances of acquisition entitled the court of impose a constructive trust on the successor in title to the licensor then a contractual licence would be binding on him, not in and of itself, but as a consequence of the constructive trust.[78] As has already been noted, this was a second ground for Lord Denning M.R.'s conclusion in *Binions v. Evans*[79] that the contractual licence of the widow should be binding on the purchaser of the estate. The Court of Appeal considered the submission that there was general rule that "when a person sells land "subject to" a contractual licence the court will impose a constructive trust upon the purchaser to give effect to the licence" but rejected it as too wide. Instead they stated:

> "The court will not impose a constructive trust unless it is satisfied that the conscience of the estate owner is affected. The mere fact that that land is expressed to be conveyed "subject to" a contract does not necessarily imply that that grantee is to be under an obligation, not otherwise existing, to give effect to the provisions of the contract. The fact that the conveyance is expressed to be subject to the contract may often . . . be at least as consistent with an intention merely to protect the grantor against claims by the grantee as an intention to impose an obligation on the grantee. The words "subject to" will, of course, impose notice. But notice is not enough to impose on somebody an obligation to give effect to a contract into which he did not enter."[80]

The Court considered the facts as if there had been a contractual licence and held that they would not have imposed a constructive trust. The major factor seems to have been the absence of any reduction in the price paid by the plaintiff's for the title to the land in consequence of their agreement to take it expressly "subject to" the defendant's rights. In contrast, the Court of Appeal considered that a constructive trust was rightly found by Lord Denning M.R. in *Binions v. Evans*[81] because it was established as a fact

[76] *Canadian Imperial Bank of Commerce v. Bello* (1992) 64 P. & C.R. 48.
[77] (1992) 90 L.G.R. 358, 373.
[78] See: *Lyus v. Prowsa Developments* [1982] 1 W.L.R. 1044.
[79] [1972] Ch. 359.
[80] [1989] Ch. 1, 25–26.
[81] [1972] Ch. 359.

that the plaintiffs had purchased the cottage from the estate at a reduced price to reflect the fact that it was sold subject to the widow's occupancy. It therefore seems possible to conclude that a person who acquires land at a reduced value to reflect the fact that they have expressly agreed to take it subject to a pre-existing irrevocable contractual licence will not be permitted to claim that the licence is not binding on them because it is incapable of existing as a proprietary interest in land, but will be subject to a constructive trust requiring them to give effect to their agreement to continue to allow the licensee to enjoy his entitlement.

ESTOPPEL LICENCES

1 Nature of a estoppel licence

It has been seen how a licence can confers a right to occupy land. An estoppel licence is a licence which arises in favour of the licensor by means of the doctrine of proprietary estoppel. The distinction between estoppel licences and the three varieties of licence which have been examined so far therefore lies in the manner by which they are brought into existence.

2 Creation of estoppel licences

(a) Remedies granted under the general doctrine of proprietary estoppel

Estoppel licences are one of a number of potential remedies which may be awarded by a court to a person who is able to show that they are entitled to an interest by way of proprietary estoppel. The principles of proprietary estoppel are founded in older equity cases[82] but have been brought to increasing prominence since the middle of this century. The general doctrine of proprietary estoppel is examined in detail in Chapter 13 as a discrete area, and only a brief summary of its requirements will be given here.

(b) Requirements of proprietary estoppel: establishing an "equity"

A person seeking to claim an interest in land by way of proprietary estoppel will have to establish that they have an "equity" which calls to be remedied. This simply means that in the circumstances they are entitled to some variety of interest in land as against the owner. An "equity" will be raised whenever it would be unconscionable[83] for the owner to land to deny an interest, and this will be so when three elements are established:

(i) A representation: The owner of land must have made some representation or assurance to the person claiming an "equity" by way of proprietary estoppel that they would be entitled to some interest in relation to his land. This representation can be made either actively, or passively by failing to prevent the claimant acting when it was

[82] *Ramsden v. Dyson* (1866) L.R. 1 H.L. 129; *Wilmott v. Barber* (1880) 15 Ch.D. 96.

[83] See: *Taylors Fashions Ltd v. Liverpool Victoria Trustees Co. Ltd* [1982] Q.B. 133; *Lim Teng Huan v. Ang Swee Chuan* [1992] 1 W.L.R. 113.

obvious that he was doing so with the expectation of enjoying some interest in the land.

(ii) Reliance: The claimant will only be able to assert an "equity" if he can demonstrate that he acted in reliance on the assurance. Thus changed conduct for reasons of love or affection may not necessarily be regarded as a consequence of the assurance.[84]

(iii) Detriment: An equity will only arise in favour of a claimant who has acted to her detriment in reliance upon the assurance. It is this element of reliance which renders it unconscionable for the owner to rely on his strict legal rights and to deny the claimant any entitlement to the land. In more recent cases it has been said that there is detriment whenever a claimant has changed her position in reliance on a representation.[85]

(c) Remedies arising by proprietary estoppel: satisfying the equity

When a claimant has established that they are entitled to an "equity" by way of proprietary estoppel this does not of itself answer the question as to the type of interest that arises in their favour. It is for the court to determine the appropriate remedy and to award the claimant what it determines, in its discretion, is the appropriate interest to "satisfy" the equity which has been raised. There is some dispute as to whether the court has a wide discretion to award whatever remedy it wishes, or whether the prime object of the court is to try to fulfil the expectations of the parties. A wide range of interests have been awarded by way of proprietary estoppel, including a transfer of the freehold ownership of the land,[86] a leasehold interest[87] and an easement.[88] In some cases a purely financial remedy has been awarded, usually because a breakdown of relationships has made it impossible for the parties to share occupation of the land in question.[89] However one common remedy has been the award of an occupational licence of the land and this is the interest with which this section is concerned.

(d) Award of an occupational licence as a remedy for proprietary estoppel

In a number of cases it has been held that the appropriate interest to satisfy the equity raised is the award of a licence entitling the claimant to occupy the land subject to the estoppel. In *Plimmer v. Mayor of Wellington,*[90] one of the oldest cases on what today would be recognised as proprietary estoppel, the claimant was held to have become entitled to an irrevocable licence to occupy a jetty and wharf when the landowner had encouraged him to make improvements to it. In *Inwards v. Baker*[91] the Court of Appeal held that a son who had been encouraged to build a bungalow on land owned by his father was entitled to an irrevocable licence to occupy the land for as long as he wanted. Similarly in *Greasley v. Cooke*[92] a maid who had cohabited with the son of the

[84] See: *Coombes v. Smith* [1986] 1 W.L.R. 808.
[85] *Grant v. Edwards* [1986] Ch. 638; *In re Basham decd* [1986] 1 W.L.R. 1498.
[86] *Pascoe v. Turner* [1979] 1 W.L.R. 431.
[87] *Griffiths v. Williams* (1977) 248 E.G. 947.
[88] *Crabb v. Arun District Council* [1976] Ch. 179.
[89] *Dodsworth v. Dodsworth* (1973) 228 E.G. 1115.
[90] (1884) 9 App.Cas. 699.
[91] [1965] 2 Q.B. 29.
[92] [1980] 1 W.L.R. 1306.

owner of a house and looked after members of his family after encouragement that she was to regard the property as her home for the rest of her life was held to be entitled to remain there as long as she wished. In *Re Sharp (A bankrupt)*[93] Browne-Wilkinson J. held that an aunt who had lent money to her nephew in return for an assurance that she would be able to live with him and his wife for life was entitled to an irrevocable licence to occupy until the loan had been repaid.

3 Revocability of an estoppel licence

Whether an estoppel licence is revocable by the licensor will depend upon the precise terms of the licence awarded by the court. As has been noted in the examples cited above the courts have awarded irrevocable licences where this was clearly the expectation of the licensee. As such, the licensor will be unable to terminate the licence and the licensee would be entitled to equitable remedies to enforce his interest.

4 Effect of estoppel licences on third party transferees of the land

(a) Differentiating between the equity and the remedy

Despite the development of the proprietary estoppel as a means of acquiring a right to occupy land as a licensee there is little authority as to the question whether an estoppel licence is capable of binding a successor in title to the licensor obliged to observe it. This problem is complicated by the theoretical question whether an interest by way of proprietary estoppel arises at the date of the events giving rise to the "equity" or at the time when the court awards the remedy to "satisfy" the equity. The better view seems to be that before the court grants a particular right in satisfaction the equity raised by the estoppel is an inchoate interest. Different considerations may apply to the question whether an inchoate equity yet to be satisfied is capable of binding a transferee of the land to which it relates than to whether a remedy granted in satisfaction of such an equity is capable of affecting successors in title.

(b) Can an inchoate equity bind a successor in title?

Despite some academic argument[94] and judicial pronouncements[95] to the contrary, there are dicta which suggest that an inchoate equity raised by way of proprietary estoppel is itself an interest capable of passing with the land, so that the claimant can obtain a remedy in satisfaction against a successor in title.[96] If this is correct then in unregistered land an estoppel will be binding on successors in title who are not protected by the doctrine of notice, since the estoppel equity is not a registrable land charge. If the successor in title was found to be subject to the estoppel equity the court would be able to award what it considered an appropriate remedy to the claimant,

[93] [1980] 1 W.L.R. 219.
[94] See: [1983] Conv. 99 (Bailey); [1990] Conv. 370 (Hayton).
[95] *Fryer v. Brook* [1984] L.S.Gaz. 2856.
[96] E R Ives Investment Ltd v. High [1967] 2 Q.B. 379, 395; *Re Sharpe* [1980] 1 W.L.R. 219, 225; *Sen v. Headley* [1991] Ch. 425, 440; *Voyce v. Voyce* (1991) 62 P. & C.R. 290, 294; *Milton v. Proctor* (1989) N.S.W. Conv.R. 55.

which might include an occupational licence, which he would be bound to observe. In registered land such an estoppel equity could perhaps rank as an overriding interest[97] although this was doubted by Dillon L.J. in *Canadian Imperial Bank of Commerce v. Bello.*[98] It might be possible to protect an estoppel equity as a minor interest on the register, but often the informal nature of the acquisition of the equity will mean that the claimant was unaware of any need to protect it. An estoppel equity was held to be binding on the personal representative of the father who was estopped from denying his son's entitlement to live in a bungalow rent free for the rest of his life in *Inwards v. Baker*[99] and against the trustee in bankruptcy of the estopped nephew in *Re Sharpe (A bankrupt),*[1] neither of whom were purchasers of the land subject to the equity.

(c) Can an estoppel licence awarded in satisfaction of an equity bind a successor in title to the licensor?

If a claimant has been awarded an irrevocable licence to occupy by the court as a remedy in satisfaction of his equity it is unclear whether it is capable of binding a third party who acquires the land from the estopped licensor. Some authorities seem to take the view that the estoppel licence is capable of binding a third party successor in title to the land. In *Re Sharpe (A Bankrupt)*[2] Browne-Wilkinson J. felt compelled to find that an estoppel licence was binding on the trustee in bankruptcy of the licensor, and potentially upon a purchaser of the legal title from the trustee, because of the authorities at that date holding that a irrevocable contractual licence was a property right binding a third party acquiring the title with notice. However, following the decision of the Court of Appeal in *Ashburn Anstalt v. Arnold*[3] an irrevocable licence is not of capable of binding a successor in title to the land in the absence of a constructive trust. The Court doubted whether there was any grounds for finding a constructive trust against the trustee or purchaser in *Re Sharpe.*[4] As a matter of theory it seems that any right which is awarded in satisfaction of an estoppel equity must from that point onwards be treated according to its nature.[5] For example, if the court awards an easement or a lease in satisfaction of an estoppel equity the question whether a successor in title to the land affected will be subject to the easement or lease must be answered by application of the appropriate priorities rules relating to easements and leases respectively. Since present authorities maintain that an irrevocable licence is only able to bind a successor in title who takes the land subject to a constructive trust, a licence generated by estoppel should only be capable of binding a successor in title to the licensor if the stringent requirement for a constructive trust are met. There is no reason why a licence arising by estoppel should be treated any more favourably than a contractual licence which is expressly granted in return for consideration provided by the licensee.[6]

[97] See for example *National Provincial Bank Ltd v. Hastings Car Mart Ltd* [1964] Ch. 665, 689 *per* Lord Denning M.R.
[98] (1992) 64 P. & C.R. 48, 52.
[99] [1965] 2 Q.B. 29.
[1] [1980] 1 W.L.R. 219.
[2] [1980] 1 W.L.R. 219.
[3] [1989] Ch. 1.
[4] *ibid.* at 25.
[5] [1991] Conv. 36 (Battersby).
[6] See also: (1994) 14 L.S. 147 (Baughen).

(d) Inappropriateness of the estoppel licence as a means of satisfying expectations of residential occupation

The problems occasioned by the non-proprietary status of licences and the fact that they will not bind successors in title to the licensor may simply mean that they are an inappropriate means of satisfying the equity raised by estoppel when the clear expectation of the claimant is that they are to be entitled to live rent free in the property for the rest of their life. The courts should perhaps avoid the use of licences altogether in such instances and award appropriate proprietary rights to achieve the same result. For example, *Griffiths v. Williams*[7] Goff J. held that the estoppel equity of a woman who had lived most of her life in her mother's house caring for her and improving the property because she expected to be entitled to live their for the rest of her life could be satisfied against the granddaughter to whom the mother had left the house on her death by the grant of a lease determinable upon death, with no power to assign, at a nominal rent. In many of the cases where an estoppel licence was found the appropriate remedy would probably have been a life interest for the claimant, which would have perfectly satisfied their expectations. However, there was a marked reluctance to grant such an entitlement in satisfaction since it would have the effect of subjecting the land in question to a strict settlement under the Settled Land Act 1925. This would have the unacceptable consequence that the life-tenant would be entitled to the legal title to the land and the concomitant powers of management and disposition, which would far exceed the scope of any expectations. However, with the abolition of the strict settlement and the introduction of the new unitary trust of land by the Trusts of Land and Appointment of Trustees Act 1996,[8] where the legal title can be retained by the trustees along with all the powers of disposition, it may be that a life-interest under such a trust of land is a much more appropriate means of satisfying the estoppel equity where the expectation is of residency for life. As proprietary interests in their own right, leases or life-interests awarded in satisfaction of an estoppel equity would certainly be capable of binding a transferee of the land.

OCCUPATIONAL RIGHTS IN THE FAMILY HOME

1 Introduction to occupational rights in the family home

In many cases today where a couple is cohabiting in residential property both partners will be entitled to occupy the premises since they will be co-owners either of the legal title or as the beneficiaries of a trust of land.[9] This reflects the modern reality that most women, whether married or cohabiting, make some form of financial contribution to the acquisition of their family home, or are more able to insist that it should be owned jointly. However, where a partner has no proprietary interest in the family home the question arises as to whether they have any rights of occupation. Such rights will prove particularly important when the relationship breaks down, since the owner may seek to

[7] (1977) 248 E.G. 947.
[8] See Chap. 8.
[9] See Chap. 7.

claim possession against the non-owning partner. The law has developed so that occupational rights arise in favour of spouses, both by common law and by statute, but not in favour of unmarried cohabitees.

2 Non-statutory occupation rights in the family home

(a) Common law right of the spouse to occupy the matrimonial home

(i) Nature of the right to occupy: In *National Provincial Bank v. Hastings Car Mart Ltd*[10] the House of Lords recognised that at common law a wife was entitled to occupy her matrimonial home, and that this right was not a form of licence but arose by virtue of her status as a wife. Lord Upjohn stated:

> "I think a great deal of the trouble that has arisen in this branch of the law is by reason of attaching to the wife the label of "licensee." But a wife does not remain lawfully in the matrimonial home by leave or licence of her husband as the owner of the property. She remains there because as a result of the status of marriage it is her right and duty so to do and if her husband fails in his duty to remain there that cannot affect her right to do so. She is not a trespasser, she is not a licensee of her husband, she is lawfully there as a wife, the situation is one *sui generis*."[11]

Although most of the cases concern the right of wives to occupy there is no reason why the principle should not extended to husbands, but it does not apply to those who are unmarried.

(ii) Status of the occupational right: The common law spousal right of occupation is a personal interest enforceable only against the other spouse. As Lord Denning M.R. stated in *Gurasz v. Gurasz:*[12] "This right is a personal right which belongs to her as a wife. It is not a proprietary right. It is not available against third persons. It is only available against the husband." The common law right of occupation is therefore incapable of binding a transferee of the land.

(iii) Preventing a transfer which would defeat the right of occupation: Although the common law spousal right of occupation is incapable of binding a transferee of the land the court will act to prevent a transfer occurring which would interfere with the right. In *Lee v. Lee*[13] the Court of Appeal held that a county court judge had the jurisdiction to order a husband who had left his wife not to take any steps by way of sale or assignment of any interest in the matrimonial home, thus preventing him from disposing of it to the prejudice of his wife's right to occupy.

(b) An equitable proprietary right to occupy

(i) The deserted wife's equity: Given the very limited nature of the common law occupation right of spouses, and in particular its inability to affect transferees of the matrimonial home, the Courts developed a species of occupational right in favour of a

[10] [1965] A.C. 1175.
[11] *ibid.* at 1232. See also: *Hall v. King* (1988) 55 P. & C.R. 307, 309 *per* Donaldson M.R.
[12] [1970] P. 11, 16.
[13] [1952] 2 Q.B. 489.

wife who had been left by her husband, known as the "deserted wife's equity."[14] This "equity" was given a proprietary status so that it could potentially bind third party transferees of the matrimonial home. In unregistered land it would bind any purchaser with notice of the equity, and in registered land it would rank as an overriding interest under section 70(1)(g) of the Land Registration Act 1925. In *National Provincial Bank Ltd v. Hastings Car Mart Ltd*[15] a husband who had left his wife subsequently transferred the title of their matrimonial home to his company, which then mortgaged the property to the bank. The Court of Appeal held that the bank took their interest subject to the wife's "equity" since she was in actual occupation of the land and it was therefore an overriding interest.

(ii) Rejection of the "equity": However, on appeal to the House of Lords under the name *National Provincial Bank Ltd v. Ainsworth*[16] the decision of the Court of Appeal was reversed and it was held that a deserted spouse has no proprietary right to occupation of the matrimonial home capable of binding a third party acquiring an interest in the land. Lord Upjohn stated:

> "The right of the wife to remain in occupation even as against her deserting husband is incapable of precise definition, it depends so much on all the circumstances of the case, on the exercise of purely discretionary remedies, and the right to remain may change overnight by the act or behaviour of either spouse. So as a matter of broad principle I am of opinion that the rights of the husband and wife must be regarded as purely personal *inter se* and that these rights as a matter of law do not affect third parties . . . I myself cannot see how it is possible for a "mere equity" to bind a purchaser unless such an equity is ancillary to or dependant upon an equitable estate or interest in land . . . a "mere equity" naked and alone is, in my opinion, incapable of binding successors in title even with notice; it is personal to the parties."[17]

This rejection of the "deserted wife's equity" ultimately ended any possibility of the judicial development of a right of occupation capable of binding transferees of land, and led to the introduction of a statutory right.

3 Statutory rights of occupation in the family home

(a) Introduction of a statutory right

In order to provide some protection for the rights of spouses with no share of the ownership of their matrimonial home the Matrimonial Homes Act 1967 introduced a statutory right of occupation. This legislation was first consolidated in the Matrimonial Homes Act 1983 and more recently in Part IV of the Family Law Act 1996.

(b) Entitlement to "matrimonial home rights"

The Family law Act 1996 introduces a new terminology for the right of occupation of the matrimonial home, namely "matrimonial home rights". A matrimonial home right will arise if the following conditions are met:

[14] See: *Bendall v. McWhirter* [1952] 2 Q.B. 466; *Ferris v. Weaven* [1952] 2 All E.R. 233; *Westminster Bank v. Lee* [1956] Ch. 7.
[15] [1964] Ch. 667.
[16] [1965] A.C. 1175.
[17] *ibid.* at 1233–1238.

(i) Spouses only entitled to matrimonial home rights: The provisions of the Act conferring matrimonial home rights operate only in favour of spouses and have no application to unmarried cohabitees who may share occupation of what is in effect a quasi-matrimonial home. Sections 30(8) and 31(8) make clear that such rights can only persist for so long as the marriage is subsisting, and that they are automatically terminated by the termination of the marriage.[18]

(ii) Spouse only entitled to matrimonial home rights if they have no legal ownership rights in the land: Section 31 provides that only a spouse with no ownership rights is entitled to matrimonial home rights:

> (1) This section applies if—
>
> (a) one spouse is entitled to occupy a dwelling-house by virtue of—
> (i) a beneficial estate or interest or contract; or
> (ii) any enactment giving that spouse the right to remain in occupation; and
>
> (b) The other spouse is not so entitled

However, this is qualified by section 31(9) which provides that a spouse with a purely equitable interest in a house or its proceeds of sale is not to be treated as entitled to occupy by virtue of that interest, solely for the purpose of determining whether they enjoy statutory matrimonial home rights. This provision is especially important in the context of unregistered land since it means that a spouse who enjoys an equitable interest can protect their matrimonial home rights by registration as a land charge, whereas their beneficial entitlement would be subject to the doctrine of notice and cannot be protected.

(iii) Entitlement conferred by statutory matrimonial home rights: Section 30(2) determines the extent of the matrimonial home rights created by the statute:

> "Subject to the provisions of this Part, the spouse not so entitled has the following rights ("matrimonial home rights") —
>
> (a) If in occupation, a right not to be evicted or excluded from the dwelling-house or any part of it by the other spouse except with the leave of the court given by an order under section 33;
> (b) If not in occupation, a right with the leave of the court so given to enter into and occupy the dwelling-house.

(c) Status of matrimonial home rights

Matrimonial home rights conferred by statute remain purely personal rights enjoyed by one spouse against another. However, by section 31(2) the statute confers on them the status of a charge on the estate or interest of the owning spouse. Section 31provides that:

[18] Except in so far as the Court has not made an order under, s.33(5) that the matrimonial home rights are not brought to an end by the termination of the marriage.

(1) Subsections (2) and (3) apply if, at any time during a marriage, one spouse is entitled to occupy a dwelling-house by virtue of a beneficial estate or interest.

(2) The other spouse's matrimonial home rights are a charge on the estate or interest;

(3) The charge created by subsection (2) has the same priority as if it were an equitable interest created at whichever is the latest of the following dates:

(a) The date on which the spouse so entitled acquires the estate or interest;
(b) The date of the marriage; and
(c) 1st January 1968 (the commencement date of the Matrimonial Homes Act 1967).

Thus by statute matrimonial home rights are deemed to enjoy the equivalent proprietary status of equitable interests in the land. Thus what judicial development was unable to achieve through the deserted wife's equity has been accomplished by legislation, namely that a personal right of occupation is capable of binding successors in title to the land.

(d) Effect of matrimonial home rights on third party transferees of the land

Although a matrimonial home right is capable of enjoying priority over the rights of a transferee of the land, or an interest in it, whether such a right is binding will depend upon the type of land concerned.

(i) Matrimonial home rights in unregistered land:[19] In unregistered land matrimonial home rights rank as Class F Land Charges. If they are properly protected they will be binding against any third party acquiring the land or any interest in the land. [20] Failure to register an appropriate land charge will mean that a purchaser will take his interest free from it, since section 4(8) of the Land Charges Act 1972 provides that:

> "A land charge of Class F shall be void as against a purchaser of the land charged with it, or of any interest in such land, unless the land charge is registered in the appropriate register before the completion of the purchase."

(ii) Matrimonial home rights in registered land: Where title to the dwelling house in which a spouse enjoys a matrimonial home right is registered section 31(10) provides that the charge thereby affecting the land can be protected by registering a notice on the register.[21] Although a notice can normally only be entered with the consent of the registered proprietor, a matrimonial home right can be protected by the entry of a notice without the production of the proprietor's land certificate.[22] Section 31(10)(b) provides that a spouses matrimonial home rights are "not an overriding interest within the meaning of that Act affecting the dwelling-house even though the spouse is in actual occupation." This means that they will not be binding as against a purchaser of an interest in the land if they have not been appropriately protected.

[19] See Chap. 17 below.
[20] *Hastings and Thanet Building Society v. Goddard* [1970] 1 W.L.R. 1544; *Perez-Adamson v. Perez-Rivas* [1987] Fam 89.
[21] See Chap. 15.
[22] See: Law of Property Act 1925, s.64; Matrimonial Homes and Property Act 1981, s.4(1).

(e) Occupation orders where a spouse is entitled to matrimonial home rights

Under section 33 of the Family Law Act 1996 the court possesses a wide jurisdiction to make an occupation order in favour of a person who "has matrimonial home rights in relation to a dwelling house."[23] Section 33(3) provides that such an order may:

(a) Enforce the applicant's entitlement to remain in occupation as against the other person ("the respondent");

(b) Require the respondent to permit the applicant to enter and remain in the dwelling-house or part of the dwelling-house;

(c) Regulate the occupation of the dwelling house by either or both parties;

(d) [inapplicable to matrimonial home rights]

(e) If the respondent has matrimonial home rights in relation to the dwelling-house and the applicant is the other spouse, restrict or terminate those rights;

(f) require the respondent to leave the dwelling-house or part of the dwelling-house; or

(g) Exclude the respondent from a defined area in which the dwelling-house is included.

Section 33(6) requires the court to take into account all the circumstances when deciding whether to grant an order, but especially:

(a) The housing needs and housing resources of each of the parties and of any relevant child;

(b) the financial resources of each of the parties;

(c) The likely effect of any order, or of any decision by the court not to exercise its powers under subsection (3), on the health, safety, or well-being of the parties and of any relevant child;

(d) the conduct of the parties in relation to each other and otherwise.

In some cases the courts have been willing to exercise their jurisdiction so as to deprive a person otherwise entitled to a matrimonial home right from asserting their entitlement to occupation against a successor in title. In *Kaur v. Gill*[24] a wife had enjoyed an occupational right in her matrimonial home which she protected by means of a notice on the land register prior to the completion of a sale by her husband to a third party. The Court of Appeal upheld the refusal of an order under the predecessor of section 33(3) of the Family Law Act 1996[25] that she should be entitled to occupy, because the purchaser was a blind man who had acquired the house because it was more convenient for him. He was only bound by notice because his solicitor had

[23] s.33(1)(a)(ii).
[24] [1988] 2 F.L.R. 328.
[25] Matrimonial Homes Act 1983, s.1(3).

conducted an inadequate telephone search of the land register. The Court held that it was perfectly legitimate to take into account the circumstances of the purchaser as well as the spouse. Dillon L.J. stated:

> "I have no doubt that the fact that a purchaser has constructive, or actual, notice of a wife's claim to rights of occupation and buys a property subject to that claim is, of itself, a highly material factor for the court to consider. Moreover, if the evidence was that the purchaser was buying by way of collusion with a husband to evict a wife, any other circumstances of merit on the purchaser's side might carry little weight in the balance. But I cannot see that the court is, without regard to merits, bound to refuse to consider the circumstances of the purchaser, or other third party deriving title under the husband subject to a wife's claim, at all."[26]

[26] [1988] 2 F.L.R. 328, 333.

Chapter 13

PROPRIETARY ESTOPPEL[1]

INTRODUCTION TO PROPRIETARY ESTOPPEL

1 A means of creating proprietary interests in land

At a number of points in earlier chapters reference has been made to the doctrine of proprietary estoppel. It has been noted that this doctrine operates as a means by which a person may acquire an interest in land, whether the freehold ownership,[2] a lease,[3] an easement[4] or a licence.[5] The essence of proprietary estoppel is that the Court may award an interests in land as a remedy against a landowner who has conducted himself in such a way that it would be unjust for him to assert his strict and unqualified right as owner to deny the claimant any entitlement because it had not been appropriately created. As Scott L.J. observed in *Layton v. Martin*:[6]

> "The proprietary estoppel line of cases are concerned with the question whether an owner of property can, by insisting on his strict legal rights therein, defeat an expectation of an interest in that property, it being an expectation which he has raised by his conduct and which has been relied on by the claimant."

Proprietary estoppel provides, along with the principles of resulting and constructive trusts, a means by which interests in land may be obtained informally. The role and operation of proprietary estoppel was summarised by Stephen Moriarty:[7]

> "The role of proprietary estoppel seems self-evident: it provides for the informal creation of interests in land whenever a person has acted detrimentally in reliance upon an oral assurance that he has such an interest. Oral grants of

[1] See: Pearce & Stevens, *The Law of Trusts and Equitable Obligations*, (1995), Chap. 30.
[2] See p. 62.
[3] See p. 93.
[4] See Chap. 9.
[5] See Chap. 12.
[6] [1986] 2 F.L.R. 227, 238.
[7] (1984) 100 L.Q.R. 376 at 381.

interests by themselves, therefore are insufficient; but act in reliance upon some such assurance, and proprietary estoppel will validate what the law of property say has no effect."

2 Elements of a claim by proprietary estoppel

Acquisition of an interest in land by way of proprietary estoppel involves two essential stages:

(a) Establishing an "equity"

First the claimant must demonstrate that in the circumstances an estoppel has arisen which requires a remedy. More recent cases have identified three elements as necessary to the establishment of a proprietary estoppel, namely: (1) a representation; (2) reliance by the claimant on the representation; (3) change of position or detriment. When these three elements are present the claimant is said to enjoy an estoppel "equity" which requires a remedy.

(b) Satisfying the "equity"

Once an equity has been established by a claimant it is for the court to award an appropriate remedy in satisfaction of it. Until such time as the equity is satisfied it remains inchoate.

3 Distinguishing the principle of proprietary estoppel from the doctrine of constructive trusts

Although proprietary estoppel shares a functionally similar role to that of constructive trusts in that it provides for the informal creation of proprietary rights in land, as English law has developed the two concepts are distinct. Three major differences may be observed:

(a) "Representation" rather than "common intention"

It has been seen that a constructive trust will only be established where it can be shown that the parties shared a "common intention" that the ownership of the land should be shared, and the constructive trust arises in fulfilment of that intention. Although common intention can be criticised as the theoretical basis for the imposition of constructive trusts on the grounds of artificiality, the central question is often whether such a common intention can be established, and it has been seen that in *Lloyds Bank plc v. Rosset*[8] the House of Lords adopted a very narrow view of the circumstances in which such an intention could be inferred from the parties conduct alone. In contrast proprietary estoppel operates on the basis of "representation" by the owner of land that the claimant is entitled to some interest in it. This operates as a lower threshold than "common intention" which means that it will sometimes be possible to establish an estoppel equity when a "common intention" cannot be established. As will be seen, a wider range of factual information about the nature of the parties conduct and their

[8] [1991] 1 A.C. 107.

relationship will be taken into account by the court in determining whether there was a representation sufficient to establish an equity, and in particular non-financial contributions are not regarded as irrelevant.

(b) A range of remedies rather then a share of the equitable ownership

Where the requirements for a constructive trust are established the only possible consequence is that the claimant will be recognised as enjoying a share of the equitable ownership of the land subject to the trust. There is no flexibility for the court to award any alternative remedy, and the land will become subject to a trust of land, and the relationship of the parties will be regulated and determined by the rules concerning concurrent ownership. However, in the case of proprietary estoppel there is no such certainty as to the nature of the remedy that will be awarded to a successful claimant. Instead, the nature of the right awarded to satisfy the estoppel equity is a matter for the discretion of the court. As far as possible the court will attempt to fulfil the reasonable expectation of the claimant, and to award the right it was represented that he would enjoy. A wide range of interests in land have been awarded on the basis of an estoppel, and the remedial flexibility is particularly apparent in the fact that on occasions the court has refused to award an interest in land at all but has simply ordered that the claimant receive financial compensation.

(c) Interest in land acquired when awarded by the court rather than at the date of the events establishing the cause of action

A third significant difference is that where an interest in land is awarded by the court to satisfy an estoppel equity that interest arises from the date of the judgment awarding it, not from the earlier date when the equity was itself raised by detrimental reliance on the relevant representation. This contrasts with a constructive trust, where the court merely recognises the existence of the trust which arises from the moment that the beneficiary acted to her detriment on the basis of the common intention that she was to enjoy a share of the ownership of the land. In essence the interest awarded as a response to satisfy an estoppel equity had no existence prior to the judgment awarding it and can properly be regarded as a remedy, whereas the constructive trust generates an equitable entitlement as soon as the appropriate triggers have occurred without the intervention of the court, so that it is not truly remedial but institutional in nature. The main significance of this difference is the extent to which the respective rights generated in the land are capable of binding third party interests arising in the intervening period between the events justifying the claim and the judgment of the court. In the case of a constructive trust, since the claimant's beneficial interest in the land arises form the moment that the common intention was acted upon, third parties subsequently gaining an interest in the land will potentially take their interests subject to the pre-existing equitable ownership generated by the constructive trust. Thus if a man who is the sole legal owner of a house, in which his partner enjoys a half-share by way of a constructive trust, subsequently mortgages the land to a bank, the bank may take its mortgage subject to the partner's beneficial interest, dependent on the applicable rules of priority. Interests awarded by the court in satisfaction of an estoppel equity are incapable of taking priority over intervening third party interests in and of themselves. The court may even take account of the existence of such intervening third party interests in determining the appropriate remedy for the estoppel. However, although the interest awarded may not be capable of binding a third party who has become entitled to intervening rights in the land it is an important question whether the estoppel "equity" calling for a remedy is itself an interest in land capable of binding a third party even while it has not yet been crystallised into a traditional proprietary right by judgement of the court. For example, if a cohabitee can establish that she is entitled to an estoppel equity, but the land has been sold to a third party, can the third party take the land subject to her right to be awarded a remedy in satisfaction of the estoppel?

ESTABLISHING AN EQUITY BY PROPRIETARY ESTOPPEL

1 Historical evolution

The doctrine of proprietary estoppel as a means of acquisition of interests in land has a long historical pedigree. In a number of cases in the Nineteenth Century it was held that a person's conduct could entitle a claimant to an interest in land despite the absence of the necessary formalities for the creation of such an interest.[9] Although some cases, such as *Ramsden v. Dyson,*[10] suggested a broad approach to determining when such an interest should be acquired, the development of a generalised principle was stultified by *Willmott v. Barber*[11] where Fry J. held that the legal owner could only be prevented from asserting his title if he had acquiesced in a mistake made by the claimant as to his rights in the land, since the foundation of the doctrine was the prevention of fraud. He laid down what have become known as the "five probanda" as pre-requisites of a successful claim:

> "A man is not to be deprived of his legal rights unless he has acted in such a way as would make it fraudulent for him to set up those rights. What, then, are the elements or requisites necessary to constitute fraud of that description? In the first place the plaintiff must have made some mistake as to his legal rights. Secondly, the plaintiff must have expended some money or must have done some act (not necessarily upon the defendant's land) on the faith of his mistaken belief. Thirdly, the defendants, the possessor of the legal right, must know of the existence of his own right which is inconsistent with the right claimed by the plaintiff. If he does not know of it he is in the same position as the plaintiff, and the doctrine of acquiescence is founded upon conduct with a knowledge of your legal rights. Fourthly, the defendant, the possessor of the legal right, must know of the plaintiff's mistaken belief of his rights. If he does not, there is nothing which calls upon him to assert his own rights. Lastly, the defendant, the possessor of the legal right, must have encouraged the plaintiff in his expenditure of money or in the other acts which he has done, either directly or by abstaining form asserting his legal right. Where all these elements exist, there is fraud of such a

[9] See: *Dillwyn v. Llewellyn* (1862) 4 De G. F. & J. 517; *Ramsden v. Dyson* (1866) L.R. 1 H.L. 129.
[10] (1866) L.R. 1 H.L. 129.
[11] (1880) 15 Ch.D. 96.

nature as will entitle the court to restrain the possessor of the legal title from exercising it, but, in my judgment, nothing short of this will do."[12]

Although these probanda have been applied in subsequent cases,[13] including *Matharu v. Matharu*[14] where Roch L.J. held that they had been satisfied on the facts, other cases seem to suggest that a less rigid approach should be taken to the question whether an equity has been established.[15] In *Ramsden v. Dyson*[16] itself Lord Kingsdown articulated a much more generalised jurisdiction for establishing an equity rooted in the concept of expectations induced by the landowner rather than mistake by the claimant:

"If a man, under a verbal agreement with a landlord for a certain interest in land, or what amounts to the same thing, under an expectation, created or encouraged by the landlord, that he shall have a certain interest, takes possession of such land, with the consent of the landlord, and upon faith of such promise or expectation, with the knowledge of the landlord and without objection by him, he lays out money upon the land, a court of equity will compel the landlord to give effect to such promise or expectation."

In the leading modern authority, *Taylor Fashions Ltd v. Liverpool Victoria Trustees Co. Ltd*[17] Oliver J. restated the requirements for a successful estoppel claim so that it is not universally necessary to meet all five of the *Willmott v. Barber* probanda. Instead he considered that the doctrine was founded upon a broad principle of unconscionability:

". . . the recent cases indicate, in my judgement, that the application of the *Ramsden v. Dyson* principle — whether you call it proprietary estoppel, estoppel by acquiescence or estoppel by encouragement is really immaterial — requires a very much broader approach which is directed rather at ascertaining whether, in particular individual circumstances, it would be unconscionable for a party to be permitted to deny that which, knowingly or unknowingly, he has allowed or encouraged another to assume to his detriment, than to inquiring whether the circumstances can be fitted within the confines of some preconceived formula serving as a universal yardstick for every form of unconscionable behaviour."

This broader approach was been approved by the Court of Appeal in *Habib Bank Ltd v. Habib Bank A.G. Zurich*[18] and was applied by the Privy Council in *Lim Teng Huan v. Ang Swee Chuan*[19] where Lord Browne-Wilkinson stated:

[12] *ibid.* at 105–106.
[13] See: *Crabb v. Arun District Council* [1976] Ch. 179; *Swallow Securities v. Isenberg* [1985] 1 E.G.L.R. 132; *Coombes v. Smith* [1986] 1 W.L.R. 808. In *Kammins Ballroom Co v. Zenith Instruments (Torquay) Ltd* [1971] A.C. 850 and *E. and L. Berg Homes Ltd v. Grey* (1979) 253 E.G. 473 claims of proprietary estoppel failed where the probanda were not satisifed.
[14] [1994] 2 F.L.R. 597; [1995] Conv. 61 (Welstead).
[15] See: *Appleby v. Cowley, The Times,* April 14, 1982; *Amalgamated Investment & Property Co. Ltd v. Texas Commerce International Bank* [1982] Q.B. 84; *Re Basham (dec'd)* [1986] 1 W.L.R. 1498.
[16] (1866) L.R. 1 H.L. 129, 170.
[17] [1982] Q.B. 133.
[18] [1981] 1 W.L.R. 1265.
[19] [1992] 1 W.L.R. 113.

> "The decision in *Taylor Fashions Ltd v. Liverpool Victoria Trustees Co. Ltd* showed that, in order to found a proprietary estoppel, it is not essential that the representor should have been guilty of unconscionable conduct in permitting the representee to assume that he could act as he did: it is enough if, in all the circumstances, it is unconscionable for the representor to go back on the assumption which he permitted the representee to make."

2 The modern requirements

Following the re-statement of principle in *Taylor Fashions Ltd v. Liverpool Victoria Trustees Co. Ltd* there are three inter-related elements that must be met to establish an estoppel equity. First, the claimant must show that there was a representation by the landowner which gave rise to an expectation that they were entitled to some interest in the land. Secondly, they must have relied on that representation. Thirdly, they must have acted to their detriment as a consequence of such reliance. Each of these requirements will be examined in turn.

3 A representation

(a) Importance of a representation

The foundation of an estoppel claim is that the claimant acted on the basis that they were entitled, or were going to become entitled,[20] to an interest in the land concerned. It is obviously not sufficient to justify a remedy if they were acting under a unilateral mistake that they were so entitled, and therefore the element of representation is the connecting factor between the expectations of the claimant and the activities of the owner of the land which call for a remedy. As Edward Nugee Q.C. stated in *Re Basham (dec'd)*[21] the essence of proprietary estoppel is that:

> "where one person, A, has acted to his detriment on the faith of a belief, which was known to and encouraged by another person, B, that he either has or is going to be given a right in or over B's property, B cannot insist on his strict legal rights if to do so would be inconsistent with A's belief."

(b) Form of representation

(i) Active representation: An active representation occurs when the owner of land by words or conduct leads the claimant to expect that they enjoy some entitlement in the land. For example, in *Pascoe v. Turner*[22] the defendant had moved in with the plaintiff first as his housekeeper and then as his lover. They moved to a new house which he purchased, but he subsequently began an affair with another woman and moved out. After he had left she remained in the house and he told her that she should not worry as the house was hers and everything in it. The Court of Appeal held that in these

[20] *Re Basham* [1986] 1 W.L.R. 1498.
[21] [1986] 1 W.L.R. 1498, 1503.
[22] [1979] 1 W.L.R. 431.

circumstances he had made a representation which was sufficient to establish a proprietary estoppel. In *Inwards v. Baker*[23] a son was intending to purchase some land on which to build a bungalow as his home. His father persuaded him to build the bungalow on land that he owned so that it would be bigger. The Court of Appeal held that this gave rise to an expectation of the son that he would be allowed to remain in the bungalow for his lifetime which entitled him to a remedy by way of estoppel. In *Griffiths v. Williams*[24] the Court of Appeal similarly held that there was a sufficient representation where a mother has assured her daughter, who was living with her and caring for her, that she would be entitled to live in the house for the whole of her life. In *Re Basham (dec'd)*[25] the plaintiff was the step-daughter of the owner of a cottage who had died intestate. Prior to his death she and her husband had helped him to run his business and looked after him and the cottage, and on a number of occasions he had made clear that she was to expect to have the house when he died. When a new room was added he had told her that it was "putting money on the property for you" and when there was a boundary dispute with the neighbours he told her to sort it out herself as she was going to be entitled to the property. Edward Nugee Q.C. held that these representations encouraged the plaintiff's belief that she was going to receive the cottage and were sufficient to give rise to an estoppel equity preventing it passing to others on his intestacy.

(ii) Passive representation: A passive representation occurs when the owner of land stands by and does nothing to disavow the claimant of a mistaken expectation that they are or will become entitled to an interest in the land. The possibility of a passive representation was raised by Lord Wensleydale in *Ramsden v. Dyson*[26] where he stated: "[If a stranger] builds on my land, supposing it to his own, and I, knowing it to be mine, do not interfere, but leave him to go on, equity considers it to be dishonest in me to remain passive and afterwards to interfere and take the profit." Although subsequent cases have made clear that it is not strictly essential to establishing an equity by proprietary estoppel that the owner knew of the claimant's mistaken belief and also of their own legal rights to intervene,[27] these are relevant factors and it will be easier to establish an equity by passive representation where they are present.

(c) Person making the representation

Although in most cases the representation will have been made by the owner of the land in which an interest is claimed, an estoppel equity will also arise if the representation was made by the owners employee or agent.[28] However a tenant cannot make a representation which will generate an equity against the freehold owner.[29]

(d) Object of the representation

A representation will only give rise to an estoppel equity if it generated an expectation in relation to specific assets. In *Layton v. Martin*[30] Scott J. held that there was no

[23] [1965] 2 Q.B. 29.
[24] (1977) 248 E.G. 947.
[25] [1986] 1 W.L.R. 498.
[26] (1866) L.R. 1 H.L. 129, 168.
[27] See: *Shaw v. Applegate* [1977] 1 W.L.R. 970; *Taylor Fashions Ltd v. Liverpool Victoria Trustees Co. Ltd* [1982] Q.B. 133. Compare: *Armstrong v. Sheppard & Short Ltd* [1959] 2 Q.B. 384.
[28] *Ivory v. Palmer* [1975] ICR 340.
[29] *Ward v. Kirkland* [1967] Ch. 194; *Swallow Securities Ltd v. Isenberg* (1985) 274 E.G. 1028.
[30] [1986] 2 F.L.R. 227.

estoppel equity where a man had given a woman who moved in with him a general assurance that he would provide for her financially. He stated that the representation must arise:

> ". . . in connection with some asset in respect of which it has been represented, or is alleged to have been represented that the claimant is to have some interest . . . The present case does not raise that question. A representation that "financial security" would be provided by the deceased to the plaintiff, and on which I will assume she acted, is not a representation that she is to have some equitable or legal interest in any particular asset of assets."[31]

However, in *Re Basham (dec'd)*[32] it was held that a representation that the plaintiff would become entitled to the whole of the representor's estate on death was sufficient to give rise to an equity and that the representation did not need to relate to a clearly identified piece of property. By analogy with the doctrine of mutual wills Edward Nugee Q.C. stated:

> "If the belief that B will leave the whole of his estate to A is established by sufficiently cogent evidence . . . I see no reason in principle or in authority why the doctrine of proprietary estoppel should not apply so as to raise an equity against B in favour of A extending to the whole of B's estate."

The case also clearly demonstrates that a representation will create an equity even if it was made in relation to the grant of future rights.

4 Reliance on the representation

The element of reliance is closely connected with the third requirement that the claimant must have acted to their detriment on the basis of the representation. Reliance is the element which connects any detriment with the representation so that the claimant can be said to have so acted because of the inducement of the representation. In *Att.-Gen. of Hong Kong v. Humphrey's Estate (Queen's Gardens) Ltd*[33] the Privy Council stated that claimants of proprietary estoppel must "show" that they had relied on the belief or expectation encouraged by the landowner. In most cases the element of reliance will be obvious, and in *Greasley v. Cooke*[34] Lord Denning M.R. considered that it should be presumed once a representation has been established. In *Lim Teng Huan v. Ang Swee Chuan*[35] the Privy Council held that reliance could be established by an inevitable inference from the facts of a case. The element of reliance will generally only be in question in extreme situations and to eliminate those cases where the claimant cannot be shown to have changed their conduct in any way as a result of the representation made. One such case where it was

[31] *ibid.* at 238–239.
[32] [1986] 1 W.L.R. 1498.
[33] [1987] A.C. 114.
[34] [1980] 1 W.L.R. 1306.
[35] [1992] 1 W.L.R. 113.

held that there was no reliance was *Coombes v. Smith.*[36] Mrs Coombes and Mr Smith became lovers while they were still married to different partners. Mr Smith purchased a house in which they intended to co-habit, and he said such things to Mrs Combes as "it'll be nice when we're living together — we'll spend the rest of our lives together." It was a new house and she decorated it. Just before she moved into the house Mrs Combes became pregnant. Initially she moved in alone and Mr Smith promised that he would join her after spending Christmas with his children, but in the event he never moved in. After three years Mrs Coombes and the daughter moved to a new house purchased by Mr Smith, which she again redecorated. He then began living with another woman. He undertook to permit them to remain in the house until the child was 17, but she claimed that she was entitled to have the house conveyed to her on the grounds of proprietary estoppel. Jonathon Parker Q.C. held that none of the elements of a proprietary estoppel claim were established, since Mrs Coombes had not been acting under a mistaken belief as to her legal rights and that her conduct did not constitute a detriment. He also held that her acts of alleged detriment, including leaving her husband and having a child, were not causally connected with any representation so that the element of reliance was absent:

> "The first act relied on by the plaintiff is allowing herself to become pregnant by the defendant. In my judgement, it would be wholly unreal, to put it mildly, to find on the evidence adduced before me that the plaintiff allowed herself to become pregnant by the defendant in reliance on some mistaken belief as to her legal rights. She allowed herself to become pregnant because she wished to live with the defendant and to bear his child . . . The second act relied on as detriment was the plaintiff's leaving her husband and moving [into the defendant's house] . . . The reality is that the plaintiff decided to [move to his house] because she preferred to have a relationship with, and a child by, the defendant rather than continuing to live with her husband. It seems to me to have been as simple as that. There is no evidence that she left her husband in reliance on the defendant's assurance that he would provide for her if and when their relationship came to an end: the idea of detriment or prejudice is only introduced *ex post facto*."

It is questionable whether this blanket rejection of reliance merely because the claimant also acted from personal feelings is correct, and the facts are not altogether dissimilar to those of *Pascoe v. Turner*[37] where it was held that the claimant was entitled to an estoppel equity and to a conveyance of the house she occupied. Jonathon Parker Q.C. distinguished the case on the grounds that in *Pascoe v. Turner* there had been a much clearer express representation that Mrs Turner was to regard the house as belonging to her, but this alone would not have been sufficient to establish the equity in the absence of reliance. The acts of Mrs Turner, such as moving into the co-habited house, could also have been explained on the basis of her affection for Mr Pascoe rather than any expectation of gaining an interest in the land, but this did not

[36] [1986] 1 W.L.R. 808.
[37] [1979] 1 W.L.R. 431.

prevent a finding that she was entitled to an equity. In reality the judgement in *Coombes v. Smith* seems to draw too categorical a distinction between motives of love and affection and the desire to acquire a proprietary interest. People act with mixed motives, and in many cases where a claim by proprietary estoppel has succeeded it could be said that the claimant was motivated by emotional attachment to a relationship.[38] The rejection of Mrs Coombes' claim may have been influenced by the fact that Mr Smith had already agreed that she and their daughter could remain in occupation until the child had grown up, a concession which made it somewhat easier to dismiss her claim for ownership. It is surely questionable whether the court would have refused her claim entirely if no such concession had been made so that she would not have enjoyed any right to occupy the house. Despite these criticisms of the decision the principle stands that in the absence of reliance there will be no estoppel equity. In *Stilwell v. Simpson*[39] it was held that a claimant who had carried out repairs on a house of which he was the tenant had not relied on an assurance of the landlady that he would have the property, or a first option to purchase it, on her death because he had carried the work out for his own benefit, knowing that she was not able to pay for it to be done.

5 Detriment or change of position by the claimant

(a) Detrimental reliance generates the estoppel

The mere fact that a representation has been made does not entitle a person to an interest in land, in just the same way that a mere promise to make a gift does not entitle the prospective donee to compel the donor to make it. A person is perfectly entitled to go back on his word. However if the person to whom the representation was made has acted in some way in reliance upon it then the representor will be estopped from denying the expectation he had generated. It is the element of detrimental reliance which renders it unconscionable[40] for the landowner to assert his strict rights against the representee. Although the language of "detriment" is common in the cases, more recent decisions have expressed the need for a "change of position"[41] by the representee. In *Lloyds Bank v. Rosset*[42] Lord Bridge stated that in order to generate a constructive trust or proprietary estoppel the claimant must:

> "show that he or she acted to his or her detriment or significantly altered his or her position in reliance on the [representation[43]]."

(b) What will constitute detriment or "significant change of position"

There is no complete catalogue of behaviour or conduct which will be regarded as constituting sufficient detriment or change of position to establish an estoppel equity.

[38] See for example, *Greasley v. Cooke* [1980] 1 W.L.R. 1306.
[39] (1983) 133 N.L.J. 894.
[40] see: *Grundt v. Great Boulder Gold Mines* (1937) 59 C.L.R. 641.
[41] See: *E R Ives Investments Ltd v. High* [1967] 2 Q.B. 379; *Re Basham (Dec'd)* [1986] 1 W.L.R. 1498.
[42] [1991] 1 A.C. 107, 132.
[43] Lord Bridge actually used the term "agreement" which was appropriate in the prime context of the case, which concerned the creation of constructive trusts.

In *Watts v. Storey*[44] the Court of Appeal said that "the categories of detriment were not closed." However certain types of conduct have come to be recognised as sufficient.
(i) Improving the representor's land: Expenditure by the representee to improve the land of the representor will constitute sufficient detriment to establish an estoppel equity against him, provided that the expenditure was incurred in reliance upon the representation.[45] In *Inwards v. Baker*[46] the son improved his father's land by building a bungalow on it in reliance on the assurance that he had received that he would be able to live there as long as he wished. In *Pascoe v. Turner*[47] the representee was held to have acted to her detriment when she spent money improving, repairing and redecorating the house of her former lover in reliance on his representation that she was entitled to an interest in it. Cumming-Bruce L.J. stated:

> "... the [claimant], having been told that the house was hers, set about improving it within and without. Outside she did not do much ... Inside she did a great deal more. She installed gas in the kitchen with a cooker, improved the plumbing in the kitchen and put in a new sink. She got new gas fires, putting a gas fire in the lounge. She redecorated four rooms ... We would describe the work done in and about the house as substantial in the sense that that adjective is used in the context of estoppel"[48]

(ii) Representee improves his own land: There will also be sufficient detriment if the representee incurs expenditure improving or changing his own land in reliance on a representation of an entitlement to the representor's land. For example, in *Rochdale Canal Co. v. King*[49] the representee built a mill on his land after applying to the canal company to draw water from their canal for his steam engines and their acquiescence in his laying of pipes for that purpose, at which their engineers were present. It was held that they were not entitled to an injunction restraining the representee form drawing water.
(iii) Representee purchases new land: A representee will have acted to his detriment if he purchases new land on the basis of a representation by representor. In *Salvation Army Trustees Co. Ltd v. West Yorkshire Metropolitan County Council*[50] the Salvation Army purchased a new site and built a replacement hall when the council represented that it would be requiring their present site for a road widening scheme. They were later informed that the scheme would not be adopted for some years. Although there had never been a binding contract for the sale of the site Woolf J. held that the Salvation Army were entitled to an equity and that the doctrine of proprietary estoppel was "capable of extending to the disposal of an interest in land where that disposal is closely linked by an arrangement that also involves the acquiring of an interest in land."

[44] [1984] 134 NLJ 631.
[45] *Voyce v. Voyce* (1991) 62 P. & C.R. 290.
[46] [1965] 2 Q.B. 29.
[47] [1979] 1 W.L.R. 431.
[48] *ibid.* 435-436.
[49] (1853) 16 Beav. 630.
[50] (1981) 41 P. & C.R. 179.

(iv) Non-financial personal disadvantage to the representee: It has been a matter of some debate whether a representee who acts to his or her personal disadvantage or changes his conduct, without any financial detriment, in reliance on a representation will be entitled to a claim by proprietary estoppel. A narrow approach was taken by Jonathan Parker Q.C. in *Coombes v. Smith,*[51] the facts of which have been discussed in detail above, where he held that the claimant's conduct in leaving her husband, having and caring for a child and redecorating the representor's house were insufficient to establish an estoppel equity. He held that becoming pregnant and giving birth was not capable of constituting detriment in the context of proprietary estoppel, and that looking after the child after it was born and redecorating the property could not give rise to "any question of prejudice or detriment." He also rejected the suggestion that her failure to take any other steps to provide for herself and her future security by looking for a job was a detriment. However, this narrow view is somewhat anomalous it the light of other cases which have taken a much more positive approach to the assessment of non-financial conduct as sufficient detriment. In *Re Basham (dec'd)*[52] Edward Nugee Q.C. stated that: "It is in my judgement established that the expenditure of A's money on B's property is not the only kind of detriment that gives rise to proprietary estoppel." He therefore held that a the step-daughter who had cared for her step-father on the basis of his representation that she would be entitled to the cottage he owned on his death was entitled to an estoppel equity:

> ". . . the [claimant] did a very great deal for the deceased, and it is clear that she did not receive any commensurate reward for this during her lifetime. There is some evidence, though not very much, of occasions when the [claimant] or her husband acted or refrained from acting in a way in which they might have done but for their expectation of inheriting the deceased's property: I refer to the occasions when the husband refrained form selling his building land, and refrained from taking a job in Lincolnshire which would have made it impossible for the [claimant] to continue caring for her mother and the deceased, and the occasions when the [claimant] instructed solicitors at her own expense in connection with the boundary dispute between the deceased and [his neighbour], and the expenditure of time and money on the house and garden and on carpeting the house, when the deceased had ample means of his own to pay for such matters. It may be that none of these incidents, taken by itself, would be very significant, but the cumulative effect of them supports the view that the [claimant] and her husband subordinated their own interests to the wishes of the deceased."

Although there was clearly some element of financial detriment on the claimants part a large number of these "cumulative" acts were non-financial and it was held that they went "well beyond what was called for by natural love and affection." In a number of other cases conduct which was not essentially financial in nature has been held to be sufficient detriment. For example, in *Jones (AE) v. Jones (FW)*[53] a son who had moved

[51] [1986] 1 W.L.R. 808.
[52] [1986] 1 W.L.R. 1498, 1509.
[53] [1977] 1 W.L.R. 438.

to a house purchased by his father so that he could live nearby was held to have acted to his detriment so as to be entitled to a claim by way of proprietary estoppel, and in *Greasley v. Cooke*[54] the Court of Appeal held a servant who looked after the members of a family and lived with one of the owner's sons had acted to her detriment, reversing the judgement at first instance where it had been held that her activities were not capable of generating an estoppel equity. However, the most important indication of the relevance of non-financial detriment was given by Browne-Wilkinson L.J. in *Grant v. Edwards.*[55] Although the case itself concerned the question whether a common intention constructive trust had arisen, he considered that useful guidance on the question of detriment could be gained from "the principle underlying the law of proprietary estoppel:

> "In many cases of the present sort, it is impossible to say whether or not the claimant would have done the acts relied on as detriment even if she thought she had no interest in the house. Setting up house together, having a baby, making payments to the general housekeeping expenses (not strictly necessary to enable the mortgage to be paid) may all be referable to the mutual love and affection of the parties and not specifically referable to the claimant's belief that she has an interest in the house. As at present advised, once it has been shown that there was a common intention that the claimant should have an interest in the house, an act done by her to her detriment relating to the joint lives of the parties is, in my judgment, sufficient detriment to qualify."[56]

The same conclusion should also be true for proprietary estoppel, so that any conduct detrimental to a claimant, irrespective of whether it was financial or non-financial, should be capable of generating an estoppel if the requisite elements of a representation and reliance are present. The central difference between the requirements of constructive trusts and proprietary estoppel is as to the circumstances which can generate the implication of a common intention. Whereas *Lloyd's Bank v. Rosset*[57] makes clear that non-financial detriment is incapable of supporting an implication of common intention in the absence of express intention, it is capable of generating an estoppel equity.

(v) Offsetting benefits derived by the representee against any detriment suffered: There is some indication that the courts are willing to weigh any benefit gained by a representee who has acted in reliance on a representation against any detriment that he has incurred, and that if there is an overall advantage that he will be unable to maintain a claim by way of proprietary estoppel. In *Watts v. Story*[58] the Court of Appeal held that a grandson who had given up his protected tenancy in Leeds to move into his grandmother's home in Nottinghamshire when she moved to the Isle of Wight, and consequently gave up any prospects of employment in Leeds, had on balance suffered no detriment:

[54] [1980] 1 W.L.R. 1306.
[55] [1986] Ch. 638.
[56] *ibid.* at 657.
[57] [1991] 1 A.C. 107.
[58] (1984) 134 N.L.J. 631.

"... when the benefits derived by him from his rent-free occupation ... are set against any detriments suffered by him as a result of making the move from his Rent Act protected flat in Leeds, he has not on balance suffered any detriment in financial or material terms."[59]

SATISFYING THE ESTOPPEL EQUITY

1 Award of an appropriate remedy by the court

A claimant who has demonstrated the requisite elements of a representation, reliance and detriment is entitled to an estoppel equity. This is not a remedy in itself, but a right to prevent the representor from asserting his strict legal rights in his land to defeat the expectation he induced. It is then for the court to determine the appropriate interest which should be awarded to the claimant in satisfaction of their inchoate equity. As the Privy Council observed in *Plimmer v. City of Wellington Corporation*[60]: "The court must look at the circumstances in each case to decide in what way the equity can be satisfied."

2 A variety of interests awarded in satisfaction

The cases demonstrate that the courts have utilised a wide variety of interests as the appropriate means for satisfying an estoppel equity. These have included interests in land, occupational rights and even monetary compensation.

(a) Conveyance of the freehold ownership

In some cases the courts have ordered that the representor transfer the legal fee simple estate in his land to the representee in satisfaction of the estoppel equity. The representee thus becomes the absolute owner of the land. Such a transfer of the freehold ownership was ordered in *Dillwyn v. Llewelyn*[61] and *Pascoe v. Turner.*[62] In some cases the court has ordered the transfer of a conditional or determinable fee simple, specifying the conditions on which the estate will come to an end.[63]

(b) Grant of a lease

In some circumstances the court has ordered the representor to grant the representee a leasehold estate in his land to satisfy the estoppel equity, as for example in *Siew Soon Wah v. Yong Tong Hong.*[64] In *Grant v. Williams*[65] a daughter who had lived for most of her life in her mother's house and had cared for her and incurred expenditure

[59] See also: *Appleby v. Cowley, The Times,* April 14, 1982.
[60] (1884) 9 App. Cas. 699, 714.
[61] (1862) 4 De G. F. & J. 517.
[62] [1979] 1 W.L.R. 431. See also: *Thomas v. Thomas* [1956] N.Z.L.R. 785; *Cameron v. Murdoch* [1983] W.A.R. 321; *Re Basham (dec'd)* [1986] 1 W.L.R. 1498; *Voyce v. Voyce* (1991) 62 P. & C.R. 290.
[63] *Williams v. Staite* [1979] Ch. 291.
[64] [1973] A.C. 836.
[65] (1977) 248 E.G. 947.

improving the property on the basis of a representation that she would be entitled to live in it for the rest of her life was held to be entitled to an interest by way of proprietary estoppel when her mother died and left the house to her granddaughter. The Court of Appeal granted her a long lease at a nominal rent of £30 per annum determinable on her death in satisfaction of her estoppel equity. It should be noted, however, that this solution was proposed by the parties themselves, but the court may also have the power to direct such a solution if considered appropriate.

(c) Transfer of a share of the equitable ownership

Where land is held on trust by tenants in common the court has ordered the representor to transfer his undivided share in the land to the representee in satisfaction of the estoppel equity, as in *Lim Teng Huan v. Ang Swee Chuan*[66] where one joint tenant of land in Brunei built on land when he mistakenly thought he had contracted to purchase the interest of the other joint tenant, who did nothing to disavow him of his belief and was therefore estopped from denying his title.

(d) Grant of a right of occupancy

In many cases the court has determined that the appropriate remedy was that the representee should enjoy a licence to occupy the representor's land, often for life. For example, in *Greasley v. Cooke*[67] the claimant was held entitled to live in the house rent free for as long as she wished, and in *Inwards v. Baker*[68] the son was similarly entitled to remain in the bungalow on his father's land as long as he wanted. In such cases the reality of the right is that it amounts to a virtual "life interest" in the land. However, the Courts have been extremely reluctant to award a life interests as an appropriate remedy because this would lead to the creation of a strict settlement under the Settled Land Act 1925, and since the claimant would become the tenant for life would vest the legal title in them and confer on them all the powers conferred by that statute on a tenant for life, including the power to sell the land. In *Grant v. Williams*[69] Goff L.J. was keen to point out that the grant of a long lease determinable on death "could not in any event give [the claimant] the statutory powers under the Settled Land Act." It may be that with the replacement of the strict settlement by the trust of land in the regime introduced by the Trusts of Land and Appointment of Trustees Act 1996, where the powers of management are retained by the trustees unless they deliberately delegate them to the life tenant, the courts will feel more able to use the life interest as a means of satisfying an estoppel equity and that the occupational licence, which as has been seen in Chapter 12 confers no interest in the land and is vulnerable to third parties subsequently acquiring ownership of the land, will fall from favour.

(e) Award of a lien over land to secure financial compensation

In a number of cases the representee has been awarded no interest in the land and no occupational right but merely financial compensation for any expenditure incurred by way of detriment in reliance on the representation. For example in *Dodsworth v.*

[66] [1992] 1 W.L.R. 113.
[67] [1980] 1 W.L.R. 1306.
[68] [1965] 2 Q.B. 29.
[69] (1977) 248 E.G. 947.

Dodsworth[70] the claimants, who were the representor's brother and sister-in-law, were given to believe that they could live with the representor in her bungalow for as long as they wished on their return from Australia. They subsequently spent some £700 on improvements to the property. Following a breakdown of relationship between the parties the court held that their estoppel interest should not be satisfied by the award of a right to live in the bungalow rent free for life, but that they should be repaid the amount they had expended, and they were awarded a lien over the bungalow to the value of the improvements made.[71]

(f) Award of an easement[72]

Where appropriate the court has awarded an easement, generally a right of way, in satisfaction of the equity raised where there was a representation that such a right would be enjoyed.[73]

(g) Award of a share of the equitable ownership by way of a constructive trust

Although there is no case where the court has awarded a representee a share of the equitable ownership of the representor's land by way of a constructive trust in satisfaction of an estoppel equity there are some indications that such an interest may be capable of being so awarded. In *Hussey v. Palmer*[74] Lord Denning M.R. raised the possibility of such an award:

> "To this I would add *Inwards v. Baker,*[75] where a son built a bungalow on his father's land in the expectation that he would be allowed to stay there as his home, although there was no promise to that effect. After the father's death, his trustees sought to turn the son out. It was held that he had an equitable interest which was good against the trustees. In those cases it was emphasised that the court must look at the circumstances of each case to decide in what way the equity can be satisfied. In some by an equitable lien, in others by a constructive trust."

This dicta has received judicial approval in New South Wales[76] and in *Re Basham (dec'd)*[77] Edward Nugee Q.C. took the view that a constructive trust was also a potential remedy for proprietary estoppel. However if such a trust were to be awarded in satisfaction of an estoppel equity it would be very different from the common intention constructive trust delimited by the House of Lords in *Lloyd's Bank v. Rosset,*[78] which is institutional and arises when the relevant requirements of a common intention and detriment are fulfilled. The court merely recognises the trust the parties have created by their conduct. A constructive trust awarded in satisfaction of an

[70] (1973) 228 E.G. 1115.
[71] See also: *Unity Joint Stock Mutual Banking Association v. King* (1858) 25 Beav. 72; *Taylor v. Taylor* [1956] N.Z.L.R. 99.
[72] See pp. 310 *et seq.*
[73] *ER Ives Investments Ltd v. High* [1967] 2 Q.B. 379; *Crabb v. Arun District Council* [1976] Ch. 179.
[74] [1972] 3 All E.R. 744, 747–748.
[75] [1965] 2 Q.B. 29.
[76] *Pearce v. Pearce* [1977] 1 N.S.W.L.R. 170.
[77] [1986] 1 W.L.R. 1498, 1503–1504.
[78] [1991] 1 A.C. 107.

estoppel equity would be remedial since it would only arise when awarded by the court and would not necessarily gain priority over intervening third party interests. The conceptual distinctions between constructive trusts and proprietary estoppel are well illustrated in *Preston and Henderson v. St Helens Metropolitan Borough Council.*[79] A house was purchased in the name of Mr Preston with the help of a mortgage, and after Mrs Henderson moved in with him she paid the mortgage instalments and other expenses of the property. It was held that at this time she had gained a half-share of the equitable ownership by way of a common intention constructive trust. He then left and represented that as far as he was concerned the house was hers. The Land Tribunal held that on the basis of this representation she had become entitled to the other half of the equitable ownership by way of proprietary estoppel.

(h) Composite remedies

In some cases the courts have awarded composite remedies in satisfaction of the estoppel equity. For example, in *Re Sharpe (a bankrupt)*[80] it was held that an aunt who had moved in with her nephew and his family and provided £12,000 of the purchase price by way of a loan was entitled to live in the house until the loan was repaid. This amounts to a composite of an occupational right and financial compensation.

(i) No remedy required

In some cases the courts have concluded that the equity raised in favour of a representee did not require the award of any remedy in satisfaction. For example, in *Appleby v. Cowley*[81] the representor had allowed a barristers' chamber to occupy a building under a licence, paying a rent of £1,500. They incurred expenditure of £7,700 on repairs and renovations. They claimed a right to occupy the premises indefinitely subject to indemnifying the representor for any expenditure incurred in relation to the building. Megarry V.-C. held that although there were circumstances where it would have been unconscionable for the representor to take the benefit of the remedial work, for example if he had evicted them soon after the works had been done, on the facts there was no requirement for a remedy:

> "When the work was being done the rental value of the premises for which some £1,500 a year had been paid for some 10 years was about £4,300 . . . In those circumstances I think [the representor] may echo the phrase of Lord Hardwicke L.C. in *Attorney-General v. Balliol College Oxford*[82] . . . and say that the plaintiff's have have had "sufficient satisfaction" for their expenditure."

He declined to debate the "nice academic point" whether the rational for the refusal of the remedy was that no proprietary estoppel had been established, or whether an equity had been established but no remedy should be granted, but the many clear statements that the court has a discretion to determine how to satisfy an estoppel equity appropriately suggest that this must include the right to refuse any remedy.

[79] (1989) 58 P. & C.R. 500.
[80] [1980] 1 W.L.R. 219.
[81] *The Times,* April 14, 1982.
[82] (1744) 9 Mod. 407 at 412.

3 Determining the appropriate satisfaction of the estoppel equity

(a) Court enjoys a broad discretion

It has been seen that the courts have awarded a wide range of remedies to satisfy an inchoate estoppel equity. This raises the question how the appropriate remedy is selected. Some cases seem to suggest that it is purely a matter for the unfettered discretion of the court to decide the appropriate interest or remedy which should be awarded to the claimant. This discretion was evident in *Plimmer v. City of Wellington*[83] where it was said that the "court must . . . in each case decide in what way the equity can be satisfied." In *Crabb v. Arun District Council*[84] Lord Denning M.R. suggested that "equity is displayed at its most flexible" in the context of determining how an established equity should be satisfied. In *Greasley v. Cooke*[85] he went on to say that: "The equity having thus been raised . . . it is for the courts of equity to decide in what way the equity should be satisfied." Goff L.J. also stressed the discretion of the court in *Griffiths v. Williams*[86] where he answered the question "what is the relief appropriate to satisfy the equity?":

> "The . . . question is one upon which the court has to exercise a discretion. If it finds that there is an equity, then it must determine the nature of it, and then, guided by that nature and exercising discretion in all the circumstances, it has to determine what is the fair order to make between the parties for the protection of the claimant."

However despite these judicial sentiments and a degree of academic support[87] it seems inappropriate that the award of a remedy should be a matter purely for the courts discretion without any principles to guide the determination of what would be appropriate. Proprietary estoppel does not yet serve as a broad remedy in the manner of the remedial constructive trust or Lord Denning's rejected "new model" constructive trust. The pure discretion theory of proprietary estoppel remedies is open to the objection of uncertainty and unpredictability. It is also inconceivable that an expectation raised of one kind of interest in land should entitle the court to award a greater interest by way of satisfaction of the estoppel equity. If the nature of the representation was that the representee should be entitled to occupy the representor's land this should not entitle the court to order the transfer of the freehold ownership to the representee which would be in excess of the expectation that had been induced.

(b) Court constrained to fulfil the representee's expectations as far as possible

The better view seems to be that the court does not possess a broad discretion to award whatever remedy it wishes in satisfaction of the estoppel equity, but that it should select the remedy best able to fulfil the reasonable expectations of the representee. This analysis explains the disparity between such cases as *Dillwyn v.*

[83] (1884) 9 App. Cas. 699, 714.
[84] [1976] Ch. 179.
[85] [1980] 1 W.L.R. 1306, 1312.
[86] (19770 248 E.G. 947.
[87] see: [1986] Conv. 406 (Thompson); (1986) 49 M.L.R. 741 (Dewar).

Llewelyn[88] and *Pascoe v. Turner*[89] where a conveyance of the freehold ownership was ordered, and *Inwards v. Baker*[90] and *Williams v. Staite*[91] where a mere right of occupancy was awarded. In the former cases the expectation raised by the representation of the owner was that the land would belong to the claimant, whereas there was no such representation in the latter cases. In *Inwards v. Baker* the father had encouraged the son to build the bungalow on his land because it would be bigger, and although there was a clear implication that he could remain on the land as long as he wanted there was nothing from which he could reasonably expect ownership of the land. In *Williams v. Staite* the representation was merely that the claimant could "live here as long as you want." Those cases where monetary compensation was payable are explicable not on the grounds that such compensation was the expectation of the claimants, but that the breakdown of the relationship between the parties had rendered fulfilment of an expectations of shared occupancy impossible. Monetary compensation is a default remedy. For example in *Dodsworth v. Dodsworth*[92] the representation was one of occupancy for as long as the representees wished but this would not have been possible when the parties had fallen out. As Russell L.J. observed, to grant a right of occupancy in such circumstances would merely lead to the representor having to "continue sharing her home for the rest of her life with the [claimants] with whom she was, or thought she was, at loggerheads." In *Burrows and Burrows v. Sharpe*[93] an equity was established where the plaintiff and her family had moved in with her grandmother. Dillon L.J. stated that the usual approach to satisfaction of the equity was to fulfil the representee's expectations: "It was often appropriate to satisfy the equity by granting the claimant the interest he was intended to have." Having emphasised the courts discretion he considered that it should be exercised "in the light of the circumstances at the date of the hearing, taking into account, if appropriate, the conduct of the parties at that date." The relationship of the parties had broken down and the Court of Appeal rejected the solution of the first instance judge who had ordered that the plaintiff be entitled to continue to live in the house as unworkable and awarded financial compensation instead. Dillon L.J. accepted that in such circumstances the court may have to satisfy the equity in a "wholly different form from what had been intended when the parties were on good terms." The fulfilment of expectations analysis has also gained academic support. Moriarty concludes that:

> "Normally . . . a remedy will be chosen which gives the party precisely what he has been led to expect, but occasionally, where joint rights to land have been represented, he may get money instead."[94]

This analysis can be criticised on the grounds that often parties' reasonable expectations cannot be easily identified because the representation made, especially if passive,

[88] (1862) 4 De G. F. & J. 517.
[89] [1979] 1 W.L.R. 431.
[90] [1965] 2 Q.B. 29.
[91] [1979] Ch. 291.
[92] (1973) 288 E.G. 1115.
[93] [1991] Fam Law. 67.
[94] (1984) L.Q.R. 376, 412.

is ambiguous. For example, it is somewhat unrealistic to characterise the expectation in *Inwards v. Baker*[95] as extending only to a right of occupation, since as Lord Westbury L.C. indicated in the factually similar case *Dillwyn v. Llwelyn*:[96]

> "No one builds a house for his own life only, and it is absurd to suppose that it was intended by either party that the house at the death of the son, should become the property of the father."

Despite these deficiencies, the fulfilment of expectations analysis offers the better practical and theoretical model for explaining how the court determines the appropriate remedy to satisfy an estoppel equity.

PRIORITY AND PROPRIETARY ESTOPPEL

1 Priority of interests in land awarded to satisfy an estoppel equity

When a claim by way of proprietary estoppel has come to court and an equity is established and a remedy granted in satisfaction of it, any subsequent issues of priority will be determined by the ordinary rules applicable to the type of interest awarded. For example, if the representor is ordered to grant the claimant a lease then any issues of priority concerning the representee's lease will be resolved by the appropriate rules for leases. If the representor subsequently transfers or mortgages the freehold reversion, the transferee or mortgagee will potentially take subject to it. Greater difficulties arise where there is an award of an occupational licence to satisfy the equity[97] since it is now clear that a licence is incapable of existing as an interest in land even if it is irrevocable. In principle a licence generated by proprietary estoppel should only be capable of binding a third party who acquires a subsequent interest in the land if it was acquired subject to a constructive trust, for example if he had expressly agreed to take the land subject to the estoppel licence and paid a lower price for the land in recognition of such concession.[98] This issue has been discussed more fully in Chapter 12. Obviously where satisfaction of the equity takes the form of an order to pay compensation to the representee no question of subsequent priorities will arise unless the order is also secured by an equitable lien on the land of the representor.

2 Priority of an inchoate estoppel equity

(a) The inchoate equity as a proprietary right

Much more difficult questions arise where third party rights have intervened after the events which would entitle a representee to an equity have occurred, but before any claim has come before the court so that the equity can be established and satisfied.

[95] [1965] 2 Q.B. 29.
[96] (1862) 4 De G. F. & J. 517, 522.
[97] See: [1991] Conv. 36 (Battersby); (1994) 14 L.S. 147 (Baughen).
[98] See: *Asburn Anstalt v. Arnold* [1989] Ch. 1.

Since, unlike a constructive trust, the mere circumstances entitling a representee to an equity do not create a specific interest in the land at that moment they occur, and it remains uncertain whether the representee will be awarded any interest in the land in satisfaction, the representee will only gain priority if the unsatisfied "equity" is itself capable of binding the third party. For example, if an equity has arisen where a representee was assured that they would own the representor's land but the land has now been transferred or mortgaged, can the transferee or mortgagee be held to have acquired his interest subject to the unsatisfied equity? The inchoate estoppel equity does not fall within the catalogue of rights and interests historically recognised as proprietary, and the recent failure to confer proprietary status on contractual licences indicates the difficulty of gaining such status for a new right. Some academics have therefore argued that the estoppel equity is incapable of binding third parties.[99] In *Pennine Railway v. Kirklees Council*[1] the Court of Appeal held that an estoppel licence to use and occupy land for motor racing was sufficient of an interest in land to entitle the representees to compensation under planning legislation, but Eveleigh L.J. expressly stated that he was not saying that "the appellant's interest is an interest in land in a strict conveyancing sense." However, there are other indications that an inchoate estoppel equity is a form of proprietary interest and therefore capable of binding third parties who subsequently gain an interest in the land to which it relates. In *Re Sharpe (a bankrupt)*[2] the question arose whether the representee's estoppel interest was binding on the representor's trustee in bankruptcy. Browne-Wilkinson J. held that it was, and stated that in such cases "it cannot be that the interest in property arises for the first time when the court declares it to exist." As a result she was entitled to be awarded an occupational licence which was binding on the trustee in bankruptcy to whom the title of the house had passed, and he was unable to complete a transfer of the house to a to a purchaser who had contracted to buy it from him. In *Voyce v. Voyce*[3] the Court of Appeal held that a man who had lived in a cottage and incurred expenditure on it was entitled to a claim by way of proprietary estoppel against the owner, his mother, who had represented that it would be his. It held that this estoppel equity bound his younger brother, to whom the mother had transferred the cottage as a gift. Dillon L.J. explained:

> "I am equally unable to accept the suggestion . . . that as the plaintiff was not the donor he is somehow in a better position that the mother, who was the donor, *vis-à-vis* his brother the defendant. It was suggested that some form of balancing exercise should be carried out between the interests of the plaintiff and the interests of the defendant. The court of equity has habitually sought to protect a purchaser for value without notice of an equitable interest, but I do not find any indication that the court has sought to protect a volunteer successor in title from a donor who has notice of the circumstances from which an equity has arisen and notice that the claimant to an equity is, and was at the time of the deed of gift to him, in occupation of the property."

99 See: [1983] Conv. 99 (Bailey); [1990] Conv. 370 (Hayton).
1 [1983] 1 Q.B. 382. See also *Plimmer v. Wellington Corporation* (1884) 9 App.Cas. 699.
2 [1980] 1 W.L.R. 219.
3 (1991) 62 P. & C.R. 290.

However, this authority is somewhat ambiguous as to the character of the estoppel right. On the one hand Dillon L.J. termed it an "equitable interest" which is consistent with the view that it is an interest in property, but he also described it as an "equity," and "mere equities" have always bound a donee of property to which they relate. However, they never bind purchasers, irrespective of whether or not the purchaser had notice of their existence, and since Dillon L.J. regarded notice as an important criteria whether a purchaser takes free from an estoppel equity on balance his comments support the view that an inchoate equity is an equitable interest in property. This view is also supported by cases where an estoppel has been held to bind the representor's personal representatives[4] and a successor in title to a representor local authority.[5] Some support can also be gained from cases which suggest that an estoppel equity is capable of being transferred by the representee to a third party who is then able to derive the benefit of it against the representor. For example in *E R Ives Investments Ltd v. High*[6] Lord Denning M.R. held that an estoppel raised when the representor acquiesced in his neighbour resurfacing a yard over which it had been represented that he would enjoy a right of way was available not only to the original representee but also to his successors in title. This transmissibility of an estoppel equity is accepted in Australia[7] and again points to a right with proprietary characteristics. However there are other cases, such as *Fryer v. Brook*,[8] which suggest that the benefit of an estoppel equity is incapable of transmission as it is purely personal to the representee.[9] Weighing all these factors the conclusion must be that the present state of the law is inconclusive concerning the status of the inchoate estoppel equity, but that the trend seems towards recognition that it is a species of proprietary interest capable of binding third parties who might acquire an interest in the land to which it relates. The Australian courts have unequivocally regarded such estoppel equities as interests in land.[10]

(b) Priority of an inchoate equity in unregistered land

If an inchoate estoppel equity is a proprietary interest in land capable of binding third parties it will only do so if he acquires his interest subject to the "equity" in accordance with the priority rules appropriate for the type of land in question. A greater number of authorities have considered the place of estoppel equities in unregistered land, and these suggest that a third party will take subject to a representee's inchoate equity unless protected by the doctrine of notice. This follows from the fact that the inchoate equity is neither a land charge under the scheme of the Land Charges Act 1972 nor an overreachable interest within section 2(1) of the Law of Property Act 1925 . In *E R Ives Investment Ltd v. High*[11] the Court of Appeal held that an estoppel interest was binding on the purchaser of the representor's land who had actual notice of the

[4] *Inwards v. Baker* [1965] 2 Q.B. 29; *Jones (A.E.) v. Jones (F.W.)* [1977] 1 W.L.R. 438.
[5] *Salvation Army Trustees Co. Ltd v. West Yorkshire M.C.C.* (1941) P. & C.R. 179.
[6] [1967] 2 Q.B. 379.
[7] *Hamilton v. Geraghty* (1901) 1 S.R.(N.S.W.) (eq.) 81; *Cameron v. Murdoch* [1983] W.A.R. 321; affirmed (1986) 63 A.L.R. 575.
[8] [1984] L.S.Gaz.R. 2856.
[9] See also: *Jones (A.E.) v. Jones (F.W.)* [1977] 1 W.L.R. 438.
[10] See: *Cameron v. Murdoch* [1983] W.A.R. 321; *Beaton v. McDivitt* (1985) 13 N.S.W.L.R. 134; *Milton v Proctor* (1989) N.S.W. Conv.R. 55–450.
[11] [1967] 2 Q.B. 379.

easement claimed. However in *Re Sharpe (a bankrupt)*[12] Browne-Wilkinson J. seemed to suggest that a third party who acquired the land with merely constructive notice would take free from the inchoate equity.[13] This is contrary to principle and it is not unreasonable to expect a potential purchaser to make enquiries of the rights of any person occupying the land and to ascertain whether they claim any entitlement therein.[14] If the potential purchaser does make appropriate enquiries he will not be affixed with constructive notice.

(c) Priority of an inchoate equity in registered land

If the inchoate equity is a proprietary interest in land and the title to which it relates is registered it should be capable of protection as a minor interest by the entry of a caution on the register.[15] This depends upon the awareness of the representee that they enjoy an entitlement in the land and, as with constructive trusts, it is more often the case that those who are most vulnerable to having their informally created rights in the land defeated are those least likely to know of the need to protect them. However, if the inchoate estoppel equity is capable of ranking as an overriding interest under section 70(1)(g) of the Land Registration Act 1925, and the representee is in "actual occupation" of the land,[16] it will be binding upon any third party purchaser or mortgagee of the land unless enquiries were made of the representee and he denied that he had any interests in the land. In *Canadian Imperial Bank of Commerce v. Bello*[17] Dillon L.J. approved the comments of the first instance judge that an estoppel was an insufficient interest in the land to be an overriding interest within the meaning of section 70(1)(g). It is suggested that this is illogical and inconsistent with the position adopted in relation to resulting and constructive trusts. If the inchoate estoppel equity is a proprietary interest there is no reason why it should not form the subject matter of an overriding interest. Although it is less certain what precise right will be conferred upon the representee when the equity is satisfied a prospective purchaser is under no greater obligation to protect himself than when there is a danger that an occupier might subsequently establish that she is entitled to a share of the equitable ownership by way of an informally created trust. Such a purchaser would be well advised to make enquiries of all persons in occupation as to whether they claim any entitlements in the land. It remains to be seen whether such an approach will be adopted.[18]

(d) Overreaching of inchoate equities

The question of whether an inchoate equity can be overreached has not arisen. If estoppel equities are recognised as proprietary rights capable of binding third parties as overriding interests, or by the doctrine of notice in unregistered land, it seems only

[12] [1980] 1 W.L.R. 219.
[13] Compare *Bristol & West Building Society v. Henning* [1985] 1 W.L.R. 778 where Browne-Wilkinson L.J. seemed to indicate that constructive notice would be sufficient.
[14] *Compare Kingsnorth Finance Co. Ltd v. Tizard* [1986] 1 W.L.R. 783.
[15] See below Chap. 15. See also: [1983] Conv. 50 (Bailey); Law Commission, *Property Law: Second Report on Land Registration (Provisional)* (1984), para. 57.
[16] Or alternatively in receipt of the rent and profits thereof.
[17] [1992] 64 P. & C.R. 48, 52.
[18] See also [1989] Conv. 418, 428 (Evans), where it is suggested that issues of priority concerning estoppel equities in registered land may be governed by the doctrine of notice.

right that they should also be subject to the possibility of overreaching. It would be anomalous if a purchaser who paid over his purchase money to two trustees of land gained automatic priority over a resulting or constructive trust interest, but not over an estoppel equity.

However, again on general principles, if the inchoate equity would have given rise to an easement or other right incapable of being overreached should the equity have been crystallised by way of court order, it would unfairly prejudice the representee to lose the right through overreaching. Whether a particular inchoate equity is overreached must therefore depend upon the nature of the underlying expectation which it protects.

Part IV

Registered Land

Chapter 14

REGISTRATION OF TITLE

INTRODUCTION TO REGISTRATION OF TITLE

1 Object of this section of the book

In the preceding sections of this book the nature of the most important rights and interests in land have been examined. It has been noted how they can be created and some attention has been devoted to how they are accommodated within the systems of registered and unregistered land. The purpose of this section of the book is to examine in detail the operation of the system of land registration. To some extent this will involve a repetition of material, but this final section aims to draw together everything which has been studied so far so as to provide a comprehensive understanding of English land law.

2 The introduction of a system of land registration

(a) Before the introduction of registration

Historically, English Land law had no system of registration of title. Ownership of land was demonstrated by means of title deeds, which were a collection of documents showing how the present claimant of ownership came to enjoy a good title to the land. In the absence of the ability to prove a good root of title ownership was constituted by mere physical possession of the land for a sufficient period of time. Land was transferred by the owner conveying his interest to the transferee and there was no state supervision or involvement in this process. Issues of priority relating to subsidiary interests in the land were governed by the doctrine of notice, so that legal interests were binding on everyone, whereas a person purchasing a legal estate in land would take it free from any pre-existing equitable interests of which they had no notice. The main problem associated with this regime was inefficiency. It complicated the acquisition of land from the perspective of a potential purchaser. For example, if Albert was wanting to purchase Wellington House from Victoria he would want to satisfy himself that she enjoyed good title to the land, so that she was entitled to sell it to him and he would himself gain a good title, and also that there were no adverse third party interests which would affect its value, or his use and enjoyment. He might not wish to purchase the land, or to pay so high a price, if it were subject to a mortgage held by the Osborne Building Society, if it had been leased to Gladstone so that Albert could not enjoy vacant possession, or if it was held on trust for Benjamin. Victoria would be under no obligation to reveal any third party interests to Albert since the rule *caveat emptor* applied to sales of land. The process of investigating and establishing a good root of title would be much more complex if there were a large number of co-owners. The potential purchaser could only protect himself against third party subsidiary interests in the land by conducting appropriate inspections of the land and the title documents, and he would be affixed with notice not only of those interests which he actually discovered, but also of those interests which he should have discovered by reasonable inspections. If, after satisfying himself of Victoria's title and of any third party interests, Albert purchased the house and it was conveyed to him and some years later he decided to sell to Isambard, the whole process would have to be repeated, so that Isambard would in turn have to investigate Albert's title and satisfy himself of the existence of any third party interests. In *Williams & Glynn's Bank Ltd v. Boland*[1] Lord Scarman commented that this system involved the "wearisome and intricate task of examining title."

(b) The advantages of registration

The chief objective of registration is that the state should provide a centrally kept register containing comprehensive details of the ownership of land and the existence of any third party interests which affect it. If such a register is maintained potential purchasers, or those interested in acquiring a subsidiary interest in land, will not need to go through the process of investigating the title to ensure themselves of whether the person they are dealing with is the genuine owner, nor will they have to rely on a physical inspection of the land and the documents relating to it to protect themselves from any third party interests which the seller has not disclosed. By simply looking at the register entry for the piece of land in which they are interested they should be able to discover exactly who owns it, who is entitled to sell it, and who enjoys any subsidiary rights over it. Under a system of registration if Albert wishes to purchase Wellington House from Victoria all he would have to do to establish that she owned it would be to check that she was registered as the owner. Similarly, the Osbourne Building Society's mortgage, Galdstone's lease and Benjamin's trust interest could also be entered onto the register enabling Albert to easily discover their existence. A key feature of such a system of registration would be that a person acquiring the land would not be subject to any interests which did had not been entered on the register, so that if the Building Society had not ensured that their mortgage was noted on the register entry for Wellington House Albert would not be bound by it if he went ahead and purchased. By such a system the rights of the owners of land, and those enjoying subsidiary interests, would be adequately protected against misappropriation and potential purchasers would be able to transact more confidently, thus promoting efficient dealing with the land. It remains to be seen whether these features of a comprehensive register have been realised by the system of land registration adopted in England.

(c) The introduction of registration in England

Although the property legislation of 1925 began the process of the introduction of a universal scheme of registration of land in England and Wales a system of registration

[1] [1981] A.C. 487.

was first introduced by the Land Registry Act 1862,[2] the pre-amble to which stated that the object was to "facilitate the proof of title." The Land Transfer Act 1897 provided for compulsory registration of title in designated areas. The present system, built upon the foundations already laid in the earlier legislation, is found in the Land Registration Act 1925. Lord Oliver noted in *City of London Building Society v. Flegg*[3] that this Act: ". . . was introduced as part and parcel of the overall property legislation enacted in that year and it introduced for the first time . . . a power in central government to designate areas in which registered conveyancing would be compulsory." As it was obviously impossible for all land to be registered immediately, land was to be registered either voluntarily by its owners or compulsorily on sale in designated geographical areas, with the object that eventually all land would be registered. For land remaining unregistered a partial scheme of registration for some important interests was introduced by the Land Charges Act 1925. It was initially anticipated that universal registration would be accomplished within thirty years of the Land Registration Act 1925, but this goal has proved impossible to attain. The final stage of the transition to such universal coverage was set in place by the Registration of Title Order 1989, under which the entire country was designated an area of compulsory registration. The Land Registration Act 1997 has recently widened the circumstances in which title to remaining unregistered land must be registered, reflecting a desire to speed the completion of the process.

(d) System of land registration not intended to be identical in effect to unregistered land

It has sometimes been thought that the legislation introducing the system of registration of title was merely intended to place the existing principles relating to unregistered land on a statutory footing, so that there would be no substantive difference in the circumstances in which a purchaser would take title free from subsidiary interests in the land. If this analysis is correct then obviously much help could be derived in interpreting the various statutory provisions by examining the pre-existing law. However, the House of Lords has made clear that there should be no presumption that the legislation intended to leave the substantive law unchanged. In *Midland Bank Trust Co. v Green*[4] Lord Wilberforce stated in relation to a question of interpretation of the Land Charges Act 1925:

> "My lords, I do not think it is safe to seek the answer to this question by means of a general assertion that the property legislation of 1922–25 was not intended to alter the law, or not intended to alter it in a particular filed, such as that relating to purchasers of legal estate. All the Acts of 1925, and their precursors, were drafted with the utmost care, and their wording, certainly where this is apparently clear, has to be accorded firm respect."

The land registration system must therefore be taken on its own terms as an integral whole transforming the law rather than codifying it.

[2] See: (1972) 36 Conv. 390 (H. W. Wilkinson).
[3] [1988] A.C. 54 at 84.
[4] [1981] A.C. 513 at 529.

3 Key features of the system of land registration

(a) A register of ownership

The system of land registration introduced in England is not one of the registration of land itself, which would mean each geographical parcel of land having an entry on a central register. Rather, the system is founded upon the registration of particular ownership rights over land. It has been seen that as a consequence of section 1 of the Law of Property Act 1925 freehold ownership (the fee simple absolute in possession) and leasehold ownership (term of years absolute) are the only two estates which are capable of existing at law. These legal estates in land must be registered as individual "titles" at the Land Registry. When registered they provide the fundamental building blocks of the system of registration, and subsidiary interests in land affecting them can be protected against their register entry.

(b) Eliminating the complexity of equitable ownership from the register

Although the register is based on the registration of legal ownership it has also been seen how a person can enjoy the equitable ownership of land through a trust. Such trust interests can be more easily created and transferred than their legal equivalents, and their existence was not generally evident from the title deeds of land. This is particularly true of resulting or constructive trusts. It would have been possible to require all such beneficial interest to appear on the register of the legal estate to which they relate, but this would have led to extreme complexity. Instead, the legislation of 1925 introduced a means by which, as far as possible, equitable ownership need not appear on the register. Overreaching provides a mechanism whereby a purchaser of land can be sure that he will acquire it free from any existing beneficial interests by paying the purchase price to at least two legal owners, who would be the trustees holding the land subject to the trust. If this condition is met the trust interests no longer affect the land and the purchaser will take his title unencumbered by them. The interests of the beneficiaries are not destroyed by overreaching, but transferred to the purchase moneys in the hands of the trustees. Overreaching has proved so effective as a means of keeping equitable ownership off the register that the majority of problems associated with trust interests in registered land have occurred where it has not taken place because a person has acquired the legal ownership from a sole proprietor.

(c) Subsidiary interests in land

(i) Some legal subsidiary interests may only be created by registration: Although only the two legal estates are capable of being registered as separate titles at the land registry some subsidiary interests in land are only capable of being created at law by registration. In particular, a charge by way of legal mortgage and a legal easement will only be created when the chargee or the proprietor of the easement is registered as such on the title to which it relates. In the absence of such registration the mortgage or easement granted be equitable only and rank alongside other subsidiary interests as a "minor interest."

(ii) Minor interests: With the exception of the two registrable interests and the legal subsidiary interests which can only be created by registration, all lesser interests in the land are incapable of independent registration. Such lesser interests are collectively termed "minor interests."[5] At the heart of the system of registration is the idea that

[5] Land Registration Act 1925, s.3(xv).

minor interests should be entered on the registered title of the land to which they relate. For example, if Kevin owns a 99 year leasehold of a Farm which is registered, and Ian is entitled to an easement to walk across one of his fields, Ian should protect his interest by means of a entry on the register of title of the leasehold estate. If Kevin then contemplates selling his leasehold estate to Robert, Robert will immediately know from the register that the land is subject to Ian's easement. More significantly, a failure to protect a minor interest should mean that a purchaser will acquire the land free from it. For example, what happens if Ian never protects his easement and Robert purchases the land having examined the register and found no mention of it? Since the cardinal principle is that a purchaser of a registered estate acquires the land subject only to those minor interests which have been properly protected, Robert should enjoy the farm free from Ian's easement. It is important to note that this leaves no continuing role for concepts of notice, as it is irrelevant whether Robert knew of the existence of Ian's easement or not. He takes the land free from it purely because Ian had not taken steps to protect it. It is therefore obvious that the burden of protecting subsidiary interests in land falls to those who hold them.

(iii) Overriding interests: Having noted the general principle that unprotected minor interests will not be binding on purchasers of the land, the Land Registration Act 1925 introduces a further category of subsidiary interests in land which are named "overriding interests." These interests are defined in section 70(1) of the Land Registration Act 1925 and their essential characteristic is that they bind a purchaser of the land even where they have not been protected on the register of the estate they affect. In a sense they are rather like "trump cards" of the registered land system, taking automatic priority to any rights which are subsequently acquired by a person in the land. The example of Ian's easement above must therefore be qualified, as by section 70(1)(a) of the Land Registration Act 1925 legal easements are defined to be overriding interests. Therefore, Ian's legal easement over the farm would be binding on Robert even though it had not been protected on the register against Kevin's leasehold estate. By far the most wide ranging of the overriding interests is found in section 70(1)(g) of the Land Registration Act 1925, which protects any subsidiary right in the land of a person in "actual occupation" of it. Overriding interests are a significant gap in the comprehensiveness of the land registration system, since they mean that a purchaser of land may find that it is subject to third party interests which were not revealed on the register. A prospective purchaser cannot therefore rely on the register alone to satisfy himself whether there might be any adverse interests affecting the land.

(d) Register maintained by the state

The Land Register of ownership of land is maintained by the state under the control of the Chief Land Registrar. The register is maintained centrally in London and by nineteen district land registries. The system is self-funding through the imposition of fees for searches and registrations. The Register is open to general public inspection.[6]

[6] Land Registration Act 1925, s.112(1) (As substituted by Land Registration Act 1988, s.1(1)).

REGISTRATION OF LEGAL OWNERSHIP OF LAND

1 Interests which must be registered

(a) Legal estates are registrable interests

It has been noted that the foundations of the land registration system are the two forms of legal ownership of land. This follows from section 2(1) of the Land Registration Act 1925 which provides:

> "After the commencement of this Act, estates capable of subsisting as legal estates shall be the only interests in respect of which a proprietor can be registered . . . ."

Since section 1(1)(a) of the Law of Property Act 1925 provides that "an estate in fee simple absolute in possession" is capable of subsisting at law, freehold ownership must be registered. Leasehold interests are also capable of existing at law as they are "a term of years absolute" within section 1(1)(b) of the Law of Property Act 1925. However, it has been seen in Chapter 5 that legal leases may take a variety of forms, ranging from fixed term leases for a long duration, to short term leases or periodic tenancies. It is obviously unfeasible to operate a system where every legal lease must be registered as an independent title at the Land Registry and therefore section 123(1) of the Land Registration Act 1925 provides that only legal leases for a period of more than twenty-one years can be registered.

(b) When must title be registered for the first time?

Registration of freehold and leasehold ownership of land was introduced on a gradual basis, by requiring compulsory registration when certain transactions were performed in relation to land which was unregistered. There was a requirement to register title whenever freehold land was conveyed from a vendor to a purchaser, a legal lease for more than 21 year was granted, or a legal lease with more than 21 years of its term remaining was assigned, in an area designated an area of compulsory registration.[7] Following the Registration of Title Order 1989 the whole of England and Wales is now designated so that title must be registered when an appropriate transaction takes place. When such a transaction occurred the estate created or transferred must have been registered within a two-month period, otherwise section 123(1) of the Land Registration Act provided that it was "void so far as regards the grant or conveyance of the legal estate in the freehold or leasehold land comprised in the conveyance, grant or assignment." The circumstances in which title to land must be registered have been recently widened by amendment to section 123 of the Land Registration Act 1925 introduced by the Land Registration Act 1997. Section 123(1) now requires compulsory registration of transactions which are a "qualifying conveyance." This includes a transfer of the freehold estate as a gift or in pursuance of an order of the court,[8] and also to any "disposition by the estate owner of unregistered land which is a legal

[7] Land Registration Act 1925, s.123(1) (prior to amendment by Land Registration Act 1997).
[8] Land Registration Act 1925, s.123(6).

mortgage," provided that the mortgage is to be protected by the deposit of title deeds and ranks ahead of any other mortgages affecting the estate.[9] Failure to register the disposition transferring or creating an interest in the land will render it void so far as regards the transfer, grant or creation of the legal estate or mortgage, but will give rise to the equitable equivalent.[10] By requiring registration whenever there are such dealings with the legal ownership of land it is inevitable that eventually title to most land will become registered and the principles of unregistered land will be redundant. However, some residue of land will remain unregistered for a long time because it is unlikely that there will be any dealing with it, for example land owned by Oxford and Cambridge colleges or the Crown. A point may be reached where in order to tidy loose ends it is appropriate to require the owners of land to register their title even though there is no transaction.

(c) Grades of title awarded on first registration of ownership

When land is registered for the first time the Land Registrar is required to investigate the title of the person seeking to be registered as owner. The registrar will then register the land with a grade of title appropriate to the degree to which the owner has been able to satisfy him of their entitlement. In the case of freehold ownership the first registration may grant absolute, possessory or qualified title. In the case of leasehold ownership the additional grade of "good leasehold title" may be awarded. The circumstances in which these various degrees of title will be awarded and their impact upon the registered owner have already been examined in the context of freehold and leasehold interests.[11] It should be remembered that registration with absolute title is effective to vest ownership in the person registered as proprietor of the estate concerned and to cure any defects in their title.[12]

(d) Subsequent dealings with the registered legal ownership

Once the freehold or leasehold ownership of land is registered, all subsequent dealings with the legal title to the land must take place through the register. Unlike the previous system where title could be transferred by the present owner executing a conveyance in favour of the transferee, a registered title can only be transferred by the registration of the transferee as the proprietor of the relevant freehold or leasehold in place of the previous proprietor. Section 19(1) of the Land Registration Act 1925 provides for the transfer of registered freeholds and section 22(1) for the transfer of registered leaseholds in almost identical terms:

> "The transfer of the registered estate in the land or part thereof shall be completed by the registrar entering on the register the transferee as the proprietor of the estate transferred, but until such entry is made the transferor shall be deemed to remain proprietor of the registered estate . . . "

Where no registration occurs the effect is not to render the transferee's interest void, but merely to prevent any disposition of the legal title to the land. The transferee will

[9] Land Registration Act 1925, s.123(2).
[10] Land Registration Act 1925, s.123A.
[11] See Chaps. 4 and 5.
[12] Land Registration Act 1925, s.5; *Re 139 High Street Deptford, ex p. British Transport Commission* [1951] Ch. 884.

enjoy either merely an equitable interest in the freehold or leasehold estate. Transfers of freehold and leasehold ownership has been examined in greater detail in Chapters 4 and 5 above.

2 Format of the register

(a) A trinity of registers

Although each registered estate, whether freehold or leasehold, has a single entry at the Land Registry, which is given an individual title number, each entry is divided into three sections detailing different aspects of the land to which it relates.

(i) Property register: The property register is the first section of the entry for any registered estate. It identifies the land in relation to which the estate exists, by means of a verbal description and reference to a map, and states whether the estate is freehold or leasehold. The property register may also contain details of benefits attached to the land, such as easements and restrictive covenants enjoyed over other land and of which the registered estate is the dominant tenement. Where the estate is leasehold the property register will also contain brief details of the lease.

(ii) Proprietorship register: The second section of the register entry is the proprietorship register, which contains the name and address of the present registered proprietor and states the quality of title with which their estate has been registered. The proprietorship register also contains details of any entries on the register which have the effect of restricting or limiting the rights of the registered proprietor to dispose of the land. These include restrictions, cautions or inhibitions which third parties may have entered onto the register to protect their minor interests.

(iii) Charges register: The third section of the register is the charges register, which contains details of third party rights which burden the land. For example the charges register may contain details of mortgages and other financial charges which are secured on the land, restrictive covenants limiting its use and easements which third parties enjoy over it.

(b) Registered proprietor entitled to a land certificate

The registered proprietor is entitled under section 63 of the Land Registration Act 1925 to a copy of the entry for his title on the Register. This copy is known as a land certificate, and although in practice it may be treated as the equivalent of title deeds it is not. The land certificate is only evidence of title, which is in fact constituted by the entry on the land register. In some circumstances when the land register entry is amended, for example where there is a disposition of the registered estate or if a restriction or notice is entered, the land certificate must also be produced for amendment.[13] Where the registered estate is subject to a mortgage or charge the land certificate must be deposited with the land registry until the mortgage or charge has been discharged.[14]

(c) Searches of the land register

(i) An "official search": Since the object of the register is to provide a definitive record of the ownership of land and the existence of subsidiaries interest which affect

[13] Land Registration Act 1925, s.64(1).
[14] Land Registration Act 1925, s.65.

it, it is important that those contemplating purchase or the acquisition of a subsidiary interest, for example a mortgage, are able to inspect it to verify the title and obtain any information they require. Rather than conducting a search in person an official search may be requested, and the land registry will then inspect the relevant title and issue an official search certificate.

(ii) A thirty day grace period after an official search: Where an official search has been requisitioned the searcher enjoys a thirty day period in which to enter into his proposed transaction in regard to the land, and no minor interests which are protected during that thirty day period will affect any estate or interest he acquires in the land.[15] For example, in *Watts v. Waller*[16] the plaintiff agreed to purchase a house from the defendant and requisitioned an official search on April 29th, with a certificate returned on the 30th which showed no entries in relation to the land. The defendant's wife, who was not in occupation, subsequently applied to register a notice of a charge against the house under the Matrimonial Homes Act 1967, which was entered on the register on May 10. The sale was completed on May 20 and a transfer of the house executed on May 24. It was held that if this transfer had been delivered to the Land Registry by the end of the priority period, which was 11 a.m. on May 25 then the plaintiff would have acquired the land free from the wife's minor interest.

(iii) Official search is not conclusive: Whilst it might be thought that a person who requisitions an official search of the register would be entitled to rely upon the contents of the official search certificate he receives from the land registry in fact it is not conclusive according to its terms. If the certificate fails to reveal the existence of a minor interest which has been properly protected on the register the searcher will take any interest he acquires in the land subject to that protected interest. However he will be entitled to an indemnity from the Land Registry compensating him for any loss he suffered as a result. Such a mistake occurred in *Parkash v. Irani Finance Ltd*[17] where Mr Kalra was the registered proprietor of freehold land subject to a caution entered on the register by the defendants who had obtained a charging order to secure a debt. The plaintiff requisitioned an official search of the register and was issued with a certificate which failed to reveal the defendant's caution. Plowman J. held that even though the plaintiff was ignorant of the existence of the charge because of the mistake of the land registry he did not take the land free from it because it had been properly protected.

CERTAIN SUBSIDIARY INTERESTS CAN ONLY BE CREATED AT LAW BY REGISTRATION

1 Reasons for requiring registration

Although the general policy of the land registration system is that only two legal estates require registration and that all other subsidiary interests in land can be

[15] The Land Registration (Official Searches) Rules 1990.
[16] [1973] 1 Q.B. 153.
[17] [1970] Ch. 101.

protected against the title to which they relate, the legislation requires that some subsidiary interests can only be created with legal status by entry on the register. In the absence of such registration they will be merely equitable and be treated as if they were ordinary minor interests. The range of such interests which require registration is very narrow, but they are also extremely important since they comprise the most significant interests likely to be acquired in land by third parties as part of a commercial transaction.

2 Mortgage by way of legal charge

In Chapter 11 it has been seen how the simplest means of creation of a mortgage over registered land is a charge by way of legal mortgage. The protection of mortgagees is crucial to the efficient operation of the property market as the majority of land owners acquire their land with the help of mortgage lending and it is important that commercial lenders feel that their loan will be secure. By sections 18(4) and 21(4) of the Land Registration Act 1925 the grant of a charge by way of legal mortgage is a registered disposition, and by section 26(1) the creation of the charge can only be completed by the registration of the chargee as the proprietor of the charge in the charges register of the title to which it relates. Although section 106(1) of the Land Registration Act 1925 provides for the creation of a mortgage or charge of registered land by any of the means permissible in unregistered land, subsection (2)(a) provides:

> "Unless and until the mortgage becomes a registered charge . . . it shall take effect only in equity."

Such an equitable charge or mortgage will rank as an ordinary minor interest, and can be protected on the register in an appropriate manner.[18]

3 Legal easements

Similarly, the grant of an easement or profit over registered land is a registered disposition and can only be completed by the registration of the easement against the registered title of the servient land to which it relates.[19] In the absence of registration the easement will rank only as an equitable easement and may be protected as a minor interest, or in some circumstances will rank as an overriding interest under section 70(1)(a) of the Land Registration Act 1925.[20]

OVERREACHING OF EQUITABLE OWNERSHIP[21]

1 What is overreaching?

(a) The philosophy which underlies the mechanism of overreaching

It has already been noted, both above and in the context of the description of equitable ownership of land in Chapter 6, one objective of the property legislation of 1925 was to

[18] Land Registration Act 1925, s.106(3).
[19] ss.19(2) and 22(2).
[20] See below p. 522.
[21] See: [1990] C.L.J. 277 (Harpum).

simplify conveyancing and transfers of the ownership of land by ensuring that potential purchasers only need to concern themselves with the legal title and not with otherwise hidden and potentially complex beneficial interests. This objective was achieved partly by a statutory limitation of the number of legal estates in land and the restriction of the maximum number of co-owners of the legal title to four.[22] However central to the removal of equitable ownership from the concern of a potential purchaser of an interest in land is the mechanism of overreaching. The essence of overreaching is that if certain statutory criteria are satisfied when a legal estate in land subject to a trust is sold, or mortgaged, any equitable ownership is removed from the land and transferred to the proceeds of sale paid to the trustees. As a consequence the beneficiaries no longer retain any equitable ownership in the land but their rights are preserved and transferred exclusively to the proceeds of sale, which the trustees who have received them continue to hold on trust for them. The purchaser of the land who has complied with the statutory criteria therefore acquires his interest in the land entirely free from the equitable ownership of the beneficiaries. Overreaching effects a substitution of the subject matter of the trust, so that whereas prior to overreaching the beneficiaries enjoyed the equitable ownership of land, after overreaching they enjoy only the equitable ownership of money. Lord Oliver explained the rationale of overreaching in *City of London Building Society v. Flegg*:[23]

> "The whole philosophy of the [Law of Property Act 1925] . . . was that a purchaser of a legal estate (which by section 205(1)(xxi) includes a mortgagee) should not be concerned with the beneficial interests of the [co-owners] which were shifted to the proceeds of sale."

He stated that overreaching was critical to achieving the legislative policy of "keeping the interests of beneficiaries behind the curtain and confining the investigation of title to the devolution of the legal estate."[24] These sentiments were more recently approved by the Court of Appeal in *State Bank of India v. Sood*[25] where Peter Gibson L.J. summarised that:

> "A principal objective of the 1925 property legislation was to simplify conveyancing and the proof of title to land. To this end equitable interests were to be kept off the title to the legal estate and could be overreached on a conveyance to a purchaser who took free from them."[26]

It had been assumed that overreaching would only occur where a transaction affecting the legal title of land held on trust resulted in the payment of capital moneys into which the beneficial interests could be transferred. However in *State Bank of India v. Sood* the Court of Appeal held that overreaching could occur even where a transaction did not produce a money substitute for the beneficiaries' equitable ownership of land. The Court regarded overreaching as a means by which a purchaser of a legal estate in

[22] See Chap. 7 above.
[23] [1988] A.C. 54 at 77.
[24] *ibid.* at 77.
[25] [1997] 1 All E.R. 169.
[26] *ibid.* at 172–173.

land or a mortgagee could gain priority over equitable interests irrespective of whether they were preserved in other property or not. Peter Gibson L.J. defined overreaching as "the process whereby existing interests are subordinated to a later interest or estate created pursuant to a trust or power."[27]

(b) An example of overreaching in practice

In *City of London Building Society v. Flegg* the House of Lords considered the effects of the statutory overreaching provisions. The case concerned a house which had been purchased in the names of Mr and Mrs Maxwell-Brown, who were the registered proprietors, but the purchase money had been partly provided by Mr and Mrs Flegg, who were Mrs Maxwell-Brown's parents, with the intention that they would be able to share occupation of the property. Mr and Mrs Flegg had in fact lived in the house from when it was purchased. The effect of their contribution was that they enjoyed a share of the equitable ownership by way of a resulting trust, and that Mr and Mrs Maxwell-Bown held the legal title as trustees for them. Unfortunately Mr and Mrs Maxwell-Brown suffered severe financial difficulties, and granted the plaintiff's a charge by way of legal mortgage over the house. The Flegg's were unaware of this transaction and did not consent to it. The plaintiff's advanced £37,500 to the Maxwell-Browns which they used to discharge their debts. Inevitably they defaulted on their mortgage repayments, and the mortgagees sought possession of the house. The main issue was whether the mortgagees took their legal mortgage subject to the Flegg's pre-existing equitable ownership. The House of Lords held that since the statutory criteria for overreaching had been satisfied the Flegg's equitable ownership had been transferred from the house to the money which had been advanced to Mr and Mrs Maxwell-Brown, and that they therefore had no interests in the land capable of taking priority to the mortgage. Lord Oliver explained the effect of overreaching on their rights in the land:

> "If, then, one asks what were the subsisting rights of [Mr and Mrs Flegg] . . . the answer must, in my judgement, be that they were rights which, *vis-à-vis* the [mortgagee], were *eo instanti* with the creation of the charge, overreached and therefore subsisted only in relation to the equity of redemption."

As a consequence the mortgagee could force a sale of their home to recover the amount of their loan and, since the trustees had dissipated the proceeds of sale, the preservation of their beneficial interests in the proceeds of sale was merely theoretical and they would only recover their initial investment into the purchase price of the house if there was sufficient capital remaining after sale and the discharge of the mortgage. Their only other remedies would lie against the trustees for breach of trust. Although this result may seem unfair, in reality they were the victims of the trustee's dishonesty, and the case demonstrates that overreaching operates primarily as a mechanism to protect the interests of purchasers not to safeguard the entitlements of beneficiaries. When one innocent party must inevitably loose out, the system favours the third party who has taken an interest in the land as any other result would act as a disincentive to those contemplating acquiring interests in land, especially mortgagees, thus affecting the stability of the housing market and the wider economy.

[27] *ibid.* at 172, citing with approval [1990] C.L.J. 277 (Harpum).

2 Statutory criteria for overreaching

(a) Interests in land which may be overreached

Only specified interests in land are capable of being overreached. Section 2(1) of the Law of Property Act 1925 makes a general assertion that: "A conveyance to a purchaser of a legal estate in land shall overreach any equitable interest or power affecting that estate, whether or not he has notice thereof . . ." The breadth of this subsection, which suggests a general overreaching of equitable interests in land, is curtailed by section 2(3) which provides that certain categories of equitable interest cannot be overreached:

> "The following equitable interests and power are excepted from the operation of subsection (2) of this section, namely —
>
> (i) equitable interest protected by a deposit of documents relating to the legal estate effected;
>
> (ii) The benefit of any covenant or agreement restrictive of the user of the land;
>
> (iii) Any easement, liberty, privilege over or affecting land and being merely an equitable interest (in this Act referred to as an "equitable easement");
>
> (iv) The benefit of any contract (in this Act referred to as an "estate contract") to convey or create a legal estate, including a contract conferring either expressly or by statutory implication a valid option to purchase, a right of pre-emption, or any other like right;
>
> (v) Any equitable interest protected by registration under the Land Charges Act 1925, other than —
>
> (a) an annuity within the meaning of Part II of that Act;
>
> (b) a limited owners charge or general equitable charge within the meaning of that Act.

This subsection excludes all the most important equitable rights in land from the consequences of overreaching, including an equitable mortgage; equitable easements; equitable restrictive covenants and estate contracts. The net impact is that overreaching operates against equitable ownership of land arising behind a trust, whether under a strict settlement which was created before January 1, 1997 and is still in existence, or a trust of land introduced by the Trusts of Land and Appointment of Trustees Act 1996.

(b) Transactions which have overreaching effect

For overreaching to occur not only must the equitable interest be capable of being overreached but the transaction must be one which is capable of having an overreaching effect. Section 2(1) provides that in four situations a conveyance of a legal estate in the land will have a potentially overreaching effect. These situations are defined by reference to the persons who are making the conveyance of the legal estate:

> (i) the conveyance is *made under the powers conferred by the Settled Land Act 1925,* or any additional powers conferred by a settlement, and the equitable interest or power is capable of being overreached thereby . . .

(ii) the conveyance is *made by trustees of land* and the equitable interest or power is at the date of the conveyance capable of being overreached by such trustees . . .

(iii) the conveyance is *made by a mortgagee or personal representative* in the exercise of his paramount powers, and the equitable interest or power is capable of being overreached by such conveyance . . .

(iv) the conveyance is *made under an order of the court* and the equitable interest or power is bound by such order . . .

By section 205(1)(ii) "conveyance" is given an extended meaning so that it includes "a mortgage, charge, lease, assent, vesting declaration, vesting instrument, disclaimer, release and every other assurance of property or of an interest therein by any instrument, except a will."

(c) Overreaching only operates in favour of the purchaser of a legal estate

By section 2(1) of the Law of Property Act 1925 overreaching will only operate in favour of a person who is a "purchaser of a legal estate of land." This means overreaching will only occur where a person purchases either the freehold of land or a legal lease. By statutory extension in section 205(1)(xxi) of the Law of Property Act 1925 "purchaser of a legal estate" includes "a chargee by way of legal mortgage" so that a mortgagee will also enjoy the benefits of overreaching, as was the case in *City of London Building Society v. Flegg.*[28] Since the overreaching provisions are found in Part 1 of the Law of Property Act 1925 section 205(xxi) defines a purchaser as "a person who acquires an interest in or charge on property for money or money's worth." There is therefore no requirement that a person seeking to take advantage of the overreaching mechanism must have acted in good faith,[29] nor must they have provided adequate consideration in return for the legal estate they acquired.[30] In *State Bank of India v. Sood*[31] the Court of Appeal expressly stated that the payment of a mere nominal consideration in money would have overreaching effect. Therefore overreaching will operate in favour of a person who purchases land at an extreme undervalue.

(d) If capital moneys arise overreaching only operates if they are applied appropriately

The central limitation to the operation of overreaching is that the purchaser of the legal estate must pay any capital moneys arising under the conveyance in the appropriate manner required by the statute. These requirements are intended to provide the persons whose interests are overreached with some measure of protection against fraud, but they are only relevant where a conveyance gives rise to capital moneys.[32]

[28] [1988] A.C. 54.
[29] Contrast *Peffer v. Rigg* [1977] 1 W.L.R. 285 in the context of minor interest.
[30] Compare *Midland Bank Trust Co v. Green* [1981] A.C. 513 in the context of the registration of land charges in unregistered land.
[31] [1997] 1 All E.R. 169.
[32] *State Bank of India v. Sood* [1997] 1 All E.R. 169.

(i) Overreaching of trusts interests behind a strict settlement: Where a conveyance is made to a purchaser of a legal estate in land subject to a strict settlement section 2(1)(i) provides that overreaching will only take place if "... the statutory requirements respecting the payment of capital money arising under the settlement are complied with." As has been seen,[33] these requirements are that the proceeds of sale must be paid either to, or at the direction, of the trustees of the settlement, or into court.[34] It should be remembered that in such cases it is the tenant for life or statutory owner who is vested with the legal title and is capable of conveying a legal estate in the land.

(ii) Overreaching of trust interests behind a trust of land: Where land is held upon a trust of land, introduced by the Trust of Land and Appointment of Trustees Act 1925 to replace both the "trust for sale" and the strict settlement, section 2(1)(ii) of the Law of Property Act 1925 provides that the beneficiaries interests will only be overreached if "... the requirements of Section 27 of this Act respecting the payment of capital money arising on such a conveyance are complied with. Section 27 provides that:

> (1) A purchaser of a legal estate from trustees of land shall not be concerned with the trusts affecting the land, the net income of the land or the proceeds of sale of the land whether or not those trusts are declared by the same instrument as that by which the trust of land is created.
>
> (2) Notwithstanding anything to the contrary in the instrument (if any) creating a trust of land or in any trust affecting the net proceeds of sale of the land if it is sold, *the proceeds of sale or other capital money shall not be paid to or applied by the direction of fewer than two persons as trustees, except where the trustee is a trust corporation*, but this subsection does not affect the right of a sole personal representative as such to give valid receipts for, or direct the application of, proceeds of sale or other capital money, nor, except where capital money arises on the transaction, render it necessary to have more than one trustee.

Although a strict reading of section 27 would seem to suggest that a transaction cannot be effective at all if the proceeds of sale are paid to less than two trustees for sale, or a trust corporation, transactions have not been held void even where the capital moneys arising on a conveyance were paid to a sole trustee, as for example in *Williams & Glynn's Bank Ltd v. Boland*[35] and *Abbey National v. Cann*.[36] However failure to pay the capital moneys arising under the conveyance to two or more trustees, or a trust corporation, deprives the conveyance of overreaching effect. In such cases the equitable ownership of the beneficiaries is not automatically deprived of priority over the legal estate of the purchaser or mortgagee. Instead, questions of priority will be determined by whether the equitable interest was properly protected as a minor interest or, if not, whether it was an overriding interest.

[33] See Chap. 8.
[34] Settled Land Act 1925, s.18.
[35] [1981] A.C. 487.
[36] [1991] 1 A.C. 56.

(iii) Overreaching of trust interests where land is conveyed by a mortgagee or personal representative: Where a conveyance of land is made by a mortgagee or personal representative by section 2(1)(iii) of the Law of Property Act 1925 overreaching will take effect provided that any capital moneys arising are paid to the mortgagee or the personal representative.

(iv) overreaching of trust interests where land is conveyed under an order of the court: A conveyance of land under an order of the court has overreaching effect under section 2(1)(iv) of the Law of Property Act 1925 provided that any capital money arising is either paid into court or in accordance with an the order of he court.

(e) Overreaching may occur where no capital moneys arise from the conveyance

In *State Bank of India v. Sood*[37] the Court of Appeal held that it was not a necessary requirement of overreaching that the conveyance with claimed overreaching effect must have resulted in the payment of capital moneys which were appropriately applied. Rather, appropriate payment of capital moneys is only requisite where the conveyance gives rise to them. The case concerned the claim of four family members that their trust interests in their home had not been overreached when the two registered proprietors, who were holding the house on trust for sale, had granted a legal charge over the property to a bank in 1989 in order to secure the present and future liabilities of a company. The bank claimed that this charge was a conveyance which had overreached their interests, which would not therefore be capable of overriding status under section 70(1)(g) of the Land Registration Act 1925. The defendants argued that their interests had not been overreached because, unlike *City of London Building Society v. Flegg* where the money raised by way of mortgage had been paid over to Mr and Mrs Maxwell-Brown, no capital moneys had arisen contemporaneously with the grant of the legal charge. Since the facts were not in dispute Peter Gibson L.J. stated the legal question which was at issue:

> "The crucial issue is the construction of the final condition of section 2(1)(ii) of the Law of Property Act 1925 relating to the statutory requirements respecting the payment of capital money. There is no dispute that if capital money does arise under a conveyance by trustees for sale to a purchaser it must be paid or applied as section 27(2) of that Act dictates. But for overreaching to occur, does capital money have to arise on and contemporaneously with the conveyance?"[38]

The Court held that as a matter of construction section 2(1)(ii) did not *require* the payment of capital moneys since the identical requirement was imposed in section 2(1)(i) in relation to Settled Land and, as capital moneys would not arise in consequence of every conveyance made under the powers conferred by the Settled Land Act 1925 the statutory requirement could only apply to those conveyances which did give rise to such capital money. The presence of the phrase "any capital money" in sections 2(1)(iii) and (iv) was not taken to indicate that the payment of capital money was itself a requirement under section 2(1)(ii). Peter Gibson L.J. pointed out that there were several types of conveyance of land which would not give rise to a

[37] [1997] 1 All E.R. 169.
[38] *ibid.* at 177.

contemporaneous payment of capital moneys other than a charge to secure existing or future indebtedness, including an exchange of land and the grant of a lease without a premium and questioned why the legislature had intended to exclude such conveyances from having an overreaching effect[39] Pill L.J. pointed out that since it was accepted that even a nominal payment of capital at the time of a conveyance would have overreaching effect this would have the effect of rendering any protection of the beneficiaries largely illusory. He therefore considered that the legislation did not require any payment on conveyance:

> "Had Parliament intended to protect those interests by requiring the contemporaneous payment of capital money if overreaching is to occur, I would have expected express and stringent provision."[40]

The Court also considered and dismissed the policy arguments against permitting overreaching where no capital moneys were paid over. Peter Gibson L.J. stated:

> "A more substantial argument of policy advanced on behalf of [the defendants] is that if overreaching occurs where no capital money arises, the beneficiaries' interests may be reduced by the conveyance leaving nothing to which the interests can attach by way of replacement save the equity of redemption, and that may be or become valueless. I see considerable force in this point, but I am not persuaded that it suffices to defeat what I see to be the policy of the legislation, to allow valid dispositions to overreach equitable interests. In my judgement, on its true construction section 2(1)(ii) only requires compliance with the statutory requirements respecting "payment of capital money if capital money arises. Accordingly, I would hold that capital money did not have to arise under the conveyance."[41]

The conclusion reached demonstrates the power of overreaching as a mechanism for defeating pre-existing equitable interests and the supremacy given to conveyancing considerations. As Peter Gibson L.J. pointed out commercial lenders have consistently acted as though such charges confer priority by overreaching and that to have allowed the defendants to succeed would have undermined a system which had proved an important means of small businessmen obtaining finance for their ventures:

> "I accept that a novel and important point of law is raised by this appeal. Lending institutions regularly take security from business men in the form of a legal charge on property (which very frequently means that the matrimonial home is charged) to secure existing and future indebtedness, and very commonly that property will be registered land held by two registered proprietors on trust for sale with no restriction registered in respect of their power to transfer or mortgage that property. It was not suggested that it had ever been the practice of mortgagees to make enquiries of occupiers of the property as to any claimed

[39] *ibid.* at 178.
[40] *ibid.* at 182.
[41] *ibid.* at 178.

rights. Yet if the [defendants] are right, that is what the mortgagees must do if they are not to take subject to the beneficial interests of the occupiers."[42]

(f) Overreaching occurs irrespective of notice

Section 2(1) stated that overreaching occurs in favour of a purchaser of a legal estate in land "whether or not he has notice thereof." It is therefore entirely irrelevant whether a purchaser of land knew that it was held on trust, and the beneficiaries' equitable ownership will be overreached provided that the statutory requirements are met. This again emphasises how overreaching is a mechanical process operating to secure conveyancing efficiency rather than as a genuine means of preserving the rights of the beneficiaries against unjust misappropriation.

3 Reform of Overreaching

(a) Criticism of the overreaching mechanism

Although the operation of overreaching manifestly achieves its objective of ensuring that those seeking to purchase a legal estate in, or to take a legal charge over, land only need to concern themselves with the legal title, the question arises whether this conveyancing efficiency is achieved at a disproportionately high cost of the unjust defeat of some beneficial interests. Overreaching places the beneficiaries in an extremely vulnerable position at the hands of their trustees, and there is little that they can do to protect themselves if the trustees act in fraud of their interests, as when Mr and Mrs Maxwell-Brown felt compelled by their financial plight to deceive their parents. In such cases should the purchaser who has dealt with the legal owners automatically take the land free from the beneficial interests, leaving the erstwhile beneficiaries with what are likely to be inadequate remedies against the trustee personally, or, in the case of land subjected to a legal mortgage, with rights only against the equity of redemption? The courts have applied the overreaching mechanism in such a way that it will defeat even the interests of a beneficiary who is in physical occupation of the land and whose presence should therefore have been obvious to the potential purchaser, and the Law of Property Act 1925 makes clear that overreaching operates irrespective of whether the purchaser has notice of the existence of the beneficial interests. The courts have systematically rejected interpretations of the legislation which would have preserved the interests of beneficiaries in possession, in *City of London Building Society v. Flegg*[43] refusing to find that occupying beneficiaries' rights could be preserved as overriding interests by operation of section 70(1)(g) of the Land Registration Act 1925 and in *State Bank of India v. Sood*[44] finding that overreaching operated even where there were no capital moneys arising on a conveyance. It seems that a purchaser will be protected by overreaching even if he was fully aware that the effect of the transaction by the legal owners would be to ensure the practical elimination of the beneficiaries' interests in the land, for example if a

[42] *ibid.* at 176.
[43] [1988] A.C. 54.
[44] [1997] 1 All E.R. 169.

purchaser acquired a freehold of land from legal owners desperate for money so that he was able to negotiate a price at a substantial undervalue whilst being fully aware of the beneficiaries interests. Criticism of the operation of overreaching was voiced by the Court of Appeal in *State Bank of India v. Sood*[45] where despite clear statements that conveyancing policy demanded that the beneficial interests of the defendants be overreached there was some reluctance to reach that conclusion. Peter Gibson L.J. summarised:

> "Much though I value the principle of overreaching as having aided the simplification of conveyancing, I cannot pretend that I regard the position in the present case as entirely satisfactory. The safeguard for beneficiaries under the existing legislation is largely limited to having two trustees or a trust corporation where capital money falls to be received. But that is no safeguard at all, as this case has shown, when no capital money is received on and contemporaneously with the conveyance. Further, even when it is received by two trustees as in *Flegg*, it might be thought that the beneficiaries in occupation are insufficiently protected."[46]

The criticisms of overreaching essentially flow from the fact that beneficiaries whose interests would have been protected by the doctrine of notice, since it is likely that a potential purchaser would at least have had constructive notice of the interests of all persons in physical occupation of the land if he did not make adequate enquiries of them, will lose priority through the application of a merely mechanical statutory process which makes no allowance for whether or not the conscience of the purchaser was affected by the existence of their interests.

(b) Beneficiaries can protect their interest on the register[47]

It might be thought that overreaching is not as unfair as first impressions may suggest on the basis that those persons enjoying equitable ownership of the land could protect their beneficial entitlements on the register of title of the estate to which they relate. This would reflect the self-help approach to registration of subsidiary interests articulated by the House of Lords in *Midland Bank Trust Co. Ltd v. Green*[48] Mr and Mrs Flegg could have demanded that they were included as proprietors of the house that was purchased and not merely relied on the honestly of their daughter and son-in-law to protect their interests. They, or the defendants in Sood, could have entered a caution[49] on the register which would have entitled them to be informed of any intended dealings in relation to the land. A caution would not protect the substantive rights of the beneficiary, but it would act as a deterrent to a third party contemplating acquiring a legal estate or interest from the registered proprietors. The strongest form of protection, placing a restriction of the register preventing the registered proprietors dealing with the land in a manner inconsistent with their interests, would probably

[45] *ibid.*
[46] *ibid.* at 180.
[47] See: Law Com. No. 188, *Transfer of Land: Overreaching: Beneficiaries in Occupation* (1989), para 2.25–2.27.
[48] [1981] A.C.
[49] See Chap. 15.

have been unavailable to them as such a restriction can only be entered with the consent of the proprietors, who must be willing to submit their land certificate to the Land Registry for alteration. However, the central flaw with this approach is that in many instances the very persons whose interests are most likely to be affected by overreaching are those who are unlikely to be aware of the need to protect them, and in some cases may not be aware of the existence of their interests at all. This is especially the case where their equitable ownership of the land has arisen by means of a resulting or constructive trust. For example, in *State Bank of India v. Sood*[50] four of the defendants claimed entitlement by way of resulting trusts and three by constructive trusts. It is unlikely that such beneficiaries even contemplated the existence of these rights until they were faced with the prospect of repossession of their home and sought legal advice to avoid it, much less that they would have considered the need to protect them against the other family members who held the legal title.

(c) No overreaching of the interests of beneficiaries in occupation without consent

The Court of Appeal in *City of London Building Society v. Flegg*[51] effectively reached the conclusion that in registered land the rights of a beneficiary in occupation could not be defeated by overreaching since they would be protected as overriding interests under section 70(1)(g) of the Land Registration Act 1925. In such circumstances priority would only be gained if the potential purchaser had made inquiries of the beneficiary in occupation and they had denied the existence of any right or if their consent had been obtained to the conveyance. Although this approach attracted much criticism[52] and was overruled by the House of Lords[53] the Law Commission in its report *Transfer of Land: Overreaching: Beneficiaries in Occupation*[54] recommended statutory reform to protect the position of a beneficiary in occupation of the land. Their principle recommendation was summarised in para 4.3:

> "A conveyance of a legal estate in property should not have the effect of overreaching the interest of anyone of full age and capacity who is entitled to a beneficial interest in the property and who has a right to occupy it and is in actual occupation of it at the date of the conveyance, unless that person consents."

Such consent could be either express or implied. This would mean that such persons as Mr and Mrs Flegg, or the defendants in *Sood* would not lose priority to a subsequent legal mortgagee without their consent, and it would impose on a person seeking to acquire a legal estate in the land or taking a legal mortgage the added burden of ensuring that the consent of all those in occupation had been received. It should be noted that this would not necessarily involve a greater degree of burden on a potential purchaser because they already have a vested interest in making inquiries of occupiers to protect themselves against interests other than beneficial interests which might form

[50] [1997] 1 All E.R. 169.
[51] [1986] Ch. 605.
[52] See: [1986] C.L.J. 202; [1986] Conv. 131; (1986) 102 L.Q.R. 349; (1986) 49 M.L.R. 519; [1987] Conv. 379.
[53] [1988] A.C. 54. See: [1987] C.L.J. 392; (1987) 103 L.Q.R. 520; [1987] Conv. 451; (1988) 51 M.L.R. 565.
[54] Law Com. No. 188 (1989).

the subject matter of a section 70(1)(g) overriding interest,[55] for example an equitable lease. Indeed the Commission stated: "we would not expect our recommendations to necessitate enquiries and inspections going beyond what is done at present."[56] It was proposed that beneficiaries in occupation could give consent by any means and that no formalities would be required, and that the court should have an unfettered discretion to dispense with the consent requirement. The proposals of the Law Commission have been subjected to criticism by Harpum[57] who makes three main objections. First, he considers that it draws an unfair distinction between the rights of beneficiaries who are in occupation of the land and of those who are not. Secondly, he argues that it would defeat the curtain principle underlying the property legislation of 1925 by forcing purchasers of legal estates to make more extensive enquiries of persons in occupation to determine whether they have beneficial rights, thus meaning that trusts would again become a matter of title and a concern for purchasers. Thirdly, he suggests that it would weaken the system of land registration by extending the breadth of the category of overriding interests to include rights which are overreachable.

(d) Limiting the powers of the trustees of land

Harpum advocates an alternative reform of the perceived defects of overreaching a restricting the legal owners' powers of disposition over land held on trust. He suggests that overreaching should continue to occur wherever there was a sale or lease of the land, but that the powers of the trustees to mortgage the land should be limited so that they would be able to raise a first mortgage to fund the purchase of property and to raise money for improvement or repair, but that they should have no power to raise a second mortgage. If the trustees were then to transact outside their powers it would require them to obtain the consent of all those beneficially entitled to the property. He concludes by summarising the perceived benefits of his alternative scheme:

> "The proposed scheme would facilitate most ordinary conveyancing transactions of sale and leasing. Purchasers and building societies would not need to investigate the rights of persons in actual occupation nor obtain their consent if there were two or more legal owners. It would protect the rights of *all* beneficiaries, whether in actual occupation or not, in the case of dispositions outside the trustees' powers. Transactions such as second mortgages, which are likely to be detrimental to beneficiaries would be voidable, unless all beneficiaries under the trust had consented. This would of course constitute an exception to the general principle that trusts are to be kept off the title, but it is an exception that exists under the 1925 legislation."[58]

However, this recommendation was not enacted in the Trusts of Land and Appointment of Trustees Act 1996 which grants the trustees of a trust of land "all the powers of an absolute owner."[59]

[55] See para. 4.24-4.26.
[56] Para 4.24.
[57] [1990] C.L.J. 275.
[58] *ibid.* at p 332.
[59] s.6(1).

(e) No legislative response

Having examined the criticisms which have been levelled against the operation of the overreaching mechanism and the proposals which have been made for reform, it is clear that no fundamental change will occur unless legislative initiative is taken. In *State Bank of India v Sood*[60] Peter Gibson L.J. referred specifically to the reforms advocated by the Law Commission and by Harpum but concluded that "whether the legislature will reform the law remains to be seen."[61] He also noted that the Trusts of Land and Appointment of Trustees Act 1996 had no effect on overreaching. It should perhaps be concluded that although the reforms which have been proposed would help protect the most vulnerable persons from the elimination of their interests in land they do not amount to a comprehensive repudiation of the philosophy of overreaching within the registered land system. They would tinker with the edges to redress the perception derived from the decision in *City of London Building Society v. Flegg*[62] that the commercially aware mortgage company was overprotected as against the naive beneficiaries. However, the judgement of the House of Lords in that case was entirely consistent with the trend of decisions relating to issues of priority in registered land which have almost unanimously favoured the position of mortgagees over beneficiaries seeking to claim priority to defeat repossession where a mortgage has been granted by the legal owner.[63] Ultimately the concerns of lenders, with concomitant effects on the property market if their security is weakened or perceived to be weakened, have been judged more important that the equitable ownership rights of individuals in hard cases.

ALTERATIONS TO THE REGISTER: RECTIFICATION AND INDEMNITY

1 Potential rectification of the register

At the heart of the system of land registration is the idea that the land is owned by the person(s) who are registered as the proprietor(s) and that their title is good against all the world, so that a person seeking to acquire ownership or an interest in the land from them can be confident that they are transacting with the person(s) entitled to make dispositions of the land. It has already been noted that registration with absolute title is sufficient to constitute the person so registered as proprietor with the ownership of the land good against the entire world,[64] even if his title was defective. The interests of the true owner are therefore defeated by such registration. However errors on the register may occur as a result of either fraud or mistake, and the Land Registration Act 1925 makes provision for the register to be corrected. Such correction is technically called rectification, and where a person has suffered any loss as a result of a rectification of an incorrect register entry they may be entitled to receive compensation for their loss by means of the payment of an indemnity.

[60] [1997] 1 All E.R. 169.
[61] *ibid.* at 180.
[62] [1988] A.C. 54.
[63] See for example: *Abbey National v. Cann* [1991] 1 A.C. 56; *Lloyd's Bank v. Rosset* [1991] 1 A.C. 107.
[64] Land Registration Act 1925, s.5.

2 Jurisdiction to rectify the register

(a) Circumstances in which rectification is possible

Section 82(1) of the Land Registration Act 1925 provides that the register may be rectified by order of the court or at the discretion of the Registrar where an error has occurred in specified circumstances:

> "The register may be rectified pursuant to an order of the court or by the registrar, subject to an appeal to the court, in any of the following cases, but subject to the provisions of this section:
>
> (a) Subject to any express provisions of this Act to the contrary, where a court of competent jurisdiction has decided that any person is entitled to any estate right or interest in or to any registered land or charge, and as a consequence of such decision such court is of opinion that a rectification of the register is required, and makes an order to that effect;
> (b) Subject to any express provision of this Act to the contrary, where the court, on the application in the prescribed manner of any person who is aggrieved by any entry made in, or by the omission of any entry from, the register, or by default being made, or unnecessary delay taking place, in the making of any entry in the register, makes an order for the rectification of the register;
> (c) In any case and at any time with the consent of all persons interested;
> (d) Where the court or the registrar is satisfied that any entry in the register has been obtained by fraud;
> (e) Where two or more persons are, by mistake, registered as proprietors of the same registered estate or the same charge;
> (f) Where a mortgagee has been registered as proprietor of the land instead of as proprietor of a charge and a right of redemption is subsisting;
> (g) Where a legal estate has been registered in the name of a person who if the land had not been registered would not have been the estate owner; and
> (h) In any other case where, by reason of any error or omission in the register, or by reason of any entry made under a mistake, it may be deemed just to rectify the register.

(b) A jurisdiction to rectify whenever "just and equitable"?[65]

The very broad wording of section 82(1), and in particular of section 82(1)(h), has given rise to the question whether there is a general jurisdiction to rectify the register whenever this is considered just and equitable. In some cases it had been held that there was a wide general discretion to rectify[66] but this approach was rejected by the

[65] See: [1992] Conv. 293 (Davis); (1993) 109 L.Q.R. 187 (Smith).
[66] See: *Orakpo v. Manson Investments Ltd* [1977] 1 W.L.R. 347, 360; *Peffer v. Rigg* [1977] 1 W.L.R. 285, 294; *Argyle Building Society v. Hammond* [1984] 49 P. & C.R. 148, 158; *Proctor v. Kidman* (1985) 51 P. & C.R. 67, 72.

Court of Appeal in *Norwich and Peterborough Building Society v. Steed.*[67] Derek Steed was the registered proprietor of a house in London, which had been purchased with the aid of a loan from a local authority which was protected in the charges register. Derek's mother, sister and her husband also lived at the house. Derek emigrated to California and granted his mother a power for attorney in relation to the house. A transfer was then executed, purportedly by Mrs Steed, transferring the title into the names of his sister and her husband, who purchased the property with the help of a building society mortgage which was protected as a legal charge. They fell into arrears on the mortgage payment and the building society sought repossession. When Derek returned he joined the proceedings for possession and claimed that he was entitled to rectification of the register as against his sister and her husband and the building society, contending that his mother's signature on the transfer was a forgery. Eventually the forgery allegation was dropped and instead Derek claimed that his mother had not know what she was signing and that the transfer was void on grounds of *non est factum.* Knox J. held that the transfer was not void but voidable because of the fraud that had been perpetrated, and he ordered that the register be rectified to restore Derek as the registered proprietor, but he did not order rectification against the building society by removal of their charge. The Court of Appeal held that the *non est factum* plea should fail for lack of evidence and that the exercise of the power of attorney was not *ultra vires.* There was no doubt that the transfer was induced by the sister's fraud and the question was whether this entitled Derek to rectification against the building society. Scott L.J. rejected the view that there was a general power to rectify the register and instead held that "if an order or rectification is to be made the case must be brought within at least one of paragraphs (a) to (h) of section 82(1)."[68] He then proceeded to summarise the intended scope of section 82(1):

> "In my opinion the scheme is reasonably clear. Paragraphs (a) and (b) give power to the court to make orders of rectification in order to give effect to property rights which have been established in an action or which are clear. Paragraph (c) enables orders to be made by consent. The remaining paragraphs, (d) to (h), are intended to enable errors to be corrected. Paragraph (d), paragraph (e), paragraph (f) and paragraph (g) each deal with an error of a particular character. But, since these paragraphs might not cover comprehensively all errors, paragraph (h) was added as a catch-all provision to cover any other errors. The breadth of the catch-all provision was, I imagine, the reason why it was thought appropriate to make the power exerciseable 'where it may be deemed just to rectify the register'."[69]

Given this analysis of the availability of rectification in its entirety he held that paragraph (h) only granted jurisdiction to rectify where a genuine mistake had occurred in registration:

[67] [1993] Ch. 116.
[68] *ibid.* at 131.
[69] *ibid.* at 134–135.

> "in order for [paragraph (h)] to be applicable some "error or omission" in the register or some "entry made under a mistake" must be shown."[70]

Since the building society's charge was not registered against the property by an error of any kind there was no grounds for rectification under paragraph (h).

(c) Examples of circumstances where rectification may be granted

(i) Court determines that a person is entitled to an estate, right or interest which does not appear on the register: Under paragraph (a) of section 82(1) the court alone has power to order rectification in favour of a person who it concludes is entitled to an estate, right or interest in the land which does not appear on the register at present. In *Norwich and Peterborough Building Society v. Steed* Scott L.J. held that this referred only to entitlements to rights under the substantive law and gave examples of where rectification would be available, including the setting aside of a transaction on grounds of misrepresentation, asserting a possessory title and the assertion by a beneficiary under a trust that they have become absolutely entitled to the land. It may also include an order to enter a subsisting overriding interest on the register.[71] What Scott L.J. made clear was that the jurisdiction under paragraph (a) does not extend to a situation where a person had no substantive right in the land, so that it does not enable a voidable transaction to be set aside against a bona fide purchaser who has acquired a legal estate by registration.

(ii) Court orders rectification where interest wrongly omitted or included on first registration: The precise scope of paragraph (b) is unclear. It seems, however, that it enables the court to order the addition of rights wrongly omitted at first registration[72] or excluding rights wrongly included. In *Norwich and Peterborough Building Society v. Steed* Scott L.J. stated that paragraph (b) could only relate to pre-existing rights and was not intended to produce new rights in relation to the registered land.

(iii) Rectification by consent: Paragraph (c) is self-explanatory and permits rectification with the agreement of all the parties involved in the land.

(iv) Entries on the register obtained by fraud perpetrated against the Registrar: Paragraph (d) permits rectification where an entry on the register was obtained by fraud. This may not necessarily include every situation in which there was an element of fraud in obtaining an interest which is subsequently registered, as in *Norwich and Peterborough Building Society v. Steed* where the mortgage was obtained by the fraudulent scheme of Derek's sister and husband. Scott L.J. considered that the paragraph only permitted rectification where the fraud was practised against the Land Registry to obtain the registration of the building society's charge. However this approach may be considered unduly narrow. In *Re Leighton's Conveyance*[73] the plaintiff claimed rectification of the register when her daughter had obtained a transfer of the registered title into her name by fraudulently misrepresenting the nature of documents that she asked her to sign. The daughter subsequently mortgaged the property and the mortgagee's interests were effected as registered charges. Luxmore J., seemingly acting

[70] *ibid.* at 135.
[71] *Chowood v. Lyall* (No. 2) [1930] 2 Ch. 156.
[72] *Calgary and Edmonton Land Co. Ltd v. Discount Bank (Overseas) Ltd* [1971] 1 W.L.R. 81.
[73] [1936] 1 All E.R. 1033.

under section 82(1)(d),[74] ordered rectification of the register so that the plaintiff was inserted as the owner of the land with absolute title, but there was no interference with the registered charges which remained enforceable against the property. It seems impossible to characterise the fraud perpetrated in that case as against the Land Registry, since it was clearly against the registered proprietor by her daughter. In *Norwich and Peterborough Building Society v. Steed,* Scott L.J. considered that the power to rectify could only have arisen under section 82(1)(a).

(v) Multiple registration: Paragraph (e) is self-evident and permits rectification where an error has occurred resulting in the registration of two or more persons as proprietors of the same estate or charge.

(vi) Mortgagee registered as proprietor of land not of charge: Paragraph (f) permits rectification in the event that a mortgagee is mistakenly registered as being the proprietor of the registered estate in the land itself and not merely of a charge over the land.

(vii) Someone else entitled to ownership of the estate: Paragraph (g) provides for registration where the person registered as proprietor of the estate in question would not have been the owner if the land had not been registered. The most likely scenario where such an error would occur is if a person was registered as the transferee from the supposed owner of the land where someone else had already acquired the land by way of adverse possession. Since the transferee would not take good title the adverse possessor would be entitled to have the register rectified against them. For example, in *Chowood Ltd v. Lyall*[75] the Court of Appeal ordered rectification where the plaintiffs had been registered as the first proprietors of land they had purchased and the defendant, who was the neighbouring landowner, had previously become entitled by adverse possession of two narrow strips of woodland. In *Norwich and Peterborough Building Society v. Steed* Scott L.J. considered that rectification could also be granted under paragraph (g) where a transfer of title was void because it was established that it had been signed *non est factum* or was a forgery.

(viii) Other mistakes: As has already been seen, it has been held that paragraph (h) does not confer a general discretion to rectify where it is thought "just and reasonable" but rather permits rectification if there was a genuine mistake in the register entry not covered by paragraphs (d) to (g).

3 Effect of rectification of the register

(a) Rectification may affect rights and interests subsisting in the land

Section 82(2) of the Land Registration Act 1925 makes clear that rectification has the capacity to affect any rights and interests which may be subsisting in relation to the registered land:

> "The register may be rectified under this section, notwithstanding that the rectification may affect any estates, rights, charges or interests acquired or protected by registration, or by any entry on the register, or otherwise."

[74] As indicated by the Editorial Note to the report.
[75] [1930] 2 Ch. 156.

This section reverses the principle of indefeasibility of registered title adopted in earlier legislation which did not permit rectification affecting estates and rights acquired by registration.

(b) Rectification may deprive a registered proprietor of title

Where the register is rectified so that there is a substitution of the registered proprietor the previous proprietor will be divested of his estate in the land which will vest in the new proprietor.[76] For example in *Chowood Ltd v. Lyall*[77] the effect of rectification was to deprive the registered proprietors of their title to the land which had been previously acquired by the defendants adverse possession.

(c) Rectification may subject the land to a previously unprotected subsidiary interest

Where rectification is ordered because of a failure to include a subsidiary interests on the register that interest will be binding on the registered estate. This can be seen in *Freer v. Unwins*[78] where the plaintiffs were the freeholders of a tobacconists shop and the defendant the lessees of a separate shop in the same parade. The plaintiffs' shop enjoyed the benefit of a restrictive covenant affecting the shop leased by the defendant preventing its use for the sale of tobacco. The burden of this covenant was protected against the freeholders of the defendant's shop under the Land Charges Act 1925. When title to the shops was registered the title of the shop occupied by the defendant did not show the benefit of the restrictive covenant. The Land Registrar subsequently rectified the register against the freehold title so that the burden of the restrictive covenant affected the land. It should be noted that this rectification was probably inconsistent with section 82(3) of the Land Registration Act 1925, which protects the rights of a proprietor in possession, but the freeholder did not appeal against it.

(d) Rectification may cause a third party to be deprived of his properly protected subsidiary interest in the land

If the register is rectified by the removal of the entry protecting a subsidiary interest of a third party which has been properly protected, the third party will be deprived of his interest. For example, in *Argyle Building Society v. Hammond*[79] the Court of Appeal held that the register could be rectified so that the registered charge of a building society would be removed. The case concerned a preliminary point in the litigation culminating in the decision of the Court of Appeal in *Norwich and Peterborough Building Society v. Steed*. As a preliminary matter the Court of Appeal held that there was jurisdiction to rectify the register so as to deprive the building society of their registered charge, even though they had taken it in good faith after the registered proprietor had obtained her title by fraud. Slade L.J. considered that whether there should be rectification in such circumstances was a matter for the court's discretion but that there was no absolute qualification preventing rectification disturbing the charge of a bona fide mortgagee.[80] This was approved by Scott L.J. in *Norwich and*

[76] s.69(1) Land Registration Act 1925.
[77] [1930] 2 Ch. 156.
[78] [1976] Ch. 288; [1976] C.L.J. 215 (Hayton); (1976) 30 Conv. 304 (Crane); (1976) 92 L.Q.R. 338.
[79] (1985) 49 P. & C.R. 148.
[80] Contra *Ruoff & Roper's The Law and Practice of Registered Conveyancing,* 4th ed, 1979, p. 789. See also the comments of Slade L.J. on the decision of Luxmore J. in *Re Leighton's Conveyance* [1936] 1 All E.R. 1033, (1985) 49 P. & C.R. 148, 159–163.

Peterborough Building Society v. Steed[81] who held that the court would have jurisdiction to order rectification even against innocent third parties, subject to the limitation that a power of rectification was only available if the case could be brought within one of the specific grounds outlined in section 82(1). If rectification is granted against the interests of an innocent third party he will be entitled to an indemnity to compensate any loss.[82]

4 Limitations to the availability and effects of rectification

(a) No rectification against an innocent proprietor in possession

Although section 82(1) provides a wide power to rectify the register the position of registered proprietors in possession of the land is protected by section 82(3) which provides:

> "The register shall not be rectified, except for the purpose of giving effect to an overriding interest, or to an order of the court, so as to affect the title of the proprietor who is in possession —
>
> (a) unless the proprietor has caused or substantially contributed to the error or omission by fraud or lack of proper care;
>
> (b) . . .
>
> (c) unless for any other reason, in any particular case, it is considered that it would be unjust not to rectify the register against him."

(i) Proprietor in possession: A proprietor in possession clearly includes a person who is registered as the proprietor of an estate who is in actual occupation of the land. However, possession is granted a wider meaning in section 3(xviii) of the Land Registration Act 1925 and includes a person "in receipt of rent and profits or the right to receive the same." This will include a registered proprietor who has leased the land.
(ii) Rectification by order of the court: Although section 83(2) excludes protection where rectification is ordered by the court it seems that this provision, which was introduced by the Administration of Justice Act 1977, was not intended to include the power of the court to rectify under section 82(1)(a) and (b). Instead it was primarily intended to permit the court to order rectification against a registered proprietor who had been registered in consequence of a transfer intended to defeat the rights of the trustee in bankruptcy of the previous proprietor.[83]
(iii) Registered proprietor caused or contributed to error on the register: Under s82(3)(a) a registered proprietor will have no entitlement to protection from rectification if the error on the register was substantially caused by his own conduct. Although deliberate fraud will not prevent rectification it is unclear whether innocent conduct will deprive him of protection. In *Re 139 Deptford High Street*[84] Wynn-Parry J. held that a person who had been registered as the first proprietor of land including a small plot

[81] [1993] Ch. 116.
[82] Land Registration Act 1925, s.83(4).
[83] See: Law Com. No. 158, *Property Law: Third Report on Land Registration* (1987) para. 3.13.
[84] [1951] Ch. 884.

belonging to the British Transport Commission was not entitled to the protection of section 82(3) because he had contributed to the error by putting forward an application for registration containing the error,[85] despite the fact that his mistake was completely innocent. However, this decision was made under an earlier version of the section and the present section 82(3)(a) requires a lack of proper care by the registered proprietor. It seems that a failure by the registered proprietor to properly investigate his title before applying for first registration would deprive him of protection.

(iv) Discretion to ignore the protection of the proprietor in possession if leaving the register unchanged would be unjust: Despite the general protection of the proprietor in possession afforded by section 82(3), paragraph (c) entitles the court to rectify the register in a manner detrimental to such a person if in all the circumstances it would be unjust not to rectify. The mere fact that rectification would be just from the perspective of the persons seeking it is insufficient. In *Chowood v. Lyall*[86] Luxmore J. held that it would be unjust not to rectify where otherwise a person who was entitled to land by adverse possession would be deprived of their ownership. However, in *Epps v. Esso Petroleum*[87] Templeman J. held that it would not have been unjust to refuse rectification against the registered proprietor. The defendants had purchased land and were registered as first proprietors of it and a strip of frontage previously conveyed to the predecessors in title to the plaintiff. When the land was conveyed to the plaintiffs they were registered as proprietors of the same strip of frontage, so that there was a double registration. Templeman J. held that since the plaintiffs' vendor had taken the land subject to a covenant to build a wall marking the boundary which they had failed to fulfil it would not be unjust to refuse rectification of the defendant's title, thus depriving them of ownership of the strip of land. he noted that there was "nothing on the register or on the ground on or before the date when the defendants became the registered proprietors of the dispute strip which put [them] on inquiry" and that the plaintiff's should have been aware of a potential dispute concerning the boundary from their vendor's documents of title. In *London Borough of Hounslow v. Hare*[88] Knox J. similarly held that a refusal to rectify would not be unjust. The defendant was granted a 125 year lease of a flat which was protected on the title of the freehold to which it related and was also registered as a title at the land registry, which lease was void since the land was owned by a charity and the consent of the Commissioners had not been obtained as required by section 29(1) Charities Act 1960. He took into account the fact that the plaintiff was entirely innocent and noted the effect that registration would have upon the nature of her interests:

> "What I primarily . . . have to look at is whether it is considered that it would be unjust not to rectify the register against Miss Hare and I cannot reach that conclusion. She has been in possession of this property for a very long time . . . it seems to me that when one is dealing with a person's home the change from the near equivalent of a freehold that a 125 year lease gives to somebody of that age

[85] See also: *Re Sea View Gardens, Warden* [1976] 1 W.L.R. 134.
[86] [1930] 1 Ch. 424.
[87] [1973] 1 W.L.R. 1071; (1973) 37 Conv. 284; [1974] C.L.J. 60.
[88] [1992] 24 H.L.R. 9; [1993] Conv. 224.

> nearing forty to that of a tenant, assured or not, is one of very considerable significance. That feature does, in my judgement, far outweigh any financial considerations that there may be the other way."[89]

(b) Rectification is within the discretion of the court

Even where rectification would be available under the various categories stipulated in section 82(1), and even if it would have no effect on the title of a proprietor in possession, it remains discretionary and the court or Registrar may refuse to rectify. It is clear from many decisions that the potential availability of an indemnity is a crucial factor to be taken into account in determining whether rectification should be granted.[90] Although in *Norwich and Peterborough Building Society v. Steed*[91] the Court of Appeal held that there was no power to rectify the register against the building society which had a registered charge, at first instance Knox J. had held that there was such a power but refused to exercise it as a matter of discretion. He held that as between the proprietor claiming rectification and the building society "all the equities are on the society's side." However, in the Court of Appeal Scott L.J. pointed out that it was not so easy to weigh the equities if the possibility of an indemnity on rectification was taken into account. He noted that: "If rectification were ordered, the loss would fall not upon the building society but upon the public purse. If rectification were refused, the public purse would be saved the burden of paying an indemnity."[92] However, having indicated that a more complex analysis was necessary he expressly stated that he was not intending to indicate disagreement with Knox J.'s conclusion that rectification should have been refused, if it had been available.

(c) Rectification does not affect third party interests acquired before it was granted

It has already been seen that in *Freer v. Unwins*[93] rectification was granted of the register of a freehold interest of a shop where the burden of a restrictive covenant had been accidentally omitted from the register. The main issue in the case was whether the title of the defendant lessee of the premises, who had acquired his tenancy before the register was rectified, should take it subject to the burden of the covenant, which would then enable the plaintiff to seek an injunction preventing him selling tobacco. The lease had been granted in 1969 and was assigned to the defendants in 1974. The register was rectified so that the restrictive covenant appeared on April 28, 1975. Walton J. held that since the covenant did not appear on the register on the date when the lease was granted section 20(1) of the Land Registration Act 1925 applied and the lessees did not take the lease subject to the restrictive covenant, which therefore did not bind the defendants as assignees. The effect of this decision was that the covenant was binding upon the freehold of the shop but not on the lessees for the duration of the lease. However it should be noted that the lease involved was for less than 21 years and did not require registration. Walton J. indicated that if the lease had itself been

[89] *ibid.* at 27.
[90] *Epps v. Esso Petroleum Co Ltd* [1973] 1 W.L.R. 1071; *Argyle Building Society v. Hammond* (1984) 49 P. & C.R. 148.
[91] [1993] Ch. 116.
[92] *ibid.* at 138.
[93] [1976] Ch. 288.

registered rectification of the relevant leasehold title might have been ordered, thus rendering the defendant subject to the restrictive covenant. In such an event he would have been entitled to an indemnity for any loss that he suffered as a consequence.

5 Payment of an indemnity where the register is rectified[94]

(a) Indemnity where the register is rectified

Section 83(1) provides that:

> "Subject to the provisions of this Act to the contrary, any person suffering loss by reason of any rectification of the register under this Act shall be entitled to be indemnified."

This means that they will be entitled to receive a compensating payment from the public purse for the extinction or diminution of the extent of their interest in the land. Such loss is to be calculated by reference to the value of the estate, interest or charge immediately before rectification took place.[95] There is no right to an indemnity if the person applying for it suffered his loss wholly or partly as a result of his own fraud or wholly as a result of his own lack of proper care.[96] If he has contributed partly to his loss by his lack of proper care any indemnity payable shall be reduced to such extent as is just and equitable having regard to his share of the responsibility for the loss.[97] Any fraud of lack of proper care by the person from whom the claimant of an indemnity derived his title is treated as if it were his own fraud or lack of care.[98] There is no right to an indemnity where the register was rectified to give effect to an overriding interest, since in such circumstances the proprietor has suffered no loss as his estate was already subject to it even though it did not appear on the face of the register.[99] However, a person who was registered as proprietor in good faith under a forged disposition is entitled to an indemnity for the loss of his estate by rectification.[1] A limitation period of six years applies to claims for an indemnity, running from the time that the claimant knew, or ought to have known, of the existence of his claim.

(b) Indemnity where rectification of the register is refused

Where rectification is available but is refused for whatever reason section 83(2) provides that an indemnity will be available:

> "Where an error or omission has occurred in the register, but the register is not rectified, a person suffering loss by reason of such error or omission shall, subject to the provisions of this Act be entitled to be indemnified under this Act."

[94] See: (1986) 39 C.L.P. 111 (Smith); [1988] Conv. 73; (1987) 284 E.G. 1437.
[95] s.83(8)(b).
[96] s.83(5).
[97] s.83(6).
[98] s.83(7).
[99] *Re Chowood's Registered Land* [1933] Ch. 574.
[1] s.83(4).

In such cases any loss is calculated by the value of the estate, interest or charge at the time when the error or omission causing it was made.[2] Again an indemnity is not available to a person who caused the loss wholly or partly by his fraud or wholly by his lack of proper care, and any indemnity may be reduced by his contributory negligence.

[2] s.83(6)(a).

Chapter 15

Minor Interests in Registered Land

Introduction to Minor Interests

1 Relationship to registered interests

In the previous chapter it has been seen how the 1925 property legislation introduced what is to become a universal scheme for the registration of title to land. The only interests in land which can be registered as individual titles are the two legal estates, namely the freehold fee simple absolute in possession and the leasehold term of years absolute for greater than twenty one years. It is obvious that there are many other interests which may be enjoyed over land, for example equitable ownership behind a trust of a legal estate, options to purchase and other estate contracts, equitable leases and restrictive covenants. It has been seen how equitable ownership behind a trust can be kept from the register of title through the overreaching mechanism. The central objective of registered land is that most other subsidiary interests should be protected by means of an entry on the register of the estate to which they relate and affect. Such subsidiary interest are termed "minor interests," not in the sense that they are unimportant, but that they are lesser interests than those which may be registered in their own right.

2 Definition of minor interests

(a) A statutory definition by inclusion and exclusion

Section 3(xv) of the Land Registration Act 1925 defines "minor interests":

> "Minor interests" mean the interests not capable of being disposed of or created by registered dispositions and capable of being overridden (whether or not a purchaser has notice thereof) by the proprietors unless protected as provided by this Act, and all rights and interests which are not registered and protected on the register and are not overriding interests, and include —
>
> (a) in the case of land subject to a trust of land, all interests and powers which are under the Law of Property Act 1925, capable of being

overridden by the trustees, whether or not such interests are so protected; and

(b) in the case of settled land, all interests and powers which are under the Settled Land Act 1925 and the Law of Property Act 1925, or either of them, capable of being overridden by the tenant for life or statutory owner, whether or not such interests and powers are so protected as aforesaid.

Although complex, this section defines minor interests both by inclusion and exclusion. Its net effect is that almost all rights and interests in land, other than the two registrable interests together with the charge by way of legal mortgage and legal easement which can only exist by appropriate registration, will constitute minor interests. This clearly includes all interests in land which are purely equitable in nature, including estate contracts and equitable ownership under either a trust of land or a strict settlement.

(b) Are "minor interests" and "overriding interests" mutually exclusive?

At first sight section 3(xv) seems to excludes "overriding interests" from the definition of minor interests, so that the two are mutually distinct categories of right subject to separate regimes. As will be seen,[1] overriding interests are defined in Land Registration Act 1925, s.70(1)(a)-(l) and the majority are specific interests which might effect the land. For example, by section 70(1)(d) a "liability in respect of embankments, and sea and river walls" is an overriding interest, as is a legal lease for less than 21 years under section 70(1)(k). However, the problem arises in relation to section 70(1)(g) which is general in its scope and does not stipulate a specific interest but rather states that "the rights of every person in actual occupation of the land" are overriding interests. The question is whether minor interests can also enjoy status as overriding interests under section 70(1)(g) when section 3(xv) seems to provide that the category of minor interests expressly excludes all overriding interests. This question was addressed by the House of Lords in *Williams & Glynn's Bank Ltd v. Boland*,[2] where it was held that an equitable beneficial interest behind a trust for sale, which would today be a trust of land as a consequence of the Trusts of Land and Appointment of Trustees Act 1996, was capable of ranking not merely as a minor interest but also as an overriding interest under section 70(1)(g). Lord Wilberforce explained why it might be thought that a minor interest cannot be an overriding interest:

> "As to structure it is said that the [Land Registration Act 1925] recognises three thing: (a) legal estates, (b) minor interests, which take effect in equity, and (c) overriding interests. These are mutually exclusive: an equitable interest which is a minor interest, is incapable of being at the same time an overriding interest . . . As to the provisions of the Act, particular emphasis is placed on section 3(xv) which, in defining "minor interests" specifically includes in the case of land held on trust for sale "all interests and powers which are under the Law of Property

[1] See below Chap. 16.
[2] [1981] A.C. 487.

> Act 1925 capable of being overridden by the trustees for sale" and excludes expressly, overriding interests . . . My Lords I find this argument formidable."[3]

However, he went on to consider the nature of equitable ownership arising under a trust for sale and concluded that such rights were capable of existing both as minor interests and overriding interests:

> "How then are these various rights to be fitted into the scheme of the Land Registration Act 1925? It is clear, at least, that the interests of the co-owners under the "statutory trusts" are minor interests — this fits with the definition in section 3(xv). But I can see no reason why, if these interests, or that any one of them, are or is protected by "actual occupation" they should remain merely as "minor interests." On the contrary, I see every reason why, in that event, they should acquire the status of overriding interests."[4]

The significance of this decision will be considered later in this chapter, and also in the next chapter, since it means that a failure to protect a minor interest appropriately will not necessarily mean that it loses priority to a purchaser of a legal estate in the land. However, at this stage it is sufficient to note the important point that the categories of minor interests and overriding interests are not mutually exclusive but to some extent overlap.

THE OPPORTUNITY TO PROTECT MINOR INTERESTS ON THE REGISTER

1 An opportunity not an obligation

Central to the operation of the registered land system is the opportunity that those persons who enjoy minor interests in land which is registered have to protect them by means of an entry on the register of the title to which they relate. This possibility of protection by registration is not an obligation, in the sense that failure to protect would mean that the minor interest will be void against a registered proprietor who granted it. Instead, a failure to protect will mean that the holder of the minor interest is extremely vulnerable if the land is transferred to a new registered proprietor, or if a legal mortgage is granted over the land, because if certain statutory criteria are met the transferee or chargee will acquire the estate or mortgage free from the unprotected minor interest. This will be so even if the transferee or chargee had actual notice of the existence of the unprotected minor interest. The policy objective enshrined in the system of protection of minor interests is that those who enjoy subsidiary interests in the land are expected to look after their own interests by taking the step of protecting them. If they fail to do so, it is their own fault that they have to concede priority to a purchaser who is entitled to rely on the face of the register to indicate whether there

[3] *ibid.* at 506.
[4] *ibid.* at 507.

are any rights and interests to which the land is subject. Sentiments to this effect were expressed by the House of Lords in *Midland Bank Trust Co. v. Green*[5] in the context of the registration of land charges in unregistered land which are roughly the equivalent to minor interests in registered land. Lord Wilberforce considered that it was not unfair that a holder of an equitable estate contract, which had not been protected by appropriate registration, should lose priority to a subsequent purchaser of the freehold ownership of the land who had actual notice of the existence of his interest. He stated that:

> "Any temptation to remould the [Land Charges Act 1925] to meet the facts of the present case, on the supposition that it is a hard one and that justice requires it is, for me at least, removed by the consideration that the Act itself provides a simple and effective protection for persons [holding such interests in the land] . . . viz. — by registration."[6]

The same could be said in relation to minor interests, so that the burden of self-protection falls on their holders. If they fail to protect themselves the balance of justice will lie with the purchaser, and unless they are binding as overriding interests or in some other way, the purchaser will take free from them.

2 Means of protecting a minor interest

The Land Registration Act 1925 provides four means by which the holder of a minor interest may protect it against the title of the estate to which it relates. These four means of protection differ in respect to the manner in which they affect the ability of the registered proprietor to deal with his land, so that some provide more protection than others. They also differ in the extent to which the consent of the registered proprietor is required before they may be obtained.

(a) Protection by entry of a restriction on the proprietorship register

Minor interests may be protected by means of the entry of a restriction[7] on the proprietorship register[8] of the estate to which it relates. The terms of a restriction impede the ability of the registered proprietor to deal with his land by preventing any transactions inconsistent with its terms. For example, a restriction may be entered preventing the registration of any disposition of the land unless specified consents have been obtained. Restrictions are particularly appropriate where the minor interest concerned is a beneficial interest behind a trust of land or under a continuing strict settlement, since it can be used to prevent a registered disposition unless any proceeds of sale are paid over to least two trustees or a trust corporation, thus effecting overreaching. Although a restriction provides one of the strongest forms of protection of minor interests it will only be available with the co-operation of the registered proprietor, or at the instance of the Registrar, because by section 64(1)(c) of the Land

[5] [1981] A.C. 513.
[6] *ibid.* at 528.
[7] Land Registration Act 1925, s.58.
[8] Land Registration Rules 1925, r.6.

Registration Act 1925 a restriction can only be entered on the register if the proprietor's land certificate is also submitted to the Registrar by the applicant for alteration. In the event that the registered estate is already subject to a mortgage the land certificate will already be lodged with the Land Registry.[9] A restriction will be entered at the instance of the Registrar where land is subject to a strict settlement[10] or if a trust of land appears on the title.[11] By section 58(3) the Registrar is not under a duty to enter any restriction he deems "unreasonable or calculated to cause inconvenience."

(b) Protection by entry of a notice on the charges register

A second means by which a minor interest may be protected is by the entry of a notice on the charges register of the title to which it relates. Under Land Registration Act 1925, s.49 a notice is the appropriate means of protection for any interests which would constitute land charges under the Land Charges Act 1925, which includes such interests as estate contracts, annuities, equitable charges and equitable easements. By section 50 a notice can also be used a means of entering the benefit of a restrictive covenant against the title which is burdened. By section 49(1)(d) the rights of the beneficiaries of a trust of land or a continuing strict settlement to require two trustees can also be entered as a notice. Entry of a minor interest by a notice on the register has no validating effect, so that the interest protected will only bind the proprietor if it was valid in itself.[12] Where a notice has been entered on the register Land Registration Act 1925, s.25(1) provides that:

> "A disposition by the proprietor shall take effect subject to all the estates, rights and claims which are protected by way of notice on the register at the date of the registration or entry of notice of the disposition, but only if and so far as such estates, rights and claims may be valid and are not (independently of this Act) overridden by the disposition."

This means that a minor interest protected by a notice will be binding on a person subsequently acquiring the land or any interest in it, except if the interest protected is otherwise overreached by the transaction, as would be the case if it were a trust interest and there was a conveyance of a legal estate or legal mortgage. In the majority of cases a notice can only be entered with the consent of the registered proprietor since the land certificate must be lodged with the registrar.[13] Notices are not merely used to protect minor interests but are also used to note the existence of a lease for more than 21 years, which would require a separate title, on the title of the estate from which it is derived.[14]

(c) Protection by entry of a caution against dealings in the proprietorship register

It has been seen how a restriction or notice can only be entered on the register if the proprietor's land certificate is made available, which will generally mean that his co-

[9] Land Registration Act 1925, s.65.
[10] Land Registration Rules 1925, rr.56–58.
[11] Land Registration Rules 1925, r.213.
[12] *Kitney v. MEPC Ltd* [1977] 1 W.L.R. 981; (1977) 41 Conv. 356; [1978] C.L.J. 13.
[13] Land Registration Act 1925, s.64(1)(c).
[14] Land Registration Act 1925, s.48.

operation is required. Where such co-operation is refused, perhaps because the proprietor disputes the existence of the claimed interest, it is possible to enter a caution in the proprietorship register. This offers a form of inchoate protection of minor interests, since the entry of a caution does not itself subject the land to the interest claimed. Instead, it enables the cautioner who has entered it to substantiate the existence of his interest in the future if the proprietor proposes to deal with the land in a manner which would otherwise affect its existence. Section 54(1) of the Land Registration Act 1925 provides that entry of a caution has the effect that: " . . . no dealing with such land or charge on the part of the proprietor is to be registered until notice has been served upon the cautioner." The serving of notice gives the cautioner an opportunity to object to the proposed transaction to the Registrar. He will adjudicate and can decide whether the caution should be removed, thus allowing the proposed transaction to go ahead. He also has the discretion to enter a notice or restriction in place of the caution, thus providing the cautioner's interest with substantive protection. The cautioner who is warned of an impending transaction has a period of 14 days in which to respond, and if he fails to do so his caution will "cease to have any effect"[15] and he is said to have been "warned-off" the register. Since the entry of a caution does not require the consent or co-operation of the registered proprietor, and will severely impede his ability to sell, it could be used maliciously by a person who wished to cause trouble for a proprietor. For this reason Land Registration Act 1925, s.56(3) provides that a person who lodges a caution without reasonable cause is liable to compensate any person sustaining damage as a result.

(d) Protection by entry of an inhibition on the proprietorship register

A final means by which a minor interests can be protected is by the entry of an inhibition on the proprietorship register of the land to which it relates. If entered it has the effect of preventing any dealings with the registered land. Section 57(1) enables the court or the registrar to enter an inhibition on the application of any person interested in the land. The section also provides that an inhibition may take a wide variety of forms since the registrar may: "make an entry inhibiting for a time, or until the occurrence of an event to be named in such order of entry, or generally until further order or entry, the restriction or entry of any dealing with any registered land or registered charge." An inhibition is not the most appropriate means of protecting a minor interest and is more commonly used where there is a possibility of fraudulent dealings with the title, for example if the land certificate has been stolen. If the holder of a minor interest seeks the entry of an inhibition the court or registrar may order a notice or restriction to be entered on the register in lieu of the inhibition.[16] An automatic inhibition is entered if a bankruptcy order has been made against the proprietor.[17]

PRIORITY BETWEEN MINOR INTERESTS

Where registered land is subject to two or more minor interests the questions arises as to which of them should enjoy priority. Although it might be thought that the first to

[15] Land Registration Act 1925, s.55(1).
[16] Land Registration Act, s.58(4).
[17] Land Registration Act 1925, s.61(3).

be created should always enjoy priority the operation of this simple rule is complicated by registration. For example if Nick owns a house and in January grants Owen an option to purchase for £100,000, which Owen does not protect until November, then in February grants Penelope an option to purchase for £90,000 which she protects immediately, which of the two options will have priority, the option registered first or the option created first? In *Re White Rose Cottage*[18] Lord Denning M.R. suggested that prima facie priority between minor interests should be governed by their respective dates of registration. However, in *Barclays Bank v. Taylor*[19] the Court of Appeal held that priority was determined by the date of creation. The registered proprietors of a house executed a legal mortgage in August 1962 to secure the indebtedness of a company. The bank did not register its charge against the title. Subsequently, in February 1968, they entered an estate contract to sell the land to the defendants, which they protected by means of a caution in August. The Bank then called in the company overdraft and sought to register their legal charge. Since the defendants had entered a caution on the register they were given notice of this intention to register, and objected. At first instance Goulding J. ordered that the charge should be registered, but subject to the defendant's contract. The Court of Appeal held that the charge should take priority over the protected estate contract:

> "In truth the bank in respect of its interest, albeit taking effect as a minor interest only in equity, did not need any protection against the subsequent equitable interest of the Taylors: it only needed protection against a registration of the Taylors as proprietors . . . or against a subsequent mortgagee whose charge was registered . . . Consequently, in our view . . . the Taylors' caution did not and could not confer on their equitable entitlement or interest any priority over the bank's equitable charge . . . [T]he ordinary rules of priority between persons equitably interested in land must apply."[20]

This approach, which affords priority between competing equitable minor interests on the basis of first creation rather than first registration, was affirmed by the Court of Appeal in *Mortgage Corporation Ltd v. Nationwide Credit Corporation Ltd.*[21] The registered proprietors granted a legal mortgage to the plaintiff's on July 10, 1994, which was not protected on the register, and a further mortgage to the defendants on July 31, which was protected by the entry of a notice on the register on August 14. The house was sold by the plaintiff's and the issue was as to which charge enjoyed priority, because the proceeds of sale of the land were insufficient to repay both mortgagees in full, and therefore the one enjoying priority would be repaid in full and the other would have to bear the full extent of the shortfall. Dillon L.J. held that the plaintiff's mortgage must take priority, because without registration a charge only took effect in equity. Since the defendant's charge also only took effect in equity the first in time took priority.[22] However, he pointed out that if the plaintiffs had registered their

[18] [1965] Ch. 940.
[19] [1974] Ch. 137. (1972) 36 Conv. 272; (1972) 88 L.Q.R. 476; (1973) 37 Conv. 203; (1973) 89 L.Q.R. 170.
[20] *ibid.* at 147.
[21] [1994] Ch. 49; [1993] Conv. 224.
[22] Citing: *Cory v. Eyre* (1863) 1 De G. J. & S. 149; *Barclays Bank v. Taylor* [1974] Ch. 137.

charge as a legal mortgage they would then have taken their interest subject to the defendant's equitable charge which had been protected on the register.[23] It is therefore somewhat ironic that the plaintiffs were in a better position never having created a legal mortgage.

STATUTORY PRIORITY OVER UNPROTECTED MINOR INTERESTS

1 Failure to protect a minor interest does not automatically mean that priority is lost

Although the system of land registration provides the opportunity for those persons who enjoy minor interests in land to protect them against the title to which they relate, a failure to protect does not mean that the minor interest is automatically void. As against the registered proprietor who granted a minor interest there is no question that his estate is subject to it. The central question is whether the minor interest is binding upon a person who subsequently acquires either an estate in the land or another minor interest. The structure of the act is such that only certain classes of persons who acquire interests in land will take free from an unprotected minor interest.

2 Statutory priority granted

(a) Statutory priority in the context of registered freehold estates

Where freehold land is registered section 20(1) of the Land Registration Act 1925 provides that:

> "In the case of a freehold estate registered with an absolute title, a disposition of the registered land or of a legal estate therein, including a lease thereof, for valuable consideration, shall, when registered, confer on the transferee or grantee an estate in fee simple or the term of years absolute or other legal estate expressed to be created in the land dealt with, together with all rights, privileges, and appurtenances belonging or appurtenant thereto, including (subject to any entry to the contrary in the register) the appropriate rights and interests which would, under the Law of Property Act 1925, have been transferred if the land had not been registered, subject:
>
> (a) *to the incumbrances and other entries, if any, appearing on the register* [and any charge for capital transfer tax subject to which the disposition takes effect under section 73 of this Act]; and
>
> (b) unless the contrary is expressed on the register, *to the overriding interests*, if any affecting the estate transferred or created,
>
> *but free from all other estates and interests whatever*, including estates and interests of His Majesty, and the disposition shall operate in like manner as if the

[23] This is the effect of Land Registration Act 1925, ss.27 and 49.

registered transferor or grantor were (subject to any entry in the register) entitled to the registered land in fee simple in possession for his own benefit.

Despite the relative complexity of the drafting of this provision, its effect is straightforward. A person meeting the statutory requirements takes his interest in the land subject only to such minor interests as have been protected on the register and any overriding interests. By exclusion he takes free from all other interests and therefore gains priority over any unprotected minor interests.

(b) Statutory priority in the context of registered leasehold estates

An almost identical provision operates in the context of the assignment or sub-lease of a registered leasehold estate. Section 23(1) provides that the transferee or underlessee only takes his interest in the land subject to properly protected minor interests and overriding interests, but also adds in section 23(1)(a) that he takes subject "to all implied and express covenants, obligations, and liabilities incident to the estate or interest transferred or created." This simply means that he is bound by the covenants of the lease which has been assigned. Again the net effect is that a person who meets the statutory criteria takes his interest free from any unprotected minor interests.

3 Essential pre-requisites for statutory priority

Whether the land concerned was freehold or leasehold statutory priority will only be granted in favour of a person who meets the two essential criteria.

(a) Registered disposition of the land or a legal estate therein

The protection afforded under sections 20(1) and 23(1) is only granted to a person who takes a registered disposition of the land or a legal estate therein. The technical nature of this terminology should not be allowed to cloud its simple meaning that statutory priority only operates in favour of a person who acquires a legal estate in the land, in other words the freehold, a legal lease or a charge by way of legal mortgage over the registered estate.[24] Thus a person who acquires a trust interest in land, or an equitable lease or equitable mortgage, cannot gain priority over any unprotected minor interests which are held by third parties.

(b) Payment of valuable consideration

The second essential requirement is that the legal estate or charge must have been acquired for valuable consideration. For the purposes of the Land Registration Act 1925 "valuable consideration" is defined by section 3(xxxi):

> " 'Valuable consideration' includes marriage, but does not include a nominal consideration in money."

This makes clear that statutory priority cannot be afforded to a person who acquires legal title to the land by succession, gift or adverse possession. It also seems clear that

[24] This is because, Land Registration Act 1925, s.3(xxii) defines a "registered disposition" as a disposition by way of "transfer, charge, lease or otherwise."

there is no need to provide "adequate consideration" in return for the acquisition of a legal estate or charge, in the sense that statutory priority will be granted even to a person who takes their interest at a gross undervalue. In the context of parallel provisions for the registration of land charges in unregistered land the House of Lords held in *Midland Bank Trust Co. v. Green*[25] that valuable consideration had been provided where a defendant purchased for £500 the freehold of land worth some £40,000. Lord Wilberforce stressed that "nominal consideration" was not synonymous with "inadequate" or even "grossly inadequate" consideration.[26] The provision of purely nominal consideration will clearly not result in statutory priority. In *Peffer v. Rigg*[27] a husband, who was the sole registered proprietor of a house in which the plaintiff enjoyed an equitable trust interest which had not been protected on the register, sold it to his wife for £1. It was held that she took the land subject to the plaintiff's unprotected minor interest as she had only provided nominal consideration and was not therefore entitled to the protection of section 20(1) of the Land Registration Act 1925.[28] However, it was also argued that the transfer had been effected as part of a divorce settlement between the wife and her husband and that therefore the consideration was in fact more than merely the £1. Goulding J. considered that it was not appropriate for him to treat the consideration as anything other than what the parties had stated in the transfer agreement itself, but he implicitly accepted the possibility that if the transfer could genuinely have been shown to comprise part of a wider arrangement between the parties then the consideration would not have been nominal. It is extremely hard to indicate what sum of money would be regarded by the court as nominal. In *Midland Bank Trust Co. v Green*[29] Lord Wilberforce considered that £500 was not nominal. It is impossible to say whether the payment of £250, or £100, or £50 or £10 or £5 would have been regarded as nominal. In most cases such a problem will simply not arise, and even if the entire purpose of a transaction was to defeat an unprotected minor interest well advised parties would be likely to pay something more than a derisory sum, albeit that it might appear paltry in comparison to the value of the interest acquired.

4 Notice is irrelevant where statutory priority is available

(a) *Irrelevance of notice stated by Land Registration Act 1925, s.59(6)*

The Land Registration Act 1925 seems to make absolutely clear that the issue of notice is entirely irrelevant to the question whether a person meeting the statutory criteria of sections 20(1) and 23(1) gains priority over unprotected minor interests. Where a person is entitled to statutory priority they should take the land free from even those unprotected minor interests of which they have actual notice. This is confirmed by section 59(6) which provides:[30]

[25] [1981] A.C. 513.
[26] *ibid.* at 532.
[27] [1977] 1 W.L.R. 285.
[28] It should be noted that the interest was not overreached because there was no conveyance of the land by two trustees, and no overriding interest because the plaintiff was not in actual occupation.
[29] [1981] A.C. 513.
[30] See also, Land Registration Act 1925, s.74.

"Subject to the provisions of this Act relating to fraud and to the title of a trustee in bankruptcy, a purchaser acquiring title under a registered disposition, shall not be concerned with any pending action, writ, order, deed of arrangement, or other document, matter, or claim (not being an overriding interest [or a charge for capital transfer tax subject to which the disposition takes effect under section 73 of this Act]) which is *not protected* by a caution or other entry on the register, *whether he has or has not notice thereof*, express, implied or constructive."

(b) Notice re-introduced by creative judicial interpretation

Despite the clear wording of the Land Registration Act 1925 that notice has been rendered irrelevant as a means of determining questions of priority as between competing rights and interests, in *Peffer v. Rigg*[31] Graham J. propounded an interpretation of the relevant statutory provisions of the Land Registration Act 1925 in such a manner that the doctrine of notice would be re-introduced. The facts were alluded to above. A house was purchased with money provided by Mr Peffer and Mr Rigg in the sole name of Mr Peffer, who was the registered proprietor. Mr Rigg therefore enjoyed a half-share of the equitable ownership by way of a resulting trust. His beneficial interest was clearly a minor interest, but he took no steps to protect it on the register. Following a marital breakdown Mr Peffer transferred the title to his wife for £1. She was fully aware of the existence of Mr Rigg's trust interest at the time that the transaction took place. As has been seen, Graham J. held that she was not entitled to statutory priority under section 20(1) because she had not provided valuable consideration. However, he went on to consider what the position would have been if he had been wrong to conclude that the transfer had not been part of a wider divorce settlement, and thus that valuable consideration had been provided. He considered the argument that Land Registration Act 1925, s.20(1) granted statutory priority to any person meeting its criteria irrespective of whether they were acting in good faith or not, and concluded that such an interpretation was unacceptable:

"This at first sight seems a remarkable proposition and though undoubtedly the property legislation of 1925 was intended to simplify such matters of title as far as possible, I find it difficult to think that section 20 of this Act can have been intended to be as broad in scope as this . . ."[32]

He noted that in section 59(6) the expression "purchaser" was used in contrast to the term "transferee or grantee" in section 20(1), and that in section 3(xxi) a purchaser is defined as a "purchaser in good faith for valuable consideration." He therefore concluded that statutory priority conferred under section 20 should also be subject to a requirement of good faith on the part of the transferee or grantee providing valuable consideration:

"It seems clear to me therefore that as a matter of construction a purchaser who is not in fact one in "good faith" *will* be concerned with matters not protected by a caution or other entry on the register, at any rate, as I hold, if he has notice

[31] [1977] 1 W.L.R. 285.
[32] *ibid.* at 293.

> thereof. If these sections 20 and 59 are read together in the context of the Act they can be reconciled by holding that if the "transferee" spoken of in section 20 is in fact a "purchaser" he will only be protected if he has given valuable consideration and is in good faith. He cannot in my judgement be in good faith if he has in fact notice of something which affects his title as in the present case. Of course if he and, a fortiori, if a purchaser from him has given valuable consideration and in fact has no notice he is under no obligation to go behind the register, and will in such a case be fully protected."[33]

If this analysis is accepted as correct the effect is a dramatic re-introduction of the doctrine of notice into the registered land system, since it means that a purchaser of a legal estate in registered land will only take free of unprotected minor interests of which he did not have notice. Although Mrs Peffer had actual notice of Mr Rigg's trust interest it is unclear that Graham J. confined his re-introduction to actual notice, or whether a purchaser with constructive notice would also be regarded as not acting "in good faith".

(c) Rejection of the proposed re-introduction of notice

(i) General criticism — the decision is inconsistent with the policy objectives of the land registration system: The approach advocated in *Peffer v. Rigg* would amount to renunciation of the recognised policy of the system of land registration of ensuring that the register operates as a mirror of all the interests affecting the land, so that a purchaser need not be concerned with any interests which have not been properly protected. Graham J. did not consider the many clear statements of the courts that the whole object of registration is to render notice irrelevant, as for example in *Strand Securities v. Casewell*[34] where Cross J stated that it is "vital to the working of the land registration system that notice of something which is not on the register of the title in question shall not affect a transferee unless it is an overriding interest."[35] Although there may be some emotional reasons for regarding as unsatisfactory the operation of statutory priority so as to defeat unprotected interests of which a transferee or grantee was aware, on the grounds that it represents the triumph of a mechanical system over the principle of conscience inculcated within the doctrine of notice, land registration has shifted the burden of responsibility from a purchaser protecting himself by adequate inquiries to investigate the existence of third party rights to the holders of such rights having to take active steps to protect their interests. Given that the rights of actual occupiers are automatically protected as overriding interests,[36] it is not unjust that those persons enjoying minor interests are required to protect themselves and in most cases where such an interest is created or acquired the assistance of a legal professional will be sought who should advise on the need to register. Mr Rigg knew perfectly well of the existence of his minor interest and should have taken legal advice when the house was acquired as to how to protect his interest. It was either a consequence of his adviser's negligence that his interest was not protected, in which

[33] *ibid.* at 294.
[34] [1965] Ch. 373.
[35] *ibid.* at 390. See also: *Hodges v. Jones* [1935] 1 Ch. 657; *Parkash v. Irani Finance Ltd* [1970] Ch. 101; *De Lusigan v. Johnson* (1973) 230 E.G. 499; [1985] C.L.J. 280 (Thompson).
[36] Land Registration Act 1925, s.70(1)(g).

case he would have been able to recover damages for negligence if he subsequently lost priority, or his own choice not to protect and to rely instead on the honesty and integrity of Mr Peffer for protection, in which case he should bear the consequences of his stupidity.

(ii) Specific criticism — the statutory interpretation employed was flawed: [37] Irrespective of the inconsistency of the result with general policy, the interpretation of the relevant sections of the statute employed by Graham J. cannot be correct. First, there is no reason why the position of a "transferee or grantee" in section 20(1) should be equated with a "purchaser" in section 59(6) and therefore that the definition of a purchaser requiring good faith should be incorporated into it. In *Midland Bank Trust Co. v. Green*,[38] a case concerning the interpretation of the Land Charges Act 1925, the House of Lords held that the omission of a requirement of "good faith" from a particular section of the act was deliberate, and that to incorporate it by constructive interpretation would violate the cannons of interpretation. The importation of good faith into section 20(1) is equally unjustified. Secondly, even if good faith were to be incorporated into section 20(1) there is no reason why it should be equated with the presence of "notice". Section 59(6) itself incorporates "good faith" as the term "purchaser" is used, but it states that notice, whether express, implied or constructive, is irrelevant. This seems to make clear that the presence of notice, even actual notice, is not synonymous with "good faith," so that a purchaser with actual notice can still enjoy the protection of section 59(6).

(iii) Status of the decision: The length of discussion devoted to *Peffer v. Rigg* is justified rather by the importance of the principle that the doctrine of notice should not be revived within the land registration system rather than by the intrinsic importance of the decision itself. The interpretation of section 20(1) propounded by Graham J. can be dismissed briefly as mere *obiter dicta* and it should not be forgotten that Mrs Peffer was in fact held bound by Mr Rigg's trust interest because she had not provided valuable consideration, depriving her of any entitlement to statutory priority. Moreover, Graham J.'s view is inconsistent with two subsequent House of Lords decisions which are amongst the most fundamental and significant in the field of land law. First, in *Midland Bank Trust Co. v Green*[39] it was held that a purchaser of the freehold of land should take free from an unprotected land charge even though she was fully aware of its existence and that the whole purpose of the transaction was to defeat it. Lord Wilberforce concluded that it was not fraud for a person to rely on legal rights conferred by an Act of Parliament.[40] If there is a right to rely on statutory priority to defeat an unprotected land charge there is no reason why the same right should not be afforded to a person acquiring land where there was an unprotected minor interest. This equivalence between unprotected land charges and unprotected minor interests was recognised by Robert Wright Q.C. in *Du Boulay v. Raggett*[41] when he concluded that there was "no material difference . . . between section 20 of the Land Registration Act 1925 and section 13 Land Charges Act 1925," which section had

[37] See: [1977] C.L.J. 227 (Hayton); (1977) 40 M.L.R. 602 (Anderson); (1977) 93 LQR 341 (Smith); (1977) 41 Conv. 207 (Crane).

[38] [1981] A.C. 513.

[39] *ibid.*.

[40] *ibid.* at 531, citing *Re Monolithic Building Co.* [1915] 2 Ch. 643.

[41] (1989) 58 P. & C.R. 138 at 154.

been at issue in *Midland Bank Trust Co. v. Green*[42] Secondly, in *Williams & Glyn's Bank Ltd v. Boland*[43] Lord Wilberforce categorically re-stated that the system of registered land was intended to eliminate the doctrine of notice from registered land:

> "Above all, the [Land Registration Act 1925] system is designed to free the purchaser from the hazards of notice — real or constructive — which, in the case of unregistered land, involved him in enquiries, often quite elaborate, failing which he might be bound by equities."[44]

In the light of such clear statements it is inconceivable that the *dicta* of Graham J. will ever be followed as good authority.

CIRCUMSTANCES IN WHICH AN UNPROTECTED MINOR INTEREST MAY BIND A PERSON ENTITLED TO STATUTORY PRIORITY

1 Introduction

Despite the general principle which has been examined that a person entitled to statutory priority under sections 20(1) and 23(1) of the Land Registration Act 1925 will not acquire his estate or interest subject to unprotected minor interests, there are a number of limited exceptions where statutory priority will not provide protection and the land will be taken subject to such an interest. This will only occur if the Land Registration Act 1925 also accords the unprotected minor interest status as an overriding interest, in which case it will be binding by virtue of its status as such; if there is an independent constructive trust arising outside of the Land Registration system; or if the transferee or grantee otherwise entitled to statutory priority has committed a recognised fraud.

2 Unprotected minor interest binding as an overriding interest

It has already been noted above that in *Williams & Glynn's Bank Ltd v. Boland*[45] the House of Lords reached the tremendously significant conclusion that a minor interest accompanied by the presence of actual occupation will enjoy status as an overriding interest under Land Registration Act 1925, s.70(1)(g). Since section 20(1)(b) provides that a transferee or grantee of an estate or registered disposition of land takes his interest subject to "the overriding interests, if any, affecting the estate transferred or created" the unprotected minor interests of persons in actual occupation[46] of land will still be binding even if they have not been protected on the register. In *Williams & Glynn's Bank Ltd v. Boland* a wife was entitled to a share of the equitable ownership of

[42] *ibid.*
[43] [1981] A.C. 487.
[44] *ibid.* at 503.
[45] [1981] A.C. 487.
[46] Or in the receipt of rent and profits form the land.

her matrimonial home by reason of a resulting trust deriving from her contribution to the purchase price. This trust interest was a minor interest capable of protection, but the wife had taken no steps to protect it by an entry on the register. Her husband granted a legal mortgage to the Bank. As he was the sole registered proprietor and the mortgage money was advanced to him alone the trust interests were not overreached. The House of Lords held that although the Bank qualified for statutory priority over unprotected minor interests under section 20(1) her trust interest had been converted into an overriding interest by her actual occupation of the house, and as such enjoyed priority over their mortgage. This result can be contrasted with *Peffer v. Rigg*[47] where Mr Rigg was neither in occupation of the house, nor in receipt of rent and profits, so that his interests were incapable of enjoying overriding status. The operation of overriding interests will be examined in detail in the next chapter, but at this stage it should be obvious that they represent a major inroad into the principle that only those interests protected on the register are binding on a transferee of the land.

3 Unprotected minor interest binding by means of an independent constructive trust

(a) *The possibility of an independent constructive trust*[48]

Although in most circumstances an unprotected minor interest which has not been protected on the register will not be binding upon a person entitled to statutory priority unless it is also an overriding interest, it seems to have been recognised that in very limited circumstances a constructive trust of such an unprotected interest can arise wholly outside of the registered land system and legislation so that it is binding upon a transferee or grantee acquiring title to the land. The possibility of such a trust was raised by Graham J. in *Peffer v. Rigg*[49] where he suggested that Mrs Peffer might be bound by Mr Riggs equitable trust interest even if his analysis of the requirement of good faith under section 20(1) was incorrect. He stated:

> "On the evidence in this case I have found that [Mrs Peffer] knew quite well that [Mr Peffer] held the property on trust for himself and [Mr Rigg] in equal shares. [Mrs Peffer] knew this was so and that the property was trust property when the transfer was made to her, and therefore she took the property on a constructive trust in accordance with general equitable principles . . . This is a new trust imposed by equity and is distinct from the trust which bound [Mr Peffer]. Even if, therefore, I am wrong as to the proper construction of sections 20 and 59, when read together, and even if section 20 strikes off the shackles of the express trust which bound [Mr Peffer], this cannot invalidate the new trust imposed on [Mrs Peffer]."[50]

This somewhat novel approach that an express trust defeated by the appropriate rules of priority is replaced by a distinct constructive trust seems inconsistent with the

[47] [1977] 1 W.L.R. 285.
[48] [1983] C.L.J. 54 (Harpum); [1983] Conv. 64 (Jackson); (1983) 46 M.L.R. 96; (1984) 47 M.L.R. 476 (Bennett).
[49] [1977] 1 W.L.R. 285.
[50] *ibid.* at 294.

traditional rule that acquisition of the legal title by a bona fide purchaser for value without notice has the effect of permanently extinguishing pre-existing equitable interests.[51] It has, however, been approved and applied in subsequent cases. In *Lyus v. Prowsa Developments*[52] Mr and Mrs Lyus had entered into a contract with a building company for the purchase of a plot of land on which they were intending to build a house. They therefore enjoyed a minor interest, namely an estate contract, against the building company who were the registered proprietor of the land. The company had previously mortgaged the land to a bank, which enjoyed a registered charge over it. The building company went into liquidation before construction had started and the land was sold by the mortgagee bank to a further building company. Although Mr and Mrs Lyus had protected their interest by means of a caution the Bank would have been able to sell the land free from their estate contract because of their prior registered charge, thus leaving them with only a personal right to prove for damages for breach of contract in the company's liquidation. However, the contract under which the bank sold the land to the second building company contained a clause that it was sold "subject to" Mr and Mrs Lyus' estate contract. Dillon J. held that in these circumstances the building company had acquired the land subject to the Lyus' estate contract by way of a constructive trust and were not entitled to rely on the provisions of the Land Registration Act 1925 granting them statutory priority.[53] He stated his reasoning as follows:

> "It seems to me that the fraud on the part of the defendants in the present case lies not just in relying on the legal rights conferred by an act of Parliament, but in the [purchaser] reneging on a positive stipulation in favour of [Mr and Mrs Lyus]. In the bargain under which [they] acquired the land. That seems to me to make all the difference. It has long since been held, for instance in *Rochefoucauld v. Boustead* [1897] 1 Ch. 196 that the provisions of the Statute of Frauds 1677 cannot be used as an instrument of fraud, now incorporated in certain sections of the Law of Property Act 1925, and that it is fraud for a person to whom the land is agreed to be conveyed as trustee for another to deny the trust and relying on the terms of the statute to claim the land for himself . . . it seems to me that the same considerations are applicable in relation to the Land Registration Act 1925."[54]

The potential for a constructive trust arising independently so as to bind the purchaser of land with an interest from which they would otherwise have taken free was also recognised by the Court of Appeal in *Ashburn Anstalt v. Arnold*[55] in the context of contractual licences. Fox L.J. stated that the rationale for the imposition of such a trust was that "the conscience of the estate owner is affected"[56] and warned that such trusts should not be easily established:

[51] *Wilkes v. Spooner* [1911] 2 K.B. 473.
[52] [1982] 1 W.L.R. 1044.
[53] See ss.20 and 34.
[54] [1982] 1 W.L.R. 1044 at 1054–1055.
[55] [1989] Ch. 1.
[56] *ibid.* at 25.

"In matters relating to title to land, certainty is of prime importance. We do not think it desirable that constructive trusts of land should be imposed in reliance on inferences from slender materials."[57]

(b) Essential requirements for the imposition of an independent constructive trust

Although the possibility of an independent constructive trust of an unprotected minor interest has been accepted it is likely that it will only be established if stringent criteria are satisfied.

(i) Independent constructive trust will not arise merely because the transferee had actual notice of the existence of an unprotected interest: It seems clear that the mere fact that a transferee of land had actual notice of the existence of an unprotected minor interest will not give rise to a constructive trust. It was implicit in *Lyus v. Prowsa Developments*[58] that the building company would not have been affected by Mr and Mrs Lyus' estate contract if they had merely purchased the land from the Bank knowing of its existence. In such circumstances they would have been entitled to rely on the statutory priority afforded by the Land Registration Act 1925 to take their title free from it.

(ii) Independent constructive trust will not arise merely because the transferee had agreed to take the land subject to interests affecting it in general: Crucial to the finding of an independent constructive trust in *Lyus v. Prowsa Developments* was that the building company had expressly agreed to take title to the land "subject to" the estate contract. Contracts of sale often contain a term that the purchaser agrees to take subject to all rights affecting the land. It seems that such general agreements are not sufficient to give rise to a constructive trust. The trust arises only because the conscience of the purchaser is affected, and this will only be so if there was an agreement to take subject to the specific interest concerned.

(iii) An independent constructive trust will not arise unless there was detrimental reliance by the transferor in consequence of the transferee's agreement to take title subject to a specific interest: In *Ashburn Anstalt v. Arnold*[59] the Court of Appeal emphasised that the mere fact that a transferee of the title of land had agreed to take it subject to a specific interest from which he would otherwise take free was not alone sufficient to give rise to a constructive trust, since it was not inevitable that the conscience of the transferee would have been affected. There may be other reasons for the inclusion of such stipulations, for example the duty of the vendor to disclose all possible incumbrances known to him. As Fox L.J. stated:

"The mere fact that land is expressly to be conveyed "subject" to a contract does not necessarily imply that the grantee is to be under an obligation, not otherwise existing, to give effect to the provisions of the contract. The fact that the conveyance is expressed to be subject to the contract may often . . . be at least as consistent with an intention merely to protect the grantor against claims by the grantee as an intention to impose an obligation on the grantee. The words

[57] *ibid.* at 26.
[58] [1982] 1 W.L.R. 1044.
[59] [1989] Ch. 1.

> "subject to" will, of course, impose notice. But notice is not enough to impose on somebody an obligation to give effect to a contract into which he did not enter. Thus, mere notice of a restrictive covenant is not enough to impose upon the estate owner and obligation to give effect to it: *London County Council v. Allen*[60]."[61]

The Court of Appeal held that a constructive trust would only arise where there was some detrimental reliance by the transferor selling the land, and a corresponding advantage to the transferee, as a consequence of his agreeing to take the land subject to the interest. Where such detriment and advantage are present the conscience of the transferee is affected so that he cannot be allowed to take the advantage flowing from his agreement only to subsequently renege on it and assert that by statute the land is not encumbered by the interest he agreed to take "subject to". The most obvious form of such advantage is a reduction in the price he paid for the land in recognition that he had agreed to abide by the interest. In *Ashburn Anstalt v. Arnold* Fox L.J. stressed that there had been no finding of fact that the purchaser had "paid a lower price in consequence of the finding that the sale was subject" to a contractual licence, and therefore there was no constructive trust. Another example of such advantage would be if the vendor had sold the land to the purchaser ahead of a rival bidder, albeit at the same price, on the grounds that he had agreed to take subject to an interest.

(c) Circumstances in which there will be an independent constructive trust of an unprotected minor interest

Drawing the strands of the authorities together it seems that an unprotected minor interest which is not also an overriding interest will only bind a transferee or grantee of land otherwise entitled to statutory priority if the transferee specifically agreed to take the land subject to it, and gained some advantage as a result, which would render it inequitable or fraudulent to rely on their statutory priority.

4 Unprotected minor interest binding because of fraud

(a) Deliberate schemes to defeat unprotected interests: a residual concept of fraud?

The question arises whether there are any other circumstances in which the conduct of a transferee or grantee is fraudulent so as to disentitle him from the protection of statutory priority under sections 20(1) or 23(1) of the Land Registration Act 1925. Several older authorities suggest that a deliberate scheme to defeat the interests of a third party in the land will be regarded as fraud. For example, in *Waimiha Sawmill Co. Ltd v. Waione Timber Co. Ltd*[62] Lord Buckmaster stated: "If the designed object of a transfer be to cheat a man of a known existing right, that is fraudulent." In *Jones v. Lipman*[63] Benny Lipman agreed to sell a house to Mr and Mrs Jones for £5,250. He subsequently refused to perform his contract and, to avoid specific performance,

[60] [1914] 3 K.B. 642.
[61] [1989] Ch. 1 at 26.
[62] [1926] 101 at 106.
[63] [1962] 1 W.L.R. 832.

transferred title to the house into the name of a company, Alamed Ltd, who were registered as proprietors. Mr Lipman and his solicitor's clerk were the sole shareholders of the company. Russell J. held that in these circumstances the company should be bound by the contract to sell and he ordered specific performance. He emphasised that:

> "The defendant company is the creature of the first defendant, a device and a sham, a mask which he holds before his face in an attempt to avoid recognition by the eye of equity. The cases cited illustrate that an equitable remedy is rightly to be granted directly against the creature in such circumstances."[64]

However it is questionable whether a general principle that a scheme to deliberately defeat the unprotected interests of a third party can survive the decision of the House of Lords in *Midland Bank Trust Co. v Green.* In the Court of Appeal Lord Denning M.R. had held that the transaction in question was fraudulent because it was "executed deliberately to deprive"[65] a person enjoying an unprotected option to purchase land of his right. This was rejected by the House of Lord, where Lord Wilberforce stated that it was not fraud for a person to rely on legal rights to which they are entitled by statute, even though the circumstances suggested a transaction arranged with the prime object of defeating the unprotected estate contract. *Jones v. Lipman*[66] can be distinguished because the rationale for finding fraud vitiating the availability of statutory priority was the absence in reality of a genuine transfer of the land. Since the company could be regarded as an extension of Mr Lipman he had in substance transferred the legal title to himself. In *Midland Bank Trust Co. v. Green* there was a genuine transfer of the legal title to the land from husband to wife and it was impossible to prove that the sole motivation was to achieve the defeat of their son's interests. As Lord Wilberforce commented:

> "Any advantage to oneself seems necessarily to involve a disadvantage for another: to make the validity of the purchase depend upon which aspect of the transaction was prevalent in the purchaser's mind seems to create distinctions equally difficult to analyse in law as to establish in fact; avarice and malice may be distinct sins, but in human conduct they are liable to be intertwined. The problem becomes even more acute if one supposes a mixture of motives. Suppose — and this may not be far from the truth — that the purchaser's motives were in part to take the farm from Geoffrey, and in part to distribute it between Geoffrey and his brothers and sisters, but not at all to obtain any benefit for herself, is this acting in "good faith" or not? Should, family feeling be denied a protection afforded to simple greed?"[67]

It may be that if it had been established that the wife had been acting solely at the direction of her husband, so that she was in effect his nominee and held the legal title

[64] *ibid.* at 836–837.
[65] [1980] Ch. 590 at 625.
[66] [1962] 1 W.L.R. 832.
[67] [1981] A.C. 513 at 530.

she acquired on a bare trust for him, that this would have constituted sufficient fraud to negate the operation of statutory priority. It is therefore possible to accept a general principle that where it can be shown that a transaction was a sham, in that the transferee of the legal title was in reality the transferor, either by the device of a company or a bare trust, that there is a fraud which vitiates the operation of sections 20(1) and 23(1) of the Land Registration Act 1925.

(b) A person who acquires land in a fiduciary capacity is not entitled to rely on statutory priority

It also seems that a person who acquires the title to land will not be entitled to statutory priority so as to defeat the unprotected interests of a third party to whom they also owed a fiduciary duty. *Du Boulay v. Raggett*[68] concerned a plot of land which had been purchased at an auction by Mr Ragget, which he had subsequently transferred to his wife. Prior to the auction Mr and Mrs Raggett had agreed with the plaintiffs that they would bid for the land for themselves and also on the plaintiffs' behalf, so that the plaintiffs would not have to bid independently, and that they would then convey parts of the plot to the plaintiffs. After the land was purchased Mr Raggett refused to convey the agreed parts to the plaintiffs, alleging that he had only said that he would consider letting them the areas they were interested in. Mr Raggett then conveyed the plot to his wife, who claimed that she had taken her title free from the agreement to convey as it had not been protected as a minor interest and she was entitled to statutory priority under Land Registration Act 1925, s.20(1). However, Robert Wright Q.C. held that as a consequence of their dealings Mr and Mrs Raggett stood in a fiduciary relationship to the plaintiffs in respect of the purchase at auction, and that Mrs Raggett was not entitled to acquire the land free from their interests. He considered the argument from *Midland Bank Trust Co. v. Green* that Mrs Raggett was entitled to rely on her statutory rights but rejected it:

> "I recognise the force of that argument but I do not think that it avails Mrs Raggett for the reason that she acquired the title already impressed with a trust . . . The question, therefore, is whether Mrs Raggett, in the light of the facts . . . had imposed upon herself a fiduciary duty to hold any title she might obtain upon trust for herself and Mr Raggett and the plaintiffs. I think the answer is yes."[69]

Although this principle is clearly similar to the imposition of an independent constructive trust, the fraud arises because the transferee enjoys a particular status in relation to the third party who enjoys an unprotected interest in the land, not because they have entered a specific agreement with the transferor that they will take the land subject to it.

REFORM OF STATUTORY PRIORITY OVER UNPROTECTED MINOR INTERESTS

In 1987 and 1988 the Law Commission published two reports[70] examining the place of minor interests within the system of registration of title and recommended reform in a number of important areas.

[68] (1989) 58 P. & C.R. 138.
[69] *ibid.* at 154.
[70] Law Com No. 158; Law Com No. 173.

1 Introduction of a statutory requirement of good faith as a pre-requisite to the availability of statutory priority

The Law Commission examined the question highlighted in *Peffer v. Rigg*[71] as to whether statutory priority under sections 20(1) and 23(1) of the Land Registration Act 1925 should be subject to a requirement of "good faith" so that a transferee or grantee of a qualifying legal estate in the land for valuable consideration will not automatically enjoy statutory priority. The Commission noted that the justification for importing "good faith" into the present sections was slender,[72] and instead recommended that the statute should be amended so that transferees and other purchasers who wish to take free from unprotected minor interests must "take in good faith and for valuable consideration."[73] The Commission felt that although this would be inconsistent with the position in unregistered land following *Midland Bank Trust Co. v. Green,*[74] the consequences of not introducing a requirement of good faith were unacceptable, thus implicitly rejecting the approach taken in that case. The central difficulty of such a reform would be to determine precisely when a person had not acted in "good faith." The Commission pointed to the guidance of case-law[75] and recommended that it be expressly enacted that "a transferee or purchaser should not be deemed dishonest merely because he had actual knowledge of the unprotected minor interest in question."

2 Ability to enter a restriction on the register without the consent of the proprietor

As was noted above, of the four means by which a minor interest can be protected on the register of title to which it relates, namely restriction, notice, caution and inhibition, only a caution can be realistically utilised by a third party entitled to a minor interest without the co-operation of the registered proprietor as the land certificate need not be submitted to the registrar for alteration. The Law Commission proposed that restrictions should be utilised where the land is held on trust, and that they should be capable of entry against the proprietor's title without the consent.[76] As a consequence there would no longer be a need to protect trust interests by the less suitable means of a notice or caution. It was proposed that a notice should be entered, with the written consent of the proprietor, if the proprietor acknowledged the existence of the interest claimed, and a caution if the proprietor disputes the alleged interest.

3 Priority between minor interest to be governed by date of registration

The Commission also recommended that issues of priority between competing minor interests should be determined by their respective dates of registration rather than by

[71] [1977] 1 W.L.R. 285.
[72] Law Com. 158, para. 4.14.
[73] Law Com. 158, para. 4.15.
[74] [1981] A.C. 513.
[75] *Waring v. London and Manchester Assurance Co. Ltd* [1935] Ch. 310; *Dowger Duchess of Sutherland v. Duke of Sutherland* [1893] 3 Ch. 169; *Middlemas v. Stevens* [1901] 1 Ch. 574.
[76] Law Com 158, para. 4.38 (v)-(vii).

their dates of creation. This would reverse the effect of *Barclays Bank v. Taylor*[77] that the priority of equitable minor interests *inter se* is governed by the temporal sequence of their creation. In order to prevent unacceptable consequences it was recommended that time of creation should continue to govern priority between rights of occupation under the Matrimonial Homes Act 1983 and other equitable minor interests.

[77] [1974] Ch. 137.

Chapter 16

OVERRIDING INTERESTS

OVERRIDING INTERESTS WITHIN THE REGISTERED LAND SYSTEM

1 Overriding interests contrasted with minor interests

In the previous chapter it has been seen how the majority of subsidiary interests in land are characterised as minor interests. They can be protected against the title of the land to which they relate, and in the absence of such registration the prima facie consequence is that a person who acquires either a legal estate or legal charge in the land for valuable consideration will take his interest free from the unprotected minor interest. However, the very sections which entitle a transferee or grantee to statutory priority over minor interests also refer to a further category of interests. Section 20(1)(b) of the Land Registration Act 1925 provides that the transferee or grantee takes his interest not only subject to those minor interests which have been entered on the register but also: "unless the contrary is expressed on the register, to the overriding interests, if any, affecting the estate transferred or created." The essence of overriding interests is, therefore, that title to the land cannot be acquired in any circumstances free from them. Irrespective of whether or not they appear on the face of the Register, and irrespective of whether or not the transferee had notice of their existence, they will continue to bind the land and any estate or interest of a transferee or chargee will be subject to them. Overriding interests therefore represent the major exception to the principle that purchasers of a legal estate or charge over land need not concern themselves with any interests which cannot be discovered from the register alone. If they are prudent they will not be content merely to rely on the register but will have to make physical inspections of the land and inquiries of any persons in actual occupation in order to attempt to discover if there are any overriding interest which will adversely affect them. As has already been suggested, overriding interests are perhaps best regarded as the trump cards of the registered land system.

2 Defining overriding interests:

(a) Defined by Land Registration Act 1925, s.70(1)

Given their almost virtual indefeasibility it is obviously important that there be clarity as to which interests in land are capable of ranking as overriding interests. A statutory catalogue is provided in section 70(1) of the Land Registration Act 1925:

"All registered land shall, unless under the provisions of this Act the contrary is expressed on the register, be deemed to be subject to such of the following overriding interests as may be for the time being subsisting in reference thereto, and such interests shall not be treated as incumbrances within the meaning of this act, (that is to say):—

(a) Rights of common, drainage rights, customary rights (until extinguished), public rights, *profits à prendre*, rights of sheepwalk, rights of way, watercourses, rights of water, and other easements not being equitable easements required to be protected by notice on the register;
(b) Liability to repair highways by reason of tenure, quit-rents, crown rents, heriots and other rents and charges (until extinguished) having their origin in tenure;
(c) Liability to repair the chancel of any church;
(d) Liability in respect of embankments, and sea and river walls;
(e) . . ., payments in lieu of tithe, and charges annuities payable for the redemption of tithe rentcharges;
(f) Subject to the provisions of this Act, rights acquired or in course of being acquired under the Limitation Acts;
(g) The rights of every person in actual occupation of the land or in receipt of the rent and profits thereof, save where enquiry is made of such person and the rights are not disclosed;
(h) in the case of a possessory, qualified, or good leasehold title, all estates, rights, interests, and powers excepted from the effect of registration;
(i) Rights under local land charges unless and until protected on the register in the proscribed manner;
(j) Rights of fishing and sporting, seignorial and manorial rights of all descriptions (until extinguished), and franchises;
(k) Leases granted for a term not exceeding twenty-one years;
(l) In respect of land registered before the commencement of this Act, rights to mines and minerals, and rights of entry, search, and user, and other rights and reservations incidental to or required for the purpose of giving full effect to the enjoyment of rights to mines and minerals or of property in mines and minerals, being rights which, where the title was first registered before the first date of January, eighteen hundred and ninety-eight, were created before that date, and where the title was first registered after the thirty-first day of December eighteen hundred and ninety-seven, were created before the date of first registration."

(b) Two conceptually distinct categories of overriding interests

(i) Specific interests enjoying overriding status: It is plain from the content of section 70(1) of the Land Registration Act 1925 that the majority of the paragraphs stipulate that specific interests enjoy overriding status. For example, paragraph (k) accords short leases overriding status and paragraph (f) rights acquired by adverse possession. Many of the other paragraphs stipulate that rights which burden the land in a manner similar to an easement, so that the land is a form of servient tenement and third parties enjoy rights to extract a payment or the performance of an obligation from the owner, are overriding interests. For example, in older villages it is relatively common for the most important properties to be subject to an obligation to repair the main part of the local parish church, an obligation which in the event of severe damage could be extremely onerous.[1] These rights are generally either of great civic importance, such as the obligation to upkeep sea walls, or those which it cannot be expected that the holder will protect, such as rights in the process of being acquired by adverse possession.

(ii) General interests capable of enjoying overriding status if the relevant statutory criteria are satisfied: It is not, however, the specifically identified overriding interests which have caused major inroads into the system of registered land. The most significant of the overriding interests in practice, and the cause of much litigation, has been section 70(1)(g) which has been held to have the effect of converting interests in land which would not otherwise fall within the scope of section 70(1) into overriding interest if the holder of the interest is in actual occupation of the land. As was noted in the previous chapter this means that a minor interest which has not been protected appropriately may yet be binding on a transferee or chargee otherwise entitled to statutory priority as an overriding interest. This principle of the conversion of minor interests into overriding interests was approved and accepted by the House of Lords in *Williams & Glynn's Bank Ltd v. Boland.*[2] The facts of that case are a very good illustration of the effects flowing from the recognition of such general overriding interests. Mr Boland was the sole registered proprietor of his matrimonial home, and he held it on trust for himself and his wife, who was entitled to a share of the equitable ownership by way of a resulting trust. He subsequently granted a mortgage of the house to a Bank, which entered its charge on the register. Mr Boland was unable to keep up the necessary mortgage payments and the Bank sought to re-posses and sell the property. Mrs Boland argued that her equitable interest under a trust for sale was binding on the Bank so that they were not entitled to possession. The House of Lords held that even though Mrs Boland's interest was a minor interest which had not been protected on the register of title, and that the Bank was otherwise entitled to statutory priority under section 20(1) of the Land Registration Act 1925, she was a person who was in "actual occupation" of the land and that her interest was binding under section 70(1)(g).

(iii) Did the statute intend to create general overriding interests under section 70(1)(g)?: Although judicial clarification has now made clear that any rights or interests in land are capable of enjoying status as overriding interests if they are coupled with the statutory magic ingredient of actual occupation it is far from clear that the draftsman intended the wide ranging impact that this has had on the system of land registration. Prior to the introduction of registration of title issues of priority were determined by the general doctrine of notice, so that a purchaser of a legal estate in land, or a legal mortgage, would only take subject to such equitable interests of which he had notice, actual or constructive. Under the doctrine of *Hunt v. Luck*[3] the purchaser of land was held to have constructive notice of the interests of a tenant who

[1] In reality such obligations are generally fulfilled by means of an insurance policy taken out by all the landowners in the area who are so affected.
[2] [1981] A.C. 487.
[3] [1901] 1 Ch. 45.

was in possession of the land, since he was expected to make inquiries of any person other than the vendor who was in occupation. Vaughan Williams L.J. explained that:

"If a purchaser or a mortgagee has notice that the vendor or mortgagor is not in possession of the property, he must make inquiries of the person in possession — of the tenant who is in possession — and find out from him what his rights are, and if, he does not choose to do that, then whatever title he acquires as purchaser or mortgagee will be subject to the title or right of the tenant in possession."[4]

If purchaser did make enquiries but the occupier failed to disclose the nature of his interests the purchaser would take free from them. It has been suggested on many occasions that section 70(1)(g) was enacted to preserve the doctrine of *Hunt v. Luck* into unregistered land, as for example by Lord Wilberforce in *Williams & Gylnn's Bank v. Boland*[5] and Lord Oliver in *Abbey National Building Society v. Cann.*[6] The language of the paragraph certainly bears remarkable similarities to it, for example the protection of the transferee or grantee if inquiries have been made and the interest has not been revealed. In *Strand Securities v. Casewell*[7] Lord Denning M.R. stated:

"It is up to every purchaser before he buys to make enquiry on the premises. If he fails to do so, it is at his own risk. He must take subject to whatever rights the occupier may have. Such is the doctrine of *Hunt v. Luck* for unregistered land. Section 70(1)(g) carries the same doctrine forward into registered land . . ."

However, he went on to recognise that section 70(1)(g) does more than merely introduce a principle identical to that in unregistered land, as it extends the doctrine to the rights of persons who are not in factual possession of the land but who are merely receiving rents and profits derived from it. In other words, not only will a tenant in possession gain protection for his rights, but the interests of his immediate landlord, to whom he is paying rent, will also be preserved. It also seems that section 70(1)(g) is not confined in scope to circumstances in which occupation would have constituted constructive notice in unregistered land. It operates mechanistically so that the criteria is essential factual, namely whether there was actual occupation or not, and not one of whether the conscience of the purchaser was affected by that occupation. However, most of the controversy associated with the operation of section 70(1)(g) has derived not from its existence *per se*, but from the massive expansion in circumstances in which it may be found that a person has gained a trust interest in land informally. As has been seen in Chapter 6, the doctrines of resulting and constructive trusts were drastically extended by the House of Lords in the early 1970's in *Gissing v. Gissing*[8] and *Pettitt v. Pettitt.*[9]

[4] *ibid.* at 433.
[5] [1981] A.C. 487, 504.
[6] [1991] 1 A.C. 56, 87.
[7] [1965] Ch. 958 at 979.
[8] [1971] A.C. 886.
[9] [1970] A.C. 777.

Since these decisions increased the likelihood that a wife or co-habitee would be entitled to a share of the equitable ownership of land registered in the sole name of their husband or partner it is unsurprising that some 10 years later the question arose whether such trust interests would be binding on subsequent purchasers, or more often mortgagees, of the title. Since such equitable ownership had arisen informally it was unsurprising that the beneficiaries had not protected their interests as minor interests as they were often unaware of their existence. Similarly, since title was usually in the name of a sole proprietor overreaching of the trust interest would not have occurred when he entered into any transactions. The context of such cases was therefore whether a professional mortgage company or Bank could enforce its security against the outwardly innocent beneficiary, who was entitled to a trust interest through her often enormous contribution to the financial purchase of the house or to the life of the family. The policy issue was whether the commercial interests of lenders, together with any knock-on consequences that a reluctance to lend would have on the property market as a whole, should prevail over the protection of the interests of the vulnerable wives and partners whose rights were only just being recognised by the law. In marked contrast with the tenor of the land registration system, which seems to favour the commercial interests of the conveyancer, the courts held that the trust interests of such persons as Mrs Boland would be binding on lenders as overriding interests. The balance of justice was felt to lie with the party who could not protect themselves rather than the commercial lender who was able to take steps to protect himself by making inquiries of any persons in factual occupation of the land to discover if they possessed adverse interests. Inevitably the major impact of these decisions was to force commercial lenders to adopt different business practices, and that they could no longer deal with a sole legal owner by examining the register of title alone. As Lord Wilberforce observed in *Williams & Glynn's Bank v. Boland*[10]:

> "What is involved is a departure from an easy-going practice of dispensing with the enquiries as to occupation beyond that of the vendor and accepting the risks of doing so. To substitute for this a practice of more careful enquiry as to the fact of occupation, and if necessary, as to the rights of occupiers, can not, in my view of the matter, be considered as unacceptable except at the price of overlooking the widespread development of shared interests of ownership."

(iv) Policy limits to the availability of section 70(1)(g) overriding interests: Although the initial balance of justice was felt to lie with persons claiming informal trusts interests in land rather than mortgage lenders, more recent judicial policy seems to have shifted in favour of protecting the security of such lenders. This probably reflects the more difficult economic climate of the 1990's, with problems of negative equity, and a sense that it may be too easy for co-habitiees to claim overriding interests only after they have fallen into financial difficulties as a way of preventing lenders from repossessing their properties. The courts seems to have taken a more overtly commercial approach and are not content to allow a couple to remain in occupation of their house, without any obligation to pay back the mortgage, because the borrower's spouse or partner claims an overriding interest. There have been various aspects of the

[10] [1981] A.C. 487 at 508–509.

requirements of section 70(1)(g) which have been interpreted more restrictively. In *Abbey National Building Society v. Cann*[11] the House of Lords emphasised that trivial acts could not constitute actual occupation, and that in the context of overriding interests claimed to arise on the purchase of a property the actual occupation must have existed at the date that the purchase was completed. An alternative approach has been to restrict the circumstances in which an occupier will be found to have enjoyed an interest in the land capable of becoming an overriding interest. *Lloyd's Bank v. Rossett*[12] can be understood in these terms, so that the House of Lords held it impossible to establish an implied common intention constructive trust in the absence of substantial financial contribution to prevent the unacceptable result that Mrs Rossett would have had an interest binding on the Bank which had made a mortgage advance to her husband. Similarly, in *City of London Building Society v. Flegg*[13] the House of Lords held that the trust interests of two actual occupiers had been overreached so that they enjoyed no rights in the land capable of forming the subject matter of an overriding interest. The courts have also developed indirect means of avoiding conceding priority to an occupier, for example by finding that a person otherwise entitled to claim an overriding interest had impliedly consented to a mortgage, thus depriving him of the right to assert a claim of priority, as in *Bristol & West Building Society v. Henning.*[14] With many more couples now owning their property jointly at law the judicial initiative has tended to shift from the exploitation of overriding interests to the doctrine of undue influence as a means of escaping the consequences of mortgages affecting the co-owned land.

SPECIFIC INTERESTS WHICH ENJOY OVERRIDING STATUS

As has already been noted, section 70(1) provides that a number of specific subsidiary interests in land enjoy overriding status. It is not the purpose of this section to examine them all in detail, but to focus on the most significant.

1 Easements

(a) Specifically identified rights

Section 70(1)(a) of the Land Registration Act 1925, which has been cited above, provides that a wide variety of rights which are analogous to easements constitute overriding interests, for example rights of sheepwalk. Profits à prendre also constitute overriding interests, whether they are legal or equitable in character.

(b) Legal easements

Section 70(1)(a) also makes a more general assertion that "other easements not being equitable easements required to be protected by registration on the register" are

[11] [1991] 1 A.C. 56.
[12] [1991] A.C. 107.
[13] [1988] A.C. 54.
[14] [1985] 1 W.L.R. 778.

overriding interests. The scope of this language clearly seems to include easements which are legal in character. This raises some difficulties because, as has been noted earlier,[15] other provisions of the Land Registration Act 1925 define the creation of an easement over registered land as a "registered disposition" which must be completed by registration on the title of the servient tenement.[16] One possible reconciliation of these seemingly inconsistent provisions is that section 70(1)(a) is only intended to protect legal easements created by operation of law, for example by prescription or Law of Property Act 1925, s.62, rather than express grants. However, the present position seems to be that all legal easements, however created, will rank as overriding interests thus rendering the requirement or registration otiose.

(c) Equitable easements

Greater difficulties have been occasioned by the question whether easements which are purely equitable in character enjoy overriding status. The language of section 70(1)(a) would seem to suggest that equitable easements are excluded from the pantheon of overriding interests since it seems to imply that equitable easements must be protected on the register as minor interests. The issue was raised in *Celsteel Ltd v. Alton House Holdings Ltd*[17] where Scott J. had cause to consider whether a purely equitable right of way providing access to a garage was binding on a subsequent lessee of the land when it had not been protected by registration. He interpreted the scope of section 70(1)(a) creatively through the mirror of rule 258 of the Land Registration Rules 1925 which provides that:

> "Rights, privileges and appurtenances appertaining or reputed to appertain to land or demised, occupied or enjoyed therewith or reputed or known as part and parcel of or appurtenant thereto, which adversely affect registered land, are overriding interests within section 70 of the Act . . ."

On the grounds that Land Registration Act 1925, s.144(2) provides that "any rules made pursuant of this section shall be of the same force as if enacted in this Act" he concluded that rule 258 was capable of rendering an equitable easement which was "at the relevant time openly exercised and enjoyed"[18] an overriding interest. The plaintiff's right of way was therefore binding on the defendant lessee.[19]

2 Rights acquired by adverse possession

By section 70(1)(f) the rights of any person who has acquired land by adverse possession rank as overriding interests. As has been seen above[20] this is important in registered land because the adverse possessor does not automatically receive good legal title on completion of the requisite period of possession as legal title only passes

[15] See Chap. 9.
[16] ss.19(2) and 22(2).
[17] [1985] 1 W.L.R. 204; see [1986] Conv. 31 (Thompson).
[18] *ibid.* at 221.
[19] The first instance decision was upheld by the Court of Appeal: [1986] 1 W.L.R. 512.
[20] See Chap. 4.

to him when he is registered as proprietor in consequence of such possession. In the meantime the registered proprietor holds the legal title on trust for the adverse possessor.[21] If the registered proprietor transfers the legal title section 70(1)(f) ensures that the rights of the adverse possessor will be binding on the transferee. The operation of these principles can seen in *Bridges v. Mees.*[22] The disputed land had been adversely possessed by the plaintiff for more than 12 years when it was sold to the defendant, who was registered as the proprietor. Harman J. held that the vendor of the land had become a trustee of it for the plaintiff, and that the plaintiff's rights were binding on the defendant as an overriding interest by section 70(1)(f). The rights of an adverse possessor who is in actual occupation of the land at the date of sale will also fall within the scope of section 70(1)(g) of the Land Registration Act 1925.

3 Short term leases

(a) Legal leases for less than 21 years

It has already been seen that leases for a term in excess of 21 years must be registered with their own independent title at the Land Registry. To prevent the unnecessary complications of registration leases for a shorter duration do not require to be so registered. By section 70(1)(k) "leases granted for a term not exceeding 21 years" rank as overriding interests. Although it has been seen that a specifically enforceable contract to grant a lease generates an equitable lease on the terms of the agreement, in *City Permanent Building Society v. Miller*[23] the Court of Appeal held that only legal leases were included within the scope of section 70(1)(k). Jenkins L.J. explained the rationale for this limitation:

> ". . . the use there of the word "granted" clearly imports the actual creation of a term of years, whether it is done by deed or by an arrangement under hand only, in that class of cases in which a legal term can be created by a document not under seal, or indeed by parol in any case in which an actual tenancy taking effect at law may be created without writing. But in my judgement the word "granted" necessarily imports the actual creation of a term, and that excludes, by force of the context, the case of a mere agreement for a lease, having no more than a contractual effect."[24]

(b) Equitable leases

Although an equitable lease created for a period of less than 21 years does not enjoy overriding status as of right under section 70(1)(k), it should not be forgotten that such a lease, or indeed an equitable lease for a longer duration, may acquire overriding status under section 70(1)(g) if the tenant is in actual occupation, or in the receipt of rent and profits from the land for example if there has been the grant of a sub-tenancy.

[21] See:, s.75 Land Registration Act 1925; *Mount Carmel Investments Ltd v. Peter Thurlow Ltd* [1988] 1 W.L.R. 1078.
[22] [1957] Ch. 475.
[23] [1952] Ch. 840.
[24] *ibid.* at 853.

GENERAL INTERESTS ATTRACTING OVERRIDING STATUS

1 Introduction

(a) Section 70(1)(g)

It has already been noted that the statutory definition of overriding interests is not confined to a relatively small number of specific rights, but that section 70(1)(g) has been interpreted as having the effect of affording overriding status to any rights where the appropriate statutory criteria are satisfied. The section is sufficiently important for the definition to be repeated. Section 70(1)(g) provides that the following are overriding interests:

> "The rights of every person in actual occupation of the land or in receipt of the rents and profits thereof, save where enquiry is made of such person and the rights are not disclosed."

(b) Three essential requirements

It should be noted that there are three essential elements to the definition of overriding interests under section 70(1)(g), two of which are positive and the third negative in nature:

(i) The existence of a right in the land: First, section 70(1)(g) only operates in relation to rights in land within the registered land system, and does not have the effect of conferring proprietary status on rights which would otherwise be purely personal in character. For example, if the criteria are met section 70(1)(g) is capable of conferring overriding status on an equitable lease. However, even if a licensee is in actual occupation of land section 70(1)(g) will have no effect upon the character of that right, so that it will remain purely personal and incapable of binding a subsequent transferee of the title.

(ii) A qualifying circumstance: The mere fact that a person enjoys a proprietary right in land is of no consequence under section 70(1)(g) unless one of the two qualifying criteria are also satisfied. A right will only acquire overriding status if either the holder is in actual occupation of the land, or in the absence of their own occupation they are presently receiving rent or profit derived from the land. If they are neither in actual occupation, nor in receipt of rent or profits, their interest will be incapable of attracting overriding status.

(iii) The existence of the right has not been concealed on inquiry: Even if a person enjoys a right in land and meets one of the two qualifying circumstances their interest will be deprived of overriding status if the person claiming priority made enquiries of them and they failed to disclose its existence.

2 Rights capable of enjoying overriding status

(a) Proprietary rights in land

It is clear from the language of section 70(1) of the Land Registration Act 1925 that only proprietary rights in the land itself are capable of constituting overriding interests.

The section refers to rights "subsisting in reference" to the land and Land Registration Act 1925, s.20(1)(b) refers to "the overriding interests, if any, affecting the estate transferred or created." By definition, therefore, rights which do not exist in relation to the land are incapable of forming the subject matter of an overriding interest. As Lord Jauncey remarked in *Abbey National v. Cann*[25] section 70(1)(g) does not "alter the scope or the character" of the rights to which it applies. For this reason in *National Provincial Bank Ltd v. Ainsworth*[26] the House of Lords held that the right of a wife to remain living in her matrimonial home even when she was not entitled to any share of the ownership, the so-called "deserted wife's equity, was incapable of constituting an overriding interest so as to bind a transferee of the legal title. In the Court of Appeal Russell L.J. had emphasised that section 70(1)(g) overriding interests did not protect actual occupation of land *per se*, but only the proprietary rights of a person in actual occupation. He stated:

> "It seems to me that section 70 in all its parts is dealing with rights in reference to land which have the quality of being capable of enduring through different ownerships of the land, according to the normal conceptions of title to real property. If . . . a right . . . is not of this quality, I would not be prepared as a matter of construction to hold that it is embraced by the language of section 70."[27]

His analysis was confirmed by the House of Lords, where Lord Wilberforce explained how the intended scope of the protection of section 70(1)(g) was to be derived when considering the argument that all rights, no matter whether they were purely personal in character, were converted into binding overriding interests by the statute:

> "To ascertain what "rights" come within this provisions, one must look outside the Land Registration Act to see what rights affect purchasers under the general law. To suppose that the subsection makes any right, of howsoever a personal character, which a person in occupation may have, an overriding interest by which a purchaser is bound, would involve two consequences: first that the Act, in this respect, brings about a substantive change in real property law by making personal rights bind purchasers; second, that there is a difference *as to the nature of the rights by which a purchaser may be bound* between registered and unregistered land, for purely personal rights including the wife's right to stay in the house cannot affect purchasers of unregistered land even with notice. One may have to accept that there is a difference between unregistered land and registered land as regards what kind of notice binds a purchaser. But there is no warrant in the terms of this paragraph or elsewhere in the Act for supposing that the nature of the rights which are to bind a purchaser is to be different, excluding personal rights in one case, including them in another."[28]

[25] [1991] 1 A.C. 56, 95.
[26] [1965] A.C. 1175.
[27] [1964] Ch. 665, 696.
[28] *ibid.* at 1261.

Since the deserted wife's right was a purely personal claim against her husband "not specifically related to the house in question" he held that it was incapable of being an overriding interest.

(b) Examples of rights held capable of constituting overriding interests under section 70(1)(g)

All rights proprietary rights which subsist in relation to land are capable of attaining overriding status under section 70(1)(g). The following examples are not intended to be exhaustive, but to illustrate the most important of such rights.

(i) Estate contracts: Although in *National Provincial Bank Ltd v. Ainsworth*[29] Lord Wilberforce indicated that a purely contractual right was a personal interest and therefore incapable of being an overriding interest, it is clear that contracts for the acquisition or grant of an estate in land create more than personal contractual rights and that the holder of the benefit of such a contract enjoys a proprietary interest in the land itself which is capable of enduring through changes in ownership of the land to which it relates. Such estate contracts are therefore capable of constituting an overriding interest under section 70(1)(g). For example, in *Webb v. Pollmount*[30] it was held that an option to purchase the freehold of land was an overriding interest, as would be an option to acquire a leasehold interest.[31] A right of pre-emption is also an estate contract capable of forming an overriding interest.[32]

(ii) Equitable leases: It has been seen how under the doctrine of *Walsh v. Lonsdale*[33] a binding contractual agreement for a lease creates an equitable lease even if the requisite formalities for a legal lease have not been fulfilled. Such an equitable lease is clearly a proprietary right in the land and is therefore capable of being an overriding interest.

(iii) An unpaid vendors lien: In *London and Cheshire Insurance Co. Ltd*[34] Brightman J. held that a lien enjoyed by a vendor over property he had sold but for which he had not yet received the purchase money was capable of forming the subject matter of an overriding interest when the vendor had remained in occupation of the property under a lease granted by the purchaser.

(iv) A right to rectification in equity: In *Blacklocks v. J B Developments*[35] Judge Mervyn Davies held that a vendor's right to have a conveyance rectified on the grounds that it had included a parcel of land, by the common mistake of the vendor and purchaser, which it had not been intended should form part of the transaction, was capable of constituting an overriding interest. Although the equitable right to rectify for mistake is often described as a mere equity, thus indicating that it does not usually survive through transfers of ownership of the property to which it relates, the judge held that in the circumstances it was an equity ancillary to an interest in land and

[29] [1965] A.C. 1175.
[30] [1966] Ch. 584; see also *Bridges v. Mees* [1957] Ch. 475.
[31] See: *Woolwich Equitable Building Society v. Marshall* [1952] 1 Ch. 1; *Grace Rymer Investments Ltd v. Waite* [1958] Ch. 831; *Ashburn Anstalt v. Arnold* [1989] Ch. 1; *Canadian Imperial Bank of Comerce v. Bello* (1992) 64 P. & C.R. 48.
[32] *Kling v. Keston Properties Ltd* (1983) 49 P. & C.R. 212.
[33] (1882) 21 Ch.D. 9.
[34] [1971] Ch. 499.
[35] [1982] Ch. 183.

therefore transmissible and enjoying the quality of durability through changes of ownership characteristic of a proprietary right. Since the equity had this character it was a right within the scope of section 70(1)(g).

(v) Equitable ownership behind a trust of land: By far the most important category of rights which have been held capable of overriding status are the interests of a beneficiary of a trust of land. Such equitable ownership is a proprietary right and therefore within the scope of section 70(1)(g). For example, in *Hodgson v. Marks*[36] the Court of Appeal held the purchaser of a house which was held on a bare trust by a sole trustee was bound by the equitable ownership of the beneficiary as she was in actual occupation and her interest was therefore overriding. Similarly, it has been seen how in *Williams & Glynn's Bank Ltd v. Boland*[37] the House of Lords held that the equitable ownership of a wife arising through a resulting or constructive trust was an overriding interest, and therefore binding on the subsequent mortgagee bank, because she was in actual occupation of the land. However, in *City of London Building Society v. Flegg*[38] the House of Lords held that where a transaction had overreaching effect the consequence was that any subsisting trust interests at the time of the transaction would be rendered incapable of forming the subject matter of an overriding interest. The overreaching mechanism has been discussed in detail,[39] and it will be remembered that Mr and Mrs Maxwell-Browne were the registered proprietors of a house which they held on trust for themselves and Mr and Mrs Flegg as co-owners in equity. They subsequently mortgaged the house without the Flegg's knowledge. Mr and Mrs Flegg claimed that since they had been in actual occupation of the house throughout their equitable interest was binding on the mortgagee as an overriding interest under section 70(1)(g) and that it could not have taken its mortgage with priority. Lord Oliver explained how the overreaching mechanisms deprived the Flegg's of any rights in the land capable of falling within the ambit of section 70(1)(g):

> "I cannot, for my part, accept that, once what I may call the parent interest, by which alone the occupation can be justified, has been overreached and thus subordinated to a legal estate properly created by the trustees under their statutory powers, it can, in relation to the proprietor of the legal estate so created, be any longer said to be a right "for the time being subsisting." Section 70(1)(g) protects only the rights in reference to the land of the occupier whatever they are at the material time — in the instant case the right to enjoy *in specie* the rent and profits of the land held in trust for him. Once the beneficiary's rights have been shifted from the land to capital moneys in the hands of the trustees, there is no longer an interest in the land to which the occupation can be referred or which it can protect. If the trustees sell in accordance with the statutory provisions and so overreach the beneficial interests in reference to the land, nothing remains to which a right of occupation can attach and the same result must, in my judgement, follow *vis-à-vis* a chargee by way of legal mortgage so long as the transaction is carried out in the manner proscribed by the Law of

[36] [1971] Ch. 892.
[37] [1981] A.C. 487.
[38] [1988] A.C.
[39] See Chap. 14.

> Property Act 1925, overreaching the beneficial interests by subordinating them to the estate of the chargee which is no longer "affected" by them . . . In the instant case, therefore, I would, for my part, hold that the charge created in favour of the [building society] overreaches the beneficial interests of the [Fleggs] and that there is nothing in section 70(1)(g) of the Land Registration Act 1925 or in *Boland's* case which has the effect of preserving against the [Building Society] any rights of the [Flegg's] . . ."[40]

In consequence, the equitable ownership of a beneficiary behind a trust of land will only be capable of overriding status if it has not been overreached, *i.e.* if the land was held by a sole trustee, as in *Williams & Glynn's Bank Ltd v. Boland.*[41]

(c) examples of rights held incapable of constituting overriding interests under section 70(1)(g)

It has already been noted how spousal rights of occupation not founded upon any share of the equitable ownership of the matrimonial home are incapable of overriding status. The most significant area of controversy concerning whether rights are proprietary and capable of existing as overriding interests, or purely personal, is that of licences.

(i) Bare licences: It is clear that a bare licence is a purely personal right granted by the licensor to the licensee, and that it is therefore incapable of constituting an overriding interest even if the licensee is in actual occupation of the land. In *Strand Securities v. Casewell*[42] Eric Casewell was the tenant of a sub-lease of a flat. He was not living there himself, but allowed his step-daughter to reside rent-free. The head-lease was then transferred to the plaintiffs. Since the step-daughter was a bare licensee of the flat she had no right which was capable of constituting an overriding interest under section 70(1)(g) despite the fact that she was in actual occupation.

(ii) Contractual licences: It seems that a contractual licence is also incapable of attaining the status of an overriding interest. This follows from the comments of the Court of Appeal in *Ashburn Anstalt v. Arnold* [43] rejecting earlier attempts by Lord Denning M.R. to accord contractual licences proprietary status, and approving the dissenting judgment of Russell L.J. in *National Provincial Bank Ltd v. Hastings Car Mart Ltd*[44] who had held that a contractual licence could not be an overriding interest.[45] The Court of Appeal did acknowledge that a contractual licence would be binding on a subsequent purchaser if it could be shown that there were grounds to impose an independent constructive trust on the purchaser, but this is a essentially different to establishing an overriding interest and has been discussed above.[46]

(iii) Licences generated by proprietary estoppel: Although bare and contractual licences cannot form the subject matter of an overriding interest it remains unclear whether a licence generated by an estoppel interest is sufficiently proprietary in

[40] *ibid.* at 90–91.
[41] [1981] A.C. 487.
[42] [1965] Ch. 958.
[43] [1989] Ch. 1.
[44] [1964] Ch. 665.
[45] See also: *Canadian Imperial Bank of Commerce v. Bello* (1992) 64 P. & C.R. 48 at 51.
[46] See Chap. 15.

character to fall within the scope of section 70(1)(g). In *National Provincial Bank Ltd v. Hastings Car Mart Ltd*[47] Lord Denning M.R. seemed to suggest that the equity of a licensee arising from his expenditure on land would be capable of existing as an overriding interest. However, in *Canadian Imperial Insurance Bank of Commerce v. Bello*[48] Dillon L.J. concluded, in the light of *Ashburn Anstalt v. Arnold,* that an estoppel would be an "insufficient interest in the property to be an overriding interest within the meaning of section 70(1)(g)."[49]

3 Qualifying circumstances which accord a proprietary right overriding status

A proprietary right in land only constitutes an overriding interest if one of the two qualifying circumstances identified in section 70(1)(g) are satisfied by the person claiming priority.

(a) Actual occupation

Of the two possible qualifying circumstances under section 70(1)(g) by far the most significant practice has been that of actual occupation of the land by the person enjoying the right claimed to have overriding status.

(i) Occupation as a straightforward question of fact: The requirement of "actual occupation" as a qualifying circumstance under section 70(1)(g) has been consistently interpreted by the Court as a simple matter of fact,[50] namely whether the person claiming entitlement to an overriding interest was physically present on the land to which that interest relates. It is not to be regarded as a term of legal art which has a peculiarly limited meaning, nor as requiring that the person factually occupying land enjoyed a legal entitlement to do so. In *Williams & Glynn's Bank Ltd v. Boland*[51] Lord Wilberforce considered the meaning of "actual occupation" and concluded:

> "The words are ordinary words of plain English, and should, in my opinion, be interpreted as such . . . Given occupation, *i.e.* presence on the land, I do not think that the word "actual" was intended to introduce any additional qualification, certainly not to suggest that possession must be "adverse": it merely emphasises that what is required is physical presence, not some entitlement in law."

This approach has been approved by subsequent cases, although it has been stressed that what will amount to sufficient physical presence to constitute actual occupation will depend on the circumstances of the land in question. In *Lloyd's Bank v. Rossett*[52] Mustill L.J. stated that:

> "For want of a better synonym, the person in occupation could be identified as the person who is "there" on the property: although what this entails will be

[47] [1964] Ch. 665.
[48] (1992) 64 P. & C.R. 48.
[49] *ibid.* at 52.
[50] In *Williams & Glynn's Bank v. Boland* [1979] Ch. 312, 322 Lord Denning M.R. stated that actual occupation "is a matter of fact, not matter of law."
[51] [1981] A.C. 487, 504–505.
[52] [1989] Ch. 350, 397.

dependent on the nature of the property and the circumstances of the individual case."

In many cases it will be clear that a person is in actual occupation of land, especially residential property, since as Nicholls L.J. observed in *Lloyd's Bank v. Rossett*[53] residential premises are occupied by "those who live in them." Most cases which have concerned straightforward situations of a person living in property have only considered the meaning of "actual occupation" because some limited interpretation was being advocated. For example, in *Hodgson v. Marks*[54] Mrs Hodgson transferred the legal title of her house into the name of her lodger, Evans, who sold the property to Marks. She had continued to live there, and when Marks came to view the property he saw her coming up a path to the house but did not ascertain who she was. The first instance judge held that she was not in "actual occupation" for the purposes of section 70(1)(g) because the word "actual" limited protection to those persons whose occupation was by an act recognisable to any person seeking to acquire an interest in the land. However, the Court of Appeal rejected this analysis and concluded that Mrs Hodgson had clearly been in actual occupation of the property at all material times as she was "de facto living in the house as her house,"[55] and it was irrelevant that the purchaser had assumed her to be Evans' wife. In *Williams & Glynn's Bank Ltd v. Boland*[56] Mrs Boland was living in the matrimonial home she shared with her husband and in which she enjoyed a share of the equitable ownership. The Bank which had granted him a mortgage argued that she was not to be regarded as enjoying "actual occupation" within section 70(1)(g) on three grounds: first because the vendor (mortgagor) was in occupation; second, because her occupation as a wife was merely a shadow of her husband's occupation; and thirdly because her occupation was not inconsistent with the title of the vendor. Lord Wilberforce rejected these proposed qualifications. He held that the occupation of a vendor does not exclude the possible occupation of others, approving comments to that effect in *Caunce v. Caunce*[57] and *Hodgson v. Marks.*[58] He rejected as obsolete the argument raised *Bird v. Syme-Thomson*[59] that the unity of a husband and wife meant that a wife's occupation was merely a shadow of her husband's. He held that there was no requirement that the occupation must be inconsistent with the title of the vendor, and concluded: "The only solution which is consistent with the Act and with common sense is to read the paragraph for what it says. Occupation, existing as a fact, may protect rights if the person in occupation has rights." Although in many cases the question of actual occupation will be straightforward because the claimant of an overriding interest clearly lives in the property to which it relates, difficulties have arisen in relation to how far the concept of occupation can be carried. As was observed by Lord Oliver in *Abbey National v. Cann*[60] the issue of whether a person was in actual occupation may essentially be a matter of fact, but:

[53] *ibid.* at 376.
[54] [1971] Ch. 892.
[55] *ibid.* at 932.
[56] [1981] A.C. 487.
[57] [1969] 1 W.L.R. 286.
[58] [1971] Ch. 892.
[59] [1979] 1 W.L.R. 440.
[60] [1991] 1 A.C. 56, 93.

"There is the serious question of what, in law, can amount to "actual occupation" for the purposes of section 70(1)(g). In *Williams & Glyn's Bank Ltd v. Boland* Lord Wilberforce observed that these words should be interpreted for what they are, that is to say, ordinary words of plain English. But even plain English may contain a variety of shades of meaning."

(ii) Presence insufficient to constitute actual occupation: In the absence of sufficient physical presence on the land it will be impossible to establish actual occupation. In *Epps v. Esso Petroleum*[61] the plaintiffs claimed that they enjoyed actual occupation of a strip of land where they had parked their car on an unidentified part for an undefined time. Templeman J. held that they had failed to establish that they were entitled to an overriding interest:

"But even if Mr Jones regularly parked his car on the disputed strip I do not consider that this constituted actual occupation of the disputed strip in the circumstances of the present case. I reach this conclusion for the following reasons; first, the parking of a car on a strip 11 feet wide by 80 feet long does not actually occupy the whole, or a substantial, or any defined part of that disputed strip for the whole or any defined time. Secondly, the parking of a car on an unidentified piece of land, apparently comprised in garage premises, is not an assertion of actual occupation of anything."[62]

(iii) Residence is not required to establish actual occupation: Although it is clear that slight physical presence will not amount to actual occupation, residence is not a necessary criteria. The level of presence necessary will depend on the nature of the land over which an overriding interest is claimed. In *Lloyd's Bank v. Rosset*[63] the question was whether a wife could claim an overriding interest against the bank which had granted a mortgage when her husband purchased a derelict farmhouse. Prior to the completion of the sale the vendors had allowed the Rossetts to begin renovation work of the property. Builders that they employed were on the premises daily and one of the men slept there most nights. The wife spent almost every day at the house, arriving at 10 a.m. and leaving just after 4 p.m., urging the builders on and decorating rooms, and also spent two nights sleeping there. The majority of the Court of Appeal held that in these circumstances she was in actual occupation of the house even though she was not resident as such. Nicholls L.J. explained and applied the principles:

" . . . I accept that in ordinary speech one normally does equate occupation in relation to a house with living there. If a person is intending to move into a house but has not yet done so, he would not normally be regarded as having gone into occupation. That is the normal position, with a house which is fit for living in. But that does not provide the answer in the present case, where the house was semi-derelict . . . If, day after day, workmen are actively building a house on a plot of land, or actively and substantially renovating a semi-derelict house, it

[61] [1973] 1 W.L.R. 1071.
[62] *ibid.* at 1079–1080.
[63] [1989] Ch. 350.

would be contrary to the principle underlying paragraph (g) if a would be purchaser or mortgagee were entitled to treat that site as currently devoid of an occupant for the purpose of the paragraph . . . In my view, the test of residence propounded by the bank is too narrow. As the judge observed, what constitutes occupation will depend upon the nature and state of the property in question. I can see no reason, in principle or in practice, why a semi-derelict house such as Vincent farmhouse should not be capable of actual occupation whilst the works proceed and before anyone has started to live in the building."[64]

The House of Lords[65] subsequently held that the wife was not entitled to any overriding interest, on the grounds that she was unable to establish that she enjoyed any share of the equitable ownership of the land by way of a constructive trust.[66] Sadly this meant that there was no need to determine if she had been in actual occupation and Lord Bridge refused to go into a question he saw as remaining only of academic interest.

(iv) Occupation by the physical presence of a representative: It seems clear that a person may be regarded as being in actual occupation of land even when they are not physically present if someone is "living there" on their behalf in a representative capacity. This was recognised by Lord Oliver in *Abbey National v. Cann,* who stated that actual occupation does not necessarily involve the personal presence of the claimant, so that a caretaker or representative of a company could occupy on behalf of his employer. Similarly in *Lloyd's Bank v. Rosset*[67] the Court of Appeal considered that builders employed to renovate a property were capable of occupying on behalf of their employers. In *Strand Securities v. Casewell*[68] the Court of Appeal held that representative occupation was possible by an agent or employee. Although the court considered that a contractual relationship was not essential for finding representative occupation, and Harman L.J. suggested that a house occupied by a wife could also be regarded as being occupied by her husband since she occupied as his representative,[69] it held that the tenant did not enjoy actual occupation of the flat in which he had allowed his step-daughter to occupy as a licensee. Lord Denning M.R. explained his reluctance at the inevitability of this conclusion:

"I would like to hold that the [father] was sharing the occupation of the flat with the [step-daughter]. But I cannot bring myself to this conclusion. The truth is that he allowed her to be in actual occupation, and that is all there is to it. She was a licensee rent free and I fear that it does not give him protection. It seems to me to be a very rare case — a case which the legislature did not think of for it is quite clear that if the [daughter] had paid a token sum as rent, or for use and occupation, to the [father], he would be "in receipt of rents and profits" and his rights would be protected under section 70(1)(g). Again if the [father] put his servant or caretaker into the flat, rent free, he would be protected because his

[64] *ibid.* at 376–377.
[65] [1991] 1 A.C. 107.
[66] See Chap. 6.
[67] [1989] Ch. 350.
[68] [1965] Ch. 958.
[69] *ibid.* at 984.

agent would have actual occupation on his behalf. It is odd that the [father] is not protected simply because he let his stepdaughter in rent free. Odd as it is, I fear the words of the statute do not cover this case . . . "[70]

(v) Actual occupation preserved through temporary absence by symbolic occupation: Although in *Abbey National v. Cann* Lord Oliver stressed that actual occupation must "involve some degree of permanence and continuity"[71] it is clear that persons who can be properly described as "living there" may not in fact enjoy continuous physical occupation of land. For example, if an MP owns a flat in London which he shares with his mistress, he may be living there during the week, but living back with his family in his constituency during the weekend. The same is true of persons who own second homes. Alternatively a co-owner of a property may be called away for a period of time on a business trip, or take a holiday for a week or so. Does their actual occupation cease during this time that they are "away"? Although with relatively short absences the answer must certainly be no, the problems posed are greater if a person is absent for a longer period of time. For example, a co-owner may decide to spend a month inter-railing in Europe, six-months sailing round the world, or be seconded by their business to Saudi Arabia for six weeks. During such an absence there may be ample opportunity for the legal owner of the land to arrange things so that there are few obvious physical signs of their occupation to a potential purchaser of an interest in the land. The question arises whether if they transact with the legal title, perhaps by mortgaging or selling the property, the co-owner's interests will be binding on the mortgagee or transferee as overriding interests. Just as was seen above that a person who is not physically present on the land can preserve their actual occupation through the occupation of a representative, so it seems a person can preserve their actual occupation through temporary absences by the continued presence of their personal belongings on the land. Such "symbolic" occupation was a factor in finding that a wife's share of the equitable ownership of her matrimonial home was protected as an overriding interest in *Chhokar v. Chhokar.*[72] As has been noted earlier,[73] Mr Chhokar was the sole legal owner of the house and he sold it to a Mr Parmar, deliberately arranging that completion of the sale should occur while his wife was in hospital giving birth to their child. Ewbank J. explained the circumstances of the transaction:

> "On 19 February, the date of completion, the husband made special arrangements to have the net proceeds of sale in cash in his hands. He paid his debts and then he set off for India. That was the last the wife saw of him for some 2 years. The wife and baby were discharged from hospital on 22 February. They went home. They found the locks had been changed . . . on 1 March 1979 Mr Parmar registered the conveyance to him at the Land Registry. The wife at that date was not in the house because he had put her out, but some of her furniture was there. I have to consider whether she was in actual occupation on the day of the registration of the conveyance. I have no difficulty in deciding that she was in

[70] *ibid.* at 981.
[71] [1991] 1 A.C. 56, 93.
[72] [1984] F.L.R. 313. See also: *Hoggett v. Hoggett* (1980) 39 P. & C.R. 121.
[73] See Chap. 7.

> actual occupation. Her interest, accordingly, in the house is an overriding interest . . ."[74]

Such symbolic occupation was also recognised in *Kling v. Keston Properties*[75] where Vinelott J. held that the plaintiff had enjoyed actual occupation of a garage partly because his wife's car had been trapped in it by the defendant parking her car across the entrance.

(vi) Is symbolic occupation alone enough to constitute actual occupation?: Although *Chhokar v. Chhokar* suggests that symbolic occupation by furniture and personal belongings may prove sufficient to preserve a pre-existing actual occupation established by physical presence, it is less certain whether alone it can establish actual occupation. This issue arose in *Abbey National v. Cann*[76] where it was argued that following the purchase of a house a mother enjoying an equitable interest in the purchase moneys was entitled to an overriding interest binding a mortgage company which had taken a security over the property, on the grounds that at the moment of completion of the purchase she had been in actual occupation. Since she had been abroad on holiday at the time that the completion occurred, her claim of actual occupation was founded on the fact that some 35 minutes before completion took place the vendors had allowed her son to begin to unload her furniture into the house and permitted carpet layers to begin laying her carpets. The House of lords held that these acts were wholly insufficient to constitute actual occupation. Lord Oliver commented that much more was required than a mere fleeting presence:

> "A prospective tenant or purchaser who is allowed, as a matter of indulgence, to go into property in order to plan decorations or measure for furnishings would not, in ordinary parlance, be said to be occupying it, even though he might be there for hours at a time. Of course, in the instant case, there was, no doubt, on the part of the persons involved in moving Mrs Cann's belongings, an intention that they should remain there and would render the premises suitable for her ultimate use as a residential occupier. Like the trial judge, however, I am unable to accept that acts of this proprietary character, carried out by courtesy of the vendor prior to completion can constitute "actual occupation" for the purposes of section 70(1)(g)."[77]

This does not, however, mean that actual occupation can never be established by purely symbolic occupancy. For example, if rather than concerning a mortgage granted at the moment of completion the case had concerned a three-year lease of the house granted by Mr Cann to a third party on the day before his mother returned from holiday, it is likely that Mrs Cann would have been able to claim an overriding interest against the lessor. The presence of her furniture and belonging would have been permanent and not merely fleeting, and not dependent on the indulgence of the vendor.

[74] *ibid.* at 317.
[75] (1985) 49 P. & C.R. 212.
[76] [1991] 1 A.C. 56.
[77] *ibid.* at 94.

(b) Receipt of rents or profits

Although actual occupation is the most significant and important of the two qualifying circumstances which accord a right overriding status, section 70(1)(g) also provides automatic protection for rights enjoyed by a person who, though not in factual possession of the land, receives payments of money or benefits in kind derived from it.
(i) Receipt of rents and profits in fact: It seems clear that the actual receipt of any such rent or profits from the land will suffice to generate an overriding interest. A common situation would be if the claimant had granted a tenancy of the land and is receiving periodic payments as consideration. However, there is no need for the rent or profit to be derived from a proprietary entitlement of the present occupier of the land. Even if the occupier is merely a licensee the payment of any consideration associated with the licence will ensure that the underlying proprietary entitlement of the licensor to the land is protected as an overriding interest. This is evident from *Strand Securities v. Casewell*[78] where it was suggested that if the step-daughter had made any payments to her father in relation to her occupancy, rather than enjoying it rent free, he would have been entitled to an overriding interest.
(ii) A right to receive rent or profits? The question has arisen whether the protection of section 70(1)(g) is limited to those in actual receipt of rent or profits or if it is capable of extension to those who are entitled to receive them but have not in fact done so. In *E.S. Schwab & Co. Ltd v. McCarthy*[79] the defendant was the freehold owner of a maisonette. He granted a 99 year lease to a tenant who secured a loan by way of a legal charge on his leasehold estate. Before the lease and charge could be registered, the tenant left and returned the keys to the defendant, thus surrendering the lease. The defendant then granted a weekly tenancy to someone else at a rent of £6.50 per week and a deposit of £420. The tenant failed to pay the rent. The legal charge created by the preceding tenant was subsequently registered and the question was whether it had priority over the defendant's interests. It was argued that the defendant was entitled to an overriding interest by section 70(1)(g) on the grounds that the "receipt of rents and profits" should be interpreted as meaning entitled to the rents and profits, even if there was no actual receipt.[80] This interpretation was rejected by Oliver J. and by the Court of Appeal. Sir John Pennycuick stated bluntly:

> "It is said that the defendant was in receipt of the rents and profits of the maisonette. In fact he was not in receipt of the rents and profits because no rent had ever been paid by him, although he retained a deposit by way of security for the rent."[81]

4 Potential purchasers can protect themselves by making enquiries

(a) A policy of self-protection

It has been seen how under section 70(1)(g) the proprietary rights of any persons who fulfil either of the two qualifying circumstances will be accorded overriding status, and

[78] [1965] Ch. 958.
[79] (1976) 31 P. & C.R. 196.
[80] *ibid.* at 202.
[81] *ibid.* at 213.

as such they will be binding on any purchaser acquiring even a legal estate in the land. Given the power of such automatic priority, the question arises as to whether potential purchasers can enjoy any protection against the existence of such interests, especially since they are in direct contradiction to the general policy of the land registration system that a purchaser should be able to readily discover all the rights and interests affecting the land which will bind him from the face of the register itself. Section 70(1)(g) therefore provides such a potential purchaser with the opportunity of protecting himself by making appropriate inquiries of all persons who he suspects could enjoy such interests. If he makes an inquiry of such a suspect, and they reveal their interest, he will be aware of how his land will be encumbered and will be able to make a decision whether to go ahead with his proposed acquisition. If, however, the rights are denied, the statute deprives the right of overriding status against him if he purchases a legal estate in the land. This policy of enabling self-protection was emphasised by the House of Lords in *Abbey National v. Cann*[82] in the context of considering the relevant date for determining the existence of an overriding interest. Lord Oliver stressed that section 70(1)(g) was clearly intended to reflect the rule in *Hunt v. Luck*[83] in unregistered land and that "the reference to inquiry and failure to disclose cannot make any sense unless it is related to a period in which such inquiry could be other than otiose," so that any interpretation which allowed overriding interests to arise under the section without allowing the purchaser opportunity to make protective inquiries would result in a "conveyancing absurdity."[84] However, protection will only be available if inquiries are made by the right person, of the right person in the right manner.

(b) Inquiry must be made by the prospective purchaser or his agent

The nature of inquiries which will be effective to protect a purchaser from an overriding interest were considered by Brightman J. in *London and Cheshire Insurance Co. Ltd v. Laplagrene Property Co. Ltd*[85] where he said: "the inquiry which paragraph (g) envisages is readily and sensibly confined to inquiry by or on behalf of the intending transferee or grantee for the purposes of the intended disposition." This suggests that the inquiries can be made either by the prospective purchaser himself, or by an agent acting on his behalf, provided that the inquiries are made in the course of the transaction. To this extent *any* inquiries made by *any* person, however disinterested in or unconnected with the property, will not suffice.

(c) Inquiry must be addressed to the person entitled to the right or their agent

An inquiry will only be effective to protect a purchaser if it was made of the person entitled to the right claimed to enjoy overriding status. For example, in *Hodgson v. Marks*[86] Russell L.J. held that a purchaser would not be protected when he had failed to make any inquiry of Mrs Hodgson as to her rights in the property he was acquiring, and that he would not be entitled to rely on the "untrue *ipse dixit* of the vendor" that she had no rights, nor on his assumption that she was the vendor's wife. In *Winkworth*

[82] [1991] 1 A.C. 56.
[83] [1902] 1 Ch. 428.
[84] [1991] 1 A.C. 56, 88.
[85] [1971] Ch. 499, 505.
[86] [1971] Ch. 892.

v. Edward Baron Developments Ltd[87] the Court of Appeal considered that an inquiry made of an agent, for example a solicitor, acting for the party entitled to a right in the land would be effective to protect a potential purchaser from an overriding interest if the agent failed to disclose its existence. However in the circumstances, where a husband mortgaged the matrimonial home of which his wife was an equitable co-owner, the court held that there had been no effective inquiry made of the wife since the solicitor acting for her and her husband was not asked to answer an inquiry on her behalf but merely to pass a letter to them, which he passed to the husband who did not pass it on to his wife but answered the inquiries falsely.

(d) Inquiry must be made as to the existence of rights in the land

An inquiry will only be effective to protect the potential purchaser if it is directed to the question whether the person of whom it is made enjoys rights in the land. If an inquiry is made as to whether the person enjoys certain specific rights in the land this will be inadequate to protect against the overriding status of other rights in relation to which no inquiry was addressed. In *Winkworth v. Edward Baron Developments Ltd*[88] the mortgage company had asked the husband and wife to acknowledge that they occupied the house as licensees and not by virtue of any tenancy or lease. Nourse L.J. held that this amounted to no more than "an inquiry as to the capacity in which the husband and wife *occupied* the property"[89] and did not provide protection against her trust interest acquiring overriding status. The Court indicated that an inquiry did not need to be specific in order to be effective and Nourse L.J. implied that a inquiry "as to their rights in the land generally" would have been sufficient to protect the mortgagee from any rights that they then failed to disclose.

(e) Adequacy of the protection available through proper inquiries

The provision of a mechanism enabling potential purchasers or mortgagees of land to protect themselves against overriding interests in section 70(1)(g) has the obvious implication that a prudent purchaser will inspect not merely the register, but the land itself, in an attempt to ascertain whether there are any persons in actual occupation of whom he ought to make appropriate inquiries, or from whom he can establish whether there are any persons receiving rent or profits in respect of the land. However, this protection is neither adequate from the perspective of such a prospective purchaser, nor fair to a person with rights in the land. Although the essence of the doctrine of *Hunt v. Luck* was that the purchaser of unregistered land was fixed with notice of the rights of persons whose existence was obvious from a physical inspection of the land, the purely factual nature of "actual occupation" and the scope that the concept has been given by the courts means that it may be virtually impossible for a potential purchaser to discover their existence, so enabling them to make inquiries. For example, if a house is owned at law by a man who is living with a partner who is a co-owner in equity, and while she is away for a two-week holiday in New Zealand he empties the house of all signs of her presence, though leaving her furniture, and executes a legal charge and runs off with the money, it seems likely that the mortgagee will be bound

[87] (1986) 52 P. & C.R. 67.
[88] *ibid.*
[89] *ibid.* at 77.

by her interest as an overriding interest despite the fact that there was almost no possibility of discovering her existence. Are the purchasers in such circumstances expected for example to ask the neighbours as to who they are aware lives in the property? The protection may operate unfairly in relation to those enjoying rights in the land, especially if such persons are unaware that they have any entitlement. Those persons entitled to informally created equitable ownership by way of resulting or constructive trusts may have no awareness of their proprietary rights and thus fail to respond when a general inquiry is made. The very ignorance which leads them to fail to protect their interest as a minor interest is likely to mean that they are unaware of the need to disclose them when an inquiry is made. Despite these inadequacies it should be recognised that such problems will only arise in exceptional circumstances and the availability of protection by inquiries to potential purchasers is an essential counterbalance to the statutory priority enjoyed by overriding interests.

THE DATE AT WHICH OVERRIDING INTERESTS GAIN PRIORITY

1 The Problem of the registration gap

(a) Identifying the problem of the registration gap

It has been seen how Land Registration Act 1925, s.70(1) accords certain rights and interests in land overriding status, and that in conjunction with sections 20(1) and 23(1) such interests will be binding on the grantee or transferee of a legal estate or charge of the land to which they relate. However it is important to establish the relevant point at which such a right acquires overriding status and therefore priority over the interest of the grantee or transferee. The problem is compounded by the fact that the acquisition of a legal estate, or a charge by way of legal mortgage, is a registered disposition, so that the purchaser or mortgagee is not vested with a legal estate until they are entered on the land register as the proprietor of the freehold of the land, the lessee of a term of years for more than 21 years, or the chargee of the charge by way of legal mortgage. This means that there is an inevitable period of time after a transaction such as sale or mortgage of registered land has been completed whilst the legal title remains with the grantor or transferor, and the purchaser or mortgagee enjoys only an equitable interest over the land. This period is known as the "registration gap" and a central question is whether overriding interests can arise during this period so that they are binding on the legal estate or charge of the grantee or transferee when perfected by registration.

(b) A practical illustration of the problems of the registration gap

The potential difficulties presented by the existence of the "registration gap" are well illustrated by the facts of the two leading cases. In *Lloyds Bank v. Rossett* [90] it should be remembered that a husband acquired the legal title to a derelict farmhouse. Prior to the completion of the purchase his wife spent a great deal of time on the premises,

[90] [1989] Ch. 350.

directing the work of builders who were employed to renovate it and decorating a number of rooms. The sale was completed on December 17, but unbeknown to the wife the husband also granted the bank a mortgage over the property which was executed that same day. Registration of the legal title and the charge occurred on February 7, at which stage Mrs Rossett was clearly in "actual occupation" of the house. When the husband was unable to continue repayments of the mortgage the wife claimed that she had an overriding interest which was binding on the Bank. The logic of this claim was explained by Nicholls L.J.:

> " . . . the wife's submission is that the bank's charge took effect subject to her beneficial interest in the property, because on 7th February she was in occupation and her interest was an overriding interest under section 70(1)(g) and on registration the bank's charge took effect subject to that overriding interest by virtue of s20(1)(b)."[91]

Similarly in *Abbey National v. Cann*[92] George Cann purchased a house in circumstances in which part of the purchase moneys were provided by his mother, so that she was entitled to a share of the equitable ownership. Completion occurred on August 13, but George granted a mortgage to the building society and kept part of the intended purchase money for himself. The charge was also executed on August 13, but it was not until September 13, that the charge was registered and George was registered as proprietor. Again by that date Mrs Cann was in actual occupation of the property, and one argument on her behalf was that she was entitled to an overriding interest taking priority to the charge of the Building Society. In both cases the question to be resolved was whether an overriding interest of the parties respective beneficial interests could arise during the registration gap.

2 Competing solutions to the problem of the registration gap

Having recognised the problem raised by the existence of the registration gap the cases have suggested a number of potential resolutions by manipulation of the date which determines whether an overriding interest enjoys priority.

(a) Date of registration of the estate or charge allegedly subject to the overriding interest

The language of the Land Registration Act 1925 seems to provide that the appropriate date for determining if a legal estate or charge is subject to any adverse overriding interests is the date at which that estate or charge was registered. Section 20(1) of the Land Registration Act states that a disposition of the registered land shall confer that estate on the transferee or grantee subject to overriding interests affecting the estate transferred or created "*when registered*". However, if this is the case transferees, grantees or chargees do not acquire the land free from overriding interests which arise during the registration gap, with the consequence that they might find themselves

[91] *ibid.* at 371.
[92] [1991] 1 A.C. 56. See also *Barclays Bank plc v. Zaroovabli* [1997] 2 All E.R. 19 (above, p. 408).

subject to third party rights when they have already irrevocably committed themselves to a transaction and having had no opportunity of protecting themselves by inquiries. In such cases as *Cann* and *Rosset* the effect of allowing the claimants to establish their overriding interests on the basis of actual occupation at the date of registration would be to render the respective mortgagees' rights valueless.

(b) Date of completion of the transaction creating or transferring the interest allegedly subject to the overriding interest

An alternative approach would be to construe the statutory provisions so that the relevant date for the establishment of an overriding interest is not that of the registration of the estate of charge allegedly subject to it, but the date of completion of the transaction creating or transferring the estate or charge. Such a construction would have the effect of eliminating the problem of the registration gap altogether, so that no overriding interest would gain priority over an estate or charge which was not already in existence when the charge was executed or the estate conveyed. This analysis was adopted by Scarlett J. at first instance in *Lloyd's Bank v. Rossett*. His approach was summarised by Nicholls L.J. in the Court of Appeal:

> "The construction of section 20(1)(b) adopted by the judge would have the consequence that on registration a transferee or mortgagee would acquire a legal estate subject to entries on the register, and to any overriding interests affecting the estate transferred or created at the time it was transferred or created, but free from all other estates and interests. On this construction he would, on registration, take free from all overriding interests, whatever their nature, which came into being after the execution of the transfer or mortgage and before registration."[93]

(c) Different dates applicable to different categories of overriding interests

Although the solution of Scarlett J. has the merit of simplicity, it was rejected by the Court of Appeal on the grounds that it involved an unsustainable construction of the relevant provisions of the Act. Instead, the Court of Appeal considered that a distinction was to be drawn between the different categories of overriding interest defined by Land Registration Act 1925, s.70(1). It held that for all but section 70(1)(g) the relevant date was the date of registration of the estate or charged alleged to be subject to it. However, it held that for overriding interests under section 70(1)(g) the relevant date could not be that of registration because this would produce a result wholly inconsistent with the object of the paragraph, where there was a emphasis on both the actual occupation of the claimant and the opportunity of the potential purchaser to protect himself by making inquiries. Nicholls L.J. explained the rationale for this differential approach:

> "Paragraph (g) is designed to protect occupants against estates or interests acquired whilst they are in actual occupation . . . Consistently with conveyancing sense and the underlying conveyancing principle which is being carried forward

[93] [1989] Ch. 350, 373.

> into paragraph (g), it seems to me that paragraph (g) is concerned with persons who are in actual occupation of the land at the time when the estate or interest which is said to be subject to the rights of the actual occupant was created. For example, on completion of a purchase or a mortgage in the usual way. This is so despite the need for a further step to be taken (registration) before the legal estate will be acquired by the purchaser or mortgagee. In line with this is the expectation provided for in paragraph (g). Explicitly the rights of an occupant are not protected if inquiry is made of him and the rights are not disclosed. That exception, implicitly, contemplates an inquiry by or on behalf of the person whose estate or interest is said to be subject to the rights of the occupant and, again, implicitly, an inquiry made before he acquired his estate or interest. Otherwise the provision makes no sort of sense."[94]

Given this interpretation of the objects of section 70(1)(g) he held that the relevant date for the establishment of an overriding interest within that category was the date of completion of the transaction creating or transferring the estate or charge:

> "If this is right, the pieces of the jigsaw fit together reasonably well. A purchaser or mortgagee inspects and inquires before completion, in the established fashion. Or if he fails to do so, at his own risk. He then completes the transaction, taking an executed transfer or mortgage. Whether or not an overriding interest under paragraph (g) subsists so far as his freehold or mortgage is concerned falls to be determined at that moment. If an overriding interest does subsist, then his estate when registered takes subject to that interest. If it does not, then subsequent entry of a person into occupation before the transfer or mortgage has been registered . . . does not have the consequence of creating an overriding interest under paragraph (g) in relation to the freehold or mortgage."[95]

3 Resolution of the problem of the registration gap by the House of Lords

A number of potential approaches to the problem of the registration gap have been outlined, but a resolution was finally provided by the House of Lords in *Abbey National v. Cann*,[96] where a symbiosis of the various alternatives was adopted.

(a) Registration is the relevant date for establishing the existence of all overriding interests

The House of Lords held that it was impossible as a matter of construction to conclude that the relevant date for the establishment of any of the overriding interests in section 70(1) was other than the date of registration of the estate or interest they were alleged to affect. In reaching this conclusion it was recognised that this inevitably means that overriding interests can arise during the registration gap. However, as Lord Oliver explained, in some circumstances this must have been the intention of the legislation,

[94] *ibid.* at 373–374.
[95] *ibid.* at 374.
[96] [1991] 1 A.C. 56.

so that under section 70(1)(i) local land charges are overriding interests which should be binding on an estate even if they are created between completion and registration. The date of registration is therefore also the relevant date for determining the existence of overriding interests under section 70(1)(g).

(b) Completion is the relevant date for establishing actual occupation

Although the House of Lords held that the date of registration was the relevant date for establishing an overriding interest it went on to hold that for the purpose of section 70(1)(g) the qualifying circumstance, which is usually actual occupation, must be established at the date of completion. In other words a distinction is drawn not between the relevant date for the establishment of different categories of overriding interests, but between determining if there was an overriding interest and if there was actual occupation. This distinction was explained by Lord Oliver:

> "The question remains, however, whether the date of registration is also the relevant date for determining whether a claimant to a right is in actual occupation. It is to be noted that it is not actual occupation which gives rise to the right or determines its existence. Actual occupation merely operates as the trigger, as it were, for treatment of the right, whatever it may be, as an overriding interest . . . The case which does give rise to difficulty if the date of registration is the relevant date for determining whether there is a claimant in actual occupation is one in which the sequence of events is that the right, unaccompanied by occupation, is created before completion and before the chargee has advanced his money and then subsequently the claimant enters into actual occupation after completion and remains in occupation up to the date when the registration of the charge is effected. The chargee in that event would have no possibility of discovering the existence of the claimant's interest before advancing his money and taking his charge, but would nevertheless be subject, on registration, to the claimant's prior equitable interest which, *ex hypothesi*, would not have been subject to the charge at its creation."[97]

He therefore concluded that to avoid a conveyancing absurdity "the actual occupation required to support such an interest as a subsisting interest must exist at the date of completion of the transaction giving rise to the right to be registered, for that is the only date at which the inquiry referred to in paragraph (g) could, in practice, be made and be relevant."

(c) Practical implications of the interpretation adopted in Abbey National v. Cann

(i) Elimination of the problem presented by the registration gap in relation to overriding interests under section 70(1)(g): The major achievement of the decision of the House of Lords was to provide a means of preventing overriding interests arising under section 70(1)(g) during he registration gap whilst respecting the language of the statute that the relevant date for establishing overriding interests is registration. In practice this means that unless the claimant of an overriding interest was in factual occupation at the date of the completion of a contract to sell or create a legal estate in

[97] *ibid.* at 87–88.

the land, or on the execution of a legal charge, there will be no overriding interest. In such cases as *Williams & Glynn's Bank v. Boland*[98] where a mortgage is granted by the legal owner of land long after it has been acquired there is unlikely to be any problem with actual occupation, unless a co-owner in equity was absent from the land when the charge was executed but has moved back prior to its completion. In cases where property is purchased and the purchasers do not already live in it, unlike for example if tenants are purchasing the freehold reversion of a house, there will be no possibility of any person establishing an overriding interest against a mortgagee who has funded the purchase unless they were established in occupation prior to completion occurring. As has already been noted Mrs Cann was held not to have been in occupation at that moment and her equitable interest did not therefore have priority over the charge of the Building Society, and her rights were confined to the equity of redemption.
(ii) Failure to resolve problems of the registration gap entirely: Despite the practical elimination of the problem of the registration gap for overriding interests within section 70(1)(g) there is still some potential for overriding interests in other categories to arise during that period, thus affecting the estate or charge when registered. In some cases, as for example with local land charges, it is entirely appropriate that such interests should be binding on the transferee or chargee. However, this should be confined to interests created by third parties external to the relationship of the transferor and transferee, or chargor and chargee, and problems remain because the transferor or chargor who retains the legal title during the period of the registration gap is thereby capable of creating interests in favour of third parties which will be binding as overriding interests. This difficulty was recognised by Lord Oliver:

> "This does, of course, give rise to the theoretical difficulty that since a transferor remains the registered proprietor until registration of the transfer, it would be possible for him, in breach of trust, to create overriding interests, for instance, by grant of an easement or of a lease, which would be binding on the transferee and against which the transferee would not be protected by an official search."[99]

For example, if the transferor were to grant a legal lease for less than 21 years, which is an overriding interest under section 70(1)(k) and not dependent on the qualifying circumstance of actual occupation, this would be binding on the transferee. However, Lord Oliver regarded such possibilities as "improbable" and as such they should not undermine an otherwise successful elimination of registration gap problems.

CIRCUMSTANCES IN WHICH AN OVERRIDING INTEREST MAY LOSE PRIORITY TO WHICH IT WAS OTHERWISE ENTITLED

Even where a person enjoys a proprietary right in land which falls within the scope of section 70(1)(g), a legal estate or charge will not be subject to it if in all the circumstances it can be shown that the person entitled to the right has expressly or

[98] [1981] A.C. 487.
[99] [1991] 1 A.C. 56, 87.

impliedly waived the right to enjoy such priority. This situation will especially occur where an equitable co-owner of land has expressly or implied agreed to the grant of a mortgage. In *Paddington Building Society v. Mendelsohn*[1] a flat was purchased with £15,500 provided by a mother and the remaining £17,000 raised by way of a mortgage by her son. As the mother was too old to obtain a mortgage herself it was agreed that the flat should be purchased in the sole name of the son. Subsequently the mother allowed the son to raise a further £6,000 on a second mortgage. When the mortgage was unpaid and the building society sought possession she claimed that since she was entitled to a share of the equitable ownership and was in actual occupation she had an overriding interest binding on the mortgagees. The Court of Appeal rejected her claim on the grounds that she had expressly agreed that the rights were subject to those of the mortgagee. Browne-Wilkinson L.J. explained:

> "The effect of section 70(1)(g) could not in my judgement have been to enlarge the mother's rights so as to give her rights in priority to the society when, under the trust deed, her rights were expressly subject to those of the society. Her rights would be "overriding interests" in that the society would have to give effect to them, but the inherent quality of the mother's rights would not have been such as to give them priority over the society's rights. So in the present case, once it is established that the imputed intention must be that the mother's rights were to be subject to the mortgage, there is nothing in section 70 of the Registration Act 1925 which enlarges those rights into any greater rights."[2]

Similarly, if the House of Lords had found in *Abbey National v. Cann*[3] that Mrs Cann had been in actual occupation of the house at completion, her overriding interest would not have bound the Building Society because they also found that she had impliedly consented to her son raising a mortgage to fund the purchase, and she would have been precluded from relying upon her interest as prevailing over the rights of the mortgagee. However, in *Woolwich Building Society v. Dickman*[4] the Court of Appeal held that express consents executed by the protected tenants of a leasehold property were incapable of estopping them from asserting an overriding interest under section 70(1)(g) against a building society which had granted a mortgage to the landlord. This seems to be a special exception, as Morrit L.J. recognised that in other circumstances such consent would operate to prevent an overriding interest being asserted:

> "In the case of registered land other than a dwelling house subject to a protected or statutory tenancy it will not matter whether the effect of the estoppel is to remove an overriding interest or merely to set up a bar as between the parties to the estoppel so as to prevent the one relying on that interest as against the other. But in the case of a dwelling house let on a protected tenancy it does not."[5]

[1] (1985) 50 P. & C.R. 244.
[2] *ibid.* at 248.
[3] [1991] 1 A.C. 56.
[4] [1996] 3 All E.R. 204.
[5] *ibid.* at 214.

REFORM OF OVERRIDING INTERESTS?

A number of difficulties connected with the place of overriding interests within the system of land registration have been noted in the course of the preceding exposition of the law. A thorough re-consideration of their role was undertaken by the Law Commission in their Third Report on Land Registration in 1987,[6] in the course of which a number of proposals for reform were made.

1 The necessity of overriding interests

Although the Commission considered the main criticisms of overriding interests, namely that they are an exception to the "mirror" principle that the land register should reflect the totality of rights and interests affecting any particular estate and the danger that an entirely innocent and properly careful purchaser for value of an "absolute" title might find his land subject to an overriding interest without any realistic means of having discovered its existence prior to his purchase and without any right to an indemnity or any compensation for his loss of user, it concluded that they had a valid place to play within registered land. It adopted two fundamental principles by which to judge the appropriateness of overriding interests:

> "(1) in the interests of certainty and of simplifying conveyancing, the class of right which may bind a purchaser otherwise than as the result of an entry in the register should be as narrow as possible *but* (2) interests should be overriding where protection against purchasers is needed, yet it is either not reasonable to expect or sensible to require any entry on the register. Thus far the welfare of the conveyancer, or rather his client, is our first but not our paramount consideration."[7]

In the light of these principles the Commission recommended a number of reforms to the present law concerning overriding interests.

2 Reduction of the number of recognised overriding interests

The Commission considered the various rights and interests which are currently defined as overriding in Land Registration Act 1925, s.70(1) and concluded that many should be abolished or have their overriding status removed. It was proposed that only five categories of right should continue to enjoy such status:[8]

(1) easements and profits à prendre

(2) rights by adverse possession

(3) short leases

[6] Law Com. No. 158.
[7] para. 2.6.
[8] para. 2.24.

(4) rights of persons in actual occupation

(5) customary rights

3 Revision of the content of some such overriding interests

As well as proposing an overall reduction in the number of overriding interests the commission proposed that the content of some of the present specific interests should be revised.

(a) Easements

The commission noted the conflict between the statutory provisions requiring easements to be "completed by registration"[9] and section 70(1)(a) which accords them overriding status. The Commission recommended that where easements are created by means of an express grant or reservation they should not be overriding interests. The nature of their creation means that there is every expectation that that should be protected by registration. Pending "completion by registration" they should rank merely as minor interests.[10] However, easements created by implied grant or reservation, by operation of Land Registration Act 1925, s.62 or by prescription should continue to be overriding interests since it would not be sensible to require entries on the register in respect of them.[11] The commission also considered the place of equitable easements and recommended that, despite the ruling in *Celsteel Ltd v. Alton House Holdings Ltd*[12] to the contrary, they should not rank as overriding interests and that it was reasonable to expect them to be protected as minor interests.[13]

(b) Short leases

Under section 70(1)(k) it has been seen that legal leases for less than 21 years are overriding interests. The Commission considered a number of possible changes. First, it was suggested that overriding status should only be accorded to legal leases not in fact created by deed, on the basis that since the formality of a deed had been used it would be reasonable to expect the formality of registration. However, this was rejected on the grounds that it is the landlord who undertakes the formality of executing the lease by deed, and that it was not sensible to require the protection of very short leases on the register.[14] Secondly, the proposal that only legal leases of a duration less than three years should be overriding interests was abandoned due to lack of support during consultation. The Commission did, however, propose that leases should only be overriding interests if they take effect in possession either immediately or within one month of creation. This would prevent the perceived problems posed by reversionary leases, the existence of which would not be ascertainable from an inspection of the land.[15]

[9] Land Registration Act 1925, ss.19(2) and 22(2).
[10] para. 2.26.
[11] para. 2.27-2.30.
[12] [1985] 1 W.L.R. 204.
[13] para. 2.31-2.33.
[14] para. 2.40.
[15] para. 2.44.

(c) Rights of actual occupiers

The Commission accepted that the rights of actual occupiers should continue to be protected as overriding interests since, especially in the case of beneficial interests in dwelling houses, they "are very often of the sort which arise without express grant, without the grantee or acquirer having the benefit of legal advice"[16] and that it is not therefore reasonable to expect their protection by registration. However, the Commission recommended that protection should not continue to be extended to the rights of persons "in receipt of the rents and profits" of land:

> "We consider it reasonable to expect and sensible to require such persons in their own interests and as against purchasers to protect themselves on the register because greater injustice lies in expecting the purchaser to be able to ascertain by enquiry of the recipient of the rents and profits."

The Commission also considered that the general exception under section 70(1)(g) that overriding interests arise "save where enquiry is made of such person and the rights are not disclosed," serves no useful purpose, and proposed instead the introduction of a general provision in relation to all overriding interests granting the court a jurisdiction to postpone them as against subsequent purchasers and lenders on the grounds of fraud or estoppel.[17]

4 The problem of the "registration gap"

The Commission also considered the potential difficulty of overriding interests under section 70(1)(g) arising during the "registration gap." At the time of their report this issue had been left open by the Court of Appeal in *Paddington Building Society v. Mendelsohn.*[18] The Commission considered that this was unsatisfactory and proposed that "for the purposes of deciding whether purchasers and lenders take subject to an overriding interest, the relevant date should be the date of the disposition, *i.e.* the date of the instrument which on registration creates or transfers the legal interest." In the following Fourth Report on Land Registration,[19] which included draft amendments to the Land Registration Act the Commission included this proposal in clause 9, and noted that it placed on a statutory footing the decision of the Court of Appeal in *Lloyd's Bank v. Rosset.*[20] This proposal has to some extent been eclipsed by interpretation adopted by the House of Lords in *Abbey National v. Cann*[21] that in general the relevant date for the determination of the existence of overriding interests is the date of registration, but that for the purposes of section 70(1)(g) actual occupation must be established at the date of completion. As has been noted, this does not provide an answer to all the difficulties raised by the registration gap under the present system, and the Law Commission's proposal would seem to provide an attractive and sensible

[16] para. 2.64.
[17] para. 2.75.
[18] (1985) 50 P. & C.R. 244.
[19] Law Com. No. 173.
[20] [1989] Ch. 350.
[21] [1991] 1 A.C. 56.

solution, particularly if the range of overriding interests is also limited, thus excluding those which the House of Lords felt bound to conclude should still gain priority even if they arose during the registration gap.

Priorities in registered land

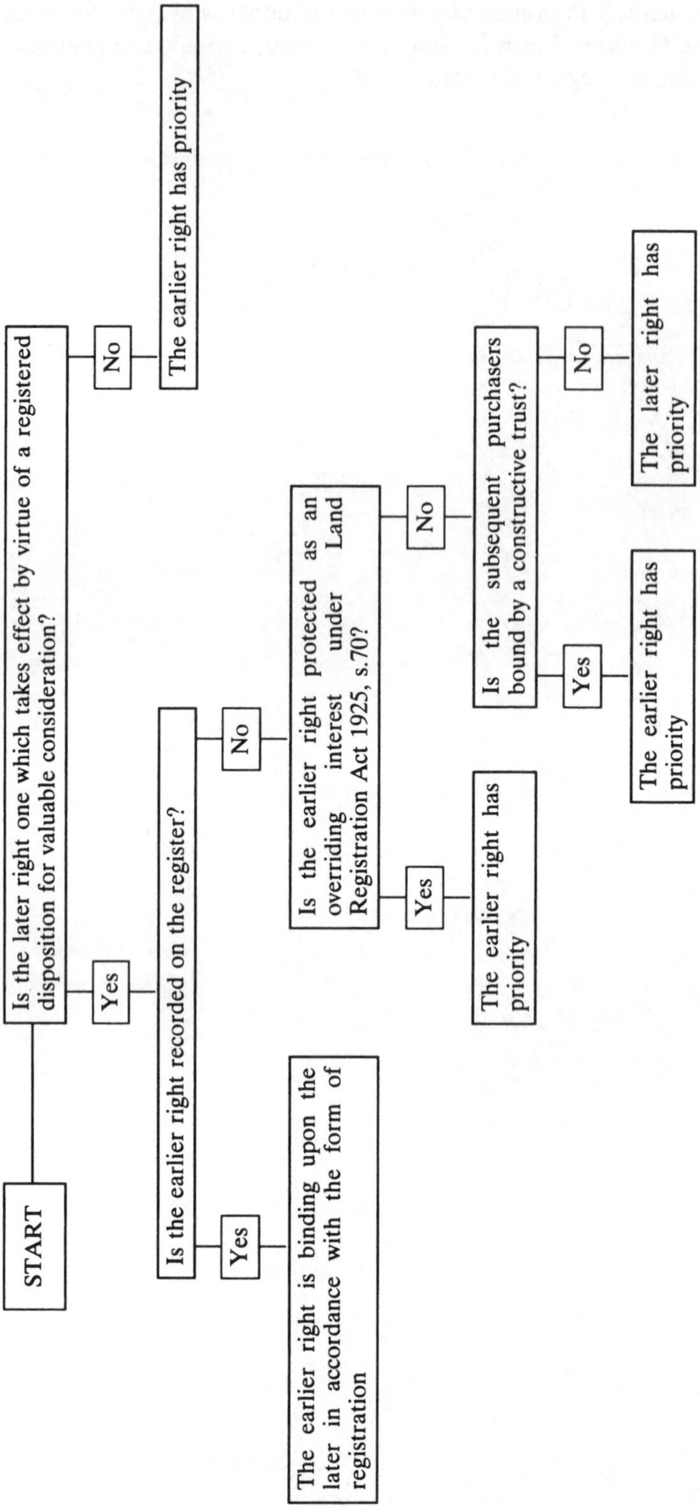

Part V

Unregistered Land

Chapter 17

UNREGISTERED LAND

THE DIMINISHING SIGNIFICANCE OF UNREGISTERED LAND

It has been seen how the central objective of the property legislation of 1925 was to introduce a universal system of registration of title for all land in England and Wales, but that this could not be accomplished immediately. Therefore much land initially remained unregistered. It has also been seen that the gradual introduction of geographical areas of compulsory registration, culminating in the Registration of Title Order 1989, has had the effect that the majority of land is either registered, or likely to become registered, within a generation. Unregistered land is therefore of constantly diminishing significance, and will ultimately become a matter of historical interest only. For this reason this book has taken the view that registered land is now the paradigm of English land law. However, the continuing residual significance of unregistered land means that some attention must be given to how the key questions of land law are addressed within it.

LEGAL TITLE IN UNREGISTERED LAND

1 The title deeds of land

In the registered land system the identity of the owner of a legal estate in land is relatively easy to establish, since the owner of the freehold or a leasehold with a duration of more than 21 years will be registered as proprietor of that estate. Thus, a potential purchaser or lender can establish that a vendor or prospective mortgagor has good title merely by examining the register. Where title is not registered any potential purchaser or mortgagor of an estate in land must satisfy themselves that the vendor or mortgagee does enjoy good title to the legal estate claimed. This is usually achieved by allowing the potential purchaser to examine the vendor's title deeds. These consist of the collection of conveyances or other deeds and documents by which the estate in issue has been created or disposed of in the past, which together provide a historical record demonstrating how the vendor has come to enjoy good title to the land.

2 Establishing a good root of title[1]

(a) *Meaning of a "good root of title"*

Where land is unregistered a prospective purchaser or mortgagee will want the vendor or mortgagor to establish that they enjoy a "good root of title." This means a document which clearly identifies the land in relation to which the legal estate is claimed and establishes the existence of the estate which can then be traced into the hands of the present vendor. Although there is no statutory or judicial definition of a "good root of title" it was described in *Williams on Vendor and Purchaser*[2] as:

> ". . . an instrument or disposition dealing with or proving on the face of it, without the aid of extrinsic evidence, the ownership of the whole legal and equitable estate in the property sold, containing a description by which the property can be identified and showing nothing to cast any doubt on the title of the disposing parties."

(b) *Establishing a good root of title to a freehold estate*

In the case of a freehold estate the best root of title is a past conveyance which was executed when the freehold estate was sold. Such a conveyance on sale indicates that the title was investigated and accepted at the date that the conveyance was made. By Law of Property Act 1925, s.44(1) the purchaser of land may require that the vendor demonstrate 15 years good title.[3] This means that he must be able to point to a conveyance on sale dating back at least 15 years. Obviously if there was such a conveyance to himself 17 years previously this will be sufficient to demonstrate good title and no further investigation need be made.[4] However, if the land had been conveyed to him 10 years ago, by a vendor who derived his own title from a conveyance made in 1930, the earlier conveyance would form the good root of title. Clearly a good title can also be acquired by adverse possession of 12 years, however, a vendor may be extremely wary about transacting with such an adverse possessor, since here will be some risk that their claim cannot be substantiated.

(c) *Establishing a good root of title to a legal leasehold estate*

If a purchaser is seeking an assignment of a leasehold estate, or a mortgagee to take a mortgage over such an estate, he will obviously wish to satisfy himself that the vendor or mortgagor is entitled to the estate claimed. To do this he must produce an abstract or copy of the lease from which his estate derives and proof of dealings with the leasehold estate dating back at least 15 years establishing that he is currently the tenant. For example, if a 99 year lease was granted in 1920 a vendor must both produce the lease itself and demonstrate that he has good title to the tenancy thereby created. If the tenancy was assigned to him 17 years ago, this will be sufficient. However, if it was assigned to him 10 years ago, by a tenant who had previous taken an

[1] For further information see *Barnsley's Conveyancing Law and Practice,* (4th ed., 1996) pp.265–331.
[2] (4th ed.) p.124.
[3] Reduced from 30 years by Law of Property Act 1969, s.23.
[4] The parties may contractually agree on a shorter period of time.

assignment in 1960, he must produce the earlier assignment in order to establish a good root of title. By Law of Property Act 1925, s.44(2) the purchaser of a leasehold estate is not entitled to require the vendor to prove the validity of the freehold title of his landlord.

ISSUES OF PRIORITY IN UNREGISTERED LAND

1 Outline of Priorities in Unregistered Land

(a) Overreaching of trust interests

The overreaching mechanism, by which if appropriate statutory criteria are fulfilled the purchasers or mortgagees of a legal estate in land acquire their interests in the land free from any pre-existing equitable trust interests, has been examined in detail in the context of registered land.[5] It operates equally in respect of land which is unregistered. Therefore if the legal title to a freehold or leasehold estate is conveyed by two or more joint tenants who hold the land on a trust of land,[6] any equitable ownership rights will be overreached and rendered incapable of binding the purchaser, who will gain priority over them. As in registered land the majority of problems concerning issues of priority where there is a trust of land occur when the legal title was transferred by a sole trustee so that the beneficial interests were not overreached, as in *Kingsnorth Finance v. Tizard*.[7]

(b) A limited scheme of registration for land charges

Although land is termed "unregistered" because there is no registration of title of legal estates, a limited system of registration was introduced for certain specified subsidiary interests in land. These interests are termed "land charges" and the Land Charges Act 1925, replaced by the Land Charges Act 1972, introduced a land charges register. In many respects the system of land charges registration equates land charges with minor interests in registered land, so that the holder of such an interest has the opportunity to protect it by means of an entry on a state maintained register. Subsequent purchasers of a legal estate will then only acquire it subject to those land charges affecting it which have been properly protected, whereas they will take free from those which have not been registered. The central difference lies in the nature of the register. Minor interests in registered land are protected on the register entry of the estate to which they relate. However in the case of unregistered land there is no such register. Instead the land charges register is a names based register, so that land charges can be protected by an entry against the name of the estate owner of the land to which they relate. This reflects the interim and short term nature of the land charges register and has inevitably lead to difficulties which will only be overcome when all land is registered.

(c) Residual operation of the doctrine of notice

Since the land charges system only applies to a limited number of rights and interests in land an alternative method of establishing priority must operate in relation to all

[5] See Chap. 14.
[6] Law of Property Act 1925, s.2.
[7] [1986] 1 W.L.R. 783.

other interests. For those rights and interests which are not land charges, issues of priority are determined by the traditional doctrine of notice. Thus, a purchaser of a legal estate in unregistered land will take his title subject to all subsisting legal interests which are not land charges, and to all equitable interests which are not land charges of which he had notice, actual, constructive or imputed.

(2) Land charges

(a) Definition of land charges

Section 2 of the Land Charges Act 1972 provides that certain interests in unregistered land are to rank as land charges. There are six basic categories of land charge, termed "classes," although within some classes there is a further sub-division. Some such land charges are uncontroversial, whereas in relation to others there has been much debate as to their precise scope.

(i) Class A land charges: Class A land charges comprise rights to receive a sum of money from the owner of land, for example an annuity, arising only by an application under an Act of Parliament to recover money spent on the land under the provisions of such an Act. An example of such a land charge is the landlord's right to compensation under the Agricultural Holdings Act 1986.[8]

(ii) Class B land charges: Class B land charges comprise rights identical to those in Class A which are not dependent for their creation on the application of any person, but which arise automatically by operation of statute, excluding local land charges. An example of such a land charge is the charge over land recovered in a legally aided action arising to recoup the client's unpaid legal aid contributions.[9]

(iii) Class C(i) land charges: Class C(i) land charges comprise the "puisne mortgage," which is defined as a "legal mortgage which is not protected by the deposit of documents relating to the legal estate affected." Such mortgages will generally be second mortgages, since the mortgagee of a first mortgage will usually insist on holding the title documents to prevent the mortgagor dealing with the legal estate. The puisine mortgage is unusual in that it is a legal subsidiary interest which ranks as a land charge. This anomaly is explicable by the importance of affording adequate protection to the mortgagee, since it is obvious that the title documents cannot be deposited with separate lenders.

(iv) Class C(ii) land charges: Class C(ii) land charges comprise the "limited owner's charge" which is defined as "an equitable charge acquired by a tenant for life or statutory owner under the Inheritance Tax Act 1984 or under any other statute by reason of the discharge by him of any capital transfer tax or other liabilities and to which special priority is given by statute." This would include, for example, the charge in favour of a tenant for life under a strict settlement who pays inheritance tax on the estate from which his life interest is derived.

(v) Class C(iii) land charges: Class C(iii) land charges consist of the "general equitable charge." This is a catch-all category which will include all equitable charges over land except those excluded by Land Charges Act 1972, s.2(4)(iii) which provides that:

[8] ss. 85 and 86.
[9] Legal Aid Act 1988, s.16(6).

"A general equitable charge is any equitable charge which —

(a) is not secured by a deposit of documents relating to the legal estate affected; and
(b) does not arise or affect an interest arising under a trust of land or a settlement; and
(c) is not a charge given by way of indemnity against rents equitably apportioned or charged exclusively on land in exoneration of other land and against the breach or non-observance of covenants or conditions; and
(d) is not included in any other class of land charge."

This category of land charge will include an equitable mortgage of a legal estate not secured by title deeds, and an unpaid vendor's lien.
(vi) Class C(iv) land charges: Class C(iv) land charges comprise "estate contracts," which are probably the single most significant category of land charge. They are defined by section 2(4)(iv):

"an estate contract is a contract by an estate owner or by a person entitled at the date of the contract to have a legal estate conveyed to him to convey or create a legal estate, including a contract conferring either expressly or by statutory implication a valid option to purchase, a right of pre-emption of any other like right."

Estate contracts will therefore include contracts for the sale of the freehold of land and contracts to grant a lease.[10] They also include the grant of an option to acquire such a legal estate.[11] An option entitles the grantee to demand that the grantor makes a conveyance of the agreed estate in the land, and since the grantor is taken to be under an obligation not to do anything which would prevent his ability to execute the agreed conveyance if the grantee chooses to exercise his option the grantee is regarded as enjoying an equitable interest in the land from the moment that the option was validly granted.[12] A right of pre-emption will also constitute a C(iv) land charge, but its nature is essentially distinct from that of an option. The grantee of a right of pre-emption merely has the right of first refusal if the grantor decides to make a conveyance of a legal estate in the land. As such, he cannot in any way demand that the estate subject to the right should be conveyed to him, and the initiative remains exclusively with the grantor. For this reason he does not gain any equitable rights in the land itself on the mere grant of the right of pre-emption. Instead his rights only crystallise in the land when the grantor decides to sell. This difference between the immediate status of the option and delayed character of the right of pre-emption as equitable rights in land is important if the same estate is subject to both an option to purchase and a right of pre-

[10] *Phillips v. Mobil Oil Co. Ltd* [1989] 1 W.L.R. 888.
[11] See: *Midland Bank Trust Co. v. Green* [1981] A.C. 513 (option to purchase freehold); *Taylor Fashions Ltd v. Liverpool Victoria Trustees Co. Ltd* [1982] Q.B. 133 (option to renew lease).
[12] See: *London and South Western Railways Co. v. Gomm* (1882) 20 Ch.D. 562; *First National Securities Ltd v. Chiltern D.C.* [1975] 1 W.L.R. 1075; *London & Blenheim Estates Ltd v. Ladbroke Retail Parks Ltd* [1992] 1 W.L.R. 1278.

emption. This issue arose in *Pritchard v. Briggs*[13] where the owners of a hotel had sold it but retained the surrounding land. The initial conveyance of 1944 granted the purchasers of the hotel a right of pre-emption in relation to the surrounding land, which was duly protected as a land charge. However, in 1959 the land was leased and the lease granted the tenant an option to purchase, which was also protected as a land charge. The land was eventually sold to the hotel owners and after the sale was completed the tenants claimed the right to exercise the option. The hotel owners claimed that their right of pre-emption took priority over the option because it had been registered earlier, but the Court of Appeal held that since only the option had existed as an interest in land prior to the decision to sell the right of pre-emption could not gain priority over it even though it had been protected by registration. This approach has been approved in subsequent cases.[14] It is also unlikely that a contract creating an agency arrangement with the owner of land will itself constitute a land charge within Class C(iv). In *Thomas v. Rose*[15] the plaintiff entered into a contract with Rose under which Rose was appointed sole agent to clear and grade the plaintiff's land in preparation for use as a building site, and he reserved the right to accept or refuse any offer for sale of the land. Rose registered this agreement as a land charge. The plaintiff subsequently sought an order that the agreement was not capable of registration as a land charge, which was granted by Megarry J. He questioned the earlier decision of *Turley v. Mackay,*[16] where Uthwatt J. had held that an agency agreement was a land charge within Class C(iv), and concluded that the contract was not an estate contract:

> "But does the contract contain any obligation on the plaintiff's part to 'create or convey' any legal estate in favour of anyone? I cannot see that it does. It gives the agent, Mr Rose, the power . . . to 'accept . . . any offer for the sale of all or any part of the area.' Let the agent do this, and there would spring into being a contract with the purchaser by the landowner, made through his agent; and doubtless that contract would be registrable. But that contract is not this contract: a contract providing for the making of a further contract to create or convey a legal estate is not itself a contract to convey or create a legal estate. I do not see how Class C(iv) can be read as embracing contracts at one remove. In my judgement, on the wording of the statute the only contracts that fall within Class C(iv) are those which *themselves* bind the estate owner (or other person entitled) to convey or create a legal estate. It is not enough for the contract merely to provide machinery whereby such an obligation may be created by some other transaction: the very contract itself must impose the obligation."[17]

Problems also arise as to whether an interest is to be regarded as a Class C(iv) estate contract when parties have entered into a specifically enforceable contract to purchase land because the contract itself gives rise to a constructive trust in favour of the

[13] [1980] Ch. 338.
[14] *Kling v. Keston Properties Ltd* (1985) 49 P. & C.R. 212; *London & Blenheim Estates Ltd v. Ladbroke Retail Parks Ltd* [1994] 1 W.L.R. 31.
[15] [1968] 1 W.L.R. 1797.
[16] [1944] Ch. 37.
[17] *ibid.* at 1804–1805.

purchaser, who thereby gains the equitable ownership. If this right is classified as an estate contract issues of priority will be governed by the relevant provisions of the Land Charges Act 1925, but if the equitable trust interest is treated as distinct from the estate contract and existing in its own right such issues will fall to be determined by the doctrine of notice. The question arose in *Lloyd's Bank v. Carrick*[18] where the defendant had entered into a contract to purchase a maisonette, moved into possession and paid the purchase price, but where title had never been conveyed to her. The owner subsequently mortgaged the property without her knowledge. She had failed to register her interests as a Class C(iv) land charge, and the bank had failed to make any inspection of the property before accepting the mortgage. The defendant claimed that since the owner held the maisonette on trust for her as a consequence of the specifically enforceable contract, the bank were bound by that trust interest as they had constructive notice of it. However the Court of Appeal held that even though she had paid the purchase price her trust interest could not be treated as existing independently of her contract, which was void as against the mortgagees. Morritt L.J. explained:

> "The source and origin of the trust was the contract; the payment of the price by [the defendant] served only to make it a bare trust by removing any beneficial interest of [the owner]. Section 4(6) of the [Land Charges Act 1972][19] avoids that contract as against the bank. The result, in my judgement, must be that [the defendant] is unable to establish the bare trust as against the bank for it has no existence except as the equitable consequence of the contract."[20]

(vii) Class D(i) land charges: Class D(i) land charges comprise the "Inland Revenue Charge," which is a charge acquired over land by the Inland Revenue Board under the Inheritance Act 1984.
(viii) Class D(ii) land charges: Class D(ii) land charges comprise restrictive covenants. However, not every restrictive covenant in unregistered land is a land charge. By Land Charges Act 1972, s.2(5)(ii) only those restrictive covenants "entered into on or after 1st January 1926" are within Class D(iv). Issues of priority relating to restrictive covenants created before that date will fall to be determined by the doctrine of notice.
(ix) Class D(iii) land charges: Class D(iii) land charges comprise "equitable easements," which are defined by section 2(5)(iii) as:

> " . . . an easement right or privilege over or affecting land created or arising on or after 1st January 1926, and being merely an equitable easement."

Although this definition seems relatively straightforward, comprising easements coming into existence after the specified date which are not legal in status, its precise scope has been the subject of some controversy. In *E R Ives Investment Ltd v. High*[21] Lord Denning M.R. adopted a restrictive interpretation that Class D(iii) only included easements which would have enjoyed legal status if they had been granted prior to 1926:

[18] [1996] 4 All E.R. 630.
[19] See below p. 564.
[20] [1996] 4 All E.R. 630, 638.
[21] [1967] 2 Q.B. 379.

> "It appears, then, that an "equitable easement" is a proprietary interest in land such as would before 1926 have been recognised as capable of being conveyed or created *at law*, but which since 1926 only takes effect as an equitable interest. An instance of such a proprietary right is a profit à prendre for life."

He therefore held that the easement claimed to have arisen in equity by reason of "mutual benefit and burden" was not a land charge requiring registration because it was not capable of being created at law prior to 1926 but would only have subsisted in equity. However, this approach was not adopted by the other two judges in the Court of Appeal, who based their decision on grounds of proprietary estoppel arising outside of the operation of the land charges system. Although Lord Denning's view has not been expressly disapproved,[22] it should be rejected as highly artificial and inconsistent with the plain meaning of the statute. All easements which are purely equitable in character created after 1926 should rank as land charges, irrespective of what their status would have been prior to that date.

(x) Class E land charges: Class E land charges comprise annuities affecting land which were created prior to January 1, 1926 but which had not been registered in a pre-existing register of annuities which was closed when the Land Charges Act 1925 was brought into force. Clearly this is a very narrow category.

(xi) Class F Land Charges: Class F land charges comprise the rights of occupation of a matrimonial home enjoyed by a spouse enjoyed by a spouse under Part IV of the Family Law Act 1996.

(b) Registration of land charges

(i) Protection by registration on the Land Charges Register: As has been noted land charges can be protected by registration on the Land Charges Register. Section 3(1) of the Land Charges Act 1972 provides that "a land charge shall be registered in the name of the estate owner whose estate is intended to be affected." The register which is maintained is therefore based on the "names" of the persons who owned the land at the date when the land charge was registered, and not on entries referenced to the land itself.

(ii) The appropriate name in which a land charge should be registered: One potential difficulty with a names based register is that many people use a number of different versions of their name. They may be known by a nick-name, or use a informal version of their name for personal relationships but the full formal version for important transactions. It is therefore important to have a standard bench mark for determining the appropriate name which should be used for the purposes of land charges registration to minimise the risk of confusion and mistakes. In *Standard Property Investment plc v. British Plastics Federation*[23] Walton J. held that the appropriate name in which a land charge should be registered was the name of the owner of the estate affected as found in the conveyance by which the estate had been conveyed to them. This would serve as a "fixed point of reference" since it would be available to any potential purchaser of the land, who would then be able to conduct a search of the land charges register with confidence that he was doing so in the correct name.

[22] See *Poster v. Slough Estates Ltd* [1968] 1 W.L.R. 1515, 1520–1521 *per* Cross J.
[23] (1985) 53 P. & C.R. 25.

(iii) Effect of registration of a land charge in the appropriate name: The correct registration of a land charge is deemed by statute to have the effect of giving everyone in the world actual knowledge of its existence. Section 198(1) of the Law of Property Act 1925 provides that:

> "The registration of any instrument or matter in any register kept under the Land Charges Act 1972 or any local land charges register, shall be deemed to constitute actual notice of such instrument or matter, and of the fact of such registration, to all persons, and for all purposes connected with the land affected, as from the date of registration or other prescribed date and so long as the registration continues in force."

In consequence any person acquiring a legal interest in the land will take their title, or mortgage, subject to the registered land charge. This deeming provisions was initially the cause of problems as a search of the land charges register would often only reveal adverse interests after contracts for the sale of the land had been exchanged. It was held that, since the purchaser was deemed by section 198(1) to have had actual notice of the existence of the land charge at the date of the contract, a subsequent revelation of its existence did not entitle him to refuse to complete the purchase.[24] This difficulty was remedied by Law of Property Act 1969, s.24(1) which provided that:

> "Where under a contract for the sale or other disposition of any estate or interest in the land the title to which is not registered . . . any question arises whether the purchaser had knowledge, at the time of entering into the contract, of a registered land charge, that question shall be determined by reference to his actual knowledge and without regard to the provisions of section 198 . . ."

This provision has the effect that a purchaser will be entitled to refuse to complete a contract if a registered land charge comes to light by search after it was entered, provided that the purchaser did not have actual knowledge of its existence at the time that he entered the contract.
(iv) Effect of registration in an incorrect name: It has already been noted that the appropriate name for registration of a land charge is that of the estate owner as revealed in the conveyance by which he derived his estate. However, it is possible that due to ignorance or mistake a person may have registered their land charge against an incorrect version of that name. This occurred in *Diligent Finance v. Alleyne*[25] where the legal title to a house was owned by a husband, whose name on the conveyance was Erskine Owen Alleyne. His wife had registered a Class F land charge against the name Erskine Alleyne. He subsequently granted a mortgage to the finance company, which requisitioned an official search against the correct name. Foster J. held that because the registration had been made in an incorrect name but the search was requisitioned in the correct name, the finance company did not take subject to the land charge. However, in some circumstances even an incorrect registration may prove effective. In

[24] *Re Forsey and Hollebone's Contract* [1927] 2 Ch. 379.
[25] (1971) 23 P. & C.R. 346.

Oak Co-operative Building Society v. Blackburn[26] the legal owner of a house was Francis David Blackburn. He entered into an estate contract to sell the property to the defendant, who registered a Class C(iv) land charge against the name *Frank* David Blackburn, since this was how he was known locally. He subsequently mortgaged the property, and before agreeing to make the loan the Building Society requisitioned an official search of the land charges register. However due to an error the search was requisitioned in the name of Francis *Davis* Blackburn. The Court of Appeal held that in these circumstances the incorrect registration should not be ineffective since the search had also been requisitioned in the wrong name. Russell L.J. stated the principle from which this conclusion was derived:

> " . . . if there be a registration in what may be fairly described as a version of the full names of the vendor, albeit not a version which is bound to be discovered on a search in the correct full names, we would not hold it a nullity against someone who does not search at all, or who (as here) searches in the wrong name."

(v) Inaccessible registrations: Another problem associated with the names based register of land charges is that since each entry is related to the name of an estate owner rather than to the land itself a prospective purchaser may need to know the names of all the estate owners after 1925 in order to be certain that there are no adverse land charges affecting the land. For example, if the freehold owner of land granted a 99 year option to purchase in 1927, which was registered as a Class C(iv) land charge, a prospective purchaser in 1997 would only be able to ascertain its existence if he knew the name of the owner against whom it had been registered. However, as has been seen above, the prospective purchaser only enjoys the statutory right to examine the title deeds establishing a good root of title dating back at least 15 years. Since he does not have the right of access to earlier documents and conveyances he may find that it is impossible to discover the names of previous estate owners in order to requisition a search against them. For example, if the land subject to the option had been sold by the subsequent estate owners in 1947, 1967 and 1987 a prospective purchaser in 1997 would have the right to examine the conveyance of 1967 to establish title. Although this might reveal the name of the transferee of the estate under the 1947 conveyance, it would not reveal the name of the person who had been the estate owner in 1927 when the estate contract had been registered. The problem is compounded by the fact that by Law of Property Act 1925, s.198 effective registration is deemed to constitute actual notice of the registered land charge. Therefore, a prospective purchaser could go ahead and acquire the land in 1997 without being able to discover the existence of the registered charge because the essential information concerning the name of the estate owner was unavailable to him, yet find that he was still bound by the option because he was deemed to have actual notice of it. Two factors have compounded this difficulty. First, it was never intended that land would remain unregistered for such a long period of time, since the legislators expected comprehensive registration within 30 years. Secondly, there has been a gradual erosion of the duration of title which a prospective purchaser is entitled to inspect, which was 60 years in 1925 and is now only 15. In order to prevent any unfairness which might

[26] [1968] Ch. 730.

arise from these difficulties the Law of Property Act 1969 introduced a right to statutory compensation for anyone who suffers loss as a result of the existence of a land charge registered against the name of an estate owner who was in no way connected with the present transaction. Section 25(1) provides:

> "Where a purchaser of any estate or interest in land under a disposition to which this section applies has suffered loss by reason that the estate or interest is affected by a registered land charge, then if —
>
> (a) the date of completion was after the commencement of this Act; and
> (b) on that date the purchaser had no actual knowledge of the charge; and
> (c) the charge was registered against the name of an owner of an estate in the land who was not an owner of any such a state a party to any transaction, or concerned in any event, comprised in the relevant title;
>
> the purchaser shall be entitled to compensation for the loss."

Statutory compensation applies where there was a sale, mortgage, or lease derived out of a leasehold interest, but not to a lease of freehold land.[27]

(c) Discovering the existence of registered land charges

(i) Searches of the land charges register: When a person is prospectively considering the acquisition of an interest in unregistered land they have the opportunity to search the Land Charges Register in order to discover whether any interests have been protected by registration. Such a search may either be undertaken personally, or alternatively an official search may be requisitioned, in which case the person searching will submit the appropriate names to the registry which will carry out the search and then issue a certificate indicating any land charges which have been registered against them. In *Oak Co-operative Building Society v. Blackburn*[28] Russell L.J. expressed the clear preference of the law in favour of an official search and regarded a personal search as "foolish."[29]

(ii) Effect of an official search certificate: When an official search is requisitioned the resulting official search certificate is of vital importance because Land Charges Act 1972, s.10(4) provides that:

> "In favour of a purchaser or an intending purchaser, as against persons interested under or in respect of matters or documents entries of which are required or allowed as aforesaid, *the certificate, according to its tenor, shall be conclusive*, affirmatively or negatively, as the case may be."

This means that if a mistake is made by the land registry, so that a land charge which had been registered was not included in the official search certificate, the purchaser is entitled to rely on the certificate and, if the other relevant statutory criteria are

[27] s.25(9).
[28] [1968] Ch. 730.
[29] *ibid.* at 744.

satisfied, will acquire the land free from the otherwise validly protected land charge. In such cases the holder of the land charge would have a remedy against the land registry for negligence, thus enabling him to recover compensation for any loss that he suffered as a result.[30]

(d) Unregistered land charges rendered void if statutory criteria satisfied

(i) Unregistered land charges of Classes C(iv) and D: In relation to estate contracts and Class D land charges Land Charges Act 1925, s.4(6) lays down the statutory criteria by which such an interest will be rendered void if unprotected:

> "An estate contract and a land charge of Class D created or entered into on or after 1st January 1926 shall be void as against a purchaser for money or moneys worth . . . of a legal estate in the land charged with it, unless the land charge is registered in the appropriate register before the completion of the purchase."

Thus if a person satisfies the two conditions set out in this subsection they will take the land free from the unprotected land charge. First, he must be a *purchaser for money of money's worth*. This means that a person acquiring title by gift, through succession, in return for marriage consideration or for nominal non-monetary consideration will not be entitled to protection and will take their interest subject even to unprotected land charges. In *Midland Bank Trust Co. Ltd v. Green*[31] the House of Lords rejected the interpretation of this requirement propounded by Lord Denning M.R. in the Court of Appeal that the consideration provided must be adequate in relation to the value of the land acquired. Lord Wilberforce stated that: "To exclude a nominal sum of money from [s.4(6)] of the Land Charges Act would be to re-write the section."[32] It was therefore held that an unprotected option was rendered void when the farm to which it related was purchased by the owner's wife for £500 when at the date of the transaction it was worth some £40,000. Secondly, he must have acquired a *legal estate* in the land subject to the unprotected charge. This means that he must have purchased either the freehold of the land, taken a legal lease or a charge by way of legal mortgage.[33] Therefore a person who has only acquired an equitable interest in the land, for example a share of the equitable ownership behind a trust or an equitable mortgage, will take their interest subject even to unprotected land charges.[34] It is also clear from the decision of the House of Lords in *Midland Bank Trust Co. Ltd v. Green*[35] that provided the appropriate statutory conditions have been satisfied it is irrelevant that the person claiming that an unregistered land charge was rendered void against them had actual notice of its existence. In the Court of Appeal Lord Denning M.R. had construed section 4(6) so as to introduce an additional requirement of "good faith," by referring to the definition of a purchaser in Law of Property Act 1925, s.205(xxi) and concluded that where a mother had purchased a farm with full knowledge that her son had been granted an option over it she could not claim the benefit of the statute to

[30] *Ministry of Housing and Local Government v. Sharp* [1970] 2 Q.B. 223.
[31] [1981] A.C. 513.
[32] *ibid.* at 532.
[33] Law of Property Act 1925, s.87(1).
[34] See: *McCarthy and Stone Ltd v. Hodge* [1971] 1 W.L.R. 1547.
[35] [1981] A.C. 513.

render the unprotected estate contract void. However the House of Lords rejected his interpretation and Lord Wilberforce held that it was entirely inappropriate to read a requirement of good faith into section 4(6) by reference to contemporaneous Acts, and that the omission of such a requirement had been deliberate. It was therefore held that the wife acquired the freehold of the farm free from the estate contract of her son, even though she knew full well of its existence at the time of the transaction.

(ii) Unregistered land charges of the other Classes: With some slight variations[36] the remaining land charges will be rendered void when unprotected if slightly lesser statutory conditions are met. The formula used is that they are void: ". . . as against a purchaser of the land charged with it, or of any interest in such land, unless the land charge is registered in the appropriate register before the completion of the purchase."[37] In comparison with section 4(6) such unprotected land charges will be rendered void even against a person who does not acquire a legal estate in the land, for example the mortgagee of an equitable mortgage. The requirement as to consideration is also different. Rather than requiring "money or money's worth" statutory protection is given to any *purchaser* a term which is defined in section 17 to mean: "any person (including a mortgagee or lessee) who, for valuable consideration, takes any interest in land or in a charge on land . . ." This will include marriage consideration and nominal consideration, but again an unprotected land charge will not be rendered void as against a person who acquires an interest in the land by way of a gift or through succession.

(d) Circumstances in which land charges rendered void by statute may still be binding on a purchaser of the land

(i) Parallels with minor interests in registered land: It has already been noted how the operation of land charges registration is similar to that of the protection of minor interests in registered land. In Chapter 15 it was noted how minor interests which have not been protected on the register of the title to which they relate may still be binding on a transferee of the land through an independent constructive trust or on the grounds of fraud. The same doctrines may also be applicable in the context of unregistered land charges so that an otherwise void land charge will still be binding. However, an important difference is that whilst unprotected minor interests may also rank as overriding interests if coupled with actual occupation under section 70(1)(g) of the Land Registration Act 1925 there is no equivalent principle in unregistered land, so that even a land charge of a person occupying land will be void if he has failed to protect it appropriately, as was the case in *Midland Bank Trust Co. Ltd v. Green.*[38] To this extent some of the problems associated with the failure to protect land charges will only be ameliorated when all land is registered and there is fuller protection for the rights of occupiers.

(ii) Statutorily void land charge binding by means of an independent constructive trust: In *Lyus v. Prowsa Develoments*[39] it was held that an unprotected minor interest in registered land was binding on a purchaser who had expressly agreed to take title

[36] Class A land charges are.

[37] See: s.4(2) (Class A charges created after December 31, 1888); s.4(3) (Class A land charges created before January 1, 1889); s.46(4) (Classes B and C(i), (ii) & (iii)); s.46(8) (Class F).

[38] [1981] A.C. 513.

[39] [1952] 1 W.L.R. 1044.

subject to it by means of a constructive trust. There is no reason why this principle should not equally apply where the purchaser of land has expressly agreed to take it subject to an unregistered land charge. The operation of this principle was discussed in detail above,[40] and it should be remembered that two criteria must be satisfied. First, the purchaser must have agreed to take the land subject to the specific interest claimed to be binding by a constructive trust. A mere general agreement to take subject to third party interests affecting the land would not be sufficient to impose a constructive trust of an unregistered land charge. Secondly, the transferor of the land must have detrimentally relied upon such an express undertaking, so as to justify the court in concluding that the transferee's conscience was affected in such a way as to call for the imposition of a constructive trust. The most common such detriment would be a reduction in the price paid for the land to reflect the promise to observe the third party right.[41]

(iii) Statutorily void land charge binding by estoppel: Even if a land charge would be rendered statutorily void by operation of the Land Charges Act 1972 it is possible that it might be binding on a purchaser who is estopped from denying its existence. Although this principle is closely related to the concept of the independent constructive trust it seems that a lower threshold would be required to establish the estoppel since there is no need to demonstrate an agreement to take the land subject to the interest. The possibility of such an estoppel seems to have been raised in *E R Ives Investments Ltd v. High*,[42] the precise ratio of which is difficult to discern because of the different approaches of the three judges who decided it. The case concerned a right of way over a yard which had never been formally granted as an easement or protected as a land charge. The owner of the land adjacent to that of the defendant had constructed a block of flats the foundations of which constituted a trespass. The owner orally agreed to allow the defendant access across his yard in return for his not taking any action in relation to the trespass. Some years later the neighbour sold the land to a purchaser who knew of the agreement. The defendant then built a garage which was dependant upon the right of way for its utility to which the new owner made no objection. Some years later the defendant resurfaced the yard and bore most of the expense incurred. The neighbouring land was subsequently purchased by the plaintiffs, and the conveyance stated that the land was subject to the right of way. As has already been noted, Lord Denning M.R. held that the right of was not an "equitable easement" within Class D(iii) and that priority was determined by the doctrine of notice. Winn L.J. held that the defendants had acquired a right of way against the first purchasers of the yard by means of estoppel, since the purchasers had over a number of years represented to them that they had a right to access, and that this estoppel right was binding on the plaintiffs since it was not registrable as a land charge and as they had actual notice of its existence they were bound by it as successors in title. Again this amounts to a finding that the easement in question was not a right requiring protection as a land charge. However, Danckwerts L.J. reached an identical conclusion that the plaintiffs were bound by the right of way for very different reasons. He held that the interest should have been protected as a land charge and would have been

[40] See Chap. 15.
[41] See: *Ashburn Anstalt v. Arnold* [1989] Ch. 1.
[42] [1967] 2 Q.B. 379.

void for non-registration, and that the mere fact of actual notice on the part of the purchasers would not alone have prevented such a conclusion. But he held that there was a separate and external principle of estoppel by which the plaintiffs would be forced to observe the defendants' right of way. He considered that as the plaintiffs had continued to enjoy the benefits of the oral agreement which the defendants had originally made, namely that the foundations of their building continued to trespass, they had to take the land subject to the burden of that agreement:

> "The plaintiffs bought the property subject to Mr High's equitable rights and the property was so conveyed to them. They had full knowledge of the situation, yet they continue to enjoy the benefits of the situation and wish to deny Mr High the benefit of what he was induced to do in reliance on the mutual arrangement. As long as the plaintiffs continue to enjoy the foundations, they must accept the terms of that enjoyment."[43]

In effect they were estopped from denying the existence of the right of way, even though it would otherwise have been rendered void by operation of the Act. This doctrine of mutual benefit and burden was also accepted as a grounds for finding the plaintiffs obliged to observe the right of way by Lord Denning M.R. The principle that an estoppel might mean that an otherwise void land charge remains binding was also accepted by Oliver J. in *Taylor fashions Ltd v. Liverpool Victoria Trustees Co. Ltd*[44] where two cases were in issue. The first plaintiff's were lessors of premises under a lease which granted them an option to renew which had not been registered as a land charge due to the parties' mistaken belief that it was not registrable. They claimed to be entitled to exercise the option as against the successors in title to the original lessees, who had purchased the freehold reversion in 1949, on the grounds of estoppel, arising from the fact that the parties were aware of the option and that they had improved the premises, including installing a lift, in reliance upon their right to exercise it. Oliver J. held that in principle an estoppel could be raised, but that it was not established in the circumstances because there was no evidence of any encouragement of the plaintiffs by the lessees as to the validity of the option, nor was there any expenditure in reliance which was not consistent with the unexpired term remaining at the date it was incurred. The option was therefore void as an unprotected land charge. The second plaintiff's had also taken a lease containing an unprotected option to renew, but in respect of this right Oliver J. held that the defendants were estopped from denying its validity because they had encouraged the seconds plaintiffs to expend large sums on the premises and to take a lease of adjoining premises upon the expectation, which they had encouraged, that the lease would be renewed. As Oliver J. stated:

> "It would, in my judgment, be most inequitable that the defendants, having put forward [the] option as a valid option in two documents, under each of which they are the grantors, and having encouraged [the plaintiffs] to incur expenditure and to alter their position irrevocably by taking additional premises on the faith

[43] *ibid.* at 400.
[44] [1982] Q.B. 133.

> of that supposition, should now be permitted to resile and to assert, as they do, that they are and were all along entitled to frustrate the expectation which they themselves created and that the right which they themselves stated to exist did not, at any material time, have any existence in fact."[45]

(iv) Statutorily void land charge binding because of the purchaser's fraud: It was also noted in the context of unprotected minor interests that a transferor could not claim the benefit of priority conferred by the Land Registration Act 1925 if he had acted fraudulently. One of the central issues in *Midland Bank Trust Co. Ltd v. Green*[46] was whether in the circumstances the mother's right to rely on section 4(6) to render her son's unprotected estate contract void was vitiated by fraud. In the Court of Appeal Lord Denning M.R. concluded that there was sufficient fraud to prevent her relying on the statutory provisions which would otherwise operate in her favour. He defined what he considered constituted vitiating fraud:

> "Fraud in this context covers any dishonest dealing done so as to deprive unwary innocents of their rightful dues. The marks of it are transactions done stealthily and speedily in secret for no sufficient consideration. All these appear in this conveyance made by [the husband] to his wife."[47]

In essence Lord Denning M.R. propounded a general doctrine that "the provisions for protecting a purchaser are of no avail when the sale to him is done in fraud of the holder of the estate contract." However, the width of this concept of fraud was rejected by the House of Lords, which held that a purchaser is fully entitled to take advantage of the legal rights granted him by a statute. Lord Wilberforce referred to the earlier Court of Appeal decision in *Re Monolithic Building Co.*[48] and the principle stated by Lord Cozens-Hardy M.R. that "it is not fraud to take advantage of legal rights, the existence of which may be taken to be known to both parties." He therefore concluded that equitable doctrines such as notice and fraud should not be read into modern Acts of Parliament, and that clear enactments as to registration and priority should be interpreted according to their tenor.[49] In the view of the House of Lords therefore, the mere fact that a person knew of a failure to register a land charge appropriately does not mean that it was fraudulent to exploit that opportunity and acquire the land free from it, even if this was the sole object of the transaction. In reality the reason why such a person would suffer the consequence that their interest was rendered void was their own failure to take steps to protect it. This may result in some seemingly harsh outcomes, but it is consistent with the policy of the 1925 legislation which shifted the emphasis from the obligation of the prospective purchaser to make adequate inquiries to protect himself to the obligation of the holder of subsidiary interests to take the necessary steps to ensure that they were protected. As Lord Wilberforce noted:

> "The case is plain: the Act is clear and definite. Intended as it was to provide a simple and understandable system for the protection of title to land, it should not

[45] *ibid.* at 158.
[46] [1981] A.C. 513.
[47] [1980] Ch. 590 at 625.
[48] [1915] 2 Ch. 643.
[49] [1981] A.C. 513 at 531.

be read down or glossed; to do so would destroy the usefulness of the Act. Any temptation to remould the act to meet the facts of the present case, on the supposition that it is a hard one and that justice requires it, is, for me at least, removed by the consideration that the Act itself provides a simple and effective protection for persons in [the son's] position, *viz* by registration."[50]

However, this does not mean that a transaction which is deliberately designed to defeat an unprotected land charge will never be regarded as fraudulent. For example it is unlikely that a land charge would be rendered void if the purported sale of the land was no real transaction at all because the purchaser was in effect the same person as the present owner subject to the unprotected interest, either because the purchaser was a nominee of the owner and held the land acquired on bare trust for him, or was a company which was a mere shell for the owner.[51] Similarly if the purchaser of the land stood as a fiduciary of the holder of the unprotected land charge it is unlikely that they would take the land free from it.[52]

(3) Subsidiary interests in unregistered land which are not land charges

(a) General principle

Whereas a special statutory regime applies for the determination of priority issues in relation to those rights in unregistered land which are defined to be land charges there is no special regime for those rights which fall outside of its scope. Instead issues of priority to such rights are resolved by the general law, namely the doctrine of notice.

(b) priority in relation to legal rights in unregistered land which are not land charges

(i) Examples of such rights: The majority of such rights are outside of the land charges system, since as has been seen the puisne mortgage is the only legal interest falling within the scope of the Land Charges Act 1972. Hence such rights as legal leases, legal easements and legal first mortgages will be governed by the general principle that "legal rights bind the world."
(ii) Determining priority issues: Legal rights in unregistered land are indestructible, in the sense that no person acquiring an interest in the land subsequent to their creation can gain priority over them, and must take subject to them. For example, if unregistered land is subject to a legal lease for 10 years and the freehold owner grants a legal mortgage to a Bank, the Bank cannot take its interest as mortgagee free from the legal lease of the tenant. Similarly if a third party enjoyed a legal easement over the land which had pre-dated the creation of the lease, the tenant would take his tenancy subject to the legal easement. The only circumstance in which a legal right can be defeated is if there is adverse possession against the freehold or leasehold so as to defeat the legal title concerned.

[50] In the event it should be noted that although the son's family failed to establish that the mother's estate was bound by the unprotected option they were able to recover damages from the son's solicitors for their negligence in not advising him to protect his option as soon as it had been granted.
[51] See: *Jones v. Lipman* [1962] 1 W.L.R. 832.
[52] See: *Du Boulay v. Raggett* (1989) 58 P. & C.R. 138.

(c) Priority in relation to equitable rights in unregistered land which are not land charges

(i) Examples of equitable rights which are not land charges: Although virtually all land charges in unregistered land are equitable in character, they are by no means comprehensive. The most important equitable right which is not a land charge is the equitable ownership which exists behind a trust of land. In *E R Ives Investments Ltd v. High*[53] the majority of the Court of Appeal held that an equitable easement in land generated by estoppel was not a land charge, and in *Shiloh Spinners Ltd v. Harding*[54] the House of Lords held that an equitable right or re-entry for breach of covenant entered into on the assignment of a lease was also outside of the land charges system. It should be remembered that some such equitable interests, and in particular equitable ownership behind a trust, are capable of being overreached if the relevant statutory conditions are met.

(ii) Determining priority issues in relation to equitable interests which are not easements: priority issues relating to equitable interests which are not land charges are resolved by application of the doctrine of notice. This means that a pre-existing equitable interest will be binding on all persons subsequently acquiring an interest in the land except someone who is a bona fide purchaser of a legal estate in the land for value without notice of the existence of the pre-existing equitable right. All the elements of this formula must be satisfied if priority is to be gained. First the requirement of bona fides means that that purchaser must have acted in good faith. Given the development of the doctrine of constructive notice this is a requirement of very little import, since the presence of notice is generally synonymous with the absence of good faith. Secondly, the doctrine of notice only operates in favour of someone acquiring a legal estate in the land, in other words the freehold title, a legal lease or a legal mortgage. Thirdly, it only operates in favour of a purchaser for value, which includes someone who provides marriage consideration but excludes purely nominal non-monetary consideration. Lastly, and most importantly, the doctrine of notice only operates in favour of a person who had no notice, actual, constructive or imputed, of the existence of the pre-existing equitable interest. Since it is this last element which is usually crucial it will be examined in more detail.

(iii) Actual notice: A person has actual notice of an interest in land when they are consciously aware of its existence. As Lord Cairns L.C. stated in *Lloyd v. Bank*[55] actual notice exists where the mind of a person:

> "... has in some way been brought to the intelligent apprehension of the nature of [an interest] which has come upon the property, so that a reasonable man, or an ordinary man of business, would act upon the information and would regulate his conduct by it."

The mother in *Midland Bank Trust Co. Ltd v. Green*[56] had actual notice of her son's option to purchase the land since she knew that he had been granted it by her

[53] [1967] 2 Q.B. 379.
[54] [1973] A.C. 691.
[55] (1868) 3 Ch. App 488, 490–491.
[56] [1981] A.C. 513.

husband. It is clear that justice demands that a person who has actual notice of an equitable interest affecting the land, which is not a land charge, should take the land subject to it. As Lord Cranworth said in *Ware v. Lord Egmont*[57]: "Where a person has actual notice of any matter of fact, there can be no danger of doing injustice if he is held to be bound by all the consequences of that which he knows to exist." In the context of claims that a person is subject to a duty to account for the value of property received which they knew to be trust property Megarry V.-C. suggested in *Re Monatgu's Settlement*[58] that a person would not be regarded as having actual knowledge if they had once known of the existence of an equitable interest but had subsequently forgotten so that they were no longer aware. The Duke of Manchester had known that certain chattels in his possession were trust property, but he sold them many years later when he had forgotten that they were not his own. It was held that he did not have actual knowledge and was not therefore liable to account for their value. Obviously, such forgetfulness must be genuine and not merely convenient.

(iv) The concept of constructive notice: Where a person is said to have constructive notice of the existence of an equitable interest in land this does not mean that they were consciously aware of its existence. Instead, constructive notice follows from the fact that prospective purchasers of land are expected to take all reasonable steps to inquire whether there are any equitable interests adversely affecting the land, and that they cannot take advantage of their failure to take such steps. Equity therefore deems them to have notice of the existence of such interests affecting the land as they would have discovered if they had made all reasonable inquiries. This principle is placed on a statutory footing in Law of Property Act 1925, s.199(1)(ii)(a) which provides that a purchaser is to be affected by notice of any instrument, matter or fact if: ". . . it is within his own knowledge, or would have come to his knowledge if such inquiries and inspections had been made as ought reasonably to have been made by him." The obligation to make reasonable inquiries and inspection has been taken to mean two things. First, he must inspect the title documents of the land, and secondly he must physically inspect the land itself.

(v) Constructive notice flowing from a failure to make a reasonable inspection of the title documents: It has been seen that in unregistered land a prospective purchaser of a legal estate is entitled to require the vendor to provide proof of title and that this will involve the production of an abstract of title. The purchaser is then expected to examine the documents provided. If he fails to do so he will be held to have notice of such interests as would have been revealed by an inspection. If the purchaser fails to make any inquiry for the title deeds at all, but allows them to remain in the hands of a third person, such as an equitable mortgagee, he will be taken to have constructive notice of the equitable interests of the possessors of the deeds.[59] If he inquires after them, but the vendor fails to produce them, he will have notice of any equitable interests which would have been revealed if the failure to secure their production was through his gross negligence.[60] Although a prospective purchaser is entitled to insist on proof of title for at least 15 years by statute, if the parties choose they can agree to a

[57] (1854) 4 De G.M. & G. 460 at 473.
[58] [1987] Ch. 264.
[59] *Walker v. Linom* [1907] 2 Ch. 104.
[60] *Oliver v. Hinton* [1899] 2 Ch. 264; *Hewitt v. Loosemore* (1851) 9 Hare 449.

lesser period in their contract. If a lesser period is stipulated the purchaser will have constructive notice of any equitable interests which would have been disclosed if he had insisted on proof of title for the whole period.[61]

(v) Constructive notice flowing from a failure to make a reasonable inspection of the land itself: A purchaser of land will be taken to have constructive notice of any equitable rights which would have been evident from a physical inspection of the land. Sometimes this principle was taken to extreme lengths, for example in *Hervey v. Smith*[62] it was held that a purchaser had notice of his neighbour's equitable easement to make use of two flues in his house because he should have noticed that he had 14 chimney pots and only 12 flues. However, as has been seen the majority of commercial equitable interests, such as equitable easements, estate contracts and restrictive covenants, have now been placed within the land charges system where notice is irrelevant and the most important interest still governed by the doctrine of notice is equitable ownership behind trusts of land. Often such interests are enjoyed by persons who are in occupation of the land together with a co-owner who holds the legal title, and therefore although the existence of the trust may be impossible to establish from the title documents, especially if it is a resulting or constructive trust, the existence of a person in occupation could be ascertained by reasonable inspection. In *Hunt v. Luck*[63] the Court of Appeal adopted the principle that:

> ". . . if a purchaser or a mortgagee has notice that the vendor or mortgagor is not in possession of the property, he must make inquiries of the person in possession...and find out from him what his rights are, and if he does not choose to do that, then whatever title he acquires as purchaser or mortgagee will be subject to the title or right of the tenant in possession."[64]

Given the state of the law at the time of the decision, and the relatively undeveloped doctrine of resulting and constructive trusts, the prime focus of the Court of Appeal was in relation to tenants. The freehold owner was not in occupation and therefore the person in occupation was either a tenant or a sub-tenant. If inquiries were not made at all the purchaser would be bound by the interests of the possessor. If inquiries revealed that the possessor was paying rent to a third party the purchaser would also be bound by the interests of that third party. In the modern law the principle remains but has been given broader force. A purchaser is expected to make reasonable inquiries of all persons who are occupying the land, whether that occupation is exclusive or contemporaneous with the occupation of the owner. In *Caunce v. Caunce*[65] Stamp J. held that a mortgagee did not have constructive notice of the trust interest of a wife who shared occupation of her matrimonial home with her husband, who was the sole legal owner and had granted the mortgage, because her occupation was "wholly consistent with the title offered." However, such sentiments were rejected by the House of Lords in *Williams & Glynn's Bank Ltd v. Boland*[66] and today no person in actual occupation of

[61] *Re Cox and Neve's Contract* [1891] 2 Ch. 109; *Re Nisbet and Pott's Contract* [1906] 1 Ch. 386.
[62] (1856) 22 Beav. 299.
[63] [1902] 1 Ch. 428.
[64] *ibid.* at 433 *per* Vaughan Williams L.J.
[65] [1969] 1 W.L.R. 286.
[66] [1981] A.C. 487.

the land can be presumed not to enjoy rights inconsistent with the title claimed by the legal owner. Clearly failure to make any inspection of the land at all will cause a purchaser to be deemed to have notice of the existence of the rights of all the persons whose existence he would have discovered by making such an inspection.[67] However even if a purchaser makes some inspection he will still be affixed with constructive notice if that inspection was inadequate. In *Kingsnorth Finance v. Tizard*[68] a matrimonial home was co-owned in equity by the husband and wife, but he was the sole legal owner. Following the breakdown of their marriage the wife slept elsewhere, but returned every day to care for their twin children, which led the judge to conclude that she was in continued occupation. The husband subsequently mortgaged the property and disappeared with the money he had raised. The mortgagees accepted the mortgage after their agent had inspected the property on Sunday shortly after lunchtime, a time arranged by the husband to ensure that his wife and children would not be present on the property. When the agent visited the house the husband told him that his wife had left many months ago and that they were separated and she was living with someone else nearby. The agent inspected the property and looked round inside and out, discovering evidence of occupation by the two children but finding no evidence of female occupation other than by the teenage daughter. Judge Finlay Q.C. held that, in the circumstances, the inspection which had been made was inadequate because it had been conducted at a time arranged by the husband to ensure that his wife would not be present. He stated:

> "... if the purchaser or mortgagee carries out such inspections "as ought reasonably to be made" and does not find the claimant in occupation or find evidence of that occupation, then I am not persuaded that the purchaser or mortgagee is in such circumstances ... fixed with notice of the claimant's rights. One of the circumstances, however, is that such inspection is made "as ought reasonably to be made." Here [the agent] carried out his inspection on a Sunday afternoon at a time arranged with Mr Tizard. If the only purpose of such an inspection were to ascertain the physical state of the property, the time at which the inspection is made and whether or not that time is one agreed in advance with the vendor or the mortgagor appears to me to be immaterial. Where, however, the object of the inspection (or one of the objects) is to ascertain who is in occupation, I cannot see that an inspection at a time pre-arranged with the vendor will necessarily attain that object. Such a pre-arranged inspection may achieve no more than an inquiry of the vendor or mortgagor and his answer to it."[69]

At first sight the decision may seem somewhat harsh, since it begs the question how a purchaser or mortgagee could protect themselves against a vendor or mortgagor who is deliberately concealing the occupation of some other person. There must clearly be limits to what an inspection can demand. For example, the judge agreed that it was not reasonable for the agent to open cupboards and draws to look for signs of occupation.

[67] See: *Lloyd's Bank v. Carrick* [1996] 4 All E.R. 630.
[68] [1986] 1 W.L.R. 783.
[69] *ibid.* at 794–795.

The central inadequacy therefore seems to have been the unusual timing of the inspection and that this should have alerted them to the possibility of concealment. However it was not merely the inadequacy of the inspection which led to a finding of constructive notice. In the course of the inspection the agent had been made aware by Mr Tizard that he was married, albeit separated, whereas on the application form for the loan he had declared himself single. Therefore when it became apparent that he was in fact married, and that a spouse was in existence, the mortgagors should have been put on notice that further inquiries were appropriate to ascertain whether the wife enjoyed any interests in the land. No reasonable mortgagor would have taken a mortgage over what had been a matrimonial home knowing of the existence of a spouse but having failed to ensure that she had no interests in the land. The decision is more easily supported on the grounds that the inspection was inadequate because it failed to investigate further into circumstances which it had revealed.

(vi) Imputed notice: by process of extension a purchaser or a mortgagee will be treated of enjoying notice of any equitable interests affecting the land of which an agent acting on their behalf had notice. This will be so whether the agent's notice was actual or constructive. This principle is again evident in *Kingsnorth Finance v. Tizard* since it was the surveyor instructed to act by the mortgagees who had constructive notice of the interests of Mrs Tizard, and the mortgagees were therefore imputed with such notice and did not acquire their legal mortgage free from her share of the equitable ownership of the house. Imputed notice was also placed on a statutory basis in Law of Property Act 1925, s.199(1)(ii)(b).

(vii) Estoppel operating where an equitable interest has not been revealed: Although a purchaser or mortgagee will be affixed with constructive notice if they have failed to make adequate inquiries it is clear that in some circumstances the holder of an equitable interest will be regarded as required to reveal its existence, and they will be estopped from asserting its priority if they fail to do so. In *Midland Bank Ltd v. Farmpride Hatcheries Ltd*[70] a man occupied a farm under a contractual licence granted by the company which owned the land, which he in turn co-owned and controlled with his wife. The company granted the Bank a mortgage of the land, and he negotiated the details of the loan acting as the agent of the company. Although the Bank was aware that he and his family occupied the land he at no point disclosed the existence of the licence to them, and it was not revealed by their negotiations. He subsequently claimed that the Bank had taken the mortgage subject to his contractual licence on the grounds that they has contractual notice of its existence. The Court of Appeal held that he could not assert the priority of his interest over the mortgage because he was estopped by his failure to disclose it. Shaw L.J. explained:

> "In my judgment Mr Willey set up a smoke-screen designed to hide even the possible existence of some interest in himself which could derogate from the interest of the company ostensibly conferred by the mortgage. To change the metaphor, he deliberately put [the bank] off the scent and the bank accepted the mortgage as a consequence. They would not have done so but for Mr Willey's subtle but positive indication that he had communicated all that had to be told which could be relevant to the bank's consideration of the company's application.

[70] (1980) 260 E.G. 493.

> This being so, I am of the opinion that Mr Willey is estopped from setting up any facts which would go to show that he held an interest which overrides or stands in priority of the company's application."[71]

The other judges of the Court of Appeal also held that since Mr Willey was acting as the agent of the company in the negotiations he was thereby representing that the company had an indefeasible title to the property, and that he enjoyed no interest in the land which was adverse to such title. The bank was therefore entitled to rely on that representation and had not failed to make reasonable inquiries by not investigating further the nature of his occupancy of the land.

(viii) Effect of acquisition of a legal estate by a bona fide purchaser without notice on the pre-existing equitable interest: Where all the criteria of the doctrine of notice are satisfied, the effect is to completely destroy the pre-existing equitable interest. The purchaser or mortgagee takes his title free from the equitable interest which is effectively rendered void, just as an unregistered land charge is rendered statutorily void if the appropriate conditions are met. Once such an equitable interest is rendered void by operation of the doctrine of notice there is no possibility of its subsequent revival, even if the land was to be conveyed to a person who did have knowledge of its prior existence.[72]

[71] *ibid.* at 497.
[72] *Wilkes v. Spooner* [1911] 2 K.B. 473.

Priorities in unregistered land

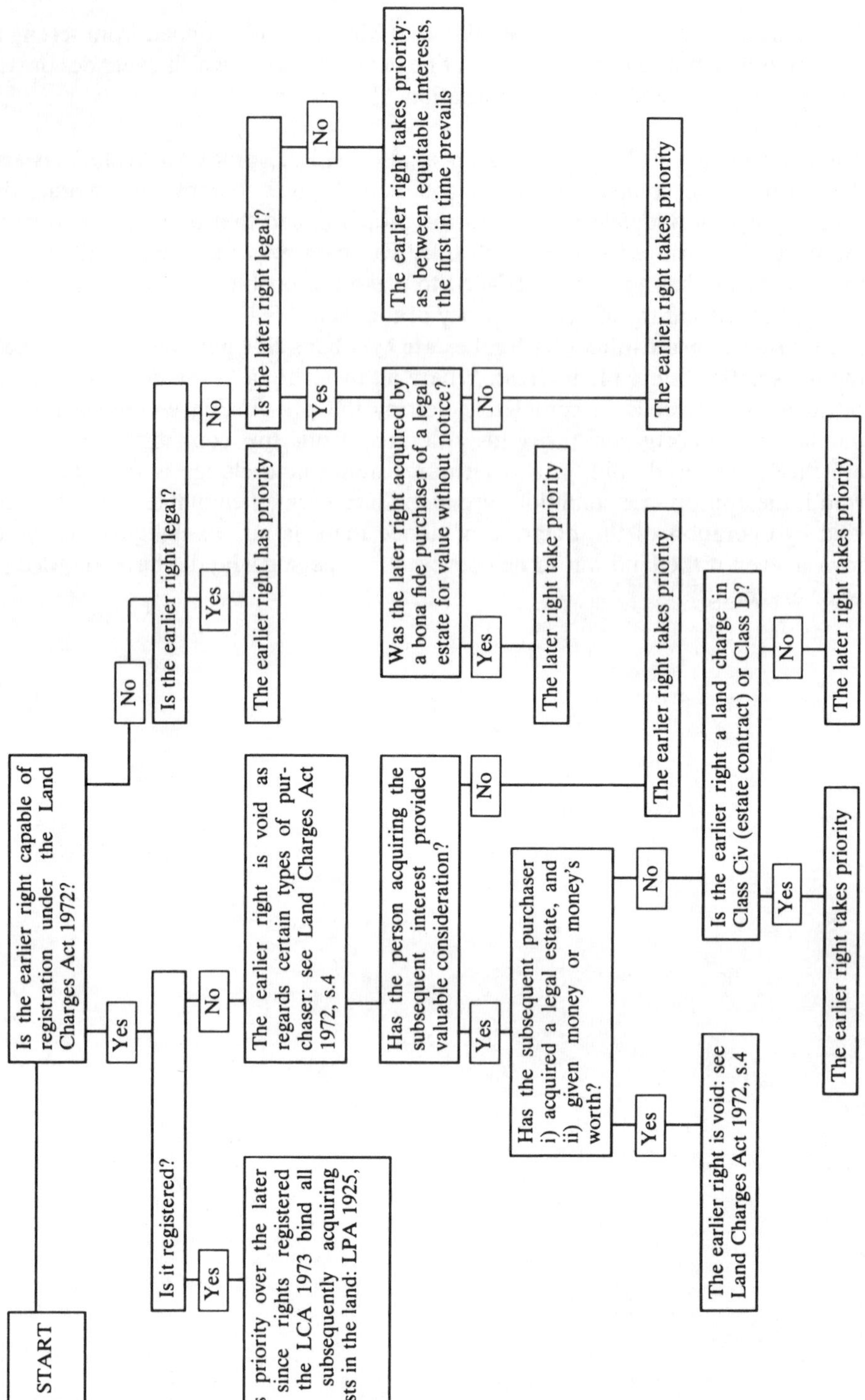

INDEX